HANDBOOK
OF
SURGERY

HANDBOOK
OF
SURGERY

SIXTH EDITION

Edited by

THEODORE R. SCHROCK, MD
University of California, San Francisco

JONES MEDICAL PUBLICATIONS 1978
Greenbrae, California

Copyright c 1978

Jones Medical Publications
355 Los Cerros Drive, Greenbrae, California 94904

JMP Handbook series
Handbook of Medical Treatment, 15th edition, 1977
        Milton J. Chatton (editor)

Previous editions copyrighted c 1960, 1963,
1966, 1973 by Lange Medical Publications,
Los Altos, California

Library of Congress Catalog Number: 78-57211

ISBN: 0-930010-02-7

Printed in USA
9 8 7 6 5 4 3

CONTENTS

PREFACE

Handbook of Surgery is a concise, portable first reference for the student, resident, and nonspecialist physician. It is intended for use on the scene to give the reader some idea of what questions to ask in taking the history, what physical signs to elicit, what tests to order, what other diagnostic possibilities to consider, and what treatment to institute immediately. This handbook is not a substitute for standard textbooks or original literature. Discussions of diagnosis and treatment are sufficient to help the nonspecialist handle problems on the spot, but it is assumed that the reader will take the earliest opportunity to consult references which discuss the topics more thoroughly.

Handbook of Surgery was edited by Dr. John L. Wilson and published by Lange Medical Publications through five editions over the past 18 years. This, the Sixth Edition, has a new editor and a new publisher. Most of the text has been rewritten by new contributors; authors in previous editions have revised and updated their material extensively. The contents have been reorganized, the format altered, and the type reset.

I am indebted to the contributors for submitting authoritative material despite the constraints imposed upon them by the style and objectives of this book. I am grateful to my publisher, Richard C. M. Jones, for his patience when the expected flood of edited manuscript proved to be a mere trickle. Both Mr. Jones and I are warmly appreciative of the close cooperation and support of Dr. Jack Lange in bringing this project to completion.

Theodore R. Schrock

San Francisco, California
July, 1978

AUTHORS

Except where noted, all authors are at University of California, San Francisco

F. WILLIAM BLAISDELL, MD, Chairman, Department of Surgery, University of California, Davis

ORLO H. CLARK, MD, Assistant Professor of Surgery

WAYNE W. DEATSCH, MD, Associate Clinical Professor, Otolaryngology

ALFRED A. deLORIMIER, MD, Associate Professor of Surgery

DENNIS J. FLORA, MD, PharmD, Valley Medical Center, Fresno, Ca

PETER H. FORSHAM, MD, Professor of Medicine and Pediatrics

NERI P. GUADAGNI, MD, Associate Professor of Anesthesia

MICHAEL R. HARRISON, MD, Assistant Professor of Surgery

EDWARD C. HILL, MD, Associate Professor of Obstetrics and Gynecology

JULIAN T. HOFF, MD, Associate Professor of Neurological Surgery

JOHN C. HUTCHINSON, MD, Clinical Professor of Medicine and Surgery

ERNEST JAWETZ, MD, PhD, Professor of Microbiology and Medicine

FLOYD H. JERGESEN, MD, Clinical Professor of Orthopedic Surgery

EUGENE S. KILGORE, JR., MD, Clinical Professor of Surgery

FRANK R. LEWIS, JR., MD, Assistant Professor of Surgery

WILLIAM J. MORRIS, MD, Associate Clinical Professor of Surgery

WILLIAM L. NEWMEYER, III, MD, Assistant Clinical Professor of Surgery

CORNELIUS OLCOTT, IV, MD, Assistant Professor of Surgery

LAWRENCE H. PITTS, MD, Assistant Professor of Neurological Surgery

CURT A. RIES, MD, Associate Clinical Professor of Medicine and Laboratory Medicine

THEODORE R. SCHROCK, MD, Associate Professor of Surgery

GEORGE F. SHELDON, MD, Associate Professor of Surgery

MURIEL STEELE, MD, Associate Clinical Professor of Surgery

EMIL A. TANAGHO, MD, Professor and Chairman, Department of Urology

ARTHUR N. THOMAS, MD, Assistant Professor of Surgery

DONALD TRUNKEY, MD, Assistant Professor of Surgery

DANIEL J. ULLYOT, MD, Assistant Professor of Surgery

FLAVIO VINCENTI, MD, Assistant Clinical Professor of Medicine

EDWIN J. WYLIE, MD, Professor of Surgery

SHOCK & TRAUMA

Donald Trunkey, MD

I. SHOCK

Shock is defined as peripheral circulatory failure causing tissue perfusion to be inadequate to meet the nutritional requirements of the cells and remove the waste products of metabolism. In the simplest terms, therefore, shock is **inadequate tissue perfusion.**

Shock may be classified as hypovolemic, septic, cardiogenic, neurogenic, or miscellaneous (e.g., anaphylactic reactions and insulin shock).

A. HYPOVOLEMIC SHOCK is the result of decreased blood volume due to acute and severe loss of blood, plasma, or body water and electrolytes. Hemorrhage, burns, bowel obstruction, peritonitis, and crush injuries are some of the common causes. A fall in venous pressure, a rise in peripheral vascular resistance, and tachycardia are characteristic of hypovolemic shock.

Factors that make a patient especially susceptible to hypovolemic shock include: **age** (the very young and the elderly tolerate loss of body water or plasma poorly); **chronic illness** (such patients often have a reduced blood volume and relatively small acute losses may precipitate shock); **anesthesia** (paralysis of vasomotor tone may cause shock in a patient who has compensated for a reduced blood volume); **adrenal insufficiency** (profound hypotension may be induced by minimal stress if corticosteroids are not supplied during and after trauma, operation, or illness).

1. Pathophysiology Events in the microcirculation progress in phases.

a. Compensation phase The first response of the circulation to hypovolemia is contraction of the precapillary arterial sphincters; this causes the filtration pressure in the capillaries to fall. Since osmotic pressure remains the same, fluid moves into the vascular space with a corresponding increase in blood volume. If this compensatory mechanism is adequate to return blood volume to normal, the capillary sphincters relax and microcirculatory flow returns to normal. If shock is prolonged and profound, the next phase is entered.

b. Cell distress phase If vascular volume has not been restored, the precapillary sphincters remain closed, and arteriovenous shunts open up to divert arterial blood directly back into the venous system, thus maintaining circulation to more important organs such as the heart and brain. The cells in the bypassed segment of the microcirculation must rely on anaerobic metabolism for energy. The amount of glucose and oxygen available for the cell decreases, and metabolic waste products such as lactate accumulate. Histamine is released, resulting in closure of the postcapillary sphincters, and this mechanism serves to slow the remaining capillary flow and hold the red blood cells and nutrients in the capillaries longer. The empty capillary bed constricts almost completely; very few capillaries remain open.

c. Decompensation phase Just before cell death, local reflexes (probably initiated by acidosis and accumulated metabolites) reopen the precapillary sphincters while the postcapillary sphincters stay closed. Prolonged vasoconstriction of the capillary bed damages endothelial cells and results in increased capillary permeability. When the capillaries finally reopen, fluid and protein are leaked into the interstitial space, the capillaries distend with red blood cells, and sludging occurs. Cells become swollen, they are unable to utilize oxygen, and they die.

d. Recovery phase If blood volume is restored at some point in the decompensation phase, the effects on the microcirculation may still be reversible. Badly damaged cells may recover, and capillary integrity may be regained. The 'sludge' in the microcirculation is swept into the venous circulation and eventually into the lungs where these platelet and white cell aggregates are filtered out and produce postshock pulmonary failure (see Chapter 2). Other capillaries may be so badly damaged and filled with sludge that they remain permanently closed; cells dependent upon these capillaries die.

Table 1-1. Clinical classification of hypovolemic shock

Mild shock (up to 20% blood volume loss)
> **Definition:** Decreased perfusion of nonvital organs and tissues (skin, fat, skeletal muscle, and bone).
> **Manifestations:** Pale, cool skin. Patient complains of feeling cold.

Moderate shock (20–40% blood volume loss)
> **Definition:** Decreased perfusion of vital organs (liver, gut, kidneys).
> **Manifestations:** Oliguria to anuria and slight to significant drop in blood pressure.

Severe shock (40% or more blood volume loss)
> **Definition:** Decreased perfusion of heart and brain.
> **Manifestations:** Restlessness, agitation, coma, cardiac irregularities, ECG abnormalities, and cardiac arrest.

Reproduced with permission from Dunphy JE, Way LW (Eds.): *Current Surgical Diagnosis and Treatment,* 3rd Ed. Lange 1977.

2. Diagnosis Clinical assessment permits classification of hypovolemic shock as mild, moderate, or severe (Table 1-1). The compensatory mechanisms act to preserve blood flow to the heart and brain at the expense of all others; thus, in severe shock, there is marked constriction of all other vascular beds.

3. Treatment Shock is an acute emergency: **act promptly!**
a. Keep the patient recumbent—do not move the patient unnecessarily.
b. Establish and maintain an airway.
c. Place one or more large intravenous catheters.
> (1) Do a cutdown in the long saphenous vein at the ankle; this method is rapid and safe.
> (2) Do a cutdown on the basilic vein in the antecubital space so that central venous pressure can be monitored.
> (3) Percutaneous insertion of subclavian or jugular catheters is not recommended because the veins are collapsed in hypovolemic shock. Femoral vein catheters may be placed percutaneously in unusual circumstances, e.g., when a single physician is available for resuscitation.

d. Parenteral fluids Begin **immediately** to restore blood volume. In mild or moderate shock, it makes little difference which fluid is used (Table 1-2). In severe shock, the choice of fluid is important because endothelial permeability may be increased throughout the body, resulting in 'capillary leak' which compounds the problems if colloid is given.

(1) *Crystalloids* are preferred in the initial treatment of shock. They are readily available and effectively restore vascular volume for brief periods. Crystalloids also lower blood viscosity and enhance resuscitation of the microcirculation. Balanced salt solutions plus judicious amounts of sodium bicarbonate correct the acidosis which invariably is present in shock. Serial blood pH measurements are a guide. Overcorrection of acidosis is more harmful than the opposite.

Table 1-2. Fluid resuscitation of shock

I. **Crystalloids**
  A. Isotonic sodium chloride
  B. Hypertonic sodium chloride
  C. Balanced salt solution
    1. Ringer's lactate
    2. *Ringer's acetate*
    3. Normosol, Plasmolyte, etc.
II. **Colloid**
  A. Blood
    1. Low-titer O negative blood
    2. *Type-specific*
    3. Typed and crossed
    4. Washed red cells
    5. Fresh red cells
  B. Plasma and its components
    1. Plasma—fresh frozen
    2. Albumin
    3. Plasmanate
  C. Plasma substitutes
    1. Clinical dextran (M.W. 70,000)
    2. Low molecular weight dextran (M.W. 40,000)

(2) *Colloids*
  (a) *Blood* is available in emergencies as low-titer O negative or type-specific. O negative blood has the theoretical disadvantage of isoimmunization or difficulty with typing and crossmatching later; this is probably not a major consideration. Type-specific blood can be used until crossmatched blood becomes available (about 45 minutes).
    If shock persists after 2 liters of crystalloid have been infused, or if shock recurs after the patient initially responds, whole blood should be transfused immediately.
  (b) *Plasma* and albumin solutions are detrimental in prolonged severe shock. These substances leak through capillary membranes taking water with them, thus exacerbating the interstitial edema. Plasma and its components should be withheld until capillaries regain their integrity (about 24 hours).
  (c) *Plasma substitutes* (dextrans) interfere with function of the reticuloendothelial system and depress the already impaired immune mechanisms in shock patients. Clinical dextran coats red cells, making typing and crossmatching difficult; low molecular weight dextran coats platelets and may contribute to bleeding.

e. The underlying cause of shock should be investigated and treated while resuscitation is underway. Failure of resuscitation almost always reflects persistent massive hemorrhage, and definitive operative treatment offers the only chance for survival.

f. Evaluation of treatment   The amount of fluid that a patient should receive is governed by the patient's response; there is no rigid formula. Constant close monitoring is essential (see Table 1-3). Atrial filling pressure and urine output are the most useful signs.

Table 1-3. Variables frequently monitored in shock

Measurement	Typical normal values	Typical values in severe shock
Arterial blood pressure	120/180	< 90 mm Hg systolic
Pulse rate	80/minute	> 100/minute
Central venous pressure	4–8 cm saline	< 3 cm
Hematocrit	35–45%	< 35%
Arterial blood:		
pH	7.4	7.3
pO_2	95 mm Hg	85 mm Hg
pCO_2	40 mm Hg	< 30 mm Hg
$-HCO_3$	23–25 mEq/liter	< 23 mEq/liter
Lactic acid	12 mg/100 ml	> 20 mg/100 ml
Urine:		
Volume	50 ml/hour	< 20 ml/hour
Specific gravity	1.015–1.025	> 1.025
Osmolality	300–400 mOsm/ kg water	> 700 mOsm/ kg water

(1) *Left atrial filling pressure* is rarely measured directly, but the pulmonary artery wedge pressure is a useful approximation, and it should be monitored in critical patients. Central venous pressure is sufficiently accurate in the majority of patients. In mild or moderate shock, resuscitation may be permitted to raise atrial filling pressure as high as 24 torr without risk. In severe shock, however, atrial filling pressure must be kept at or near normal (3–8 torr) because higher pressures aggravate interstitial edema.

(2) *Urine output* should be monitored; this usually requires a urinary catheter. Urine output greater than 0.5 cc/kg/hour is a good index of visceral blood flow, specifically renal blood flow.

(3) Additional signs of successful resuscitation include an alert, oriented patient and adequate peripheral perfusion as judged by clinical criteria.

(4) Blood pressure, pulse rate, and respiratory rate should be recorded every 15–30 minutes.

(5) Hematocrit should be measured every few hours if continued bleeding is suspected. The hematocrit usually falls gradually over a period of 24–48 hours because of hemodilution even if bleeding has stopped.

(6) Blood gases should be determined repeatedly (see Table 1-3).

(7) Other measurements, obtained in certain circumstances, include cardiac output and oxygen consumption.

g. Failures of resuscitation

(1) If both atrial filling pressure and urine output are increased, too much fluid is being given, and the infusion rate should be slowed immediately.

(2) If both atrial filling pressure and urine output are below normal, more volume is required.

(3) When atrial filling pressure is elevated and urine output is low, measurement of cardiac output is useful.

    (a) High atrial filling pressure, low urine output, and high cardiac output indicate deficient renal function. (i) Give mannitol (12.5-25 gm IV) followed by infusion of mannitol 50 gm in 500-1000 ml of balanced salt solution. No more than 75-100 gm of mannitol should be given. (ii) If there is no response to mannitol, give small doses of furosemide (10-20 mg IV) or ethacrynic acid (50 mg IV). These diuretics may cause vasodilatation and redistribution of blood flow within the kidney.

    (b) High atrial filling pressure, low urine output, and low cardiac output suggest that an inotropic agent is needed (Table 1-4). (i) *Dopamine hydrochloride,* 200 mg in 500 ml of sodium injection USP (400 μg/ml), is given initially at a rate of 2.5 μg/kg/minute. These doses stimulate both the dopaminergic receptors, which increase the renal blood flow and urine output, and the beta-adrenergic cardiac receptors, which increase the cardiac output. Higher levels stimulate alpha receptors to cause systemic vasoconstriction, and doses above 20 μg/kg/minute reverse the vasodilatation of the renal vessels achieved at lower levels. (ii) *Isoproterenol,* a beta-adrenergic stimulator, increases cardiac output by its action on the myocardial contraction mechanism, and it also produces peripheral vasodilatation. Give 1-2 mg in 500 ml of 5% dextrose in water IV. Isoproterenol should not be used if the heart rate is greater than 100-120/minute lest cardiac arrhythmias develop. (iii) *10% calcium chloride* (10 cc) may be administered directly IV over 2-3 minutes provided there is continuous cardiac monitoring for arrhythmias. Although calcium may produce an instant inotrophic effect, it is usually not sustained, and repeated doses are required. Measurement of ionized calcium levels are prudent in such instances.

(4) There is no convincing evidence that corticosteroids or ganglionic blocking drugs are of value in hypovolemic shock.

B. SEPTIC SHOCK is most often due to gram-negative septicemia, although infection by gram-positive bacteria can also cause shock. Trauma, diabetes mellitus, hematologic diseases, corticosteroid therapy, immunosuppressive drugs, and radiation therapy increase susceptibility to infection and thus predispose to septic shock. Precipitating events are often operations on the urinary, biliary, or gynecologic systems.

    1. Pathophysiology

    a. Gram-negative septicemia causes a generalized increase in capillary permeability, loss of fluid from the vascular space, and pooling of blood in the microcirculation. All of these mechanisms contribute to hypovolemia. There may also be a direct toxic effect on the heart, with depression of myocardial function. Peripheral vascular resistance usually is lowered as the result of arteriovenous shunting.

    b. Gram-positive septicemia occasionally produces hypovolemia, but the loss of fluid from the vascular space usually is limited to the area of infection.

    c. Disseminated intravascular coagulation (DIC) may develop in septic shock (see pages 49 and 84).

    2. Diagnosis

    a. Symptoms and signs (1) The inciting infection may be obscure. (2) Confusion and restlessness are early indications. (3) The skin is warm and the

Table 1-4. Adrenergic drugs used in hypotensive states.
(Effects graded on a scale of 0-5.)

Drug	Vasomotor Effect		Cardiac Stimulant (Inotropic Effect)	Cardiac Output	Renal and Splanchnic Blood Flow
	Vaso-constriction	Vaso-dilatation			
Alpha-adrenergic					
Phenylephrine (Neo-Synephrine)	5	0	0	Reduced	Reduced
Mixed alpha- and beta-adrenergic					
Norepinephrine (Levophed)	4	0	2	Reduced	Reduced
Metaraminol (Aramine)	3	2	1	Reduced	Reduced
Epinephrine (Adrenalin)	4	3	4	Increased	Reduced
Dopamine (Intropin)*	2	2	2	Usually increased	Increased
Beta-adrenergic					
Isoproterenol (many trade names)	0	5	4	Increased	Usually reduced

*Claimed to have a special (dopaminergic) receptor.

Reproduced with permission from Krupp, MA, Chatton, MJ (Eds.): *Current Medical Diagnosis & Treatment.* Lange, 1977.

pulses full initially; vasoconstriction develops later. (4) Pulmonary hypertension and hyperventilation. (5) Urine output is normal at first, then it slows rapidly.

    b. Laboratory tests (1) Inability to metabolize glucose (glucosuria, hyperglycemia) is an early finding. (2) Respiratory alkalosis. (3) Hemoconcentration is common. (4) Early leukopenia followed by leukocytosis; usually the leukocyte count is 15,000 or more with a shift to the left. (5) Identification of the

Table 1-5. Biochemical and metabolic effects
of corticosteroids

---

1. ↑ Hepatic glucose output

2. Hyperaminoacidemia

3. ↑ Secretion of glucagon

4. Inhibition of lipogenesis—selective

5. Induces negative calcium balance

6. Blocks ↑ capillary endothelial permeability

7. Markedly inhibits exudation of inflammatory cells

8. May maintain plasma membrane integrity

9. Suppresses T helper cell

10. Stabilizes lysosome membrane

11. Exhibits myocardial inotropism

---

responsible organism(s) is urgent. Obtain cultures on samples of blood, sputum, urine, drainage fluid, and any other suspicious site. A gram-stained smear of infected fluid may suggest the origin of the problem and guide emergency therapy.

    3. Treatment As in other forms of shock, the objective of treatment is to improve tissue perfusion. In addition, the underlying infection must be treated.

    a. Volume replacement The initial fluid should be balanced salt solution; colloids are particularly prone to leak from capillaries and aggravate interstitial edema in septic shock. Fluid volume is adjusted by close monitoring as described for hypovolemic shock.

Table 1-6. Acute complications of corticosteroid therapy
in the shock patient

---

1. Peptic ulceration

2. Intestinal perforation

3. Pancreatitis

4. Sodium and water retention

5. Impaired wound healing

6. Suppression of the immune response

---

    b. Antibiotic therapy Large doses of specific antibiotics should be given if the organism is known; if not, a 'best guess' should be made as to the responsible bacteria, and antibiotics are given accordingly (see Table 4-1).

    c. Surgical drainage If an abscess or other accessible focus of infection is identified, it should be drained, debrided, or decompressed promptly. Antibiotics and fluid resuscitation will not salvage the patient if the source of infection is not found and drained.

    d. Supportive measures Close attention should be paid to maintenance of ventilation. Accompanying disorders must be treated. If the patient continues to deteriorate, cardiovascular support with inotropic agents may be required as in hypovolemic shock.

    e. Corticosteroid therapy Corticosteroids have both beneficial and deleterious effects in septic shock (Tables 1-5 and 1-6). Because the disadvantages outweigh the advantages, the use of corticosteroids in septic shock cannot be recommended.

    f. Treatment of DIC (see page 84) If hemorrhagic manifestations of DIC develop, **heparin** should be given (100 units/kg IV initially, then 1000–3000 units/hour by continuous IV infusion). Response to heparin is indicated by improvement of bleeding and a rise of factors 5 and 7 and fibrinogen within 12 hours. Platelets may increase at a slower rate. Discontinue heparin therapy when the cause of DIC has been corrected and coagulation factors have returned to hemostatic levels.

C. CARDIOGENIC SHOCK Some degree of cardiac failure, usually left ventricular, can be detected in 20–50% of patients with acute myocardial infarction.

    1. Diagnosis Clinical findings are often absent or minimal. Dyspnea, pulmonary rales, diastolic gallop, accentuated pulmonary second sound, pulsus alternans, and pulmonary venous congestion on chest x-ray may or may not be present. The radiographic changes take time to develop and are slow to resolve, so they are not very helpful acutely. Hypotension is often the first sign that cardiac failure is more severe than suggested by the other parameters.

    2. Treatment

    a. Treatment of *mild left ventricular failure* consists of oral diuretics (e.g., hydrochlorothiazide 50–100 mg), oxygen, and limitation of sodium intake.

    b. More aggressive treatment is required for *severe left ventricular failure.* Such patients should have monitoring of arterial pressure, pulmonary artery wedge pressure, and cardiac output. The stroke work index can be computed, and rational therapy is based on the specific hemodynamic abnormality found.

        (1) Low left ventricular filling pressure (less than 12 torr), normal cardiac output, and low arterial pressure indicate hypovolemia. Replace volume, beginning with 100 ml of saline or balanced salt solution. If cardiac output does not increase as left ventricular filling pressure rises to 15–20 torr, stop volume replacement to avoid pulmonary edema which may occur abruptly.

        (2) Elevated left ventricular filling pressure, normal cardiac output, and normal blood pressure suggest that vigorous diuresis should be attempted with large doses of furosemide. Avoid volume depletion from excessive diuresis.

        (3) Normal left ventricular filling pressure, normal cardiac output, and low arterial pressure reflect a failure of compensatory peripheral vasoconstriction. Give epinephrine or dopamine to stimulate beta-adrenergic receptors. These drugs should be infused slowly to avoid tachycardia, hypertension, and ventricular arrhythmias. The goal is to maintain blood pressure but not increase the stroke work index.

        (4) Elevated left ventricular filling pressure (more than 20 torr), low cardiac output, and arterial blood pressure at or above 90 torr, is a pattern for which vasodilator therapy can be given. Drugs such as sodium nitroprusside, phentolamine, or nitroglycerine infused slowly IV, decrease the impedance to left ventricular ejection. Re-

duced left ventricular volume and filling pressure may improve the left ventricular stroke work index, lower the myocardial oxygen consumption (MVO_2), and improve perfusion to the brain, heart, and kidneys. The arterial blood pressure should be 90 torr or more before vasodilators can be given safely; if vasopressors cannot be used to raise blood pressure without elevating left ventricular filling pressure and aggravating cardiac failure, aortic balloon counter pulsation may be useful as a temporary aid to make vasodilator therapy possible.

D. NEUROGENIC SHOCK is due to a failure of arterial resistance from nervous or psychic stimulation (e.g., sudden pain or fright), vasodilator drugs (nitrites), spinal anesthesia, or spinal trauma. Blood pools in dilated capacitance vessels, and blood pressure falls. Cardiac activity increases to fill the dilated vascular bed and preserve tissue perfusion.

Prodromal symptoms and signs are pallor, cold sweat, weakness, light headedness, and occasionally nausea. Fainting is accompanied by transient hypotension and bradycardia.

Neurogenic shock is self-limiting. Resting in a recumbent or head-down position with the legs elevated for a few minutes is usually sufficient. If the patient is sitting down, and reclining is not possible, have him bend forward with his head between his knees. When faintness or prostration persists, other types of shock must be considered.

High spinal anesthesia induces neurogenic shock by paralyzing the vasoconstrictor nerves. Treatment consists of placing the patient in the head-down (Trendelenburg) position and administering a vasopressor agent. Acute traumatic paraplegia or quadriplegia causes neurogenic shock; however, associated injuries are common in these patients, and hypovolemia must be assumed to be responsible for shock until proved otherwise.

E. ANAPHYLACTIC REACTIONS These catastrophic allergic reactions may occur within seconds or minutes after the parenteral administration of animal sera or drugs; rarely, anaphylaxis develops after oral ingestion of drugs or foods. Anaphylaxis represents hypersensitivity induced by previous injection or ingestion, although occasionally no history of earlier exposure can be obtained.

    1. Diagnosis The most conspicuous clinical feature may be laryngeal edema, bronchospasm, or vascular collapse. Symptoms and signs include apprehension, generalized urticaria or edema, a choking sensation, wheezing, cough, or status asthmaticus. In severe cases, hypotension, loss of consciousness, dilatation of pupils, incontinence, convulsions, and death occur suddenly.

    2. Treatment Anaphylaxis is a life-threatening emergency. **Act immediately!**

        a. Position the patient for comfort and ease of respiration.

        b. Establish an airway and maintain oxygenation. If respirations have ceased, give artificial respiration by the mouth-to-mouth, mask, or endotracheal tube technics (see Chapter 3).

        c. Drug therapy Epinephrine is the drug of choice for emergency use. It may be necessary to give intravenous antihistaminics, steroids, and aminophylline also.

           (1) *Epinephrine hydrochloride:* give 1 ml of 1:1000 solution IM; repeat dose in 5-10 minutes and later as needed. For more rapid effect, give 0.1-0.4 ml of 1:1000 solution in 10 ml of saline slowly IV.

           (2) *Antihistaminics:* give diphenhydramine hydrochloride (Benadryl) or tripelenamine hydrochloride (Pyribenzamine) 10-20 mg IV if the response to epinephrine is not prompt and sustained.

           (3) *Steroids:* give hydrocortisone hemisuccinate (Solu-Cortef) 100-250 mg or prednisolone hemisuccinate (Meticortelone Soluble) 50-100

mg IV over 30 seconds. The dosage depends upon the severity of the patient's condition. Repeat the drug at increasing intervals (1, 3, 6, 10 hours, etc.) as indicated.

(4) *Aminophylline* injection, 0.25-0.5 gm in 10-20 ml of saline is given slowly IV if bronchospasm is severe. The dose may be repeated in 3-4 hours.

3. Prophylaxis   Avoid using potentially dangerous drugs or sera if possible. Be particularly cautious when administering parenteral medications to patients with a history of allergy or previous reaction. Give injections slowly and keep such individuals under close observation for an hour or more thereafter.

Always perform a sensitivity test (intradermal or conjunctival) before injecting animal sera or other agents to which a hypersensitivity reaction may occur. When sensitivity is demonstrated by a positive test or is suggested by the history, the patient must be desensitized by the administration of a series of divided doses.

II. FIRST AID

A. GENERAL PRINCIPLES

1. Determine the extent of injury quickly.

2. Treat all life-threatening conditions immediately. Assessment and treatment often must be done simultaneously.

3. Control hemorrhage, splint fractures, and arrange transportation so that definitive treatment may be given promptly.

B. EVALUATION OF THE PATIENT

1. If possible, obtain a history to ascertain the degree and type of damage and any serious underlying medical problems (e.g., cardiac disease or diabetes mellitus). The family or rescue personnel may be able to provide useful information, such as amount of blood at the scene or whether a steering wheel injury occurred. Rescue personnel can also describe the condition of the patient during transportation.

2. Examine the patient thoroughly after major trauma with special attention to the following:

a. Quickly undress the patient and roll him or her from side to side to check for posterior wounds. Assess peripheral perfusion by examining the skin of the extremities.

b. Respiratory distress   Assess adequacy of ventilation. Stridor and suprasternal or intercostal retraction indicate airway obstruction. Cyanosis is due to poor oxygenation until proved otherwise. Shortness of breath may reflect chest injury, shock, or head injury. In respiratory arrest, begin mouth-to-mouth resuscitation immediately (see Chapter 3).

c. Cardiac arrest   Check for carotid pulses immediately; if absent, start cardiopulmonary resuscitation (see page 64).

d. Shock   If peripheral perfusion is diminished, quickly examine the neck veins. If the neck veins are distended, shock is due to cardiac failure. Assume that hypovolemia is the cause of shock if the neck veins are flat. Additional criteria for the assessment of shock are described in Section I.

e. External wounds and bleeding   Control bleeding promptly, using direct pressure and apply a sterile dressing.

f. Neurological injuries   Evaluate by repeated examination of state of consciousness, cranial nerve signs, gross skin sensation, ability to move extremities, rectal examination, and peripheral reflexes (see Chapter 16).

g. Fractures and dislocations   Palpate carefully from head to foot; move all joints cautiously and exert gentle pressure on the spine, chest, and pelvis. Pain, swelling, ecchymosis, deformity, and limitation of motion are classical signs of fracture and dislocation. Splint all fractures as quickly as possible to prevent further soft tissue and neurovascular damage.

h. Internal injury Overt localizing signs are often minimal. Hypovolemic shock in the absence of external bleeding indicates internal hemorrhage. Chest films may localize blood in one or the other hemithorax. Repeated abdominal examination, serial hematocrit, and serial leukocyte counts are helpful in localizing visceral injury.

Pull Out Tongue   Pull Jaw Forward

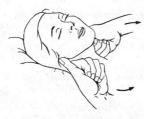

Lift Jaw Forward

Figure 1-1. Relief of airway obstruction. (Reproduced, with permission, from Dunphy JE, Way LW (Eds.): *Current Surgical Diagnosis and Treatment,* 2nd Ed. Lange, 1975.

C. EMERGENCY TREATMENT
1. Respiratory distress
a. When due to airway obstruction (see Figure 1-1) (1) Quickly clear the airway by suctioning secretions and removing foreign material from the mouth and pharynx. (2) Hold up the patient's chin, pull out his tongue, or force the mandible forward by pressure behind the angle of the jaw to overcome soft tissue obstruction of the hypopharynx. Oral pharyngeal airways may be useful in the unconscious patient. (3) A bag and mask are often sufficient to ventilate the patient initially. Endotracheal intubation may be required in some instances (see Figure 3-1). (4) Tracheostomy as an emergency is rarely indicated, but it may be necessary if the upper airway is obstructed by edema or a foreign body (see Figure 6-1).
b. When due to other causes: maintain a clear airway, treat the underlying cause, and increase the inspired oxygen concentration if possible.
c. Respiratory arrest Clear the airway and institute mouth-to-mouth resuscitation (see Figure 3-2).
2. Cardiac arrest See Chapter 2.
3. Shock Anticipate and prevent shock by the measures outlined below:

a. Control hemorrhage and such contributing causes as exposure and pain. Reduce anxiety by reassurance and explanations to the patient.

b. Keep the patient comfortable, warm, and in a recumbent position. Avoid rapid changes of position.

c. Splint all fractures and apply traction if necessary to relieve pain and reduce soft tissue injury.

d. Transport as quickly as possible to a hospital. Provide prior warning to the hospital when possible.

e. For definitive treatment see Section I.

4. External bleeding

a. Venous and minor arterial bleeding can be controlled by direct pressure on the wound with sterile gauze or a clean cloth; elevate the bleeding extremity if possible.

b. Major arterial bleeding Compression of the major artery proximal to the wound plus direct pressure on the wound controls almost all external arterial hemorrhage.

A tourniquet is rarely necessary. Traumatic amputation and uncontrolled hemorrhage when only one person is available for resuscitation may require the use of a tourniquet. **Caution:** faulty use of a tourniquet may cause irreparable vascular or neurological damage. Tourniquets should not be left on longer than 30 minutes.

A MAST suit may be very helpful in controlling hemorrhage from the lower abdomen, pelvis, and lower extremities. It is particularly useful in patients with compound fractures and if it will take longer than 15 minutes to transport the patient to a hospital. Great care must be exercised to prevent 'declamping' shock when the suit is removed. Access to the circulation must be achieved and adequate volume resuscitation begun before the compression is relieved.

5. Pain Distinguish fear and excitement from real pain. Severe injuries cause surprisingly little discomfort. Immobilization of injured parts often relieves distress.

When pain is severe, give morphine sulfate, 2–4 mg IV every hour. **Caution:** narcotics are contraindicated in coma, head injuries, respiratory distress, and hypovolemia. The IV route is quick and sure. Peripheral vasoconstriction may delay absorption of a subcutaneous injection and will lead to overdosage if multiple injections are later absorbed at the same time. Inform the patient that he has received morphine and record the time and dosage on a note or tag affixed to his wrist, ankle, or forehead.

6. Open wounds

a. Remove gross foreign debris. Apply sterile dressing or a clean cloth and secure firmly in place.

b. Do not place antiseptic solutions or antibacterial powders in the wound. It is not necessary to cleanse the skin around the wound with soap or antiseptic.

c. Arrange for the earliest possible cleansing, debridement, and closure under aseptic conditions.

7. Fractures Splint all fractures as quickly as possible to prevent further soft tissue and neurovascular damage. (See Figure 1-2).

8. Transportation of the injured patient Improper methods of moving patients can cause further injury. Lift severely injured patients with care, and improvise stretchers (blankets, boards, and doors) when necessary. Transport patients in the recumbent position on a stretcher, preferably in an ambulance.

The physician administering first aid is morally, and in some areas legally, responsible for the patient until care is assumed by another physician.

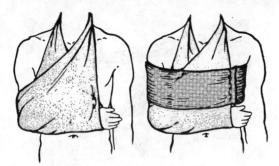

Method of Application of Sling and Swathe

Keller–Blake Half-ring Splint for Transportation of Patient With Fracture of Thigh or Leg. Spanish windlass on a Collins hitch.

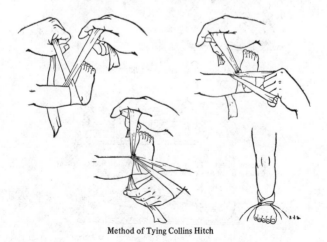

Method of Tying Collins Hitch

Figure 1-2

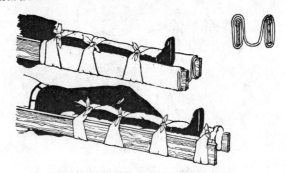

Padded Board Splints for Transportation of Patient With Fracture of Thigh and Leg. Outer board extends to axilla.

Method of Application of Pillow Splints

Reinforcement of Pillow Splint for Transportation of Patient With Injury of Ankle and Foot

Board or Door Used for Transportation of Patient With Injured Spine

Figure 1-2 (cont.)

III. BURNS

Burns may be caused by heat, ultraviolet light, x-rays, nuclear radiation, electricity, chemicals, and mechanical abrasions. Thermal injury from fire, steam, or scalding liquids is the most common type of severe burn.

A. STRUCTURE AND FUNCTION OF THE SKIN

1. Structure The skin is the largest organ in the body; it ranges from $0.25 \ m^2$ to $1.8 \ m^2$ and is divided into 2 layers, the epidermis and the corium or dermis.

a. The epidermis is a very thin layer of epithelial cells. The outermost cells are cornified dead cells which provide protection against the environment.

b. The corium is a thicker layer composed of fibrous connective tissue containing blood vessels, nerves, and the epithelial appendages (hair follicles, sebaceous glands, and sweat glands).

2. Function The skin is a physical barrier to penetration of the body by microorganisms. The small numbers of bacteria that penetrate intact skin are destroyed by immunological cells in the corium.

The skin (especially the corium) prevents excessive loss of body fluids by evaporation.

Sweat glands help regulate body temperature by increasing or decreasing the amount of water of evaporation.

Sweat glands also act as crude excretory organs by eliminating excess water, small amounts of sodium, chloride, and cholesterol compounds, and traces of albumin and urea.

The skin is a sensory organ; it allows a person to recognize and adapt to changes in the physical environment and thus provides important protection.

The skin serves as a person's identity (color, texture, grain, fingerprints, etc.)

The skin synthesizes vitamin D by the effects of sunlight on certain cholesterol compounds in the corium.

B. DETERMINANTS OF SEVERITY OF INJURY

1. Depth The depth of a burn significantly affects its healing. It may be difficult to evaluate depth, especially in infants whose skin is very thin. Certain symptoms and signs are helpful, but frequently the exact depth of injury can be determined only by observation over a period of days or weeks.

a. First degree burns involve only the epidermis, and are usually caused by sunlight or brief scalding. Tissue damage is minimal. Pain is the predominant symptom. The burned skin is erythematous, and there may be very mild edema. Systemic effects are rare. Pain resolves in 48-72 hours, and healing takes place uneventfully in 5-10 days.

b. Second degree burns involve all of the epithelium and much of the corium. The burn is characterized by redness and blisters. **Superficial** second degree burns usually heal with minimal scarring in 10-14 days unless they become infected. **Deep** second degree burns extend to the depths of the corium, and the dead covering resembles a third degree burn except that it is usually red and may blanch when touched. Healing occurs by regeneration of epithelium from sweat glands and hair follicles, this process takes 25-35 days. Dense scarring is common. Deep second degree burns become full thickness if they become infected. Fluid losses and metabolic effects are the same as in third degree burns.

c. Third degree (full thickness) burns are characterized by a dry, tough, leathery surface that is usually brown, tan, or black, although it may even be white or red. Blisters are uncommon. These burns are anesthetic because pain receptors have been destroyed. If pressure is applied to the burn, the surface will not blanch and refill because the tissue is dead and the blood vessels are thrombosed.

2. Surface area   The size of a burn is usually expressed as a percentage of the total body surface area and is most accurately estimated from age-related charts (Figure · 1-3). Accurate determination of the percentage of total body burn is useful because it directly relates to severity of injury, it is a good prognostic index, and helps determine which patients should be treated in specialized burn facilities. Fluid replacement is often governed by the burn size.

3. Age   Burns of any given depth and surface area inflict higher mortality in children under 2 years and adults over age 60. The mortality in infants is attributed to immature immune competence; older adults often have associated diseases that increase mortality.

4. Associated diseases   Diabetes, congestive heart failure, pulmonary disease, and chronic treatment with immunosuppressive drugs are among the conditions that make patients less able to tolerate burns.

5. Location of the burn is another determinant of severity. For example, burns of the hands, even if only second degree, may result in scarring and contractures which render the hand useless unless expert treatment is started early. Further, even minor burns of both hands may make it impossible for the patient to care for himself outside the hospital. Patients with perineal burns should be hospitalized because of the high incidence of infection.

6. Associated injuries   Inhalation injury, fractures, head injuries, and other trauma contribute to the impact of a burn on the patient.

7. Type of burn   Patients with certain types of burns should always be admitted to a specialized facility. Electrical or chemical burns may appear, superficially, to be quite minor injuries, but they often involve deep structures and are difficult to manage.

8. Pediatric burns   Burned children should be admitted to the hospital when the physician doubts that the parents have the ability to care for what appears to be a simple wound. Neglect can result in disability from relatively minor initial injuries. If suspicion exists that the burn might have been intentional, the child must be admitted to the hospital, a fact that cannot be overemphasized.

C. OUTPATIENT CARE OF BURNS   General guidelines for admission to specialized facilities are outlined in Table 1-7. Before treating a burn victim as an outpatient, however, the physician should have a clear understanding of the family situation and whether or not the patient or the family can take care of the burn wound.

The best first-aid for a minor burn wound at home is immersion in cold tapwater; no other agents are necessary, and some may be damaging. Following initial assessment, wounds should be cleansed and debrided with a cool physiological saline solution.

Controversy exists regarding debridement of blisters. Debridement leaves a cleaner wound with less chance of infection to develop in the blister fluid. The disadvantage is that the wound is more painful. All blisters that involve joint spaces on the hand should be debrided, and very large blisters in any location are best treated by debridement.

Tetanus prophylaxis (see Chapter 4).

The use of antibiotics immediately after a burn is controversial. Penicillin prevents the development of streptococcal wound infections, but these infections occur in only 5% of patients. If penicillin is given, it should be discontinued after 48 hours; in no case should broad-spectrum antibiotics be used.

The wound should be covered with a bulky dressing. The patient is instructed to remove the dressing, wash the wound with mild soap and tepid water, and replace the dressing at least daily. The pain caused by dressing changes is reduced by soaking the dressing with tepid water prior to removal or by using a nonadherent gauze impregnated with a bland emulsion.

Xenograft (pigskin) is very useful in treating some minor wounds.

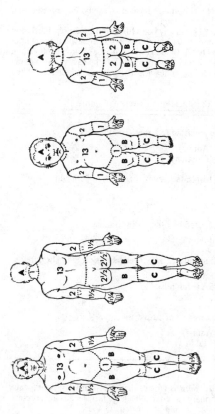

Relative Percentages of Areas Affected by Growth

Area	10	Age 15	Adult
A = half of head	5½	4½	3½
B = half of one thigh	4¼	4½	4¾
C = half of one leg	3	3¼	3½

Relative Percentages of Areas Affected by Growth

Area	0	Age 1	5
A = half of head	9½	8½	6½
B = half of one thigh	2¾	3¼	4
C = half of one leg	2½	2½	2¾

Figure 1-3. Table for estimating extent of burns. In adults, a reasonable system for calculating the percentage of body surface burned is the 'rule of nines': each arm equals 9%, the head equals 9%, the anterior and posterior trunk each equal 18%, and each leg equals 18%; the sum of these percentages is 99%. Reproduced, with permission, from Dunphy JE, Way LW (Eds): *Current Surgical Diagnosis & Treatment*, 3rd Ed, Lange, 1977.

Topical antibacterial agents in the outpatient care of burns is the subject of debate. There are no well-controlled studies that demonstrate significant improvement with these compounds.

In most instances, wounds will heal in 15–20 days; grease and flame burns may require longer.

D. ACUTE RESUSCITATION   Hospitalized patients should be assessed and treated rapidly as with any other major injury.

1. Airway maintenance   The airway takes first priority.   Smoke inhalation should be suspected if fire occurred in a closed space or if there are thermal injuries to the face, nares, or upper torso. Blood gases, including carboxyhemoglobin, should be determined. Oxygen should be administered. If the patient has extreme air hunger or is in critical condition, endotracheal intubation is indicated. When in doubt intubate.

TABLE 1-7. Classification of severity of burns

Major burn injury: Must be admitted to a specialized facility

> $2°$ burn > 25% BSA* (Adults)
> $2°$ burn > 20% BSA   (Children)
> $3°$ burn > 10% BSA
> Most burns involving hands, face, eyes, ears, feet, or perineum
>
> Most patients with:
> > Inhalation injury
> > Electrical injury
> > Burn injury complicated by other major trauma
>
> Poor risk patients with burns

Moderate uncomplicated burn injury: May need admission to the hospital

> $2°$ burn of 15–25% BSA (Adults)
> $2°$ burn of 10–20% BSA (Children)
> $3°$ burn < 10% BSA

Minor burn injury: Usually treated as outpatient

> $2°$ burn < 15% BSA (Adults)
> $2°$ burn < 10% BSA (Children)
> $3°$ burn < 2% BSA

*Body Surface Area

2. Fluid therapy.   If the burn is greater than 10% third degree or greater than 20% second degree, a urinary catheter and a large intravenous line, preferably a central venous pressure line, should be inserted.

Crystalloid solution is preferred during the first 24 hours, followed by colloid and water in the second 24 hours. The amount of crystalloid solution administered depends upon the response of the individual; formulas are useful guidelines but should not be adhered to rigidly if circumstances dictate otherwise. The **Baxter formula** is recommended among the various ones available: First 24 hours—balanced salt solution (lactated Ringer's injection), 4cc/kg/% burn; give half of this during the first 8 hours and the other half over the next 16 hours; Second 24 hours—5% dextrose in water (2000cc maintenance) and plasma in sufficient amounts to restore normal plasma volume.

Monitoring of fluid resuscitation: atrial filling pressure is the best index. Since left ventricular end diastolic filling pressure is impractical to obtain, central venous pressure is usually used. Urine output also reflects adequacy of volume replacement; 0.5 cc/kg/hour is the acceptable minimal output. Other parameters such as peripheral perfusion and sensorium should be followed.

In patients with inhalation injury, minimal administration of fluid is prudent, but fluid should not be restricted at the expense of renal function since the combination of inhalation injury and renal failure carries a high mortality.

Children may require more free water than older patients. This requirement can be monitored by frequent determinations of serum osmolality or serum sodium. Urine specific gravity can also be used to assess the amount of free water needed.

3. Tetanus toxoid (0.5cc) should be administered to all patients. If the wound is greater than 50% of the body surface area, 250 units of tetanus immune globulin (human) should also be administered.

4. Give intravenous narcotic (morphine 0.1 mg/kg or meperidine 1-2 mg/kg) to relieve pain. Avoid combinations of sedatives and analgesics. Give all medications intravenously.

5. Penicillin may be given to prevent infection by beta hemolytic streptococci. Penicillin should be discontinued after 48 hours.

E. CARE OF THE BURN WOUND   There are 3 methods of caring for the burn wound: the exposure method, occlusive dressings, and primary excision.

1. The exposure method is used on areas that are conveniently left exposed, such as the face. The burn is initially cleansed and allowed to dry. A second degree burn forms a crust that usually brushes off after 2-3 weeks leaving minimal scarring. The advantage of exposure treatment is that the patient is not immobilized in bulky dressings. The disadvantage is that the protection against infection afforded by sterile dressings is absent.

2. Occlusive dressings, nearly always combined with topical antibacterials, are the most common methods of burn care. The ointment or cream may be applied to the patient or to the gauze. The antibacterial agent most frequently used today is silver sulfadiazine. Other compounds are listed in Table 1-8.

3. Primary excision of the burn is gaining popularity. Methods include tangential excision, excision with special knives such as the laser or plasma scalpel, and primary excision down to fascia. In most instances, the wound is covered with autograft, homograft, or xenograft, depending on availability of these tissues.

Regardless of the method of wound care, patients are usually bathed daily in a Hubbard Tank where the dressings or cream are washed off. Debridement of all loose tissues is performed during the bath.

Debridement with proteolytic enzymes, such as sutilains (Travase), may be used to remove the tough eschar. Unfortunately, enzymatic debridement may predispose to burn wound sepsis since it allows rapid entry of bacteria into tissue planes and the blood stream.

Circumferential burns of the extremity or the trunk may require escharotomy to prevent venous obstruction from edema beneath the constricting eschar. Longitudinal escharotomy, or incision of the burn wound, may decompress these compartments. An escharotomy on the chest may relieve tightening and restriction of ventilation.

Another form of wound incision is the grid escharotomy. This is indicated if there is gross infection beneath the eschar; it serves to drain the wound and aid in debridement. The procedure is a series of multiple parallel incisions made diagonally across the burn with other multiple incisions made at right angles to them, thus dividing the wound into a grid with squares of about 2 cm^2.

The therapeutic objective in third degree burns is to remove all dead skin and to cover the defects with autografts. Multiple operations may be required. If insufficient skin is available for autografting, xenograft or homograft is an acceptable substitute temporarily.

Table 1-8. Comparison of common topical agents

	Mafenide	Silver nitrate	Silver sulfadiazine	Povidine-iodine ointment
Spectrum	Antibacterial	Antibacterial	Antibacterial	Antibacterial Antifungal
Penetration of wound	Good	Poor	Fair	Good
Effect on eschar	Results in delayed separation	Dries eschar	Softens eschar for easy debridement	Tans eschar making it tough and dry
Allergy	Common in children	None	Rare	Relatively uncommon in children
Pain	About 40% of patients	Painless	Painless	Burning sensation in approximately 11%
Type of dressing	Exposure or dressings	Thick-occlusive dressings	Exposure or dressings	Usually dressings
Mobility	Motion of joints maintained	Impedes movement of joints	Motion of joints maintained	Impedes movement of joints
Ease of use	Easy	Difficult because of attention to dressing	Easy	Easy
Metabolic changes	Carbonic anhydrase inhibitor	Electrolyte deficiencies and methemaglobinemia	None known	Elevation of PBI

The maintenance of joint motion during burn care is important. Loss of motion is related to two factors: immobilization and pain. The use of splints and elevation to maintain functional position of hands and feet, followed by aggressive physical therapy, will minimize these undesirable sequelae.

F. NUTRITION IN THE BURN PATIENT Metabolic requirements are increased 2–4 fold after thermal injury. Nutrition may be maintained by oral feedings, tube feedings, or total parenteral nutrition in descending order of preference.

Positive nitrogen balance is the goal; if it cannot be achieved with oral feedings, supplemental tube feedings or parenteral nutrition is necessary.

A daily count of caloric intake is mandatory; daily weight should be recorded, and nitrogen balance studies are obtained as indicated.

Tube feedings are given in the form of a blenderized diet or commercial preparations. The latter may be hyperosmolar, and care must be taken to avoid hyperosmolar coma and diarrhea.

Management of total parenteral nutrition is described on page 112.

Antacids should be given to prevent stress ulcers.

Supplemental vitamins and iron are required by most patients.

G. COMPLICATIONS

1. Sepsis is the most common cause of morbidity and mortality in the burn patient, particularly pneumonia.

a. Pneumonia should be prevented, if possible, by vigorous pulmonary toilet and frequent assessment of tracheobronchial flora. If the patient has sustained an inhalation injury, gram stains of the sputum should be obtained daily. If polymorphonuclear leukocytes or overgrowth of organisms is seen, appropriate antibiotics should be instituted and changed if necessary when results of cultures and sensitivities are available. X-rays should be used as corroborative evidence.

b. The burn wound is also a source of infection. The wound should be cultured, preferably by quantitative methods, at least twice a week. If burn wound sepsis occurs, systemic antibiotics should be given based on cultures and sensitivities. Subeschar injections of antibiotics should also be considered.

2. Bleeding from stress ulcers is a common complication of major burns, but can be prevented by routine administration of antacids. If bleeding occurs, the problem is evaluated and treated like upper gastrointestinal bleeding in any patient (see Chapter 10).

3. Unique complications in children include: seizures from electrolyte imbalance, hypoxemia, infection and drug administration; gastric dilatation, treated by nasogastric tube decompression; and hypertension, which occurs in approximately 30% of children and may require treatment with vasodilators.

H. RESPIRATORY FAILURE IN BURNS Inhalation injuries are caused by 3 mechanisms: heat, carbon monoxide poisoning, and inhalation of noxious gases. About 60% of burn fatalities are directly or indirectly due to inhalation injury.

1. Direct inhalation of heat was considered to be a rare cause of damage below the vocal cords because of the efficient way the upper airway cools inspired gases. Recently, however, it has been shown that inspiration of hot droplets and soot particles causes direct damage to the tracheobronchial mucosa, setting the stage for further damage by pneumonia and tracheobronchitis.

2. Carbon monoxide poisoning should be suspected in any patient with inhalation injury. Carbon monoxide poisoning is confirmed by measurement of carboxyhemoglobin levels. Symptoms are listed in Table 1-9. Treatment is by administration of 100% oxygen until blood gases return to normal.

3. The kinds of noxious chemicals inhaled in smoke depend upon the type of materials that are burning (Table 1-10).

4. Treatment, in addition to the measures listed above, consists of humidifying the inspired gases, tracheobronchial toilet, bronchial dilators in some cases, and mechanical ventilation if necessary. In general, the following criteria are used for institution of mechanical ventilation:

a. Inability to oxygenate arterial blood as shown by arterial oxygen tension of less than 60 mm Hg on room air or an alveolar–arterial oxygen difference of 300 on 100% inspired oxygen.

Table 1-9. Carbon monoxide poisoning

HbCO level	Severity	Symptoms
20% HbCO	Mild	Headache, mild dyspnea, visual changes, confusion
20-40% HbCO	Moderate	Irritability, diminished judgement, dim vision, nausea, easy fatigability
40-60% HbCO	Severe	Hallucinations, confusion, ataxia, collapse, coma
60% HbCO	Fatal	

b. Inability to ventilate adequately as shown by an arterial pCO_2 greater than 50 mm Hg.

c. Vital capacity that is less than 10 cc/kg body weight or less than 3 times normal tidal volume.

5. The use of steroids in patients with inhalation injury is a controversial issue. At the present time, the disadvantages appear to outweigh the advantages, and steroids are not recommended.

I. ELECTRICAL INJURIES are divided into 3 categories: true electrical current injury, electrothermal burns caused by arcing of the current, and flame burns resulting from ignition of clothing.

Tissues in the body vary in their resistance to passage of electrical current. Bone has the highest resistance. Heat is stored and dissipated into the surrounding muscle causing myonecrosis and subsequent myoglobinuria which may lead to renal failure.

Blood and nerve are the least resistant. Current passing through vessels may damage the intima and cause thrombosis; gangrene of extremities or intestine may be the consequence. Current passing through the brain may cause seizures or apnea. Ventricular fibrillation may result from electrical current passing through the chest.

Alternating current has an additional hazard as compared to direct current, since it may cause tetanic contractions and severe muscle and bony injuries. The heart is very sensitive to 60 cycle AC.

Almost all patients with electrical burns should be admitted to the hospital because the injury is often underestimated and sequelae are common.

Cutaneous burns are treated as other burns.

Myoglobinuria is treated by alkalinizing the urine and giving an osmotic diuretic (e.g., mannitol).

Late sequelae such as thrombosis of vessels are treated as they appear.

In injuries from high tension electrical sources, the amputation rate is at least 50%.

J. REHABILITATION OF THE BURN PATIENT includes treatment of both psychological and physical problems. Patients should be informed that achievement of optimal results may require years. The physician should be realistic as to what the 'optimal' results are.

The patient must take special care of the healed skin. Direct exposure to sunlight should be avoided; screening agents are useful on areas such as the hands and face. Creams and lotions to prevent drying and cracking are required. Lanolin, A & D ointment, and Eucerin are all effective.

Hypertrophic scar and keloid formation are common; they may be minimized by pressure dressings for 6 months following the injury.

Physical therapy is essential to restore motion to joints injured by the burn or immobilized in dressings.

The family of a burn victim undergoes extreme stress. There are often feelings of guilt. An experienced psychiatric nurse is an integral member of the burn team.

Table 1-10. Sources of noxious chemicals in smoke

Polyethylene	Clean burning
Polypropylene	Combustion to CO_2, and H_2O
Polystyrene	Copious black smoke and soot—CO_2, H_2O, some CO
Wood	Aldehydes
Cotton	(Acrolein)
Polyvinylchloride	Hydrochloric acid
Acrylonitrile	
Polyurethane	Hydrogen cyanide
Nitrogenous compounds	
Fire retardants may produce toxic fumes	Halogens (F_2, Cl_2, Br_2) Ammonia

IV. MISCELLANEOUS INJURIES

A. COMMON SOFT TISSUE INJURIES

1. Abrasion Loss of superficial epithelium caused by friction. The abraded surface bleeds from exposed capillaries. Treatment consists of cleansing the wound and application of sterile dressings; alternatively, abrasions may be left undressed.

2. Contusion (bruise) Interstitial hemorrhage and tissue damage from blunt trauma. Superficial contusions are minor, but fractures of underlying bones and injuries of internal organs must be ruled out. Application of an ice pack within the first few hours may limit the interstitial hemorrhage and subsequent ecchymosis.

3. Hematoma Liquid or clotted blood in the subcutaneous or intramuscular spaces. Hematoma is usually associated with contusion. Most hematomas will be resorbed, and surgical evacuation is seldom necessary. Clotted blood cannot be aspirated through a needle; incision, with careful aseptic technic, is the best method of evacuation.

4. Laceration A tear or cut in soft tissues. The basic steps in management are debridement, irrigation, and wound closure, usually under local anesthesia. Always examine for damage to nerves and tendons and for the presence of foreign material. Lacerations of the hand, the face, the scalp, and those associated with loss of skin require special care (see Chapters 14, 15, and 16).

a. Wound closure *Primary closure* is immediate suture of a wound. Absorbable material is used in the deeper layers and fine nonabsorbable sutures are placed in the skin. Lacerations that occur under relatively clean conditions may be closed primarily up to 24 hours after injury. Primary closure is used whenever possible for lacerations of the head and neck where the blood supply is excellent and the cosmetic result is important.

Delayed primary closure is used for contaminated wounds or those seen after 24 hours. A single layer of petrolatum gauze is placed in the wound and covered with fluffed gauze. The wound is examined in 48–72 hours and loosely closed with sutures or adhesive tape if it appears clean.

Secondary closure is suture closure of heavily contaminated wounds after several days. Many times it is better to allow such a wound to heal spontaneously by second intention than to attempt suture approximation of granulating surfaces.

b. Antibiotics Most small or clean lacerations do not require antibiotic therapy. When contamination is marked or when delayed primary closure is contemplated, systemic penicillin therapy is justified.

c. Tetanus prophylaxis This is recommended if contamination by soil is suspected (see Chapter 4).

5. Penetrating wound The chief complications of penetrating wounds are perforation of a viscus, introduction of bacteria, and retained foreign body. Treatment must be individualized. Clean puncture wounds and through-and-through missile wounds that cause no serious damage may require only observation. Penetrating injuries that drive clothing or other foreign material into the wound must be explored and debrided. Tetanus prophylaxis is usually indicated.

6. Foreign body Any open wound may contain a foreign body. Small, inert foreign bodies less than 1 cm beneath the skin can usually be left alone and checked by x-ray several months later. A foreign body should be removed if it protrudes through the skin; if it causes pain; if it consists of or is contaminated by dirt, cloth, wood, or other material likely to cause infection or reaction; if the wound is infected or draining; or if the foreign body may migrate to or impinge upon important structures. Tetanus prophylaxis should be given as indicated in Chapter 4. Exploration of a wound to extract a foreign body should be performed only after the foreign material has been localized by (a) x-rays in 2 or more planes with lead markers on the skin, (b) placing identifying marks on the skin under fluoroscopy, or (c) inserting a needle down to the foreign body under fluoroscopy.

B. BITES AND STINGS

1. Human bites (see also Chapter 15) Human bites are serious because of the virulence of aerobic and anaerobic organisms in the mouth. These bacteria are already proliferating under human conditions when they are implanted in the bite wound. Deep penetrating wounds of the knuckles incurred by fighting are especially serious due to frequent involvement of the metacarpophalangeal joint and extensor tendon. When the hand is opened, the glide of the extensor tendon carries infecting organisms proximally into anaerobic sites on the back of the hand. Cellulitis appears within 24–72 hours and may extend rapidly. Marked pain and swelling due to necrosis and abscess formation are the typical findings in the advanced case.

Emergency treatment of the fresh human bite wound consists of irrigation and debridement, extending the wound as required. Aerobic and anaerobic cultures should be taken and tests made for antibiotic sensitivity. **Do not suture the wound;** cover it with petrolatum gauze and dry dressing and splint the hand and wrist as necessary. Observe for infection, and administer full doses of penicillin pending the results of antibiotic sensitivity tests. Tetanus prophylaxis should be given.

If a human bite wound is seen late, obtain cultures, drain abscesses, place the patient at bed rest with the part elevated, apply hot moist packs, and give penicillin until the antibiotic of choice can be chosen on the basis of sensitivity studies.

2. Animal bites (see also Rabies in Chapter 4)

a. Dog bites Small penetrating wounds should be thoroughly irrigated and left open. Lacerations are debrided, irrigated, and sutured according to the usual principles. Tetanus prophylaxis is usually indicated.

b. Cat bites and scratches Cat bites are more likely to cause infection than dog bites. Cleanse the area thoroughly with soap and water, apply a dry sterile dressing, splint the part if possible, and observe for infection. Administer penicillin pending antibiotic sensitivity studies. Tetanus prophylaxis is given as indicated.

Cats may also transmit a condition known as cat-scratch fever. At the wound site there is localized cellulitis followed by regional lymphadenopathy; the nodes may suppurate. Encephalitis or pneumonitis occurs rarely.

3. Snake bites Nonpoisonous snake bites may cause pain but are otherwise minor. Four types of poisonous snakes are found in the USA: rattlesnake (several species), copperhead, cottonmouth moccasin, and coral snake. The venom of poisonous snakes contains proteolytic enzymes that are neurotoxic or hemotoxic. Neurotoxins cause respiratory failure; hemotoxic venoms cause hemolysis, local hemorrhage, and bleeding from mucous membranes.

The manifestations of poisonous snake bites are severe and persistent local pain, redness, and swelling followed rapidly by nausea, vomiting, and collapse. About 15% of adults bitten by rattlesnakes will die.

Treatment is outlined below.

a. Determine if the bite was made by a poisonous snake Poisonous snakes have fangs that make 2 puncture wounds where they enter the skin. Nonpoisonous snakes lack fangs, and the bite leaves semicircular rows of tooth marks.

b. Immobilization and transportation Keep the patient recumbent and quiet; muscular action tends to spread venom. Transport the patient by stretcher to a hospital at once. Give barbiturates for restlessness. **Do not give alcohol.**

c. Tourniquet Apply a tourniquet proximal to the bite. The tourniquet should be loose enough to permit insertion of a finger between it and the skin. It can be left continuously in place for 1 hour.

d. Cold pack Application of an ice pack to the wound will slow absorption of the venom and relieve pain. Packing of the entire extremity in ice is not advised.

e. Care of the wound (1) Wash the wound thoroughly with soap and water to remove venom from the skin. (2) Prepare the skin with antiseptic and make longitudinal incisions through the fang marks. Suction is applied by a suction device (or by mouth, if necessary, spitting out the venom and washing out the mouth frequently with water). Up to 50% of the venom can be removed in this manner if tourniquet, incision, and suction are used within the first 3 minutes. The method is useful up to 1 hour after the bite. (3) If appropriate facilities are available within the first half-hour (or 1½ hours if a tourniquet has been in place), the bite wound can be elliptically excised with a 1-inch margin to the depth required to remove the venom, which may be down to the fascia or into the muscle. This will remove 90% of the venom.

f. Antivenin Species-specific antivenin should be administered as soon as possible, after testing for sensitivity to horse serum. (Follow printed instructions in the package.) Identification of the snake is important in order to choose the correct antivenin. Polyvalent pit viper antivenin and coral snake antivenin are available from Wyeth Laboratories or from the National Center for Disease Control, Atlanta, Georgia, and from other sources in southeastern USA.

g. Other measures (1) Treat respiratory failure by oxygen administration and artificial ventilation (see Chapter 2). (2) Treat shock (see Section I). (3) Antibiotics have no value. (4) Corticosteroids relieve symptoms temporarily but do not lower mortality. Do not give steroids if the patient is receiving antivenin. (5) Extensive tissue necrosis requires debridement. (6) Fasciotomy may be necessary if severe edema compresses nerves or vessels in an extremity.

4. Spider bites and scorpion stings Bites and stings of many spiders and scorpions cause only local pain, redness, and swelling. Several species are quite venomous however. The toxin of the black widow spider (*Latrodectus mactans*) causes severe systemic symptoms, including generalized muscular pains, abdominal cramps, nausea, vomiting, and collapse. The abdominal muscles may become rigid, resembling an acute abdominal emergency.

If symptoms are severe, give specific spider or scorpion antiserum after skin testing. For convulsions or muscle cramps, give calcium gluconate, 10 ml of 10% solution IV, and repeat as needed. Additional measures include hot baths and control of restlessness with barbiturates. Treat the local wound by application of cold compresses. If the skin becomes necrotic, excision and grafting may be indicated.

C. BLAST AND CRUSH INJURY

1. Blast injury The blast force from an explosion can damage lungs and abdominal viscera. Localizing symptoms and signs frequently are delayed.

Diffuse alveolar hemorrhage with dyspnea and frothy hemoptysis is typical of blast injury to the lungs. Tracheal intubation or tracheostomy may be required to remove secretions and administer oxygen. Do not overlook pneumothorax or hemothorax.

Mild contusions of the abdominal viscera cause moderate discomfort and occasionally colicky pain which subsides in 48–96 hours. More serious injuries with impending or actual perforation produce signs of peritoneal irritation or shock.

Rupture of the ear drum causes severe pain and often deafness. No local treatment is required. Packs and ear drops are contraindicated.

2. Crush injury The crush syndrome is compression injury, shock, and acute renal insufficiency. Shock results from extravasation of blood and plasma into injured tissues after release of compression that has lasted for an hour or more. Renal failure is a consequence of prolonged shock and the nephrotoxic effect of myoglobin released from ischemic or dead muscle. Dark, brownish-red urine should make one suspicious of myoglobinuria; it must be treated promptly with an osmotic diuretic and alkalinization of the urine (see page 73).

D. THERMAL INJURIES OTHER THAN BURNS

1. Heat stroke About 4000 Americans die of heat stroke each year. The great majority of these victims are over 50 years old.

Early clinical symptoms include headache, dizziness, nausea, and visual disturbances. The skin is hot, flushed, and dry; absence of sweating is an important sign. The skin loses its vascular resistance, and cutaneous vasodilatation is prominent. Conversely, pulmonary vascular resistance is usually increased with high normal or elevated central venous pressure. A hyperdynamic state is common; heart rate and cardiac output are increased.

Renal problems result from decreased perfusion and myoglobinuria; the latter is due to rhabdomyolysis and disseminated intravascular clotting. Rectal temperatures may be as high as 42–44°C. Confusion, ataxia, seizures, and coma are common neurologic manifestations.

The objective of treatment is rapid lowering of body temperature by means of ice packs and cold water. The rectal temperature should be reduced to 39°C, after which one should proceed more slowly. Intravenous fluids and support of respiration may also be necessary, and heparin should be given for disseminated intravascular clotting.

2. Heat cramps are painful spasms of the voluntary muscles of the abdomen and extremities due to depletion of body salt by profuse sweating. Heavy manual labor in a hot environment may result in the loss of 3-4 liters of sweat (containing 0.2-0.5% sodium chloride) per hour. Persons working in high temperature areas should drink fluids liberally and should add 1 level teaspoon of salt to each quart of water, or they should take a sodium chloride tablet (1gm) with each 1-2 glasses of water.

In addition to cramps, there may be muscle twitchings. The skin is moist and cool, and body temperature is normal or only slightly elevated. Laboratory studies show a low serum sodium.

The condition is treated by moving the victim to a cool place. Cramps will frequently subside on rest alone. Give sodium chloride, 1 gm, by mouth every hour with 1-2 glasses of water, until 15 doses have been administered. In severe cases, 1-2 liters of physiologic saline should be given IV.

3. Cold injury The fundamental pathologic process is the same in all types of cold injury: arterial and capillary spasm, ischemia, and tissue damage. Blistering and edema due to plasma leakage through capillary endothelium is characteristic. The most serious destruction occurs in the skin and subcutaneous tissue, since cooling is greatest in these superficial structures. In the great majority of cold injuries, the tissues are not actually frozen. Freezing injury (frostbite) does not occur until the skin temperature drops to -4 to -10°C.

The likelihood of cold injury is increased by immobility, venous stasis, occlusive arterial vascular disease, previous cold injury, and a high wind-chill index.

a. Prevention 'Keep warm, keep dry, and keep moving'. Wear windproof and water repellant clothing, change wet garments and foot gear as quickly as possible, and maintain the circulation by frequently exercising the arms, legs, fingers, and toes. Avoid constrictive clothing and shoes and prolonged dependency of the feet. Head gear is mandatory because more body heat is lost from the head than from any other site. Protect the ears; they are the most commonly injured structures.

b. Trenchfoot (immersion foot) is the mildest form of cold injury. It usually results from exposure of wet feet to temperatures of 0-4°C for several hours. The first symptom is an uncomfortable coldness followed by numbness. Throbbing, aching, or burning and varying degrees of redness, cyanosis, edema, blistering, and skin necrosis occur after rewarming. The tissues may become gangrenous in severe cases of trenchfoot.

c. Chilblain (pernio) is the second most severe type of cold injury. It develops after prolonged exposure to temperatures below -6°C. It commonly affects the dorsum of the hand, but it may also involve the legs, particularly the anterior tibial surfaces in young women. Chilblain is characterized by a transient bluish-red caste to the skin with mild edema and pain, but blisters seldom form.

Treatment consists of rewarming the affected area promptly. Avoid trauma, massage, and excessive heat. Elevate the part if edema is present. Protect from infection by gentle cleansing and placement of a sterile, dry dressing over open vesicles and ulcers. The area may be sensitive to cold and painful after it heals. Hyperhidrosis can also result.

d. Frostbite is the most severe form of cold injury and is due to actual freezing of the tissue fluid. The length of exposure necessary to produce frostbite varies from a few seconds to several hours, depending upon the temperature of the environment and the wind-chill index.

Symptoms and signs: Local sensations of coldness or stinging give way to numbness, and the skin becomes pale. Hyperemia may occur after rewarming; during this phase the skin is acutely painful, warm, and red or bluish. These changes are followed by varying degrees of edema, blistering, and skin necrosis, depending upon the depth of injury. The phase of hyperemia and local warmth gives way to cyanosis, hyperhidrosis, and coldness with persistent burning pain. Prenecrotic skin becomes dark brown and finally black. These areas of dry gangrene eventually mummify and separate in 1–2 months.

Immediate treatment: (1) Rewarm rapidly by immersion in water at 40–42°C, with body heat, or by exposure to warm air. Do not expose to an open fire. Maintain general body warmth. (2) Avoid trauma. All casualties with foot involvement are litter cases; do not massage the affected part. (3) Prevent infection. Cleanse the part gently with bland soap. Dressings are not necessary if the skin is intact. (4) If blistering has occurred, debridement and placement of a biological dressing such as pigskin may be helpful.

General treatment: (1) Absolute bedrest is required when the feet are involved. (2) Slight elevation of the part may control edema but marked elevation diminishes the blood flow and is contraindicated. (3) Expose closed lesions to room air at a temperature of 21–23°C. (4) Rigid asepsis is mandatory in dressing open lesions. Use loosely-applied sterile dry gauze or xenograft. (5) Heparin may be of some value in preventing secondary thrombosis in surrounding areas if it is begun within 24 hours after thawing and continued for 1 week. (6) Tetanus prophylaxis (see Chapter 4). (7) Regional sympathectomy performed as early as possible after a severe full thickness cold injury appears to conserve tissue, promote rapid demarcation and healing, diminish pain, and minimize or eliminate some late sequelae.

Surgical treatment: Debride conservatively. Amputate only when demarcation is definite. Remove superficial necrotic tissue with aseptic precautions and cover large open areas with skin grafts as early as possible. In general, the tissue loss in cold injury will be less than appears likely initially. Necrosis may be superficial, and the underlying skin may heal well.

Treatment of sequelae: (1) Neurological measures: late sequelae such as hyperhidrosis, coldness, cyanosis, edema, chronic ulcers, and pain may be palliated by sympathectomy. (2) Orthopedic measures: pain in the feet on weight-bearing should be treated with well-fitted shoes and the use of pads, supports, and other orthopedic devices. Contractures due to fibrosis of muscles may require surgical release.

E. DROWNING Respiratory obstruction is the primary disturbance in drowning. Spasm of the larynx usually develops, and this leads to acute oxygen deprivation and respiratory arrest. Only a small amount of water may be aspirated, but the stomach is often filled with water. The body is cold, and the face is cyanotic and congested.

1. Emergency treatment

a. Clear the airway Remove mucus and foreign matter manually from the nose and throat, and drain water from the respiratory tract by gravity. Use suction if available. If possible, insert an endotracheal tube and inflate the lungs with oxygen, using an anesthesia bag.

b. Begin mouth-to-mouth respiration immediately (see Figure 3-2) and continue until spontaneous respiration returns or until death is absolutely certain.

c. If heart action fails, combine mouth-to-mouth breathing with closed chest massage. If ventricular fibrillation is suspected, attempt external defibrillation if equipment is available (see Chapter 2).

d. Loosen or remove constricting clothing.

e. Keep the patient comfortably warm.

f. In cases of near drowning in salt water, blood studies may indicate the need for intravenous infusions to correct hemoconcentration, electrolyte disturbances, or hypovolemia.

2

PREOPERATIVE &
POSTOPERATIVE CARE

Evaluation and preparation of patients preoperatively and care for them postoperatively share equal importance with events in the operating room. The operation itself is but one phase in a continuum of care that begins when the surgeon and the patient first meet and continues long after the last suture is placed.

Diagnostic evaluation of diseases requiring operation is described in appropriate chapters elsewhere in this book. This chapter discusses subjects that pertain to all patients with major surgical problems.

PREOPERATIVE EVALUATION AND PREPARATION*

I. EVALUATION

The primary purpose of preoperative evaluation is to identify problems that affect surgical risk. (See also specific sections later in this chapter). In addition, however, hospitalization provides the opportunity to identify other health problems that need attention, whether or not they have a bearing on the proposed operation.

A. HISTORY A complete health history should be obtained, including the present illness, past illnesses, and associated diseases. Inquire about bleeding tendencies, current medications, and allergies. Psychiatric history is important.

B. PHYSICAL EXAMINATION Thorough examination is mandatory. The cardiorespiratory system deserves careful attention. Do not overlook peripheral pulses, rectal examination, sigmoidoscopy (if indicated), and pelvic examination (unless contraindicated by age, marital status, or other reasons).

C. LABORATORY TESTS A complete blood count and urinalysis are required in every patient. Serology is also advisable. In hospitals with automated laboratories, a battery of 12 or more blood chemistry tests can be obtained rapidly and inexpensively; if these batteries are not available, serum creatinine and blood glucose are recommended. Stool should be tested for occult blood. Papanicolau smear of the cervix should be obtained in women over age 30. Infections should be cultured. Blood should be grouped and typed if the need for transfusion is anticipated.

D. X-RAYS Chest x-rays should be obtained in all adults.

E. OTHER STUDIES Electrocardiogram (ECG) is essential in all patients over age 40.

---

*By Theodore R. Schrock, MD

II. PREPARATION

A. CORRECT DISORDERS that affect surgical risk as much as possible. These problems are discussed in more detail below. Shock, hypovolemia, anemia, electrolyte imbalance, respiratory infection, cardiac decompensation, diabetic acidosis, renal insufficiency, and hyperthermia must be treated (or the operation postponed) in elective cases; in emergencies, the need for operation immediately may dictate that complete correction cannot be achieved.

B. INFORMED CONSENT   The patient and the family should be advised of alternative forms of therapy. The nature of the operation and its risks must be outlined and the signature of the patient or legal guardian obtained on the operative permit. In emergencies, with the patient unconscious and the family unavailable, operation may have to be done without a permit. The surgeon should know and follow local legal requirements.

C. PREOPERATIVE NOTE   The surgeon should enter a note into the record summarizing the history, findings, and indications for operation. The statement should include the fact that informed consent has been obtained.

D. PREOPERATIVE ORDERS   Orders are written on the day before operation to complete the preparation of the patient.
    1. Skin preparation   The area to be shaved is specified. Preferably, shaving is done immediately prior to operation, not the day before. The patient should bathe thoroughly the night before operation. The umbilicus is a repository for desquamated epithelium and dirt; it should be cleansed by the patient or the nursing staff. One-time use of hexachlorophene in detergent has no advantage over other soaps or detergents.
    2. Diet   No solid food should be taken for 12 hours and no liquids for 8 hours preoperatively. Infants having operation first thing in the morning should have the 4 am feeding omitted.
    3. Intravenous fluids   Consideration should be given to intravenous fluid administration **before** operation. IVs are unnecessary in many elective cases, but elderly or debilitated patients, patients given vigorous bowel preparation, patients having operations late in the day, patients having major vascular reconstruction, etc. may benefit from maintenance fluids starting the night before operation.
    4. Bowel preparation   Laxatives and enemas need not be given routinely to all surgical patients. Thorough mechanical (and antibacterial) preparation is essential if colorectal surgery is planned (see Chapter 4). Other indications for preoperative laxatives or enemas include: chronic constipation; recent barium studies of the gastrointestinal tract; ingestion of antacids containing aluminum or calcium; operations frequently followed by delayed bowel function (i.e., most abdominal operations). Partial evacuation of the colon is achieved by bisacodyl (Dulcolax) tablets (2-3) orally, or bisacodyl (10 mg) rectal suppository. More thorough cleansing is obtained by enemas with lukewarm physiologic saline or tap water (500-1500 ml). Saline is preferred, except in patients with risk of cardiac decompensation from absorption of salt.
    5. Medications   Bear in mind that the patient will be NPO for about 8 hours preoperatively. Medications during that time must be given IV or IM.
    Anesthetic premedications, including sedatives at bedtime, are usually ordered by the anesthesiologist (see Chapter 3).
    Medications currently taken by the patient may or may not be continued up to the time of operation. No rules can be stated that cover all possibilities, and each drug should be decided upon individually. Insulin, corticosteroids, digitalis and antihypertensive medications require special attention (see below in this chapter).

Antibiotics should be started preoperatively if they are used as prophylaxis against infection (see Chapter 4).

Low-dose heparin should be given preoperatively to some patients (see page 86).

6. Laboratory tests   Blood should be drawn for tests in the morning before operation in certain patients. Examples include blood glucose in diabetics, serum potassium in patients with renal failure, hematocrit if large blood loss is anticipated.

7. Blood transfusion   Blood should be cross-matched with the patient if the need for transfusions is anticipated. Blood components (e.g., platelets) must be arranged for in advance if they will be needed.

8. Activity   Ambulatory patients should be awakened and instructed to walk before sedation is given preoperatively.

9. Bladder   If a urinary catheter will not be used, the patient should void before anesthetic premedications are given. A Foley catheter is used in pelvic surgery, lengthy operations, operations with large blood loss, etc; it is kinder to insert the catheter after the patient is anesthetized, rather than before.

10. Respiratory   Patients with pulmonary disease should have a brief session of coughing and deep breathing with the incentive spirometer before sedation to clear secretions accumulated during the night.

11. Nasogastric tube   Unless the patient has gastrointestinal obstruction, a full stomach, or some other special reason, a nasogastric tube can be inserted after induction of anesthesia if a tube is required.

12. Venous and arterial catheters   A venous line is inserted the night before operation if preoperative IV fluids are required. Large-bore venous catheters should be inserted percutaneously or by cut-down, on the ward or in the operating room, if large blood loss is expected or if cardiac compensation is marginal. It is probably safer to place percutaneous subclavian lines on the ward, so that a chest film can be obtained to detect pneumothorax. Arterial catheters are used with increasing frequency in very ill patients or in those undergoing extensive operations; this can be done in the operating room as a rule.

13. Special   Complex operations may have special requirements not listed here.

POSTOPERATIVE CARE*

I. POSTOPERATIVE ORDERS

An operation automatically cancels all previous orders in most institutions. Postoperative orders must be written to cover all aspects of care.

A. The **TYPE OF OPERATION** should be stated so that the nursing staff and physicians unfamiliar with the patient will know what problems to look for.

B. VITAL SIGNS   The surgeon should specify acceptable limits for each vital sign; if a limit is exceeded, the surgeon should be notified (e.g., 'notify surgeon if pulse is <60 or >100'). The limits are different for each patient.

1. Blood pressure, pulse, and respiratory rate should be recorded every 15 minutes—more often in some cases—until the patient is stable. Thereafter, vital signs should be recorded hourly for several hours, then every 4 hours. The frequency of these observations obviously depends upon the nature of the operation and the patient's condition. Temperature usually is recorded every 4 hours, but

*By Theodore R. Schrock, MD

some patients become hypothermic during operation and others have fever before operation: these people are monitored more frequently.

2. Central venous pressure is measured along with the other signs. Be certain to specify the lower and upper limits that are acceptable for the individual patient.

3. Arterial pressure lines should be maintained once established. The line should be flushed with physiologic saline every 30 minutes. Arterial pressure usually is displayed continuously on an oscilloscope.

4. Pulmonary arterial pressure is measured in certain critical patients: a left atrial catheter is placed during certain cardiac operations for postoperative monitoring.

5. Continuous monitoring of ECG is advisable in ill patients.

C. ACTIVITY AND POSITION These orders depend entirely upon the patient's condition and the operation performed. The patient should be kept at bed rest until stable. For routine cases, patients are allowed to walk with assistance the evening of operation: or at least, male patients may stand to void.

Position is usually supine initially, but patients should be turned from side to side every 30 minutes while unconscious and hourly thereafter. Order active and passive motion of lower extremities every hour until ambulatory. Special precautions are required if the extremities are paralyzed from spinal anesthesia.

Position should be specified, e.g., supine, foot of bed elevated, sitting, etc.

D. DIET Nothing is permitted by mouth after most major operations: in other cases, a specific diet can be ordered immediately. In patients who are NPO initially, liquids are permitted when intestinal function resumes, and food is allowed once liquids are known to be tolerated. 'Full liquid' diet is an unnecessary step in dietary progression: sweet milkshakes and other items in a full liquid diet often are unpalatable to the postoperative patient. As a rule, solid food is permissible after clear liquids are tolerated.

Tube feedings and IV feedings are discussed in the section on Nutrition in this chapter.

E. RESPIRATORY CARE Patients on ventilators should have the pressure, volume, and oxygen concentration specified. Patients who are breathing spontaneously should be urged to cough and hyperventilate every hour or two to prevent atelectasis. An incentive spirometer is useful to encourage deep breathing. (See Pulmonary Complications in this chapter).

F. INTRAVENOUS FLUIDS Orders are written for the type of fluids and the rate of infusion (see Fluids and Electrolytes in this chapter). Be certain that an order is written for every venous line: unnecessary lines should be removed. Blood transfusions are ordered if necessary.

G. URINARY SYSTEM The rate of urine flow in catheterized patients is monitored as the vital signs are, usually hourly. If no catheter is present, the surgeon should be notified if the patient does not void by a certain time, preferably 6 hours after operation.

H. INTAKE AND OUTPUT of fluids from all sources should be recorded at intervals. usually every 8 hours, and body-weight is recorded daily following major operations. Minor procedures do not require such close monitoring.

I. TUBES, PACKS, AND DRAINS Care of each of these items should be specified (see below).

J. MEDICATIONS
1. Analgesics Narcotics are required for relief of pain in most patients. Morphine and meperidine (Demerol) are used commonly. In the recovery room

or intensive care unit, where the patient is monitored closely, narcotics are best given in small doses IV (e.g., morphine sulfate 1-2 mg) every 1-2 hours. On the ward, narcotics are given in larger doses IM (e.g., morphine sulfate 5-8 mg) every 3-4 hours. Doses vary with the patient; if more is needed, give it. But remember that narcotics depress respiration and that the most common cause of postoperative restlessness is hypoxemia, not pain: **narcotics given to the restless hypoxemic patient may be fatal.**

2. Antibiotics should be continued if necessary.

3. Other medications Insulin, corticosteroids, digitalis, antihypertensives, etc. should be prescribed as indicated. Scrutinize the list of preoperative medications and make a decision whether or not each is essential immediately postoperatively. Drugs must be given parenterally in patients who are NPO. Other medications not taken previously may be required by the nature of the disease or the operation.

K. LABORATORY TESTS AND X-RAYS The need for these studies varies. Hematocrit, serum electrolytes, urinalysis, arterial blood gases, ECG, and chest x-rays are among those frequently ordered. Do not order routine laboratory tests thoughtlessly.

L. SPECIAL Orders should be written to observe for developments that pertain to the particular operation performed, (e.g., neurologic signs after a neurosurgical procedure, pulses distal to arterial reconstruction, etc.)

II. DAILY ORDERS

New orders must be written and old ones renewed. IV fluids, medications, activity, diet, laboratory tests, x-rays, removal of drains and tubes, frequency of vital signs, etc. should be changed as necessary. Orders often remain in force long after they become obsolete because no one remembers to cancel them. Review orders each day and cancel those that are no longer essential. This relieves the nursing staff of unnecessary burdens and frees their time for more important tasks.

III. PROGRESS NOTES

A. DAILY PROGRESS NOTES provide a record of the patient's recovery. Like all entries into the medical record, these notes should be factual, concise, and dispassionate. The following parameters should be listed daily in the immediate postoperative period:

1. General description: mental alertness, mood, tolerance to pain, etc.
2. Vital signs.
3. Activity.
4. Diet (e.g., tolerance of liquids or food).
5. Respiratory status.
6. Intake and output: note output of tubes and drains specifically.
7. Intestinal function (flatus or stool per rectum, abdominal distention).
8. Wound.
9. Laboratory tests.
10. Special observations relevant to the operation.
11. Complications not mentioned earlier.
12. Plans for changes in treatment.

B. PROBLEM-ORIENTED RECORD The problem-oriented (Weed) system of medical records requires that a progress note be made daily for each active problem. For example, an active problem may be 'cholecystectomy'. Information is listed under each of 4 headings for each active problem: Subjective, Objective, Assessment, Plans (SOAP). This method helps ensure that recognized problems are not forgotten postoperatively, and it helps the surgeon to think logically about the patient's condition.

IV. CARE OF PACKS, DRAINS, AND TUBES

A. PACKS Certain wounds are packed with gauze of various types because they are infected, they are too large to close primarily, they are bleeding, or for other reasons. Packed wounds drain fluid and should be covered with absorbent dressings that must be changed when they become saturated. An effort is made to keep some packed wounds sterile in anticipation of delayed primary closure; others are obviously unsuited for sterile precautions. Packs should be removed as soon as possible; the timing is dependent entirely upon the circumstances in each case.

B. DRAINS are placed to permit egress of fluids that are already present or are anticipated to accumulate in the future. Some surgeons use drains rarely, others place them frequently. Drains in body cavities quickly become sealed off so that they are effective in only a local area; drainage of the entire peritoneal cavity is impossible.

1. Types of drains

a. Soft rubber strips or tubes Fluid travels by capillary action and gravity along the outside of these drains; fluid does not usually flow through the lumen. Penrose drains are a popular type of soft rubber hollow tube. If gauze is placed within the lumen of a Penrose drain, it is termed a 'cigarette drain'; the gauze offers no additional advantages over the rubber alone.

b. Gauze Strips of gauze provide a wick, and fluid moves by capillary action. The gauze ceases to be effective when its interstices are saturated. Gauze drains usually are used only in superficial locations.

c. Sump drains Sump drains have 2 lumens; one is for the egress of fluid and is placed on suction, and the other allows air to enter from the outside to maintain patency. Sump drains are available commercially or they can be constructed by the surgeon. They are useful if large volumes of drainage are expected over prolonged periods, and they are preferable for drainage of recesses of the body where gravity works against exit of fluid through simple rubber drains.

2. Management

a. The skin opening or the drains themselves must be covered with sterile dressings or arranged to empty into a collecting device (e.g., a temporary stoma appliance). The dressings should be changed sterilely, unless, of course, the drainage is already infected; in this case, care should be taken to avoid spreading contamination to other patients.

b. Sump drains can be irrigated through the air vent. Simple rubber drains cannot usually be irrigated effectively.

c. Drains should be removed as soon as possible. Long drains should be shortened and removed step-wise over a period of about 3 days to allow the tract to close from the depths. Some drains (e.g., those placed in subphrenic abscesses), are removed very gradually over many days to avoid leaving residual pockets of infection along the tract.

3. Complications

a. Drains are foreign bodies They incite inflammation, and fluid will emerge alongside drains for this reason alone. It is unnecessary, therefore, to wait until all drainage ceases before drains are removed; essentially, drains never stop draining.

b. Infection in the tract, and within the body cavity as far as the drain extends, is a problem if drains are left in for more than a few days or if sterile precautions are not observed in the care of dressings. Drains placed to remove fluid and prevent infection may in fact cause infection by bacteria entering from the skin surface.

c. Drains interfere with healing of incisions if they exit through the operative wound.

d. Drains placed in proximity to intestinal anastomoses interfere with the defenses of the peritoneal cavity against infection, they prevent adherence of omentum to the anastomosis, and they contribute to leakage of anastomoses.

e. Abdominal drains cause adhesions that may lead to intestinal obstruction.

f. Drains may erode into adjacent structures, (e.g., the intestine). Rigid sump drains are more likely to erode, but even soft rubber (Penrose) drains will do so if left for a week or more.

g. Drains may recede into the body cavity They should be fastened securely to the skin at all times. Drains sometimes break, leaving a portion of the foreign body in the wound when it is withdrawn. Persistent infection and drainage is the consequence. Examine removed drains to be certain they are intact.

h. The wound through which the drain is placed may not be large enough so that fluid accumulates inside rather than emerging to the outside.

C. TUBES

1. Nasogastric tubes are used to remove gas and fluid from the stomach. Soft rubber (Levine) tubes are the least irritating, but plastic sump tubes maintain patency with less care. Size 16 French is sufficient for most purposes; size 18 French is required in some cases.

a. Insertion

(1) Inform and reassure the patient.

(2) The tube is easier to insert if it is stiffened by cooling it in ice for a few minutes.

(3) Estimate the proper length to be inserted as follows: hold the distal end of the tube at the xiphoid; measure with the tube to the tip of the nose, then back to the ear and around the ear once. Mark this spot on the tube.

(4) Lubricate the tube.

(5) With the patient sitting up and with head tilted slightly back, slide the tube gently through the nares into the pharynx. Remember that the floor of the nasal passage courses inferiorly; if the tube is oriented superiorly, it will injure the turbinates.

(6) Plastic tubes have a curve from being packaged in a coil; when the tip of the tube is in the pharynx, rotate it 180° so that the tip points posteriorly. This will help avoid insertion into the trachea.

(7) Have the patient swallow (sips of water may help) as the tube is slowly and gently advanced through the esophagus. Coordinate gentle advancement with swallowing until the tube enters the stomach. Advance until the previously marked point in the tube is at the anterior nares.

(8) Gastric contents can be aspirated easily when the tube is properly positioned. Air can be injected through the tube and borborygmi heard over the stomach; this test is not entirely reliable. A better test is irrigation with saline; most of the irrigant should be retrievable with aspiration on the syringe if the patient is supine and the tube is well situated.

(9) Secure the tube to the nose. Take care not to wrap tape tightly around the nose lest pressure necrosis occur. The tube should emerge forward and downward from the nares in a straight line, not pressed upward against the nose as it is when taped to the forehead.

b. *Management*

(1) *Suction* Intermittent low vacuum should be used for simple tubes. Sump tubes can be connected to higher suction because the continual ingress of air through the vent prevents occlusion of the lumen by gastric mucosa.

(2) *Irrigation* Simple tubes must be irrigated with 30 ml of air every hour. Sump tubes do not require irrigation as frequently, although the tips of some models of nasogastric tube can become occluded even though the sump mechanism continues to function.

(3) *Removal* The tube is removed as soon as it is no longer needed.

c. *Problems and complications*

(1) *Discomfort* Nasogastric tubes are uncomfortable nuisances. Often a patient is more distressed by the tube than by the painful incision. Many surgeons reserve the right to remove nasogastric tubes for themselves; patients are very grateful.

(2) *Respiratory* Nasogastric tubes interfere with ventilation of the lungs and coughing to clear secretions. Removal of the tube helps atelectasis to resolve.

(3) *Drying of the mouth* and pharynx results from mouth-breathing. Lubricants to the lips, and mouthwashes help.

(4) *Necrosis* of the nares was mentioned above. This problem is preventable.

(5) *Esophagitis* This results from reflux around the tube which lies across the gastroesophageal junction and breaks the barrier normally provided by the lower esophageal sphincter. Prolonged nasogastric intubation can lead to esophageal stricture for this reason, and in some cases the stricture presents a therapeutic challenge for months after operation. Swallowing of antacids around the tube may help to prevent this complication.

(6) *Vomiting* around the tube usually results from poor placement; the tube should be repositioned.

(7) *Fluid depletion* and electrolyte derangement from nasogastric suction can be significant. H^+, Cl^-, K^+, and Na^+ may be lost in large amounts and must be replaced by IV fluids. Electrolyte losses through the tube are exaggerated if the patient takes water or ice chips by mouth.

(8) Other complications include nasal bleeding, sinusitis, otitis media, parotitis, laryngitis, necrosis of the pharynx, and retropharyngeal abscesses.

2. Long intestinal tubes are used to decompress the small bowel proximal to an obstruction. Nasogastric tubes do just as well if secretions and gas above an obstruction can reflux back into the stomach where the tube resides. Long tubes also are used by some surgeons to 'splint' the intestine and (it is hoped) permit adhesions to form without causing obstruction after extensive abdominal operations. Occasionally a tube is passed preoperatively so that the proximal bowel can be identified more readily. Surgeons vary greatly in their fondness for long intestinal tubes; some use them regularly and others very rarely find them necessary or even helpful.

a. *Types of tubes*

(1) *Single-lumen* These tubes have a balloon at the distal tip into which 2 ml of mercury are injected, (e.g., Cantor tube), or the tip has a steel weight instead (e.g., Johnston tube). Other single-lumen tubes have no balloon or weight; they are usually intended for insertion during operation, with the surgeon guiding the tip of the tube through the upper gastrointestinal tract. An example is the Leonard tube.

(2) *Double-lumen* One lumen is for aspiration of intestinal contents and the other permits inflation of the balloon at the distal end with air, saline, or mercury after the tube is inserted. A disadvantage is the small lumen for suction; it occludes easily. An example is the Miller–Abbott tube.

b. Insertion Most long tubes are passed nasally, but sometimes a tube is placed through the mouth during an operation. Still another route is through a jejunostomy constructed at operation; this method was described by Baker. The following procedure is used for nasal insertion:

(1) Measure the distance to the stomach as described for nasogastric tubes. Inform and reassure the patient.

(2) Lubricate the tube and pass it through the nares into the pharynx.

(3) If the tube has a balloon that requires direct instillation of mercury (e.g., Cantor tube), grasp the tip of the tube in the pharynx, pull it through the mouth, and add the mercury. It is advisable to make a pinhole perforation of the balloon to avoid progressive distention by gas that diffuses into the rubber bag.

(4) Replace the balloon into the pharynx and advance it into the stomach.

(5) Progression of the tube into the duodenum is facilitated by placing the patient on the right side, with the head of the bed elevated 30°. Fluoroscopy may be necessary to assist in this step.

(6) Once the tube enters the duodenum, the balloon of a Miller–Abbot type tube is inflated. It should not be taped to the nose or elsewhere at this point; it will advance slowly by peristaltic action. The tube should be lubricated frequently at the nares. X-rays record the progress. When properly positioned, the tube is taped to the nose.

c. Management Low vacuum suction is used. All long tubes, including the double-lumen types, must be irrigated frequently.

d. Removal Long intestinal tubes are withdrawn slowly, a few inches at a time, at intervals of about an hour. Tape the tube to the nose after each withdrawal so that this length of tube cannot move distally again. When the balloon reaches the pharynx, withdraw it through the mouth and cut it off; remove the tube through the nose. If the tube cannot be withdrawn from above, sever the tube at the nose and allow it to pass per rectum.

e. Problems and complications

(1) Distention of the balloon by gases diffusing into the balloon is prevented by making a pinhole opening as described above.

(2) Rupture of the balloon, even those containing mercury, is usually not serious.

(3) With double-lumen tubes, irrigating fluid can be instilled inadvertently into the balloon instead of the lumen. This can overdistend and rupture the balloon; very rarely, the balloon will distend so greatly that the intestinal wall is perforated. Be certain to mark the 2 channels before inserting the tube.

(4) Reverse intussusception during removal is avoided by slow stepwise withdrawal as described.

(5) Because long tubes decompress obstructed intestine and thus relieve pain, obstructions can proceed to strangulation without the surgeon's awareness of this development until it is too late. This is a complication of misuse of long tubes.

3. Bile duct tubes Straight or T-shaped, rubber or plastic tubes are placed into the extrahepatic bile ducts for external drainage, for decompression, and sometimes as an internal stent through a bile duct anastomosis.

T-tubes are the most common bile duct tubes. Long-armed T-tubes have one limb that passes through the ampulla into the duodenum; these tubes may obstruct the pancreatic duct and should not be used.

A circular or U-tube is a special form of biliary tube that is used to decompress obstructed ducts above an unresectable bile duct tumor. The U-tube enters the common bile duct, lies in the duct lumen through the obstructing lesion, and exits through the surface of the liver. Both ends are brought through the abdominal wall and connected together externally. If it becomes occluded by debris, this kind of tube can be changed without another operation.

  a. Management
  (1) The skin around the tube should be cleansed daily and covered with a sterile dressing at all times.
  (2) The tube is sutured to the skin at operation; in addition, it should be securely taped to the skin to avoid accidental withdrawal.
  (3) The tube is connected to gravity drainage.
  (4) Irrigation of the tube with saline or antibiotic solution is advocated by some surgeons; others believe that irrigation may introduce bacteria, raise the pressure in the biliary tree, and cause cholangitis.
  (5) Tubes are removed at varying intervals after operation, depending on the indication for placement of the tube. Tubes used for decompression after routine bile duct exploration are usually removed 10–12 days later, after a T-tube cholangiogram shows that the duct is normal. Tubes placed for other reasons are left for weeks, months, or even permanently. Tubes are removed by gentle steady traction.

  b. Problems and complications
  (1) The tube may be accidentally withdrawn, partially or completely. If the tube is partially removed and bile still drains through or around it, leave the tube in. If the tube is completely withdrawn, one may try to pass a straight catheter through the tract; this must be done immediately, and even then it may be impossible to reinsert the tube in the first few days after operation because a firm tract has not yet formed. Watch these patients closely for bile peritonitis or subhepatic collection.
  (2) Tubes may become occluded by blood clot or sludge. Irrigation may be attempted to dislodge the occluding material. If left for long periods, all bile duct tubes become occluded by debris.
  (3) Cholangitis is a risk if high pressure develops in ducts contaminated by bacteria. Such pressure may result from occlusion of the tube or forceful irrigation.

  4. Other tubes Chest tubes are discussed in Chapter 8. Sengstaken–Blakemore tubes are discussed in Chapter 10.

GENERAL CONDITIONS AFFECTING SURGICAL RISK*

Specific nonsurgical diseases affecting surgical risk are discussed in the next Section. General conditions affecting risk are considered here.

A. AGE Patients at the extreme ages of life have a greater risk of complications or death from operation because they have a narrow margin of safety; small errors that might be well-tolerated by a young adult are quickly compounded in the child or geriatric patient, sometimes with catastrophic consequences.

*By Theodore R. Schrock, MD

1. Infants   Special problems in pediatric surgical patients are discussed in more detail in Chapter 18.

a. Infants become severely hypovolemic from small losses of blood or fluid.

b. Vitamin K deficiency in neonates may result in bleeding from hypoprothrombinemia; give water soluble Vitamin K, 2 mg IM, 1 dose only.

c. Fever may cause convulsions or cardiovascular collapse; temperature should be lowered preoperatively by sponging with water and alcohol or by application of ice packs. An elective operation should be postponed if the child is febrile.

2. The elderly

a. Operative risk should be judged on the basis of physiologic rather than chronologic age. Do not deny the elderly patient a needed operation because of age alone. The hazard of the average major operation for the patient over 60 is increased only slightly provided there is no cardiovascular, renal, or other serious systemic disease.

b. Assume that every patient over 60, even in the absence of symptoms and physical signs, has generalized arteriosclerosis and potential limitation of myocardial and renal reserve. Accordingly, the preoperative evaluation should be comprehensive.

c. Occult cancer is not infrequent in this age group; investigate suggestive gastrointestinal and other complaints, even though they might be minor.

d. The elderly patient is apt to develop cardiac failure if the circulation is overloaded with excessive fluids. Monitor intake, output, body weight, vital signs, and serum electrolytes closely.

e. Elderly people generally require smaller doses of narcotics, sedatives, and anesthetics than younger patients. Respiratory depression may result from narcotics; barbiturates often cause mental confusion.

B. OBESITY   Obese surgical patients have a greater than normal tendency to serious concomitant disease and a higher incidence of postoperative wound and thromboembolic complications. Obesity also increases the technical difficulty of surgery and anesthesia. It may at times be advisable to delay elective surgery until the patient loses weight by appropriate dietary measures.

C. COMPROMISED OR ALTERED HOST   A patient is a 'compromised or altered host' if his or her capacity to respond normally to infection and trauma has been significantly reduced by some disease or agent. Obviously, preoperative recognition and special evaluation of these patients is important. Increased susceptibility to infection and delayed wound healing are the major postoperative problems.

Increased susceptibility to infection may arise from:

1. Drugs, such as corticosteroids, immunosuppressive agents, cytotoxic drugs, and prolonged antibiotic therapy. Infections in these patients may be caused by common bacteria, but sometimes fungi and other organisms that are rarely pathogenic are responsible.

2. Malnutrition.

3. Renal failure.

4. Granulocytopenia and diseases which produce immunologic deficiency (e.g., lymphomas, leukemias, and hypogammaglobulinemia).

5. Uncontrolled diabetes mellitus.

D. ALLERGIES AND SENSITIVITIES   A history of untoward reaction or sickness after injection, oral administration, or other use of any of the following substances should be noted so that these materials may be avoided:

1. Penicillin or other antibiotics, including sulfonamides.

2. Narcotics.

   3. Aspirin or other analgesics.
   4. Procaine or other anesthetics.
   5. Barbiturates.
   6. Tetanus antitoxin or other sera.
   7. Iodine or other antiseptics.
   8. Any other medications.
   9. Food (e.g., chocolate, milk, eggs).
   10. Adhesive tape.

E. CURRENT DRUGS   Drugs currently taken by the patient should be considered for continuation, discontinuation, or dosage adjustment. Medications such as digitalis, insulin, and cortisone must usually be maintained and their dosage carefully regulated during the operative and postoperative periods. Anticoagulants are an example of medication to be strictly monitored or eliminated preoperatively.

   The anesthesiologist is concerned with the long-term preoperative use of CNS depressants (e.g., barbiturates, opiates, alcohol), which may be associated with increased tolerance for anesthetic drugs, and with tranquilizers (e.g., phenothiazine derivatives such as chlorpromazine) and antihypertensive agents (e.g., rauwolfia derivatives such as reserpine), which may be associated with hypotension in response to anesthesia.

NONSURGICAL DISEASES AFFECTING SURGICAL RISK

I. CARDIAC DISEASE*

Cardiac conditions severe enough to impair the capacity of the heart to respond to stress can increase operative risk. Myocardial failure, ischemia, or serious arrhythmia may be precipitated by operation or its complications in patients who have minimal or absent cardiac symptoms under normal conditions. Cardiovascular function may be adversely affected by such common sequelae of surgery as apprehension, severe pain, fluid and electrolyte imbalance, infection, hypoxemia, hypercapnia, hypovolemia, altered peripheral resistance, hypotension, tachycardia, bradycardia, and arrhythmia. The cardiac patient, therefore, requires careful preoperative evaluation and close observation during and after operation. A cardiologist should be consulted if a significant cardiac condition is present preoperatively or if it develops in the postoperative period.

   Cardiac conditions most commonly associated with increased surgical risk are as follows: cardiac failure or limited myocardial reserve; coronary heart disease with a history of myocardial infarction or angina pectoris; major arrhythmia (fibrillation, flutter, or block); hypertension associated with coronary artery disease, cardiac failure, or renal insufficiency; valvular heart disease; and congenital heart disease.

A. PREOPERATIVE EVALUATION

   1. History and physical examination   The most common symptoms of heart disease are dyspnea, fatigue, chest pain, and palpitation. Signs include cardiac enlargement, murmurs, hypertension, arrhythmias, and such evidence of cardiac failure as distention of neck veins, dependent edema, rales, liver enlargement, and ascites. A past history of angina pectoris, myocardial infarction, Stokes-Adams attacks, stroke, cerebral ischemic attacks, intermittent claudica-

---

*By John C. Hutchinson, MD

tion, or previous treatment for heart disease or hypertension should alert the surgeon to the possibility of a cardiac abnormality requiring special study.

Conditions that contraindicate elective surgery because of increased risk are a recent occurrence of angina pectoris, a crescendo change in the pattern of angina pectoris in recent weeks or months, preinfarction angina, acute myocardial infarction, severe aortic stenosis, and a high degree of atrioventricular block.

2. Special examinations If symptoms, signs, or past history are suggestive of heart disease, the following examinations may further clarify the diagnosis and the functional state of the heart.

a. Electrocardiography The ECG is useful diagnostically and as a baseline for evaluating subsequent changes in the myocardium and conduction system. It may provide evidence of arrhythmia, myocardial hypertrophy or strain, coronary artery disease, digitalis effect, or electrolyte disturbance. The ECG has its limitations, however. Some patients with known previous myocardial infarction or, more importantly, with preinfarction angina, may have a normal ECG, while, in other patients, grossly abnormal changes may be due to an old infarct that has healed and is therefore of lesser significance.

In general, a stable abnormality in the ECG, in the absence of cardiac failure or angina pectoris, indicates that the operative risk is probably only slightly increased. A patient with a healed myocardial infarction has an added mortality factor of about 3–5%. Assessment of the stability of the current ECG pattern requires comparison with past tracings, if at all possible.

b. Chest x-ray This should be checked for abnormalities in the size and shape of cardiac and vascular contours and for evidence of valvular calcifications and pulmonary vascular congestion. Again, serial films are helpful.

c. Central venous pressure Elevations above 10 cm H_2O demonstrate right ventricular failure. Normal CVP does not exclude left ventricular failure, however.

d. Cardiac catheterization and angiography These examinations are rarely required except in preparation for cardiac surgery. However, if a patient with serious congenital or coronary heart disease is under consideration for elective surgery, it may be necessary to complete one or both of these studies in order to decide whether corrective cardiac surgery should take precedence.

e. Determination of *pulmonary arterial wedge pressure* is possible by use of the Swan-Ganz flow-directed catheter, and indicates left ventricular filling pressure. Serial values can guide fluid therapy, even in the presence of left ventricular failure. Values below 10 mm Hg may be associated with shock; above 25 mm Hg, with pulmonary edema.

f. Exercise tolerance tests Rarely, an exercise ECG test may be warranted if the diagnosis of coronary heart disease is seriously in doubt. Do not do an exercise test unless the resting ECG is normal, the patient has had no digitalis for 3 weeks, and the onset of pain of an anginal type is not of recent origin. A simple but adequate exercise tolerance test is to have the patient walk up 3 flights of stairs. If this can be accomplished without precipitating angina and without stopping because of dyspnea, there probably is no significant deficit in cardiopulmonary function.

B. PREOPERATIVE PREPARATION The cardiac patient should achieve the best possible cardiac status before surgery. Special attention should be paid to correction of electrolyte imbalance, fluid excess, and anemia (with packed red cells rather than whole blood). Alert all those concerned with the patient's care during and after the operation to the importance of avoiding hypotension, hypoxia, excessive sodium, fluid, and blood administration, and undue pain or excitement. These stresses may precipitate major cardiac complications.

1. Cardiac failure Cardiac failure should be treated before surgery. It is desirable to have the patient stabilized for at least 1 month preoperatively, with special care to avoid digitalis toxicity and potassium depletion from diuretics. If the patient is well-controlled for a month, digitalis and diuretics can be avoided for a few days before surgery. In the presence of such symptoms and signs as dyspnea when walking on level ground, orthopnea or nocturnal dyspnea, gallop rhythm, increased venous pressure, and rales, the risk of surgery is significantly increased and the operation should be delayed if possible. Patients with mild cardiac failure whose symptoms and signs are controlled with digitalis and diuretics have only a slightly increased surgical risk, provided that they are able to perform ordinary activities without symptoms.

2. Coronary artery disease Many surgical patients, most of whom are in the older age group, have either occult or symptomatic coronary artery disease. A history of previous myocardial infarction or angina is frequently obtained and its implication must be assessed. Important danger signals, indicating markedly increased surgical risk, are crescendo in the character of the anginal pain, pain at rest, and the possibility of preinfarction angina or actual recent myocardial infarction. Under these circumstances, elective surgery should be deferred.

When emergency surgery must be done in spite of recent myocardial infarction, the mortality rate has been 30-50%. Surgery that is important but not urgent should be delayed at least 3 weeks if possible following myocardial infarction. Elective surgery should be postponed 6 months. If at least 6 months have elapsed following a myocardial infarction, if the coronary artery disease is stable as evidenced by no change in pattern of pain or in the serial ECG, if there are no signs of cardiac failure, and if the indications for surgery are definite, operation can be undertaken.

3. Arrhythmias Atrial premature beats occur more frequently in diseased hearts and may forebode supraventricular arrhythmias, for which monitoring is indicated. Occasional ventricular premature beats generally have no definite significance; they may respond to treatment with phenobarbital. When ventricular premature beats are frequent and arise from multiple foci, when they occur with rapid ventricular rates or in runs, or when they appear during digitalis administration, they may be an indication of severe myocardial disease or digitalis toxicity and thus may require preoperative study and treatment. Partial (second degree) or complete (third degree) heart block indicates organic heart disease. The patient should be monitored; prior to a surgical procedure, it may be advisable to insert a transvenous electrode catheter into the right ventricle and have a pacemaker available in case ventricular standstill occurs. These patients are candidates for permanent pacemakers.

4. Hypertension Moderate hypertension alone does not affect the surgical risk significantly unless renal or cardiac complications are present. Patients with uncomplicated chronic hypertension, even with left ventricular hypertrophy and an abnormal ECG, tolerate surgery well if there is no evidence of coronary heart disease or cardiac failure and if renal function is normal. Operative risk is minimized by controlling the blood pressure into the range 140-160/85-95. This control may require the continuation of antihypertensive drugs through the entire operative period. If thiazides have been used, be certain that the body potassium level is normal. Catechol depletion following reserpine, methyldopa, and guanethidine can be managed satisfactorily if the anesthesiologist is forewarned and is prepared to give vasopressors if hypotension occurs. If the blood pressure rises out of control in the operative period, sodium nitroprusside, by carefully regulated IV infusion, is a useful and powerful temporary measure.

5. Valvular heart disease Acquired valvular conditions that affect operative risk adversely are severe aortic stenosis and tight mitral stenosis. An aortic systolic murmur without significant valvular disease or important left ventricular hypertrophy does not increase the mortality rate. Mitral insufficiency is usually well-tolerated, but tight mitral stenosis may result in pulmonary edema, especially if the patient has sinus rhythm and if there is abrupt fibrillation during surgery. Severe coronary ostial involvement from syphilitic aortitis considerably increases the hazard of operation. Assessment of the severity of valvular heart disease by echocardiography is currently widely available.

6. Congenital heart disease Uncomplicated ventricular or atrial septal defect does not usually increase surgical risk. Coarctation of the aorta and patent ductus arteriosus should usually be repaired before other kinds of elective surgery. Patients with tetralogy of Fallot are poor surgical risks because of polycythemia and the probability of contraction of the infundibulum and decreased cardiac output; corrective surgery should be considered before major elective surgery. Pulmonic stenosis, if mild, does not contraindicate elective surgery, but severe pulmonic stenosis does; it should probably be corrected first because of the danger of acute right heart failure or a reversed shunt through a patent foramen ovale or atrial septal defect. Pulmonary hypertension with Eisenmenger's syndrome significantly increases mortality and is a contraindication to surgery unless the need is urgent.

In all cyanotic heart conditions the danger of emboli, such as clots or bubbles, crossing to the arterial circulation is very high. Extreme caution should be exercised with all IV injections.

C. PROGNOSIS Generalizations about the cardiac patient's prognosis for survival of surgery are difficult. Large series of cardiac patients have shown an average mortality of only 3% after major abdominal and thoracic surgery. Certain cardiac conditions, however, are associated with an inherently greater surgical risk. Coronary heart disease is the commonest of these encountered in practice. In general, surgical mortality for major procedures is doubled by congestive failure or angina with mild exertion. Risk is further increased in the presence of serious arrhythmia or a history of myocardial infarction within 6 months. Angina at rest quadruples the risk and recent myocardial infarction raises the risk to a practically prohibitive level.

II. PULMONARY DISEASE*

Operative morbidity and mortality are adversely affected by acute and chronic diseases of the respiratory tract. The extent of preoperative assessment that is required depends upon the patient's age, evidence of preexisting disease, and the type of operation to be performed. Operations under local anesthesia generally require minimal respiratory evaluation. Any procedure involving general anesthesia requires more attention to pulmonary risk. Patients over age 60 and patients with chronic pulmonary disease should have brief mechanical pulmonary function testing (vital capacity and forced expiration volume) and preoperative arterial blood gas determinations. Patients in the highest risk groups and those who are to undergo thoracotomy, particularly if pulmonary resection is contemplated, should have extensive testing of pulmonary function.

Acute respiratory conditions affecting operative risk are mainly infections. Any respiratory infection (e.g., pharyngitis, bronchitis, or pneumonitis) is a contraindication to elective surgery and should be resolved for 1-2 weeks before operation is done. If emergency operation is required in the presence of acute respiratory infection, inhalation anesthetics should be avoided if possible, and antibiotic therapy should be administered if a bacterial cause is evident.

Most pulmonary conditions that present a significant risk are chronic and involve some degree of airway obstruction. Chronic bronchitis, bronchiectasis, emphysema, and asthma are the usual conditions seen today. Smoking is a common accompaniment of these disorders and is a significant risk factor in itself. Assessment of chronic pulmonary disease requires evaluation of airway obstruc-

*By Frank R. Lewis, Jr. MD

tion and vital capacity. This will be discussed in detail in the following section. A history of sputum production should be obtained, and, if present, sputum should be studied by smear and culture. Purulent sputum is an indication for specific antibiotic treatment preoperatively, usually for a period of 1-2 weeks until the sputum is no longer purulent and the amount of sputum decreases. Copious production of sputum should raise the possibility of bronchiectasis or lung abscess. Smokers should abstain for 2 weeks before elective operations.

A. PREOPERATIVE EVALUATION   Initial assessment of the patient for pulmonary disease is based on information obtained from the history, physical examination, and any exercise testing carried out. In patients who will undergo minor surgical procedures, and in those who are at minimal risk even if major procedures are planned, the assessment may stop at this point. If a question is raised, or if obvious pulmonary problems exist, clinical evaluation is not enough, and specific laboratory tests must be done to categorize the pulmonary dysfunction and its severity.

1. History   The essential features to be elicited are a history of known pulmonary disease or symptoms, positional or exercise limitations that produce shortness of breath, respiratory difficulties with previous operations, smoking, sputum production, and hemoptysis. Any positive items in the history must be followed up in detail and the cause specifically determined.

2. Physical examination   Physical findings to be noted are the rate and character of respirations, thoracic anatomy, presence or absence of respiratory distress, use of accessory muscles of respiration, and evidence of restriction of rib cage motion on one or both sides.

a. Patients with chronic bronchitis and emphysema often have an increased anterior-posterior thoracic diameter and a noticeably prolonged expiratory phase to their breathing. In severe cases, the use of accessory muscles of respiration may be marked with the patient laboring, even at rest, to exchange adequate amounts of air.

b. Tachypnea is an often overlooked symptom of respiratory problems, especially acute ones. If the patient is unable to breathe deeply enough, he compensates by breathing more rapidly.

A second cause of tachypnea is increased stiffness of the lungs; this usually occurs with acute conditions. When the lungs become stiff (decreased compliance), the elastic work of breathing is accentuated, and less energy is expended if the tidal volume is small and the rate is high.

A third reason for tachypnea is a marked increase in physiologic dead space which results in an increased fraction of wasted ventilation with each breath. In order to achieve a given amount of alveolar ventilation, the rate or depth must be increased.

All of these problems represent significant pulmonary disease and increased surgical risk. Tachypnea (greater than 25 respirations per minute) in any patient signals the need for intensive investigation of the cause.

3. Exercise tests   Simple exercise testing is a rough indication of the patient's functional reserve. The ability to walk vigorously on the level for about 100 meters, and the ability to climb 2 flights of stairs without pausing, are commonly used exercise tests. If the patient about to undergo thoracic or major abdominal surgery is unable to do these tests, further pulmonary function studies must be obtained.

B. PULMONARY FUNCTION TESTS

1. Physiology   The transport of oxygen from the external environment to the intracellular organelles which utilize it in metabolism may be analyzed in 5 steps: (a) Physical exchange of air in the environment with gas in the alveoli of the lung. (b) Diffusion of oxygen from the alveoli into the pulmonary capillaries.

(c) Transport of oxygenated blood from pulmonary capillaries to peripheral tissue beds. (d) Diffusion through the peripheral capillary walls and the interstitial space into oxygen-consuming cells. (e) Intracellular utilization by mitochondria.

The first 2 steps in this cycle are ordinarily evaluated with pulmonary function tests. The third step is evaluated by studies of cardiac function and oxygen-carrying capacity of the blood. The last 2 steps are assessed by usual clinical methods, but they may be investigated by certain research procedures which measure tissue P_{O_2} tensions.

2. Ventilation

a. Physical exchange of gas from the environment to the alveolar space is defined as ventilation. The total volume of gas exchanged per minute is termed the minute ventilation. A portion of this goes to ventilate the physiologic dead space and is termed the wasted ventilation or dead space ventilation, and the remainder goes to ventilate alveolar spaces which are perfused with blood and is defined as **alveolar ventilation.** Only the latter is effective in gas exchange.

b. Mechanical breathing function relates generally to 3 factors: the relative stiffness of the lungs, the muscle power which is available to overcome this resistance and move gas in and out of the lungs, and the resistance of the airways through which the air moves.

c. The vital capacity is defined as the maximal amount of air which a patient can move from full inspiration to full expiration; it provides a measure of the first 2 factors. If the lungs are excessively stiff (low compliance), or if the intercostal muscles and diaphragm are weak, vital capacity is reduced. Normal vital capacity is 65-70 ml/kg of body weight. One must have a vital capacity of at least 10-15 ml/kg of body weight, or approximately 15-20% of normal, in order to maintain spontaneous ventilation.

d. In patients who are intubated, the relative stiffness of the lungs may be assessed directly by measuring the volume of gas which can be exchanged with a given pressure change. This is defined as **compliance** (the inverse of stiffness) and is expressed as ml/cm H_2O pressure.

e. Airway resistance is determined by measuring the volume of gas which can be exhaled forcibly in 1 second (FEV_1). Normally more than 80% of vital capacity can be exhaled in 1 second. If less than 70% is exhaled, some degree of obstruction is present. If less than 60% can be exhaled in 1 second, the obstructive disease is severe. If the FEV_1 is reduced, more sophisticated tests of pulmonary function are indicated, including measurement of maximal expiratory flow rates, flow volume curves, airway resistance, and changes in these measurements after the use of bronchodilators.

f. The arterial carbon dioxide tension (P_{CO_2}) provides an index of the adequacy of alveolar ventilation. Normal values are 38-42 mm Hg. Elevation of the P_{CO_2} under resting conditions reflects compromised pulmonary function, usually obstructive in nature, and must be evaluated.

3. Alveolar-capillary diffusion The second phase of oxygen transport is the diffusion of oxygen from the alveoli into the blood in the pulmonary capillaries. Diffusion is evaluated by measuring arterial oxygen tension (P_{O_2}). Under normal conditions, breathing room air, the arterial oxygen tension will be greater than 95 mm Hg in patients under 40 years of age. Normal values decline approximately 5 mm Hg for each decade of additional age. Pulmonary parenchymal diseases (e.g., atelectasis, pneumonia, aspiration, fat embolism, or pulmonary embolism) can cause marked hemoglobin desaturation, and the arterial P_{O_2} while breathing room air may be as low as 40 or 50 mm Hg. Any reduction below 70 mm Hg while breathing room air is an indication of significant parenchymal disease. An effort should be made at all times to maintain the arterial P_{O_2} above 60 mm Hg by increasing the concentration of inspired oxygen, either by mask, or, if necessary, by endotracheal intubation.

C. PREOPERATIVE PREPARATION   After the extent of pulmonary disease has been defined, a decision must be made about the risk it poses for the patient. In certain cases, the risk may be sufficiently great to contraindicate the proposed operation, e.g., when a pneumonectomy might make it impossible for the patient to ventilate adequately with the remaining lung. In most circumstances, however, preoperative preparation improves respiratory function to the point that the patient can tolerate the operation. If emergency surgery is necessary for a life-threatening condition, one obviously must accept whatever risk is present and attempt to treat the pulmonary disease in the postoperative period.

  1. Acute respiratory conditions   When respiratory problems are due to acute infections, the patient should be treated with antibiotics and the operation postponed. Emergency operations must be done despite respiratory infection. Specific antibiotics are chosen initially on the basis of a gram stain of the sputum or pharyngeal swab and changed if necessary when results of culture and sensitivity tests become available.

  2. Chronic respiratory conditions   Patients who have chronic lung disease cannot be returned to a normal state, and some compromise must be reached which represents the best achievable pulmonary function. Such patients should be hospitalized for 1-2 weeks and treated with antibiotics, nebulized bronchodilators, intermittent positive pressure ventilation, postural drainage, and respiratory exercises. With significant pulmonary impairment, planned postoperative endotracheal intubation and mechanical ventilation may be necessary.

III. RENAL DISEASE*

A. CAUSES OF CHRONIC RENAL FAILURE include the following:

  1. Primary glomerular diseases (e.g., glomerulonephritis).

  2. Renovascular diseases, including nephrosclerosis from hypertension. Hypertension plays a dual role in chronic renal disease. It may be the primary problem leading to renal failure, or it may occur in the course of other renal diseases and accelerate the progression to renal failure.

  3. Metabolic diseases with renal involvement, such as diabetes and amyloidosis.

  4. Interstitial nephrides, including nephrotoxic diseases.

  5. Obstructive uropathy.

  6. Chronic nonobstructive pyelonephritis (at present a rare cause of renal failure.

  7. Polycystic kidney disease.

B. MANIFESTATIONS OF CHRONIC RENAL FAILURE   Symptoms and signs of renal disease frequently reflect the degree of renal failure; on the other hand, it is not uncommon for patients with marked impairment of renal function to be essentially asymptomatic. The progression of chronic renal disease may be divided into 3 phases:

  1. Diminished renal reserve   Although renal reserve is diminished, the excretory and regulatory functions of the kidney are still adequate.

  a. Creatinine clearance is greater than 30 cc/minute.

  b. The blood urea nitrogen (BUN) rises, but the value may still be within the normal range.

  c. Symptoms are usually absent except for nocturia, which is an early manifestation of the loss of concentrating ability

  2. Renal failure

  a. Creatinine clearance is less than 30 cc/minute and the BUN is distinctly elevated (azotemia).

*By Flavio Vincenti, MD

b. A variety of symptoms, such as fatigue, poor appetite, and pruritus may occur.

c. Anemia, acidosis, hyperphosphatemia, hypocalcemia and hyponatremia can develop.

d. Significant hyperkalemia is absent unless the intake of potassium is greatly exaggerated.

3. Uremia is the terminal phase of renal failure and is present when the creatinine clearance is less than 10 cc/minute; the BUN is usually well above 100 mg/100 ml. Symptoms and their severity vary greatly.

a. CNS dysfunction may be manifested by the loss of higher integrative functions, memory loss, personality changes, and alteration in consciousness.

b. Peripheral nervous system disease includes sensory and motor neuropathy, the restless leg syndrome, fasciculations, and asterixis.

c. Hypertension, congestive heart failure, and edema are frequently present.

d. Pericarditis and pericardial effusion may occur in the terminal stages of uremia; these signs were ominous in the predialysis era.

e. Gastrointestinal symptoms include nausea, vomiting, anorexia, weight loss, metallic taste, and enterocolitis.

f. Hematologic disorders Anemia, bleeding tendency due to platelet dysfunction, and impaired immunological function.

g. Endocrine-metabolic Impaired carbohydrate tolerance, hyperlipidemia, abnormal thyroid function tests, hyperuricemia, infertility, and sexual dysfunction.

h. Musculoskeletal Bone pain, pathologic fractures, hypocalcemia, hyperphosphatemia, hyperparathyroidism, osteomalacia, and metastatic soft tissue calcification.

C. PREOPERATIVE EVALUATION

1. Laboratory tests

a. Determination of the BUN, the serum creatinine, and routine urinalysis are adequate screening tests for renal disease.

b. A freshly voided urine sample may yield much information about the renal disease. Hematuria may be secondary to glomerular disease or to a lesion in the collecting system. Different types of casts are found in the urine of advancing renal disease. Red-cell casts are very strongly suggestive of an inflammatory glomerular lesion (glomerulonephritis), and white cell casts, especially in the presence of bacteria, are indicative of acute pyelonephritis.

c. In patients with reduced muscle mass, serum creatinine can remain within the range of normal even though creatinine clearance is no more than 20% of normal.

d. A BUN : creatinine ratio well above 10 : 1 may reflect prerenal azotemia, GI bleeding, enhanced catabolic states, or the catabolic effect of drugs (e.g., tetracycline, steroids).

2. X-rays Chest x-rays in patients with chronic renal disease frequently show an enlarged cardiac silhouette, prominent pulmonary vasculature, and, in later stages, pleural or pericardial effusions. Even in advanced renal disease, an infusion intravenous pyelogram may establish kidney size and the presence of urinary obstruction, cysts, and calcifications. Renal arteriograms and retrograde pyelography are needed occasionally. Renal scans are not very helpful diagnostic tools in chronic renal disease.

D. PREOPERATIVE PREPARATION

1. Evaluate renal function carefully.

2. Correct electrolyte imbalance. In severe renal failure, hemodialysis may be advisable.

3. Anemia is a frequent finding. Hemodialysis patients adapt to hematocrits in the range of 20% and do not need transfusions unless significant losses occur. Blood transfusions should be given cautiously to avoid cardiac decompensation.

4. Patients with severe renal failure may have bleeding because of platelet dysfunction. Elective surgery should be delayed until platelet dysfunction has been reversed by hemodialysis.

5. Antihypertensive medication should be stopped prior to surgery. However, discontinuation of clonidine may result in paroxysmal hypertension, and abrupt withdrawal of propranolol may precipitate cardiac arrhythmias.

6. Avoid nephrotoxic drugs whenever possible and be alert to medication that may accumulate because of decreased renal excretion (see Table 2-1).

Table 2-1. Dosage reduction of antibiotics in renal failure

None or minor	Moderate	Major	Avoid
Cephalothin	Amphotericin B	Aminoglycosides	Methenamine
Cephapirin	Ampicillin	Carbenicillin	Nalidixic Acid
Chloramphenicol	Cefazolin	5-Fluorocytosine	Nitrofurantoin
Clindamycin	Cephalexin		Sulfonamides
Doxycycline	Cephradine		Tetracycline
Erythromycin	Ethambutol		Aminosalicylic Acid
Ethionamide	Methicillin		
Isoniazid	Metronidazole		
Isoxazolyl penicillins	Penicillin G		
(dicloxacillin,	Trimethoprim-		
nafcillin)	Sulfamethoxazole		
Lincomycin			
Rifampin			

E. POSTOPERATIVE CARE

1. Record daily weights, input, and output.

2. Determine BUN, creatinine, and electrolytes daily.

3. Maintain fluid and electrolyte balance   If in doubt, measure urinary electrolytes. Severe hyperkalemia may occur within hours after operation in previous normokalemic patients. Be careful with potassium supplementation.

4. Acidosis should be corrected gradually and carefully. Rapid correction of acidosis may lead to respiratory alkalosis, CNS depression, and decreased oxygen delivery to tissues.

5. Postoperative hypertension frequently is related to excessive fluid replacement. Antihypertensive therapy should be initiated with a diuretic agent. In renal failure, furosemide is more effective than thiazides and can be used in doses ranging from 40-200 mg, orally or IV. In addition, the daily dose of the following antihypertensive medications may be used: alpha-methyldopa, 1-2 gm; propranolol, 40-120 mg; and hydralazine, 25-200 mg. Refractory hypertensive crises should be treated with IV diazoxide, 300-600 mg, or nitroprusside by constant IV infusion.

6. Diet   Restrict proteins to 0.75-1 gm/kg/day in moderately azotemic patients. The diet should include adequate calories. Most patients with chronic renal failure can ingest a diet containing normal amounts of sodium and potassium. Patients with salt-wasting diseases, such as medullary cystic disease, may need to be supplemented with additional sodium chloride. Those with the nephrotic syndrome or hypertension may need salt restriction.

IV. DISORDERS OF HEMOSTASIS*

Patients with preexisting hemostatic defects are more frequently undergoing operations today than in the past. Since specific replacement therapy is now available, it is essential to identify the exact defect preoperatively whenever possible. Occasionally, the first sign of a hemostatic defect will be excessive bleeding at operation; this distressing situation will seldom arise from a preexisting disorder if a bleeding history and screening laboratory tests are obtained prior to surgery.

A. SCREENING PROCEDURES

1. History   Any of the following patients should be suspected of having a hemostatic defect. Consultation with a hematologist is advised.

a. Patients with a personal or family history of abnormal bleeding or bruising, especially abnormal bleeding following previous surgery, dental extractions, or trauma.

b. Patients with known predisposing conditions such as hematological malignancies or liver disease.

c. Patients who are taking drugs which are known to adversely affect clotting and/or platelet function.

2. Laboratory tests   Screening laboratory tests useful for detecting or excluding hemostatic defects include the prothrombin time (PT), activated partial thromboplastin time (PTT), platelet count (PC), and template bleeding time (BT). The PT and/or PTT is abnormal in patients with deficiencies of any of the clotting factors (except factor XIII). The platelet count detects quantitative platelet abnormalities, and the bleeding time detects qualitative platelet defects.

If all 4 of these tests are normal, it is very unlikely that a significant hemostatic defect exists. If any of the tests are abnormal, hematology consultation should be obtained to identify the exact defect so that specific replacement therapy can be given if necessary.

Examples of how these 4 basic screening tests differ in various hemostatic defects are shown in Table 2-2.

B. CLOTTING DISORDERS may be congenital or acquired, or they may be due to anticoagulant drugs. All patients with clinically significant clotting defects have prolongation of the PT and/or the PTT (whole-blood clotting times may also be prolonged).

1. Congenital defects   Hemophilia A (factor VIII deficiency), hemophilia B (factor IX deficiency), and von Willebrand's disease are by far the most common congenital hemostatic defects.

a. The hemophilias occur only in males and are characterized by deep tissue bleeding (hemarthroses, muscle hematomas, retroperitoneal bleeding, etc.) spontaneously or after minimal trauma. Hemophilia patients have a prolonged PTT, with a normal PT and normal platelet function.

b. Patients with von Willebrand's disease have a combined clotting and platelet defect, with a low factor VIII level and a prolonged BT. In contrast to hemophilia, von Willebrand's disease occurs in both sexes and is characterized primarily by mucocutaneous bleeding and purpura, similar to patients with thrombocytopenia.

c. Surgery on patients with hemophilia or von Willebrand's disease should only be performed in coordination with hematology consultation. Severe deficiencies must be replaced before, during, and after operation.

Patients with hemophilia A should be given cryoprecipitate or lyophilized concentrates of factor VIII.

Patients with hemophilia B may be given fresh frozen plasma (FFP) or concentrates rich in factors II, VII, IX, and X; however, the factor IX concentrates have a very high risk of hepatitis.

*By Curt A. Ries, MD

Patients with von Willebrand's disease should receive either FFP or cryo-precipitate.

Blood levels of clotting factors in the range of 20-30% of normal for 1-3 days are satisfactory for minor surgery, but levels of 50-100% of normal should be maintained for as long as 10 days for major surgery.

If emergency surgery is necessary on a patient with a congenital hemostatic defect, but the exact nature of the defect is unknown, the patient should be given FFP, which will provide all the clotting factors (but not platelets).

Table 2-2. Screening tests in various hemostatic disorders.

Disorder	PT	PTT	PC	BT
Hemophilia A & B	-	+	-	-
Other congenital clotting disorders	+ and/or	+	-	-
von Willebrand's disease	-	+/-	-	+
Liver disease	+	+/-	-	-
Disseminated intravascular coagulation (DIC)	+/-	+/-	+	+
Oral anticoagulants & vitamin K deficiency	+	+/-	-	-
Heparin	+/-	+	-	-
Thrombocytopenias	-	-	+	+
Qualitative platelet defects	-	-	-	+

+ Abnormal test; - normal test

2. Acquired defects

a. Liver disease is the most common cause of an acquired clotting disorder. Usually there is clinical and/or laboratory evidence of liver disease, but occasionally gross abnormalities of liver function, except for the abnormal clotting tests, are not apparent. Patients with liver disease, those with vitamin K deficiency, and people who are taking oral anticoagulants all have similar clotting abnormalities; the PT is much more prolonged than the PTT, and the platelet count is normal unless there is concurrent hypersplenism or disseminated intravascular coagulation (DIC). Patients with significant clotting abnormalities associated with liver disease should be given FFP before operation.

b. Vitamin K deficiency occurs in patients with malabsorption, in biliary tract disease, in patients who are not eating, and in patients taking broad-spectrum antibiotics. Administration of parenteral vitamin K rapidly corrects clotting defects due to vitamin K deficiency, provided liver function is normal. FFP can also be given if emergency operation is necessary.

c. Disseminated intravascular coagulation (DIC) is usually an acute or sub-acute syndrome, but occasionally it can be chronic, associated with metastatic tumor, chronic liver disease, etc. In chronic DIC, the PT and PTT are usually normal, but the platelets and fibrinogen are low, and the fibrin split products (FSP) are elevated. For a more detailed discussion of DIC, including treatment, see page 84.

d. Other rare acquired defects of clotting, such as endogenous circulating anticoagulants, may be encountered by the surgeon. Hematology consultation is essential in such patients.

3. Anticoagulants   Most patients receiving chronic anticoagulation therapy are treated with one of the coumarin derivatives, usually sodium warfarin. These drugs inhibit the vitamin K dependent clotting factors II, VII, IX, and X. The anticoagulant effect can be rapidly reversed when vitamin K is given parenterally.

a. For elective surgery, warfarin should be discontinued 3-4 days before operation to allow the PT to gradually return toward normal. The PT does not need to return completely to normal, but it should not be greater than 15-16 sec. Warfarin can be resumed 2-3 days after surgery. Low-dose heparin may be given to these patients during the operative period when they are not anticoagulated with warfarin.

b. For emergency surgery, vitamin K should be given; FFP should also be given if operation must be done immediately. Large doses of vitamin K will correct the PT within a few hours, but the patient may be relatively refractory to re-anticoagulation with warfarin for as long as a week afterward. Heparin can be given in the interim if the risk of thromboembolism is high.

c. Heparin is rarely used for chronic anticoagulation therapy. Unlike the oral anticoagulants, heparin affects the PTT more than the PT. Heparin effect disappears with a half-life of 1-2 hours, so operation can be performed safely within 6-12 hours after stopping standard doses of IV heparin. Small doses of subcutaneous heparin do not appear to increase the risk of bleeding with most surgical procedures. For emergency operations in the fully heparinized patient, protamine sulfate can be used to reverse the heparin effect immediately.

C. PLATELET DISORDERS Abnormal formation of platelet plugs may be due to quantitative or qualitative defects. Most clinically significant platelet disorders are acquired, although rare examples of serious bleeding due to congenital abnormalities have been described. Patients with platelet defects tend to have mucocutaneous bleeding, with petechiae and purpura, rather than deep tissue bleeding. They characteristically have a prolonged BT, with or without an abnormal platelet count, and normal clotting times (PT, PTT, etc.).

1. Thrombocytopenias may be due to increased platelet destruction or decreased platelet production. *Increased platelet destruction* occurs in idiopathic thrombocytopenic purpura (ITP), secondary and drug-induced immune thrombocytopenias, thrombotic thrombocytopenic purpura (TTP), hemolytic-uremic syndrome (HUS), disseminated intravascular coagulation (DIC), and vasculitis. *Decreased platelet production* is responsible for thrombocytopenia in aplastic anemia, leukemias, other bone marrow failure states, and following cytotoxic chemotherapy.

It is important to understand the mechanism of thrombocytopenia in a particular patient, not only to predict the possible effect of the underlying disease on the proposed operation, but also to determine the potential usefulness of platelet transfusions before and after surgery. Platelet survival in ITP and related disorders may be markedly shortened, with transfused platelets circulating for less than an hour in some patients, so platelet transfusions are often of limited value in these disorders. Platelet survival is usually normal in patients with decreased platelet production, and platelet counts and bleeding times can usually be maintained at normal or near-normal levels by platelet transfusions. Patients with splenomegaly and hypersplenism have an enlarged splenic platelet pool; transfused platelets are preferentially pooled in the spleen rather than circulating in the peripheral blood. The platelet count and BT can often be improved in such patients, however, if 2-4 times the usual number of platelet packs are transfused.

Excessive bleeding during and after operation is unlikely unless the platelet count is less than 60-100,000/mm³. Severe bleeding is likely if the platelet count is less than 20-30,000/mm³.

Patients with moderate to severe thrombocytopenia due to lack of platelet production should be given platelet transfusions to increase the platelet count to about 100,000/mm² 12-24 hours prior to elective operation. This usually requires transfusion of 8-12 units of platelet packs in an average sized adult.

Patients with ITP and other thrombocytopenias due to increased platelet destruction should not be given prophylactic platelet transfusions preoperatively unless there is life-threatening bleeding. Corticosteroids often raise the platelet count in these patients so that elective operation can be safely performed; steroids can be tapered rapidly after surgery. When ITP is refractory to steroids, and splenectomy is necessary for treatment of the ITP, platelet transfusions should be available in the operating room and should be infused as soon as the splenic artery is clamped. Platelet survival and hemostasis usually improves rapidly after the spleen has been isolated from the general circulation.

2. Thrombocytosis (platelet count greater than $600,000/mm^3$) often occurs transiently after splenectomy and other major operations, and it may be seen in patients with chronic inflammatory and neoplastic diseases. Such 'reactive' thrombocytoses rarely cause clinical difficulties, and treatment is generally not indicated.

Clinically significant thrombocytosis tends to occur with myeloproliferative syndromes: polycythemia vera, chronic myelogenous leukemia, myeloid metaplasia, and essential thrombocytosis. These patients often have qualitative platelet abnormalities in addition to thrombocytosis, and both excessive bleeding and thrombosis can occur simultaneously. Patients with polycythemia vera also have an increased risk of bleeding and thrombosis due to their increased red cell mass, even when the platelet count is normal. Operations on patients with myeloproliferative disorders that are not well-controlled have high morbidity and mortality rates. Hematology consultation should be obtained, and the platelet count and red cell mass should be controlled before elective operation is undertaken.

3. Qualitative platelet defects A qualitative platelet defect is defined as abnormal platelet function with a normal platelet count. These patients have prolonged BT and abnormal platelet function in vitro as determined by platelet aggregation and other special tests. Qualitative platelet defects may be congenital or acquired.

a. von Willebrand's disease is both a clotting disorder and a congenital qualitative platelet disorder. It is essential to distinguish between von Willebrand's disease, which is due to lack of a humoral plasma factor, and intrinsic qualitative platelet defects; von Willebrand's disease must be treated with cryoprecipitate or FFP to control or prevent bleeding, and true platelet defects must be treated with platelet transfusions. Patients with significant prolongation of the BT should be given replacement therapy prior to surgery.

b. Acquired platelet dysfunction is caused by aspirin and other antiinflammatory drugs, certain other unrelated drugs, IV dextran, uremia, and hyperglobulinemic states (Waldenstrom's macroglobulinemia, multiple myeloma, etc.). The BT is only modestly prolonged in these situations, and operation can usually be performed safely without special precautions, provided there are no other hemostatic defects. Patients with underlying diseases such as hemophilia, von Willebrand's disease, or ITP should not be given aspirin or other drugs which inhibit platelet function, since the combined defects could lead to serious bleeding. Patients with myeloproliferative disorders may have severe acquired platelet dysfunction with a markedly prolonged BT, with or without thrombocytopenia; these patients should receive platelet transfusions in preparation for operation. When severe platelet dysfunction is the result of an abnormal plasma protein, such as in Waldenstrom's macroglobulinemia, plasma exchange or plasmapheresis must be performed to prevent bleeding. Likewise, dialysis is necessary to control the qualitative platelet defect associated with uremia.

V. ENDOCRINE DISORDERS*

A. DIABETES MELLITUS Well controlled diabetes does not by itself increase operative risks; however, the diabetic patient is always physiologically some 8 to 10 years older than his chronological age and tends to develop atherosclerosis earlier. Thus, the anesthesia should be kept as light as possible and mobility should not be limited for too long in order to minimize the possible cardiac, peripheral vascular, renal, and cerebral complications. In the uncontrolled state, the diabetic is much more susceptible to infection, which aggravates his metabolic disorder. He must be protected by receiving bactericidal antibiotic treatment whenever infection begins—the reason being that the phagocytosis is impaired by hyperglycemia. This and the poor wound-healing are reasons for maintaining euglycemia as closely as possible. This is made difficult by the excitement and stress of surgery, anesthesia, nutritional derangement, and inflammation. To minimize these disturbances, early diagnosis and maintenance of euglycemia is essential. It is advisable to ask an internist in consultation for the management of the diabetic.

In order to control the diabetic, one has to use simple devices for urine glucose testing such as TesTape or Klinistix or Diastix tape. Also, to control the severity of ketoacidosis, one may use Ketodiastix. Blood glucose measurements are well standardized today and can be obtained within minutes either from the laboratory or from special ward equipment.

1. Preoperative preparation of the diabetic It is imperative to find out what type of diabetes the patient is suffering from.

10% of the diabetic population are **insulinopenic** and prone to ketoacidosis with wide swings of blood glucose (± 100 mg/100 ml); they comprise most children and young adults, although occasionally older subjects are thus afflicted. 10% are of the **insulinotardic** type; these patients are of normal weight but have a sluggish discharge of insulin when taking food. The **insulinoplethoric** type make up approximately 80–85% of the adult diabetic population; these are obese diabetics who have large amounts of insulin in their plasma. A small percentage of obese diabetics happen to become insulinopenic after long periods of insulinoplethora, but they will have shown recent weight loss.

Table 2-3. Calculation of IV insulin dose per hour

Insulinopenic diabetic	$\dfrac{\text{Blood sugar}}{150}$ = Units/hour
Diabetic on Glucocorticoids	$\dfrac{\text{Blood sugar}}{100}$ = Units/hour

Thus, it is important to question patients at once to determine: (1) whether they show any of the classical symptoms of uncontrolled diabetes (i.e., thirst, frequent urination, and hunger with weight loss); (2) whether they have a hypoglycemic reaction some 4 hours after a meal (indicating the insulinotardic type of diabetes appearing as late hypoglycemia); and (3) whether they are overweight and not ketoacidotic. Depending on the findings, the preoperative preparation differs.

2. The insulinopenic diabetic The ongoing insulin regimen is followed the morning preceding the day of surgery. If there is any insulin injection the afternoon before surgery, the intermediate-acting (NPH or lente) insulin is cut in half, while the rapid-acting insulin (regular) is kept the same.

---

*By Peter Forsham. MD

Nothing is given by mouth after midnight. In the morning, the diabetic patient on insulin should be operated on as the first or early case. Premedication should be kept to a minimum. Prior to, and during, surgery, the patient should receive, IV, 100ml/hour of 5 or 10% dextrose in water containing an amount of regular insulin determined from Table 2-3. Two units per hour is prepared by adding 20 units of regular insulin to 1000 ml IV solution and allowing some 20 ml to run out of the needle to saturate the container and tubing with insulin (which will preclude any further losses by absorption). The material is infused at the rate of 100 ml/hour, and this can be continued for as long as oral intake is contraindicated. By this means, a reasonable blood glucose level of between 100 and 300 mg/100 ml will be maintained in the plasma. Ketoacidosis is not present under these circumstances. This is much preferable to giving subcutaneous injections determined by the concentrations of urine or blood glucose found.

Postoperative care If the procedure allows for food intake the afternoon of surgery, one should give fruit juices and Jello and other easily digestible carbohydrate materials for the first afternoon and evening and then resume the old diet and insulin management the next day. If there is nothing given by mouth for 2 or 3 days, the insulin/glucose infusion may be continued—provided that one adds 30 mEq potassium chloride to 1000 ml of half-normal saline solution in 5% dextrose with 20 units of regular insulin added. Obtain a blood glucose value before surgery, 1 hour and 6 hours after the end of surgery, and again the next morning (in the fasting state) to ascertain the dosage of insulin and glucose. Should it prove necessary to increase or decrease the insulin, the infusion rate may be altered by a new water solution of 1000 ml of base glucose and electrolyte prepared to which one adds 10-30 units of regular insulin/1000 ml (see Table 2-3) in order to vary the amount per hour. When using this simple intravenous method of insulin and glucose infusion, ketoacidosis is generally kept to a minimum.

Table 2-4. Action of insulin in the diabetic

Product	Action		
	Onset	Maximum	Total duration
Short-acting insulins			
Regular, IV	Immediate	1 hour	
Regular, subcut.	½ hour	3 hours	6 hours
Intermediate insulins			
NPH	3 hours	8-9 hours	16-17 hours
Lente (30% semi and 70% ultra)	3 hours	8-9 hours	16-18 hours

3. The insulinotardic diabetic Whether the regimen for such a patient is just diet or diet and sulfonylurea, one need only give the sulfonylurea dosage prior to surgery and infuse IV 5% dextrose in water at a rate of about 100 ml/hour throughout surgery and recovery. If the type of anesthesia precludes oral medication, 1 gm tolbutamide (Orinase) can be given IV preoperatively, or insulin can be used.

4. The insulinoplethoric, obese diabetic For those not on insulin, no special maintenance is required during surgery; those on oral agents are treated as the insulinotardic group; and those receiving small amounts of insulin are put on the treatment outlined for the insulinopenic diabetic. In any event, the appearance of ketonuria calls for an increase in both insulin and glucose administration.

Generally speaking, local anesthesia is preferred to general anesthesia.

To follow patients undergoing either minor or major surgery, blood glucose determinations should be obtained at frequent intervals (the method of choice for following the metabolic stability of the patient). Also, one should be guided by urine samples; however, if urine cannot be obtained, refrain from catheterizing a patient, since urinary tract infections are common after this procedure.

PATIENTS ON CORTICOSTEROID THERAPY This group comprises patients that at one time or another had glucocorticoid therapy for the treatment of collagen and other diseases as well as patients still on glucocorticoids. The ever-present danger in such patients is that they might go into postoperative adrenal insufficiency and shock in the absence of continuing corticoid support.

It is most important to ascertain whether the patient has been on glucocorticoids in the past or at present. If in the past, consider the possibility of adrenal insufficiency even in cases that have had a relatively short duration of small dosage of glucocorticoids. On the other hand, as a rule, 2 or 3 days of glucocorticoids will not lead to adrenal insufficiency in the future and may well be disregarded provided that one watches during the postoperative period for any signs of impending adrenal cortical insufficiency.

The postoperative adrenal cortical crisis is characterized by a fall in systolic and diastolic blood pressure; a relative ineffectiveness of the usual pressor agents that show decreased activity in the absence of adequate glucocorticoid levels in the system (permissive function of glucocorticoids); and often by nausea, vomiting, and fever.

The **treatment** differs in three classes of patients:

1. In those who have been **on more than 2 days of glucocorticoid therapy in the past** the simplest precaution is to give some glucocorticoid substitution during surgery and thereby prevent any shock prophylactically. There is little risk from prophylactic glucocorticoid administration. Tests devised to evaluate adequate ACTH reserve and adrenal cortical function preoperatively have been shown not to correlate completely with the subsequent onset of adrenal cortical insufficiency.

At time of incision, give hydrocortisone phosphate or hemisuccinate IM, 100 mg/70-kg person (50 mg in lighter weight people), then 50 mg every 6 hours for 3 doses; then twice daily ending on the third postoperative day with 50 mg in the morning. These dosages may be halved if good facilities for following the patient are available.

2. Patients on glucocorticoid therapy should be left on this therapy up to the night before surgery and then should be carried through surgery with the same regimen outlined for the prophylactic type therapy. The only difference in the morning is that the patient on a fairly high dosage of glucocorticoids should receive 100 mg hydrocortisone phosphate or hemisuccinate IM at the time of induction and should then be treated by 50 mg doses every 6 hours reducing dosage gradually over a total 4-day period prior to resuming the former glucocorticoid dosage used in treating the primary disease.

3. Those undergoing removal of adrenals or pituitary adenoma for Cushing's syndrome or for any other reason, are treated like patients on previous glucocorticoid therapy during the surgical period, then maintenance of hydrocortisone, 20 mg in the morning, 10 mg in the afternoon, and 10 mg before bedtime; reducing this eventually to 20 mg in the morning, 5 mg in the afternoon, and 5 mg before bedtime in the 70-kg adult. In cases of complete adrenal insufficiency postoperatively, give also 0.1 mg orally of fluorohydrocortisone as a sodium retainer. In addition it may be desirable to increase sodium chloride intake to regulate the patient's weight.

HYPOTHYROIDISM   This disease is established preoperatively by the following symptoms: fatiguability, somnolence, cold and dry skin, hair loss (particularly the outer third of the eyebrows), and in some cases, puffy skin (especially the face, hands, and legs).

   1. Laboratory tests that confirm the diagnosis are: a serum thyrotropin (TSH) level elevated beyond the upper limit of $10 \mu U/ml$ by radioimmunoassay; a thyroxine (T_4) level below the normal range of 5-15 mcg/100 ml; and a value for triiodothyronine (T_3) uptake below the normal range of 25-30%. In addition, the serum cholesterol value is usually elevated, more so in primary than in secondary (pituitary-type) hypothyroidism.

   2. Preoperative management   If at all possible, the metabolic rate should be increased to near normal prior to surgery, inasmuch as wound healing and cardiovascular respiratory function are markedly delayed in the hypothyroid state. However, many of these patients have angina (or a tendency toward it), and the overly rapid administration of thyroid hormone (Synthroid or Letter) may put them in danger of a coronary infarct.

   3. For elective surgery, it is best to administer L-thyroxine (0.05 mg) for the first 5 days, increasing the dosage in 0.05-mg increments every 5 days up to 0.2 mg just before surgery. The maintenance dosage lies between 0.1 and 0.2 mg. In severe myxedema and in the presence of heart disease, one has to start with a smaller dosage and increase regularly on a weekly basis until the optimal effect is obtained.

   4. For immediate surgery, sodium liothyronin (Cytomel) must be used. Begin with $12.5 \mu g$ daily and increase this amount every 2 days. The maintenance dosage for this short-acting drug is between 37.5 and $50 \mu g$ per day. The $25-\mu g$ dosage of Cytomel is equivalent to approximately 60 mg of dessicated thyroid or 0.1 mg of L-thyroxine.

VI. PREGNANCY*

Surgical procedures on the pregnant patient should be carried out promptly if the diagnosis of an acute surgical disease is made. Elective operations for conditions that do not threaten the pregnant woman's life should be postponed until the postpartum period. Special considerations in surgery on the pregnant patient are as follows:

A. ABORTION OR PREMATURE LABOR   Abortion will ensue if the ovary containing the corpus luteum is removed prior to the 20th day of pregnancy, unless progesterone is administered. After the second month of pregnancy, the placental production of hormones is sufficient to maintain the pregnancy.

   The risks of abdominal surgery can be minimized by manipulating the uterus as little as possible during the procedure and avoiding episodes of prolonged hypotension or hypoxemia.

   The supine position in the third trimester may produce hypotension from compression of the vena cava by the gravid uterus. This can be prevented by providing external lateral pressure against the uterus, displacing it to the left away from the vena cava (left lateral displacement). Operating-table attachments are available for this purpose.

B. ANESTHETICS AND DRUGS   Although systemic anesthetic agents cross the placenta and gain access to the fetal circulation, they are metabolized in the usual fashion and excreted by the mother. There are no known lasting effects on the fetus once organogenesis is complete. Before this stage, general anesthetics may be teratogenic and are best avoided if possible. The abortion rate among operating

---

*By Edward C. Hill, MD

room nurses is approximately twice as high as in the general population, and this is thought to be related to casual exposure to anesthetic gases.

Because of possible teratogenicity, there are certain drugs commonly used in preoperative medication that should be avoided during the first 20 weeks of pregnancy. Among them are chlordiazepoxide (Librium), diazepam (Valium), and meprobamate (Equanil and Miltown).

POSTOPERATIVE COMPLICATIONS

I. NONSPECIFIC COMPLICATIONS*

A. FEVER

1. Causes

a. Pulmonary Atelectasis is the most common cause of fever in the first 2 days after major abdominal or thoracic operations. Typically, the pulse and respiratory rates are elevated along with the temperature ('triple response'). Pneumonitis seldom develops before the third postoperative day unless pulmonary disease was present at the time of operation or the patient aspirated.

b. Wound infection caused by β-hemolytic streptococci or clostridia can appear within hours after operation. Other bacterial wound infections require several days before they develop sufficiently to cause fever.

c. Urinary In general, cystitis alone does not cause fever, but infection of the upper urinary tract does.

d. Operative site Infection in the operative site (deep to the incision) can cause fever. Examples are abdominal abscess, empyema, meningitis, vascular graft infection, etc.

e. Intravenous catheters IV plastic catheters quickly become infected unless rigid aseptic precautions are used during and after insertion.

f. Drugs Reactions to drugs, notably antibiotics, may cause fever.

2. Diagnosis The extent to which fever is investigated by laboratory tests and x-rays depends upon the interval from operation to appearance of fever, the severity of fever, and the physician's certainty about the cause based on the history and physical examination.

a. Symptoms Question the patient about symptoms (e.g., dysuria, unusual pain) that might be clues to the source of fever.

b. Signs Do a physical examination, including auscultation of the chest, inspection of the wound, and examination of IV sites.

c. Laboratory tests Leukocyte count and urinalysis are ordered in nearly every case. Cultures of urine, sputum, blood, and drainage fluid may be indicated.

d. X-rays Chest x-ray is not necessary in patients with a clinical diagnosis of atelectasis in the first day or two after operation. Persistent fever of suspected pulmonary origin requires a chest x-ray, and x-rays of other areas (e.g., the abdomen) are obtained as indicated.

e. Special tests The search for deep infections may require special tests such as gallium scan or liver scan.

3. Treatment Postoperative fever is best treated by correction of the underlying cause. Since high fever (>38.5°C) is itself debilitating, antipyretic drugs (e.g., Tylenol 0/300-0/600, aspirin 0/300-0/600) can be given by mouth or by rectal suppository while investigation of the cause is under way. Applications of ice packs, or 70% alcohol to the skin surface, or placement of the patient on a refrigerated blanket are other methods of lowering body temperature.

If the cause of fever is not clear, IV catheters should be removed and new ones placed, and possibly causative drugs should be discontinued.

---

*By Theodore R. Schrock, MD

B. VOMITING immediately after operation may be an effect of the anesthesia, or may be due to gastric distention (see Gastrointestinal Complications). Regardless of the cause, the best management is nasogastric intubation to keep the stomach empty for 12-24 hours. Drugs to suppress nausea are less effective and have untoward side-effects such as vasodilatation.

Vomiting later in the postoperative period may be due to drugs, ileus, mechanical obstruction of the gut, or many other problems that must be investigated.

C. HICCUP (SINGULTUS)   Although hiccup is usually self-limited (disappearing within a few minutes to an hour), it can be sufficiently persistent and exhausting to endanger life in a debilitated patient. It may be produced by any condition which irritates the afferent or efferent phrenic nerve pathways. The causes therefore are quite varied: CNS, cardiopulmonary, gastrointestinal, renal failure, infectious diseases, etc.

Treatment should be directed at the cause when possible, but therapy must frequently be symptomatic. Breath-holding, drinking a large glass of water, or gastric lavage with a warm 1% solution of sodium bicarbonate may be effective. Rebreathing into a paper bag, or administration of 10-15% CO_2 by face mask, induces hyperventilation and may interrupt the reflex. Tranquilizing drugs such as chlorpromazine hydrochloride (Thorazine) or other phenothiazine preparations are worthy of trial in prolonged hiccup. Barbiturate sedation may also be tried.

D. PSYCHOSIS   Elderly patients, and those who are acutely and severely ill, may become psychotic postoperatively. Causative factors include pain, sleep deprivation, isolation, and unfamiliar surroundings. The patients become disoriented, hallucinatory, agitated, combative, and fearful of personnel who are caring for them, particularly at night. The derangements are transient, and the patient usually regains his or her former mental status as recovery from operation progresses.

Make certain that the patient is not hypoxemic; hypoxemia is a common cause of postoperative restlessness, and the administration of analgesics or sedatives to a hypoxic patient may be lethal.

Simple measures that help include keeping a light on in the room and provision of a companion (family member, nurse, sitter). Mechanical restraints should be avoided unless the patient threatens self-injury by attempting to climb out of bed, pulling out tubes and catheters, etc. Tranquilizers (e.g., chlorpromazine hydrochloride) should be used cautiously, especially in the elderly patient with impaired cardiovascular function.

E. DECUBITUS ULCERS are caused by sustained pressure on the skin, usually over bony prominences such as the sacrum, ischium, trochanter, and heel. They occur in bedridden patients who are weak, aged, malnourished, or paralyzed and who are receiving poor nursing care. Soiling of the bed by incontinence of stools or urine frequently leads to skin irritation. Unrelieved pressure of only a few hours may be sufficient to produce a decubitus ulcer in a susceptible individual. Decubiti characteristically begin as small areas of redness and tenderness which soon break down to form indolent ulcers unless protected from further pressure. In neglected cases, large defects in skin and soft tissues may result from the combined effects of pressure, infection, and poor healing power. Osteomyelitis of underlying bone may occur.

1. Prevention   The most important elements in prevention are good nursing care, early mobilization, and good nutrition. Bedridden patients should be inspected frequently for areas of skin damage which might progress to ulceration. Prevent soiling in incontinent patients. An alternating pressure or foam rubber mattress is useful. Special washable sponge pads under pressure points are protective.

2. Treatment

a. General measures Relieve pressure by frequent change of position and protection of the involved area by pillows, pads, and rubber rings. Bed-clothing and skin must be kept clean and dry. Correction of malnutrition and anemia and control of infection are often essential to healing.

b. Local measures Decubitus ulcers should be kept clean, well-drained, debrided, and either exposed or covered with dry sterile dressings. Topical applications have little value. Invasive local infection is treated by drainage, saline compresses, and systemic antibiotics as indicated.

c. Surgical treatment Surgical treatment in large, resistant lesions consists of complete debridement, including removal of any bony prominences or sequestra, and closure of the wound by a local rotation flap. This will provide an adequate pad over the bone and avoids suture lines over the critical area of pressure. The donor area may frequently be closed by direct approximation, but a split-skin graft may be required.

II. WOUND COMPLICATIONS*

A. DELAYED HEALING AND DEHISCENCE

1. Causes Many systemic factors contribute to failure of wound healing by altering collagen metabolism or impairing delivery of oxygen to the wound. Local and technical problems may impair blood supply or may provide inadequate resistance to mechanical forces.

a. Altered collagen metabolism Malnutrition (especially protein depletion and deficiency of ascorbic acid); corticosteroids; cytotoxic drugs (by inhibiting proliferation of fibroblasts or synthesis of collagen); infection (increases collagenolysis).

b. Impaired oxygen delivery Hypovolemia, hypoxemia, increased blood viscosity; irradiated tissues; infection; technical errors.

c. Technical errors Wounds may dehisce because tissue is devitalized by the dissection or is strangulated by placement of too many sutures or by tying sutures too tightly. This is the most common technical cause of dehiscence and is confirmed when intact sutures are found to have cut through the tissue on one side of the wound. Less commonly, too few sutures are placed, sutures are placed too far apart, sutures break, sutures become untied, or sutures are removed too soon. Absorbable sutures (e.g., catgut, polyglycolic acid) may not remain strong long enough for secure healing, especially in debilitated patients.

d. Mechanical forces Patients with the predisposing systemic or technical factors described above are more likely to dehisce an abdominal wound if they are obese, have a postoperative cough, vomit, become distended, or develop ascites.

2. Diagnosis Dehiscence of skin is apparent on inspection. Abdominal fascial dehiscence is manifested by spontaneous drainage of **serosanguinous fluid** from the wound. One must assume that fascia has dehisced when this type of drainage appears, especially when it persists. Fluid from a seroma or hematoma is not serosanguinous and it does not continue to drain. In major abdominal dehiscences, the patient may **eviscerate** varying amounts of intestine and omentum.

3. Treatment Obvious major dehiscence of fascia should be treated by resuture under anesthesia in the operating room. Often, large sutures must be placed through all layers of the abdominal wall because the fascia is too soft to hold sutures.

Minor disruptions of fascia may be managed without resuture; however, the extent of fascial disruption is often underestimated until the skin is opened and the wound explored. It is best to do this under aseptic conditions in the operating room.

*By Theodore R. Schrock, MD

Incisional hernias result from untreated or recurrent fascial dehiscence.

B. BLEEDING from the wound usually is apparent within minutes to hours after the operation is completed. The bleeding vessel(s) may be in the skin, in the subcutaneous fat, or at the fascial level. Unless the patient has a generalized bleeding problem, the wound should be explored to control persistent bleeding. Many times this can be accomplished simply by removing a few skin sutures and ligating the bleeding point(s) with sutures or metal clips without returning the patient to the operating room.

C. HEMATOMA is a collection of clotted and/or liquid blood in or beneath the wound. A visible and palpable mass, ecchymosis, and pain are the manifestations. Large hematomas should be evacuated; usually it is necessary to open the wound widely under aseptic conditions.

D. SEROMA   Serous fluid collects gradually over several days when a space has been left beneath a wound, particularly if large skin flaps have been created. A seroma is a fluctuant mass and is usually nontender. Small seromas may be aspirated through a needle. Large seromas, or those that recur after 1 or 2 needle aspirations, require placement of a soft rubber (Penrose) drain through a small incision; the drain can be removed after a few days.

E. INFECTION   See Chapter 4.

F. SUTURE SINUSES   Sutures are foreign bodies which can serve as niduses for infection. Tiny abscesses form about the fascial and subcutaneous sutures in some patients. These abscesses may drain through the skin surface spontaneously or by surgical incision, thus relieving pain but resulting in persistent intermittent drainage of small amounts of pus. In time, the suture is extruded ('spit'), or the surgeon can grasp and remove the offending suture(s) by probing the wound; a crochet hook is a useful device for this maneuver. Once a suture sinus begins, it does not heal until the foreign body is removed. Sutures may be extruded for weeks, months, or even years after they were placed. Rarely, it is necessary to do a formal operation to open the wound widely and remove all of the infected sutures. Silk has a great propensity to formation of suture sinuses; inert materials (e.g., stainless-steel wire) seldom cause this problem.

III. CARDIAC COMPLICATIONS*

A. CARDIAC ARREST is the cessation of effective heart beat. The surgical patient is at risk of developing this complication during or after operation. Cardiac arrest occurs once in every 750-1000 operations, one-third of which are minor procedures.

   1. Causes   Special circumstances leading to cardiac arrest are electrocution, drowning, air embolism, poisoning with carbon monoxide and other gases, cardiac contusion or manipulation, and overdose of arrhythmogenic agents such as digitalis and sympathomimetics.

   In the surgical patient, cardiac arrest is due to an underlying cardiac condition plus a precipitating cause. The commonest underlying condition is coronary artery disease. The commonest precipitating causes are: shock; hypoventilation; anesthetic overdose; drug effect or idiosyncrasy; vaso-vagal reflex; myocardial infarction; hypothermia.

   Effective heart-beat ceases because of arrhythmia (ventricular fibrillation or asystole) or because of marked reduction in ventricular contractility with preserved rhythm ('electromechanical dissociation').

   a. Ventricular fibrillation has numerous causes including increased sympathetic stimulation, hypoxia, drug effects, electrolyte imbalances, and myocardial

*By John C. Hutchinson, MD

disease. These factors, singly or together, may cause the disordered intraventricular propagation of depolarization and/or repolarization which leads to reentry pathways. Simple reentry pathways produce premature ventricular contractions (commonly described as 'irritability'); complex or multiple reentry pathways may result in ventricular fibrillation.

　　b. Asystole occurring as the first rhythmic abnormality ('primary asystole') generally represents the progression of prior partial atrioventricular or fascicular block.

　　c. Electromechanical dissociation most commonly results from profound global ventricular ischemia.

　　2. Prevention　Electrocardiographic monitoring should be used during all surgical procedures to detect signs of impending danger and to recognize the rhythmic nature of the arrest should it occur.

　　Maintain arterial oxygen tension over 80 mm Hg and Pco_2 at 30-45 mm Hg.

　　Maintain mean blood pressure between 60 and 100 mm Hg.

　　Prevent vagal overactivity with atropine (0.4-1 mg IV).

　　In the presence of increasing numbers of premature ventricular contractions, look for light anesthesia, CO_2 retention, myocardial ischemia due to hypotension, or the combination of hypertension and tachycardia which causes increased myocardial oxygen utilization.

　　In the presence of bradycardia, look for anesthetic excess, hypoxia, A-V block, or vagal stimulation by visceral traction, carotid sinus compression, traction on extraocular muscles.

　　In the presence of falling blood pressure, look for anesthetic excess, myocardial ischemia, or inadequate blood volume due to blood or fluid losses, obstruction of venous return, or vasodilation.

　　3. Diagnosis　Signs in the **surgical field** are cessation of bleeding, dark arterial blood, agonal breathing, and pulseless arteries.

　　Signs for the **anesthesiologist** are absent carotid pulse, absent heart tones by esophageal stethoscope, absent blood pressure, and ventricular fibrillation or asystole on the ECG monitor.

　　In the **postoperative patient,** the signs are absence of blood pressure, carotid pulse, or respiration.

　　4. Treatment　Step-wise treatment of cardiac arrest is detailed in Table 2-5. The following comments are supplementary.

　　a. Remove the underlying cause if recognizable.

　　b. Correct the fundamental abnormality as soon as possible: (1) Ventricular fibrillation requires electrical defibrillation. (2) Asystole requires cardiac massage, vagolytic or sympathomimetic drugs, or cardiac pacing. (3) Electromechanical dissociation is treated with inotropic drugs (calcium, epinephrine, or dopamine).

　　c. Cardiopulmonary resuscitation is used immediately and during the removal of the underlying cause and correction of the fundamental abnormality. **Act immediately!** Absence of blood flow to the brain results in a progressive ischemic injury which is fatal in about 4 minutes. Prior inadequacies in blood flow and oxygenation to the brain further shorten the time available for successful correction.

　　d. Open chest cardiac massage　Closed chest massage is the initial method of choice because it can be started quickly. Open chest cardiac massage is undertaken only when an operating room is available for subsequent closure. Open chest massage may be more effective and therefore is indicated when: the chest is already open; there is trauma to the chest with pneumothorax, cardiac tamponade, or cardiac perforation; or the thorax is deformed.

　　(1) *To open the chest:* Establish positive pressure ventilation immediately. No skin preparation is necessary—speed is essential. Use gloves if available. A knife is the only necessary instrument, but a rib-spreader is desirable.

Make a bold submammary incision through the fourth or fifth interspace from sternum to posterior axillary line.

(2) *To massage heart:* Compress the heart rhythmically 70-80 times a minute, either against the sternum or between the thumb and fingers. Compress with a vigorous impulse, then quickly relax pressure to allow filling. Open the pericardium longitudinally if response is not immediate, especially if heart trauma may have occurred. If manual compression is effective, a distinct peripheral pulse is felt and should be monitored at the femoral or carotid artery by an assistant. The pupils should remain constricted if blood flow to the brain is adequate.

Fatigue of the hands will occur quickly, especially in the absence of a rib-spreader, and may require changes of hand position or of operator. These changes must be made quickly as possible.

(3) *Supportive measures during open chest massage*   Be sure that the lungs are ventilating.

Intracardiac drugs   For the soft flabby heart (with or without fibrillation), inject epinephrine into the left ventricle; inject 0.5-1.5 mg as a 1:10,000 solution, and repeat every 3-5 minutes prn. If epinephrine is

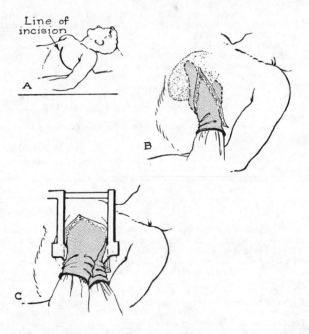

Fig. 2-1. Open chest cardiac massage. (A) Position of patient for cardiac massage. (B) and (C) Insertion of 1 hand or 2 hands for rhythmic compression of heart

ineffective in the dilated, weakly beating heart, inject calcium gluconate or chloride, 300-1000 mg of a 1:10 solution into the left ventricle.

IV drugs   As soon as possible, an IV infusion should be started by cutdown or femoral, subclavian, or internal jugular vein catheterization. Cardiac arrest and inadequate tissue perfusion during massage are accompanied by rapid development of metabolic acidosis. Correction of acidosis may have a beneficial effect on cardiac function. As soon as the IV route is open, treat metabolic acidosis with 1 mEq/kg of sodium bicarbonate. Repeat the injection every 5 minutes as long as cardiac massage is necessary. Determination of arterial pH and Pco_2 will allow calculation of the 'base deficit' by the method of Sigaard Anderson. Full correction of base deficiency is found by multiplying the base deficit (in mEq/liter) by 30% of the body weight (in liters). The resulting number of mEq of sodium bicarbonate may be given, with the measurement and calculation repeated in 10-15 minutes.

(4) *Defibrillation during open chest massage*   Ventricular fibrillation may be present at the onset or may develop during manual compression. It is rarely reversible except by electric shock. Proceed as follows: Attempt defibrillation with 20-60 watt-seconds of direct current discharge as soon as the defibrillator can be readied. Apply defibrillator electrodes firmly on opposite surfaces of the heart. If this attempt is unsuccessful, use cardiac compression, ventilation, and cardiotonic drugs to develop an oxygenated (pink) myocardium with good tone. Then try defibrillation again. Sometimes IV lidocaine may be helpful in achieving defibrillation. The dose should be 1 mg/kg given rapidly and repeated to a maximum total dose of 3-5 mg/kg. If digitalis intoxication is possibly the cause of the arrest, avoid calcium, but guarantee that the serum potassium level is in the high-normal range.

(5) *Continuation of resuscitative efforts* are indicated as long as the heart maintains tone, color, and responsiveness and as long as there is no evidence of irreversible brain damage, such as widely dilated pupils, flaccid paralysis, and absence of spontaneous respiration. Resuscitation may rarely be successful after as long as 6 hours of manual compression. Recurrent ventricular fibrillation may require repeated resuscitations and may be controlled by a continuous lidocaine infusion at 1-4 mg/minute (10-40 gm/kg/minute).

(6) *Chest closure* is routine. Begin intensive IV antibiotic therapy.

5. Care after resuscitation by closed or open method   Post-resuscitative care should, if possible, be carried out in an intensive care unit where continuous monitoring of ECG and frequent determination of central venous and arterial blood pressures are feasible. Equipment for external defibrillation should be immediately available. Recurrent cardiac arrest is common. Hypoxia and hypercapnia should be avoided by administration of oxygen and, if necessary, by ventilatory assistance with mask or endotracheal or tracheostomy tube. Determinations of arterial pH, Po_2, and Pco_2 are valuable when there is question of acidosis or inadequate ventilation. If acidosis is present, sodium bicarbonate may be indicated (see above). Hypovolemia is corrected by administration of blood and fluids as needed and urinary output is watched and maintained. Neurologic status must be closely followed, since cerebral damage is frequent. Treatment of prolonged coma must be individualized. Sternal and rib fractures, ruptured liver, pneumothorax, or other complication of overly vigorous external massage should not be overlooked.

6. Prognosis   Good results are proportional to the speed and skill of resuscitative efforts. When arrest occurs in the operating room, it is possible to save about 75% of patients. The percentage of successful resuscitations outside the operating room in cardiac arrest due to myocardial infarction and other causes is

Table 2-5. Technic of heart-lung resuscitation (modified after Safar)

Phase 1: First aid (emergency oxygenation of the brain) Must be instituted within 3-4 minutes for optimal effectiveness and to minimize the possibility of permanent brain damage.

Step 1   Place patient in a supine position on a firm surface. A 2x3 foot sheet of plywood should be available at emergency care stations, or use a food tray.

Step 2   Tilt head backward and maintain in this hyperextended position. Keep mandible displaced forward by pulling strongly at the angle of the jaw.

If victim is not breathing

Step 3   Clear mouth and pharynx of mucus, blood, vomitus, or foreign material.

Step 4   Separate lips and teeth to open oral airway.

Step 5   If steps 2-4 fail to open airway, forcibly blow air through mouth (keeping nose closed) or nose (keeping mouth closed) and inflate the lungs 3-5 times. Watch for chest movement. If this fails to clear the airway immediately and if pharyngeal or tracheal tubes are available, use them without delay. Tracheostomy may be necessary.

Step 6   Feel the carotid artery for pulsations.

a. If carotid pulsations are present

Give lung inflation by mouth-to-mouth breathing (keeping patient's nostrils closed) or mouth-to-nose breathing (keeping patient's mouth closed) 12-15 times per minute--allowing about 2 seconds for inspiration and 3 seconds for expiration—until spontaneous respirations return. Continue as long as the pulses remain palpable and previously dilated pupils remain constricted. Bag-mask technics for lung inflation may be substituted. If pulsations cease, follow directions as in 6b, below.

b. If carotid pulsations are absent

Alternate cardiac compression (closed heart massage) and pulmonary ventilation as in 6a, above. Place the heel of one hand on the sternum just above the xiphoid. With the heel of the other hand on top of it, apply firm vertical pressure sufficient to force the sternum about 2 inches downward (less in children) about once every second. After 15 sternal compressions, alternate with 3-5 deep lung inflations. Repeat and continue this alternating procedure until it is possible to obtain additional assistance and more definitive care. Resuscitation must be continuous during transportation to the hospital. Open heart massage should be attempted only in a hospital. When possible, obtain an ECG, but do not interrupt resuscitation to do so. Have an assistant monitor the femoral or carotid pulse, which should be palpable with each cardiac compression as an indication of cardiac output.

Table 2-5 (cont.) Technic of heart-lung resuscitation

Phase II: Restoration of spontaneous circulation. Until spontaneous respiration and circulation are restored, there must be no interruption of artificial ventilation and cardiac massage while steps 7-13 (below) are being carried out. Three basic questions must be considered at this point:

    (1) What is the underlying cause, and is it correctable?
    (2) What is the nature of the cardiac arrest?
    (3) What further measures will be necessary? The physician must plan upon the assistance of trained hospital personnel*, an ECG, a defibrillator, and emergency drugs.

Step 7 If a spontaneous effective heartbeat is not restored after 1-2 minutes of cardiac compression, have an assistant give epinephrine (adrenaline), 1 mg (1 ml of 1 : 1000 or 10 ml of 1 : 10,000 aqueous solution) IV or 0.5 mg (5 ml of 1:10,000 aqueous solution) by the intracardiac route. Repeat larger dose at 3-5 minute intervals if necessary. The intracardiac method is not without hazard. Inject at the cardiac apex directed toward the right scapula. Aspirate bright red blood before injecting.

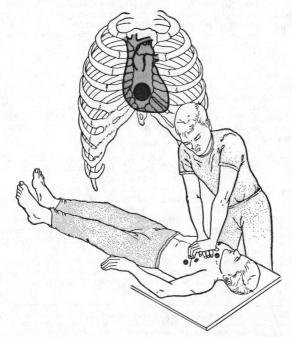

Technic of closed chest cardiac massage. Heavy circle in heart drawing shows area of application of force. Circles on supine figure show points of application of electrodes for defibrillation.

Table 2-5 (cont.) Technic of heart-lung
resuscitation

Step 8	Promote venous return and combat shock by elevating the legs or placing the patient in the Trendelenburg position, and give IV fluids as available and indicated.
Step 9	If the victim is pulseless for more than 5 minutes, give sodium bicarbonate solution, 1 mEq/kg IV to combat impending metabolic acidosis. Repeat every 5–10 minutes as indicated.
Step 10	If pulsations still do not return, suspect ventricular fibrillation. Obtain ECG.
Step 11	If ECG demonstrates ventricular fibrillation, maintain cardiac massage until just before giving an external defibrillating shock of 4 watt-seconds/kg of DC current with one electrode firmly applied to the skin over the apex of the heart and the other over the right sub-clavicular area. Monitor with ECG. If cardiac function is not restored, resume massage and repeat shocks at intervals of 1–3 minutes. If cardiac action is reestablished but remains weak, give calcium chloride or calcium gluconate, 5–10 ml (0.5–1 gm) of 10% solution IV; it probably should not be used in patients who have been taking digitalis. Calcium must be given if hyperkalemia is suspected as cause of the arrest.
Step 12	Thoracotomy and open heart massage may be considered (see text).
Step 13	If cardiac, pulmonary, and CNS functions are restored, the patient should be carefully observed for shock and complications of the precipitating cause.

Phase III: Follow-up measures. When cardiac and pulmonary function have been reestablished and satisfactorily maintained, evaluation of CNS function deserves careful consideration. Decision as to the nature and duration of subsequent treatment must be individualized. The physician must decide if he is 'prolonging life' or simply 'prolonging dying.' Complete CNS recovery has been reported in a few patients unconscious up to a week after appropriate treatment.

Step 14	If circulation and respiration are restored but there are no signs of CNS recovery within 30 minutes, hypothermia at 32°C for 2–3 days may lessen the degree of brain damage.
Step 15	Support ventilation and circulation. Treat any other complications which might arise. Do not overlook the possibility of complications of external cardiac massage (e.g., broken ribs, ruptured viscera).
Step 16	Meticulous postresuscitation care is required, particularly for the first 48 hours after recovery. Observe carefully for possible multiple cardiac arrhythmias, especially recurrent fibrillation or cardiac standstill.
Step 17	Consider the use of assisted circulation in selected cases. A few patients who cannot be salvaged by conventional cardiopulmonary resuscitation may be saved by the addition of partial cardiopulmonary bypass measures.

---

*In the hospital, a physician able to intubate the trachea will quickly visualize the larynx, suck out all foreign material, pass a large, cuffed endotracheal tube, and attach the airway to an IPPB or anesthesia machine for adequate ventilation. Serial arterial blood gas, pH, and bicarbonate determinations are important.

increasing with the wider application of closed chest massage. It is the responsibility of every physician to acquire the judgment, skill, and decisiveness needed to accomplish cardiac resuscitation. It is the responsibility of the hospital to provide resuscitation equipment, which should include a laryngoscope, endotracheal tubes, a mask and bag for artificial ventilation, and a DC defibrillator. Along with the necessary cardiac drugs, this equipment can be conveniently stored in a special cart. The cart can be kept available in the operating suite, or in those hospital units concerned with emergency, intensive, and coronary care.

B. ACUTE PULMONARY EDEMA (acute congestive failure) is a grave emergency. **Act Immediately.** It is often precipitated by stress, transfusion of too much blood, or excess IV administration of sodium-containing fluids. Myocardial infarction or an attack of atrial fibrillation with a rapid ventricular rate may be the precipitating factor.

    Treatment

    a. Position Place the patient in a sitting position in bed or in a chair in order to decrease venous return to the heart.

    b. Morphine sulfate, 10-15 mg IV or IM every 2-4 hours, depresses pulmonary reflexes, relieves anxiety, and induces sleep.

    c. Give oxygen in high concentrations, preferably by mask. Positive pressure breathing for short periods may be of value. Monitor CO_2 retention.

    d. Vasodilation using nitroglycerin 0.4 mg sublingually, allows prompt peripheral pooling of blood volume and is immediately helpful if blood pressure does not fall below 90/60. If hypertension is present, vasodilation is particularly effective and may be achieved by longer-acting agents (Isosorbide) or nitroprusside infusion.

    e. Reduction of blood volume is accomplished in 1 of 2 ways: (1) By application of rubber tourniquets or BP cuffs to 3 extremities with sufficient pressure to obstruct venous but not arterial flow. Rotate the tourniquets every 10-15 minutes by placing a tourniquet on the fourth extremity and releasing one of the others. (2) By venesection of 300-700 ml of blood in successive bleedings.

    f. Rapid digitalization This is of great value. Extreme care is necessary in giving digitalis IV to a previously digitalized patient. If undigitalized, give Digoxin 1 mg/m² body surface area in divided doses, giving 50% as the first dose, then 30% and 20% at 6-hour intervals.

    g. Rapid diuresis may be useful in some circumstances. This may be accomplished with ethacrynic acid (Edecrin), 25-100 mg orally or 25-50 mg IV, or furosemide (Lasix) 40-80 mg orally or IV.

C. SUBACUTE OR CHRONIC CONGESTIVE FAILURE Symptoms and signs include dyspnea, orthopnea, rales at lung bases, venous and hepatic engorgement, dependent edema, prolonged circulation time, and increased venous pressure.

    Treatment

    a. Eliminate or control precipitating factors such as stress, sepsis, anemia, excess sodium administration, arrhythmias, and thyrotoxicosis.

    b. Rest in bed or chair with appropriate sedation decreases the work required of the heart.

    c. The diet should be low in sodium (less than 0.6 gm of sodium or 1.5 gm of sodium chloride). With sodium restriction, fluids may be allowed ad lib.

    d. Digitalis (see above).

    e. Diuretics (see above).

    f. The patient will lose weight and dyspnea will subside as improvement occurs. Activity can then be resumed gradually within appropriate limits.

D. ACUTE MYOCARDIAL INFARCTION Prolonged, usually severe precordial or substernal pain, sometimes radiating to the neck or upper extremities, is typical, but these symptoms may be masked by anesthesia or narcotics. Infarction is often associated with shock, congestive failure, and arrhythmias. Other manifestations include fever, leukocytosis, and elevation of sedimentation rate and the serum levels of glutamic-oxaloacetic transaminase (SGOT), lactic dehydrogenase (LDH), and creatine phosphokinase (CPK). There are characteristic ECG changes (which may be delayed). During the acute stage, the patient's ECG, pulse, and possibly the venous and arterial pressures should be continuously monitored in a coronary care or equivalent unit.

Treatment

a. Rest Complete bed rest for 1-4 weeks is advocated, with gradual resumption of activity as tolerated. Use sedatives as required.

b. Relief of pain Give morphine sulfate, 10-15 mg subcut, IM, or slowly IV, or choose an alternative narcotic.

c. Oxygen therapy is usually necessary.

d. Shock If cardiac shock is present, treat with an inotropic drug, such as dopamine, and with cautious digitalization. Vasopressor drugs such as metaraminol (Aramine) or levarterenol (Levophed) are thought by some clinicians to be helpful, but inotropic drugs are usually more helpful.

e. Digitalis and drugs to control arrhythmia are prescribed for specific indications.

E. CARDIAC ARRHYTHMIAS Treatment of the major arrhythmias is a complex problem calling for the close collaboration of the internist and surgeon. However, the surgeon may be required to give emergency treatment or initiate treatment until the services of an internist can be obtained. The final diagnosis of the type of arrhythmia present is made from the ECG.

1. Atrial fibrillation Rapid atrial fibrillation decreases the efficiency of the heart and may lead to congestive failure. Emergency treatment consists of slowing the rate by adequate digitalization. Conversion to normal sinus rhythm by quinidine or DC countershock may be urgently required if shock or pulmonary edema ensue. Propranolol may be used IV to slow the rate more quickly than is possible with digitalis, but it may give rise to shock or pulmonary edema unless very carefully titrated.

2. Atrial flutter Rapid atrial flutter may lead to congestive failure. Digitalization will slow the rate, either by increasing the degree of block or by converting the flutter to sinus rhythm or atrial fibrillation. The final conversion is best supervised by one familiar with the treatment of this condition. DC countershock may be the treatment of choice, especially if the rhythm is poorly tolerated. Propranolol is useful in this arrhythmia also.

3. Paroxysmal supraventricular tachycardia Paroxysmal atrial tachycardia is the most common paroxysmal tachycardia. Other types are paroxysmal nodal tachycardia and a group of tachycardias in which the source of the ectopic focus cannot be determined. Supraventricular tachycardias often occur in patients with otherwise normal hearts. In the absence of heart disease, serious effects are rare. Remedies that are more dangerous than the disease should be avoided. Rule out digitalis toxicity as a cause of the tachycardia. Vagus stimulation (carotid sinus pressure, gagging, Valsalva's maneuver) should be tried initially. If mechanical measures fail, drugs should be used. Sedation alone may be sufficient. There is no unanimity regarding the most effective cardiac medication, but the following may be tried: (a) Edrophonium (Tensilon) initially 2.5 mg IV, with doubling of the dose every 5 minutes until abdominal cramps or retching occur, or until the rhythm slows or subsides. Side-effects are very brief, making this a very useful drug. (b) Digitalis orally or, if no digitalis has been given in the preceding 2 weeks, IV. (c) Vasopressor agents. (d) Procainamide hydrochloride. Continuous ECG monitoring of heart rate and monitoring of BP are essential. (e) Propranolol (Inderal), 10-30 mg 3 times a day before meals and at bedtime, or 1 mg IV slowly, and with continuous clinical and ECG monitoring, until therapeutic effect begins. If necessary (and there have been no untoward effects) a subsequent dose of 1 mg may be given every 2-5 minutes, to a total of 10 mg. Atropine, 0.5-1 mg should be given IV if excessive bradycardia occurs.

Rarely, cardioversion by DC countershock may be required if the patient's condition deteriorates in spite of the above measures.

4. Ventricular tachycardia This arrhythmia is usually associated with myocardial damage, especially myocardial infarction. Digitalis toxicity may cause this arrhythmia. Lidocaine (Xylocaine) is the drug of choice for emergency treatment because of its short duration of action and infrequent hypotensive effect. Give 1 mg/kg IV as a bolus and repeat the injection if the initial bolus is not effective. If the arrhythmia recurs, an IV infusion of 1-3 mg/kg/hour may be given or the IV injection repeated twice at 20-minute intervals. If lidocaine is without effect, cardioversion by DC countershock is preferred to additional pharmacologic methods of treatment.

5. Ventricular fibrillation produces cardiac arrest and requires electric shock defibrillation with cardiopulmonary resuscitation if fibrillation persists.

6. Electrical cardioversion Conversion to normal sinus rhythm by depolarization of the entire heart with a DC shock is an important method of therapy in arrhythmias. Initial energy settings of 25 watt-seconds are employed for atrial flutter and supraventricular tachycardias, and 50 watt-seconds for atrial fibrillation and ventricular tachycardia. If the initial energy is ineffective, sequential increases in energy may be required. Brief anesthesia is desirable and is induced with sodium thiopental (1.5-3 mg/kg) with preoxygenation and attention to the adequacy of ventilation.

IV. PULMONARY COMPLICATIONS*

A. VENTILATORY FAILURE Some degree of ventilatory impairment is universal after abdominal and thoracic surgical procedures. In most instances, the impairment is not sufficient to prevent resumption of spontaneous breathing by the patient. However, if the operative procedures are extensive, if there has been massive trauma, if the patient is elderly, or if the patient has preexistent chronic disease or malnutrition, the ventilatory impairment may be so great that a period of mechanical ventilation is necessary.

A critical period in which acute ventilatory failure most commonly occurs is the first few hours after operation, when the effects of muscle relaxants have not worn off and muscular weakness results in reduced vital capacity. Later, during the second or third postoperative days, abdominal distention, with restriction of chest wall motion and elevation of the diaphragm, is the usual cause of ventilatory compromise. If a respiratory complication develops, decreased compliance of the lungs may contribute to inadequate ventilatory function.

1. Diagnosis In all instances, assessment of ventilatory adequacy is best made by measurement of forced vital capacity. As noted earlier, normal values are 65-70 ml/kg of body weight. Vital capacity less than 12-15 ml/kg of body weight indicates borderline function. When vital capacity is less than this, the patient will not be able to breathe deeply enough to prevent atelectasis, or to cough vigorously enough to clear airway secretions.

Another test often used to evaluate mechanical lung function is the maximal inspiratory force (MIF). This measurement is carried out in the intubated patient by asking the patient to inhale as forcefully as possible after normal expiration, with the endotracheal tube occluded. Under normal circumstances, a negative pressure of greater than -200 cm H_2O can be generated. In the patient with ventilatory compromise, values less than -25 to -30 cm H_2O indicate inadequate mechanical function.

*By Frank Lewis, Jr., MD

2. Treatment If inadequate ventilation is indicated by the patient's clinical status and the tests described, a nasotracheal tube should be inserted and the patient placed on mechanical ventilation until the cause of the problem resolves. The nasal and pharyngeal mucosa is anesthetized with cocaine or Pontocaine, and insertion of the nasotracheal tube can be accomplished with minimal discomfort in the awake patient.

B. ASPIRATION In patients undergoing surgery, aspiration of gastric contents is most likely to occur during the induction or termination of the general anesthetic. During the procedure itself, an endotracheal tube with a distensible cuff which seals against the tracheal wall is normally inserted, and this prevents regurgitation and aspiration.

1. Prevention The patient undergoing elective surgery should have no oral intake for 6-8 hours prior to the procedure and may be assumed to have an empty stomach at the time of induction. Patients who require emergency operation should have a nasogastric tube inserted while awake to empty the stomach as completely as possible. Anesthesia induction technics in patients suspected of having food in the stomach are modified to minimize the hazard of aspiration. Either 'awake' intubation or 'crash' induction, with an assistant maintaining tracheal compression until insertion of the endotracheal tube, is commonly employed. In patients emerging from general anesthesia, the endotracheal tube is left in place until the patient has begun to react to it by coughing or straining, thus evidencing return of protective airway reflexes.

2. Treatment If aspiration is observed, immediate endotracheal intubation, suctioning of the airways, and lavage with saline should be done. Within 10 minutes of gastric acid aspiration, the resultant bronchorrhea will neutralize the acidic pH, so lavage after an interval longer than this is probably of no benefit. Treatment otherwise is supportive, with monitoring for the development of pulmonary infiltrates, hypoxemia, and pneumonia. Steroids have been advocated but there is no clear evidence of their benefit. Antibiotics should be reserved for treatment of specific organisms and not used prophylactically. If aspiration of solid material is suspected, bronchoscopy is indicated for inspection of the tracheobronchial tree and removal of any foreign material.

C. PNEUMOTHORAX is a relatively uncommon complication in elective surgical procedures but should be considered in any patient who develops sudden respiratory distress or sudden deterioration intraoperatively. The principal cause of pneumothorax in the hospitalized patient today is iatrogenic puncture of the lung while attempting percutaneous placement of a subclavian or internal jugular venous catheter. It may also occur in the patient being anesthetized who coughs or 'bucks' on the endotracheal tube, causing rupture of a pulmonary bleb.

1. Diagnosis is classically made by a decrease in, or absence of, breath sounds on the affected side with hyperresonance to percussion and a tracheal shift away from that side. X-ray is confirmatory.

2. Treatment Any patient who develops severe respiratory distress after insertion of a subclavian or jugular catheter should be presumed to have a pneumothorax, and a chest tube should be inserted immediately without waiting for an x-ray. If pneumothorax is suspected but the patient is comfortable, one should get the chest x-ray first and insert a chest tube if needed.

D. ATELECTASIS is the most common complication in the first 2 or 3 postoperative days. It is a direct result of underexpansion of portions of the lung. In the most dependent segments of the lung, and in those segments adjacent to the diaphragm (after abdominal surgery), ventilation is impaired to the greatest extent and collapse is most probable. For these reasons, the inferior and posterior portions of the lung most often become atelectatic.

1. Diagnosis Clinical signs are fever, tachypnea, and tachycardia which develop simultaneously within the first 2 or 3 postoperative days. Chest x-ray usually shows a linear density in dependent segments or an area of lobar or sublobar collapse. There is often radiographic evidence of volume loss in the affected lung. Atelectasis may also be diffuse and miliary, in which case minimal x-ray signs will be present.

2. Treatment consists of maneuvers which cause the patient to breathe more deeply and/or cough in order to expand underventilated segments of the lung. The most conservative treatment methods consist of an aggressive 'stir-up' regimen plus verbal encouragement and supervision of the patient in deep breathing and coughing. The patient should be ambulated at least every 2 hours if there are no contraindications. If the patient cannot walk, useful measures include turning every hour from supine to prone or to left and right lateral positions in bed, and if possible sitting up in a chair for short periods.

Often direct coaching of a patient, with reassurance that the abdominal incision won't be harmed by coughing, will improve the ability to ventilate. If incisional pain is severe, holding a pillow tightly against the abdomen to support it during coughing is helpful. A variety of mechanical devices, such as the incentive spirometer, blow bottles, and Triflow incentive flowmeter are available to give the patient a visual indication of the adequacy of breathing.

Intermittent positive pressure breathing (IPPB) has been advocated for the prophylaxis and treatment of atelectasis, but in the nonintubated patient it does not achieve the objective. Simpler, more direct, and less expensive modalities are more effective. IPPB has no role in the care of the postoperative nonintubated patient.

If the above measures prove ineffective in treating atelectasis, direct stimulation of tracheal mucosa may be used to induce involuntary coughing and deep breathing. This is most commonly done by passing a small (size 14 French) suction catheter through the nose and into the trachea. In the awake patient, passage of the catheter into the trachea can be immediately recognized by the induction of coughing and the inability to phonate because the catheter separates the vocal cords. A similar effect is produced by the instillation of 5 ml of sterile water into the trachea by percutaneous tracheal puncture with a #22 needle, or by percutaneous insertion of a plastic catheter into the trachea. These methods have risks: the posterior tracheal wall may be lacerated when the needle is inserted, and subcutaneous emphysema may be produced from air leaking through the puncture wound in the trachea. Since these methods have no advantage over passage of a nasotracheal suction catheter, there is little justification for their use.

If all the above methods fail to reverse the atelectasis, bronchoscopy may be indicated to suction secretions out of the atelectatic segment. Another alternative is to insert an endotracheal tube and ventilate the patient, thus allowing passive expansion of the collapsed areas of lung. These modalities are rarely necessary and should be used only when the atelectasis is severe, involving an entire lobe or more, or the patient is developing respiratory distress or deteriorating blood gases.

E. PULMONARY EDEMA   Acute interstitial and alveolar edema is most likely to develop in the elderly patient with compromised cardiac function or the occasional younger patient with significant cardiac disease. It often develops on the second or third postoperative day as fluid is mobilized from third-space depots, although it can occur with excessive administration of fluid during or immediately after an operation if the patient's cardiac or renal function is compromised. The healthy patient with normal cardiac and renal function can usually tolerate fluid overload, with prompt diuresis and no pulmonary symptoms.

1. Diagnosis   The diagnosis is made by the presence of tachypnea, tachycardia, shortness of breath and orthopnea, coupled with an elevated central venous pressure, distended neck veins, and wet rales in the basilar lung segments.

A diastolic 'gallop' may be heard. The sputum is often frothy and pink. Chest x-ray shows symmetrical perihilar fluffy infiltrates, cardiac enlargement, prominent pulmonary vascular shadows, and lymphatic congestion in the costophrenic angles (Kerley's B lines).

Pulmonary edema is often difficult to diagnose in marginal cases, and confusion with bronchial asthma occurs. Pulmonary edema has been referred to as 'cardiac asthma' because the findings of respiratory distress and wheezing are similar. The two conditions may be distinguished by the presence of wet rales with 'cardiac asthma'; rales are heard bilaterally at the lung bases, and they may extend half to two-thirds of the way up the lung apex.

   2. Treatment of pulmonary edema is described in the Cardiac Complications Section.

F. PNEUMONIA in the postoperative patient is usually a sequela of inadequately treated atelectasis, gross airway contamination, or preexistent pulmonary disease, most commonly from smoking. It rarely develops earlier than 4-5 days after operation unless an unusual event, such as aspiration, occurs. The cause is nearly always bacterial, and if the patient has been given prophylactic or therapeutic antibiotics from the time of surgery, one may assume that the organism causing the pneumonia is resistant to the antibiotics being used.

   1. Diagnosis   The diagnosis is made by the presence of fever, leukocytosis, increased sputum production, consolidation and/or rales on physical examination, and a localized or diffuse infiltrate on x-ray. Gram stain of the sputum usually reveals heavy colonization by a single organism, and a large number of polymorphonuclear leukocytes are present. If few bacteria of mixed types are seen, and if there are minimal numbers of PMNs, the diagnosis is open to question. It should be emphasized that the gram stain is more valid as an index of pulmonary infection than the culture, as it is possible to culture some organism from the trachea in virtually everyone.

   2. Treatment   If pneumonia is diagnosed, antibiotic therapy is begun immediately based on the gram stain. Confirmatory culture is obtained and the antibiotic sensitivities are checked. Therapy otherwise should be supportive and if possible directed at the underlying cause of the pneumonia. Blood gases should be monitored and nasotracheal intubation and ventilation carried out if the patient's status deteriorates. If the patient is unable to eat or has had minimal caloric intake for more than 1 week, IV hyperalimentation should be considered. Starvation causes some degree of immunologic depression within 1-2 weeks and nutritional support is mandatory if the patient is depleted or has undergone major trauma or extensive surgery.

G. ADULT RESPIRATORY DISTRESS SYNDROME   In unusual instances, after extensive surgery or massive trauma, patients develop tachypnea, hypoxemia, diffuse pulmonary infiltrates, and decreased compliance of the lungs. Physical examination does not disclose rales, bronchospasm, or evidence of alveolar edema. This syndrome may be differentiated from pneumonitis by the absence of signs of infection and the absence of significant organisms or leukocytes on gram stain of the sputum.

Adult respiratory distress syndrome appears in many cases to be related to pulmonary microembolism, and the findings are similar to those which have been described for fat embolism (see next section). Evidence of intravascular coagulation is a common accompaniment of this syndrome, but the role of intravascular coagulation as a specific cause has not been proved. The most common associated condition is systemic sepsis, often from intraabdominal foci following intestinal surgery or massive trauma. Severe pancreatitis is also a common antecedent cause.

   1. Diagnosis   Adult respiratory distress syndrome is diagnosed by the findings described above and the exclusion of other more specific pulmonary entities. It normally does not develop until 3-4 days postoperatively, and it is usually associated with other complications, particularly sepsis.

2. Treatment When the disease is mild to moderate, supportive care with administration of increased concentrations of oxygen by mask may be sufficient treatment. In most cases, the symptoms are relatively severe, and the degree of arterial hypoxemia necessitates endotracheal intubation and mechanical ventilation. Mechanical ventilation is indicated if the arterial Po_2 cannot be maintained above 70 mm Hg with the administration of supplemental oxygen by mask.

Nasotracheal intubation in the awake patient is carried out with local anesthesia as described previously, and mechanical ventilation using a volume cycled ventilator is instituted. In severe cases, positive end expiratory pressure should be used to improve oxygenation.

The patient should be closely monitored for the development of secondary pulmonary infection and should be treated with appropriate antibiotics if infection occurs. The development of intravascular coagulation should be closely monitored by standard tests, and anticoagulation with systemic heparin should be carried out if there is evidence of this disorder.

Steroids have been advocated but have not been shown to be beneficial. Potent diuretics and salt-poor albumin have also been advocated; these agents are controversial, and their effects appear to be transient at best.

Insertion of a pulmonary artery catheter to monitor pulmonary wedge pressures is mandatory for careful titration of IV fluid replacement. Because of the high mortality associated with the development of renal failure in addition to respiratory failure, one should make every effort to preserve renal function by adequate hydration of the patient but should avoid over-hydration which increases the degree of pulmonary interstitial edema. The pulmonary arterial wedge pressure should be kept as low as possible consistent with adequate peripheral perfusion and urine output of 0.5 ml/kg/hour. In no case should wedge pressure be elevated above 15 mm Hg.

H. FAT EMBOLISM SYNDROME has been described in the past as a specific entity occurring after extensive trauma with fractures of pelvis or long bones. It was said to result from the venous embolization of marrow fat, which travels to the pulmonary capillaries and produces symptoms by a combination of mechanical obstruction and inflammatory reaction. The symptoms are similar to those of the adult respiratory distress syndrome—tachypnea, hypoxemia, diffuse pulmonary infiltrates, and decreased lung compliance. The only difference clinically has been a higher reported incidence of cerebral symptoms with fat embolism, usually consisting of disorientation, confusion, or delirium, and often progressing to obtundation without localizing signs.

The true cause of the syndrome is unclear, as the pathologic findings of fat in pulmonary, renal, and cerebral capillaries may be seen in traumatized patients who do not have long bone fractures or any clinical manifestations of the fat embolism syndrome. At present, it seems best to consider fat embolism as being indistinguishable from the adult respiratory distress syndrome, because the symptoms, findings, and treatment are essentially the same.

I. PULMONARY EMBOLISM (See Section VII).

V. ACUTE RENAL FAILURE*

Acute renal failure is the rapid onset of impaired renal function. The hallmark is **rapidly progressive azotemia**, usually, but not always, accompanied by oliguria (urine output less than 400 cc/24 hours).

Causes of acute renal failure are listed in Table 2-6. Prerenal azotemia and acute tubular necrosis (ATN) are the most common types. Laboratory findings in these 2 entities are listed in Table 2-7.

*By Flavio Vincenti, MD

A. PRERENAL AZOTEMIA is the result of renal hypoperfusion because of volume depletion (dehydration or blood loss) or decreased cardiac output from pump failure without volume depletion (congestive heart failure). The glomerular filtration rate is decreased, and there is enhanced reabsorption of sodium, water, and urea in the tubules in patients with prerenal azotemia.

It is important to diagnose prerenal azotemia because it may be easily reversible and also because persistence of renal hypoperfusion may lead to the development of ATN.

1. Diagnosis Assess the volume status (fullness of neck veins, skin turgor, orthostatic changes in blood pressure and heart rate, peripheral perfusion). Note that central redistribution of the intravascular volume from acidosis-induced venoconstriction may result in prominent neck veins despite extracellular fluid depletion.

Examine the heart and lungs. The findings may indicate congestive heart failure.

Catheterize the urinary bladder to obtain a urine specimen and to monitor urine output during treatment.

Send blood for BUN, creatinine, electrolytes, and osmolality, and measure urine electrolytes and osmolality. Examine the urine sediment (see Table 2-7).

These steps should lead to a diagnosis of prerenal azotemia on the basis of hypovolemia or congestive heart failure. In patients with borderline cardiac function, measurement of central venous or even pulmonary arterial pressures may be necessary before treatment is instituted.

2. Treatment of congestive heart failure is discussed in Cardiac Complications section above.

Hypovolemic patients should be given 0.9% saline solution IV at a rate of 100-500 cc/hour, depending upon the severity of volume depletion.

Do **not** give diuretics prior to correction of hypovolemia. If there is no improvement in urine output **after** blood volume has been replenished, a bolus of furosemide (80-200 mg IV) or mannitol (12.5-25 gm IV) may be administered. **Caution** must be observed in the use of mannitol infusions since, if oliguria persists, failure to excrete mannitol may lead to volume expansion and pulmonary edema.

If there is no response to these diuretics, ATN or obstructive uropathy is probably present.

Table 2-6. Causes of acute renal failure

1. Prerenal azotemia
2. Renovascular disease
   A. Arterial occlusion
      1. Major emboli or thrombi
      2. Vasculitides and bilateral cortical necrosis
   B. Venous thrombosis
3. Parenchymal renal disease
   A. Acute Tubular Necrosis (ATN)
      1. Renal ischemia
      2. Nephrotoxins
      3. Mixed (1 + 2)–unknown
   B. Other causes
      1. Glomerulo and interstitial nephritides
      2. Disorders of calcium and uric acid homeostasis
4. Postrenal azotemia (obstructive)

B. ACUTE TUBULAR NECROSIS may be a consequence of **ischemia** (usually due to hypotension), **nephrotoxins** (e.g., $HgCl_2$, CCl_4, methoxyflurane, or antibiotics—especially the aminoglycosides), or **mixed** (or unknown) **mechanisms** (e.g., hemoglobinuria, myoglobinuria, radiographic contrast media).

1. Course The course of ATN may be divided into 3 phases:

a. Pre-ATN phase The findings are similar to those in prerenal azotemia, and prompt treatment may prevent progression to ATN. Pre-ATN is usually a retrospective diagnosis.

b. Oliguric phase ATN is fully established in this phase. Oliguria usually lasts 7-21 days.

c. Diuretic phase The urine output gradually increases as the kidneys recover. In some cases, the postoliguric diuresis may be massive. The creatinine clearance returns to 80% of the baseline level in 6-12 weeks.

2. Diagnosis ATN, despite its name, is not usually associated with necrosis of tubular cells that can be seen histologically. Renal biopsy, therefore, is not usually obtained.

The clinical setting and the laboratory tests, especially the urine findings (see Table 2-7), are usually sufficient to establish the diagnosis of ATN.

Table 2-7. Laboratory guidelines in the diagnosis of oliguria

	Prerenal azotemia	ATN
BUN/creatinine	> 20/1	< 10/1
Urine Sp. Gr.	≥ 1.020	≤ 1.012
U/P Osm*	≥ 1.5	< 1.5
Urine Na	<10 mEq/liter	>20 mEq/liter
Urine sediment	Unremarkable	Hematin (pigmented) casts

*U/P Osm = urine to plasma osmolality

The severity of renal damage varies; in mild cases, there may be high urinary output rather than oliguria (nonoliguric ATN).

Anuria is rare in ATN; bilateral cortical necrosis, acute glomerulonephritis, urinary obstruction, and thrombosis of the major renal vessels are more likely to cause anuria.

3. Complications The abnormalities described in chronic renal failure (see Section III in this chapter) occur in acute renal failure, frequently with greater severity because of the acuteness of the renal dysfunction. Fluid and electrolyte abnormalities are invariably present, and profound acidosis and severe hyperkalemia are common. Infection and gastrointestinal bleeding are the major complications associated with ATN, and infection is the principal cause of death.

4. Treatment of ATN is supportive and is directed at preventing or treating complications until renal function returns to normal.

There is no evidence that the course of established ATN is modified by the administration of furosemide or mannitol. Diuretics should not be given.

a. Fluids and electrolytes

Fluid Measurable fluid losses (urine, gastrointestinal fluids) and insensible losses (400-500 ml/day) should be replaced. Carefully record intake, output, and body weight daily.

Sodium Replace losses of sodium from urine or other measurable sources. *Hyponatremia* developing in the course of ATN is usually indicative of fluid excess, rather than sodium deficit, and is best treated by fluid restriction.

Potassium *Hyperkalemia* commonly occurs in these patients. A variety of factors contribute to hyperkalemia, including acidosis and potassium release from tissues secondary to excessive catabolism, trauma, or hemolysis. Be aware of the potassium content of potassium penicillin G (1.7 mEq/million units) and salt substitutes. Monitor serum potassium concentration and the ECG.

Ion exchange resin (Kayexalate) administered orally (25 gm Kayexalate and 50 gm of Sorbitol) or as a retention enema (50 gm Kayexalate and 50 gm of Sorbitol with 100 cc of tap water) reduce serum potassium levels over several hours. Potential side-effects include excessive sodium retention and heart failure.

More urgent treatment of hyperkalemia (serum potassium greater than 7 mEq/liter) requires administration of sodium bicarbonate (44-88 mEq of sodium bicarbonate IV) or hypertonic glucose solution and regular insulin (100 cc of 50% glucose plus 10 units of regular insulin).

Life-threatening cardiac arrhythmias due to hyperkalemia are treated by IV calcium gluconate or calcium chloride (5-10 ml of 10% solution over 5 minutes with ECG monitoring).

Dialysis may be required to remove excess potassium.

Restrict *magnesium* (e.g., in antacids) and watch for low *calcium* levels in the blood.

Acidosis Acidosis in ATN may result from acid produced by normal metabolic processes or in association with hypercatabolic states. Acidosis may be treated by administration of sodium bicarbonate, but this may result in sodium excess and heart failure. Acidosis associated with volume overload is best treated by dialysis.

b. Diet Adequate nutrition is fundamental in the treatment of ATN (see Nutrition Section in this chapter).

c. Drugs Dosages of drugs, including antibiotics (see Chapter 4), digoxin, and magnesium-containing antacids must be modified in ATN. If a nephrotoxin is suspected of having caused the ATN, the nephrotoxic drug must, of course, be discontinued.

d. Dialysis Uncontrollable hyperkalemia or acidosis, overhydration, and the development of uremic symptoms are indications for dialysis. Peritoneal and hemodialysis are equally efficacious. Early and aggressive dialysis seems to result in improved survival in patients with ATN.

e. Diuretic phase Careful observation of blood volume and electrolytes is important through the diuretic stage because the creatinine clearance may lag behind the increase in urine volume. Measurement of urine output, urine electrolyte concentrations, and serial body weights are helpful.

5. Prognosis ATN has an overall mortality rate of 50%. Mortality is about 80% in patients with burns, trauma, or surgical procedures and only 30% in 'medical ATN' (usually due to nephrotoxins) because there are more complications of the underlying condition in the surgical group.

C. POSTRENAL AZOTEMIA Obstruction of the urinary tract should be suspected if the patient is **anuric.** Obstruction of the upper tract must be bilateral for azotemia to occur; renal hippurate scan, infusion IVP, and retrograde ureteral catheterization are important diagnostic tests. Severe obstruction of the lower tract is easily recognized by the inability to insert a Foley catheter.

VI. URINARY RETENTION*

Inability to urinate after surgery is a frequent problem. It may be seen after any operation, but it is particularly common after pelvic or perineal procedures.

1. Causes

a. Reflex spasm of the voluntary sphincter because of pain or anxiety.

b. Medication—usually anticholinergics and narcotics.

c. Preexisting partial bladder outlet obstruction—commonly an enlarged prostate.

d. Detrusor atony as result of surgery and manipulation, (e.g., after recto-perineal or pelvic surgery.

e. Overdistention during surgery, due to diuresis or prolonged operation.

f. Mechanical obstruction by expanding hematoma or fluid collection.

2. Prevention

a. Voiding patterns should be evaluated carefully preoperatively if one suspects bladder outlet obstruction. Obstruction can be corrected before operation, or catheter drainage may be instituted immediately after surgery.

b. Avoid excessive use of narcotics and parasympatholytic drugs.

c. Patients scheduled for lengthy operations should be catheterized preoperatively and the bladder drained throughout the procedure.

d. Avoid excessive IV fluids during and immediately after the operation. This is a common factor contributing to retention after brief, relatively minor operations (e.g., inguinal hernia repair) done under spinal anesthesia that lasts for hours after the operation is completed.

3. Diagnosis If a patient is unable to pass urine for several hours postoperatively and there is no desire to urinate, one must explore the possibility of **oliguria** as a consequence of diminished fluid intake (see above). Sometimes a heavily sedated patient does not recognize the sensation of fullness and does not urinate for that reason.

A **palpable bladder** in the midline above the symphysis pubis is an almost sure sign of acute retention. Every patient should be examined if he does not urinate for 6 hours after operation. In this way, overdistention of the bladder, which might induce bladder atony and perhaps myogenic damage to the bladder wall (in some cases permanent), could be avoided.

4. Treatment

a. Conservative (1) Relieve local pain, if any, by narcotics or sedatives. (2) If the patient's condition permits, he should urinate in the standing or sitting position instead of the supine position. (3) Turning on a water faucet within the patient's hearing encourages voiding. (4) Sitting in a tub of warm water is possible after some operations, and this may make it possible to urinate. (5) Cholinergic drugs such as bethanechol chloride (Urecholine) should be given (2.5 mg subcutaneously, followed in 1 hour by another injection of 5 mg). (6) If there is no effect, the bladder should be catheterized.

b. Catheterization When all other measures fail, the bladder is markedly distended, and the patient is experiencing severe bladder contractions without voiding, catheterization should be performed. Preferably, catheterization should be done only once and the patient then encouraged to void on his own accord. A preoperative history of any voiding difficulty is very important to help decide on the duration of catheter drainage. If there was no or only minimal preoperative obstruction, the patient should be able to resume normal voiding spontaneously.

---

*By Emil Tanagho, MD

VII. BLEEDING AND THROMBOSIS*

One of the fundamental problems of surgery is hemostasis. The surgeon must have knowledge of the diagnosis and treatment of abnormal bleeding and abnormal clotting during and after operation.

A. FACTORS IN HEMOSTASIS In the fresh surgical wound, 3 factors contribute to spontaneous cessation of bleeding: blood vessel contraction; platelet adhesion and aggregation; and coagulation. Bleeding problems are minimal if 2 of these 3 factors are functional, but if 2 of the 3 are inactive, diffuse bleeding is likely to result.

  1. Blood vessel contraction (vascular reactivity) When small blood vessels are divided, the local action of catecholamines and of the sympathetic nervous system constricts the injured vessels. Injury to larger blood vessels results in contraction with telescoping of the layers so that the intima and media are retracted inward and the adventitia is pulled over the end of the severed vessel. Cold and ganglionic blocking agents tend to interfere with vascular reactivity, while heat and sympathetic stimulation tend to increase the local vascular spasm.

  2. Platelet adhesion and aggregation Exposed collagen at the site of vascular injury causes activation and adhesion of platelets to the area of injury. This triggers a secondary reaction, releasing substances such as ADP and thrombin which cause aggregation of additional platelets to those already adherent. Thus, a **platelet plug** or platelet thrombus forms rapidly. This plug is the primary factor in vascular hemostasis and results in the cessation of bleeding. Subsequent incorporation of fibrin into the platelet plug (due to the release of thrombin from aggregating platelets) consolidates the plug and prevents its dissolution. If fibrin is not incorporated, on the other hand, the platelet plug is reversible and platelets break loose and return to the circulation. This leads to recurrent hemorrhage from the end of the injured vessel.

  Platelet adhesion and aggregation are promoted by heat, exposed collagen, catecholamines, acidosis, and stasis. Depression of platelet function interferes with formation of the platelet plug. There are more than 200 drugs that are capable of interfering with platelet adhesion or aggregation (see Table 2-8).

  3. Coagulation The third phase of hemostasis involves the conversion of fibrinogen to fibrin. The coagulation mechanism has been described as a waterfall effect in which there is progressive activation of clotting factors, the ultimate result being generation of fibrin (Fig. 2-2). The system is activated through 2 alternate pathways: the extrinsic and the intrinsic systems.

  a. Extrinsic system The extrinsic system represents a short-circuiting of the usual pathway; activation occurs through a lipoprotein moiety released from damaged cells (tissue thromboplastin). Defects in the extrinsic system prolong the prothrombin time (PT).

  b. Intrinsic system The intrinsic system, starting with factor XII (Hageman), is activated by a foreign surface (e.g., exposed collagen), by substances within the body (e.g., circulating collagen), or by exposed basement membranes. Defects in the intrinsic system result in prolongation of the partial thromboplastin time (PTT).

  c. Final common pathway Defects in the final common pathway at the level of factor X or below result in prolongation of both PT and PTT.

B. OPERATIVE AND POSTOPERATIVE BLEEDING Excessive bleeding during or immediately after an operation may be 'surgical' (i.e., the surgeon failed to ligate or cauterize large vessels), or it may reflect some type of hemostatic defect. The differential diagnosis of hemostatic defects is listed below.

*By F. William Blaisdell, MD

1. Platelet defects

a. Manifestations The primary manifestation of a preexisting platelet defect, such as might occur in association with drugs that suppress platelet function, is **oozing**; it is noted when the initial incision is made, and it recurs during the operation whenever a fresh wound is made. If the coagulation mechanism is normal, this slow bleeding eventually ceases. Thus, defective platelet function rarely results in complications more serious than increased blood loss or a greater incidence of wound hematomas.

If platelets were normal preoperatively, a defect may develop during the operation as a result of drugs administered by the anesthesiologist or because of depletion of platelets during shock or major tissue dissection, or as a result of massive transfusion.

b. Treatment When this type of bleeding is recognized and the nature of the operation dictates that it be treated to prevent morbidity, the administration of **platelet transfusions** is specific therapy. One platelet pack contains the platelets from 1 unit of blood. Since the normal adult human has a blood volume equivalent to 10–12 units of blood, 4–6 platelet packs should correct the defect. If utilization of platelets is concurrent with platelet transfusion, the required number of platelet packs cannot be predicted.

2. Coagulation defects

a. Manifestations Coagulation defects cause secondary bleeding from wounds. Initial hemostasis due to platelet aggregation is adequate, but massive, uncontrollable hemorrhage develops subsequently as the platelet plugs deaggregate. The classical example of a coagulation defect is hemophilia.

b. Differential diagnosis Coagulation defects may be due to: (1) Preexisting congenital hematologic abnormalities. (2) Anticoagulant drugs given deliberately or inadvertently. (3) Depletion of clotting factors as a result of intravascular coagulation. (4) Massive transfusion (rarely). (5) Liver disease: the ability to replace coagulation factors is limited, and defects are generated by the normal consumption of these factors during the operation.

c. Treatment Coagulation defects are treated by the administration of fresh frozen plasma or, if a congenital defect is present, specific factor concentrates are given.

3. Combined defects–consumption coagulopathy

Combined defects in platelet function and coagulation are rare. They are usually acquired secondary to intravascular coagulation. Emergency operations, particularly those associated with shock, massive transfusion, and soft-tissue injury, may be complicated by intense intravascular activation of the coagulation mechanism with a resulting depletion of platelets and coagulation factors. These combined depletion defects produce the hemorrhagic syndrome of disseminated intravascular coagulation, the **'consumption coagulopathy.'**

a. Manifestations The principal manifestation is massive, uncontrollable, life-threatening bleeding, not only from the operative wound but also from cut-down incisions, the nose, or any other site of minor trauma.

b. Treatment (1) Correct the factors responsible for intravascular activation of the coagulation mechanism. This may entail discontinuing a mismatched blood transfusion, debriding devitalized tissue, or correcting shock. When the cause is gram-negative sepsis, identification of the source of infection is imperative to permit surgical drainage and specific antibiotic treatment. (2) **Heparinize** with an IV bolus of 10,000–20,000 units to slow down utilization of clotting factors in vivo so that spontaneous regeneration of these factors can occur. In addition, transfuse platelets and replace clotting factors with fresh frozen plasma. If fresh, warm blood is available, it may be used instead of platelets and plasma.

C. SYSTEMIC CLOTTING SYNDROMES

Surgical trauma, the stress of operation, shock, and blood loss all increase the tendency of blood to coagulate. Tis-

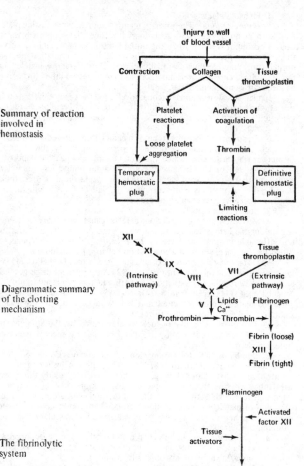

Summary of reaction involved in hemostasis

Diagrammatic summary of the clotting mechanism

The fibrinolytic system

Fig. 2-2.

(Drawings on this page modified and reproduced with permission, from Deykin: Thrombogenesis. New England J. Med. **276**:622, 1967.)

sue trauma releases factors (e.g., collagen and fragments of fat) into the bloodstream where they act as procoagulants and activate the clotting mechanism. Acidosis and release of catecholamines also increase the clotting tendency.

Clotting problems, therefore, may arise within the vascular system; they may be categorized as 'mild clotting tendency' ('hypercoagulability'), 'moderate intravascular coagulation', and 'disseminated intravascular coagulation.'

1. Hypercoagulability

a. Pathogenesis　The increased clotting tendency in certain types of patients (e.g., the elderly, orthopedic patients in traction, and the critically ill) is well known to the clinician. A classic example of someone at increased risk for clotting complications is the older patient with a hip fracture.

Low-grade clotting occurs as a result of surgical trauma. Small amounts of fibrinogen are converted into fibrin. Then, if there are insufficient amounts of circulating fibrin, a fibrin strand that has been formed is not able to link up with other molecules of fibrin; instead, it forms soluble complexes with molecules of fibrinogen, or it forms fibrin degradation products. The presence of soluble fibrin monomer complexes results in a blood composition that might be considered to be a supersaturated solution, so that a little bit of additional clotting, or the action of local factors such as stasis, may precipitate frank intravascular clotting.

Hypercoagulability has also been defined as a 'depletion of antithrombin III,' a substance which circulates in the blood and neutralizes small amounts of thrombin inevitably forming as a result of mild trauma. Depletion of antithrombin III leads to thrombin activation of the clotting cascade at the factor X level, with the generation of large quantities of thrombin, and frank intravascular coagulation is the outcome.

b. Diagnosis　Although there is little question that hypercoagulability exists, it has been difficult to identify by standard laboratory tests. Two tests, fibrin monomer assessment and antithrombin III assay, are now available to help make the diagnosis of hypercoagulability.

c. Treatment　The rationale for low-dose heparin to prevent clotting complications is based on the concept of hypercoagulability. Small amounts of heparin activate and improve the efficiency of antithrombin III so that thrombin can be neutralized before it initiates the clotting cascade. Low-dose heparin therapy consists of 5000 units of heparin administered subcutaneously 2 to 3 times daily.

2. Moderate intravascular coagulation

a. Pathogenesis　Moderate intravascular coagulation is the result of trauma or shock, and it leads to the formation of moderate to large quantities of fibrin in the microcirculation. This fibrin occludes the microcirculation or is swept into the systemic circulation where it can damage critical organs such as lung, kidney, and liver. The adult respiratory distress syndrome, renal failure, hepatic injury, and stress ulceration are complications of intravascular coagulation which develop by this mechanism. The fibrin also may precipitate in areas of stasis such as leg veins.

b. Diagnosis　It is difficult to document the presence of moderate intravascular coagulation. The partial thromboplastin time and the prothrombin time are slightly prolonged, and tests for fibrin degradation products are often positive. Following the administration of radioactive fibrinogen, there is evidence of increased radioactivity in the legs in many surgical patients, and the results of this test correlate well with the presence of clot as confirmed by phlebographic studies. Most patients with positive radioactive fibrinogen tests are clinically asymptomatic, but they are at risk of subsequent pulmonary embolism nevertheless (see Thrombophlebitis, below).

c. Treatment　includes restoration and maintenance of circulatory blood volume and, when not contraindicated, anticoagulation. **Heparin** should be administered IV as a 20,000-unit bolus followed by 1500-2000 units/hour. The circulatory status should be monitored carefully and respiratory and renal support provided as necessary.

Table 2-8. Drugs which may affect platelet function*†

Acedyne	**Chlordiazepoxide**	Duadacin
Acetax	**Chloroquine**	Duradyne
Acetonyl	**Chlorpheniramine**	Duragesic
Acetycol	**Chlorpromazine**	Ecotrin
Acetylsalicylic Acid	Chlor-PZ	Elavil
Actifed	Chlor-Trimeton	Emphaseem
Actol	Cirin	Empiral
Adrenalin	Citra	Empirin Compound
Alka-Seltzer	**Clofibrate**	Emprazil
Allerest	Coastalgesic	Endotussin
Alphaprodine	Cocaine	Entex
Alprine	ColBenemid	**Epinephrine**
Alva-Tranquil	**Colchicine**	Epitrate
Amesec	Coldene	Equagesic
Amidopyrine	Combid	Esgic
Aminophylline	Compazine	Eskatrol
Amitriptyline	Compoz	Ether
Anacin	Congespirin	Etravon
Anacin Arthritis Formula	Contac	Excedrin
Ana-Kit	Copavin	Exna-R
Analgin	Cope	Expectico
Anexsia	Co-Pyronil	Expectran
Anodynos	Coriciden	Exgendryl
Antagonate	Coryban	Fedahist
Antipyrine	Counterpain	Femicin
Anturane	Covanamine	Fiorinal
A.P.C.	Cyclopropane	Fletcher's Cough Syrup
Aralen	**Cyproheptadine**	Fluothanex
Arrestin	Dallergy	**Furosemide**
Arvin	Darvon Compound	GG-Cen
A.S.A.	Dasin	Ginsopan
Asbron	Decagesic	**Glyceryl Guaiacolate**
As-Ca-Phen	Deconamine	Glyceryl Trinitrate
Ascodeen	Defensin	Glycotuss
Ascriptin	Dehist	**Guaifenesin**
Asperbuf	Demazin	Guistreyx
Aspergum	Derfule	**Halothanex**
Asphac-B (and G)	**Desipramine**	Hasacode
Aspirin	**Dextran**	**Heparin**
Athemol	Devarex	Histabid
Atromid	**Diazepam**	Histadyl
Aventil	Dibenzylene	Histalet
Axatal	**Dibucaine**	Histaspan
Azolid	**Diethyl-ether**	Historal
Bayer Cold Tablet	**Dihydroergotamine**	Hycomine
Benadryl	Dimacol	Hycotuss
Brondecon	Dimetane	Hytuss
Bronkolixir	**Diphenhydramine**	Hydromox
Bronkotabs	Dipyridamole	Hydropres
Buff-A (Compound)	Ditazol	Hydrotensin
Buffadyne	Diupres	**Hydroxychloroquine**
Bufferin	Diutensen	Imavate
Butazolidin	Dolor	**Imipramine**
Butiserpazide	Donatussin	Indocin
Cafergot	Dondril	**Indomethacin**
Caffeine	Dorcol	Intensain
Cama Inlay-Tabs	Dormin	Iproveratril
Cerebid	Dralserp	Isoclor
Cerespan	Drinus	**Isoxuprine**
Cheracol	Dristan	Janimine

Table 2-8 (cont.) Drugs which may affect platelet function*†

Kavrin	Pavabid	San-Man
Kiddisan	Pavacap	Sansert
Lasix	Pavacen	Sedagesic
Librax	Pavadel	Ser-Ap-Es
Libritabs	Pavakey	Serpasil
Librium	Pavased	Sinarest
Lidocaine	Pavatran	SK-Pramine
Lixaminol	Pava-Wol	Sleep-Eze
Lufyllis–EPG and GG	Penthrane	Slo-Phyllin
Marhist	Percobarb	Soma
Matropinal	Percodan	Somicaps
Measurin	Periactin	Sominex
Mefenamic Acid	Persantine	Somophyllin
Menrium	Persistin	Sorbutuss
Metatensin	Pertofrane	Sta Kalm
Methadilazine	Phenaphen	Stanback
Methapyrilene	Phenergan	Stelazine
Methergoline	**Phenothiazine**	Sterazolidin
Methoxyflurane	**Phenoxybenzamine**	**Sulfinpyrazone**
Methysergide	Phensal	Supac
Micronefrin	**Phentolamine**	Super Aspirchews
Midol	**Phenylbutazone**	Sure Sleep
Migral	Phrenilin	Sus-Phrine
Mr. Sleep	Pirseal	Sustaverine
Mudrane	Plaquenil	Synalgos
Myobid	Plexonal	Synophylate
Naldecon	Polaramine	Tacaryl
Napril	Polyvinylpyrrolidone	Tandearil
Naproxen	Ponstel	Tedral
Naquival	Predisal	Teldrin
Narine	Presamine	Temaril
Narspan	Priscoline	**Theobromine**
Nasahist	**Prochlorperazine**	Theocalcin
Neocylate	**Promethazine**	Thorazine
Neo-Nyte	**Propranolol**	Tofranil
Neotap	**Prostaglandine E_1**	Tolazoline
Neothylline	Pseudo-Hist	Triaminic
Nialamide	**Pyrazole**	Triaminicin
Nicergoline	**Pyrilamine**	Triavil
Nilcol	Quadnite	Trigesic
Nisentil	Quelidrine	**Trimeprazine**
Nitroprusside	Quibron	Trind
Nolamin	Quinamm	Tus-Oraminic
Norepinephrine	Raused	Tusquelin
Norpramin	Regitine	Tussend
Nortryptiline	Regroton	Tussi-Organidin
Novahistine	Renese-R	Tussi-Ornade
Nupercaine	Repan	Unproco
Nytol	**Reserpine**	Valium
Oralen	Rhinex	Vaponefrin
Oraminic	Robaxisal	Vasal
Ornade	Robitussin	Vasodilan
Oxalid	Romilar	Vasospan
Oxyphenbutazone	Rynatan	Verequad
Pabirin	Rynatuss	Vesprin
PAC	Ryna-Tussadine	**Warfarin**
Panalgesic	S.A.C.	Wesprin
Panwafarin	Salpix	Xylocaine
Papaverine	Salutensin	Zactirin
Paracetamol	Sandril	Zipan

*Generic drug names are printed in boldface type.
†Reproduced, with permission, from Blaisdell FW, Lewis F R *Respiratory Distress Syndrome of Shock and Trauma.* Saunders, 1977.

3. Disseminated intravascular coagulation

a. Manifestations Disseminated intravascular coagulation is inevitably associated with diffuse bleeding and multiple organ failure. Septic shock and hemorrhagic shock with massive soft tissue injury are predisposing conditions.

b. Treatment is similar to that of moderate intravascular coagulation and consists of resuscitation and careful monitoring of the circulation, anticoagulants (if not contraindicated), and removal of the predisposing factor by treatment of infection, cessation of transfusion, adequate debridement of damaged or devitalized tissue, resection of dead bowel, etc.

D. THROMBOPHLEBITIS Venous thrombosis may be categorized as **phlebothrombosis** (asymptomatic, nonobstructive clot) or **thrombophlebitis** (inflammatory, thrombotic obstruction of veins.) Since one tends to blend into the other, the general term 'thrombophlebitis' is often used to denote all venous clotting conditions.

Hypovolemia and recumbency during and after operation result in circulatory stasis in the lower extremities. Stasis and hypercoagulability contribute to platelet aggregation and fibrin formation, initially in valve pockets, and eventually extending to involve major segments of the veins. The use of radioactive fibrinogen has documented that most thrombophlebitis starts in veins of the calf and progresses proximally into the pelvis and abdomen.

1. Phlebothrombosis is the formation of clot in leg veins and in other areas of stasis. Initially, the clot is not circumferentially attached to the wall of the vein and therefore does not produce venous obstruction. It usually causes no symptoms or signs. In most instances, the asymptomatic clot lyses and disappears, but in some patients the clot embolizes to the lungs (see Pulmonary Embolism).

As many as 30-40% of patients with major medical or surgical illnesses have clots in the veins of the legs detectable by radioactive fibrinogen studies. Preventive measures include low-dose heparin therapy and avoidance of circulatory stasis by promoting active exercise of the legs or by external pneumatic compression of the legs.

2. Superficial thrombophlebitis is inflammatory thrombosis in subcutaneous veins.

a. Causes Superficial thrombophlebitis can be precipitated by trauma or by stasis in preexisting varices. If there has been no break in the skin, it is safe to assume that there is no bacterial infection despite the signs of inflammation. Superficial thrombophlebitis also can be secondary to the placement of IV catheters. When the vein has been violated in this fashion, associated infection is probable (**septic thrombophlebitis**).

b. Diagnosis The subcutaneous vein is a palpable, tender cord with erythema and edema of the overlying skin and subcutaneous tissue. The findings resemble those in lymphangitis. Superficial thrombophlebitis does **not** produce swelling of the limb. In fact, it is considered a benign condition and is not associated with significant risk of embolism.

c. Treatment Warm moist compresses are usually sufficient treatment. Anticoagulants are **not** necessary ordinarily. Activity is not restricted.

Septic thrombophlebitis is treated with specific antibiotics, usually the antistaphylococcal agents. Occasionally it is necessary to excise an infected vein.

If thrombophlebitis progresses toward the junction of superficial veins with the deep veins (e.g., the saphenofemoral junction), the involved superficial vein should be ligated and divided near the junction to avoid propagation of clot into the deep venous system.

3. Deep thrombophlebitis is inflammatory thrombosis of deep veins producing **obstruction** of venous return. Deep thrombophlebitis damages the veins and sets the stage for further propagation of clot and pulmonary embolism. **Postphlebitic syndrome** is a frequent sequela (see Chapter 13).

a. Diagnosis The primary manifestations are pain and tenderness over the involved vein and edema distal to the proximal extent of clotting. Swelling of the calf and foot is characteristic of thrombosis in the superficial femoral vein; swelling of the entire lower extremity results from thrombosis of the iliac or common femoral veins.

b. Treatment Deep thrombophlebitis is always serious and should be treated vigorously.

Systemic anticoagulation should be instituted unless there are definite contraindications. Heparin is given in an initial bolus of 10,000 units IV followed by 1000-1500 units/hour by continuous IV infusion.

The extremity should be elevated and immobilized until pain and swelling disappear. At this point, the patient can be progressively mobilized.

If ambulation is tolerated without recurrence of symptoms, the patient is converted to oral anticoagulants.

When the patient is able to remain upright for an hour or two without pain and swelling, discharge from the hospital is permissible.

Elastic support from metatarsals to tibial tubercle should be used for several weeks thereafter.

In most instances, oral anticoagulation should be continued for 6 weeks to 3 months, and, if episodes recur, permanent oral anticoagulation should be seriously considered.

Postphlebitic syndrome should be prevented (see Chapter 13).

4. Phlegmasia alba dolens and phlegmasia cerulea dolens Phlegmasia alba dolens is the term for deep thrombophlebitis with swelling; the term simply means 'painful white inflammation of veins'. Phlegmasia cerulea dolens is massive venous thrombosis associated with the bluish discoloration of impending gangrene. If all venous return from the extremity is obstructed, for arterial inflow is decreased reflexly, the limb becomes cyanotic, and gangrene follows. Thrombophlebitis associated with carcinoma is apt to be of this severe type.

Phlegmasia cerulea dolens is immediately life-threatening and should be treated with full doses of anticoagulants and elevation of the limb. If there is a contraindication to anticoagulation, or if the condition fails to respond promptly to conservative management, surgical intervention (thrombectomy) may be indicated.

E. PULMONARY MICROEMBOLISM AND FAT EMBOLISM Following extensive soft tissue injury, fragments of collagen, fat, and bone marrow can be identified in the circulation. These tissue fragments activate the clotting mechanism with aggregation of platelets and formation of fibrin. This material is filtered out by the pulmonary vascular bed. In most circumstances, platelet aggregates and fibrin are rapidly disposed of by lysis and by pulmonary macrophages, resulting in little disability. When there is a deficit in circulating blood volume, or when massive amounts of clot are generated by extensive soft tissue injury, hemolytic blood transfusion or sepsis, the load on the pulmonary circulation may be overwhelming. Development of secondary changes in the lungs is responsible for the adult respiratory distress syndrome. Treatment of this syndrome is discussed under Pulmonary Complications in this chapter.

F. PULMONARY EMBOLISM Embolism of organized clot from large systemic veins obstructs the pulmonary arteries. Manifestations depend upon the amount of pulmonary vasculature that is obstructed.

1. Diagnosis Small emboli may be completely asymptomatic; multiple microemboli may cause respiratory failure as described above.

Massive embolism (occluding two-thirds of the pulmonary vasculature) causes acute pulmonary hypertension and right ventricular strain and failure. Findings are hypotension, hypoxemia, and arrhythmias; death may occur within minutes to days.

About 10% of patients with clinical evidence of pulmonary embolism develop **pulmonary infarction.** Dyspnea, pleuritic chest pain, and hemoptysis are classical symptoms. Examination may reveal decreased breath sounds, a rub, or pleural effusion. Chest x-ray shows a wedge-shaped density. The ECG often indicates right ventricular strain. Lung scan contains areas of decreased perfusion. Pulmonary angiogram shows obstruction of large pulmonary arteries and is the most accurate diagnostic tool.

2. Differential diagnosis   Myocardial infarction, asthma, pneumonia, congestive heart failure.

3. Treatment   Pulmonary embolism with circulatory instability requires large doses of heparin (initial bolus of 20,000 units followed by 2000–4000 units/hour for the first 24–48 hours).

Ligation or plication of the inferior vena cava is required if anticoagulants are contraindicated, if bleeding complications develop on anticoagulants, or if pulmonary embolism recurs in a fully anticoagulated patient. The optimal site for ligation is just below the renal veins. The vena cava can either be narrowed (with a plastic clip or sutures) or ligated. The rationale for narrowing (plicating) the cava is to filter out large clots while avoiding obstruction. Ligation provides better protection against recurrent embolism; edema of the lower extremities is an acceptable sequela of this life-saving procedure.

G. ANTICOAGULATION

1. General considerations   Anticoagulation means suppression of the coagulation mechanism. The term is used loosely in clinical practice, however, and it may refer to the suppression of clotting or the inhibition of platelet aggregation.

The **only absolute anticoagulant is heparin,** a physiologic substance that is present in the mast cells of the body and which suppresses thrombin formation. The oral anticoagulating agents are less effective; they indirectly block coagulation by depressing certain of the coagulation factors. Antiplatelet-aggregating agents interfere with the platelet contribution to coagulation.

Since the greater portion of clot in the venous system is composed of fibrin, anticoagulants (heparin or oral agents) are optimal for the prevention or treatment of venous thrombosis. The major portion of clot in the arterial system is made up of platelets; hence, the antiplatelet-aggregating drugs are often used to prevent arterial thrombosis.

2. Heparin   With the discovery and isolation of heparin in 1935, a potent therapeutic agent was made available for specific treatment of major life-threatening thrombotic conditions; heparin also has made possible the use of cardiopulmonary bypass for open heart surgery.

a. Routes of administration   Heparin can be administered either subcutaneously or intravenously. Intramuscular injections of heparin carry an unacceptable risk of local hemorrhage. The subcutaneous route is used when only small amounts of heparin are required, most often for prophylaxis against clotting; slow absorption from the subcutaneous tissues produces, in theory, continuous low levels of activity in the vascular system. Larger doses of heparin required to treat thrombotic states should be administered intravenously.

b. Dosage   Doses of heparin are measured in units; 100 units are roughly equivalent to 1 mg of heparin.

Low-dose heparin therapy   Sufficient amounts of heparin are administered to decrease the coagulation tendency without producing alterations in laboratory clotting tests. This (in theory) avoids the risk of systemic anticoagulation. Doses generally administered for prophylaxis in a low-dose heparin regimen are 5000 units given subcutaneously 2 or 3 times daily.

Systemic heparin anticoagulation requires the IV administration of 10,000 to 20,000 units as an initial bolus followed by 1000–4000 units/hour, depending upon the severity of the patient's condition. Lower doses of heparin (1000-1500 units/hour) are administered for non-life-threatening conditions such as thrombophlebitis, while doses of 2000-4000 units of heparin are given for various life-threatening problems such as massive pulmonary embolism with cardiovascular instability.

c. Monitoring of anticoagulation   The best means of monitoring the anticoagulant effect of heparin is controversial. Clotting tests such as the Lee White clotting time, the activated partial thromboplastin time, or the activated clotting time, may demonstrate the need for increased amounts of heparin.

Lee White clotting time   Three test tubes of blood are drawn, and all of the tubes are repeatedly tipped in sequence until clotting is observed. The presence of clotting in the third test tube is the end point. The Lee White time is less than 10 minutes normally and should be 20-30 minutes on full anticoagulation. This test must be done at the bedside and is time-consuming, so other tests are usually used instead.

Activated partial thromboplastin time   Blood is collected in a citrated tube, the plasma is isolated, calcium is added, and the clotting time is measured after the addition of extrinsic thrombin. The activated partial thromboplastin time is normally under 40 seconds; full anticoagulation is present when the activated partial thromboplastin time is 1½ to 2 times normal (60-80 seconds).

Activated clotting time (ACT)   Diatomaceous earth is placed in a test tube to which blood is then added. The surface area of the tube is immeasurably increased by the presence of the foreign substance, and the clotting time normally is 2 minutes or less. Full anticoagulation exists when the activated clotting time is greater than 4 minutes.

d. Reversal of anticoagulation   The half-life of heparin is such that a dose of heparin is metabolized in 4-8 hours. In the presence of bleeding complications, however, it may be necessary to reverse the heparin effect immediately by giving protamine sulfate. Approximately 1.25 mg of protamine will neutralize 100 units of heparin in a test tube, but in the patient not more than 1 mg of protamine should be given for each 100 units of heparin previously administered. Too much protamine may cause hypotension or it may in itself produce bleeding complications. For this reason, protamine should be administered slowly and carefully. Give half of the calculated amount of protamine initially and observe for formation of clot in the wound; then administer half of the remaining calculated dose every 5 minutes until clot is observed or until tests of clotting become normal.

e. Complications   Anaphylactic reaction to heparin has been described but is very rare.

Hemorrhage is the primary complication. Patients should have hematocrit determination at least daily. Usually bleeding occurs into wounds or into the retroperitoneum and is not serious if recognized promptly. Cerebral hemorrhage is the most serious complication; fortunately, it is rare.

Depression of platelet function occurs in some patients after 3-4 days of heparin therapy. The risk of hemorrhage is greatest in these patients. This can be anticipated, since it is usually preceded by a fall in the platelet count below 100,000.

Heparin should be given in adequate doses. There is probably a greater risk in the administration of marginally therapeutic amounts of heparin, which may not be sufficient to prevent clotting complications but which may still be capable of producing hemorrhage. In patients who are systemically anticoagulated, there is no correlation between the amount of heparin administered and the incidence of bleeding complications.

3. Oral anticoagulants   Spontaneous hemorrhage in cattle was noted when they ate spoiled clover. From this observation has come the isolation of the oral coumarin derivatives, the principal one of which is warfarin (Coumadin). This drug is less effective than heparin, but it is practical for prophylaxis, and it is especially useful in outpatients because it is administered orally.

a. Dosage The dosage required in individual patients varies considerably. The preferred regimen for initiation of oral anticoagulation in patients of average size is 10 mg of warfarin orally, daily until anticoagulation is obtained. The daily dose is then adjusted to maintain a prothrombin time of 1½ to 2½ times normal. About 5 mg/day is the average maintenance dose. In some instances, an initial dose of 20 mg/day is required to achieve anticoagulation with as much as 10-12 mg daily required subsequently.

b. Monitoring of anticoagulation Warfarin anticoagulation is monitored by the prothrombin time, an assessment of the extrinsic clotting system. The normal prothrombin time is 10-12 seconds; anticoagulated patients should be maintained at around twice normal. Prothrombin times in excess of 2½ times normal are associated with a high incidence of bleeding complications. The prothrombin time should be measured daily initially, then at weekly intervals, and, if the patient is stable, they can eventually be measured once every 2-4 weeks.

c. Reversal of anticoagulation The prothrombin time returns to normal within 3-4 days after warfarin is discontinued. Rapid reversal is obtained by administering 5-10 mg of vitamin K_1 IV.

d. Complications of oral anticoagulation are those of hemorrhage, most frequently into the retroperitoneum or into the urinary or GI tracts. The urine and stool should therefore be monitored for the presence of blood. Abdominal pain suggests the possibility of retroperitoneal hemorrhage.

4. Antiplatelet-aggregating drugs The antiplatelet-aggregating agents are most often used to treat arterial thrombotic conditions. In special circumstances, patients who have mild venous clotting tendencies may be treated with antiplatelet-aggregating agents. These agents carry less risk of hemorrhage than do the anticoagulants, but they probably are not as effective.

Aspirin, dipyridamole, indomethacin, and related drugs depress platelet aggregation for the life of the platelet. Therefore, reversal of the drug effect depends upon generation of new platelets. The half-life of platelets is approximately 4 days, so these agents are effective for 1-2 days. The dosage of aspirin is 0.6 gm given once to twice daily.

The dextrans (plasma volume expanders) also depress platelet aggregation. Low molecular weight dextran reduces viscosity, increases microcirculatory flow, and decreases the tendency toward platelet aggregation. This agent is often used postoperatively. Two units are administered IV as an initial priming dose in the average adult, followed by 1 unit daily during the period of risk.

Table 2-8 lists many other drugs that affect platelet function.

H. FIBRINOLYTIC AGENTS AND ANTIFIBRINOLYTIC AGENTS

1. Fibrinolytic agents dissolve clot in vivo. At the present time, fibrinolytic agents are just becoming commercially available in the USA. These include urokinase and streptokinase, both of which convert plasminogen into its active clot-dissolving component, plasmin. These agents have the promise of clearing clots from the vascular system more rapidly than would occur naturally. In life-threatening conditions (e.g., pulmonary embolism), they may ultimately prove to be valuable. However, they have a risk of hemorrhage which exceeds that associated with heparin therapy, and acceptance of these agents has consequently been slow.

2. Antifibrinolytic agents Activation of natural fibrinolysis can be demonstrated in a number of bleeding disorders. Since fibrinolysis is primarily activated by intravascular clotting, the administration of an antifibrinolytic agent runs the risk of leaving intravascular clotting unchecked. Thus, while decreasing the tendency to bleeding, antifibrinolytic agents may actually increase the risk of organ failure due to propagation of thrombi in the microcirculation. Epsilon aminocaproic acid (EACA) is available commercially in the USA, but enthusiasm for its use has waned for the reasons mentioned.

VIII. GASTROINTESTINAL COMPLICATIONS*†

A. GASTRIC DISTENTION AND GASTRIC DILATATION

1. Gastric distention   The stomach frequently becomes distended with gas during induction of anesthesia, and further quantities of air are swallowed in the postoperative period. Gastric juice and duodenal secretions that reflux into the stomach contribute to distention also. Marked gastric distention often results in nausea and vomiting; occasionally the distended stomach impairs diaphragmatic excursion and causes tachypnea. Nasogastric intubation for 12-24 hours is usually sufficient treatment; intubation for longer periods is sometimes necessary.

2. Gastric dilatation   If the stomach becomes massively distended, hemorrhage from the gastric mucosa will develop. This uncommon complication of abdominal or extraabdominal surgery is an occult cause of **shock** in the first few hours after operation. Aspiration may occur if the fluid is vomited. The distended tympanitic stomach may be visible in the epigastrium on physical examination or x-ray.

Nasogastric intubation returns large quantities (sometimes several liters) of dark brownish-green or black fluid containing occult blood. The losses of fluid and electrolytes must be replaced. **Acute gastric dilatation is fatal** if not recognized; prompt treatment brings dramatic improvement.

B. PARALYTIC ILEUS

B. PARALYTIC ILEUS is the cessation of effective gastrointestinal motility following trauma, severe illness, or operations on the abdomen or elsewhere (e.g., chest, back). Ileus is probably a gastric phenomenon primarily; the remainder of the gut is able to handle fluids much earlier than the stomach.

Vomiting and abdominal distention are the main manifestations. Quiet bowel sounds are an unreliable observation. Abdominal x-rays show gas in the stomach, small bowel, and colon. Mechanical bowel obstruction must be ruled out (see Chapter 10).

A nasogastric tube should be inserted and left in place until the ileus resolves.

C. CONSTIPATION

C. CONSTIPATION   Many factors contribute to postoperative constipation:

Nothing by mouth eliminates gastrocolic reflexes and reduces fecal bulk.

Dehydration encourages absorption of fluid from colonic contents, thus dessicating the stool.

Ileus perhaps has a component of impaired colonic motility.

Incisional pain makes the patient unwilling to increase intraabdominal pressure, so an important force contributing to defecation is impaired.

Physical inactivity removes important stimuli to movement of feces through the colon, i.e., positional change and the effects of gravity.

Opiates and antacids containing calcium or aluminum contribute to constipation.

Attempts to defecate on a bedpan are often unsuccessful because the patient is semirecumbent; the normal sitting or squatting position raises abdominal pressure and helps evacuate the rectum.

Lack of privacy is often a factor.

1. Manifestations   The patient may complain of abdominal distention, cramping pain, and a sensation of pressure in the rectum. **Fecal impaction** may

---

*By Theodore R. Schrock, MD
†See Chapter 6 for Parotitis; See Chapter 10 for Intestinal Obstruction; Pancreatitis; and Stress Ulcer.

be evidenced by frequent passage of small amounts of liquid stool around a mass of feces in the rectum; severe rectal pain or pressure may also be noted, and the patient may be incontinent from the fecal mass pressing on the anal canal from above; as the patient strains to defecate, hemorrhoids may prolapse acutely.

2. Treatment

a. A bulk agent is added to the diet as soon as the patient can eat. Bulk agents (e.g., methylcellulose, 1 tablespoon in water or juice 1-3 times daily) are more effective 'stool softeners' than the emollients (e.g., mineral oil).

b. Ambulation, regular diet, hydration, limitation of narcotics, and bathroom privileges are sufficient to reestablish bowel habits in most patients.

c. A digital rectal examination should be done if constipation appears to be a problem. If a fecal impaction is found, it must be extracted digitally; sedation or even anesthesia may be necessary. High fecal impaction may be relieved by oil-retention enema.

d. Laxatives are contraindicated in patients with a recent colonic anastomosis and should never be given until a rectal examination has been done to exclude impaction. Milk of Magnesia (30 ml) should be tried initially and more potent laxatives used thereafter if necessary.

e. Enemas are usually unnecessary and are contraindicated after colonic surgery. Oil-retention enemas help evacuate impacted feces. Saline or tap water (500-1500 ml) is effective in removing stool from the left colon and sometimes more proximally. Commercially available phosphosoda enemas (100-150 ml) usually reach only the rectum and sigmoid colon. Soapsuds enemas should **not** be used because they damage the colonic mucosa.

D. DIARRHEA   The first few stools after an ileus resolves may be more liquid— or more frequent—than usual, and both of these changes are interpreted as 'diarrhea' by the patient. True diarrhea, the frequent passage of large quantities of liquid stool, usually has a specific cause. Loss of absorptive surface (as after right hemicolectomy), bacterial overgrowth (e.g., pseudomembraneous enterocolitis), and drug effects (e.g., magnesium-containing antacids) are among the possibilities. Persistent diarrhea should be investigated.

E. HEPATIC COMPLICATIONS

1. Jaundice   The differential diagnosis includes all of the causes of jaundice seen in the nonsurgical patient. Especially common are hepatitis (late), hemolysis, and cholestasis from shock or drugs; anesthetic toxicity or hypersensitivity (e.g., halothane) is unusual. Postoperative common duct obstruction should not be overlooked.

2. Hepatitis appears in the late postoperative period, usually 4-12 weeks after transfusion of blood.

3. Hepatic abscess (see Chapter 10).

FLUID AND ELECTROLYTE THERAPY*

I. WATER METABOLISM

A. BODY WATER AND ITS DISTRIBUTION   Total body water comprises 40-65% of total body weight (mean of 55% for adult men and 45% for adult women). Body water is distributed throughout 2 main compartments: the **extracellular** compartment (plasma and interstitial fluid), which contains about one-fourth of the total body water, and the **intracellular** compartment, which contains about three-fourths of the total body water. (Table 2-9).

*By Donald D. Trunkey, MD

The considerable variation in percentage of body weight which is made up by water is due mainly to differences in body composition. The higher the fat content of a given subject, the smaller the percentage of body weight which is water. The total body water in various subjects is relatively constant when expressed as a percentage of the so-called lean body mass, i.e., the sum of the fat-free tissue. Consideration should be given to this fact when calculating fluid requirements on the basis of body weight in order to avoid excessive administration of water to obese patients.

B. NORMAL WATER LOSSES AND WATER REQUIREMENTS Water is lost from the body by 4 routes: from the **skin**, as sensible and insensible perspiration; from the **lungs**, as water vapor in the expired gas; from the **kidneys**, as urine; and from the **intestines**, with the feces. In the absence of visible perspiration, the total losses from the skin and the lungs are generally referred to as the 'insensible loss.' In adults, this loss is about 0.5 ml/kg/hour (12 ml/kg/day), i.e., approximately 800 ml/day for the average adult. In children, the insensible loss is somewhat higher when estimated on the basis of body weight, varying from 1.3 ml/kg/hour in infants to 0.6 ml/kg/hour in the older child.

Table 2-9. Distribution of body water in the male

Fluid compartment	% body weight	ml of water in a 154 lb (70 kg) man
Extracellular water		
Plasma	4-5%	3,200
Interstitial fluid	11-12%	7,300
Intracellular water	40-45%	31,500

The normal daily water losses and water requirements are summarized in Table 2-10.

C. ADDITIONAL WATER REQUIREMENTS IN DISEASE Insensible losses may rise much higher than normal postoperatively or in febrile or debilitated states. The quantity of fluid lost from the surface of the body may also be very large in the extensively burned patient.

When visible sweating occurs because of high environmental temperatures or other reasons, additional water must be provided to replace these losses. Moderate sweating results in the additional loss of about 300-500 ml/day, but with profuse sweating the losses may exceed 2000-3000 ml/day.

Water loss from the GI tract is negligible normally, but may assume great importance with prolonged diarrhea, vomiting, nasogastric suction, or drainage from fistulas or an ileostomy.

If the kidneys' ability to concentrate urine is impaired (e.g., chronic nephritis, nephrosclerosis, or pyelonephritis), it may be necessary to provide additional fluid.

D. ESTIMATION OF WATER LOSSES An accurate record of the quantity of fluid lost by all routes is of utmost importance for replacement therapy. This ordinarily includes daily measurement of urinary excretion and gastrointestinal losses. It is difficult to measure fluid losses from perspiration, exudation (as in burns), diarrhea, or fluid lost into dressings. If there are major losses of these types, daily weighing of the patient is of great value. In many hospitals special bedside scales are available for patients who cannot be weighed on the usual scales.

Table 2-10. Daily water losses and water requirements
for normal individuals who are not working or sweating

	Losses				Requirements	
	Urine (ml)	Stool (ml)	Insensible (ml)	Total (ml)	ml/person	ml/kg
Infant (2-10 kg)	200-500	25-40	75-300 (1.3 ml/kg/hr)	300-840	330-1000	165-100
Child (10-40 kg)	500-800	40-100	300-600	840-1500	1000-1800	100-45
Adolescent or adult (60 kg)	800-1000	100	600-1000 (0.5 ml/kg/hr)	1500-2100	1800-2500	45-30

Patients maintained on parenteral fluids (excluding total parenteral nutrition) do not gain weight unless they are overhydrated. Properly hydrated adults receiving only IV fluids should lose 0.25-0.5 kg/day. If rapid weight losses occur, the patient must be presumed to be dehydrated. (Patients with receding edema and those who have received diuretics are exceptions to this rule). Table 2-11 shows the relationship between the extent of rapid weight loss and the degree of dehydration.

The amount of fluid to be replaced can be estimated from the amount of weight loss; each kg of weight loss is equivalent to 1 liter of fluid.

Table 2-11. Relationship of acute weight loss
to degree of dehydration

Weight loss expressed as % of normal (or Preoperative) body weight	Degree of Dehydration
Loss of 4% body weight	Mild
Loss of 6% body weight	Moderate
Loss of 8% body weight	Severe

E. INTERNAL LOSSES OF FLUID AND ELECTROLYTES Extracellular fluid and electrolytes may be lost into fluid spaces newly created by a disease process. Examples are the accumulation of fluid in the edema of burns, in an area of infection, in the intestine during ileus, or intracellular shifts during severe shock. These losses are termed 'third space' losses. Unless promptly replaced the effect of third space losses on the circulating plasma volume will be just as serious as if the losses had been external.

Fluids lost into the third space are eventually reabsorbed unless they have been removed (as by nasogastric suction in a case of ileus), and the administration of fluid and electrolyte must be reduced to compensate. In burned patients, diuresis of fluid pooled outside the circulation usually begins after 48-72 hours; a longer interval is required in cases of infection or trauma.

II. ELECTROLYTE METABOLISM

A. ELECTROLYTE COMPOSITION OF BODY FLUIDS Table 2-12 lists the concentrations of inorganic salts (electrolytes) in the plasma and in the cells. The electrolyte composition of intracellular fluid differs from that of the plasma in

Table 2-12. Normal electrolyte composition of body fluids

	Atomic or Radicular weight	mEq wt (mg)	Extracellular fluid (Plasma)			Intracellular fluid (muscle) mEq/liter (avg)
			mEq/liter		mg/100 ml	
			(avg)	(range)		
Cations						
Na^+	23	23	143	135–147	310–340	13
K^+	39	39	5	4.6–5.6	18–22	140
Ca^{++}	40	20	5	4.5–5.5	9–11	Trace
Mg^{++}	24	12	2	1.5–3.0	1.8–3.6	45
Total			155			198
Anions						
Cl^-	35	35	103	100–112	350–390	3
(As NaCl)	(58)	(58)			(590–660)	
HCO_3^-*	–	–	27	25–30	56–65†	10
$HPO_4^{=}$ (as P)††	31	17.2	2	1.8–2.3	3–4	100
SO_4 (as S)	32	16	1			20
Org. acids §	–	–	6			Trace
Protein §	–	–	16			65
Total			155			198

*HCO_3^- is measured as CO_2 content and frequently reported in Vol. % (ml/100 ml plasma). To convert Vol. % of CO_2 to mEq/liter. HCO_3^-, divide Vol. % by 2.24.
†Vol. %.
††The inorganic phosphorus in the serum exists as a buffer mixture in which approximately 80% is in the form of $HPO_4^{=}$ and 20% as $H_2PO_4^-$. For this reason the mEq weight is usually calculated by dividing the atomic weight of phosphorus by 1.8. Thus, the mEq weight for phosphorus in the serum is taken as 31/1.8 = 17.2.
§The organic acids and the proteins are expressed in terms of their combining power with cations. For protein, the cation equivalence in mEq is calculated by multiplying the number of grams of total protein/100 ml by 2.43.

that potassium (rather than sodium) is the principal cation, and phosphate (rather than chloride) is the principal anion. There is also more protein within the cell than in the extracellular fluid.

The chemical reactivity of electrolytes in the body fluids cannot be evaluated when their concentrations are expressed as weight per volume (e.g., mg/100 ml) any more than work performance (horsepower) of an electric motor can be expressed merely in terms of its weight. For this reason, electrolyte concentrations are usually expressed in mEq per volume (mEq/liter most commonly). The mEq weight of an element is simply its atomic weight divided by its valence (number of electric changes carried by the element). In Table 2-12 the mEq weights of the electrolytes are listed. To convert a concentration of an electrolyte from mg/100 ml to mEq/liter, the formula shown below is used:

$$\frac{\text{mg}/100 \text{ ml} \times 10}{\text{mEq weight}} = \text{mEq/liter}$$

For example, if the concentration of plasma sodium is reported as 322 mg/100 ml:

$$\frac{322 \times 10}{23} = 140 \text{ mEq/liter}$$

B. COMPOSITION OF GASTROINTESTINAL SECRETIONS AND SWEAT

The volume and composition of gastrointestinal secretions and sweat are shown in Table 2-13. Large quantities of fluid and electrolyte are secreted into the GI tract, but almost all are reabsorbed, mainly in the colon and there are minimal losses of fluid and electrolyte in the feces. Vomiting, diarrhea, obstruction, fistulas, nasogastric suction, and an ileostomy are abnormalities that can lead to rapid depletion of fluid and electrolyte. **Note:** In surgical patients, gastrointestinal losses are the principal cause of severe dehydration and electrolyte depletion.

Table 2-13. Volume and composition
of gastrointestinal secretions and sweat*

Fluid	Avg. volume (ml/24 hr)	Electrolyte concentrations (mEq/liter)			
		Na$^+$	K$^+$	Cl$^-$	HCO$_3^-$
Blood plasma†		135–150	3.6–5.5	100–105	24.6–28.8
Gastric juice	2500	31–90	4.3–12	52–124	0
Bile	700–1000	134–156	3.9–6.3	83–110	38
Pancreatic juice	>1000	113–153	2.6–7.4	54–95	110
Small bowel (Miller-Abbott suction)	3000	72–120	3.5–6.8	69–127	30
Ileostomy Recent	100–4000	112–142	4.5–14	93–122	30
Adapted	100–500	50	3	20	15–30
Cecostomy	100–3000	48–116	11.1–28.3	35–70	15
Feces	100	<10	<10	<15	<15
Sweat	500–4000	30–70	0–5	30–70	0

*After J.S. Lockwood and H.T. Randall, Bull. New York Acad. Med. **25**:228, 1949; and H.T. Randall, S. Clin. North America **32**:3, 1952.
†Blood plasma included for purposes of comparison.

III. VOLUME DISORDERS

A. VOLUME DEPLETION is common in surgical patients. A systematic approach to diagnosis and treatment should be developed.

    1. Clinical manifestations include low blood pressure, narrow pulse pressure, tachycardia, poor skin turgor and dry mucous membrane.

    2. History may suggest the reason for volume depletion. Records of intake and output, changes in body weight, urine specific gravity, and analysis of the chemical composition of the urine are confirmatory.

    3. Treatment must aim to correct the volume deficit and associated aberrations in electrolyte concentrations.

B. WATER DEFICIT The simplest form of volume depletion is water deficit without accompanying solute deficit. In surgical patients, water and solute depletion more often occur together. Pure water deficits can develop in patients who are unable to regulate intake; examples include debilitated or comatose patients or those that have increased insensible water loss from fever. Patients given tube feedings without adequate water supplementation and those with diabetes insipidus may also develop this syndrome.

1. Pure water deficit is reflected biochemically by hypernatremia. The magnitude of the deficit can be estimated from the serum sodium. Other findings are an increase in the plasma osmolality, concentrated urine, and low urine sodium concentration (less than 15 mEq/liter) despite the hypernatremia.

2. Clinical manifestations include depression of the CNS (lethargy or coma) and muscle rigidity, tremors, spasticity and seizures.

3. Treatment (1) Enough water must be given to restore the plasma sodium concentration to normal. In addition to correcting the existing water deficit, on-going obligatory water losses (due to diabetes insipidus, fever, etc.) must be satisfied. (2) Treat the patient with 5% dextrose and water unless hypotension has developed, in which case hypotonic saline should be used. Rarely, isotonic saline may be indicated to treat shock from dehydration even though the patient is hypernatremic.

C. VOLUME AND ELECTROLYTE DEPLETION Combined water and electrolyte depletion may occur from gastrointestinal losses due to nasogastric suction, enteric fistulas, intestinal stomas, or diarrhea. Additional causes include excessive diuretic therapy, adrenal insufficiency, profuse sweating, burns, and body fluid sequestration (third space) following trauma or surgery.

1. Clinical findings are similar to those of pure volume depletion, but hypernatremia is not so marked or the patient may be hyponatremic. The urine sodium concentration is often less than 10 mEq/liter, a manifestation of renal sodium conservation. The urine is usually hypertonic (specific gravity greater than 1.020), with an osmolality greater than 450-500 mOsm/kg.

The decreased blood volume diminishes renal perfusion and produces prerenal azotemia. The BUN:creatinine ratio is increased up to 20-25:1 (see Acute Renal Failure in this chapter).

2. Treatment Replacement therapy should be planned as follows: Calculate the sodium deficit. If serum sodium is normal, the fluid and electrolyte losses are isotonic. If serum sodium is low, subtract the sodium value from 140 and multiply by total body water (in liters) to obtain the sodium deficit in mEq.

Estimate the volume deficit from clinical signs and changes in body weight.

The volume deficit is replaced as isotonic saline containing added sodium chloride to correct the sodium deficit.

Monitor clinical signs and serum electrolytes. Central venous or pulmonary arterial pressure should be monitored in critical cases.

D. VOLUME OVERLOAD Hormonal and circulatory responses to surgery result in postoperative conservation of sodium and water by the kidneys independent of the adequacy of the extracellular fluid volume. Antidiuretic hormone released during anesthesia and surgical stress promotes water conservation by the kidneys. Renal vasoconstriction and increased aldosterone activity reduce sodium excretion. Consequently, if fluid intake is excessive in the immediate postoperative period, volume overload may occur.

1. Clinical manifestations of volume overload include edema of the sacrum and extremities, jugular venous distention, tachypnea (if pulmonary edema develops), increased body weight, and elevated pulmonary arterial and central venous pressures.

2. Volume overload may precipitate prerenal azotemia and oliguria. Examination of the urine usually shows low sodium and high potassium concentrations consistent with enhanced tubular reabsorption of sodium and water.

3. Treatment depends upon the severity of the volume overload: For mild overload, sodium restriction is usually adequate. If hyponatremia is present, water restriction may also be necessary. Diuretics must be used for severe volume overload. In the presence of cardiac failure, digitalis is indicated.

4. Inappropriate secretion of antidiuretic hormone may occur after head injury and in some patients with cancers or burns. This syndrome is characterized by hyponatremia, concentrated urine, elevated urine sodium concentration, and a normal or mildly expanded ECF volume. Treatment with water restriction is usually successful. In some cases, diuretics and isotonic saline infusion simultaneously are necessary.

IV. SPECIFIC ELECTROLYTE DISORDERS

A. SODIUM   Regulation of the sodium concentration in plasma or urine is intimately associated with regulation of total body water. Clinically, this reflects the balance between total body solute and total body water.

   1. Hypernatremia represents, chiefly, loss of water.

   2. Hyponatremia may be dilutional, or it may result from isotonic dehydration. An apparent hyponatremia may be related to marked hyperlipemia or hyperproteinemia because fat and protein contribute to plasma bulk even though they are not dissolved in plasma water. The sodium concentration in plasma water in these situations is usually normal.

   3. Hyponatremia in severe hyperglycemia results from the osmotic effect of the elevated glucose concentration, which draws water from the intracellular space and dilutes the sodium in the extracellular fluid. The magnitude of this effect can be estimated by multiplying the blood glucose concentration in mg/100 ml by 0.016 and adding the result to the existing serum sodium concentration. The sum represents the serum sodium concentration if hyperglycemia were not present.

   4. Hyponatremia can be treated by administering the calculated sodium needs as isotonic solutions.

B. POTASSIUM   The potassium in extracellular fluid constitutes only 2% of total body potassium. The remaining 98% is within body cells. The serum potassium concentration is determined primarily by the pH of extracellular fluid and the size of the intracellular potassium pool.

   With extracellular **acidosis**, a large proportion of the excess hydrogen is buffered intracellularly by an exchange of intracellular potassium for extracellular hydrogen ion. This movement of potassium may produce dangerous **hyperkalemia.** Alkalosis has an opposite effect; as the serum pH rises, potassium moves into cells, and **hypokalemia** appears.

   In the absence of an acid base disturbance, serum potassium reflects the total body pool of potassium. With excessive external losses (e.g., from the GI tract), the serum potassium falls. A loss of 10% of total body potassium drops the serum potassium from 4 to 3 mEq/liter at a normal blood pH.

   1. Hyperkalemia may prove fatal if not treated. Patients who may develop hyperkalemia include those with severe trauma, burns, crush injuries, renal insufficiency, or marked catabolism from other causes. It can also be found in Addison's disease.

   a. Diagnosis   There are usually *no symptoms* associated with hyperkalemia, but nausea, vomiting, colicky abdominal pain, and diarrhea may occur.

   ECG changes are the most helpful indicators of the severity of hyperkalemia. Early changes include peaking of the T waves, widening of the QRS complex, and depression of the ST segment. With further elevation of the blood potassium level, the QRS widens to such a degree that the tracing resembles a sine wave; this is a premonitory sign of cardiac standstill.

   Etiologic factors other than those mentioned above must be considered in hyperkalemic patients, including hemolysis, leukocytosis, or thrombocytosis. Platelet counts greater than 1 million may elevate the serum potassium. The acid-base status should be assessed.

b. Treatment There are 3 general approaches to the treatment of hyperkalemia: (1) IV infusion of 100 ml of 50% dextrose solution containing 20 units of regular insulin lowers extracellular potassium by promoting its transport into cells in association with glucose. IV bicarbonate solution lowers serum potassium as acidosis is corrected. Calcium is a specific antagonist to the effects of potassium on tissues. An infusion of calcium chloride transiently reverses cardiac depression from hyperkalemia without changing the serum potassium concentration. (2) A slower method of controlling hyperkalemia is to administer the cation exchange resin sodium polystyrene sulfonate (Kayexalate) orally or by an enema at a rate of 40-80 gm/day. (3) If hyperkalemia is a manifestation of renal failure, dialysis is often necessary.

2. Hypokalemia may be associated with alkalosis through either of 2 mechanisms: intracellular shifts of potassium in exchange for hydrogen, or renal wasting of potassium.

a. Clinical manifestations reflect neuromuscular dysfunction (decreased muscle contractility and muscle cell potentials). In extreme cases, death may result from paralysis of the muscles of respiration.

b. Treatment consists of correcting the cause of hypokalemia and administering potassium. Potassium is given orally if the patient is able to eat; otherwise it should be given IV. Potassium concentrations in IV solutions usually should not exceed 40 mEq/liter.

In mild hypokalemia (potassium between 3 and 3.5 mEq/liter) potassium should be replaced slowly to avoid hyperkalemia.

In moderate to severe hypokalemia (potassium less than 3 mEq/liter), potassium may be administered at a rate of 20-30 mEq/hour.

C. CALCIUM is an important mediator of neuromuscular function and cellular enzymatic processes even though most of the body calcium is contained in the skeleton. The usual dietary intake of calcium is 1-3 gm/day, most of which is excreted, unabsorbed, in the feces.

1. The normal serum calcium concentration (8.5-10.5 mg/100 ml or 4.25-5.25 mEq/liter) is maintained by humoral factors, mainly vitamin D, parathyroid hormone, and calcitonin.

Approximately half of the total serum calcium is bound to plasma protein, chiefly albumin. A small amount is complexed to plasma anions such as citrate, and the remainder (approximately 40%) of the total serum calcium is free or **ionized calcium** which is the fraction responsible for the biologic effects.

Acidemia increases and alkalemia decreases the serum ionized calcium concentration.

2. Hypocalcemia occurs in hypoparathyroidism, hypomagnesemia, severe pancreatitis, chronic or acute renal failure, severe trauma, crush injuries, necrotizing fasciitis, burns and septic shock.

a. Clinical manifestations are neuromuscular: hyperactive deep tendon reflexes, a positive Chvostek sign, muscle and abdominal cramps, carpopedal spasm, and, rarely, convulsions. Hypercalcemia is reflected in the ECG by a prolonged Q-T interval.

b. Treatment The initial step is to check the whole blood pH and correct alkalosis if it is present. IV calcium, as calcium gluconate or calcium chloride, may be needed for the acute problem.

3. Hypercalcemia is caused by hyperparathyroidism, cancer with bony metastases, ectopic production of parathyroid hormone, vitamin D intoxication, hyperthyroidism, sarcoidosis, milk-alkali syndrome, or prolonged immobilization. It is also a rare complication of thiazide diuretics.

a. Symptoms of hypercalcemia are fatiguability, muscle weakness, depression, anorexia, nausea, and constipation. Severe hypercalcemia can cause coma and death; a serum concentration above 12 mg/100 ml should be regarded as a medical emergency.

b. With severe hypercalcemia (calcium greater than 14.5 mg/100 ml) IV isotonic saline should be given to expand the extracellular fluid, increase urine flow, enhance calcium excretion, and reduce the serum level of calcium.

c. Furosemide and IV sodium sulphate are other methods of increasing renal calcium excretion. Mithramycin is particularly useful for hypercalcemia associated with metastatic cancer. Adrenal corticosteroids are useful for hypercalcemia associated with sarcoidosis, vitamin D intoxication and Addison's disease. Calcitonin is indicated in patients with impaired renal and cardiovascular function. If renal failure is present, hemodialysis may be required.

D. MAGNESIUM is largely found in bones and in cells where it has an important role in cellular energy metabolism. Normal plasma magnesium concentration is 1.5-2.5 mEq/liter. Magnesium is excreted primarily by the kidneys. The serum magnesium concentration reflects total body magnesium.

1. Hypomagnesemia occurs with poor dietary intake, intestinal malabsorption, or excessive losses from the gut (enteric fistulas, the use of purgatives, or nasogastric suction). It may also result from excessive urinary losses, chronic alcoholism, hyperaldosteronism, and hypercalcemia. It occasionally develops in acute pancreatitis, diabetic acidosis, in burn patients, or after prolonged total parenteral nutrition with insufficient magnesium supplementation.

a. Clinical manifestations resemble those of hypocalcemia: hyperactive tendon reflexes, positive Chvostek sign, and tremors which may progress to delirium and convulsions.

b. The diagnosis is based on a strong index of suspicion and confirmed by measurement of the serum magnesium level.

c. Treatment consists of administering magnesium, usually as the sulfate or chloride orally or, in serious deficiencies, IV (40-80 mEq of $MgSO_4$/liter of IV fluid). When large doses are infused intravenously there is a risk of producing hypermagnesemia with tachycardia and hypotension. The ECG should be inspected for prolongation of the Q-T interval.

2. Hypermagnesemia usually occurs in patients with renal disease and is rare in surgical patients; it may develop in hypovolemic shock as magnesium is liberated from cells. Patients with renal insufficiency should have their serum magnesium level monitored closely.

a. The initial signs and symptoms of hypermagnesemia are lethargy and weakness.

b. ECG changes resemble those in hypercalcemia (widened QRS complex, S-T segment depression and peaked T waves). When the serum level reaches 6 mEq/liter, deep tendon reflexes are lost. With levels above 10 mEq/liter, somnolence, coma, and death may ensue.

c. Treatment of hypermagnesemia includes IV isotonic saline to increase the rate of renal magnesium excretion and may be accompanied by slow IV infusion of calcium (calcium antagonizes some of the neuromuscular actions of magnesium). Patients with hypermagnesemia and severe renal failure may need dialysis.

E. PHOSPHORUS is mainly a constituent of bone, but it is also an important intracellular ion with a role in energy metabolism. The serum phosphorus level is an approximate indicator of total body phosphorus and can be influenced by a number of factors including the serum calcium concentration and the pH of blood.

1. Hypophosphatemia usually is associated with poor dietary intake (especially in alcoholics), hyperparathyroidism, and antacid administration. At one time it was a frequent complication of total parenteral nutrition until phosphate supplementation became routine.

a. Clinical manifestations include lassitude, fatigue, weakness, convulsions and death. Red cells may hemolyze, thus impairing oxygen delivery to tissues. White cell phagocytosis is also depressed.

b. Treatment is principally with oral phosphorus placement. In patients receiving total parenteral nutrition, 20–40 mEq of potassium dihydrogen phosphate should be given IV for every 1000 Cal infused.

2. Hyperphosphatemia most often develops in severe renal disease, after trauma, or with marked tissue catabolism. It is rarely caused by excessive dietary intake. Hyperphosphatemia is usually asymptomatic.

Treatment is by diuresis, to increase the rate of urinary phosphorus excretion. Aluminum-containing antacids bind phosphate and prevent absorption from the gut.

In patients with renal disease, dialysis may be required.

V. ACID-BASE BALANCE

A. PHYSIOLOGY The daily metabolism of protein and carbohydrate generates approximately 70 mEq (or 1 mEq/kg of body weight) of hydrogen ion. In addition, a large amount of carbon dioxide is formed which combines with water to make carbonic acid (H_2CO_3).

Hydrogen ions generated from metabolism are buffered through 2 major systems. The first involves intracellular protein (e.g., the hemoglobin in red blood cells). More important is the bicarbonate/carbonic acid system, which can be understood from the Henderson–Hasselbalch equation:

$$pH = pK + \log \frac{(HCO_3^-)}{0.03 \times P_{CO_2}} \qquad \ldots Eq(1)$$

where pK for the HCO_3^-/H_2CO_3 system is 6.1.

Hydrogen ion concentration is related to pH in an inverse logarithmic manner. The following transformation of Eq(1) is easier to use because it eliminates the logarithms:

$$H^+ = \frac{24 \times P_{CO_2}}{HCO_3^-} \qquad \ldots Eq(2)$$

There is an approximately linear inverse relationship between pH and hydrogen ion concentration over the pH range of 7.1–7.5: for each 0.01 decrease in pH, the hydrogen ion concentration increases 1 nmol. Remembering that a normal blood pH of 7.40 is equal to a hydrogen ion concentration of 40 nmol/liter, one can calculate the approximate hydrogen ion concentration of any pH between 7.1 and 7.5. For example, a pH of 7.30 is equal to a hydrogen ion concentration of 50 nmol/liter. This estimation introduces an error of approximately 10% at the extremes of this pH range.

A consideration of the right-hand side of Eq(2) demonstrates that hydrogen ion concentration is determined by the ratio of the P_{CO_2} to plasma bicarbonate concentration. In body fluid, CO_2 is dissolved and combines with water to form carbonic acid, the acid part of the acid-base pair. If any 2 of these 3 variables are known, the third can be calculated using this expression.

Equation (2) also illustrates how the body excretes acid produced from metabolism. Blood P_{CO_2} is normally controlled within narrow limits by pulmonary ventilation. The plasma bicarbonate concentration is regulated by the renal tubules by 3 major processes: (1) Filtered bicarbonate is reabsorbed, mostly in the proximal tubule, to prevent excessive bicarbonate loss in the urine; (2) hydrogen ions are secreted as titratable acid to regenerate the bicarbonate that was buffered when these hydrogen ions were initially produced and to provide a vehicle for excretion of about one-third of the daily acid production; and (3) the kidneys also excrete hydrogen ion in the form of ammonium ion by a process which regenerates bicarbonate initially consumed in the production of these hydrogen ions. Volume depletion, increased Pco_2, and hypokalemia all favor enhanced tubular reabsorption of HCO_3.

B. ACID-BASE ABNORMALITIES The management of clinical acid-base disturbances is facilitated by the use of a nomogram (Fig. 2-3) which relates the 3 variables in Eq(2).

Primary respiratory disturbances cause changes in the blood Pco_2 (the numerator in Eq(2)) and produce corresponding effects on the blood hydrogen ion concentration. Metabolic disturbances primarily affect the plasma bicarbonate concentration (the denominator in Eq(2)). Whether the disturbance is primarily respiratory or metabolic, some degree of compensatory change occurs in the reciprocal factor in Eq(2) to limit or nullify the magnitude of perturbation of acid-base balance. Thus, changes in blood Pco_2 from respiratory disturbances are compensated for by changes in the renal handling of bicarbonate. Conversely, changes in plasma bicarbonate concentration are blunted by appropriate respiratory changes.

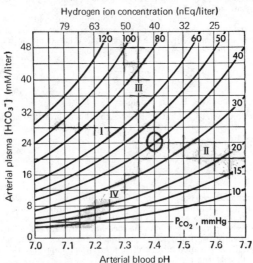

Fig. 2-3. Acid-base nomogram for use in evaluation of clinical acid-base disorders. (Courtesy of Anthony Sebastian, MD, University of California Medical Center, San Francisco.) Hydrogen ion concentration (top) or blood pH (bottom) is plotted against plasma HCO_3^- concentration; curved lines are isopleths of CO_2 tension (Pco_2, mm Hg). Knowing any 2 of these variables permits estimation of the third. The circle in the center represents the range of normal values ; the shaded bands represent the 95% confidence limits of 4 common acid-base disturbances: I, acute respiratory acidosis; II, acute respiratory alkalosis; III, chronic respiratory acidosis; IV, sustained metabolic acidosis. Points lying outside these shaded areas are mixed disturbances and indicate 2 primary acid-base disorders.

(Reproduced, with permission, from Dunphy JE, Way LW (eds): *Current Surgical Diagnosis & Treatment,* 3rd Ed. Lange 1977.)

Because acute changes allow insufficient time for compensatory mechanisms to respond, the resulting pH disturbances are often great and the abnormalities may be present in pure form. By contrast, chronic disturbances allow the full range of compensatory mechanisms to come into play, so that blood pH may remain near normal despite wide variations in the plasma bicarbonate or blood Pco_2.

C. RESPIRATORY ACIDOSIS

1. Acute respiratory acidosis occurs when respiration is suddenly inadequate. CO_2 accumulates in the blood (the numerator in Eq(2) increases), and hydrogen ion concentration increases. This occurs most often in acute airway obstruction, aspiration, respiratory arrest, certain pulmonary infections, and pulmonary edema with impaired gas exchange. There is acidemia and an elevated blood Pco_2 but little change in the plasma bicarbonate concentration. Over 80% of the carbonic acid resulting from the increased Pco_2 is buffered by intracellular mechanisms: about 50% by intracellular protein and another 30% by hemoglobin. Because relatively little is buffered by bicarbonate ion, the plasma bicarbonate concentration may be normal. An acute increase in Pco_2 from 40 to 80 mm Hg will increase the plasma bicarbonate by only 3 mEq/liter. This is why the 95% confidence band for acute respiratory acidosis (I in Fig. 2-3) is nearly horizontal, i.e., increases in Pco_2 directly decrease pH with little change in plasma bicarbonate concentration.

Treatment involves restoration of adequate ventilation. If necessary, tracheal intubation and assisted ventilation or controlled ventilation with morphine sedation should be employed.

2. Chronic respiratory acidosis arises from chronic respiratory failure in which impaired ventilation gives a sustained elevation of blood Pco_2. Renal compensation raises plasma bicarbonate to the extent illustrated by the 95% confidence limits in Fig. 2-3 (the area labelled III). Rather marked elevations of Pco_2 produce small changes in blood pH because of the increase in plasma bicarbonate concentration. This is achieved primarily by increased renal excretion of ammonium ion, which enhances acid excretion and regenerates bicarbonate, which is returned to the blood. Chronic respiratory acidosis is generally well tolerated until severe pulmonary insufficiency leads to hypoxia. At this point, the long-term prognosis is very poor. Paradoxically, the patient with chronic respiratory acidosis appears better able to tolerate additional acute increases in blood Pco_2.

Treatment of chronic respiratory acidosis depends largely on attention to pulmonary toilet and ventilatory status. Rapid correction of chronic respiratory acidosis, as may occur if the patient is placed on controlled ventilation, can be dangerous since the Pco_2 is lowered rapidly and the compensated respiratory acidosis may be converted to a severe metabolic alkalosis.

D. RESPIRATORY ALKALOSIS

1. Acute hyperventilation lowers the Pco_2 without concomitant changes in the plasma bicarbonate concentration and thereby lowers the hydrogen ion concentration (II in Fig. 2-3). The clinical manifestations are paresthesias in the extremities, carpopedal spasm, and a positive Chvostek sign. Acute hyperventilation with respiratory alkalosis may be an early sign of bacterial sepsis.

2. Chronic respiratory alkalosis occurs in pulmonary and liver disease. The renal response to chronic hypocapnia is to decrease the tubular reabsorption of filtered bicarbonate, increasing bicarbonate excretion with a consequent lowering of plasma bicarbonate concentration. As the bicarbonate concentration falls, the chloride concentration rises. This is the same pattern seen in hyperchloremic acidosis, and the two can only be distinguished by blood gas and pH measurements. Generally, chronic respiratory alkalosis does not require treatment.

E. METABOLIC ACIDOSIS is caused by increased production of hydrogen ion from metabolic or other causes, or from excessive bicarbonate losses. In either case, the plasma bicarbonate concentration is decreased, producing an increase in hydrogen ion concentration (see Eq(2)).

With excessive bicarbonate loss (e.g., severe diarrhea, diuretic treatment with acetazolamide or other carbonic anhydrase inhibitors, certain forms of renal tubular disease, and in patients with ureterosigmoidostomies), the decrease in plasma bicarbonate concentration is matched by an increase in the serum chloride, so that the anion gap (the sum of chloride and bicarbonate concentrations subtracted from the serum sodium concentration) remains at the normal level, below 15 mEq/liter.

Metabolic acidosis from increased acid production is associated with an anion gap exceeding 15 mEq/liter. Conditions in which this occurs are renal failure, diabetic ketoacidosis, lactic acidosis, methanol ingestion, salicylate intoxication, and ethylene glycol ingestion. The lungs compensate by hyperventilation, which returns the hydrogen ion concentration toward normal by lowering the blood Pco_2. In long-standing metabolic acidosis, minute ventilation may increase sufficiently to drop the Pco_2 as low as 10-15 mm Hg. The shaded area, marked IV on the nomogram (Fig. 2-3) represents the confidence limits for sustained metabolic acidosis.

    Treatment   Identifying the underlying cause and correcting it is often sufficient treatment.

In some conditions, particularly when there is an increased anion gap, alkali administration is required. The amount of sodium bicarbonate required to restore the plasma bicarbonate concentration to normal can be estimated by subtracting the existing plasma bicarbonate concentration from the normal value of 24 mEq/liter and multiplying the resulting number by half the estimated total body water. This is a useful empirical formula. In practice, it is not usually wise to administer enough bicarbonate to return the plasma bicarbonate completely to normal. It is better to raise the plasma bicarbonate concentration by 5 mEq/liter initially and then reassess the clinical situation. The administration of sodium bicarbonate may cause fluid overload from the large quantity of sodium and may overcorrect the acidosis.

The long-term management of patients with metabolic acidosis entails providing adequate alkali, either as supplemental sodium bicarbonate tablets or by dietary manipulation. In all cases, attempts should be made to minimize the magnitude of bicarbonate loss in patients with chronic metabolic acidosis.

F. METABOLIC ALKALOSIS is probably the most common acid-base disturbance in surgical patients. In this condition, the blood hydrogen ion concentration is decreased as a result of accumulation of bicarbonate in plasma. The pathogenesis is complex but involves at least 3 separate factors: loss of hydrogen ion, usually as a result of loss of gastric secretions rich in hydrochloric acid; volume depletion, which is often severe; and potassium depletion, which almost always is present.

HCl secretion by the gastric mucosa returns bicarbonate ion to the blood. Gastric acid, after mixing with ingested food, is subsequently reabsorbed in the small intestine, so that there is no net gain or loss of hydrogen ion in this process. If secreted hydrogen ion is lost through vomiting or drainage, the result is a net delivery of bicarbonate into the circulation. Normally, the kidneys are easily able to excrete the excess bicarbonate load. However, if volume depletion accompanies the loss of hydrogen ion, the kidneys work to preserve volume by increasing tubular reabsorption of sodium and whatever anions are also filtered. Consequently, because of the increased sodium reabsorption, the excess bicarbonate cannot be completely excreted. This perpetuates the metabolic alkalosis. At first, some of the filtered bicarbonate escapes reabsorption in the proximal tubule and reaches the distal tubule. Here it promotes potassium secretion and enhanced potassium loss in the urine. The urine pH will be either neutral or alkaline because of the presence of bicarbonate. Later, as volume depletion becomes more severe, the reabsorption of filtered bicarbonate in the proximal tubule becomes virtually complete. Now, only small amounts of sodium, with little bicarbonate, reach the distal tubule. If potassium depletion is severe, sodium is now reabsorbed in exchange for hydrogen ion. This results in the paradoxically acid urine sometimes observed in patients with advanced metabolic alkalosis.

1. Assessment should involve examination of the urine electrolytes and urine pH. In the early stages, bicarbonate excretion will obligate excretion of sodium as well as potassium, so the urine sodium concentration will be relatively high for a volume-depleted patient, and the urine pH will be alkaline. In this circumstance, the urine chloride will reveal the extent of the volume depletion: a urine chloride of less than 10 mEq/liter is diagnostic of volume depletion and chloride deficiency. Later, when bicarbonate reabsorption becomes virtually complete, the urine pH will be acid, and urine sodium, potassium, and chloride concentrations will all be low. The ventilatory compensation in metabolic alkalosis is variable, but the maximal extent of compensation can only raise the blood Pco_2 to about 55 mm Hg. A Pco_2 greater than 60 mm Hg in metabolic alkalosis suggests a mixed disturbance also involving respiratory acidosis.

2. Treatment To treat metabolic alkalosis, fluid must be given, usually as sodium chloride. With adequate volume repletion, the stimulus to tubular sodium reabsorption is diminished, and the kidneys can then excrete the excess bicarbonate. Most of these patients are also substantially potassium-depleted and will require potassium supplementation. This should be administered as KCl, since chloride depletion is another hallmark of this condition and potassium given as citrate or lactate will not correct the potassium deficit.

G. MIXED ACID-BASE DISORDERS In many situations, mixed disorders of acid-base balance develop. The most common example in surgical patients is metabolic acidosis superimposed on respiratory alkalosis. This problem can arise in patients with septic shock or hepatorenal syndrome. Since the 2 acid-base disorders tend to cancel each other, the disturbance in hydrogen ion concentration is usually small. The reverse situation, i.e., respiratory acidosis combined with metabolic alkalosis, is less common. Combined metabolic and respiratory acidosis occurs in cardiorespiratory arrest and obviously constitutes a medical emergency. Circumstances involving both metabolic and respiratory alkalosis are rare.

The clue to the presence of a mixed acid-base disorder comes from plotting the patient's acid-base data on the nomogram in Fig. 2-3. If the set of data falls outside one of the confidence bands, then by definition the patient has a mixed disorder. On the other hand, if the acid-base data fall within one of the confidence bands, it suggests (but does not prove) that the acid-base disturbance is pure or uncomplicated.

BLOOD AND BLOOD PRODUCTS (HEMOTHERAPY)*

Modern surgery would be impossible without the capability of restoring blood volume by transfusion. Blood and blood components vary considerably from the blood which perfuses the arteries and veins of the human body. Blood products should be considered to be drugs, biological products, or transplants. This section will review available blood products, indications for their use, and metabolic consequences of the infusion of liquid preserved blood.

*By George F. Sheldon, MD·

A. STORAGE All blood products undergo changes during storage. The citrate preservative of the past, Acid Citrate Dextrose (ACD), has largely been replaced by Citrate Phosphate Dextrose (CPD). A unit of whole blood contains 450-500 ml of donor blood and 63 ml of CPD anticoagulant.

1. Changes during storage CPD preservative causes less of a storage lesion than ACD, but important changes still occur.

a. Potassium, lactate, and ammonia values rise.

b. Particulate matter and plasticizers increase.

c. Labile clotting factors (V, VIII) diminish.

d. Diphosphoglycerate (2, 3 DPG) levels remain adequate for 14 days but are virtually absent by the end of 21 days of storage. 2, 3 DPG regulates the loading and unloading of oxygen from hemoglobin; if levels of 2,3 DPG are low, oxygen does not dissociate from hemoglobin and therefore is not available to tissues perfused by such red cells.

e. Donor blood mixed with CPD preservative has an acidic pH (initially about 7), and pH falls still further to 6.5 at the end of 2 weeks in storage.

f. Platelets become functionally inadequate as soon as blood is stored at 4° C (necessary to minimize growth of bacteria), and after 3 days of preservation in CPD, virtually no platelets remain.

2. Component therapy Many of the undesirable preservation-related changes in whole blood can be avoided by precise transfusion therapy in the form of components. For that reason, most blood banks in recent years have urged conversion from frequent use of whole blood to reliance on components.

B. RED BLOOD CELLS

1. Whole Blood is the transfusion product most familiar to physicians and is the standard against which components are judged.

At present, whole blood is indicated only for resuscitation of acutely bleeding patients in whom there is a need for replacement of both red cells and plasma. Because it is less viscous, whole blood can be infused more rapidly than red cell concentrates, and this is an advantage in emergency situations.

2. Red cell concentrates (packed red cells) In this product, 60-80% of the plasma is removed immediately after collection. Red cell concentrates are metabolically similar to whole blood, except that less citrate, antigenic debris, potassium, sodium, plasma protein, and microaggregates are present. There is a lower risk of hepatitis also. Red cell concentrates are preferred for transfusion in anemic patients who are not acutely hypovolemic.

3. Washed red cells are an improved form of red cell concentrate in which most of the plasma fraction is removed by washing. Washed red cells eliminate many of the potential hazards of the plasma fraction, including transfusion of red cell antigens and transmission of bacterial and viral diseases.

4. Frozen red cells Freezing preserves the characteristics of the red cells at the time they are frozen. Frozen cells must be washed to remove the cryopreservative before administration. Advantages include the ability to store for long periods. This method of preservation is so expensive that at present it is limited to rare cell types.

5. Red cell rejuvenation It is possible also to freeze red blood cells which are approaching the dating period (21 days after collection), treat the cells with inosine, glucose, and phosphate to restore the 2, 3 DPG and the ATP levels, and thus 'rejuvenate' a unit destined to be discarded.

C. PLATELET CONCENTRATES are obtained by centrifugation at the time of donation and can be stored up to 48 hours at room temperature, although usually they are used within 24 hours of collection. The advantage is provision of functional platelets in a small total volume of transfused fluid.

Platelets are dispensed in several different preparations. **Single unit packs** contain the platelets from one donor and are stored in 50 ml of plasma from that donor. **Platelet concentrates** may contain the platelets from 8 donors in a single unit. HL-A typing reduces immunization of the recipient and probably results in longer survival of the infused platelets. When facilities for plasmapheresis are available, large quantities of platelets from a single matched donor can be given to one recipient with less destruction from isoimmunization. If platelet transfusions are anticipated over long periods, plasmapheresed platelets are preferred.

D. LEUKOCYTE CONCENTRATES This product is being evaluated as an aid to control of infection in patients with neutropenia.

E. CRYOPRECIPITATE is rich in factor VIII and is specific therapy for patients with hemophilia. Cryoprecipitate can be stored for long periods, and the risk of transmitting hepatitis is low.

F. PLASMA

1. Pool plasma has been removed from the market in the USA because of the high risk of hepatitis and the availability of alternatives.

2. Fresh frozen plasma contains factors V and VIII in normal concentrations, and is frequently used to reverse the coagulopathy of patients receiving massive transfusion.

3. Albumin and plasma protein fractions (PPF) are used interchangeably as volume expanders and for restoration of colloid oncotic pressure. Plasma protein fractions may have alpha and beta globulins as well as albumin. Both products are stored at $60°C$ for 10-12 hours to eliminate the risk of hepatitis.

G. METABOLIC CONSEQUENCES OF TRANSFUSION

1. Hyperkalemia Stored blood is acidic and hyperkalemic, but transfusion seldom causes hyperkalemia in the recipient. Transfused citrate is rapidly metabolized to yield bicarbonate, and metabolic alkalosis is the result. Metabolic alkalosis in the presence of sodium retention after injury contributes to renal excretion of potassium.

2. Loss of 2, 3 DPG Deterioration of 2, 3 DPG in preserved red cells results in blood in which hemoglobin has a high affinity for oxygen. The deleterious effects of transfusing such blood into hypoxic, hypotensive patients may be more theoretical than real, perhaps because 2, 3 DPG values are restored to normal within 12-24 hours after transfusion.

3. Hypothermia is a common complication of massive transfusion of liquid blood stored at $4°C$. Hypothermic patients are less able to metabolize acid and potassium; further, hypothermia increases the affinity of hemoglobin for oxygen, thus adding to the possible consequences of low 2, 3 DPG values. Blood should be warmed before administration, but commercial blood warmers are frequently unable to cope when large volumes of blood must be given rapidly.

4. Hypocalcemia Citrate is a chelating agent which binds ionized calcium in the recipient and is a potential cause of hypocalcemic cardiac arrhythmia. Normothermic adults can metabolize the citrate contained in 1 unit of blood every 5 minutes without the need for exogenous calcium. However, since calcium is so essential, and because ionized calcium is difficult to measure, the current recommendation is to give 13.5 mEq of calcium for every 5 units of blood if that amount of blood must be transfused in less than 30 minutes. Hypercalcemia is potentially lethal, and calcium administration should be monitored carefully with a continuous ECG.

5. Defective hemostasis is a complication of massive transfusion, although the exact mechanism is incompletely defined. The labile factors (V and VIII) are the only coagulation factors which decay to any great extent during preservation of liquid blood. Moreover, in the patient who has been resuscitated adequately, factor VIII levels actually rise to higher than normal because of accelerated manufacture of factor VIII by the liver. Therefore, factor V is the only clotting factor which is significantly lowered by massive transfusion. Fresh frozen plasma provides clotting components, but its effectiveness in correcting the hemostatic defect caused by massive transfusion has not been established.

It should be assumed that all blood routinely dispensed from the blood bank lacks functioning platelets. Platelets lose their aggregability in cold storage, and preservatives do not maintain platelet viability beyond 72 hours. In addition, most blood banks with component programs remove the platelets from the donated unit as a routine procedure. Absent or nonfunctioning platelets contribute to posttransfusion bleeding, and the magnitude of the problem is roughly proportional to the number of units of blood administered. It is a good policy to give platelet concentrates (or platelet packs) to patients who receive 10 units of blood or more in less than 1 hour.

H. COMPLICATIONS OF TRANSFUSION Blood is the most dangerous drug used by most physicians. Complications are common and potentially fatal.

1. Infections Transmission of syphilis, malaria, bacteria, and viruses are infrequent with current banking practices. **Hepatitis,** however, remains a problem. Blood products carry a hepatitis risk proportional to the number of donors contributing blood to the pool. Recently available assays for hepatitis have greatly reduced the potential of dispensing blood from hepatitis carriers, but most cases of hepatitis which follow transfusion in the USA are not due to hepatitis B or other known viruses and may represent infection by an unidentified hepatocellular virus. The statistical risk of hepatitis is unknown because many cases are subclinical. Blood acquired from volunteer donors has a lower risk of hepatitis than blood from paid donors.

2. Isoimmunization Blood is an allograft, and the recipient may become immunized against HLA antigen, platelet antigens, and red cell antigens.

Reactions to leukocyte antigens are the probable cause of many febrile responses to transfusions. Reactions to transfusions of proteins, especially IgA, are frequently severe and may be hemolytic in nature.

3. Mismatched blood Administration of blood to the wrong recipient is the most common immunologic complication; usually it is due to incorrect labelling of blood specimens.

Massive hemolysis may occur, leading to renal failure and death. Symptoms of early hemolysis are chills, fever, back pains, circulatory collapse, or hemorrhage. Delayed hemolysis occurs from several days to 1 month after transfusion and is manifested by anemia or mild jaundice.

4. Management of transfusion reactions

a. Stop the transfusion and send the remaining blood to the blood bank for investigation of the appropriateness of the cross match, Rh compatibility, and Coombs test.

b. Maintain hydration.

c. Send samples of plasma and urine for hemoglobin determination; hemoglobin in these fluids implies that hemolysis has occurred.

d. Obtain cultures of the recipient's blood and the donor blood.

e. If a severe reaction has occurred, renal function should be evaluated and protected by giving mannitol and bicarbonate.

f. Febrile reactions, without hemolysis, are treated with antihistamines.

g. Isoimmunized patients who require subsequent transfusions should receive washed red cells.

I. HEMOTHERAPY IN SURGICAL PRACTICE Surgical patients usually receive blood transfusions for the restoration of red cell mass or blood volume.

1. Preoperative anemia Anemic patients who are asymptomatic are able to tolerate operations of almost any magnitude if operative blood loss is minimal. If a surgical procedure commonly associated with large losses of blood is planned, anemia should be corrected 1–2 days prior to operation so that the storage-related defects of transfused blood can be restored to normal. Moreover, preoperative transfusion permits transfusion reactions to be detected, a difficult task in an anesthetized patient.

Red cell concentrates are preferred for correction of preoperative anemia in stable patients.

2. Postoperative anemia The need for transfusion to correct postoperative anemia is assessed by measurement of the reticulocyte count; if it is elevated, and if the patient does not have postural hypotension or dyspnea, transfusion is unnecessary. If the reticulocyte count is low, the response to oral or parenteral iron should be determined before concluding that transfusions must be given. Chronically ill patients (e.g., those with persistent sepsis) frequently have aregenerative anemia and may require periodic transfusion of blood. Red cell concentrates are recommended for this purpose.

3. Exsanguinating hemorrhage Whole blood is the transfusion product of choice; red cell concentrates are too viscous to be administered rapidly.

4. Autotransfusion There are two forms of autotransfusion. In one type, a patient donates blood 2 weeks in advance of elective operation, and this blood is stored for transfusion back into the donor should it be required. This practice permits stimulation of erythropoiesis and results in restoration of red cell mass nearly to normal by the time of operation. A further advantage is the availability of the safest possible blood when the patient needs it (i.e., the patient's own blood).

The other kind of autotransfusion is useful in emergencies. Blood lost by the patient is collected into apparatus designed for this purpose, anticoagulated, and returned immediately to the circulation. The method is more complicated than it appears at first glance, and this fact makes autotransfusion impractical for wide use. It is most applicable in cases of bleeding into the pleural space, and it may be life-saving when compatible blood is unavailable. Coagulopathies may develop with reinfusion of large amounts of blood.

METABOLISM AND NUTRITION*

Increased attention to nutrition and the development of methods of nutritional support are among the most important surgical advances in recent years. The fundamentals of surgical metabolism and nutrition are discussed briefly in this section. Table 2-14 lists some useful numerical constants. Daily nutritional requirements for normal children and adults are listed in Table 2-15.

A. METABOLIC EFFECTS OF STARVATION AND INJURY

1. Starvation During a brief period of starvation (less than 3 days), muscle protein is catabolized to fulfill energy requirements by gluconeogenesis. About 10-15 gm of nitrogen are excreted in the urine daily during this phase.

By the end of 2 weeks of starvation, lipolysis has increased 7-fold, and fat is the primary source of energy. Ketosis is present, and the brain and heart adapt to utilize ketones as the energy substrate. Minimal amounts of nitrogen (less than 2 gm daily) are excreted in the urine. The basal metabolic rate is lowered. Death occurs after 2-3 months of total starvation.

During starvation, the provision of small amounts of carbohydrate orally or IV has a remarkable sparing effect on protein in the body, and the feeding of a balanced diet results in rapid resynthesis of tissue. These effects are in sharp contrast to those seen in injured patients.

2. Injury Accidental or planned surgical injury causes profound metabolic alterations which are different from the changes in simple starvation.

---

*By George F. Sheldon, MD

Table 2-14. Some numerical constants useful in
estimates of metabolic changes.

Protein catabolized = urinary nitrogen X 6.25
Wet lean tissue broken down = urinary nitrogen X 30 or
protein X 4.75
Wet lean tissue is assumed to be 73% water and 27% protein

In muscle tissue:
Extracellular potassium = 3.8–4.3 mEq/liter
Intracellular potassium = 148–155 mEq/liter
Potassium content = 100 mEq/kg wet weight

Energy considerations:
Caloric equivalents of nutrients:

Carbohydrate	= 4 Cal/g
Fat (triglycerides)	= 9 Cal/g
Protein	= 4 Cal/g
Ethyl alcohol	= 7 Cal/g

Respiratory quotient (RQ) = CO_2/O_2 ratio
RQ for oxidation of carbohydrate = 1.00
RQ for oxidation of fat = 0.70
When carbohydrate is being converted to fat, RQ is > 1.00
On the usual mixed diet, RQ = 0.75–0.85
Basal Metabolic Rate (adults) = 36–41 Cal/sq m/hour (approximately 1600–1800 Cal/day)
For 1800 Cal energy expenditure, oxygen consumption = 250 ml/min

Carbohydrate consumption	=	400 Cal (100 g)
Fat consumption	=	1160 Cal (130 g)
Protein consumption	=	240 Cal (60 g)
Total	=	1800 Cal/day

(Reproduced with permission from Dunphy JE, Way LW (Eds.): *Current Surgical Diagnosis & Treatment*, 3rd Ed. Lange 1977)

The metabolic rate is normal or high, protein catabolism is immediate and rapid, and although oxidation of fat occurs promptly, the body does not adapt to the use of lipid for energy. Infusion of small amounts of glucose has little sparing effect on protein, and oral or IV feedings of protein alone are ineffective because carbohydrate is the preferred source of energy.

Accelerated protein catabolism from trauma, particularly if the injury was a thermal burn or if there is associated sepsis, can result in the loss of 30% of lean body mass within a month if nutritional support is not provided. Lean body mass is protein which is essential for structure and function. If 30–50% of lean body mass is catabolized to supply energy, death usually ensues.

The consequences of these metabolic changes depend upon the severity and duration of the illness. Routine major operations are followed by a transient phase of protein catabolism, but if food can be taken orally within a few days, metabolism returns toward normal, and the patient recovers. Multiple injuries, sepsis, malignancy, inability to resume eating, malabsorption, and other complications allow the metabolic derangements to persist and worsen.

B. ASSESSMENT OF NUTRITION Pronounced malnutrition is clinically obvious, but evidence of less severe nutritional deprivation may be subtle.

1. History Duration of illness, weight loss, eating habits, age, habitus, and economic status are important data in assessing adequacy of nutrition.

2. Hospital course Hospitalized patients may become nutritionally depleted while undergoing diagnostic or therapeutic procedures. Patients of different nationalities and backgrounds may not eat institutional diets, and they may become malnourished in the hospital.

3. Weight Weight loss reflects changes in body water and/or tissue mass. Weight should be obtained daily during acute illness and at least weekly in more stable disease states.

a. Starvation alone results in the loss of about 0.5 kg/day; in the early stages of starvation, 0.2–0.3 kg of this loss is protein.

b. Stress (infection, injury) increases losses of protein by 4–10 fold.

4. Laboratory tests Hemoglobin, serum albumin, serum iron, and serum transferrin levels reflect the nutritional state.

Nitrogen balance is a useful test for protein catabolism.

a. Measure urea nitrogen in a 24-hour collection of urine. Add an arbitrary 2 gm nitrogen to the total urinary loss to allow for unmeasured protein byproducts.

b. Measure the amount of protein taken orally or IV during the same period. Divide the protein by 6.25 to determine nitrogen intake.

c. The nitrogen balance is positive if more nitrogen is taken in than is excreted during the 24-hour period.

C. NUTRITIONAL SUPPORT

1. Indications Nutritional support should be provided by enteric and/or parenteral feeding if the postoperative or postinjury patient is not expected to resume a normal diet within 5 days. A patient who has lost 10% of body weight or has a serum albumin level below 3 gm/100 ml should receive total parenteral nutrition for 2–3 weeks before major elective surgery. Other indications for nutritional therapy are loosely defined; in general, if a question arises about the adequacy of nutrition in an acutely ill patient it is advisable to provide nutritional support.

2. Caloric requirements The patient's caloric needs should be estimated.

a. About 1800 Cal/day is required to support biochemical functions; less than 1000 Cal/day results in gradual starvation.

b. Add 12% for each degree of fever above 37°C.

c. Allow for caloric expenditure from muscular activity; in general, this raises total requirements to about 2500–3000 Cal/day.

d. Septic or burned patients may need as much as 6000 Cal/day.

e. Malnourished patients, e.g., those about to undergo elective surgery, require 45 Cal/kg/day to establish positive nitrogen balance.

3. Selection of method If the absorptive surface of the small intestine is intact and functional, enteric feeding is preferred. If caloric requirements exceed what can be delivered into the gut, total parenteral nutrition is necessary.

D. ENTERIC FEEDING (TUBE FEEDING)

1. Types of diets Commercially available liquid diets for tube feeding are listed in Table 2-16. These diets fall into three categories: balanced formulas, low-residue balanced formulas, and elemental diets (requiring no digestion). The balanced formulas are preferred unless the patient has special features that make the low-residue or elemental diets a better choice.

2. Insertion of tube A polyethylene feeding tube (2–3 mm diameter) and a 16 French nasogastric tube are introduced together, with the tips of both

Table 2-15. Recommended daily dietary allowances.[1] (Revised 1974.)

	Age (years)	Weight (kg)	Weight (lbs)	Height (cm)	Height (in)	Energy (kcal)[2]	Protein (g)	Fat-Soluble Vitamins Vitamin A Activity (RE)[3]	Vitamin A Activity (IU)	Vita-min D (IU)	Vita-min E Activity[4] (IU)	Water-Soluble Vitamins Ascorbic Acid (mg)	Fola-cin[5] (µg)	Nia-cin[6] (mg)	Ribo-flavin (mg)	Thia-mine (mg)	Vita-min B6 (mg)	Vita-min B12 (µg)	Minerals Cal-cium (mg)	Phos-phorus (mg)	Iodine (µg)	Iron (mg)	Mag-nesium (mg)	Zinc (mg)
Infants	0.0–0.5	6	14	60	24	kg × 117	kg × 2.2	420[7]	1400	400	4	35	50	5	0.4	0.3	0.3	0.3	360	240	35	10	60	3
	0.5–1.0	9	20	71	28	kg × 108	kg × 2.0	400	2000	400	5	35	50	6	0.6	0.5	0.4	0.3	540	400	45	15	70	5
Children	1–3	13	28	86	34	1300	23	400	2000	400	7	40	100	9	0.8	0.7	0.6	1.0	800	800	60	15	150	10
	4–6	20	44	110	44	1800	30	500	2500	400	9	40	200	12	1.1	0.9	0.9	1.5	800	800	80	10	200	10
	7–10	30	66	135	54	2400	36	700	3300	400	10	40	300	16	1.2	1.2	1.2	2.0	800	800	110	10	250	10
Males	11–14	44	97	158	63	2800	44	1000	5000	400	12	45	400	18	1.5	1.4	1.6	3.0	1200	1200	130	18	350	15
	15–18	61	134	172	69	3000	54	1000	5000	400	15	45	400	20	1.8	1.5	2.0	3.0	1200	1200	150	18	400	15
	19–22	67	147	172	69	3000	54	1000	5000	400	15	45	400	20	1.8	1.5	2.0	3.0	800	800	140	10	350	15
	23–50	70	154	172	69	2700	56	1000	5000		15	45	400	18	1.6	1.4	2.0	3.0	800	800	130	10	350	15
	51+	70	154	172	69	2400	56	1000	5000		15	45	400	16	1.5	1.2	2.0	3.0	800	800	110	10	350	15
Females	11–14	44	97	155	62	2400	44	800	4000	400	12	45	400	16	1.3	1.2	1.6	3.0	1200	1200	115	18	300	15
	15–18	54	119	162	65	2100	48	800	4000	400	12	45	400	14	1.4	1.1	2.0	3.0	1200	1200	115	18	300	15
	19–22	58	128	162	65	2100	46	800	4000	400	12	45	400	14	1.4	1.1	2.0	3.0	800	800	100	18	300	15
	23–50	58	128	162	65	2000	46	800	4000		12	45	400	13	1.2	1.0	2.0	3.0	800	800	100	18	300	15
	51+	58	128	162	65	1800	46	800	4000		12	45	400	12	1.1	1.0	2.0	3.0	800	800	80	10	300	15
Pregnant						+300	+30	1000	5000	400	15	60	800	+2	+0.3	+0.3	2.5	4.0	1200	1200	125	18+[8]	450	20
Lactating						+500	+20	1200	6000	400	15	80	600	+4	+0.5	+0.3	2.5	4.0	1200	1200	150	18	450	25

Reference: *Recommended Dietary Allowances*, 8th rev ed. Food and Nutrition Board, National Research Council–National Academy of Sciences, 1974.

[1] The allowances are intended to provide for individual variations among most normal persons as they live in the USA under usual environmental stresses. Diets should be based on a variety of common foods in order to provide other nutrients for which human requirements have been less well defined. See text for more detailed discussion of allowances and of nutrients not tabulated.

[2] Kilojoules (kJ) = 4.2 × kcal.

[3] RE = Retinol equivalents.

[4] Total vitamin E activity, estimated to be 80% as α-tocopherol and 20% other tocopherols. See text for variation in allowances.

[5] The folacin allowances refer to dietary sources as determined by *Lactobacillus casei* assay. Pure forms of folacin may be effective in doses less than one-fourth of the recommended dietary allowance.

[6] Although allowances are expressed as niacin, it is recognized that on the average 1 mg of niacin is derived from each 60 mg of dietary tryptophan.

[7] Vitamin A activity is assumed to be all as retinol in milk during the first 6 months of life. All subsequent intakes are assumed to be half as retinol and half as β-carotene when calculated from international units. As retinol equivalents, three-fourths are as retinol and one-fourth as β-carotene.

[8] This increased requirement cannot be met by ordinary diets; therefore, the use of supplemental iron is recommended.

Table 2-16. Commercial preparations for tube-feeding a balanced diet.

Preparation	Percent by Weight			Cal/g N	Na⁺/K⁺ (mEq/liter)	Cal/ml	Osmolality (mOsm/kg)	Remarks*
	Carbohydrate	Fat	Protein					
Balanced tube feeding formulas								
Complete-B	60	20	20	156	60/37	1	468	Blenderized meat, vegetable and milk base.
Ensure	66	17	17	168	32/32	1	450	No lactose. Carbohydrate as sucrose. Fat as corn oil. Soy and casein protein.
Isocal	63	21	16	192	22/32	1.04	350	No lactose. Fat as MCT and soy oil. Soy and casein protein.
Nutri-1000	54	28	17.6	181	23/31	1.06	500	Skim milk, casein, corn oil, sucrose.
Portagen	58	24	17.7	178	22/32	1	236	No lactose. Fat as MCT.
Low-residue formulas								
Precision LR	84	0.3	9.1	263	27/20	1.08	600	Protein as egg albumin. Fat as soybean oil. Carbohydrate as maltodextrin (44%) and sucrose (6%).
Precision HN	75	0.2	16.6	150	41/22	1	580	
Precision MN	64	13.2	15.2	192	37/19	1.12	475	
Elemental diets								
Vivonex Std	85	0.54	(20.4)	300	37/30	1	500	Carbohydrate as glucose. Nitrogen as synthetic essential and nonessential amino acids.
Vivonex HN	79	0.33	(41.7)	150	34/18	1	844	
Flexical	78	15	22.5	277	15/32	1	724	Fat as soy oil and MCT. Protein as casein hydrolysate plus L-Met, L-Trp, L-Tyr.

*MCT = medium chain triglycerides.
(Reproduced with permission from Dunphy, JE, Way LW (Eds.): *Current Surgical Diagnosis & Treatment*, 3rd Ed. Lange 1977)

tubes inserted into one gelatin capsule. After the tubes have been passed through the nose into the stomach, wait 30 minutes for the capsule to dissolve, then remove the nasogastric tube. Tape the feeding tube to the side of the face.

3. Technic of administration

a. Begin tube feeding with a balanced or low-residue diet. Dilute the formula to 1/3 Cal/ml and infuse at the rate of 50 ml/hour. After 500 ml have been given, aspirate the contents of the stomach; if most of the administered volume is still in the stomach, reduce the rate of infusion.

b. Tube feedings should be delivered with an infusion pump at a constant rate over 24 hours. Boluses of fluid often cause vomiting and aspiration.

c. Observe the patient for glycosuria, gastric distention, and diarrhea. If the patient tolerates the dilute formula, increase the concentration to 2/3 Cal/ml and then to 1 Cal/ml; this is the maximal concentration that is tolerated by most patients.

d. Maintain a balance sheet to record the amounts of fluid and calories administered. It is seldom possible to deliver more than 3000 Cal daily by tube feeding. Larger requirements must be met by supplementary parenteral nutrition.

4. Other enteric routes

a. Tube gastrostomy is useful for prolonged feeding in patients with neurological disease or other causes of inability to swallow.

b. Tube jejunostomy is constructed by inserting a 14 French catheter into the proximal jejunum. If operation is performed for another purpose, the jejunostomy can be established at the same time. In general, the availability of total parenteral nutrition makes it unnecessary to operate solely to construct a feeding jejunostomy.

5. Dietary supplements Commercially available preparations can be used to supplement the diets of patients who are eating food but need to take in more nutrition than is provided by standard hospital diets. Examples are Citrotein, Lanolac, Meritene, and Sustecal.

E. TOTAL PARENTERAL NUTRITION (TPN) (also termed intravenous hyperalimentation) is the IV administration of solutions containing amino acids and large amounts of calories.

1. Clinical application The clinical application of TPN is empirical, and it is used in the treatment of many illnesses that are complicated by nutritional deprivation, enhanced catabolism, or loss of gastrointestinal function. Prevention of muscle breakdown, rather than treatment of fully developed malnutrition, is the goal in patients who are well-nourished when the illness or injury strikes.

2. Solutions Table 2-17 lists the composition of typical TPN solutions. These solutions should be prepared by a trained pharmacist under a laminar flow hood.

a. Protein Commercially-available protein sources are either hydrolysates of casein or fibrin (supplied as 5% or 10% solutions) or synthetic L-amino acids (prepared as 3.5-8.5% solutions). The hydrolysates contain large amounts of oligopeptides and various amounts of nonessential amino acids. Except for the conditions described below, any of the preparations may be used with no particular advantage of one over another.

b. Dextrose is added to the protein base in concentrations of 20-50%. Nitrogen balance is a function of the calorie : nitrogen ratio in the solution. This ratio should be 100-150 : 1 nonprotein Cal/gm of nitrogen in most patients who receive TPN.

c. Electrolytes and vitamins are added to the desired concentrations.

d. Special considerations Patients in acute renal failure are both catabolic and unable to excrete urea. TPN decreases urea production by providing amino acids and dextrose. Because hydrolysates contain excess nitrogen, a solution of amino acids (preferably essential amino acids, e.g., Nephramine) should be used

Table 2-17. Average daily composition of
adult TPN solution.*

Water	2500–3000 ml
Protein hydrolysate (amino acids)	100–130 g
Nitrogen	12–18 g
Carbohydrate (dextrose)	525–625 g
Calories	2500–3000
Sodium	125–150 mEq
Potassium	75–120 mEq
Phosphorus	20–25 mEq/1000 Cal
Magnesium	4–8 mEq

*Calcium is added to the solution when indicated. Iron is added to the solution, or given intramuscularly in depot form as iron dextran injection, or given as blood transfusion if indicated. Vitamin B_{12}, vitamin K, and folic acid are given intramuscularly or added for intravenous administration as indicated. Trace elements such as zinc, copper, manganese, cobalt, and iodine are added only after total intravenous therapy exceeds 1 month.

(Reproduced with permission from Dunphy JE, Way LW (Eds.): *Current Surgical Diagnosis & Treatment*, 3rd Ed. Lange 1977)

instead. Limitations on the amount of fluid that can be safely infused in renal failure are met by increasing the dextrose concentration to 50%. A calorie : nitrogen ratio of 800–900 : 1 is required to suppress urea formation.

Patients with hepatic disease should receive amino acid solutions, because the protein hydrolysates provide excessive nitrogen.

3. Technic of administration

a. TPN should be administered into a large central vein because the solutions are hypertonic. The **subclavian vein** is the preferred site. Sterile precautions should be observed during percutaneous insertion of the catheter. Povidone-iodine ointment is applied after insertion, and the area is dressed sterilely. The catheter site should be inspected under aseptic conditions and cleansed with povidone-iodine solution every other day.

b. The IV tubing should contain a bacterial filter, and the tubing connecting the bottle to the subclavian catheter should be changed daily. The tubing used for delivery of TPN must **not** be used for any other purpose (e.g., drawing blood samples, administration of drugs). A constant infusion pump is recommended for administration.

c. Studies to be obtained before starting TPN and parameters to monitor are listed in Table 2-18.

d. The amount of glucose infused should be increased gradually. One method is to keep the dextrose concentration constant in the TPN solution, and slowly increase the volume of solution. A recommended program of this type is to give 2 liters of solution containing 25% dextrose each day for 3 days initially, then increase the volume as the patient's condition warrants. Additional fluid should be given through a peripheral vein to meet basal fluid requirements until the volume of TPN solution reaches about 3000 ml/day.

    e. Do not discontinue TPN suddenly; taper the infusion gradually over 12 hours to avoid hypoglycemia.

    4. Mechanical complications Complications of inserting the subclavian catheter include air embolism, hemothorax, pneumothorax, hydrothorax, and injury to any of the other structures in the vicinity of the subclavian vein.

    5. Septic complications With strict aseptic precautions, the incidence of infection in the IV catheter is about 3%. If a fever develops, the IV catheter should be removed and cultures should be obtained of the catheter tip, TPN solution, and blood. Another catheter should be inserted in a new site 48 hours later, and new solution and tubing should be used. Indiscriminate use of antibiotics contributes to fungemia (e.g., candidiasis).

Table 2-18. Monitoring protocol for total parenteral nutrition

---

1. **Baseline studies before starting TPN:** electrolytes, hemoglobin, hematocrit, BUN, creatinine, bilirubin, SGOT, alkaline phosphatase, blood glucose, calcium, phosphorous, magnesium, albumin, prothrombin time.

2. **Daily studies until the patient is stable (5–7 days):**
    (a) Fractional urine for glucose every 6 hours.
    (b) Blood sugar.
    (c) Electrolytes.
    (d) Accurate intake and output recording.
    (e) Body weight.
    (f) Nitrogen balance.

3. **Routine studies after the patient is stable:**
    (a) Daily: Intake and output, body weight, fractional urines for glucose.
    (b) 2–3 times weekly: electrolytes.
    (c) Once a week: CBC, platelet count, prothrombin time, BUN, creatinine, calcium, phosphorous.
    (d) Pooled nitrogen balance twice a week.

---

6. Metabolic complications

    a. Hyperosmolar nonketotic dehydration and coma is the result of infusion of dextrose at a rate which exceeds the ability of endogenous insulin to cope with it. Careful monitoring of glucose in blood and urine will avoid this complication; if glycosuria appears, measure blood osmolarity. About 15% of patients receiving TPN require exogenous insulin; it is added directly to the solution. Diabetics can receive TPN safely. Sudden hypoglycemia in a previously stable patient suggests resistance to insulin caused by infection; chromium deficiency may also be responsible.

    b. Azotemia results from administering hypertonic solutions to dehydrated patients or infusing a solution with a low (>50 : 1) calorie-nitrogen ratio. Azotemia from osmotic dehydration may occur if the infusion is too rapid.

    c. Electrolyte abnormalities can develop from the intracellular shift of potassium, magnesium, phosphate, and calcium as anabolism begins. Hyperkalemia results from acidosis or sudden cessation of the infusion. Hypocalcemia is unusual if calcium is given routinely. Hypercalcemia occurs if excessive amounts of vitamin D are administered.

    d. Hypophosphatemia Deficiency of inorganic phosphate develops within 10 days after starting TPN if supplemental phosphate is not provided. Hypophosphatemia decreases levels of ATP and 2, 3-DPG in red cells and causes impaired delivery of oxygen to tissues. The problem is prevented by including 20–25 mEq of phosphate/1000 Cal in the TPN solution.

7. Home parenteral nutrition   Chronic TPN in ambulatory patients is available at several centers. Patients with short bowel syndrome are prime candidates; they can receive TPN at home through a special type of subclavian catheter (Broviac shunt). Solution is infused at night or around the clock, depending upon the patient's requirements. Special training and surveillance of these patients is essential.

F. INTRAVENOUS FAT EMULSION (Intralipid 10%) is prepared from soybean oil. It contains 11 Cal/gm and can be infused through a peripheral vein. Intralipid should not comprise more than 60% of the daily caloric input. The principal use of this preparation is to prevent deficiency of essential fatty acid which begins within 3 days after initiation of TPN and is clinically evident within 10 days. Patients who receive TPN should be given 500 ml of Intralipid 10% every other day for this reason.

3

ANESTHESIA

Neri P. Guadagni, MD

The conduct of an anesthetic procedure begins with the preoperative visit to the patient and ends after the patient has completely recovered from the anesthetic and any postanesthetic complications.

Anesthetic management thus includes: (1) Evaluation and preparation of the patient; (2) familiarity with the action of the drugs to be given; (3) ability to use the recommended technics; (4) ability to administer supportive measures as necessary, e.g., maintenance of adequate pulmonary ventilation; and (5) care of the patient in the postanesthetic period.

I. EVALUATION OF THE PATIENT

Except in emergencies, patients should be examined by the anesthetist on the day before the proposed procedure. A thorough review of the history, physical examination, and laboratory findings is essential to ensure proper preparation of the patient, to aid in the selection of the agent and type of anesthetic procedure, to anticipate complications, and to suggest postanesthetic care.

A. HISTORY   In taking the preanesthetic history special emphasis should be placed on the cardiorespiratory system. Question the patient about the following:

1. History of previous anesthesia: agents and methods which have caused difficulties or complications in the past.

2. History of drugs used by the patient.

a. CNS depressants   Barbiturates, opiates, and alcohol may alter tolerance to anesthetic drugs.

b. Tranquilizing drugs   Preoperative use of these drugs lowers the required dosage of general anesthetics. The important groups are as follows: (1) Dicarbamates (meprobamate, etc.), these have little effect on the conduct of anesthesia. (2) Rauwolfia derivatives (reserpine, etc.), prolonged use may lead to epinephrine depletion, but this does not occur with the usual clinical doses. (3) Phenothiazine derivatives (chlorpromazine, etc.), these drugs predispose to hypotension during anesthesia.

c. Corticosteroids   Prolonged use of cortisone impairs the physiological response of the adrenal cortex to the stress of anesthesia and surgery. Cortisone should be given immediately before, during and after surgery (see Chapter 2).

d. Any drugs which may have to be continued during anesthesia or which may have a bearing on prognosis and complications (e.g., insulin, nitroglycerin, digitalis).

3. History of allergies: asthma and drug sensitivities play an important role in the choice of agents used.

4. Presence of food in stomach: note the interval since food was last taken. Pain and anxiety may delay the emptying time of the stomach. Regurgitation and aspiration are frequent and serious complications of general anesthesia.

B. PHYSICAL EXAMINATION   The preanesthetic physical examination should be complete, with special emphasis on the following:

 1. Mental and emotional status.
 2. Cardiac status (e.g., decompensation, cyanosis, edema).
 3. Status of the respiratory system, with particular reference to (1) obstruction of the airway; (2) conditions which may lead to obstruction of the airway (foreign bodies, such as dentures); and (3) other disorders which may hinder gas exchange, such as pneumothorax, emphysema, and abdominal distention.
 4. Physical deformities or abnormalities which complicate or contraindicate specific technics. For example, the patient should be examined for spinal or sacral deformities if spinal or caudal anesthesia is contemplated; and ankylosis and other mandibular and oral pathology may render tracheal intubation difficult.

C. LABORATORY TESTS   The minimum preanesthetic laboratory evaluation should include urinalysis and Hgb or Hct. Individual patients may require chest x-rays, serum electrolyte determinations, arterial blood gas values, electrocardiograms, and other tests aimed at the diagnosis or evaluation of disorders which must be treated before anesthesia can proceed safely.

II. PREPARATION OF THE PATIENT

A. MEDICAL PREPARATION   The patient should be in the best physical condition possible within the limits of medical treatment and with consideration for the urgency of the surgery. The following conditions must be treated prior to anesthesia in all except emergencies: shock; hypovolemia; electrolyte imbalance; cardiac decompensation; diabetic acidosis; and acute inflammation of the respiratory system.

 The stomach must be allowed to empty itself or must be emptied by gastric tube or induced vomiting.

 Patency of the airway must be assured. Tracheostomy made necessary by severe upper respiratory obstruction should be performed under local anesthesia; general anesthesia must not be induced until the tracheostomy has been done.

B. PSYCHOLOGIC PREPARATION   The anesthetist must gain the patient's confidence and make every effort to allay his or her fears. A personal relationship should be established. The calm, reassured patient is more easily anesthetized.

C. PHARMACOLOGIC PREPARATION   Preanesthetic medications are given, to: ensure a good night's rest; diminish anxiety; produce a mild euphoria; produce amnesia; decrease metabolism and anesthetic requirements; decrease secretions in the mouth and respiratory tract; decrease autonomic reflexes (e.g., cardiac irregularities); counteract toxic manifestations of local anesthetics; minimize postanesthetic nausea and vomiting.

 The patient should arrive at the operating room in a drowsy but cooperative state with minimal respiratory depression.

 1. Drugs for preanesthetic medication   Tables 3-1 and 3-2 list common drugs and doses which should be modified according to age (elderly patients require little or no premedication), physical condition and mental status, and the choice of anesthetic agent.

 a. Barbiturates   For general sedation, relief of anxiety, hypnosis, and protection against local anesthetic reactions.

 b. Narcotics   For analgesia, euphoria, and general sedation.

 c. Belladonna derivatives (scopolamine, atropine)   For drying secretions and other vagolytic effects. Scopolamine also produces sedation and amnesia.

 d. Tranquilizers   Major tranquilizers such as chlorpromazine or other phenothiazines may be used. They produce drowsiness, are antiemetic, and their vascular effects facilitate hypotension and hypothermia. Chlorpromazine (Thorazine) may be given orally (25-50 mg) or IM (25 mg) in place of or in addition to a barbiturate or other sedative. Promethazine (Phenergan) or promazine (Sparine) may also be used in the same dosages. Innovar—a combination of a narcotic (fentanyl) and a tranquilizer (droperidol)—can be a useful premedication and induction agent for balanced anesthesia.

Table 3-1. Average doses of common drugs for premedication in adults[1]

Drug	Dosage	Route and time
Barbiturates		
Pentobarbital (Nembutal)	50-200 mg	Give orally 1½-2 hours before induction; or IM 30 minutes before induction; or IV 15 minutes before induction
Secobarbital (Seconal)	50-200 mg	
Amobarbital (Amytal)	50-200 mg	
Diazepam (Valium)	2-10 mg (orally); 2-5 mg (IV or IM)	
Narcotics		
Morphine sulfate	5-15 mg	Give subcut. 1 hour before induction; or IM 45 minutes before induction; or IV 15 minutes before induction
Meperidine (Demerol)	50-150 mg	
Alphaprodine (Nisentil)	30-60 mg	
Belladonna alkaloids		
Atropine	0.2-0.6 mg	Give subcut. with the narcotic before induction
Scopolamine	0.2-0.6 mg	

[1] Dosage of barbiturates and narcotics should be reduced when premedication includes tranquilizers.

III. SELECTION OF ANESTHETIC AGENTS AND TECHNICS

Many factors must be considered in deciding what type of anesthesia will be used.

A. PATIENT FACTORS Patient's preferences and prejudices and patient's condition.

B. SURGICAL REQUIREMENTS Individual skill and experience of the anesthetist with the agents and equipment at his disposal. Speed and skill of the surgeon. Site of surgery and position of patient. Use of electrocautery. Need for muscle relaxation. Open chest.

IV. TYPES OF GENERAL ANESTHESIA

General anesthesia is a state of drug-induced CNS depression characterized by (1) analgesia and amnesia, (2) unconsciousness, and (3) loss of reflexes and muscle tone. Drugs producing this state must cause no permanent tissue change, must be reversible in action by excretion or destruction, and must have minimal side-effects.

Different methods of administration all serve the same purpose, i.e., to introduce the agent into the blood stream for transport to the CNS. The route of administration (inhalation, gastrointestinal absorption, or injection into veins or tissues) depends upon the physical properties of the agent.

A. INHALATION ANESTHESIA (See Table 3-3) Inhalation anesthesia is used to administer gases and volatile liquids.

Table 3-2. Pediatric premedication*

Age	Average weight (lb)	Pentobarbital (Nembutal) or secobarbital (Seconal) mg	Atropine or scopolamine mg	Comparable doses of narcotics		
				Morphine mg	Meperidine (Demerol) mg	Alphaprodine (Nisentil) mg
Newborn	7	–	0.1	–	–	–
6 months	16	30	0.2	–	–	–
1 year	21	50	0.2	1	10	4
2 years	27	60	0.3	1.5	20	8
4 years	35	90	0.3	3	30	12
6 years	45	100	0.4	4	40	15
8 years	55	120	0.4	5	50	20
10 years	65	150	0.4	6	60	25
12 years	85	150	0.6	8	80	30

The above dosage scale is for well developed children of average weight. Reductions must be made for underweight or poorly developed patients. No barbiturate is given to infants under 6 months of age; no narcotic to patients under 1 year of age. Barbiturates are given rectally at least 90 minutes before operation. Dissolve barbiturate in 10 ml of water and insert rectally. Morphine and atropine are given subcut. 45 minutes before operation.

*Modified and reproduced, with permission, from R. M. Smith, Anesthesia for Infants and Children. Mosby, 1959.

1. Technics

a. Open drop This is the simplest and oldest method and requires the least equipment. A volatile liquid (ethers, chloroform) is administered drop by drop onto the gauze or cloth covering of a wire frame mask applied over the mouth and nose. The inhaled concentration is controlled by the rate of drip. Induction is accomplished with a slow rate of drip, and the rate is increased to the patient's tolerance. When the desired depth of anesthesia is reached, the rate of administration is slowed.

b. Insufflation This method consists of blowing anesthetic vapors or gases into the mouth, pharynx, or trachea. Some type of anesthesia machine is required. Insufflation has its greatest usefulness in operations for which a mask cannot be used (e.g., tonsillectomy).

c. Nonrebreathing Nonrebreathing anesthesia supplies a continuous fresh quantity of anesthetic agent with adequate oxygen through an apparatus which evacuates each exhalation to the atmosphere. Leigh valves and Ayre's T pieces are examples of these apparatus.

d. Partial and total rebreathing These methods require anesthesia machines and are named according to the amount of exhalation the patient is required to rebreathe. A means of absorbing the exhaled CO_2 must be provided in all instances except where the rebreathing is minimal.

2. Anesthesia machines make possible (1) use of anesthetic gases and oxygen supplied in compressed form in tanks; (2) accurate metering of these gases; (3) vaporization of volatile liquids; (4) absorption of CO_2; (5) conservation of expensive agents; (6) artificial respiration (by using the reservoir bag as a bellows for inflation of the lungs).

B. INTRAVENOUS ANESTHESIA

1. Advantages Ease of administration with a rapid and pleasant induction.

2. Disadvantages Lack of control after administration. The duration of action depends upon the destruction or renal excretion of the agent.

3. Common agents

a. Barbiturates Thiopental (Pentothal) or thiamylal (Surital) is administered slowly in 2.5% solution until loss of consciousness occurs. Dosage is limited by respiratory depression. Increments may be added as needed.

b. Narcotics.

C. RECTAL ANESTHESIA

1. Advantages Ease of administration with pleasant induction when the intravenous approach is impractical (children, obese patients).

2. Disadvantages Same as for intravenous anesthesia; in addition, the rate of absorption is slow and the amount of anesthetic which can be absorbed in this way is difficult to predict.

3. Common agents Barbiturates, tribromoethanol (Avertin).

D. BALANCED ANESTHESIA
In balanced anesthesia several agents are administered by 1 or more of the above methods. Each agent is used for its most desirable properties, and none is given in toxic amounts. By variations in the dose of different agents the anesthetic is made to suit the surgical requirements. A typical example is the combination of (1) an intravenous barbiturate for induction, (2) nitrous oxide by inhalation for maintenance of light anesthesia, (3) supplementation of nitrous oxide with an intravenous narcotic or potent inhalation agent (e.g., halothane), and (4) muscle relaxants to diminish or abolish muscle tone. Innovar is useful for induction of balanced anesthesia; it is a mixture of a neuroleptic (droperidol) and a narcotic analgesic (fentanyl).

E. DISSOCIATIVE ANESTHESIA
Ketamine (Ketaject, Ketalar), a nonbarbiturate general anesthetic administered intravenously or intramuscularly, rapidly produces somatic analgesia and anesthesia without respiratory depression or

Table 3-3. Inhalation agents for general anesthesia

	Diethyl ether ($C_2H_5)_2O$	Chloroform $CHCl_3$	Divinyl ether (Vinethene) ($C_2H_3)_2O$	Methoxyflurane (Penthrane) $CHCl_2CF_2OCH_3$	Trichloroethylene (Trimar) C_2HCl_3
Concentration in inspired mixture for:					
Analgesia	<1%	0.25-0.75%	0.2%	0.2-0.8%	0.5-1.5%
Anesthesia	3.5-4.5%	0.75-1.65%	2-4%		5-7.5%
Respiratory Arrest	6.7-8%	2%	10-12%		
Use With Soda Lime	Yes	Yes	Yes	Yes	Dangerous
Depth and Use	Any depth required for surgery	Rarely used. Light anesthesia	Light anesthesia for short procedures	Light to moderate anesthesia	Analgesia only
Cardiac Effects: Arrhythmias					
Myocardium	Occasional Depressed	Frequent Markedly depressed	Occasional Depressed	Sinus bradycardia Depressed; hypo-tension	Frequent Depressed
Use with epinephrine or norepinephrine	Yes	Dangerous	Yes	Heart sensitized to pressor amines	Dangerous
Respiratory Effects					
Irritating to respiratory passages	Yes	Not in recommended concentrations	Yes	No	No
Secretions	Increased	Slightly increased	Increased	Not increased	Slightly increased
Respiration	Stimulated, then depressed	Depressed. Circu-lation may fail be-fore respiration	Stimulated, then depressed	Depressed	Tachypnea with increasing depth
Liver Toxicity	Depression of function	Marked	Prolonged anesthe-sia causes central necrosis. Less toxic than chloroform	None reported	Yes
Renal Toxicity				Nephrotoxic	
Muscle Relaxation	Excellent	Excellent	Not used for relaxation	Good	Poor
Explosive	Yes	No	Yes	No	Not in anesthetic concentrations
Recovery	Slow. Nausea and vomiting frequent	More rapid than ether. Nausea and vomiting common	Rapid. Nausea and vomiting uncom-mon	Slow. Nausea and vomiting less than ether	Rapid. Nausea and vomiting less than with ether

	Halothane (Fluothane) $CF_3CHBrCl$	Nitrous Oxide* N_2O	Ethylene* C_2H_4	Cyclopropane C_3H_6	Enflurane (Ethrane) $CHClF\text{-}CF_2\text{-}O\text{-}CH_2$
Concentration in inspired mixture for					
Analgesia	<0.5%	20-40%	20-25%	3-5%	
Anesthesia	0.4-1.6%	85-90%	80-90%	5-23%	1.5-3.0%
Respiratory Arrest				23-40%	
Use with Soda Lime	Yes	Yes	Yes	Yes	Yes
Depth and Use	Light to moderate depth anesthesia	1st plane anesthesia	1st plane anesthesia	Moderate depth	Light to moderate depth
Cardiac effects					
Arrhythmias	Infrequent bradycardia	Rare	Rare	Frequent	Infrequent
Myocardium	Depressed; hypotension	Slight depression	Slight depression	Moderate depression	Depressed
Use with epinephrine or norepinephrine	Heart sensitized to pressor amines	Yes	Yes	Dangerous. May produce ventricular fibrillation	Yes
Respiratory Effects					
Irritating to respiratory passages	No	No	No	Nonirritating with <50%	No
Secretions	Not increased	Not increased	Not increased	Minimal	No
Respiration	Depressed; tachypnea	Normal	Normal	Depressed	Depressed
Liver Toxicity	†Hepatoxic	No	No effect	Not significantly depressed	Not reported
Muscle Relaxation	Good	No relaxation	Poor	Good	Good
Explosive	No	No, but supports combustion	Yes	Yes	No
Recovery	Moderately rapid. Nausea and vomiting infrequent	Rapid. Nausea and vomiting uncommon	Rapid. Nausea and vomiting less than with ether	Rapid. Nausea and vomiting frequent	Moderately rapid. Nausea and vomiting infrequent

*Should not be administered with less than 20% oxygen. The real danger in their use is from hypoxia and not from the gases themselves.
† Not clearly established whether this effect is due to sensitization or direct toxicity.

Table 3-4. Muscle relaxants commonly used in anesthesia

	Tubocurarine chloride	Gallamine triethiodide (Flaxedil)	Pancuronium bromide (Pavulon)	Succinylcholine chloride (Anectine, Quelicin, Sucostrin)
How supplied	10 ml vials, 3 mg/ml	10 ml vials, 20 mg/ml	2 ml ampuls, 2 mg/ml. 10 ml vials, 1 mg/ml. 5 ml ampuls, 2 mg/ml	10 ml vials, 20 mg/ml. 10 ml ampuls, 100 mg/ml
Dose				
Initial	3-15 mg IV	40-100 mg IV	2-5 mg IV	20-60 mg IV
Subsequent	1/2-1/3 previous IV dose	1/2 previous IV dose	1-2 mg IV	Same as initial IV
Continuous drip	Not used	Not used	Not used	0.1-0.2% solution
Onset of action	3-5 minutes	2-5 minutes	1-3 minutes	1-3 minutes
Duration of action of single paralyzing dose	30-60 minutes	25-30 minutes	30-60 minutes	2-5 minutes
Side effects	Histamine release, hypotension	No histamine effect; tachycardia	Slight rise in pulse rate	Muscle fasciculation with rapid injection. Salivation. Increases intraocular tension.
Other effects	Cumulative action. Additive with ether and certain antibiotics, e.g., neomycin	Same as tubocurarine chloride	None	Not additive with ether. Bradycardia. May produce anti-depolarizing type block.
Contraindications	Myasthenia gravis	Myasthenia gravis	Myasthenia gravis. Impaired renal function (drug excreted in urine)	Severe liver disease. Increased intraocular tension.
Antidote	(1) Edrophonium chloride (Tensilon): 10-20 mg IV, may be repeated once. (2) Neostigmine (Prostigmin): 0.5 - 2.5 mg IV slowly. Bradycardia caused by neostigmine should be prevented or treated with atropine sulfate, 0.4-1 mg IV	Same as curare and gallamine		After large total dosage a prolonged apnea may be reversed by neostigmine (Prostigmin). Transfusion.

loss of motor tone. The patient appears to be in a catatonic trance. Circulation is well maintained, and blood pressure may be elevated. The duration of action is brief (5–15 minutes). Repeated injections may be administered. This agent is useful when inhalation or the intravenous route is not easily available (e.g., severe burn cases) and when respiratory depression might be particularly hazardous. Unpleasant postanesthetic hallucinations are the principal disadvantage.

F. MUSCLE RELAXANTS Curare and allied drugs are listed in Table 3-4. These agents act at the myoneural junction to diminish or abolish the action of skeletal muscle. In sufficient doses they paralyze all voluntary muscles, including those of respiration.

Caution: Succinylcholine administered intravenously to infants may produce bradycardia and sinus arrest. Curare and allied drugs must never be used unless the means for effective artificial respiration (preferably with oxygen) are available. Following the administration of these agents, the patient must be observed until the return of muscular strength demonstrates a reserve well beyond the minimum requirements for ventilation and maintenance of the airway.

V. MANAGEMENT OF GENERAL ANESTHESIA

A. REGULATION OF DEPTH OF ANESTHESIA By 'depth of anesthesia' is meant the degree of depression produced by the anesthetic agent. Increasing doses of anesthetic agents progressively depress physiologic functions such as respiration, cardiac action, muscle tone, and reflexes. Changes in these functions are the signs of anesthesia. Different agents depress these functions in a different order and to different degrees. For example, at the same level of respiratory depression, the muscle relaxant and circulatory effects of ether, chloroform, cyclopropane, and halothane are very different. The clinical signs at various stages and planes of ether anesthesia were classically described by Guedel (Table 3-5). All of these signs are useful in monitoring a patient's response to any agent, but their significance in determining the depth of anesthesia will vary with the agent. By observing these signs one strives to provide satisfactory surgical conditions with minimal depression of those functions which are vital.

B. CARE OF THE UNCONSCIOUS PATIENT The nervous system depression produced during anesthesia permits painless surgery but deprives the patient of important protective reflexes and homeostatic responses. The anesthetist must compensate for these undesirable effects. The most serious are those which interfere with supply of oxygen to the tissues, i.e., hypoxia. Prevention of hypoxia is the most important task of the anesthetist.

C. HYPOXIA DURING ANESTHESIA may be due to inadequate alveolar oxygen or to circulatory deficiencies. The diagnosis should be established by arterial blood gas determinations.

1. Inadequate alveolar oxygen

a. Signs Early—Cyanosis and tachycardia. Late—Bradycardia, failing circulation, dilated pupils, and cardiac arrest.

b. Etiology (1) Insufficient oxygen tension in the inspired gases. (2) Insufficient total pulmonary ventilation due to central depression by narcotics or anesthetics; weakness or paralysis of respiratory muscles caused by muscle relaxants or deep anesthesia; or obstruction of the air passages. (3) Maldistribution of the inspired gases due to obstruction of selected air passages, or due to atelectasis which may involve a lung, a lobe, or be patchy. This permits some venous blood to shunt through the lung.

Note: Obstruction is the most common cause of hypoxia during general anesthesia. The signs of obstruction: noisy respiration; increased muscular effort

Table 3-5. Stages and planes of anesthesia

The 4 small black rectangles represent zones, as follows:

1. Conjunctival column—Disappearance and reappearance of lid reflex.
2. Pharyngeal column—Appearance of swallowing (upper border of plane i) and of vomiting (lower border of Stage II).
3. Laryngeal column—Disappearance of carinal reflex.

The large plus and minus signs refer to the presence or absence of the indicated reflex.

Respiration column

Thoracic and abdominal inspiration is shown moving away from the mid-line; expiration, toward the mid-line. Regularity, rate, and depth are shown for each stage and plane, in comparison with the normal.

(Modified and reproduced, with permission, from Goodman and Gilman, The Pharmacological Basis of Therapeutics, 2nd Ed., Macmillan, 1955, as modified from Guedel, Inhalation Anesthesia, Macmillan, 1951.)

STAGES OF ANESTHESIA	RESPIRATION (Thoracic / Abdominal)	PUPIL SIZE (No Medication / 15 mg Morphine and 0.4 mg Atropine / 15 mg Morphine)	EYE-BALL ACTIVITY	Corneal	Conjunctival	Pharyngeal	Laryngeal	Cutaneous	Peritoneal	SOMATIC MUSCLES
I — ANALGESIA	(regular waves)	(pupil graphics)	VOLUNTARY	+	+	+	+	+	+	NORMAL TONE
II — DELIRIUM	(irregular waves)	(pupil graphics)	+++++	+	+	+	+	+	+	UNINHIBITED ACTIVITY
III SURGICAL — PLANE i	(waves)	(pupil graphics)	+++	+	+ ¦	■ +	+ +	+ ¦	+	RELAXATION • SLIGHT
PLANE ii	(waves)	(pupil graphics)	FIXED	+ ¦	−	+ ¦	+	−	+ ¦	• MODERATE
PLANE iii	(waves)	(pupil graphics)	FIXED	−	−	−	−	−	−	• MARKED
PLANE iv	(waves)	(pupil graphics)	FIXED	−	−	−	■	−	−	• MARKED
IV — MEDULLARY PARALYSIS	(flat lines)	(pupil graphics)		−	−	−	−	−	−	• EXTREME

during inspiration; indrawing of the soft tissues of the thorax, such as the suprasternal notch, the supraclavicular fossae, and the intercostal spaces; and diminished gas movement for the effort involved. The volume can be assessed by observation of the rebreathing bag of the anesthesia machine or by listening with the ear close to the patient's mouth.

Obstruction of the airway may occur anywhere from the nose and lips to the pleurae (pneumothorax). Hundreds of causes have been reported, including foreign bodies, inflammatory disorders, and neoplasms. The 3 most common causes of obstruction are: (1) Relaxation of the mandibular and lingual muscles,

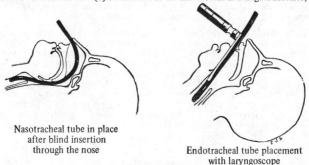

Nasotracheal tube in place
after blind insertion
through the nose

Endotracheal tube placement
with laryngoscope

Fig. 3-1. Tracheal intubation*

so that the tongue blocks the pharynx. (2) Laryngospasm—This is the reflex closure of the glottis when stimulated during light anesthesia. Thiopental, which does not suppress the laryngeal reflex, predisposes to severe laryngospasm. (3) Vomitus in the throat or trachea.

   c. Treatment

   (1) Low inspired oxygen tension—Increase oxygen concentration.

   (2) Respiratory depression—Lighten anesthesia and assist respirations.

   (3) Muscle weakness or paralysis—Assist or control respirations until muscle power returns.

   (4) Obstruction of respiratory passages. *Relaxation of mandibular and lingual muscles*—This is treated by pulling the mandible forward, inserting an oropharyngeal airway, or both. The airway must reach behind the tongue and not push the tongue farther back. *Laryngospasm*—Removal of the stimulus, deepening the anesthetic level if possible, or the use of some form of positive pressure to assist respiration, may relieve the spasm. Succinylcholine, 10-20 mg IV or IM may be resorted to if other methods fail. *Vomiting*—This is best treated prophylactically by emptying the stomach before general anesthesia. Aspirated vomitus must be suctioned out. Bronchoscopy is sometimes necessary. *Tracheal intubation* (Fig. 3-1) must be resorted to if treatment by the above measures is not successful.

   2. Circulatory deficiencies

   a. Signs   Falling BP, weak pulse, ashen gray color, altered central venous pressure (normal: 4-14 cm H_2O).

   b. Etiology   Diminished cardiac output brought on by (1) Myocardial depression—diseased myocardium, arrhythmias, anesthetic drugs (e.g., halothane), or hypoxia. Suggested by rising central venous pressure. (2) Poor venous return

---

*Reproduced, with permission, from Dunphy and Way: Current Surgical Diagnosis and Treatment. Lange, 1975.

caused by incorrect posture, loss of peripheral venous tone, increased intrathoracic pressure, manipulation of major vessels during surgery, etc.

Diminished circulating blood volume relative to capacity of vascular bed (e.g., hemorrhage, peripheral vasodilatation). Central venous pressure low.

Diminished peripheral arteriolar resistance, most often caused by the depressant actions of many anesthetic drugs on the sympathetic nervous system.

c. Treatment   Reduce depth of anesthesia. Be certain that oxygenation is adequate. Replace blood volume. Change position (Trendelenburg) to aid venous return. Vasopressor drugs—Ephedrine or other vasopressor drugs should be used as adjuncts to other methods of treatment as indicated. Digitalis for myocardial failure; lidocaine for reduction of cardiac irritability.

D. TRACHEAL INTUBATION (Fig. 3-1)   Obstruction of the upper respiratory passages may best be treated or prevented by inserting an endotracheal tube. This is done by exposing the larynx with a laryngoscope and inserting the tube into the trachea. Muscle relaxant drugs or deep anesthesia may be used to facilitate intubation. The tube should not reach the carina (teeth to carina in adults is 24-26 cm), and must be narrow enough to enter the glottis with ease.

Intubation is indicated (1) in upper respiratory obstruction, (2) to remove the anesthetic mask from the vicinity of the surgical field, (3) to facilitate controlled respiration (e.g., open chest operations), and (4) prophylactically, when emergency intubation would be difficult during surgery (e.g., when the facedown position is necessary).

VI. RESUSCITATION

The above outline of the management of the patient under general anesthesia is equally applicable when a patient's unconsciousness has other causes, such as drowning, shock, drug overdosage, diabetic coma, hypoglycemia, increased intracranial pressure (trauma, neoplasms), poisonings, etc. Tissue oxygenation must be maintained before and during the definitive treatment (e.g., transfusion, craniotomy, insulin) and as long as necessary. Though ventilation with equipment delivering oxygen is preferable if immediately available, mouth-to-mouth ventilation (Fig. 3-2) or manual ventilators (Fig. 3-3) are life-saving measures.

VII. REGIONAL ANESTHESIA (Local anesthesia)

Regional anesthesia is used to render a selected part of the body insensitive to pain and, if necessary, incapable of muscular action; the patient remains conscious. Regional anesthesia is achieved by blocking the conduction of nerve impulses from and to a well-defined area. Nerve impulses may be interrupted anywhere along the length of the peripheral nerves from their motor or sensory endings to their entry into the CNS in the spinal canal or skull.

A. AGENTS   Drugs for regional anesthesia must have a limited duration of action and must not cause permanent damage to the nerves blocked or to other tissues. Their therapeutic dose must be well below the toxic dose. Table 3-6 lists the local anesthetic drugs commonly employed.

B. TOXIC EFFECTS OF LOCAL ANESTHETICS   Local tissue toxicity is rare. Systemic toxicity is more common and may be a direct toxic effect of the drug or an allergic reaction to it. Toxic concentrations are absorbed from the site of topical application or injection if there is accidental intravascular injection or rapid rate of absorption. The rate of absorption is increased if the total dose is large or if the site of injection has a rich blood supply (reduce absorption by adding epinephrine to the anesthetic).

1. CNS reactions Twitches and tremors, first seen about the mouth and eyes, progress to convulsions which so impair the coordination of respiratory efforts that severe hypoxia ensues. The prognosis depends upon the severity and duration of hypoxia and the physical condition of the patient. Varying degrees of permanent brain damage may occur, or the patient may die in convulsions.

The hypoxia caused by convulsions is prevented or corrected by adequate pulmonary ventilation, preferably with oxygen. Intravenous barbiturates, by their central effect, or intravenous muscle relaxants, by their peripheral effect, may be used to control convulsions. Oxygenation is more important and takes precedence. **Caution:** Small doses (100 mg of thiopental, pentobarbital, or amobarbital) are adequate and more should not be given; large doses may synergize with postconvulsive depression and lead to severe central respiratory depression.

2. Cardiovascular reactions Tachycardia, palpitation, and anxiety are more likely to be caused by the epinephrine which is added to the local anesthetic.

3. Allergic manifestations in susceptible individuals include skin manifestations and bronchospasm. Treatment is with epinephrine or antihistamines.

4. Anaphylactic shock (see Chapter 1) is a rare complication of regional anesthesia and requires vigorous measures. The sudden cardiovascular collapse with absent BP and pulse and ashy pallor may require cardiac massage.

C. TECHICS OF REGIONAL ANESTHESIA

Precautions Use aseptic technic. Do not inject into an infected area. Aspirate the syringe before injecting to avoid intravascular injection.

1. Topical Application of readily absorbed local anesthetic agents (cocaine, tetracaine, lidocaine) on mucous surfaces.

2. Infiltration Injection of local anesthetic into tissues, e.g., into the fracture site for Colles' fracture, around a laceration to be sutured, around donor areas before taking skin grafts, etc.

3. Field block Injection of local anesthetic into tissues surrounding the area to be made insensitive without infiltrating the area itself, e.g., for excision of sebaceous cysts or lipomas and for herniorrhaphies.

4. Nerve blocks Injection of anesthetic agent to permeate nerves at some point proximal to the area to be anesthetized. Almost any peripheral nerve in the body may be blocked if the anatomy of the region is known. In many cases, eliciting paresthesia with the injecting needle helps locate the nerve to be blocked. Figs. 3-4 and 3-5 show some common nerve blocks useful in outpatient practice.

5. Intravenous block 50-100 ml of 0.5% lidocaine may be injected into the vein of a limb drained of blood by an elastic bandage and kept avascular by a pneumatic cuff inflated to a pressure above systolic. Complete anesthesia of the limb is achieved below the cuff and lasts until the cuff is deflated. Reactions to the lidocaine may occur on deflation of the cuff.

6. Spinal anesthesia In spinal anesthesia the spinal nerves are blocked between their emergence from the cord and their exit from the spinal canal through the intervertebral foramina. This may be done in the **subarachnoid space** by injecting a local anesthetic agent into the CSF or in the **epidural space** at any level of the vertebral column, including the sacral hiatus. Table 3-6 gives the doses of drugs used for spinal anesthesia.

a. Subarachnoid spinal anesthesia Sterile technic is used; ampuls must be autoclaved, not kept in alcohol or other disinfectants. With the patient in either the lateral decubitus or sitting position, lumbar puncture is done at any level between the second and fifth lumbar vertebrae. When a free flow of CSF is obtained, the anesthetic is injected into the subarachnoid space. This blocks all spinal nerves below the site of injection as well as those above the site of injection which are reached by the anesthetic solution in its upward spread. This upward spread can be controlled by limiting the volume and concentration of the injection and by judicious use of posture and the curves of the spinal canal to

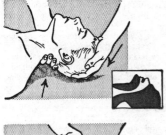

(1) The operator takes his position at the patient's head.

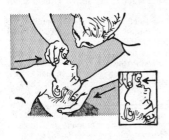

(2) With the right thumb and index finger he displaces the mandible forward by pressing at its central portion (or by forward pressure at the angle of the jaw on both sides), at the same time lifting the neck and tilting the head as far back as possible. The tongue should be pulled forward and the mouth and throat cleared of secretions and debris.

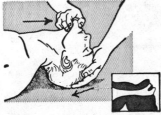

(3) The victim's mouth is opened by pulling down slightly on the jaw or by pulling down the lower lip.

(4) After taking a deep breath, the operator immediately seals his mouth around the mouth (or nose) of the victim and exhales until the chest of the victim rises.

Fig. 3-2. Technic of mouth-to-mouth insufflation

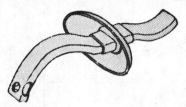

Airway for use in mouth-to-mouth insufflation. The larger airway is for adults. The guard is flexible and may be inverted from the position shown for use with infants and children.

Fig. 3-3. Portable manual resuscitator

The manual resuscitator consists of a pliable bag, nonrebreathing valve, and face mask. Effective positive pressure ventilation can be achieved by applying the mask firmly over the nose and mouth and squeezing the bag, which recoils promptly to the full position when released. Oxygen can be administered if desired by attaching the oxygen tubing to the air intake valve at the end of the bag. The manual resuscitator should be available in ambulances, coronary care and intensive care units, and wherever there might be victims of heart attack, cardiac arrest, suffocation, drowning, etc.

Instructions for use of manual resuscitator

1. Lift the victim's neck with one hand.
2. Tilt head backward into maximum neck extension. Remove secretions and debris from mouth and throat, and pull the tongue and mandible forward as required to clear the airway.
3. Hold the mask snugly over the nose and mouth, holding the chin forward and the neck in extension as shown in diagram.
4. Squeeze the bag, noting inflation of the lungs by the rise of the chest wall.
5. Release the bag, which will expand spontaneously. The patient will exhale and the chest will fall.
6. Repeat steps 4 and 5 approximately 12 times per minute.

Table 3-6. Drugs used for local anesthesia

	Cocaine	Procaine (Neocaine, Novocaine)	Tetracaine (Pontocaine)	Lidocaine (Xylocaine)	Bupivicaine (Marcaine)	Mepivacaine (Carbocaine)
Potency*	3	1	10	1.5-2	10	1.5-2
Toxicity*	4	1	10	1-1.5	3	1-1.5
Stability	Cannot be auto-claved	Stable	Stable	Stable	Stable	Stable
Recommended concentration for anesthesia						
Caudal-epidural	Do not use	2%	0.2%	1.2-2%	0.25-0.75%	1-2%
Nerve blocks	Do not use	1-2%	0.1-0.2%	1-2%	0.25-0.50%	1-2%
Infiltration	Do not use	0.25-0.5%	0.05-0.1%	0.5%	0.25%	0.5%
Topical						
Eye	2-10%	Not effective	0.5%	0.5%	Not used	Not established; probably same as lidocaine
Nose and throat	4-10%	Not effective	2%	4%	Not used	
Urethra	Absorption rapid	Not effective	Too toxic	4%	Not used	
Onset of action	Immediate	5-15 minutes	10-20 minutes	5-10 minutes		5-20 minutes
Duration of action ‡	30-60 minutes	45-60 minutes	1/2-3 hours	1-2 hours		1 1/4-3 hours
Total Maximum Dose†	100-200 mg.	1 gm	50-100 mg	500 mg		500 mg
Spinal Anesthesia						
Recommended conc.	Do not use	3-5%	0.3-0.5%	1.5-5%	Not used	Not commonly used
Dose range		50-200 mg	5-20 mg	30-75 mg		
Onset of action		3-5 minutes	5-10 minutes	3-5 minutes		
Duration of action		45-60 minutes	1 1/2-2 hours	45-75 minutes		

*Potency and toxicity relative to procaine = 1.
† Maximum dose administered at one time.
‡ Duration of anesthesia can be prolonged by using epinephrine or phenylephrine (Neo-Synephrine),
(a) For epidural and nerve blocks, use epinephrine with resultant concentration of 1:200,000.
(b) For spinal anesthesia use epinephrine, 0.1-0.3 mg, or phenylephrine (Neo-Synephrine), 2-4 mg.
AUTOCLAVE all drugs used for epidural or spinal anesthesia. DO NOT COLD STERILIZE.
Solutions for spinal anesthesia are made hyperbaric by using 10% dextrose as the diluent.

'float' or 'sink' an anesthetic solution which is heavier (hyperbaric) or lighter (hypobaric) than the CSF. Dilution by the CSF also limits the effective spread. After 20 minutes the solution is 'fixed' and further spread is unlikely.

A 'high spinal' (reaching the upper thoracic nerves) is obtained by injecting a large volume of a hypobaric solution with the patient sitting or with a hyperbaric solution with the patient placed in 5-10° of Trendelenburg.

Duration of subarachnoid spinal anesthesia depends upon the agent selected:

Procaine	30-75 minutes
Tetracaine (Pontocaine)	1-2 hours

Increased dosages increase the duration of anesthesia only slightly. The addition of 0.2-0.4 ml of 1:1000 epinephrine or 3 mg of phenylephrine (Neo-Synephrine) increases the duration of anesthetic effect 30-50%.

b. Epidural spinal anesthesia A needle is introduced into the epidural space in the lumbar area or into the sacral canal through the sacral hiatus. In the lumbar area the space is recognized by advancing the needle in the same manner as for a lumbar puncture, but stopping when resistance to injection is no longer felt even though no CSF can be aspirated. A test dose of local anesthetic sufficient to achieve subarachnoid spinal anesthesia (e.g., 5 ml of 1% lidocaine) but insufficient for epidural anesthesia proves in 5 minutes that the subarachnoid space has not been entered. The anesthetic dose is then given either by single injection or through a plastic catheter advanced through the needle for continuous epidural anesthesia. (**Caution:** Catheters should never be withdrawn through the needle for fear of shearing the catheter).

The concentrations used and the rates of onset of the block are the same as in peripheral blocks of large nerves. Lidocaine (Xylocaine), 1-2%, tetracaine (Pontocaine), 0.1-0.2%, or mepivacaine (Carbocaine), 1-2%, may be used. Since the epidural space extends from the foramen magnum to the sacral hiatus, the area anesthetized is limited only by the spread of the injected solution and is subject to considerable individual variation. The dangers of toxicity must be borne in mind because the total dose required may be quite large.

(1) Caudal approach   20 ml for sacral nerves for perineal surgery; 30-35 ml for lumbar and lower thoracic nerves.

(2) Lumbar approach   20-25 ml for lower abdominal surgery; 25-30 ml for upper abdominal surgery.

(3) Repeat doses by catheter require half the initial dose.

c. Advantages of subarachnoid block   (1) Technically easier; (2) more rapid onset; (3) smaller drug doses with less chance of toxic reactions.

d. Advantages of epidural block   (1) Fewer postoperative complications, such as spinal headaches; (2) less patient prejudice against this technic.

e. Effects of spinal anesthesia

(1) Analgesia over distribution of the spinal nerves anesthetized.

(2) Paralysis of muscles innervated by the spinal nerves anesthetized. If the anesthetic reaches the level of the fourth cervical segment in sufficient concentration, all respiratory muscles are paralyzed and respiration ceases.

(3) Sympathetic paralysis (thoracolumbar outflow from T1 to L2) causes the following: (a) Loss of vasomotor tone in the affected area, with peripheral vasodilatation, diminished vascular resistance, and loss of ability to control blood distribution. This impairment leads to a fall in BP which is particularly severe in hypertensive patients and in hypovolemic states. (b) Active intestinal peristalsis. (c) Warmth and dryness of skin, which is easily distinguished from the damp pallor seen in shock.

f. Management of patients during spinal anesthesia

(1) Prevent hypoxia by the administration of oxygen or assisted respiration.

(2) Support circulation by: (a) Positioning patient to promote venous return (head down). (b) Use of vasopressors. When high spinal anesthesia is planned, an intravenous infusion should be started before the spinal anesthetic for easy administration of vasopressors. Vasopressors may be given prophylactically before the spinal is injected. (c) Infusing fluids IV.

g. Sequelae of spinal anesthesia

(1) 'Spinal headache' Occurs during the first week after subarachnoid block and may last several days. Treatment consists of keeping the patient flat in bed for the first 24 hours to diminish CSF loss at the site of the puncture of the dura. Severe cases may require injection of saline or blood into the epidural space. The incidence is 1-15% depending on the age of the patient (low in the elderly) and the size of the needle used for lumbar puncture.

(2) Nerve injuries and transverse myelitis may cause transient or permanent disabilities ranging from minor paresthesias to paraplegia. These sequelae are rare, but their tragic impact gives them notoriety out of proportion to their frequency. They may be due to contaminants, drug sensitivities, or excessive dosages. Cases have been reported following epidural as well as subarachnoid spinal anesthesia.

VIII. POSTANESTHESIA CARE

Anesthesia does not end with closure of the incision; its termination depends upon elimination of the anesthetic agent by pulmonary or renal excretion or by metabolic destruction. The time required for recovery varies with the agents and technics used. During this period the protective reflexes and homeostatic responses which control respiration and circulation return gradually. The anesthetist must continue to provide the same care as during surgery until the patient is conscious and his vital signs have stabilized. Above all, **the patient must not be left unattended.** Respiration, circulation, and state of consciousness must be monitored at frequent intervals.

The most serious postanesthetic hazards are hypoxia and hypotension.

A. HYPOXIA is one of the most frequent causes of postoperative restlessness. Analgesics must not be given for restlessness until **hypoxia** is excluded.

Respiratory depression may be due to the prolonged effect of the anesthetic agents or may be caused by postoperative pain medication. Respiratory depression may worsen as the painful stimuli of surgery subside. Obstruction may be due to secretions, tight dressings, or casts, etc. Hematomas, pneumothorax, and atelectasis must be kept in mind also as causes of hypoxia.

Treatment of hypoxia is by removal of all impediments to respiration; oxygen therapy, and assisted respiration if necessary.

B. HYPOTENSION Postoperative hypotension may be caused by bleeding, drugs, sudden elimination of excess CO_2, and hypoxia.

Treatment consists of placing the patient in the shock position (elevate foot of bed); oxygen therapy, fluid replacement, and blood transfusion as necessary.

Surgical bleeding must be suspected and treated promptly. Vasopressors are rarely indicated; they may mask and compound the problem.

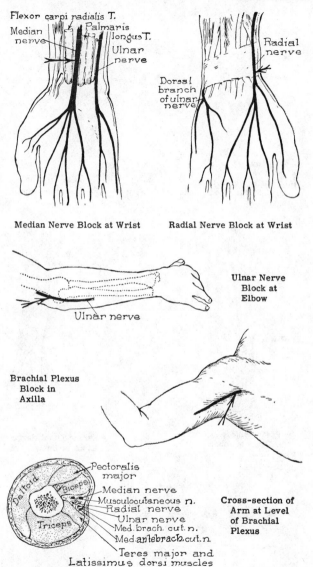

Median Nerve Block at Wrist

Radial Nerve Block at Wrist

Ulnar Nerve Block at Elbow

Brachial Plexus Block in Axilla

Cross-section of Arm at Level of Brachial Plexus

Fig. 3-4. Nerve blocks. (Heavy arrows show point of injection of anesthetic agent.)

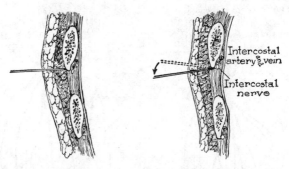

Intercostal Nerve Block. Left: Needle locating lower edge of rib. Right: Needle under edge of rib for injection of anesthetic agent.

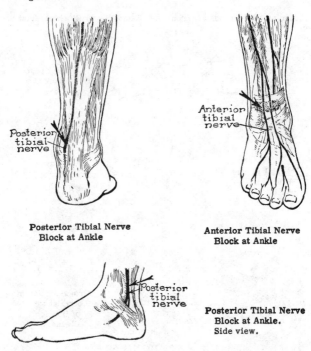

Posterior Tibial Nerve Block at Ankle

Anterior Tibial Nerve Block at Ankle

Posterior Tibial Nerve Block at Ankle. Side view.

Fig. 3-5. Nerve blocks. (Heavy arrows show point of injection of anesthetic agent.)

4

SURGICAL INFECTIONS

Ernest Jawetz, MD, PhD
Dennis J. Flora, MD

I. STERILIZATION AND ANTISEPSIS

Protection of the surgical patient from infection is a primary consideration throughout the preoperative, intraoperative, and postoperative phases of care. Host resistance which determines the individual patient's susceptibility to infection is discussed in Chapter 2. The incidence and severity of infection, particularly wound sepsis, are related also to the hospital environment and to the care with which basic principles of asepsis, antisepsis, and surgical technic are implemented.

A. STERILIZATION The only completely reliable methods of sterilization in wide use currently are steam under pressure (autoclaving), dry heat, and ethylene oxide gas.

1. Autoclaving Saturated steam at a pressure of 750 mm Hg at a temperature of 120°C destroys all vegetative bacteria and most resistant dry spores in 13 minutes. Additional time (usually a total of 30 minutes), must be allowed for the penetration of heat and moisture into the centers of packages. Modern high-vacuum or high-pressure autoclaves markedly shorten sterilization time.

2. Dry heat Exposure to continuous dry heat at 170°C for 1 hour will sterilize articles which would be spoiled by moist heat or which are more conveniently kept dry. If grease or oil is present on instruments, safe sterilization calls for 4 hours of exposure at 160°C.

3. Gas sterilization Liquid and gaseous ethylene oxide destroys bacteria, viruses, molds, pathogenic fungi, and spores. It is also flammable and toxic and will cause severe burns if it comes in contact with the skin.

Gas sterilization with ethylene oxide is the method of choice for most materials that cannot withstand autoclaving (e.g., telescopic instruments, plastic and rubber goods, sharp and delicate instruments, electric cords, sealed ampuls). Some materials (acrylics, polystyrene, pharmaceuticals) interact chemically with the ethylene oxide mixture and may be damaged, so alternative methods of sterilization must be used.

Gas sterilization requires 1 hour and 45 minutes in a gas autoclave using a mixture of 12% ethylene oxide and 88% dichlorodifluoromethane (Freon 12) at a temperature of 55°C and a pressure of 410 mm Hg. Following sterilization, a variable period of time is required for dissipation of the gas from the materials.

4. Boiling Instruments should be boiled only if autoclaving, dry heat, or gas sterilization is not available. The minimum period for sterilization in boiling water is 30 minutes at altitudes less than 300 meters. At higher altitudes, the period of sterilization must be increased. The addition of alkali to the sterilizer increases bactericidal efficiency so that sterilization time can safely be decreased to 15 minutes.

5. Soaking in antiseptics Sterilization by soaking is rarely indicated and should never be relied upon if steam autoclaving, dry heat, or gas sterilization is suitable and available. Under some circumstances, it may be necessary or more convenient to sterilize lensed or delicate cutting instruments by soaking in a liquid germicide. A variety of such germicides is available. The liquid disinfectant of current choice for lensed instruments and certain other critical items is glutaraldehyde in 2% aqueous alkaline concentration. This solution is bactericidal and virucidal in 10 minutes and sporocidal within 3 hours.

B. ANTISEPSIS Antiseptics are chemical agents which kill bacteria or arrest their growth; they may or may not be sporocidal. Antiseptics (with the possible exception of the iodophors) must not be placed in wounds because their toxicity to host cells far outweighs the possible advantages of their antibacterial effects.

1. Antiseptics for general purposes These antiseptics are used for cleaning floors, furniture, and operating room equipment and for soaking contaminated articles.

a. Soap solution One of the best all-purpose cleansing agents, but a weak antiseptic.

b. Phenol compounds Phenol and cresol are potent bactericidal chemicals but are too caustic for safe use. They have been superseded by synthetic phenolic germicides such as Lamar SP-63, Vestal Vasphene, and Western Polyphene. They kill gram-positive and gram-negative bacteria (including tubercle bacilli) and fungi. Surfaces treated with these compounds may retain antibacterial properties for 10-14 days, but this must not be relied upon as a substitute for routine frequent disinfection. Synthetic phenolic compounds, like PBS (below), are compatible with many other anionic and alkaline agents used in hospitals, and they resist deactivation by organic matter.

c. Polybrominated salicylanilide (PBS) This is a new class of antimicrobial chemicals. They are similar to synthetic phenolics with respect to antimicrobial spectrum, residual surface action, compatibility with other anionic and alkaline agents, and resistance to deactivation by organic matter. When PBS preparations are used in laundries, textiles take on a self-sanitizing antibacterial finish. A disadvantage of PBS is the white powdery film which remains on metal and other surfaces. PBS is the essential ingredient in Lamar L-300.

d. Iodophors In these chemicals, iodine is combined with a detergent (Wescodyne, Surgidine) or with polyvinylpyrrolidone (Betadine, Prepodine, Isodine). The toxicity of the iodine is practically eliminated, but surface and skin disinfection is efficient. Iodophors are rapidly diminished in activity by anionic or alkaline materials and are subject to a certain degree of volatilization.

e. Alcohols 70% ethyl alcohol is a powerful germicide. Isopropyl alcohol should be used as a 70-90% solution. Neither of these alcohols is effective against spores.

f. Quaternary ammonium compounds These are less effective and are inactivated by soap and adsorbed by fibers. Benzalkonium chloride is the prototype. It has given rise to outbreaks of gram-negative sepsis.

g. Formaldehyde and glutaraldehyde Aqueous solutions of 40% formaldehyde (20% formalin) are effective but irritating. A combination of 8% formaldehyde (20% formalin) in 70% alcohol is even more rapidly bactericidal and is sporocidal within 3 hours. Glutaraldehyde has the germicidal properties of formaldehyde but has a low tissue toxicity and no irritating odor. Glutaraldehyde in 2% aqueous alkaline concentration (Cidex) is equivalent to 8% formaldehyde in alcohol and is a good agent for soaking instruments, cleaning of anesthesia equipment, etc.

h. Other chemicals Hypochlorites, chloramine, mercury salts, and solutions of azo dyes have been replaced by more reliable compounds.

2. Skin antisepsis The most important applications of skin antisepsis are the hand scrub of the operating team and the preparation of the operative field.

a. Skin antiseptics

Tincture of iodine is 1-2% iodine in 70% ethyl alcohol. It is the most efficient and economical skin antiseptic, but it occasionally causes skin reactions and should not be used on irritated or delicate skin.

Iodophors (see above) are useful for the hand-scrub and for preparation of the operative site in situations where tincture of iodine is inadvisable.

Hexachlorophene in combination with a detergent (e.g., pHiso-Hex) or soap (Septisol, Gamophen, Dial) is also used for the hand-scrub and sometimes for the operative site. Daily use produces a sustained lowering of the bacterial count on the skin. 4% chlorhexidine in soap is equally effective and is less toxic if absorbed. Alcohol dissolves hexachlorophene and should not be applied if a prolonged surface effect is desired.

b. Hand-scrub Put on a cap and mask. Wash hands and forearms thoroughly with an iodophor or hexachlorophene preparation. Clean fingernails.

Scrub for 8 minutes (5 minutes between clean cases) with a sterile brush, covering the hands and forearms repeatedly. Most institutions use brushes impregnated with antiseptic and packaged individually; it is not possible to change brushes without contaminating the hands, so it is best to use just one brush and add more antiseptic from a dispenser.

Dry with a sterile towel and immediately don gown and gloves aseptically.

c. Preparation of the operative field The patient should bathe the evening before operation using soap and water. The umbilicus should be cleansed with particular care in abdominal cases, for it can be the repository of dirt, desquamated skin, and lint.

Shaving is required if hair is present at the operative site. It should be done **immediately** before operation; if skin is shaved the evening before, folliculitis or infection in nicks and scratches may develop.

After the patient is anesthetized and positioned, the operative site is painted with antiseptic. Tincture of iodine is used in most cases; it is not necessary to remove the iodine with alcohol until the operation is completed. Iodophors are preferable on the face, perineum, or on delicate skin (e.g., in small children). Hexachlorophene compounds are used if the patient is sensitive to iodine. 70% alcohol is another alternative in iodine-sensitive patients.

II. ANTIMICROBIAL THERAPY OF SURGICAL INFECTIONS

Microbial infection has always been an accompaniment of surgical procedures, and has often delayed or prevented successful results. Conversely, localized infections of many types—ranging from simple pus collections to infected prosthetic heart valves—have required surgery for cure. The first major development in the control of infectious complications of surgery was the concept of antisepsis, sterilization of instruments, and asepsis. The second was the development of effective antimicrobial drugs which could be used for the control of infections.

A. PRINCIPLES OF ANTIMICROBIAL CHEMOTHERAPY Antimicrobial drugs never are a substitute for sound surgical technic but they can be of help in the management of local infections, and they may be lifesaving in systemic disseminated infections. Improper application of antimicrobials may contribute to patient morbidity and mortality.

1. Selection of an antimicrobial drug on clinical grounds For optimal treatment of an infectious process, a suitable antimicrobial must be administered as early as possible. This involves a series of decisions:

a. The surgeon decides, on the basis of a clinical impression, that a microbial infection probably exists.

b. Analyzing the symptoms and signs, the surgeon makes a guess at the most likely microorganism causing the suspected infection; i.e., he attempts an etiologic diagnosis on clinical grounds.

c. The surgeon selects the drug most likely to be effective against the suspected organism; i.e., he aims a specific drug at a specific organism.

d. Before starting the drug, the surgeon must secure specimens which are

Table 4·1 Drug selections, 1977–1978

Suspected or proved etiologic agent	Drug(s) of first choice	Alternative drug(s)
Gram-negative cocci		
Gonococcus	Penicillin[1], ampicillin	Tetracycline[2], spectinomycin
Meningococcus	Penicillin[1]	Chloramphenicol, sulfonamide
Gram-positive cocci		
Pneumococcus	Penicillin[1]	Erythromycin[3], cephalosporin[4]
Streptococcus, hemolytic groups A,B,C,G	Penicillin[1]	Erythromycin[3]
Streptococcus viridans	Penicillin[1] plus aminoglycoside	Cephalosporin, vancomycin
Staphylococcus, non-penicillinase-producing	Penicillin[1]	Cephalosporin, vancomycin
Staphylococcus, penicillinase-producing	Penicillinase-resistant penicillin[5]	Cephalosporin, vancomycin, lincomycin
Streptococcus faecalis (enterococcus)	Ampicillin plus aminoglycoside	Vancomycin
Gram-negative rods		
Enterobacter (Aerobacter)	Kanamycin or gentamicin	Chloramphenicol
Bacteroides (except B fragilis)	Penicillin[1] or chloramphenicol	Clindamycin
B fragilis	Clindamycin	Chloramphenicol
Brucella	Tetracycline plus streptomycin	Streptomycin plus sulfonamide[6]
Escherichia		
E coli sepsis	Kanamycin or gentamicin	Cephalosporin, ampicillin
E coli urinary tract infection (first attack)	Sulfonamide[7] or co-trimoxazole	Ampicillin, cephalexin[4]
Haemophilus (meningitis, respiratory infections)	Chloramphenicol	Ampicillin, co-trimoxazole
Klebsiella	Cephalosporin or kanamycin	Gentamicin, chloramphenicol
Mima-Herellea (Acinetobacter)	Kanamycin	Tetracycline, gentamicin
Pasteurella (Yersinia) (plague, tularemia)	Streptomycin or tetracycline	Sulfonamide[6],
Proteus		
P mirabilis	Penicillin or ampicillin	Kanamycin, gentamicin
P vulgaris and other species	Gentamicin or kanamycin	Chloramphenicol, tobramycin
Pseudomonas		
Ps aeruginosa	Gentamicin or polymyxin	Carbenicillin, amikacin

Table 4-1. Drug selections, 1977–1978 (cont'd.)

Suspected or proved etiologic agent	Drug(s) of first choice	Alternative drug(s)
Ps pseudomallei (melioidosis)	Tetracycline	Choramphenicol
Ps mallei (glanders)	Streptomycin plus tetracycline	Chloramphenicol
Salmonella	Chloramphenicol or ampicillin	Co-trimoxazole[8]
Serratia, Providencia	Gentamicin, amikacin	Co-trimoxazole[8] plus polymyxin
Shigella	Ampicillin or chloramphenicol	Tetracycline, co-trimoxazole
Vibrio (cholera)	Tetracycline	Co-trimoxazole
Gram-positive rods		
Actinomyces	Penicillin[1]	Tetracycline, sulfonamide
Bacillus (eg, anthrax)	Penicillin[1]	Erythromycin
Clostridium (eg, gas gangrene, tetanus)	Penicillin[1]	Tetracyline, erythromycin
Corynebacterium	Erythromycin	Penicillin, cephalosporin
Listeria	Ampicillin plus aminoglycoside	Tetracycline
Acid-fast rods		
Mycobacterium tuberculosis	INH plus rifampin or ethambutol[9]	Other antituberculosis drugs
Mycobacterium leprae	Dapsone or sulfoxone	Other sulfones, amithiazone
Mycobacteria, atypical	Ethambutol plus rifampin	Rifampin plus INH
Nocardia	Sulfonamide[6]	Minocycline
Spirochetes		
Borrelia (relapsing fever)	Tetracycline	Penicillin
Leptospira	Penicillin	Tetracycline
Treponema (syphilis, yaws)	Penicillin	Erythromycin, tetracycline
Mycoplasma	Tetracycline	Erythromycin
Chlamydiae (agents of psittacosis, LGV, and trachoma)	Tetracycline, sulfonamide	Erythromycin, chloramphenicol
Rickettsiae	Tetracycline	Chloramphenicol

[1] Penicillin G is preferred for parenteral injection; penicillin G (buffered) or penicillin V for oral administration. Only highly sensitive microorganisms should be treated with oral penicillin.
[2] All tetracyclines have the same activity against microorganisms and all have comparable therapeutic activity and toxicity. Dosage is determined by the rates of absorption and excretion of different preparations.
[3] Erythromycin estolate and troleandomycin are the best absorbed oral forms.
[4] Cephalothin and cefazolin are the best accepted parenteral cephalosporins; cephalexin or cephradine the best oral forms.
[5] Parenteral methicillin, nafcillin, or oxacillin. Oral dicloxacillin or other isoxazolylpenicillin.
[6] Trisulfapyrimidines have the advantage of greater solubility in urine over sulfadiazine for oral administration; sodium sulfadiazine is suitable for intravenous injection in severely ill persons.
[7] For previously untreated urinary tract infection, a highly soluble sulfonamide such as sulfisoxazole or trisulfapyrimidines are the first choice. Cotrimoxazole is acceptable.
[8] Co-trimoxazole is a mixture of 1 part trimethoprim plus 5 parts sulfamethoxazole.
[9] Either or both.

Table 4-2. Use of antibiotics in patients with renal failure

	Principal mode of excretion or detoxification	Approximate half-life in serum		Proposed dosage regimen in renal failure		Significant removal of drug by dialysis (H=hemodialysis; P=peritoneal dialysis)
		Normal	Renal failure[1]	Initial dose[2]	Give half of initial dose at interval of	
Penicillin G	Tubular secretion	0.5 hour	6 hours	6 gm IV	8–12 hours	H, P no
Ampicillin	Tubular secretion	1 hour	8 hours	6 gm IV	8–12 hours	H yes, P no
Carbenicillin	Tubular secretion	1.5 hours	16 hours	4 gm IV	12–18 hours	H yes, P no
Methicillin	Tubular secretion	0.5 hour	6 hours	6 gm IV	8–12 hours	H, P no
Cephalothin	Tubular secretion	0.8 hour	8 hours	4 gm IV	18 hours	H, P yes
Cephalexin	Tubular secretion & glomerular filtration	2 hours	15 hours	2 gm orally	8–12 hours	H, P yes
Cefazolin	(Tubular secretion & glomerular filtration)	2 hours	30 hours	2 gm IV	24 hours	H, P yes
Streptomycin	Glomerular filtration	2.5 hours	3–4 days	1 gm IM	3–4 days	H, P yes[3]
Kanamycin	Glomerular filtration	3 hours	3–4 days	1 gm IM	3–4 days	H, P yes[3]
Gentamicin	Glomerular filtration	2.5 hours	2–4 days	3 mg/kg IM	2–3 days	H, P yes[3]
Vancomycin	Glomerular filtration	6 hours	6–9 days	1 gm IV	7–8 days	H, P no
Polymyxin B	Glomerular filtration	6 hours	2–3 days	2.5 mg/kg IV	3–4 days	P yes, H no
Colistimethate	Glomerular filtration	4 hours	2–3 days	5 mg/kg IM	3–4 days	P yes, H no
Tetracycline	Glomerular filtration	8 hours	3 days	1 gm orally or 0.5 gm IV	3 days	H, P no
Chloramphenicol	Mainly liver	3 hours	4 hours	1 gm orally or IV	8 hours	H, P poorly
Erythromycin	Mainly liver	1.5 hours	5 hours	1 gm orally or IV	8 hours	H, P poorly
Clindamycin	Glomerular filtration and liver	2.5 hours	4 hours	600 mg IV or IM	8 hours	H, P no

[1] Considered here to be marked by creatinine clearance of 10 ml/minute or less.
[2] For a 60 kg adult with a serious systemic infection. The 'initial dose' listed is administered as an intravenous infusion over a period of 1–8 hours, or as 2 intramuscular injections during an 8-hour period, or as 2–3 oral doses during the same period.
[3] Aminoglycosides are removed irregularly in peritoneal dialysis. Gentamicin is removed 60% in hemodialysis.

Reproduced, with permission, from Krupp and Chatton, Current Medical Diagnosis and Treatment. Lange 1977.

likely to reveal the etiologic agent by laboratory examination.

e. He observes the clinical response to the prescribed antimicrobial. Upon receipt of laboratory identification of a possibly important microorganism, he weighs this new information against his original 'best guess.'

f. The surgeon may choose to change his drug regimen then or upon receipt of further laboratory information on drug susceptibility of the isolated organism. However, laboratory data need not always overrule a decision based on clinical and empiric grounds, especially when the clinical response supports the initial etiologic diagnosis and drug selection.

2. Selection of an antimicrobial by laboratory tests When an etiologic pathogen has been isolated from a representative specimen, it is often possible to select the drug of choice on the basis of current clinical experience. A listing of drug choices is given in Table 4-1. At other times, laboratory tests for antimicrobial drug susceptibility are necessary, particularly if the isolated organism is of a type which varies greatly in response to different drugs.

The most common laboratory test for antimicrobial susceptibility is the disk test. In general, quantitatively controlled disk tests give valuable results. At times, however, there is a marked discrepancy between the results of the test and the clinical response of the patient treated with the chosen drug. Some possible explanations for such discrepancies are listed below.

a. The organism isolated from the specimen may not be the one responsible for the infectious process.

b. Failure to drain a collection of pus, debride necrotic tissue, or remove a foreign body. Antimicrobials can never take the place of these essential surgical procedures.

c. Sometimes, two or more microorganisms participate in an infectious process but only one may have been isolated from the specimen. The antimicrobial drug in use may be effective only against the less virulent organism.

d. Superinfection occurs fairly often in the course of prolonged chemotherapy. New microorganisms may have replaced the original infectious agent. This is particularly common with open wounds or sinus tracts.

e. The drug may not reach the site of active infection in adequate concentration. Certain drugs penetrate poorly into abscesses, phagocytic cells, the eye, CNS, and pleural or joint spaces unless they are injected directly into the area.

3. Assessment of drug and dosage Clinical response is an important but not always sufficient indication that the right drug is being given in the right dosage. Proof of drug activity in serum or urine against the original infecting organisms may provide important support for a selected drug regimen even if fever or other signs of infection are continuing. If drug therapy is adequate, the patient's serum will be markedly bactericidal in vitro against the organism isolated from that patient prior to therapy. In infections limited to the urinary tract, the patient's urine must exhibit marked activity against the original organism.

4. Determining duration of therapy The duration of drug therapy is determined in part by clinical response and past experience, and in part by laboratory indications of suppression or elimination of infection. Ultimate recovery must be verified by careful follow-up. In evaluating the patient's clinical response, the possibility of adverse reactions to antimicrobial drugs must be kept in mind. Such reactions may mimic continuing activity of the infectious process by causing fever, skin rashes, CNS disturbances, and changes in blood and urine. In the case of many drugs, it is desirable to examine blood and urine and to assess liver and kidney function at intervals. Abnormal findings may force the surgeon to reduce the dose or even discontinue a given drug.

5. Impaired renal function has an important influence on antimicrobial drug dosage, since many of these drugs are excreted by the kidneys. Only minor adjustment in dosage or frequency of administration is necessary with relatively nontoxic drugs (e.g., penicillins) or with drugs that are detoxified or excreted mainly by the liver (e.g., erythromycins or chloramphenicol). On the other hand, aminoglycosides, polymyxins, tetracyclines, and vancomycin must be drastically reduced in dosage or frequency of administration if toxicity is to be avoided in the presence of impaired renal function. Some general guidelines for the administration of such drugs to patients with renal failure are given in Table 4-2. The administration of particularly nephrotoxic antimicrobials, such as aminoglycosides, to patients in renal failure may have to be guided by frequent direct assay of drug concentration in serum.

In the newborn or premature infant, excretory mechanisms for some antimicrobials are poorly developed and special dosage schedules must be used in order to avoid toxic accumulation of drugs.

B. PROPHYLAXIS IN SURGERY   The incidence of postoperative infections is not diminished by the administration of antimicrobials in "clean" elective procedures. In compound fractures, penetrating wounds of body cavities, operation on a ruptured abdominal viscus, and other "contaminated" procedures, antimicrobial drugs are aimed at the organisms most likely to produce serious infections. A penicillin and an aminoglycoside, or a cephalosporin are often administered in such situations. A cephalosporin (e.g., cefazolin, 1 gm) given 2 hours before operation and again 2, 10, and 18 hours after operation may be useful "prophylaxis."

Before elective operations on the lower intestinal tract, the bowel flora can be reduced by the preoperative oral administration of phthalylsulfathiazole or neomycin-kanamycin. These oral insoluble drugs suppress the bowel flora only transiently and partially. The lowest number of bacteria are present within 2 days after neomycin, 1 gm every 4-6 hours.

In cardiovascular surgery, endothelial damage predisposes to endocarditis due to viridans streptococci. When penicillin G is given for 3 days postoperatively, this complication is virtually unknown, although endocarditis and pericarditis due to staphylococci and gram-negative bacteria may develop. Specific drugs directed against staphylococci (methicillin) or gram-negative rods (gentamicin) may prevent infection by these particular bacteria but favor the selection of other resistant microorganisms (serratia, fungi).

In many operations on the colon or the biliary tract or in repair of a ruptured viscus, contamination with members of the normal bowel flora occurs frequently. The administration of cefazolin, 4 gm in 24 hours, or of gentamicin, 7 mg/kg/24 hours—beginning 2 hours before surgery to establish tissue levels—can reduce postoperative peritonitis and tissue infection. Clindamycin may be added when contamination with anaerobic organisms from the colon or the female genital tract is likely. High tissue concentration of the drug must exist at the time of surgery, and "prophylactic" drug administration should not continue for more than 24-48 hours after surgery.

III. ANTIMICROBIAL DRUGS

A. PENICILLINS   All penicillins share a common chemical nucleus (aminopenicillanic acid) and a common mode of antibacterial action—the inhibition of cell wall mucopeptide (peptidoglycan) synthesis. The penicillins can be arranged according to several major criteria: (1) Susceptibility to destruction by penicillinase. (2) Susceptibility to destruction by acid pH (i.e., relative stability to gastric acid). (3) Relative efficacy against gram-positive versus gram-negative bacteria.

1. Antimicrobial activity   All penicillins specifically inhibit the synthesis of rigid bacterial cell walls which contain a complex mucopeptide. Most penicillins are much more active against gram-positive than against gram-negative bacteria. Penicillins are inactive against bacteria which are not multiplying and thus not forming new cell walls ('persisters').

One million units of penicillin G equal 0.6 gm. Other penicillins are prescribed in grams. A serum level of 0.01–1 μg/ml penicillin G or ampicillin is lethal for a majority of susceptible microorganisms; methicillin and isoxazolyl penicillins are 5–50 times less active.

2. Resistance to penicillins falls into 3 different categories:

a. Certain bacteria (e.g., some staphylococci, gram-negative bacteria) produce enzymes (penicillinases, β-lactamases) which destroy penicillin G, ampicillin, and other penicillins. Clinical penicillin resistance of staphylococci falls largely into this category.

b. Certain bacteria are resistant to some penicillins although they do not produce enzymes destroying the drug. Clinical methicillin resistance falls into this category.

c. Metabolically inactive organisms which make no new cell wall mucopeptide are temporarily resistant to penicillins. They can act as 'persisters' and perpetuate infection during and after penicillin treatment. L-forms are in this category.

3. Indications, dosages, and routes of administration The penicillins are by far the most effective and the most widely used antimicrobial drugs. All oral penicillins must be given away from meal times.

a. Penicillin G This is the drug of choice for infections caused by pneumococci, streptococci, meningococci, non-β-lactamase-producing staphylococci, and gonococci. Treponema pallidum and other spirochetes, Bacillus anthracis and other gram-positive rods, clostridia, listeria, and bacteroides (except B. fragilis).

Intramuscular or intravenous Most of the above-mentioned infections respond to aqueous penicillin G in daily doses of 0.6–5 million units (0.36-3 gm) administered by intermittent IM injection every 4–6 hours. Much larger amounts (6-120 gm daily) can be given by continuous IV infusion in serious or complicated infections due to these organisms. Sites for such intravenous administration are subject to thrombophlebitis and superinfection and must be rotated every 2 days and kept scrupulously aseptic. In enterococcus infections and some gram-negative sepsis, aminoglycosides are given simultaneously.

Oral Penicillin V is indicated only in minor infections (e.g., of the respiratory tract or its associated structures) in daily doses of 1-4 gm (1.6-6.4 million units). About one-fifth of the oral dose is absorbed, but oral administration is subject to so many variables that it should not be relied upon in seriously ill patients.

Intrathecal With high serum levels of penicillin, adequate concentrations reach the central nervous system and cerebrospinal fluid for the treatment of meningitis. Therefore, and because of the danger of injection into the subdural space of more than 10,000 units of penicillin G (which can give rise to convulsions), intrathecal injection has been virtually abandoned.

Topical Penicillins have been applied to skin, wounds, and mucous membranes by compress, ointment, and aerosol. These applications are highly sensitizing and rarely warranted. Rarely, solutions of penicillin (e.g., 100,000 units/ml) are instilled into joint or pleural spaces infected with susceptible organisms.

b. Benzathine penicillin G This penicillin is a salt of very low water solubility. It is injected IM to establish a depot which yields low but prolonged drug levels. A single injection of 1.2 million units IM is satisfactory for treatment of beta-hemolytic streptococcal pharyngitis. An injection of 1.2-2.4 million units IM every 3-4 weeks provides satisfactory prophylaxis for rheumatics against reinfection with group A streptococci. There is no indication for using this drug by mouth. Early syphilis can be treated with benzathine penicillin 2.4 million units IM once weekly for 2-4 weeks. Procaine penicillin G is another repository form for maintaining drug levels for up to 24 hours; for highly susceptible infections, 300-600 thousand units IM are usually given once daily.

c. Ampicillin, carbenicillin These drugs differ from penicillin G in having greater activity against gram-negative bacteria, but, like penicillin G, they are destroyed by penicillinases. Ampicillin can be given orally in divided doses, 2-4 gm daily, to treat urinary tract infections with coliform bacteria, enterococci, or Proteus mirabilis. It is ineffective against enterobacter and pseudomonas. In symptomatic salmonella enteric fever, ampicillin, 4-12 gm daily orally, can effectively suppress clinical disease (second choice to chloramphenicol in acute typhoid or paratyphoid) and may eliminate salmonellae from some chronic carriers. Ampicillin is somewhat more effective than penicillin G against enterococci and may be used in such infections in combination with an aminoglycoside. Hetacillin is converted in vivo to ampicillin and should not be used. Carbenicillin is relatively active against proteus and pseudomonas. Carbenicillin 12-30 gm/day together with an aminoglycoside is used in gram-negative sepsis in burns or leukemias.

d. Penicillinase-resistant penicillins Methicillin, oxacillin, cloxacillin, dicloxacillin, nafcillin, and others are relatively resistant to destruction by β-lactamase. The only indication for the use of these drugs is infection by β-lactamase-producing staphylococci.

Oral Oxacillin, cloxacillin, dicloxacillin (the isoxazolyl-penicillins), or nafcillin may be given in doses of 0.25-0.5 gm every 4-6 hours in mild or localized staphylococcal infections (50-100 mg/kg/day for children). Food must not be given in proximity to these doses because it will seriously interfere with absorption.

Intravenous For serious systemic staphylococcal infections, methicillin or nafcillin, 6-12 gm is administered IV, usually by injecting 1-2 gm during 20-30 minutes every 2 hours into a continuous infusion of 5% dextrose in water or physiologic salt solution. The dose for children is methicillin, 100 mg/kg/day, or nafcillin, 50-100 mg/kg/day.

4. Adverse effects The penicillins undoubtedly possess less direct toxicity than any other antibiotics. Most side-effects are due to hypersensitivity.

a. Allergy All penicillins are cross-sensitizing and cross-reacting. Any preparation containing penicillin may induce sensitization, including foods or cosmetics. In general, sensitization occurs in direct proportion to the duration and total dose of penicillin received in the past. Skin tests with penicilloyl-polylysine, with alkaline hydrolysis products, and with undegraded penicillin will identify many hypersensitive individuals. Although many persons develop antibodies to antigenic determinants of penicillin, the presence of such antibodies does not appear to be correlated with allergic reactivity (except rare hemolytic anemia), and serologic tests have little predictive value. A history of a penicillin reaction in the past is not reliable; however, in such cases the drug should be administered with caution or a substitute drug used.

Allergic reactions may occur as anaphylactic shock (rare—0.05%), serum sickness (urticaria, fever, joint swelling, angioneurotic edema, intense pruritus, and respiratory embarrassment occurring 7-12 days after exposure), and a variety of skin rashes, oral lesions, fever, nephritis, eosinophilia, hemolytic anemia, other hematologic disturbances, and vasculitis. LE cells are sometimes found. The incidence of hypersensitivity to penicillin is estimated to be 5-10% among adults in the U.S.A., but is negligible in small children.

Individuals known to be hypersensitive to penicillin can at times tolerate the drug during corticosteroid administration.

b. Toxicity The toxic effects of penicillin G are due to the direct irritation caused by IM or IV injection of exceedingly high concentrations (e.g., 1 gm/ml). Such concentrations may cause local pain, induration, thrombophlebitis, or degeneration of an accidentally injected nerve. All penicillins are irritating to the central nervous system. There is little indication for intrathecal administration at present. In rare cases, a patient receiving more than 50 gm of penicillin G daily parenterally has exhibited signs of cerebrocortical irritation. Direct cation toxicity (Na^+, K^+) can also occur with very large doses. Potassium penicillin G contains 1.7 mEq. of K^+ per million units (2.8 mEq/gm), and potassium may accumulate in the presence of renal failure.

Large doses of penicillins given orally may lead to nausea and diarrhea. Oral therapy may also be accompanied by luxuriant overgrowth of staphylococci, pseudomonas, proteus, or yeasts, which may occasionally cause enterocolitis. Superinfections in other organ systems may occur with penicillins as with any antibiotic therapy.

Methicillin and isoxazolyl-penicillins can cause granulocytopenia and interstitial nephritis; carbenicillin can cause bleeding defects.

B. CEPHALOSPORINS are a group of compounds closely related to the penicillins.
   1. Antimicrobial activity Cephalosporins, like penicillins, inhibit the synthesis of bacterial cell wall mucopeptide. They are resistant to destruction by some β-lactamases, but they can be hydrolyzed by others. The cephalosporins are bactericidal in vitro in concentrations of 1-20 μg/ml against most gram-positive microorganisms, except Streptococcus faecalis, and in concentrations of 5-30 μg/ml against many gram-negative bacteria, except pseudomonas, herellea, proteus, and enterobacter. There is at least partial cross-resistance between cephalosporins and β-lactamase-resistant penicillins. Thus, methicillin-resistant staphylococci are also resistant to cephalosporins.
   2. Indications, dosages, and routes of administration
   a. Oral Cephalexin or cephapirin, 0.5 gm 4 times daily orally, yields urine concentrations of 50-500 μg/ml—sufficient for treatment of urinary tract infections due to coliform organisms. They can be used to treat respiratory tract infections due to susceptible organisms.
   b. Intravenous Cephalothin (Keflin), 6-12 gm daily (for children, 50-100 mg/kg/day) by continuous drip, gives serum concentrations of 5-20 μg/ml. This is adequate for the treatment of gram-negative bacteremia or staphylococcal sepsis, or as a substitute for penicillin in serious infections caused by susceptible organisms in persons allergic to penicillin. Cefazolin 4 gm daily IV (for children, up to 100 mg/kg/day), gives serum levels of 20-25 μg/ml. It is used for the same indications and has little nephrotoxicity.
   3. Adverse effects
   a. Allergy A variety of hypersensitivity reactions occur including anaphylaxis, fever, skin rashes, granulocytopenia, and hemolytic anemia. Cross-allergy also exists with penicillins and can produce the same hypersensitivity reactions. Perhaps 6-18% of penicillin-allergic persons are also hypersensitive to cephalosporins.
   b. Toxicity Local pain after intramuscular injection, thrombophlebitis after intravenous injection. Cephaloridine can cause renal tubular necrosis and has been abandoned.

C. ERYTHROMYCIN GROUP (Macrolides) The erythromycins are a group of closely related compounds that inhibit protein synthesis and are active against gram-positive organisms (especially pneumococci, streptococci, staphylococci, and corynebacteria) in concentrations of 0.02-2 μg/ml. Neisseriae and mycoplasmas are also susceptible. Resistant mutants occur in most microbial populations and tend to emerge during prolonged treatment. There is complete cross-resistance among all members of the erythromycin group. Absorption varies greatly. Basic erythromycins are destroyed by gastric acid, but stearates are somewhat resistant. The propionyl ester of erythromycin (erythromycin estolate) and the triacetyl ester of oleandomycin are among the best absorbed oral preparations. Oral doses of 2 gm/day result in blood levels of up to 2 μg/ml, and there is wide distribution of the drug in all tissues except the central nervous system. Erythromycins are excreted largely in bile; only 5% of the dose is excreted into the urine.

Erythromycins are the drugs of choice in corynebacterial infections (diphtheroid sepsis, erythrasma). They are also effective in mycoplasmal pneumonia and Legionnaire's disease. They are most useful for streptococcal and pneumococcal infections in persons who are allergic to penicillin.

For oral administration, give erythromycin stearate, erythromycin estolate, or troleandomycin, 0.5 gm every 6 hours (for children, 40 mg/kg/day). For intravenous administration, give erythromycin lactobionate or gluceptate, 0.5 gm every 12 hours.

Such adverse effects as nausea, vomiting, and diarrhea may occur after oral intake. Erythromycin estolate or troleandomycin can produce acute cholestatic hepatitis. It is probably a hypersensitivity reaction, and most patients recover completely.

D. TETRACYCLINE GROUP The tetracyclines constitute a large group of drugs with common basic chemical structures, antimicrobial activity, and pharmacologic properties. Microorganisms resistant to this group show complete cross-resistance to all tetracyclines.

1. Antimicrobial activity Tetracyclines are inhibitors of protein synthesis and are bacteriostatic for many gram-positive and gram-negative bacteria, including anaerobes, and are strongly inhibitory for the growth of mycoplasmas, rickettsiae, chlamydiae (psittacosis-LGV-trachoma agents), and some protozoa (e.g., amebas). Equal concentrations of all tetracyclines in blood or tissue have approximately equal antimicrobial activity. However, there are great differences in the susceptibility of different strains of a given species of microorganisms, and laboratory tests are therefore important. Because of the emergence of resistant strains, tetracyclines have lost some of their former usefulness. Proteus and pseudomonas are regularly resistant; among coliform bacteria, pneumococci, and streptococci, resistant strains are increasingly common.

2. Indications, dosages, and routes of administration At present, tetracyclines are the drugs of choice in cholera, mycoplasmal pneumonia, infections with chlamydiae (psittacosis-LGV-trachoma), and infections with some rickettsiae. They may be used in various bacterial infections provided the organism is susceptible, and in amebiasis.

a. Oral Tetracycline hydrochloride, oxytetracycline, and chlortetracycline are dispensed in 250 mg capsules. Give 0.25–0.5 gm orally every 6 hours (for children, 20–40 mg/kg/day). In acne vulgaris, 0.25 gm once or twice daily for many months is prescribed by dermatologists.

Demeclocycline and methacycline are slowly excreted. Give 0.15–0.3 gm orally every 6 hours (12–20 mg/kg/day for children). Doxycycline is available in capsules of 50 or 100 mg. Give 100 mg every 12 hours on the first day, then 100 mg/day. Give minocycline 200 mg daily for 5 days in meningococcus prophylaxis.

b. Intramuscular or intravenous Several tetracyclines are formulated for IM or IV injection. Give 0.1–0.5 gm every 6–12 hours in individuals unable to take oral medication (for children, 10–15 mg/kg/day).

c. Topical Topical tetracycline, 1% in ointments, can be applied to conjunctival infections.

3. Adverse effects

a. Allergy Hypersensitivity reactions with fever or skin rashes occur.

b. Gastrointestinal side-effects Diarrhea, nausea, and anorexia, are common. These can be diminished by reducing the dose or by administering tetracyclines with food or carboxymethylcellulose, but sometimes they force discontinuance of the drug. After a few days of oral use, the gut flora is modified so that drug-resistant bacteria and yeasts become prominent. This may cause anal pruritus or even enterocolitis.

c. Bones and teeth Tetracyclines are bound to calcium deposited in growing bones and teeth, causing fluorescence, discoloration, enamel dysplasia, deformity, or growth inhibition. Therefore, tetracyclines should not be given to pregnant women or children under age 6.

d. Liver damage Tetracyclines can impair hepatic function or even cause liver necrosis, particularly during pregnancy, in the presence of preexisting liver damage or with doses of more than 3 gm IV.

e. Other Tetracyclines, principally demeclocycline, may induce photosensitization, especially in blonds. Intravenous injection may cause thrombophlebitis, and intramuscular injection may induce local inflammation with pain. Minocycline can produce severe vestibular reactions.

E. CHLORAMPHENICOL is a synthetic drug which inhibits the growth of many bacteria in concentrations of 0.5-10 μg/ml. There is no cross-resistance with other drugs.

Because of its potential toxicity, chloramphenicol is at present a possible drug of choice only in the following cases: (1) symptomatic salmonella infection, e.g., typhoid fever; (2) Haemophilus influenzae meningitis, laryngotracheitis, or pneumonia that does not respond to ampicillin; (3) occasional gram-negative bacteremia; (4) meningococcal infection in patients hypersensitive to penicillin. It is occasionally used topically in ophthalmology.

In serious systemic infection, the dose is 0.5 gm orally every 4-6 hours (for children, 30-50 mg/kg/day) for 7-21 days. Similar amounts can be given intravenously.

Nausea, vomiting, and diarrhea occur infrequently. The most serious adverse effects pertain to the hematopoietic system. Adults taking chloramphenicol in excess of 50 mg/kg/day regularly exhibit disturbances in red cell maturation after 1-2 weeks of blood levels above 25 μg/ml. There is anemia, rise in serum iron concentration, reticulocytopenia, and the appearance of vacuolated nucleated red cells in the bone marrow. These changes regress when the drug is stopped and are not related to aplastic anemia.

Serious aplastic anemia is a rare consequence of chloramphenicol administration and represents a specific, probably genetically determined individual defect. It is seen more frequently with either prolonged or repeated use. It tends to be irreversible and fatal. Fatal aplastic anemia occurs 13 times more frequently after the use of chloramphenicol than as a spontaneous occurrence. Hypoplastic anemia may be followed by the development of leukemia.

Chloramphenicol is specifically toxic for newborns, producing the highly fatal 'gray syndrome' with vomiting, flaccidity, hypothermia, and collapse. Chloramphenicol should only rarely be used in infants, and the dose must be limited to less than 50 mg/kg/day in full-term infants and less than 30 mg/kg/day in prematurely born infants.

F. AMINOGLYCOSIDES are drugs with similar chemical, antimicrobial, pharmacologic, ototoxic, and nephrotoxic characteristics.

1. Streptomycins Streptomycin can be bactericidal for gram-positive and gram-negative organisms and tubercle bacilli. The prevalence of resistance is high; even susceptible strains contain some bacteria which are chromosomally resistant or which carry plasmids that control the production of enzymes capable of destroying the drug.

a. Indications (1) Plague, tularemia, or other gram-negative sepsis. (2) In conjunction with a penicillin which favors penetration of the aminoglycoside (e.g., in enterococcus endocarditis and gram-negative sepsis). (3) An alternative drug in tuberculosis, together with INH, rifampin, or ethambutol.

b. Dosages (1) In tuberculosis: 1 gm, IM daily or twice weekly. (2) In nontuberculous infections: 0.5 gm IM every 4-6 hours.

c. Adverse effects Allergic reactions, including skin rashes and fever, may occur upon prolonged contact with streptomycin (e.g., in personnel preparing solutions). The principal side-effects are nephrotoxicity and ototoxicity.

Renal damage occurs mainly after prolonged high doses or in persons with pre-existing impairment of renal function. Damage to the eighth nerve manifests itself mainly by tinnitus, vertigo, ataxia, loss of balance, and occasionally loss of hearing. Chronic vestibular dysfunction is most common after prolonged use of streptomycin. Streptomycin, 2-3 gm/day for 4 weeks, has been used to purposely damage semicircular canal function in the treatment of Meniere's disease. Dihydrostreptomycin is no longer used because of excessive ototoxicity.

Streptomycin should not be used concurrently with other aminoglycosides, and great caution is necessary in persons with impaired renal function (see Table 4-2).

2. Kanamycin and neomycin These two aminoglycosides are comparable in most ways.

a. Antimicrobial activity These drugs are bactericidal for many gram-positive organisms (except streptococci) and many gram-negative bacteria in concentrations of 1-10 µg/ml. Most strains of pseudomonas and serratia and some strains of proteus are resistant. Resistant organisms produce enzymes which destroy the drugs; the enzymes are under the control of plasmids which are transmitted by conjugation or transduction. In the presence of these drugs, selection pressure favors the emergence of the resistant organisms which then prevail. Resistant staphylococci emerge after prolonged oral administration of neomycin or kanamycin in preparation for intestinal surgery; outbreaks of pseudomembranous enterocolitis have resulted. There is complete cross-resistance between kanamycin and neomycin and occasional cross-resistance with gentamicin, tobramycin, and amikacin.

b. Absorption and excretion Kanamycin and neomycin are not absorbed from the gut in significant amounts. After injection (15 mg/kg/day IM) serum levels reach 5-15 µg/ml. The drugs do not reach therapeutic levels in the cerebrospinal, joint, or pleural fluids unless they are injected locally. Some drug is excreted in the bile, but most is filtered into the urine where levels of 20-80 µg/ml occur. The dose or frequency must be reduced in patients with renal failure (Table 4-2).

c. Indications, dosages, and routes of administration Neomycin is used only topically or orally; kanamycin may be given systemically because it is somewhat less toxic.

Topical Solutions containing 1-5 mg/ml are used on infected surfaces or injected into joints, the pleural cavity, tissue spaces, or abscess cavities. The total amount of drug must be kept below 15 mg/kg/day because absorption can give rise to toxicity. Ointments containing 1-5 mg/gm are applied to infected skin lesions or to the nares for suppression of lactamase-producing staphylococci. Some ointments contain polymyxin and bacitracin in addition to neomycin. Aerosols of kanamycin (1 mg/ml) have been used in lower respiratory infections (e.g., bronchiectasis associated with susceptible microorganisms).

Oral Neomycin or kanamycin can be used as part of the 'bowel prep' for intestinal surgery (see Chapter 10). In hepatic coma, ammonia production is diminished by suppressing the coliform flora for prolonged periods with neomycin, 1 gm every 6-8 hours; protein intake should be reduced also. Paromomycin (Humatin) 1 gm every 6 hours orally for 2 weeks has been effective in acute intestinal amebiasis. Neomycin taken orally can suppress Escherichia coli diarrhea but is not effective in the treatment of shigella or salmonella infections.

Parenteral Kanamycin 15 mg/kg/day given in divided doses IM (e.g., 0.5 gm every 8 hours) may be effective in the treatment of bacteremia caused by gram-negative enteric organisms. It has been popular in the treatment of neonatal gram-negative sepsis. It is sometimes combined with clindamycin in penetrating abdominal wounds. Particularly serious infections of the urinary tract with indole-positive proteus or enterobacter may respond to IM kanamycin.

d. Adverse effects

Nephrotoxicity Impairment of renal function occurs commonly, particularly in patients with preexisting kidney damage. Renal function should be monitored and the dose or frequency adjusted as required (Table 4-2). These toxic effects usually reverse when the drugs are discontinued.

Ototoxicity The auditory portion of the eighth nerve can be selectively and irreversibly damaged by neomycin and kanamycin. The development of deafness is proportionate to the dosage and the duration of administration, but it can occur unpredictably even after short-term administration. Loss of perception of high frequencies as shown on audiograms may be a warning sign. Ototoxicity is a particular risk in patients with impaired kidney function and consequent accumulation of the drug.

Neuromuscular blockade The sudden absorption of neomycin or kanamycin can lead to respiratory arrest from neuromuscular blockade. Muscle-relaxing drugs used by the anesthesiologist may act in concert with the antibiotic to produce paralysis lasting many hours. Neostigmine is usually an ineffective antidote in these cases.

3. Amikacin This semisynthetic derivative of kanamycin is relatively resistant to enzymes which inactivate other aminoglycosides. It can be employed against gram-negative enteric bacteria, including strains of proteus, pseudomonas, enterobacter and serratia. Many of these organisms are inhibited by 1-20 µg/ml amikacin in vitro. Such concentrations are reached after IM injection of 0.5 gm amikacin (15 mg/kg/day) every 8-12 hours. CNS infections require intrathecal or intraventricular injection of 1-10 mg amikacin daily. Like all aminoglycosides, amikacin is nephrotoxic and ototoxic.

4. Gentamicin is an aminoglycoside which shares many properties with kanamycin but differs in its antimicrobial activity. In concentrations of 0.5-5 µg/ml, gentamicin is bactericidal not only for staphylococci and coliform organisms but also for many strains of pseudomonas, proteus, and serratia. Gentamicin is not significantly absorbed after oral intake.

Gentamicin is used in severe infections caused by gram-negative bacteria which are likely to be resistant to other, less toxic drugs. Indications include septicemia, infected burns, pneumonia, and other infections due to coliform organisms, klebsiella-enterobacter, proteus, pseudomonas, and serratia. The dosage is 5-7 mg/kg/day IM in 3 equal doses for 7-10 days. In urinary tract infections caused by these organisms, 0.8-1.2 mg/kg/day is given IM for 10 days or longer. For infected burns or skin lesions, creams containing 0.1% gentamicin are available.

Nephrotoxic effects must be monitored by periodic creatinine clearance tests. About 2-3% of patients develop vestibular dysfunction, and occasional cases of loss of hearing have been reported.

5. Tobramycin This aminoglycoside greatly resembles gentamicin in antibacterial and pharmacologic properties. However, tobramycin may be effective against some gentamicin-resistant gram-negative bacteria, especially pseudomonas. The daily dose is 3-6 mg/kg/day given IM in 3 equal doses at 8-hour intervals. In uremia, the suggested dose is 1 mg/kg IM every (6 times the serum creatinine level [in mg%]) hours. Blood levels should be monitored. Nephro- and ototoxicity are similar to other aminoglycosides.

6. Spectinomycin This aminocyclitol antibiotic is an alternative to penicillin in the treatment of gonococcal infection, especially if the gonococci produce β-lactamase. Inject 2 gm of spectinomycin IM in a single dose. Local pain, fever, and nausea may be side-effects.

G. POLYMYXINS

The polymyxins are basic polypeptides. They are bactericidal for most gram-negative bacteria (except proteus), and they are especially useful against pseudomonas. Only two of the polymyxins are used: polymyxin B sulfate, and colistin (polymyxin E) methanesulfonate.

1. Indications, dosages, and routes of administration Polymyxins are indicated in serious infections due to pseudomonas and other gram-negative bacteria which are resistant to other antimicrobial drugs.

a. Intramuscular The injection of polymyxin B is painful. Colistimethate (which contains a local anesthetic and is more rapidly excreted in the urine) is given IM, 2.5 mg/kg/day for urinary tract infection.

b. Intravenous In pseudomonas sepsis, polymyxin B sulfate, 2.5 mg/kg/day, is injected by continuous IV infusion.

c. Intrathecal In pseudomonas meningitis, give polymyxin B sulfate, 2-10 mg once daily for 2-3 days, then every other day for 2-3 weeks.

d. Topical Solutions of polymyxin B sulfate, 1 mg/ml, can be inhaled as aerosols, applied to infected surfaces, or injected into joint or pleural spaces or beneath the conjunctivae. Ointments containing 0.5 mg/gm polymyxin B sulfate in a mixture with neomycin or bacitracin are often applied to infected skin lesions. Solutions containing polymyxin B, 20 mg/liter, and neomycin, 40 mg/liter, can be used for continuous irrigation of the bladder with an indwelling catheter and a closed drainage system.

2. Adverse effects The toxicities of polymyxin B and colistimethate are similar. With the usual blood levels there are paresthesias, dizziness, flushing, and incoordination. These symptoms disappear when the drug has been excreted. With unusually high levels, respiratory arrest and paralysis can occur. All polymyxins are nephrotoxic. Proteinuria, hematuria, and cylindruria tend to be reversible, but azotemia may force reduction in dosage or discontinuance of the drug. In individuals with preexisting renal insufficiency, kidney function must be monitored and the dose reduced.

H. ANTITUBERCULOSIS DRUGS Tuberculosis and other mycobacterial infections tend to be exceedingly chronic but may give rise to hyperacute lethal complications. The organisms are frequently intracellular, have long periods of metabolic inactivity, and tend to develop resistance to any one drug. Combined drug therapy is often employed to delay the emergence of this resistance.

1. Isoniazid (INH) is the most active and the most widely used drug. INH inhibits most tubercle bacilli in a concentration of 0.2 µg/ml or less. Most 'atypical' mycobacteria are resistant, and in large populations of Mycobacterium tuberculosis, INH-resistant mutants also occur; their emergence is delayed in the presence of a second drug. There is no cross-resistance between INH, rifampin, or ethambutol.

In active, clinically manifest disease, INH is given in conjunction with rifampin or ethambutol. The initial dose is 8-10 mg/kg/day orally; later, the dosage is reduced to 5-7 mg/kg/day.

Children (or young adults) converting from a tuberculin-negative to a tuberculin-positive skin test may be given 10 mg/kg/day (maximum: 300 mg/day) for 1 year as prophylaxis against the 5-15% risk of meningitis or miliary dissemination. For this 'prophylaxis', INH is given as the sole drug.

Toxic reactions to INH include insomnia, restlessness, dysuria, hyperreflexia, and even convulsions and psychotic episodes. Many of these effects are attributable to peripheral neuritis from relative pyridoxine deficiency and can be prevented by the administration of pyridoxine, 100 mg/day.

2. Rifampin This derivative of rifamycin inhibits RNA synthesis in bacteria and chlamydiae. It is well-absorbed orally and is widely distributed in tissues. A single daily oral dose of 600 mg is combined with INH or ethambutol. Rifampin imparts a harmless orange color to the urine and sweat.

3. Ethambutol This synthetic drug is well-absorbed from the gut and is widely distributed (including the CNS and CSF). Ethambutol 15 mg/kg is given as a single daily dose for months, combined with either rifampin or INH, in the treatment of tuberculosis or infections with atypical mycobacteria. The commonest side-effects are visual disturbances (optic neuritis) that regress when the drug is stopped.

4. Streptomycin 1-10 μg/ml, is inhibitory and bactericidal for most tubercle bacilli. Most 'atypical' mycobacteria are resistant, and resistant strains of tubercle bacilli emerge within 2-4 months if streptomycin is used alone. Therefore it is used in combination with the other antituberculosis drugs. Doses and adverse effects of streptomycin are listed above (see Sections F.1. b and c). Streptomycin penetrates poorly into cells and exerts its action mainly on extracellular tubercle bacilli.

5. Alternative drugs Aminosalicylic acid (PAS), cycloserine, ethionamide, pyrazinamide, and viomycin are used in cases of resistance to 'first line' drugs. Expert guidance is necessary for the safe administration of these drugs.

I. SULFONAMIDES More than 150 different sulfonamides have been used at some time; the modifications are designed principally to achieve greater antibacterial activity, a wider antibacterial spectrum, greater solubility, or more prolonged action.

1. Antimicrobial activity The action of sulfonamides is bacteriostatic and is reversible upon removal of the drug or in the presence of an excess of *p*-aminobenzoic acid (PABA). Susceptible microorganisms require extracellular PABA in order to synthesize folic acid, an essential step in the formation of purines. Sulfonamides are structural analogues of PABA, can enter into the reaction in place of PABA competing for the enzyme involved, and can form nonfunctional analogues of folic acid. As a result, further growth of the microorganisms is inhibited. Animal cells and some sulfonamide-resistant microorganisms are unable to synthesize folic acid from PABA but depend on exogenous sources of preformed folic acid.

2. Indications The increasing emergence of sulfonamide resistance (e.g., among streptococci, meningococci, and shigellae) and the higher efficacy of other antimicrobial drugs have drastically curtailed the number of specific indications for sulfonamides as drugs of choice.

a. First (previously untreated) infection of the urinary tract due to coliform organisms.

b. Bacterial infections caused by pneumococci, staphylococci, shigellae, and meningococci. Resistance of these organisms to sulfonamides is widespread.

c. Chlamydial infections of trachoma-inclusion conjunctivitis-LGV group.

d. Certain parasitic and fungal diseases.

3. Dosages and routes of administration

a. Topical Topical application of sulfonamides is highly sensitizing. Current uses include sodium sulfacetamide solution (30%) or ointment (10%) to the conjunctivae, and mafenide actate (Suifamylon) or silver sulfadiazine to burns.

b. Oral For systemic diseases, the soluble, rapidly excreted sulfonamides (e.g., sulfadiazine, sulfisoxazole, trisulfapyrimidines) are given in an initial dose of 2-4 gm (40 mg/kg) followed by a maintenance dose of 0.5-1 gm (20 mg/kg) every 4-6 hours. Urine must be kept alkaline to avoid precipitation of crystals.

For first urinary tract infections, trisulfapyrimidines or sulfisoxazole are given in the same (or somewhat lower) doses as shown above. Following one course of sulfonamides, resistant organisms usually prevail. Simultaneous administration of a sulfonamide (2 gm/day orally) and trimethoprim (400 mg/day orally) may be more effective in urinary, respiratory, or enteric tract infections than sulfonamide alone.

Salicylazosulfapyridine (6 gm/day) is commonly used in inflammatory bowel disease.

'Long-acting' and 'intermediate-acting' sulfonamides (e.g., sulfamethoxypyridazine, sulfamethoxazole) can be used in doses of 0.5-1 gm/day (10 mg/kg) for prolonged maintenance therapy or for the treatment of minor infections.

These drugs have a significantly higher rate of toxic effects than the 'short-acting' sulfonamides.

c. Intravenous Sodium sulfadiazine and other sodium salts can be injected intravenously in 0.5% concentration in 5% dextrose in water for a total dose of 6-8 gm/day (120 mg/kg/day). This route is reserved for individuals unable to take oral medication.

4. Adverse effects Sulfonamides produce a wide variety of side effects, due partly to hypersensitivity and partly to direct toxicity.

a. Systemic side-effects Fever, skin rashes, urticaria, nausea, vomiting, or diarrhea; stomatitis, conjunctivitis, arthritis, exfoliative dermatitis; hematopoietic disturbances, including thrombocytopenia, hemolytic (in G-6-PD deficiency) or aplastic anemia, granulocytopenia, leukemoid reactions; hepatitis, polyarteritis nodosa, vasculitis, Stevens-Johnson syndrome; psychosis; and many others.

b. Urinary tract disturbances Sulfonamides may precipitate in urine, especially in neutral or acid pH, producing hematuria, crystalluria, or even obstruction. They have also been implicated in various types of nephritis and nephrosis.

5. Precautions in the use of sulfonamides

a. There is cross-allergenicity among all sulfonamides. Obtain a history of past administration or reaction. Observe for possible allergic responses.

b. Keep the urine volume above 1500 ml/day. Check urine pH; it should be 7.5 or higher. Give alkali by mouth (sodium bicarbonate or equivalent, 5-15 gm/day). Examine fresh urine for crystals and red cells every 2-4 days.

c. Check hemoglobin, white blood cell count, and differential count every 3-5 days to detect possible disturbances early.

d. If symptoms or signs of adverse effects appear, discontinue the sulfonamide drugs.

J. SPECIALIZED DRUGS AGAINST GRAM-POSITIVE BACTERIA

1. Bacitracin This polypeptide antibiotic is selectively active against gram-positive bacteria, including penicillinase-producing staphylococci, in concentrations of 0.1-20 units/ml. Bacitracin is very little absorbed from gut, skin, wounds, or mucous membranes. Topical application results in local effects without significant toxicity. Bacitracin, 500 units/gm in ointment base, is often combined with polymyxin or neomycin for the suppression of mixed bacterial flora in surface lesions. Systemic administration of bacitracin has been abandoned because of its severe nephrotoxicity.

2. Lincomycin and clindamycin These drugs resemble erythromycin and are active against gram-positive organisms (except enterococci) and against certain anaerobic gram-negative bacteria in concentrations of 0.5-5 μg/ml. Lincomycin, 0.5 gm orally every 6 hours (30-60 mg/kg/day for children), or clindamycin, 0.15-0.3 gm orally every 6 hours, yields serum concentrations of 2-5 μg/ml. The drugs are widely distributed in tissues. Excretion is through bile and urine. Clindamycin, 0.6 gm, can be injected IV every 8-12 hours. The principal indication for clindamycin is abdominal or pelvic sepsis due to the anaerobe, Bacteroides fragilis.

Common side-effects are diarrhea and colitis. Impaired liver function and neutropenia have been noted. Cardiorespiratory arrest may occur if 3-4 gm are given rapidly IV.

3. Vancomycin This drug is bactericidal for most gram-positive organisms, particularly staphylococci and enterococci, in concentrations of 0.5-10 μg/ml. Resistance is rare, and there is no cross-resistance with other antimicrobial drugs.

The only indications for vancomycin are serious staphylococcal sepsis or enterococcal endocarditis intractable to penicillins. It is given IV, 0.5 gm over a 20-minute period every 6-8 hours (for children, 20-40 mg/kg/day). Vancomycin is not absorbed from the gut; it is given orally (3-4 gm/day) only for the treatment of staphylococcal enterocolitis.

Vancomycin is intensely irritating to tissue. Chills, fever, and thrombophlebitis commonly follow IV injection. It is both nephrotoxic and ototoxic.

K. URINARY ANTISEPTICS These drugs exert antimicrobial activity in the urine but have little or no systemic antibacterial effect.

1. Nitrofurantoin (Furadantin) is bacteriostatic and bactericidal for both gram-positive and gram-negative bacteria in concentrations of 10-500 µg/ml. The activity of nitrofurantoin is greatly enhanced at pH 6.5 or lower.

Nitrofurantoin is rapidly absorbed from the gut. It has no systemic antibacterial activity. In kidney tubules, the drug is separated from carrier protein and excreted in urine where concentrations may be 200-400 µg/ml.

The average daily dose in urinary tract infections is 100 mg orally 4 times daily (for children, 5-10 mg/kg/day) taken with food. If oral medication is not feasible, nitrofurantoin can be given by continuous IV infusion, 180-360 mg/day.

Oral nitrofurantoin often causes nausea and vomiting. Hemolytic anemia occurs in G-6-PD deficiency. Hypersensitivity may produce skin rashes and pulmonary infiltration.

2. Nalidixic acid (NegGram) This synthetic urinary antiseptic inhibits many gram-negative bacteria in concentrations of 1-50 µg/ml but has no effect on pseudomonas. In susceptible bacterial populations, resistant mutants emerge fairly rapidly.

Nalidixic acid is readily absorbed from the gut. In the blood, virtually all the drug is firmly bound to protein and there is no systemic antibacterial action. About 20% of the absorbed drug is excreted in the urine in active form to give urine levels of 10-150 µg/ml.

The dose in urinary tract infections is 1 gm orally 4 times daily (for children, 55 mg/kg/day). Adverse reactions include nausea, vomiting, skin rashes, drowsiness, visual disturbances, and (rarely) convulsions.

3. Methenamine mandelate and methenamine hippurate These are salts of methenamine and mandelic acid or hippuric acid. The action of the drug depends on the liberation of formaldehyde and acid in the urine. The urinary pH must be below 5.5, and sulfonamides must not be given at the same time. The drug inhibits a variety of different microorganisms except those (e.g., proteus) which liberate ammonia from urea and produce strongly alkaline urine. The dosage is 2-6 gm orally daily.

4. Acidifying agents Urine with a pH below 5.5 tends to be antibacterial. Many substances can acidify the urine, including ammonium chloride, methionine, mandelic acid, and ascorbic acid (e.g., in cranberry juice). The dose has to be established for each patient by testing the urine for acid pH at frequent intervals.

L. ANTIFUNGAL DRUGS

1. Amphotericin B (Fungizone) 0.1 µg/ml, inhibits in vitro several organisms producing systemic mycotic disease in man, including histoplasma, cryptococcus, coccidioides, candida, blastomyces, sporotrichum, and others.

Amphotericin B solutions, 0.1 mg/ml in 5% dextrose in water, are given IV by slow infusion. The initial dose is 1-5 mg/day, increasing daily by 5 mg increments until a final dosage of 0.4-1 mg/kg/day is reached. Treatment is usually continued for many weeks. In fungal meningitis, amphotericin B (0.5 mg) is injected intrathecally 3 times weekly; continuous treatment for many weeks with an Ommaya reservoir is sometimes employed.

The IV administration of amphotericin B usually produces chills, fever, vomiting, and headache. Tolerance may be enhanced by temporary lowering of the dose or administration of corticosteroids, aspirin, phenothiazines, or antihistaminics. Therapeutically active amounts of amphotericin B commonly impair kidney and liver function and can produce anemia, hypokalemia, shock, and a variety of neurologic symptoms.

2. Griseofulvin (Fulvicin, Grifulvin) is an antibiotic that can inhibit the growth of some dermatophytes but has no effect on bacteria or on the fungi that cause deep mycoses. Absorption of microsized griseofulvin, 1 gm/day, gives blood levels of 0.5-1.5 μg/ml. Ultramicrosized griseofulvin (Gris-Peg) is absorbed twice as well. The absorbed drug has an affinity for skin and is deposited there, bound to keratin. Thus, it makes keratin resistant to fungal growth and the new growth of hair or nails is first freed of infection. As keratinized structures are shed, they are replaced by uninfected ones. Topical application of griseofulvin has little effect.

Oral doses of 0.5-1 gm/day (for children, 15 mg/kg/day) must be given for 6 weeks if only the skin is involved and for 3-6 months or longer if the hair and nails are involved. Griseofulvin is most successful in severe dermatophytosis, particularly if caused by trichophyton or microsporon.

Side-effects include headache, nausea, diarrhea, photosensitivity, fever, skin rashes, and disturbances of nervous and hematopoietic systems. Griseofulvin increases the breakdown of coumarin anticoagulants.

3. Nystatin (Mycostatin) inhibits Candida species upon direct contact. The drug is not absorbed from mucous membranes or the gut. Nystatin in ointments, suspensions, etc. can be applied to buccal or vaginal mucous membranes to suppress a local candida infection. Oral nystatin suppresses candida in the gut, but because overgrowth of candida in the intestine rarely causes disease, there is little indication for this route of administration.

4. Flucytosine (Ancobon) (150 mg/kg/day) orally has been used in yeast meningitis or sepsis. It can produce bone-marrow depression and loss of hair.

IV. SPECIFIC TYPES OF SURGICAL INFECTIONS

A. CELLULITIS, LYMPHANGITIS, AND LYMPHADENITIS Cellulitis is a common infection of the skin and subcutaneous tissues, with prominent infiltration of polymorphonuclear leukocytes but no gross suppuration except, perhaps, at the portal of entry. **Lymphangitis** is nonsuppurative infection of the lymphatic vessels that drain an area of cellulitis. **Lymphadenitis** is infection of the regional lymph nodes as a result of cellulitis and lymphangitis; rarely, these nodes suppurate and form abscesses.

Most cases are caused by aerobic hemolytic streptococci. Staphylococcus aureus and Staphylococcus epidermidis as well as anaerobic streptococci also can be responsible. Diabetics, alcoholics, and patients with postphlebitic syndrome are particularly susceptible to these infections.

1. Diagnosis

a. Symptoms and signs (1) There may be a surgical wound, puncture, skin ulcer, or a patch of dermatitis, but often a portal of entry is not seen. (2) Moderately high fever. (3) Cellulitis on an extremity is a rapidly advancing, warm, tender, red or reddish-brown area of edematous skin. (4) Lymphangitis produces red, tender, warm streaks 1-2 cm wide leading from the cellulitis toward the regional lymph nodes. (5) Lymphadenitis is diagnosed by the presence of enlarged, tender regional lymph nodes. (6) **Erysipelas** is a severe form of cellulitis, actually an acute lymphangitis of the skin, with a well-demarcated, raised advancing edge. It is caused by Group A beta-hemolytic streptococci and is most common in children and in the elderly. (7) **Acute streptococcal hemolytic gangrene** is a rare intense form of streptococcal cellulitis which progresses to necrosis of the skin and subcutaneous tissues. It is most likely to occur if the blood supply to the part is diminished.

b. Laboratory tests (1) Leukocytosis is usually present. (2) Material for culture is difficult to obtain from the infected area; blood cultures may be positive.

2. Differential diagnosis

  a. Thrombophlebitis can resemble cellulitis; swelling is usually greater in phlebitis and tenderness may be localized over a vein. Fever is higher in cellulitis.

  b. Contact allergy such as poison oak or ivy may be indistinguishable from cellulitis in its early phase; nonhemorrhagic vesiculation is characteristic of the allergic process later.

  c. Chemical inflammation can mimic cellulitis.

  d. Cat scratch fever can cause local inflammation, lymphangitis, and suppuration of regional lymph nodes.

  e. Intense pain with marked edema, with or without hemorrhagic bullae and skin necrosis, suggests necrotizing fasciitis as the correct diagnosis (see Section IV.F).

3. Treatment The affected part is immobilized and elevated, and hot packs are applied. Antibiotic therapy is based on gram-stain and culture if available; usually, however, the surgeon must select an antibiotic without this information.

  a. Clear-cut streptococcal cellulitis (1) Mild disease: 2.4 million units of procaine penicillin G, IM daily or penicillin V 1-4 gm/day orally. (2) Moderate or severe disease (including all patients with lymphangitis or lymphadenitis): 1.5-20 million units of aqueous penicillin G IV daily.

  b. Staphylococcal cellulitis (localized, spreads slowly, tends to suppurate) alone or mixed with streptococcal infection: penicillinase-resistant penicillin orally or IV, depending upon the severity of the infection.

  Examine the patient one or more times daily to look for hidden abscess and to determine response to treatment.

B. FURUNCLE A furuncle or boil is an abscess of a sweat gland or hair follicle. Furuncles can be serious when multiple and recurrent (furunculosis). This condition usually occurs in adolescents or in uncontrolled diabetics and is due to dermatologic disease, altered glandular secretions, or impaired resistance to common skin organisms. Staphylococcus aureus and diphtheroids are the organisms recovered from furuncles most commonly.

1. Diagnosis Furuncles produce pain and itching. The skin is red and indurated initially and then turns white over the center of the abscess. Systemic symptoms are rare except cases of furunculosis in poorly controlled diabetics.

2. Differential diagnosis Gout, bursitis, inflammed Baker's cyst, fungal infections, malignant skin tumors, and inflamed sebaceous or inclusion cysts.

3. Complications Suppurative thrombophlebitis may develop when furuncles are located near major veins. Furuncles on the face may lead to intracranial venous thrombosis.

4. Treatment Hot packs and then incision and drainage after the process has localized. Squeezing or incision before localization must be avoided. Antibiotics are rarely indicated except in patients with large furuncles on the nose or face. An appropriate antibiotic in this instance would be dicloxacillin 500 mg orally every 6 hours. The antibiotic regimen should be altered depending on sensitivities of the organism(s).

  Patients with furunculosis should be checked for diabetes or immune deficiencies. Have the patient bathe all over once or twice daily with soap containing hexachlorophene or other antiseptics.

C. CARBUNCLE A carbuncle is an infection which dissects through the dermis and subcutaneous tissue to form a myriad of connecting tunnels. Some of the small extensions open to the surface, giving the appearance of partially confluent furuncles with many pustular openings. There is considerable surrounding induration. The back of the neck is a common site. Carbuncles are more common in diabetics. Staphylococcus aureus is the most common organism.

The patient usually has fever and malaise. Carbuncles can be quite extensive locally and may endanger life in debilitated or diabetic patients by progressing to disseminated staphylococcal infection. Carbuncles on the back of the neck may lead to epidural abscess and meningitis.

1. Treatment

a. Carbuncles are best treated by excision of the entire process including all of the sinus tracts; these tracts usually extend far beyond the cutaneous evidence of suppuration. A large open wound results, but failure to excise all of the sinuses allows infection to persist.

b. Specific antibiotic therapy directed against penicillinase-producing staphylococci frequently helps localize the process and reduces the extent of surgical excision. Antibiotic therapy is indicated in the compromised host (i.e., diabetics and immunosuppressed patients) with or without systemic manifestations.

c. Diabetes mellitus must be sought and treated.

D. HIDRADENITIS Simple hidradenitis is a localized dermal-subcutaneous infection involving apocrine and, rarely, eccrine sweat glands. **Hidradenitis suppurativa** is a chronic, indolent disease of the skin and subcutaneous tissues in apocrine gland-bearing areas, principally the axillae, areola of the nipple, groin, perineum, perianal and periumbilical regions. The disease occurs in both sexes, but women develop the axillary form of the disease more frequently and men show a greater tendency toward perianal involvement. Hidradenitis appears after puberty; obesity and a genetic tendency to acne are apparent predisposing factors.

1. Diagnosis The involved area is diffusely indurated and fibrotic, with multiple intercommunicating sinuses that drain pus. In the acute phase of the disease, Staphylococcus aureus is the commonest organism; Escherichia coli and alpha-streptococcus are recovered occasionally. Chronic cases usually culture proteus or pseudomonas.

2. Differential diagnosis Hidradenitis suppurativa is differentiated from furunculosis by skin biopsy. Dissecting cellulitis of the scalp (Perifolliculitis chronica abscedens et suffodiens) is a disease entity of the scalp similar to hidradenitis. Hidradenitis in the perianal area mimics complex anorectal fistulas. Fistulas have a primary orifice in the anal canal, one or more secondary openings on the perianal skin, and firm tracts connecting the primary and secondary orifices.

3. Treatment

a. Unless an abscess is pointing, incision and drainage of individual lesions should be avoided to minimize the formation of draining sinuses. Warm moist compresses and antibiotics may allow the process to resolve.

b. Pointing abscesses are incised and drained. Regular cleansing, avoidance of shaving the axillary hair, and discontinuance of topical deodorants and powders may be helpful.

c. Advanced cases may require excision of **all** affected apocrine-bearing tissue with primary closure or skin grafting.

d. Perianal hidradenitis may need preliminary diverting colostomy followed by excision of the infected tissue.

4. Prognosis is good after excision of all affected areas.

E. POSTOPERATIVE WOUND INFECTION Bacterial contamination of surgical wounds during or immediately after the procedure is a common event. The size of the bacterial inoculum, the pathogenicity of the organisms, and the resistance of the host determine whether infection will develop. Diseases (e.g., diabetes) and medications (e.g., immunosuppressants) may compromise host resistance systemically; wound resistance is impaired locally by unnecessary trauma to the tissues, devitalized tissue, foreign bodies, and dead space. These contributory factors are minimized by gentle, precise surgical technic. Bacterial contamination is minimized by skin antiseptics and strict surgical asepsis. The value of prophylactic antibiotics is discussed briefly in Section IIB. Postoperative care must emphasize maintenance of blood volume and oxygenation to preserve the wound's defenses against infection.

In 'clean' operations, the incidence of infection is about 1%. In 'clean contaminated' procedures (e.g., biliary or upper gastrointestinal), wound infection rates of 5-15% are reported. Heavily contaminated wounds (e.g., perforated colon) may become infected in 20-30% of cases and are best managed by leaving the skin and subcutaneous fat open for 4-5 days, then approximating the skin with paper tapes if the wound has no signs of infection (delayed primary closure).

1. Diagnosis   Wound infections usually occur in the subcutaneous tissues; seldom do they develop in or deep to the muscle and fascia. Streptococcal and clostridial wound infections cause symptoms and signs as early as 24 hours postoperatively. The majority of infections, those due to staphylococci and gramnegative organisms, become evident 4-10 days after operation. Occasionally, an infection will not appear until weeks or months have elapsed.

The first sign is fever, and the patient may complain of excessive pain in the wound. Streptococcal cellulitis is evident on inspection, but the wound may not appear grossly inflamed in the other types of infection. The wound is edematous, indurated, and tender; sometimes, fluctuance or crepitus will be palpable. Subfascial infection is difficult to detect but should be suspected with persistent fever, pain, and localized tenderness.

2. Treatment

a. Streptococcal cellulitis is treated as other cellulitis. It is wise to open the wound to prove that no pus is present.

b. Other infections require opening the wound and allowing it to drain.

c. A culture for aerobes and anaerobes should be obtained. Before the antibiotic era, aerobic streptococci and staphylococci were predominant. After the introduction of penicillin, penicillin-resistant Staphylococcus aureus infections became common. Wound infections currently are often caused by gramnegative bacteria.

d. Antibiotics are not required if subcutaneous infections are drained promptly. Deep or extensive infections or compromised hosts are indications for antibiotics.

F. NECROTIZING FASCIITIS is a relatively rare, aggressive, invasive infection which has been variously described in the older literature as 'acute streptococcal gangrene' and 'hospital gangrene'. This infection is characterized by thrombosis of vessels passing from the deep circulation to the skin, producing necrosis of the skin, subcutaneous tissue, and fascia. It is more common in patients with ischemic small vessel disease (e.g., in diabetics).

Most fasciitis is caused by a mixture of bacteria, including Group A betahemolytic streptococcus, anaerobic streptococcus, microaerophilic streptococcus, Staphylococcus aureus, coliforms, Bacteroides fragilis, and Fusobacterium.

1. Diagnosis   Puncture wounds, leg ulcers, or perforating injuries of hollow viscera often precede the development of fasciitis. The infection spreads extensively through skin and it undermines along fascial planes causing necrosis of skin, fat, and fascia; muscle and bone remain viable. The appearance in the early stages resembles cellulitis, but there is edema, hypesthesia, and marked tenderness well beyond the erythematous area. Marked edema and hemorrhagic blebs signify death of the skin; fascial necrosis is even more extensive than the cutaneous changes. Crepitus is present if gas-forming organisms are involved. The patient is febrile and toxic. Blood cultures are positive in 10% of patients. X-rays may show gas in the soft tissues, but they are seldom necessary or helpful. The operative findings confirm the diagnosis: edematous, dull grey, necrotic fascia and subcutaneous fat with viable muscle. Thrombi are often visible in penetrating veins.

2. Differential diagnosis

a. Cellulitis, abscess, and phlebitis are usually localized, they are not as rapidly progressive, and there is less systemic toxicity than in fasciitis.

b. Clostridial myositis and gangrene from arterial occlusion are associated with necrosis of muscle.

3. Treatment

a. Correct deficiencies of fluids, electrolytes, and red cell mass; these may be severe.

b. Treat hyperthermia.

c. Obtain aerobic and anaerobic cultures of the wound, do a gram-stain on the wound exudate, and draw blood for culture.

d. Intravenous antibiotics are begun immediately after obtaining specimens for culture. Initial treatment should be: (1) Penicillin G, 1.5-4 million units IV every 4 hours. (2) Clindamycin, 600 mg IV every 6 hours (to cover Staphylococcus aureus and Bacteroides fragilis). (3) Gentamicin, 2 mg/kg IV initially followed by 1.5-1.7 mg/kg in divided doses (up to 5 mg/kg) each day.

e. Change antibiotic regimen according to culture results and response of the patient.

f. Surgical debridement and drainage under general or regional anesthesia is mandatory. Excision must extend beyond the fascial involvement. Where necrotic fascia undermines viable skin, longitudinal skin incisions permit debridement of fascia without sacrificing skin. Necrotic muscle is **not** a feature of necrotizing fasciitis.

•   *g.* The wound must be inspected repeatedly after operation, and further debridement is performed if necessary.

h. Skin grafts may be placed on the defects after the infection is under control and all necrotic tissue has been removed.

4. Prognosis   The mortality rate is 25-30%; with early recognition and prompt therapy, few patients die of this disease.

G. TETANUS is caused by the neurotoxin of Clostridium tetani which reduces inhibitory activity in the central nervous system. Tetanus bacilli are ubiquitous in nature and can easily contaminate even minor wounds. Punctures and wounds containing devitalized tissue or foreign bodies provide favorable conditions for the proliferation of these anaerobic organisms. The incubation period for tetanus averages 8 days (1-50 days).

1. Diagnosis   The diagnosis is based on a history of injury followed by development of one of the three clinical forms of tetanus. Laboratory tests are of little value.

a. Local tetanus   Persistent, unyielding rigidity of the group of muscles in close proximity to the injury. Symptoms may continue for weeks. It may progress to generalized tetanus.

b. Generalized tetanus   This is the most common form. Trismus (lockjaw) and spasms of the facial muscles (risus sardonicus) are the initial manifestations in over 50% of patients. Tonic contractions of the face, neck, back, and abdomen are common; severe spasms of the back muscles may produce opisthotonos. Difficult swallowing, laryngospasm, and hesitant micturition occur later. Trivial stimuli may elicit gross spasms or seizures. Temperature may rise 2 to 4° C during these spasms; profuse sweating is common. Tachycardia is a grave sign.

c. Cephalic tetanus   In this unusual form of tetanus, there is dysfunction of multiple cranial nerves. The incubation period is short, and it develops after otitis media or injuries to the scalp. The prognosis is extremely poor.

2. Prevention   Tetanus is a preventable disease. All persons should be immunized against tetanus, and additional prophylactic measures should be taken when tetanus-prone injuries occur.

a. Previously immunized individuals   (1) If immunized within the past 10 years, give 0.5 ml of refined tetanus toxoid IM. This booster is unnecessary if it is certain that one was given within the last 3-5 years. (2) If immunized more than 10 years previously, give 0.5 ml of adsorbed tetanus toxoid IM. If a tetanus-prone wound occurred more than 24 hours before, give also 250 units of tetanus immune globulin (human) IM and consider penicillin in addition.

b. Individuals not previously immunized (1) If tetanus is unlikely because the wound is clean and minor, give 0.5 ml of adsorbed tetanus toxoid IM. The immunization schedule should be completed as follows: second injection 4-6 weeks after the initial one, and a third injection in 6-12 months. (2) All other wounds require 0.5 ml of adsorbed tetanus toxoid IM plus 250-350 units of tetanus immune globulin (human) IM. Use different syringes and inject at different sites to avoid suppressing the development of active immunity. Consider the use of penicillin. The immunization schedule should be completed as above.

c. Tetanus antitoxin Equine antitoxin should be used prophylactically only if tetanus immune globulin (human) is not available and only if the possibility of tetanus exceeds the danger of allergic reaction. If the patient is not sensitive to horse serum by history and by testing, give 3000-6000 units of antitoxin IM. Give large doses of penicillin and no antitoxin if the patient is sensitive to horse serum.

d. Actively immunized patients may not have the usual anamnestic response to tetanus toxoid in the following situations: agammaglobulinemia, exposure to acute doses of radiation, immunosuppressive drugs (including chloramphenicol), and carcinoma of the breast (these patients may not respond to injections of tetanus toxoid in the ipsilateral upper extremity).

e. Debridement and gentle cleansing of wounds with saline solution or dilute peroxide (use no antiseptics) remove the conditions that favor the growth of tetanus bacilli.

3. Treatment Tetanus is a true emergency, and therapy should be instituted at once. A team of surgeon, internist, and anesthesiologist provides optimal care.

a. Neutralize the toxin by injecting 3000-6000 units of tetanus immune globulin (human) into the muscle in the region of the wound or further proximal in the extremity. Do **not** inject this material intravenously.

b. Debride the wound about 1 hour after serotherapy. Leave the wound open.

c. Control the muscle spasms and/or seizures by isolating the patient in a dark, quiet room. Diazepam, chlorpromazine, and short-acting barbiturates are used cautiously to avoid respiratory and cardiac depression.

d. Intravenous aqueous *penicillin* G, 10-20 million units/day in divided doses, may kill the vegetative clostridia and prevent release of more neurotoxin. Tetracycline or clindamycin are alternatives in the patient who is allergic to penicillin.

e. Respiratory problems usually require tracheostomy because mechanical ventilation must be continued for weeks once it is begun.

4. Prognosis The mortality rate is inversely proportionate to the length of the incubation period and directly proportionate to the severity of symptoms. Active immunization should be completed in survivors; an attack of tetanus does not confer permanent immunity.

H. OTHER CLOSTRIDIAL INFECTIONS
Clostridium perfringens (welchii), Cl. novyi, Cl. septicum, and other clostridial species are ubiquitous in soil and in the intestinal tracts of animals and man. These organisms elaborate toxins which destroy tissue and produce a spectrum of diseases ranging in severity from minor to fulminating. An anaerobic environment is required for these bacteria to proliferate; devitalized tissue, pyogenic infections, and foreign bodies provide suitable conditions.

1. Diagnosis

a. Simple contamination Infection of superficial necrotic tissue is the least serious of the clostridial infections. The surrounding tissues are healthy, there is no invasion, and there are no systemic symptoms or signs. Debridement of dead tissue is curative. If untreated, it can progress to one of the severe infections listed below.

   b. Gas abscess (Welch's abscess)   This is a localized infection without muscle involvement. There is little pain or systemic toxicity. A foul, brown, seropurulent exudate and gas in tissues some distance from the local infection are characteristic.

   c. Anaerobic clostridial cellulitis   This invasive infection remains superficial to the deep fascia but spreads through subcutaneous tissue at an alarming rate. There is little pain and mild to moderate toxicity (compared with myositis). The tissue is edematous, crepitant, and discolored. There may be cutaneous bullae.

   d. Clostridial myositis and myonecrosis   These infections may be localized or diffuse. The classical diffuse form (gas gangrene) has an acute onset (incubation period less than 3 days) and a fulminating course. Profound toxemia appears early and progresses to delirium. The wound is severely painful and has shiny edematous skin with bullae and patchy necrosis in some cases. There is a serosanguinous discharge which has a characteristically sweet odor; gram stain shows a few inflammatory cells and large gram-positive rods. Gas in the tissues is a late finding and may be so finely distributed that it cannot be detected.

   2. Differential diagnosis

   a. The absence of muscle involvement excludes clostridial myositis. The other clostridial infections spare the fascia as well, while in necrotizing fasciitis the fascia is nonviable.

   b. Other infections can produce gas, e.g., anaerobic-aerobic mixed cellulitis. Treatment is less radical in these infections. The differential diagnosis is made by gram stain of the exudate.

   3. Prevention   Clostridial infections are preventable by early debridement of dirty wounds and those with foreign bodies or devitalized tissue, especially muscle. Prophylactic penicillin is useful, but the emphasis must be on surgical debridement.

   4. Treatment

   a. Surgical   (1) Radical debridement of all necrotic and damaged tissue is **mandatory**. Tight fascial compartments must be decompressed. Multiple debridements are often required. (2) Amputation is necessary when there is diffuse muscle necrosis and loss of blood supply to the limb. (3) Clostridial cellulitis requires aggressive debridement but not amputation. If muscle bleeds well and contracts when stimulated, it should not be excised. (4) Diverting colostomy should be performed in cases of clostridial infections originating in perforating wounds of the colon or rectum.

   b. Antibiotics   Penicillin G, 20-40 million units, is given IV each day. Chloramphenicol or clindamycin are alternatives if penicillin cannot be used.

   c. Polyvalent antitoxin   An IV dose of 75,000 units repeated every 6 hours (for a total of 4 doses) is given only if surgical debridement cannot encompass the infection (e.g., infections in brain, spinal cord, and some abdominal wounds). The effectiveness of this antitoxin is uncertain.

   d. Hyperbaric oxygenation   This modality has equivocal value and it is rarely used at present. Aggressive debridement and antibiotics were probably responsible for some of the successes credited to hyperbaric oxygenation.

I. SUPPURATIVE THROMBOPHLEBITIS   Suppurative (septic) thrombophlebitis is infection in a thrombosed vein and usually is associated with intravenous catheters (especially in burn patients) or drug abuse. It may be a cause of persistent sepsis in patients with anaerobic pelvic infections. The incidence of septic thrombophlebitis of the subclavian and great veins has increased since the advent of intravenous hyperalimentation.

The microorganisms most commonly recovered from burn patients with septic thrombophlebitis are Klebsiella, Staphylococcus aureus, Pseudomonas, and Candida albicans. S. aureus is usually responsible in drug abusers and in non-burn patients. Candida and S. aureus are the most common offenders associated with hyperalimentation therapy.

1. Diagnosis The usual presentation is unrelenting septicemia (bacteremia) of unknown etiology, sometimes following the removal of a plastic intravenous catheter. The diagnosis is established by persistent fever, repeatedly positive blood cultures, and pus within the involved vein on aspiration or incision. Local signs of inflammation are apparent on the extremities but often absent when the subclavian or great veins are involved.

2. Differential diagnosis Undrained abscesses, endocarditis, or (rarely) infected arterial catheters may be responsible for fever and positive blood cultures.

3. Complications Septic shock and death. Extension of septic thrombosis into the great veins of the mediastinum. Bacterial endocarditis. Septic pulmonary emboli.

4. Treatment

a. Antibiotic therapy directed against the organism recovered by blood culture or from the vein.

b. If the diagnosis is suspected, an exploratory venotomy should be done proximal to the venopuncture site. Pus in the vein requires **complete** excision of the involved vein; the contaminated wound is left open for delayed primary closure or healing by second intention.

c. Septic thrombophlebitis of the subclavian or innominate veins or superior vena cava requires anticoagulation and specific antibiotics. Occasionally, a thrombus localized by venography can be extracted by passing a Fogarty catheter through an axillary venotomy.

J. INFECTIONS RESULTING FROM DRUG ABUSE Drug abuse produces a number of challenging atypical infections. The source of organisms most often is the skin, but unsterile equipment and contaminated drug mixtures also contribute.

1. Diagnosis Most of these infections occur on the extremities at sites of intravenous or extravascular injection. The drug mixtures are often irritating or necrotizing, creating a favorable environment for proliferation of contaminating bacteria. Various types of infections may occur.

a. Cutaneous and subcutaneous These infections vary from simple cellulitis or abscess to extensive spreading infections. Large areas of necrosis, multiple abscesses, foul discharge, and gas formation are characteristic. Suppurative thrombophlebitis is very common.

b. Fascial and subfascial The needle may penetrate the fascia, causing infection in the deep spaces; the external signs of abscess may be absent or minimal. A bizarre type of cellulitis, probably a fasciolitis, appears as a wooden-hard tenseness which progresses rapidly.

c. Tetanus Female addicts are prone to this disease because they more often take drugs by 'skin-popping' (extravascular injection), and they are less apt to be immunized against tetanus. Inclusion of quinine in the drug mixture creates an anaerobic environment which promotes the growth of tetanus bacilli.

d. Cardiovascular Infected arteritis and mycotic aneurysms may develop, especially in amphetamine users. Bacterial or fungal endocarditis may occur. Staphylococcus aureus, gram-negative aerobes, and Candida albicans are common organisms.

e. Pulmonary Septic pulmonary emboli, empyema, and aspiration pneumonia due to overdose are among the pulmonary infections in these patients.

f. Malaria Shared needles may transmit this disease.

g. Hepatitis Shared needles may transmit this disease.

2. Treatment Bacterial infections in the soft tissues must be incised, pus evacuated, and necrotic tissue debrided. The deep fascial compartments must be opened if the abscess is not discovered more superficially. Antibiotic therapy is advisable. Coexisting endocarditis should be considered if fever does not subside after adequate care of the wound. Involvement of joint spaces should be suspected if soft tissue infections occur nearby; this is especially true in the hand.

K. PILONIDAL SINUS is a chronic infection caused by penetration of a foreign body (hair) into the subcutaneous tissues. The sinus is lined by granulation tissue, and it often leads to a cavity filled with granulation tissue and hair. If the sinus closes temporarily, a pilonidal **cyst** remains in the deeper tissues; acute exacerbation of the chronic infection produces a pilonidal **abscess**. Most patients are young hirsute males; sedentary occupations and constant mild trauma to the sacral skin (e.g., driving a truck) are contributory factors. Pilonidal sinus is not a congenital anomaly.

1. Diagnosis Most pilonidal sinuses are in the posterior midline over the sacrum or sacrococcygeal junction; similar lesions occur in web spaces on the hands of barbers, and in the umbilicus. Acute infection is usually the first manifestation. After spontaneous or surgical drainage, the sinus discharges pus intermittently.

Examination reveals an abscess or one or more sinuses, often with hair projecting from them. The process can be extensive, with multiple, complex, intercommunicating sinuses over a large area. Aerobic and anaerobic fecal flora can be cultured.

2. Differential diagnosis

a. Anorectal fistulas usually open closer to the anus and have a palpable tract extending toward a primary orifice in the anal canal.

b. Perianal hidradenitis suppurativa also involves the groins and/or axillae. Pilonidal sinus and hidradenitis usually can be differentiated by clinical examination.

c. Osteomyelitis of the sacrum is uncommon; lateral x-rays may demonstrate it.

d. Simple furuncles or even carbuncles are very unusual in this location; a sinus with projecting hair is characteristic of pilonidal disease.

3. Complications Malignancy arising in chronic pilonidal sinuses has been reported.

4. Treatment

a. Drain acute abscesses, usually under local anesthesia. It may be possible to curette the cavity to remove hair and thus accomplish definitive treatment at the same time.

b. The vast majority of sinus tracts and cysts respond to unroofing, curettage of the contents, and packing. The surrounding hair should be shaved weekly even after healing occurs to avoid recurrence.

c. In exceptional patients (e.g., those with recurrent sinuses), the involved area can be excised and closed primarily, marsupialized, or left to heal secondarily.

L. ACTINOMYCOSIS This chronic, suppurative and granulomatous disease progresses slowly to form multiple sinuses. The causative organisms are true bacteria.

Actinomycetes are gram-positive filamentous organisms. They are strict anaerobes and are found commonly in the pharynx. The head and neck are the most common sites of actinomycosis; about 20% have involvement of the chest and an equal proportion have abdominal lesions (usually in the cecum and appendix).

1. Diagnosis There may be no systemic symptoms. Firm, nontender, nodular masses with abscesses and multiple draining sinuses are characteristic. 'Sulfur granules'—tiny yellowish masses that microscopically consist of threads enveloped by dark-staining clubs—appear in the pus. Secondary bacterial infection is common.

Pulmonary lesions cause fever, cough, pleuritic pain and weight loss. The sinuses may eventually penetrate through the chest wall. Abdominal actinomycosis mimics appendicitis or may perforate to form sinuses of the abdominal wall.

2. Treatment Surgical excision or drainage is required. Actinomycetes usually are sensitive to penicillin (5-20 million units/day) given over many weeks.

M. NOCARDIOSIS The localized form of nocardiosis resembles actinomycosis. Systemic nocardiosis begins in the lungs and spreads hematogenously to distant sites. It is prone to develop in immunodeficient patients.

Surgical drainage and excision of accessible lesions are essential. Sulfonamides (e.g., sulfisoxazole, 6-8 gm/day orally), are given for many weeks. Minocycline (200-400 mg/day orally) may be a useful adjunct.

VI. FUNGAL DISEASES*

A. BLASTOMYCOSIS is the name given to systemic fungal diseases which occur in endemic areas in America.

1. North American blastomycosis The primary lesion is pulmonary. It resembles other granulomatous diseases, and it often is asymptomatic. Skin lesions are chronic papulo-pustules with thick crusts. Destructive osteomyelitis and male genitourinary lesions may occur.

Diagnosis rests on isolation of Blastomyces dermatitidis from drainage or biopsy material. Dihydroxystilbamidine and amphotericin B are the most effective drugs. Surgical drainage or biopsy may be needed.

2. South American blastomycosis This disease, also called paracoccidioidomycosis, occurs in Colombia, Brazil, and other parts of South America. The organism (Paracoccidioides braziliensis) forms pulmonary granulomas or abscesses; another variety of the disease begins in the small intestine.

The diagnosis is made by culture, skin tests, or serologic tests. Sulfonamides are effective; amphotericin B is used in severe cases.

B. CANDIDIASIS Candida albicans may be cultured from the mouth, vagina, and feces of many persons. Thrush, vaginitis, cutaneous lesions in intertriginous areas, onychia, and paronychia are common. Systemic infection is usually found in patients with diabetes mellitus, general debility, or immunosuppression. Candida is also a frequent secondary invader in other types of infection.

Systemic infection is of two types. Endocarditis usually follows heart surgery or inoculation by contaminated needles or catheters. In the other type of systemic infection, the kidneys, myocardium, and brain are involved; this type frequently follows antibiotic and corticosteroid therapy for serious debilitating disease.

It is doubtful if primary bronchial or pulmonary infection occurs. Infection in these areas is nearly always superimposed on other serious underlying diseases.

Intravenous administration of amphotericin B 0.4-1 mg/kg/day is necessary in serious systemic infections. When combined with flucytosine, 150 mg/kg/day orally, lower doses of this toxic drug may be used. Local application of nystatin, amphotericin B, or gentian violet 1%, may help to control thrush, vaginitis, or candidal skin lesions.

Response to chemotherapy is poor in endocarditis. Valve resection and insertion of a prosthesis is usually necessary. In other systemic infections the prognosis is better if the underlying predisposing factors are corrected.

---

*Coccidioidomycosis and histoplasmosis are discussed in Chapter 8.

VII. RABIES

Rabies is a viral encephalitis transmitted to humans through infected saliva of animals; domestic dogs and cats are rarely involved. Prompt prophylactic treatment is necessary; if rabies becomes established, fever, irritability, spasms of the muscles of swallowing, and convulsions occur, and death is inevitable.

1. Prevention

a. The animal should be confined and observed for 10 days. If it becomes rabid or dies, the brain should be studied for rabies antigen by immunofluorescence.

b. The wound should be washed thoroughly, and repeatedly, with soap and water. Tetanus prophylaxis should be given.

c. Postexposure vaccine and immune globulin are administered according to the guidelines in Table 4-3.

Table 4-3. Guidelines for postexposure rabies treatment

(The following suggestions must be modified according to the circumstances of the bite or exposure, the presence of rabies in the area, and the vaccination status of the animal.)

Species of animal	Condition of animal at time of attack	Treatment of exposed human (scratched, bitten)
Skunk, fox, bat, coyote, raccoon, wolf	Regard as rabid	RIG[1] + Vaccine[2]
Dog, cat	Healthy Unknown (escaped) Suspected rabid	None RIG[1] + Vaccine[2] RIG + Vaccine[3]

[1]RIG Rabies immune globulin, Human. Concentrated from plasma of hyperimmunized human donors, contains 150 IU/ml. Inject 20 units/kg, infiltrating half around the wound, the rest intramuscularly. Use antirabies serum (ARS) (horse) only if RIG is not available. ARS frequently produces serum sickness or anaphylaxis.

[2]Vaccine Presently available is DEV, a vaccine from embryonated duck eggs, infected with rabies virus and inactivated with beta-propiolactone. Single doses are supplied lyophilized with an ampul of diluent. Injections are usually given daily for 14–23 days. Fever, malaise, and myalgias are common after 5–8 doses and neuroparalytic reactions have occurred. A new inactivated vaccine, of greater potency, is made from rabies virus grown in human diploid cells (WI38). The immunogenicity of this new vaccine is greater and the chance for reactions less. At present it is available only from the Rabies Investigation Unit, Center for Disease Control, Atlanta, Georgia, USA.

[3]If circumstances of exposure make rabies doubtful and if the fluorescent antibody determination is negative, vaccine administration is stopped.

5

ENDOCRINE SURGERY

Orlo H. Clark, MD

I. THYROID

A. THYROID FUNCTION

1. Physiology   The human thyroid gland consists of two functionally separate but structurally intermixed populations of endocrine cells: the **follicular** cells, which concentrate iodide, synthesize thyroglobulin, and secrete the thyroid hormones thyroxine (T_4) and triiodothyronine (T_3); and the **parafollicular** cells (C cells), which synthesize, store, and secrete calcitonin.

Iodide is absorbed from the gastrointestinal tract, actively trapped by the follicular cells, oxidized, and combined with tyrosine in thyroglobulin to form monoiodotyrosine (MIT) and diiodotyrosine (DIT). MIT and DIT are coupled to form the active hormones T_4 and T_3 which are stored in the colloid until released into the bloodstream.

Circulating T_4, the primary secretory product of the thyroid, and T_3, most of which arises from conversion of T_4 to T_3 in the liver, are bound to plasma proteins, chiefly to thyroxine-binding globulin (TBG) and to a lesser degree to thyroid-binding pre-albumin (TBPA). Free T_3 and T_4 are the substances that are responsible for the physiological effects of thyroid hormones.

Under normal conditions, the hypothalamus secretes thyrotropin-releasing hormone (TRH), which stimulates the anterior pituitary to secrete thyroid stimulating hormone (TSH). The secretion of T_4 and T_3 is regulated by a feedback mechanism that involves the hypothalamus and pituitary. An increase in circulating free thyroid hormone levels inhibits the pituitary's production of TSH, whereas a decrease stimulates TSH production.

Calcitonin inhibits bone resorption and acts in conjunction with parathyroid hormone (PTH) to protect against fluctuations in ionized calcium levels in the blood. PTH increases serum calcium levels while calcitonin lowers them.

2. Thyroid function tests

a. T_4 (CPB) or T_4D (Normal: 5.3–14.5 µg/dl). This test measures total thyroxine by competitive protein binding (CPB) or displacement (T_4D) and has replaced PBI and BEI since it is unaffected by exogenous iodides. Measurements of T_4 are influenced by altered thyroxine binding. Thus, increased levels are found in pregnancy and in women taking birth control pills; decreased levels occur in patients receiving anabolic steroids or androgens, and in patients with nephrosis. Salicylates, sulfonamides, and dilantin (dephenylhydantoin) also lower T_4(CPB) levels.

Analysis of serum T_4 levels is an excellent, simple screening test for hyperthyroidism or hypothyroidism and is 90% accurate in diagnosing these conditions. Measurement of T_4 by radioimmunoassay (T_4RIA) may eventually replace T_4(CPB).

b. TSH (RIA) (Normal: less than 6–10 µU/ml; varies with laboratory). This test measures TSH in the serum by radioimmunoassay and is the best test for primary hypothyroidism, in which TSH levels are elevated. Serum TSH concentrations are low in secondary hypothyroidism (pituitary hypothyroidism) and tertiary hypothyroidism (hypothalamic hypothyroidism). Determination of TSH levels is especially helpful when the serum T_4 is low or borderline.

c. T_3 (RIA) (Normal: 60–190 ng/dl; varies with laboratory). This test measures total circulating T_3 by radioimmunoassay. It is unaltered by iodide and is increased in hyperthyroidism, T_3 toxicosis, and in patients with stimulated thyroid glands. It decreases with advancing age, in severe systemic illness, and after corticosteroid administration. T_3(RIA) is very useful if T_4 levels are at the upper limit of normal or the patient has symptoms or signs of thyrotoxicosis.

d. Radioactive T_3 uptake of red cells or resin (T_3RU) (Normal: varies with laboratory). This test indirectly measures the concentration of unsaturated thyroid-binding globulin (TBG). When thyroxine-binding proteins in the blood increase, the proportion of free or unbound thyroxine decreases. When used with T_4, T_3RU corrects for an abnormal concentration of serum proteins. T_3RU values generally parallel the serum T_4 level; i.e., they are increased in hyperthyroidism and decreased in hypothyroidism. During pregnancy or in women taking birth control pills, however, T_4 levels are falsely high due to increased TBG, while T_3RU levels are low. In contrast, low concentrations of T_4 and high T_3RU levels are found in patients receiving diphenylhydantoin, salicylates, phenylbutazone, anticoagulants, cortisone, androgens, anabolic steroids, or large doses of penicillin, and in patients with nephrosis or severe liver disease.

3. Thyroid scanning Several scanning techniques are used.

a. Radioiodine scan is useful in determining whether thyroid nodules are single or multiple and whether they are functioning (warm or hot) or nonfunctioning (cold). Hot nodules may cause hyperthyroidism but are rarely malignant, whereas approximately 20% of cold nodules are malignant.

b. Radioiodine uptake The normal uptake of radioactive iodine is 10–30% at 24 hours. I^{123} has recently replaced I^{131} because of its lower radiation hazard. The uptake of radioactive iodine by the thyroid demonstrates iodide clearance from the plasma. Uptake is increased in hyperthyroidism, glandular hormone depletion, iodine depletion, and in conditions of excessive hormonal losses. Uptake is low in primary and secondary hypothyroidism, conditions of increased dietary or medicinal iodine (including contrast media), and patients receiving exogenous thyroid hormone. Uptake is also low or absent in patients with subacute thyroiditis.

c. Technetium^{99} rectilinear scanning is more sensitive than radioiodine in detecting small nodules. The vascularity of a nodule may be estimated by this technique, but no differentiation is made between hypo- or hyperfunctioning thyroid nodules.

d. Fluorescent scanning with Americium^{241} In this test a columinated source of radiation activates iodine stores within the thyroid. It is used to differentiate benign from malignant thyroid nodules. Since no radioactive materials are introduced into the body, the total radiation received is small (approximately 50 m rads). Fluorescent scans are useful during pregnancy or in patients who recently received iodine-containing substances.

4. Serologic tests Antibodies against human thyroglobulin and against subcellular thyroid components are found in high titers in patients with Hashimoto's disease, but not in patients with dyshormonogenetic or iodine-deficient goiters. Low titers of antithyroglobulin and antimicrosomal antibodies are observed in about 60% of patients with Graves' disease. Serum thyroglobulin levels, as determined by radioimmunoassay, are useful in the posttreatment follow-up of patients with differentiated thyroid cancer; patients with elevated levels often have metastatic thyroid cancer.

5. Other tests

a. TSH response to TRH (200 µg IV) is useful in diagnosing subclinical primary hypothyroidism (the TSH response to TRH is increased) and subclinical hyperthyroidism (the TSH response to TRH is decreased or absent).

b. T₃ suppression test (75–100 μg of T_3 daily for 10 days) helps determine whether the thyroid gland or a thyroid nodule is functioning autonomously. After T_3 is given, the thyroid I^{123} uptake decreases to less than half its initial value in normal individuals but not in patients with hyperthyroidism.

c. Serum cholesterol levels (Normal: 150–280 mg/dl) are often elevated in hypothyroidism and low in hyperthyroidism.

d. A relative *lymphocytosis* and relative *monocytosis,* with normal or slightly low total leukocyte count, are the characteristic blood findings in hyperthyroidism.

e. Human thyroid-stimulating immunoglobulins (HTS) have been found in the plasma of patients with Graves' disease; they correlate well with the early uptake of radioiodine by the thyroid.

B. HYPERTHYROIDISM

is due to excess circulating thyroid hormone. Diffuse toxic goiter (Graves' disease) and toxic nodular goiter (Plummer's disease) account for most cases. There are a variety of other (rare) causes.

Graves' disease may be an autoimmune disease. Increased levels of HTS are found in many of these patients. Hyperthyroidism is 6 times more common in women than in men. A few patients with hyperthyroidism have normal serum T_4 levels, normal radioiodine uptakes, and normal protein binding, and are toxic due to increased serum T_3 levels (T_3 toxicosis).

1. Diagnosis Virtually every organ system is affected by hyperthyroidism. The clinical manifestations may be subtle or marked, and they tend to exacerbate and remit. Many cases are easily diagnosed on the basis of symptoms and signs, but others (mild or apathetic hyperthyroidism) are recognized with difficulty. Graves' disease usually causes more severe hyperthyroidism than does toxic nodular goiter.

a. Symptoms Nervousness; irritability; sweating and heat intolerance; palpitations; muscular weakness and increased fatigue; increased frequency of bowel movements; polyuria; menstrual irregularities and infertility; eye irritation; weight loss (despite an increased appetite).

b. Signs Staring appearance; warm, thin, moist skin; fine hair or alopecia; a goiter; tachycardia or atrial fibrillation; weight loss; shortened Achilles' reflex time.

Extrathyroidal manifestations are almost exclusively limited to Graves' disease: exophthalmos; pretibial myxedema; vitiligo; onycholysis (longitudinal striation and flattening of nails); thyroid acropathy (clubbing of digits); gynecomastia.

c. Laboratory tests T_4 and T_3 levels are increased; radioactive iodine uptake is usually increased; T_3RU is increased; TSH response to TRH is absent; thyroidal radioactive iodine uptake does not suppress with exogenous T_3 administration; hypercalciuria and occasional hypercalcemia; blood TSH is low; blood cholesterol level may be low.

2. Differential diagnosis Anxiety neurosis, heart disease, anemia, cirrhosis, and pheochromocytoma may be difficult to distinguish from hyperthyroidism. Tachycardia at rest, a goiter, increased serum T_4, and increased radioactive iodine uptake make the diagnosis of hyperthyroidism a certainty.

3. Complications

a. Hyperthyroid crisis (thyroid storm) is characterized by fever and exaggerated thyrotoxic manifestations involving the cardiovascular, gastrointestinal, and central nervous systems. Hypotension, coma, and jaundice may occur. Storm is usually precipitated by some form of physical stress such as surgery, infection, or trauma.

Treatment must begin immediately and includes: (1) diagnosis and treatment of any underlying illness. (2) General supportive measures: oxygen, sedatives, intravenous fluids and corticosteroids (hydrocortisone 200–500 mg parenterally daily). (3) Sodium iodide USP 1-2 gm IV every 8 hours. (4) High doses of antithyroid drugs (propylthiouracil 600-1000 mg or methimazole 60-100 mg) given orally or by nasogastric tube. (5) Propanolol (1-2 mg IV for a total dose of 2-10 mg) controls the cardiac and psychomotor abnormalities within 10 minutes; its effects last for 3-4 hours.

b. Severe exophthalmos (1) Ocular manifestations of Graves' disease may be mild or severe. The mild form is due to hyperactivity of the sympathetic nervous system, and the severe type is due to infiltration of the retroorbital tissues. The infiltrative form is uncommon. Progressive ophthalmopathy occurs more frequently, and is more severe in men than in women. It is usually bilateral. Patients usually improve, but the course is unpredictable. (2) *Symptoms and signs:* edema of the orbital contents and periorbital tissues; chemosis (protrusion of edematous, injected scleral conjunctiva); excessive lacrimation; photophobia; protrusion of the eyes (exophthalmos); paresis or paralysis of the ocular muscles causing diplopia, squint, and loss of convergence; visual loss. (3) *Treatment* depends upon the severity of the ophthalmopathy, (ophthalmologic consultation is recommended); maintain the patient in a euthyroid state; protect the eyes from light and dust with dark glasses and eyeshades; elevate the head of the bed; methylcellulose eyedrops; corticosteroids (60 mg prednisone) for several weeks; retroorbital radiation; lateral tarsorrhaphy or retroorbital surgical decompression. (4) In patients with *severe* or *progressive exophthalmos,* subtotal thyroidectomy should be delayed until the eyes have stabilized.

4. Treatment Hyperthyroidism may be treated by antithyroid drugs, radioactive iodine therapy, or subtotal thyroidectomy. The choice of treatment depends upon the patient's age and the size and consistency of the goiter.

a. Antithyroid drugs Reliable patients with mild hyperthyroidism and small diffuse goiters are good candidates for antithyroid medications. (1) Use propylthiouracil (PTU), 100-300 mg orally every 8 hours or methimazole (Tapazole), 10-30 mg orally every 8 hours. (2) About 50% of patients will remain euthyroid if the drug is discontinued after 18 months. (3) Severely toxic patients should be started on these antithyroid drugs as well as on the beta-adrenergic blocking agent propanolol, 5-40 mg orally 4 times daily, before other forms of definitive therapy are instituted.

Patients receiving PTU or Tapazole should be warned to discontinue these medications and see their doctor immediately if they develop a sore throat, since granulocytopenia and fatal agranulocytosis may develop. If the leukocyte count falls below 4500 or if there are fewer than 45% granulocytes, the drug should be discontinued.

b. Radioiodine (I¹³¹) is the treatment of choice for recurrent hyperthyroidism, poor risk patients, and patients older than 45 years of age with diffuse thyroid enlargement. The treatment is effective and avoids an operation. Radioiodine should not be used in children or in pregnant women because of the radiation hazard. Radioiodine should not be used in a toxic patient with a nonfunctioning nodule within the hyperfunctioning gland because the nodule may be malignant. The incidence of hypothyroidism after radioiodine therapy is approximately twice that after subtotal thyroidectomy.

c. Subtotal thyroidectomy is the recommended form of treatment in: (1) patients with very large goiters, especially if multinodular or with low radioiodine uptake; (2) children and pregnant women; (3) patients with a thyroid nodule that may be malignant; (4) psychologically or mentally incompetent patients in whom long-term follow-up will be difficult to obtain. The advantages are the rapid return to the euthyroid state and a lower incidence of hypothyroidism than can be achieved with radioiodine treatment.

Preparation for surgery includes administration of PTU or one of its derivatives until the patient becomes euthyroid. 10-15 days before operation, potassium iodide solution or Lugol's solution (2-5 drops, orally, 3 times daily) are started and given in conjunction with PTU until the time of operation. Propanolol (5 – 40 mg, orally, 4 times daily) used to prepare severely toxic patients for operation should be continued for about 4 days after thyroidectomy because circulating levels of thyroid hormone remain elevated for several days after subtotal resection of the gland. Propanolol should not be used in patients with asthma or congestive heart failure because of the risk of precipitating bronchospasm or heart failure.

The mortality rate of subtotal thyroidectomy is less than 0.1%. Permanent injuries to the parathyroid glands or to the recurrent laryngeal nerves occur in fewer than 2% of cases. Recurrent hyperthyroidism develops in about 5% of patients.

5. Prognosis Untreated thyrotoxicosis causes progressive and profound catabolic disturbances and cardiac damage resulting in death by thyroid storm, heart failure, or cachexia. Any patient with hyperthyroidism may eventually become hypothyroid, therefore yearly thyroid function tests are advisable.

C. HYPOTHYROIDISM The clinical manifestations of hypothyroidism may be subtle, and the diagnosis is often overlooked.

1. Diagnosis

a. Symptoms Weakness; intolerance to cold; dry skin; alopecia; menometrorrhagia; constipation; periorbital swelling. There may be a history of previous treatment for hyperthyroidism.

b. Signs Rough, dry skin; yellow pallor; coarse hair; hoarse voice; some patients become comatose (myxedema coma).

c. Laboratory tests In primary hypothyroidism, serum T_4 is low and TSH levels are increased; the response of TSH to TRH is increased. In secondary (pituitary) and tertiary (hypothalamic) hypothyroidism, serum T_4 and TSH levels are low. Elevated blood cholesterol, hyponatremia, hypoxemia, and CO_2 retention are often present.

2. Treatment

a. Myxedema coma 500 µg of thyroxine IV should be given immediately, followed by 100 µg of T_4 daily. Hydrocortisone (100 µg IV every 8 hours) should also be given in this life-threatening condition.

b. Patients with severe hypothyroidism and heart disease without coma should be started on very low doses of L-sodium thyroxine (25 µg orally, daily). The dose is increased by 25 µg·every 2 weeks until euthyroidism is achieved. EKGs and myocardial enzymes should be obtained before the initial dose, and before each increase.

D. NONTOXIC NODULAR GOITER is a compensatory response to inadequate production of thyroid hormones. It may stem from a congenital defect (dyshormonogenesis); it also occurs in people living in endemic (iodine-poor) regions, or it may result from prolonged exposure to goitrogenic foods or drugs. If not treated, the goiter may become multinodular. The incidence of carcinoma in multinodular goiters is less than 1%.

The symptoms are awareness of a neck mass, dyspnea, or dysphagia. T_4, T_3, TSH, and T_3RU measurements are usually normal but radioiodine uptake and TSH levels may be slightly increased.

The differential diagnosis includes physiologic enlargement of the thyroid during puberty or pregnancy, inflammatory thyroid disease, hyperthyroidism, and thyroid tumors.

The goiter usually responds favorably to administration of thyroid hormone. Indications for removal of a nontoxic nodular goiter are: suspicion of malignancy; history of radiation to the head or neck; pressure symptoms; substernal extension; progressive enlargement; cosmetic deformity.

E. INFLAMMATORY THYROID DISEASE (Thyroiditis) Inflammatory disease of the thyroid may result in acute, subacute, or chronic thyroiditis. These conditions are of surgical importance because they sometimes are confused with thyroid cancer.

1. Acute suppurative thyroiditis is rare; it is characterized by the sudden onset of severe neck pain, dysphagia, and fever, and usually follows an upper respiratory illness. The treatment is surgical drainage.

2. Subacute thyroiditis causes pain, swelling, generalized weakness, malaise, and weight loss. The erythrocyte sedimentation rate and serum gamma globulin are almost always elevated, and radioiodine uptake is low or absent. Serum T_4 levels may be increased. Salicylates and steroids effectively relieve the symptoms. This disease is self-limited, and thyroid function returns to normal. The acute symptoms last about 10 days.

3. Hashimoto's thyroiditis is a chronic inflammation that is believed to be an autoimmune phenomenon. Patients have high levels of antimicrosomal and antithyroglobulin antibodies. About 25% become hypothyroid. Hashimoto's thyroiditis occurs almost exclusively in women and is characterized by a firm, diffusely enlarged, nontender thyroid gland. Treatment consists of full replacement doses of thyroid hormone. Operation is indicated only if a malignant tumor is suspected or if pressure symptoms are severe. Surgical division of the isthmus provides dramatic relief of pressure symptoms.

4. Reidel's stroma is a rare form of chronic thyroiditis. It appears as a hard, woody mass with tracheal compression and infiltration into the adjacent muscles, thus making it difficult to differentiate clinically from anaplastic thyroid cancer. It is sometimes associated with retroperitoneal fibrosis. Patients are usually hypothyroid. Surgical treatment is necessary to relieve tracheal or esophageal obstruction or to rule out carcinoma.

F. THYROID TUMORS Most benign or malignant thyroid tumors occur in euthyroid patients who are asymptomatic. Solitary nodules are more likely to be malignant (5-35%) than are multinodular glands (1-5%), and 'cold' thyroid nodules are more often malignant than functioning nodules. Thyroid cysts are rarely malignant and can be accurately diagnosed by echography. Although thyroid disease and thyroid malignancy are more common in women, a solitary nodule is more likely to be a cancer in a man. About 50% of solitary cold thyroid nodules in children are malignant. Exposure to ionizing radiation in infancy or childhood doubles the possibility of a nodule being malignant. No preoperative test reliably distinguishes benign from malignant in patients with solid, solitary thyroid tumors.

G. BENIGN TUMORS Benign thyroid nodules are follicular adenomas, involutionary nodules, cysts, or localized thyroiditis. Adenomas are firm, nontender, discrete, encapsulated, and slowly-growing; they may compress the adjacent thyroid or other structures. The major reasons for removal are a suspicion of malignancy, functional overactivity producing hyperthyroidism, or cosmetic disfigurement.

H. ECTOPIC THYROID The thyroid develops from a pharyngeal outpocketing that migrates caudally. Aberrant development or migration may result in: agenesis of one or both lobes of the thyroid; a lingual thyroid protruding from the base of the tongue; thyroglossal ducts (midline cysts) located anywhere from the foramen cecum of the tongue to the thyroid; or thyroid rests. In 70% or more of patients with a lingual thyroid, this is the only thyroid tissue present and removal results in hypothyroidism. Thyroglossal duct cysts occasionally must be excised for cosmetic or diagnostic reasons or because of infection. Thyroid rests are situated in the midline, whereas laterally located thyroid tissue (lateral aberrant thyroid) is metastatic follicular carcinoma in most cases.

I. THYROID CARCINOMA Primary malignant thyroid tumors are classified into 2 major types, differentiated and undifferentiated. Lymphoma and sarcoma are in another category of lesion that occurs occasionally. Differentiated carcinomas include papillary, mixed papillary and follicular, follicular, and medullary.

Cancers of the lung, breast and kidney may metastasize to the thyroid, but metastatic lesions are rarely solitary, and the primary tumor is usually apparent.

1. Differentiated carcinomas

a. Papillary adenocarcinoma accounts for 60-70% of all thyroid malignancies. It tends to occur in young adults. This lesion grows slowly and spreads via the intra- and extrathyroidal lymphatics, so that involvement of the contralateral thyroid lobe and ipsilateral thyroid lymph nodes occurs in 30-85% of patients. Growth is stimulated by TSH secretion. Mixed papillary-follicular thyroid carcinoma is usually classified with papillary carcinoma.

b. Follicular carcinoma Approximately 20% of malignant thyroid tumors are follicular. The patients are older than those with papillary cancer. Clinically, the lesion is rubbery or soft, smooth, nontender, and encapsulated; it spreads via the bloodstream to bone, lungs, or other sites. Metastatic follicular cancer usually takes up radioiodine.

c. Medullary carcinoma accounts for 2-5% of malignant thyroid tumors. It arises from the C cells (calcitonin cells) or parafollicular cells. It may occur sporadically or in association with hyperparathyroidism, pheochromocytoma, ganglioneuromatosis, and neurofibromatosis (Sipple's syndrome or type II multiple endocrine adenomatosis). Premedullary carcinoma (presumably a premalignant condition) has been diagnosed in family members of patients with Sipple's syndrome and increased serum calcitonin levels. Medullary carcinoma is more aggressive than papillary or follicular carcinoma and metastasizes early via the lymphatics.

2. Undifferentiated carcinomas include small cell, giant cell, spindle cell, and squamous cell types. They occur principally in elderly women and comprise 5% of thyroid malignancies. They grow and invade rapidly and are rarely curable. In contrast to differentiated tumors, they often cause symptoms in the neck. Cervical lymphadenopathy and pulmonary metastases are common. These tumors do not take up radioiodine.

3. Treatment

a. Cold solitary thyroid nodules should be removed by total lobectomy. If papillary or follicular cancer is diagnosed, total or near total thyroidectomy is advised, preserving parathyroid function.

If lymph node metastases are present, a conservative neck dissection preserving the sternocleidomastoid muscle is performed. Bilateral cervical node involvement requires limited dissection of the contralateral side (preserving the jugular vein) after an interval of 6 weeks.

T_3 is given postoperatively (75 µg orally daily) for 3 months, and a low iodine diet is prescribed. T_3 is then discontinued and after 10 days a radioiodine total body scan is performed. Possible persistent tumor revealed by scan is ablated with a therapeutic dose of radioiodine. The patient is then treated with suppressive doses of L-sodium thyroxine 0.2-0.3 mg orally daily.

Determination of serum thyroglobulin levels is useful. If thyroglobulin levels are increased after thyroid resection, residual thyroid cancer is usually present.

b. Medullary carcinoma is treated by total thyroidectomy and prophylactic neck dissection, especially if calcitonin levels remain elevated after the thyroid is removed.

c. Undifferentiated thyroid tumors are rarely curable by operation. The bulk of tumor should be removed and the patient treated with external radiation therapy. Radioiodine therapy is ineffective in patients with undifferentiated thyroid malignancy.

4. Prognosis Average survival rates after treatment of various forms of thyroid cancer are shown in Table 5-1. The prognosis is better in women and in patients under age 60. Locally invasive tumors have a more ominous prognosis

than tumors that have metastasized to regional lymph nodes. Medullary carcinoma is more aggressive than papillary or follicular carcinoma, although the clinical course is variable. Most patients with undifferentiated thyroid tumors are dead within a year of diagnosis.

Table 5-1. Survival rates after treatment for thyroid cancer

	Survival Rate (%)		
Years	Papillary	Follicular	Undifferentiated
10	81	58	11
20	61	48	8

II. PARATHYROID

A. HYPERPARATHYROIDISM is the excessive secretion of parathyroid hormone (PTH). It may be **primary**, caused by adenoma (87%), hyperplasia (12%), or cancer of the parathyroids (1%); **secondary**, due to diseases that lower plasma concentrations of ionized calcium; **tertiary**, a consequence of secondary hyperparathyroidism (hyperplastic glands fail to regress in the presence of hypercalcemia); or **ectopic** (pseudo) hyperparathyroidism, due to secretion of PTH or PTH-like polypeptides by nonparathyroid tumors. Serum calcium levels are elevated in all but secondary hyperparathyroidism.

B. PRIMARY HYPERPARATHYROIDISM Parathyroid adenomas are usually solitary, but multiple adenomas are common in patients with multiple endocrine adenomatosis or familial hyperparathyroidism. Primary parathyroid hyperplasia is also frequent in patients with these familial syndromes. Hyperparathyroidism is unusual in children; it is most common in women between age 30 and 60.
 1. Diagnosis The diagnosis is made by eliminating other causes of hypercalcemia and by carefully evaluating the clinical picture and laboratory tests.
 a. Symptoms and signs No symptoms: hypercalcemia detected on routine screening tests. Nonspecific symptoms: polydipsia, weight loss, muscular weakness and pain, lethargy, depression, anorexia, constipation. Other: nephrolithiasis, nephrocalcinosis, hypertension, peptic ulcer disease, pancreatitis, gout or pseudogout; clinically evident bone disease is now distinctly uncommon. Parathyroid adenomas are palpable in only 4% of patients; carcinomas are palpable in 50%. Band keratopathy occurs in approximately 25% of patients with hypercalcemia (including hyperparathyroidism); it is best seen with a slit lamp.
 b. Laboratory tests The classical biochemical abnormalities in primary hyperparathyroidism are hypercalcemia, hypophosphatemia, hyperchloremia, hypercalciuria, and increased serum PTH levels. However, one or more of these tests may be normal in an individual patient.
 The chloride-to-phosphate ratio in the serum is useful. The ratio is greater than 33 in most patients with hyperparathyroidism who have not been vomiting and are not in renal failure. The ratio is less than 33 in patients with hypercalcemia from other causes.
 Other tests: alkaline phosphatase (increased), blood pH (decreased), serum uric acid (increased), urinary cyclic AMP (increased), serum magnesium (decreased), tubular reabsorption of phosphate (below 80 in 80% of patients).
 Renal function (BUN, creatinine), serum electrophoresis, sedimentation rate, hemoglobin, hematocrit, and urinalysis help rule out other causes of hypercalcemia.
 Special tests may be required in patients with renal stones and suspected normocalcemic hypercalciuria. Since hypoalbuminemia, impaired renal function, excessive dietary phosphate intake, acute pancreatitis, and magnesium or vitamin

D deficiency may decrease serum calcium concentration, these conditions should be considered and corrected if possible. The ionized calcium should be measured; sometimes it is increased when total calcium is normal. The phosphate deprivation test is helpful also. A trial of thiazide diuretics, which decrease urinary calcium excretion and 'unmask' hypercalcemia, is also useful.

c. X-rays Osteoporosis, subperiosteal resorption or osteitis fibrosa cystica (bone cysts) are found in about 10% of cases. Subperiosteal resorption is best seen on the radial aspect of the index finger; it is rare unless the alkaline phosphatase is increased. An abnormal sella turcica may be found in patients with primary hyperparathyroidism associated with multiple endocrine adenomatosis type I. Abdominal x-rays may reveal renal or pancreatic calcifications. Intravenous urogram and chest x-ray help exclude other causes of hypercalcemia.

2. Differential diagnosis

a. Malignancy (breast, multiple myeloma, metastatic cancer, leukemia, PTH-secreting tumors of the lung, kidney, or other organs) is the most common cause of hypercalcemia in hospitalized patients. Bone pain, a mass lesion, a lung or renal lesion, increased sedimentation rate, hematuria, proteinuria, a low serum chloride level, normal phosphorus level, and increased alkaline phosphatase levels without subperiosteal resorption all suggest malignant disease.

b. Hyperparathyroidism is the second most common cause of hypercalcemia; it occurs in about 1 of every 1000 hospitalized patients.

c. Other causes of real or apparent hypercalcemia: laboratory error, venous stasis due to a tight tourniquet, immobilization, idiopathic hypercalcemia of infancy, hyperthyroidism, hypothyroidism, thiazide diuretics, milk-alkali syndrome, sarcoidosis, Vitamin D or A overdosage, Paget's disease, Addison's disease, dysproteinemias.

3. Complications
Untreated hyperparathyroidism eventually results in renal failure, hypertension, mental depression, or hypercalcemic crisis. Death is the usual outcome. Renal failure, once established, is sometimes progressive despite successful parathyroidectomy, emphasizing the importance of early diagnosis.

Hypercalcemic crisis Symptoms include nausea and vomiting, drowsiness, stupor, weakness, or coma. Treatment includes: (a) Hydration with saline, up to 2 liters IV in 3 hours, and 8 liters/day. (b) Diuresis with furosemide (Lasix) 40-100 mg or ethylenediamine tetraacetate (EDTA) 50 mg/hour over 4-6 hours. Do **not** use thiazide diuretics. (c) Correct electrolyte abnormalities (hypokalemia, hypomagnesemia, hypophosphatemia). (d) Avoid immobilization. (e) If patients fail to respond, give hydrocortisone 200 mg IV daily, calcitonin 0.5-5 MRC units/kg/hour IV, or mithramycin 25 μg/kg IV. Corticosteroids are effective in patients with vitamin D intoxication, sarcoidosis, and Addison's disease, but they are effective in only 50% of patients with hypercalcemia of malignancy and in 10% of those with hyperparathyroidism.

4. Treatment
Operation is the treatment of choice for primary hyperparathyroidism. It should be performed only after the diagnosis is firmly established. At operation, all 4 parathyroids must be identified. 80% of patients have 4 glands, 6% have 5 or more, and 14% have fewer than 4. If an adenoma is present, it is removed. If there is hyperplasia of all 4 glands, 1 gland should be subtotally resected and the others removed completely.

Experienced surgeons successfully identify and remove the hypersecreting gland(s) in more than 90% of patients. The hyperparathyroidism disappears rapidly.

Transient hypoparathyroidism with hypocalcemia and hypomagnesemia causes periorbital numbness and positive Chvostek and Trousseau signs. This condition most often develops about 48 hours after operation in patients with generalized decalcification of the skeleton, or in patients treated by subtotal parathyroidectomy. Treatment of hypoparathyroidism is discussed in a subsequent section.

C. SECONDARY-TERTIARY HYPERPARATHYROIDISM Secondary hyperparathyroidism occurs most often in patients with renal failure, but it may stem from any situation which results in low plasma concentrations of ionized calcium. Hypocalcemia causes stimulation of PTH secretion, and if the stimulation is prolonged, chief cell hyperplasia results. In secondary hyperparathyroidism due to renal failure, the serum phosphorus is usually high, whereas with malabsorption, osteomalacia, or rickets, phosphorus is normal or low.

The clinical manifestations of secondary hyperparathyroidism include bone pain, pruritus, metastatic calcification and, rarely, calciphylaxis. The majority of patients with secondary hyperparathyroidism may be treated medically: lower serum phosphate levels by the administration of aluminum carbonate or hydroxide gel 30 ml, 3 times daily with meals; increase the calcium concentration in the dialysis solution (this decreases serum PTH levels); prescribe vitamin D in high doses.

Indications for subtotal parathyroidectomy in patients who have been well-managed medically are: severe bone pain and progressive osteitis fibrosa cystica, a calcium-phosphate product of 70 mg/dl or greater, metastatic calcification, and severe pruritus. Dramatic and rapid improvement of these conditions usually follows surgical treatment.

Occasionally, a patient with secondary hyperparathyroidism develops parathyroid hyperplasia that behaves autonomously. This is tertiary hyperparathyroidism. It appears in patients on chronic hemodialysis or following a renal transplant. In most cases, serum calcium will return to normal within 6 months of transplantation. Subtotal parathyroidectomy is rarely indicated.

D. HYPOPARATHYROIDISM Parathyroid insufficiency is most commonly a complication of thyroidectomy. Permanent hypoparathyroidism is unusual after parathyroidectomy, although transient hypocalcemia due to 'hungry bones' is not uncommon in young patients with elevated serum alkaline phosphatase levels.

1. Diagnosis

a. Symptoms and signs (1) Postoperative hypoparathyroidism: latent tetany (paresthesias, positive Chvostek or Trousseau signs), anxiety, depression, muscle cramps, carpopedal spasm, laryngeal stridor, convulsions, papilledema. (2) Idiopathic hypoparathyroidism: malformation of the nails, poor dentition, thin dry hair, congestive heart failure. (3) Chronic hypoparathyroidism of any cause: cataracts, convulsive disorders, intestinal dysfunction, malabsorption, anxiety, chorea, paralysis agitans, retarded physical development, and mental deterioration; these manifestations are related both to the degree and duration of hypocalcemia.

b. Laboratory tests Hypocalcemia, hyperphosphatemia, low or absent PTH and urinary phosphate, high tubular resorption of phosphate, low urinary calcium, and systemic alkalosis. Serum alkaline phosphatase, BUN, and creatinine levels are normal. The Q-T interval of the EKG may be prolonged.

c. X-rays Calcification of the basal ganglia, arteries, and external ear may be present.

2. Differential diagnosis A history of thyroid or parathyroid surgery is most important. Tetany may develop from the alkalosis of hyperventilation. Tetany after parathyroid operations may result from hypomagnesemia; this possibility should be considered in symptomatic patients who do not respond to calcium supplementation. Patients with renal failure also have hyperphosphatemia and hypocalcemia, but renal function tests are abnormal, PTH levels are increased, and these patients are acidotic, not alkalotic. Hypocalcemia occurs in rickets and osteomalacia due to vitamin D deficiency or resistancy, renal tubular dysfunction, or malabsorption. These conditions are implicated by a careful history revealing lack of exposure to sunshine (chronic invalidism), pancreatitis, or steatorrhea.

3. Treatment The goals of therapy are to bring the patient out of tetany, to increase serum calcium concentration, and to lower serum phosphate to prevent metastatic calcification.

a. Emergency treatment of postoperative tetany

(1) Reassure the anxious patient to avoid hyperventilation. Have the patient breathe into a bag or balloon if necessary.

(2) Obtain a blood sample for calcium, phosphorus and magnesium concentrations.

(3) If patient is very symptomatic, give calcium chloride or calcium gluconate, 10-20 ml of 10% solution **slowly** IV, until tetany disappears. (Rapid infusion of calcium may cause a cardiac arrest, especially in patients receiving digitalis.) Avoid extravasation since these solutions cause tissue necrosis.

(4) 10-50 ml of 10% calcium chloride may then be added to 1 liter of saline or 5% dextrose solution and administered slowly IV. Adjust the infusion rate so that the symptoms are controlled and serum calcium levels remain normal.

(5) If the hypocalcemia and tetany are severe, vitamin D therapy may be necessary. Thyroid function should be assessed and appropriately treated, since vitamin D is more effective in euthyroid than in hypothyroid patients.

b. Maintenance therapy

(1) Once tetany is controlled, change from IV calcium to an oral calcium preparation. Use calcium glubionate (Neo-Calglucon) 30 cc orally 3 times daily; or calcium carbonate 250 mg/tab, 1 or 2 tabs 4 times daily; or calcium lactate 2-4 gm orally 3 times daily; or calcium gluconate 8 gm orally 3 times daily.

(2) Begin a high calcium, low phosphorus diet.

(3) Vitamin D: give dihydrotachysterol (Hytakerol, AT I0) 0.8-2.4 mg daily for several days and then reduce to 0.1-1 mg daily. Calciferol (vitamin D_2) 80,000-160,000 units (2-4 mg) daily is as effective as dihydrotachysterol but is slower to act. The response to vitamin D therapy is slow, and generally 7-10 days elapse before the serum calcium is raised; effects persist for weeks to months after administration is stopped.

(4) Aluminum hydroxide with magnesium hydroxide or magnesium trisilicate, 15 ml (or 20.5 gm tablets) 3 times daily with meals, reduces serum phosphorus levels.

4. Prognosis The management of hypoparathyroid patients is difficult because the difference between the controlling and intoxicating dose of vitamin D is often small. Episodes of hypercalcemia in treated patients may occur after months or even years of good control, and therefore serum calcium and phosphorus should be determined periodically.

E. PSEUDOHYPOPARATHYROIDISM AND PSEUDOPSEUDOHYPOPARA-THYROIDISM

1. Pseudohypoparathyroidism is characterized by hypocalcemia, hyperphosphatemia, and variable somatic and skeletal abnormalities including a round face, a short thick body, shortened metacarpal and metatarsal bones, mental deficiency, and x-ray evidence of soft tissue and cerebral calcification. It is inherited as an X-linked autosomal syndrome. These patients have an end-organ resistance to parathyroid hormone. PTH levels are increased and parathyroid glands are normal or hyperplastic, whereas in hypoparathyroidism, parathyroid tissue is lacking or defective and serum PTH levels are absent or low. Treatment is similar to that described for hypoparathyroidism. Smaller doses of vitamin D usually are effective, and resistance to vitamin D is uncommon.

2. Patients with **pseudopseudohypoparathyroidism** resemble those with pseudohypoparathyroidism in body habitus, chondrodystrophy, and subcutaneous calcifications, but they have normal serum calcium and phosphorus levels.

III. ADRENALS

The adrenal glands are composed of an outer cortex and inner medulla which are distinct from one another in their origin and function. Increased adrenal hormone secretion may be due to hyperplastic or neoplastic change; the clinical manifestations depend upon the type and amount of adrenal secretion. Decreased hormone production may result from hypoplasia, atrophy, destruction, or surgical removal.

A. PHYSIOLOGY The adrenal cortex is essential to life. It has a major role in intermediary metabolism and in resistance of the body to stress and a subsidiary role in sexual development and function. ACTH secreted by the pituitary regulates the secretion of cortisol, corticosterone, androgens and possibly estrogens, and has a trophic effect upon the adrenal cortex. It also has a minor effect on aldosterone secretion. Corticotropin-releasing factor from the hypothalamus and the plasma-free cortisol level regulate ACTH secretion.

  There are three major types of adrenocortical hormones.

  1. Glucocorticoids Cortisol and related steroids: (a) Play, a vital role in response to stress. (b) Promote the catabolism of protein and formation of glucose (gluconeogenesis), and inhibit tissue utilization of glucose, thereby increasing blood sugar. (c) Encourage deposition and redistribution of body fat (high levels cause lipolysis, hyperlipidemia, and hypercholesterolemia). (d) Have a weak aldosterone effect (decrease urinary excretion of sodium and increase potassium and hydrogen excretion, but unlike aldosterone, they increase water excretion). (e) Increase the number of red cells and neutrophils and decrease the number of eosinophils and lymphocytes in the blood.

  2. Mineralocorticoids Aldosterone is the most potent endogenous salt-retaining steroid. It causes retention of sodium and excretion of potassium and hydrogen ions, and it also helps to regulate extracellular fluid volume and blood pressure. Several mechanisms control aldosterone secretion: (a) Renin-angiotensin system (volume depletion increases and volume expansion suppresses). (b) Serum potassium level (hyperkalemia increases and hypokalemia decreases). (c) ACTH (increases). (d) Serum sodium concentration (hyponatremia increases and hypernatremia decreases).

  3. Sex hormones The normal adrenal cortex secretes small amounts of testosterone as well as a number of less potent androgenic substances including 17-ketosteroids (17-KS), dehydroepiandrosterone (DHEA), etiocholanolone, androsterone and the 11-oxy-derivatives. Excess androgens and estrogens may be produced by adrenocortical tumors (usually carcinoma) or hyperplasia.

B. PRIMARY HYPERALDOSTERONISM In primary hyperaldosteronism, excessive secretion of aldosterone independent of renin-angiotensin and ACTH regulation causes sodium retention, potassium depletion, and hypertension in nonedematous patients. This syndrome accounts for 1% of all cases of hypertension. Primary aldosteronism is twice as common in women as in men. The adrenal lesion is an adenoma in 75%, bilateral nodular hyperplasia in 25%, and carcinoma rarely. Patients with atypical clinical syndromes are more likely to have bilateral hyperplasia or carcinoma.

  In **secondary hyperaldosteronism,** aldosterone secretion is increased in response to overactivity of the renin-angiotensin system. Plasma renin levels are invariably increased in these cases, whereas they are low in patients with primary hyperaldosteronism.

  1. Diagnosis

  a. Symptoms and signs Hypertension, usually persistent and mild; headache, muscle weakness, polydipsia, nocturnal polyuria; edema is absent.

  b. Laboratory tests Hypokalemic alkalosis, normal or elevated serum sodium, decreased serum chloride and magnesium. Plasma aldosterone levels are elevated and plasma renin levels are low; low sodium diets and diuretics must be discontinued before these tests are obtained. Inappropriately high urinary potassium (greater than 30-40 mEq/liter) despite hypokalemia. Correction of hypokalemia after 100 mg of spironolactone (Aldactone) 4 times daily for 3 days (a dose that does not raise serum potassium in normal subjects). Urinary excretion of more than 20 μg of aldosterone daily in a sodium and potassium repleted patient. Low plasma renin level despite at least 4 hours of ambulation while on a low sodium diet, in a patient who also has elevated aldosterone levels while on a high sodium diet (2 gm sodium per meal for 3 days).

c. Other tests EKG may show the changes of hypokalemia and chronic hypertension. Adrenal scan with 19-iodocholesterol may localize a small adrenal tumor; CT scan has been used for the same purpose.

2. Differential diagnosis Primary hyperaldosteronism should be considered in any hypertensive patient with muscular weakness or hypokalemia. Diuretic drugs are the most common cause of hypokalemia, and their effects may persist for several weeks after they are discontinued.

Secondary hyperaldosteronism, with or without hypertension, may occur with renal or renovascular disease, cirrhosis, congestive heart failure, renin-secreting tumors, Bartter's syndrome, orthostatic hypotension, diabetes mellitus, or contraceptive steroid therapy.

3. Complications of primary hyperaldosteronism are related to prolonged hypertension and hypokalemia. Hypertension leads to cardiac and renal dysfunction, and hypokalemia increases the risk of developing cardiac arrhythmias, especially in patients taking digitalis.

4. Treatment

a. Medical Mild disease can be managed with spironolactone and methyldopa. These drugs have side-effects, however, and most patients are treated surgically.

b. Surgical Preparation: The potassium depletion should be corrected by prescribing a low sodium diet with potassium supplements (8 gm potassium chloride daily) and giving spironolactone. Antihypertensive medication is discontinued about 1 week before operation.

Operation is performed through a posterior incision if an adenoma has definitely been localized to one gland. Otherwise, an anterior transabdominal approach is required to explore both adrenals. An adenoma is excised; hyperplasia is treated by bilateral total or subtotal adrenalectomy.

Postoperative care: Glucocorticoids are not required if only 1 gland was removed. Transient postoperative aldosterone deficiency is treated by saline IV initially, then liberal sodium intake orally. Fludrocortisone (50-100 μg/day orally) may be needed for about 1 month.

5. Prognosis The response to removal of an adenoma is excellent, although blood pressure may not fall for weeks or months. Surgical treatment of hyperplasia is less successful, and some degree of hypertension usually remains. Overall, about 70% of patients with primary hyperaldosteronism become normotensive and the hypertension is improved in others after operation.

C. HYPERADRENOCORTICISM
Increased secretion of cortisol may be classified as Cushing's disease or Cushing's syndrome. **Cushing's disease** signifies pituitary hypothalamic-dependent ACTH excess which causes bilateral adrenocortical hyperplasia. **Cushing's syndrome** refers to hypercortisolism of any origin (administration of exogenous corticosteroids, steroid-producing adrenal adenoma or cancer, adrenal rest tumor of the gonads, or cancer of nonendocrine or endocrine tissues which elaborate on ACTH-like polypeptide).

In patients with primary cortisol-secreting adrenal tumors, hypothalamic corticotropin-releasing factor (CRF) and pituitary ACTH are suppressed and the uninvolved adrenal is atrophic. In patients with adrenal rest tumors, both adrenals and ACTH production are suppressed, while patients with ectopic or pituitary ACTH-producing neoplasms have bilateral adrenal hyperplasia.

Cushing's syndrome is 3 times more common in women than in men, and it occurs most often in patients between 20 and 40 years of age. Most cases of hyperadrenocorticism are due to administration of exogenous corticosteroids. Of the remaining cases, about 70% are due to hypothalamic or pituitary disorders, 10% are caused by ectopic ACTH-producing tumors, and 20% are due to adrenal neoplasms. Approximately 75% of the adrenal tumors are benign; malignant tumors are more common in children. About 98% of tumors are unilateral.

1. Diagnosis and differential diagnosis

a. Symptoms and signs Gradual or fulminant onset. Change in menstrual cycle, often progressing to amenorrhea. Virilization (hirsutism, balding) in women if androgens are among the hormones secreted excessively. Weight gain, lassitude, muscular weakness, psychiatric disturbance, polyuria, hypertension, easy bruisability, edema, 'buffalo hump', purple striae. Pituitary tumors and ectopic ACTH-secreting tumors usually also secrete melanotropins (MSH), which increase skin pigmentation. Obesity and growth retardation in children. The rapid onset of hypercortisolism with hypokalemic alkalosis, hypertension, and edema suggests an ectopic ACTH-producing tumor.

b. Laboratory tests These tests are performed sequentially to confirm the diagnosis of Cushing's syndrome and to identify the cause.

(1) Plasma cortisol levels are normally highest upon awakening (5-30 μg/dl at 8 am) and lowest (<10 μg/dl) at bedtime. This circadian rhythm is lost in Cushing's disease.

(2) Low-dose dexamethasone suppression test: 1 mg of dexamethasone is given at 11 pm, and plasma cortisol is measured at 8 am the next day. If the cortisol is not suppressed (<5 μg/dl), the next test is required.

(3) Urinary free cortisol excretion (normal 80-400 μg/day) is elevated in virtually all patients with Cushing's syndrome. If this value is high in a patient whose plasma cortisol did not suppress in test (2), the diagnosis of Cushing's syndrome is confirmed.

(4) The cause of Cushing's syndrome is sought by plasma ACTH assay and the high-dose dexamethasone suppression test (dexamethasone 8 mg orally over 24 hours, then urinary 17-hydroxycorticosteroids (17-OHCS) are measured for 24 hours). (a) High ACTH, no 17-OHCS suppression: ectopic source of ACTH. (b) Low ACTH, no 17-OHCS suppression: adrenal tumor. (c) Normal to high ACTH, 17-OHCS suppression: Cushing's disease.

(5) Metapyrone test is sometimes helpful. Metapyrone blocks conversion of 11-deoxycortisol compounds to cortisol; normal subjects and some with Cushing's disease respond by producing more ACTH which is reflected in increased urinary excretion of 17-OHCS. Patients with adrenal neoplasms or ectopic ACTH syndrome do not show this response.

c. Other tests Nephrotomograms, CT scan, I-19 iodocholesterol scan, and occasionally angiography are used to localize adrenal tumors.

2. Complications of the hormone excess are those of diabetes mellitus, hypertension, and severe weakness.

3. Treatment

a. Medical therapy with metapyrone, aminoglutethimide, or o,p'DDD (a derivative of DDT) controls Cushing's syndrome in a few patients, but side-effects and escape from control are common. o,p'DDD is useful for treatment of unresectable adrenocortical carcinoma.

b. Cushing's disease can be treated by radiation to the pituitary; as long as 18 months may elapse before a response is seen, however, and recurrences are frequent. Transsphenoidal hypophysectomy is a preferable method of pituitary ablation at present.

c. Adrenalectomy is the treatment of choice for Cushing's syndrome and for some patients with Cushing's disease.

Preparation: Electrolyte disorders (especially hypokalemia) must be corrected and diabetes mellitus should be controlled. Exogenous corticosteroids must be provided (see below).

Operation: Unilateral adrenalectomy is performed for adenoma or carcinoma; total adrenalectomy is recommended for bilateral hyperplasia.

Postoperative care: Cortisol hemisuccinate is given intravenously initially (100 mg every 8 hours). After total adrenalectomy, permanent replacement therapy is necessary (cortisol 30 mg daily orally, 20 mg in am and 10 mg in pm); fludrocortisone 0.1 mg/day orally provides mineralocorticoid. After unilateral adrenalectomy, the dose of cortisol is tapered to physiologic levels (30 mg/day orally) and further reduced gradually; alternate-day treatment minimizes inhibition of endogenous ACTH.

Postoperative complications frequently develop in patients with Cushing's syndrome: wound infection, wound dehiscence, bleeding, peptic ulcer, and pulmonary problems.

4. Prognosis Nelson's syndrome occurs in 15% of patients after total bilateral adrenalectomy; it is due to excessive pituitary secretion of ACTH. Hyperpigmentation, headaches, exophthalmos, and an enlarged sella turcica (occasionally leading to blindness) are present. It may be prevented by irradiation of the pituitary before adrenalectomy.

Hypoadrenocorticism and panhypopituitarism are chronic complications of total adrenalectomy or pituitary ablation, respectively.

The prognosis of adrenocortical carcinoma is poor.

D. VIRILIZING AND FEMINIZING CONDITIONS
1. Virilizing conditions

a. Congenital adrenal hyperplasia (adrenogenital syndrome) is due to deficient steroidogenesis; as a result of abnormally low cortisol production, ACTH is increased, and the adrenals are stimulated to secrete androgens. If this occurs during fetal development, female infants have ambiguous genitalia (pseudohermaphroditism) and males have macrogenitosmia. The condition may become apparent during childhood or adult life as well. Treatment consists of replacement with glucocorticoids and mineralocorticoids.

b. Cushing's syndrome may include virilizing manifestations if androgens are secreted excessively.

c. Enzymatic blockers (e.g., metapyrone, o,p'DDD) may cause virilization.

d. Androgen-secreting tumors The adrenal cortex ordinarily secretes the 17-ketosteroids, androstenedione and estrone, and only small amounts of androgens and estrogens; the gonads primarily secrete the 17-hydroxy steroids, testosterone, and estradiol. Thus, high 17-ketosteroid levels in a masculinized female generally suggest an adrenal source, and elevated 17-hydroxysteroids with normal or only slightly increased urinary 17-ketosteroids suggest a gonadal origin.

2. Feminizing tumors of the adrenal are rare. They produce tender gynecomastia and testicular atrophy in the male, and sexual precocity (breast development, uterine bleeding, pubic and axillary hair, and advanced bone age) in prepubital females. 90% are due to adrenocortical carcinomas.

E. PHEOCHROMOCYTOMA
Pheochromocytomas are catecholamine-producing tumors that arise from chromaffin cells in the adrenal medulla or elsewhere in the sympathetic nervous system in the abdomen, thorax, pelvis, neck, or urinary bladder. They are characterized by excessive production, storage, and release of epinephrine and norepinephrine. These tumors account for 0.1-0.2% of all patients with hypertension. 10% of pheochromocytomas are malignant, 10% are bilateral, and 90% occur in the adrenal or periadrenal area.

1. Diagnosis

a. Symptoms and signs depend upon the amount and type of catecholamines secreted. (1) Sustained or paroxysmal hypertension. (2) Development of hypertension during anesthetic induction or operative procedures. (3) Paradoxical increases in blood pressure when treated with catecholamine-releasing antihypertensive agents (e.g., guanethidine, methyldopa). (4) Excessive perspiration, pallor, flushing, palpitations, chest pain, trembling, weakness, anxiety, nausea; fever of unknown origin occasionally. (5) Patients with neurocutaneous syndromes (cafe-au-lait spots, neurofibromatosis, Von Hippel–Lindau's disease, Sturge–Weber disease, tuberous sclerosis, Sipple's syndrome) have an increased incidence of pheochromocytoma. Sipple's syndrome, or multiple endocrine adenomatosis II (MEA-II), includes medullary carcinoma of the thyroid, hyperparathyroidism, neurofibromatosis, and ganglioneuromatosis.

b. Laboratory tests (1) Test the urine for metabolites of catecholamines, e.g., vanillyl mandelic acid (VMA), normetanephrine, and metanephrine. One or more of these screening tests is positive in more than 90% of patients. Spurious elevations of VMA occur with coffee, tea, chocolate, vanilla extract, and bananas. Drugs such as glycerol quaiacolate, chlorpromazine, and nalidixic acid also increase urinary VMA. Normetanephrine and metanephrine are falsely increased by methyldopa (Aldomet).

(2) If the screening test is positive, measure urinary free epinephrine and norepinephrine. These values may be falsely elevated by methyldopa, sympathomimetic nasal sprays, quinidine, vitamin preparations, tetracyclines and other fluorescent compounds, and acute stress.

(3) Blood and urine glucose levels often are elevated.

(4) Provocative tests are potentially dangerous and rarely necessary. If other tests are equivocal, the glucagon test is the safest method of stimulation, and phentolamine (Regitine) is the best method of suppression.

c. X-rays Abdominal x-rays and nephrotomography often reveal a suprarenal mass or displacement of the kidney. CT scans are even more accurate. Arteriograms should be done only in patients whose hypertension has been well-controlled medically, since a hypertensive crisis may be provoked.

2. Differential diagnosis includes all causes of hypertension, hyperthyroidism, carcinoid syndrome, and intracranial lesions causing psychologic disturbances.

When epinephrine constitutes 20% or more of the total catecholamine secretion, the tumor is either in the adrenal medulla or the organ of Zuckerkandl; norepinephrine-secreting tumors may be found in the adrenal or in other sites anywhere from the neck to the pelvis. Malignant chromaffin tumors are more likely to produce catecholamine precursors than are benign pheochromocytomas.

3. Complications include any of the consequences of hypertension. Pheochromocytomas occasionally bleed or infarct resulting in hypotension and death.

4. Treatment Surgical removal of the tumor is the treatment of choice.

a. Preparation with pharmacologic agents and by restoration of blood volume is essential. (1) The alpha-adrenergic blocking agent phenoxybenzamine (Dibenzyline) should be given in doses of 10–80 mg every 12 hours, for at least 10–12 days and longer if cardiomyopathy is suspected. Phentolamine (Regitine) is a shorter acting alpha-blocker, but Dibenzyline is generally preferred because of its longer duration of action, better hypertensive control, and fewer side-effects. (2) Propanolol, a beta-blocker, is used only for the treatment of arrhythmias and should never be given before Dibenzyline as it may precipitate a hypertensive crisis.

b. Operation (1) Careful intraoperative monitoring (central venous pressure, arterial pressure, EKG) is vital. (2) The patient should be well-anesthetized and thoroughly alpha-blocked (e.g., with phentolamine 10 mg in 100 ml saline slowly IV); probably a beta-block should be established as well (e.g., propanolol

1-3 mg IV). (3) An anterior abdominal approach is recommended because tumors may be multiple or ectopic. Before the adrenal is excised, blood volume should be carefully replaced to avoid hypotension once the source of excessive catecholamines is removed.

   5. Prognosis   If all tumor has been successfully removed, urinary catecholamines should return to normal in 1 week. Periodic evaluation thereafter is recommended, especially in young patients and in those with familial syndromes, since additional pheochromocytomas may develop. In patients with malignant disease, chronic administration of phenoxybenzamine and propanolol is helpful.

6

HEAD & NECK

Wayne W. Deatsch, MD

I. TRAUMA* TO THE NECK

A. PENETRATING TRAUMA All penetrating wounds of the neck are potentially serious because of the large number of vital structures in this relatively
small space.
   1. Diagnosis
      a. Symptoms and signs depend on the structures that are injured: **Larynx
and trachea**—hoarseness, dyspnea, stridor, subcutaneous emphysema. **Blood vessels**—hematoma, external bleeding, shock. Neurologic deficit may result from injury to the carotid artery. **Pharynx and esophagus**—no symptoms initially; later
dysphagia, hematemesis, and infection in the neck or mediastinum. **Cervical
spine and spinal cord**—see Chapters 16 and 17. **Nerves**—Mirror examination of
the larynx shows recurrent laryngeal nerve injury. Cranial nerves, phrenic nerves,
and the cervical and brachial plexuses may be injured. **Salivary glands**—leakage of
saliva. Associated **head** and **thoracic** injuries must be sought in all patients with
penetrating wounds of the neck.
      b. X-ray findings X-rays of the soft tissues and the cervical spine are
essential. **Arteriography** is required for suspected vascular injuries at the base of
the neck or above the angle of the jaw.
   2. Treatment
      a. General measures An **airway** must be established by oropharyngeal,
nasopharyngeal, or orotracheal intubation (see Chapter 3). Tracheostomy (Fig.
6-1) should **not** be attempted by inexperienced physicians in emergencies;
cricothyrotomy (placement of a tube through the cricothyroid membrane) is
more rapid and safer in desperate situations.
      Do not attempt to pass a nasogastric tube in the emergency room lest
coughing and gagging cause further bleeding.
      Treat shock (see Chapter 1).
      b. Surgical Surgical exploration of the neck, in the operating room and
under general anesthesia, is mandatory if the platysma has been penetrated.
A generous oblique incision along the anterior border of the sternocleidomastoid
muscle gives good exposure and can be extended if necessary.
      Laryngeal and **tracheal** injuries are sutured; an intralaryngeal stent may
be necessary; tracheostomy is required.
      Major **arterial** injuries may require median sternotomy to gain proximal
control. Management is discussed in Chapter 13.
      Injuries to the internal jugular or other **veins** are treated by ligation. Keep
the patient's head lowered to avoid **air embolism** until the vein is controlled.

---

*Injuries to the cervical spine and spinal cord are covered in Chapters 16 and 17. Injuries to
the scalp, face, and maxillofacial bones are discussed in Chapter 14. Injuries to the head are
covered in Chapter 16.

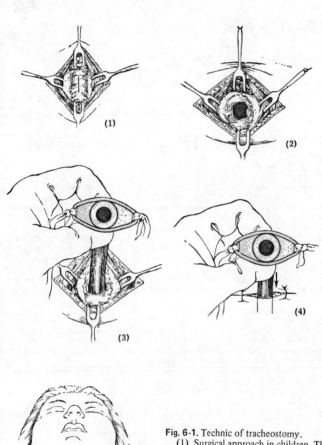

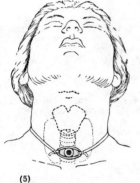

Fig. 6-1. Technic of tracheostomy.
 (1) Surgical approach in children. Third and fourth tracheal rings split in midline. No cartilage removed.
 (2) Surgical approach in adults. Anterior section of third tracheal ring removed.
 (3) Insertion of tracheostomy tube.
 (4) Loose suturing of both ends of wound.
 (5) Tube tied in place.
 Note: Use endotracheal intubation or cricothyrotomy in emergencies.

Esophageal perforations are repaired with absorbable suture, and external drainage of the sutured area is provided. Systemic antibiotics are required. Parenteral feeding for 10 days is advisable.

Nerve injuries are repaired if possible. The great auricular nerve provides a suitable graft to bridge extensively damaged motor nerves.

Salivary gland injuries are debrided and closed. Major ducts can be repaired with fine silk sutures over a ureteral catheter stent. Associated injury of the major **facial nerve** trunk in the parotid gland should be identified and repaired. Postoperative salivary fistula may require intratympanic section of Jacobsen's nerve and/or chorda tympani to decrease salivary flow, rerouting of Stensen's duct, excision of the submaxillary gland, or radiation to a salivary gland or glands.

3. Prognosis The mortality rate depends on the extent of damage and the structures injured. The overall mortality rate is about 5%.

B. BLUNT TRAUMA to the neck may involve any of the structures discussed above, but vertebral and spinal injuries (Chapters 16 and 17) and fracture of the larynx are especially frequent.

C. FRACTURE OF THE LARYNX The thyroid cartilage is usually fractured; in severe cases, the cricoid cartilage, hyoid bone, and tracheal rings can be fractured and the arytenoid cartilages dislocated.

1. Diagnosis

a. Symptoms and signs Pain, swelling, hoarseness, hemoptysis, airway obstruction (dyspnea, stridor), subcutaneous emphysema. Direct laryngoscopy or mirror laryngoscopy reveal mucosal lacerations and blood in the larynx.

b. X-ray findings Fracture of the larynx is diagnosed on clinical grounds, but x-rays may show dislocation of laryngeal structures, narrowing of the airway, and edema and emphysema of the soft tissues. Xeroradiography is a very good technic in these cases.

2. Treatment Maintain the **airway.** Orotracheal intubation may be impossible and tracheostomy may be life-saving. Operative treatment is preceded by direct laryngoscopy to assess the injury fully. Then open laryngotomy is performed, mucosal lacerations are sutured, and the laryngeal fractures are reduced and splinted internally with a plastic stent or tube. The splint is removed 3-6 months later.

3. Prognosis Laryngeal stenosis and voice disturbances result if fractures are not recognized and repaired.

II. EPISTAXIS (NASAL BLEEDING)

Epistaxis usually results from erosion of a superficial blood vessel in the mucosa overlying the cartilaginous nasal septum (Kiesselbach's area). Trauma (external or digital) and inflammation (infection or allergy) are common causes. Other diseases associated with epistaxis include nasal or sinus neoplasms, acute infectious diseases of childhood, hypertension, arteriosclerosis, and coagulation defects.

1. Diagnosis

a. Symptoms and signs If the first symptom is blood coming from the anterior nares, the bleeding site is probably anterior. Initial bleeding into the nasopharynx and pharynx usually indicates a posterior nose-bleed. The treatment is different for anterior and posterior epistaxis (see below). Systemic manifestations of severe blood loss may be present.

b. Laboratory tests should evaluate the extent of blood loss, the presence of infection, and coagulation disorders.

c. X-rays of the sinuses may show neoplasm or infection.

2. Complications Hemorrhagic shock and aspiration are life-threatening complications.

3. Treatment

a. General measures Treat shock with infusion of crystalloid and transfusion of blood. Treat underlying systemic disease that may contribute to nasal bleeding. Mild sedation relieves anxiety; do not sedate heavily if the patient is elderly or hypotensive, or if the bleeding is posterior.

b. Local measures The patient should sit upright and lean forward to minimize aspiration and swallowing of blood. Good illumination (head mirror or headlight) and suction are needed.

Anterior epistaxis Clear the nose of clots by suction or vigorous nose blowing. A bleeding vessel is usually seen on the anterior part of the nasal septum; other locations are the anterior end of the inferior turbinate or the floor of the nose. A cotton pledget the size of the distal phalanx of the patient's fifth finger is moistened in saline or a vasoconstrictor (0.25-0.5% phenylephrine or 1:1000 epinephrine); the pledget is placed in the anterior nose and the nares are pinched together for 5-10 minutes. After the bleeding has stopped, apply a cotton pledget soaked in topical anesthetic (4% lidocaine or 1% tetracaine); the vessel can then be cauterized with silver nitrate (for small superficial erosions), a chromic acid bead, trichloracetic acid, or electrocautery. Lubricate the cauterized area with petrolatum or other ointment several times daily.

If bleeding cannot be stopped or the bleeding site is not seen, an **anterior nasal pack** must be inserted. The nasal mucosa must be anesthetized and shrunken first. Cotton pledgets moistened and compressed, half-inch gauze lubricated with petrolatum, or half-inch Adaptic gauze is inserted in the nasal chamber in layers taking care to fill the spaces below the turbinates and adjacent to the septum. As much as 4 yards of half-inch gauze can be placed in each side of the nasal cavity. The packing can remain for 7 or more days if antibiotics are given to prevent sinusitis and otitis media.

Posterior epistaxis A **posterior pack** usually is required for bleeding from the nasopharynx or the posterior choanae.

Gauze 3-string pack Sew 3 strings (braided '0' silk) through the center of a rolled 4 x 4 gauze sponge. Anesthetize the nose and nasopharynx and inject an analgesic (morphine or meperidine) intramuscularly. A soft rubber catheter is inserted through the nostril, and the tip is withdrawn through the mouth. Two strings are tied to the oral end of the catheter; the nasal end of the catheter is then pulled, bringing the two strings through the mouth and nasopharynx and out the nose. The gauze is then manipulated into the nasopharynx taking care not to roll the uvula up into the nasopharynx. The third string is cut short at the level of the incisor teeth and allowed to dangle in the pharynx. It is used for later removal of the pack. The anterior nasal cavity is packed as described above. The 2 nasal strings are tied over a bolster at the anterior nares.

A 12-14 F **Foley catheter** with a 30 cc bag is a simple pack that often is effective. The catheter is inserted into the nose, the tip is positioned in the nasopharynx, and the bag is inflated with water to the point that the soft palate bulges slightly. Traction on the catheter provides a 'backstop' for anterior packing. The catheter is secured with an umbilical clamp over a bolster at the anterior nares.

With either type of pack, the patient must be followed closely to detect recurrent bleeding, otitis media, and pressure necrosis of the skin of the anterior nares.

Persistent or recurrent bleeding may require replacement of the pack under general anesthesia. Arterial ligation is necessary in some cases.

When the gauze pack is removed after 4-7 days, the third string in the pharynx should be grasped firmly before the anterior strings are cut. This will avoid the pack falling into the larynx and obstructing the airway.

4. Prognosis The prognosis of epistaxis is usually good, although control of bleeding in some patients can tax the skills of the expert. Systemic diseases, cirrhosis, coronary artery disease, coagulation disorders, and delirium tremens greatly worsen the prognosis.

III. INFECTIONS

A. ACUTE EXTERNAL OTITIS is a diffuse infection of the skin of the external ear canal. It often is a secondary infection of eczematoid or seborrheic dermatitis aggravated by scratching. Foreign bodies (cotton swabs, water) causing local trauma are common causes. Gram-positive and gram-negative bacteria and, infrequently, fungi may be cultured.

1. Diagnosis Itching, pain, and discharge are the usual symptoms. There is pain with motion of the pinna. Erythema and edema of the skin of the canal are seen; occasionally the canal is occluded completely. Fever and regional lymphadenopathy indicate severe infection.

2. Differential diagnosis Myringitis bullosa is identified by typical blebs. Acute otitis media causes conductive hearing loss, and little or no hearing loss indicates otitis externa; nevertheless, it may be difficult to distinguish the two conditions if edema obscures the tympanic membrane.

3. Treatment The canal should be cleansed with suction or fine cotton applicators and cotton wicks medicated with topical antibiotic-steroid combinations (e.g., neomycin-polymyxin, bacitracin-hydrocortisone) or Burrow's solution (aluminum acetate) should be inserted for 24 hours. After the wick is removed, antibiotic-steroid ear drops are used for 5-7 days. Systemic antibiotics (penicillin, tetracycline, erythromycin) are required for severe infections. Analgesics often are necessary.

4. Prognosis 'Malignant' external otitis in elderly diabetics is life-threatening and requires intensive treatment in the hospital. External otitis may be refractory to treatment and recurrences are frequent.

B. ACUTE SUPPURATIVE OTITIS MEDIA Acute infection of the middle ear is most common in children, often in association with upper respiratory infection. Streptococcus, staphylococcus, and Hemophilus influenzae are the offending organisms.

1. Diagnosis Pain, fever, deafness, and a full feeling in the ear are the usual symptoms. Purulent discharge indicates spontaneous perforation. The tympanic membrane at first is hyperemic and retracted; later it is red, dull, swollen and bulging as evidenced by loss of visibility of the short process of the malleus. Leukocytosis is common.

2. Differential diagnosis External otitis is discussed above. Pain in the ear (reflex otalgia) may be associated with pharyngitis, laryngitis, dental disease, or temporomandibular joint disease; there are no acute inflammatory changes in the ear canal or tympanic membrane in these conditions.

3. Complications include perforation of the tympanic membrane, acute mastoiditis, labyrinthitis, meningitis, and facial nerve paralysis.

4. Treatment Systemic antibiotics (oral penicillin, tetracycline, erythromycin) must be given for 7-10 days; topical antibiotics have limited value. Analgesics and nasal decongestants usually are needed also. Myringotomy is indicated if the ear drum is bulging or if infection does not resolve promptly. Myringotomy must be done in the posterior-inferior quadrant of the drum.

Frequent recurrent episodes of acute otitis media may require tonsillectomy and adenoidectomy or adenoidectomy alone as prophylaxis.

5. Prognosis With rare exceptions, acute otitis media resolves if treatment is begun promptly. After the acute infection clears, however, fluid may persist in the middle ear; follow-up examination is necessary to prevent chronic hearing loss.

C. SEROUS OTITIS MEDIA   Serous fluid in the middle ear causes a full feeling in the ear and conductive hearing loss. The middle ear is completely filled with fluid or a fluid level is seen behind the tympanic membrane. Antibiotics and decongestants usually resolve the problem, but refractory cases require tonsillectomy, adenoidectomy, myringotomy, and placement of plastic drainage tubes.

D. ACUTE MASTOIDITIS is a complication of acute otitis media that necroses the bony cellular structures of the mastoid, usually in the second or third week. Continued otorrhea, temporal headache, fever, mastoid tenderness, and post-auricular swelling are indications of mastoiditis. X-rays (basal skull view or Towne view) show clouding of the mastoid air cells and destruction of bony trabeculae leading to coalescent abscesses. Culture must be obtained from spontaneous drainage or fluid release by myringotomy.

Treatment must be instituted to prevent serious complications of labyrinthitis, meningitis, intracranial abscess, lateral sinus thrombosis, or facial nerve paralysis. Myringotomy is essential. Antibiotic therapy is guided by culture, but intravenous penicillin, ampicillin, or cephalosporin should be started while awaiting results. Early cases may resolve completely. Simple mastoidectomy is required for bony involvement or persistence of drainage.

E. ACUTE SINUSITIS   Pyogenic infection of any of the paranasal sinuses (frontal, ethmoid, sphenoid, maxillary) usually follows upper respiratory infection, dental infection, nasal allergies, or swimming.

1. Diagnosis   Local pain, tenderness, swelling over the involved sinus, nasal congestion and purulent nasal discharge are common manifestations. Pain is usually greater during the day. Frontal sinus infection causes pain and swelling in the medial roof of the orbit. The pain of ethmoid sinusitis is medial to and behind the eye and is aggravated by eye motion. Maxillary sinusitis causes a feeling of 'long teeth'. Fever and systemic symptoms vary with the severity of the infection. There is usually leukocytosis and culture reveals the infecting organism. Transillumination and x-ray show clouding of the involved sinus, often with an air-fluid level.

2. Differential diagnosis   Acute dental infection causes tender swelling lower in the cheek and greater tenderness to percussion of the involved tooth than does maxillary sinusitis.

3. Complications   Chronic sinusitis is the commonest complication. Frontal and ethmoid sinusitis can lead to intracranial infection (meningitis, and abscesses), osteomyelitis of the frontal bone, orbital cellulitis and abscess, and cutaneous fistula. Maxillary sinusitis can result in oroantral fistula, and all acute sinus infections can cause cavernous sinus thrombosis.

4. Treatment

a. Medical treatment is sufficient for most patients. Systemic antibiotics, oral decongestants (e.g., phenylpropanolamine 25–50 mg), analgesics, topical nasal decongestants (0.25%–0.5% phenylephrine), and local heat usually give prompt results. Mild infections can be managed on an outpatient basis. More severe infections (especially frontal and ethmoid) or complications require hospitalization and large doses of parenteral antibiotics.

b. Surgical treatment of persistent infection or complications should be delayed until medical therapy has been underway for a few days. Irrigation of the maxillary sinus through the inferior meatus, incision and drainage of an orbital abscess, trephine of a frontal sinus, and definitive sinusotomy are among the surgical procedures used in some cases.

F. CHRONIC SINUSITIS often produces few symptoms other than a mild postnasal drainage and nonproductive cough. Nasal obstruction and purulent rhinorrhea may occur. A complication of extension of infection intracranially may be the presenting symptom. X-rays show diffuse clouding of the involved sinus, often with an air-fluid level, and with disruption of the mucoperiosteal line.

Systemic antibiotic treatment, based on culture and antibiotic sensitivity tests if possible, followed by drainage procedures such as repeated maxillary sinus irrigations or intranasal suction may clear a chronic infection. Conservative operative approaches (nasal polypectomy, correction of nasal septal deformities, or intranasal antrotomy) may be helpful. If these forms of treatment are ineffective, external surgical procedures should be done.

G. ACUTE PURULENT SIALADENITIS is infection of the ducts and later the acini by pyogenic bacteria. It usually follows obstruction of the duct by stricture, calculi, or mucous plugs; the submaxillary glands are especially prone to infection from these causes. Decreased production of saliva in debilitated dehydrated patients can also result in acute sialadenitis, particularly of the parotid glands.

1. Diagnosis Unilateral pain, swelling, tenderness, fever, and sometimes septicemia are symptoms of this disease. Pus may be expressed from the duct orifice by pressure on the gland. There is leukocytosis and x-rays may reveal calculi. Mumps, cervical adenitis, and infection of cervical fascial spaces must be differentiated.

2. Complications include extension of infection into the deep fascial spaces of the neck.

3. Treatment in the early stages (before abscess formation) is with antibiotics in large doses (penicillin, methicillin, or cephalosporins), hydration, and local heat. Antibiotic sensitivity tests from cultures of the salivary secretion may alter later treatment. Low dosage x-ray therapy early in the disease (600 R in 4-5 days) has been used. If resolution does not occur in 4-6 days, abscess formation will require external incision and drainage.

4. Prognosis in the severely debilitated elderly patient can be very poor and vigorous treatment is necessary.

H. CHRONIC SIALADENITIS Recurrent infections by pyogenic bacteria cause repeated swelling, destruction, and scarring of ducts and acini with ductal dilation as the consequence. The patient complains of recurrent pain and swelling, especially with meals, but has no systemic symptoms. The gland is enlarged, tender, and the secretions are tenacious or purulent. X-rays may show calculi, and sialography (injection of contrast medium through the duct orifice) often reveals strictures and dilation of the duct.

Dilation of the ducts, antibiotics for acute episodes, intraoral extraction of calculi, meatotomy, and hydration may relieve symptoms. Total excision of the involved gland is indicated if prolonged medical therapy is inadequate.

I. SIALOLITHIASIS Salivary calculi occur most frequently in the submaxillary gland and duct (Wharton's duct). The stones are salts of calcium, sodium and potassium in an organic matrix. About 75% are radioopaque.

Obstruction of the duct by calculi frequently causes swelling of the involved gland with eating. Infections can occur. Glandular enlargement with a stone in the duct is diagnostic. Stones may be palpated or demonstrated by x-ray.

Complications of calculi include secondary infection both acute and chronic (see above).

Slitting the orifice or excision of the papilla often permits complete removal of small stones near the duct orifice. Larger stones in the terminal third of Stensen's duct, and terminal two-thirds of Wharton's duct may be removed intraorally by incising through buccal mucosa into the duct; there is no need to repair the duct. Symptomatic stones in the proximal third of Wharton's duct or in the submaxillary gland should be removed by total external excision of the submaxillary gland.

J. PERITONSILLAR ABSCESS is a complication of acute tonsillitis that occurs when infection extends into the fascial space between the tonsillar capsule and the pharyngeal constrictor muscles. Culture usually shows streptococci, staphylococci, or pneumococci.

1. **Diagnosis**

a. Symptoms Sudden increase in pain, progressive dysphagia, and trismus a few days after the onset of ordinary tonsillitis.

b. Signs Asymmetrical swelling of the pharynx and tonsils with fullness of the anterior pillar and soft palate on the affected side and deviation of the uvula to the opposite side. There is often cervical adenitis.

2. **Differential diagnosis** includes tonsillar abscess or neoplasm, retropharyngeal abscess and deep neck abscess (parapharyngeal abscess).

3. **Treatment** Attention to nutrition and hydration, oral or parenteral antibiotics, analgesics, and warm saline throat irrigations usually produce resolution if started within the first 1–2 days of the peritonsillar infection. Abscesses often form, requiring intraoral incision and drainage. This is done with the patient sitting, and leaning forward; minimal topical anesthesia should be used, and care taken to avoid injury to the deeper vascular structures and to avoid aspiration. The incision should be reopened every day for several days to prevent re-forming the abscess. Peritonsillar abscess is a firm indication for tonsillectomy 1 month or longer after resolution.

K. RETROPHARYNGEAL ABSCESS occurs in the fascial space between the posterior pharyngeal wall and the prevertebral fascia as a result of suppurative lymphadenitis. Since the retropharyngeal lymph nodes are prominent in infants and children and usually atrophy with growth, this disease is more common in children than adults.

1. **Diagnosis** Symptoms are fever, pain, dysphagia, and at times difficulty breathing. Examination reveals cervical adenitis with swelling and even fluctuance of the posterior pharyngeal wall. A lateral soft-tissue x-ray of the neck shows widening of the retropharyngeal space.

2. **Differential diagnosis** Tuberculous involvement of the cervical spine, trauma, foreign body, tonsillitis, adenoiditis, and peritonsillar abscess.

3. **Complications** Airway obstruction, spread of infection to the fascial spaces of the neck, erosion of blood vessels, and aspiration of abscess contents.

4. **Treatment** Large doses of antibiotics may resolve retropharyngeal cellulitis, but an abscess must be drained with local anesthesia (or none), with the patient in deep Trendelenburg position. Adequate lighting and suction are essential. The surgeon must be prepared to do a tracheostomy if necessary.

L. PARAPHARYNGEAL ABSCESS This is an infection of the potential space bound by the pharyngeal constrictor muscles internally and the superficial layer of the deep cervical fascia externally. The space contains the carotid sheath and extends from the base of the skull to the superior mediastinum. The source of infection is usually tonsillitis, peritonsillitis, or dental abscess.

1. **Diagnosis** Pain, fever, dysphagia, and trismus with diffuse swelling in the neck are the usual symptoms. The lateral wall of the pharynx is swollen with displacement of the tonsil and lateral wall medially; later there is brawny swelling of the neck behind and below the angle of the jaw. The veins of the neck and scalp may be distended from pressure on the jugular vein. The differential diagnosis includes infection of other neck spaces, cervical adenitis, tuberculous adenitis, tonsillitis, neoplasm, and branchial cysts.

2. **Complications** can be very severe including airway obstruction due to edema of the neck and larynx, extension of the infection into the mediastinum, involvement of carotid sheath structures with hemorrhage or septic jugular vein thrombosis, and meningitis and intracranial abscess.

3. **Treatment** If the infection does not respond to large doses of antibiotics within 2–4 days or if it is progressing, external incision and drainage should be done. One should not wait for fluctuance because the tough, deep cer-

vical fascia prevents the appreciation of this sign. General anesthesia can be dangerous due to sudden airway obstruction. Local anesthesia or preliminary tracheostomy for general anesthesia can be considered. External incision and drainage at the angle of the jaw should be done with blunt dissection deep to the deep cervical fascia.

4. Prognosis is good with adequate treatment and avoidance of complications. If complications occur, the prognosis is very poor.

M. LUDWIG'S ANGINA is a pyogenic infection of the sublingual and submaxillary spaces of the floor of the mouth and upper neck.

1. Diagnosis Patients have pain on moving the tongue and swallowing and swelling of the floor of the mouth and submental area. Motion of the tongue and mandible is limited, and the tongue is elevated to the roof of the mouth causing airway obstruction at times. Leukocytosis is usually present. X-rays are not helpful unless they show dental infection or salivary calculi. Differential diagnosis includes sialadenitis, dental abscess, and neoplasm of the tongue.

2. Complications Rapidly developing airway obstruction requiring emergency tracheostomy.

3. Treatment Large doses of antibiotics (penicillin or cephalosporin), analgesics, and hydration usually resolve the infection. If the process continues for 3–5 days or if fluctuance develops, external incision and drainage may be necessary. Local anesthesia can be used. The fascial spaces above and below the hyoglossus muscle must be opened by blunt dissection. Large quantities of free pus are seldom obtained.

4. Prognosis Good if the bacteria are sensitive to the antibiotics used and if airway obstruction can be avoided.

N. ACUTE CERVICAL LYMPHADENITIS is the most common infection in the neck of children and adults. Usually it is secondary to infection in the scalp, facial skin, ear, or nasal or oral cavity.

1. Diagnosis The symptoms vary in severity from mild enlargement of the lymph nodes to marked enlargement with pain, tenderness, fever, and symptoms of systemic sepsis. Enlarged tender nodes in the posterior triangle suggest primary infection in the scalp or nasopharynx. Adenitis in the anterior triangle results from infection in the mouth, pharynx, or face. If no primary source of infection is evident, defects in the patient's immune mechanisms should be sought. The differential diagnosis includes infected branchial cleft cyst, infectious mononucleosis, salivary gland infection, and neoplasm.

2. Treatment Antibiotic therapy of the primary infection. Incision and drainage are needed if the nodes suppurate. Superficial abscesses may be drained by sharp dissection, but deep abscesses are more safely entered by blunt dissection after the skin and platyoma are incised. The abscess wall should be biopsied to identify infected branchial cleft cysts.

O. TUBERCULOSIS

1. Cervical tuberculous lymphadenitis Tuberculosis of the cervical lymph nodes may result from tuberculosis in the gums, tonsils, or distant sites (e.g., lung). Painless swelling is the initial symptom, followed by sinus formation and drainage later. The superior cervical nodes are affected first and the more inferior ones later. Multiple matted, firm nodes and draining sinuses are evident. Mycobacteria can be identified in the draining fluid. In arrested cases, calcification is seen by x-ray.

Antituberculous chemotherapy (see Chapter 4) often heals the lesions. Surgical excision is required in some cases.

2. Laryngeal tuberculosis is a complication of pulmonary tuberculosis. Hoarseness, pain, and dysphagia are the symptoms. Inflammation usually affects the posterior half of the glottic area, although any part of the larynx and epiglottis can be involved. Biopsy reveals typical granulomata. Smears and cultures of sputum identify the organism. Chest lesions are seen on x-ray. The differential diagnosis includes carcinoma, syphilis, and other granulomatous diseases.

Treatment requires antituberculous drugs. The laryngeal infection clears readily with appropriate chemotherapy; the pulmonary tuberculosis is more significant in determining prognosis.

IV. FOREIGN BODIES OF THE NOSE AND EAR*

A. FOREIGN BODIES OF THE NOSE are a common problem that physicians often take too lightly. Although many nasal foreign bodies are removed easily, these objects can be dangerous and difficult to extract.

Endogenous foreign bodies include supernumerary teeth and bone and pieces of cartilage from intranasal surgery or facial trauma. Exogenous foreign bodies can be any objects small enough to fit into the nose. Children and mentally-deficient patients often put objects into their own noses. Foreign bodies in adults are usually accidental. Insects and fly larvae can be especially troublesome. Objects present in the nose for years may become encrusted with calcium deposits forming a rhinolith.

1. Diagnosis

a. Symptoms   Small, inert foreign bodies can remain asymptomatic, but persistent unilateral nasal obstruction, discharge and infection are the hallmarks of most. Larval infestations can be bilateral. Pain, bleeding, and sneezing also occur. Destruction and infection of bone and cartilage can develop.

b. Signs   Examination is facilitated by a headlight and by shrinkage of the nasal mucosa with topical 0.25-0.5% phenylephrine and 1% tetracaine or 10% cocaine. The nasal mucosa is swollen and there is serosanguinous or purulent drainage. Palpation with a fine probe confirms the presence of a hard object, but often misses a soft piece of sponge or paper. Mirror examination of the nasopharynx is helpful. X-rays reveal radiopaque foreign bodies and radiopaque material instilled in the nose may outline a radiolucent object.

2. Differential diagnosis   Purulent rhinitis and unilateral sinusitis are most often considered. Nasal polyps and neoplasms produce similar findings.

3. Complications   Persistence of infection before the foreign body is diagnosed is the commonest complication. Larval infestation may cause extensive bony and cartilaginous damage with severe sepsis. Posterior dislodgement either spontaneously or by manipulation can produce airway obstruction and death.

4. Treatment   After topical anesthesia and mucosal shrinkage, vigorous nose blowing may expel the object. Most others can be removed instrumentally under topical anesthesia. An uncooperative child, or very large foreign bodies are indications for general anesthesia.

Some objects can be extracted with forceps. Great care must be taken with hard round objects to avoid pushing them further into the nose. A blunt hook can often be passed behind the object and withdrawn together with it. A suction tip will effectively remove small soft objects. With either local or general anesthesia, care must be taken to avoid dislodgement into the larynx, lower airway, or digestive tract. Very large or severely impacted objects may require lateral rhinotomy for removal.

5. Prognosis   If foreign bodies are diagnosed and removed, subsequent treatment for infection is usually satisfactory. Failure to remove a foreign body results in persistence of infection.

B. FOREIGN BODIES OF THE EAR   Children frequently put small objects into their ears. Foreign bodies in adult ears are more often accidental. Objects in the cartilaginous canal are less painful and easier to remove than those in the

---

*Foreign bodies of the tracheobronchial tree are covered in Chapter 8.

bony canal. Foreign bodies may be animate (small insects) or inanimate (any small object). Beans and seeds are hygroscopic and likely to swell.

1. Diagnosis A foreign body in the ear can be asymptomatic. A feeling of fullness, decreased hearing, tinnitus and itching may occur. A live insect can create an intolerable noise. Pain is due to secondary infection or burns from hot or acidic foreign material. Otoscopy reveals the object, but it may be difficult to identify if it is encased in cerumen. The differential diagnosis includes external otitis and otitis media.

2. Complications are chiefly related to trauma to the skin of the ear canal, tympanic membrane, and middle ear structures caused by inexpert attempts at removal.

3. Treatment depends more on the age and behavior of the patient than on the type and location of the foreign body. In adults and cooperative children, the object often can be removed without anesthesia. Topical anesthesia by iontophoresis may be helpful, but a general anesthetic is necessary for the crying, uncooperative child.

Instrumental removal should not be attempted by a person unfamiliar with the anatomy of the ear. It is essential that the foreign body not be pushed farther into the ear canal. This can impact it in the bony canal making removal much more difficult, or the tympanic membrane and middle ear structures can be damaged.

Some foreign bodies can be removed by irrigation with warm water directed not at the object but at the wall of the ear canal. This is the safest method for the nonspecialist. In the case of vegetable foreign bodies (beans, seeds, etc.) or if there is any question of tympanic membrane perforation, the ear canal should not be irrigated with water but with warm oil or 95% alcohol instead. Insects should be rendered inactive by instilling alcohol or oil before removal.

Small hard objects are extracted with a small blunt hook or a dull ring curette slid past the foreign body and withdrawn. A suction tip retrieves some objects. Only in the most unusual circumstances is it necessary to surgically enlarge the bony ear canal or approach the canal through a mastoid incision.

4. Prognosis With care almost all foreign bodies are satisfactorily removed. Middle ear damage is infrequent.

V. TRACHEAL STENOSIS

Tracheal stenosis is most commonly caused by cicatrix at the site of tracheal mucosal ulceration from pressure necrosis by the balloon cuff of an endotracheal or tracheostomy tube. It also occurs at the site of tracheostomy if an excessive amount of tracheal cartilage is removed. External trauma and complications of surgery for neoplasms or tracheoesophageal fistula can produce stenosis. Partial asymptomatic obstructions can become severe rapidly and cause death if only a small amount of tracheal edema is added to the stenosis.

Dyspnea, stridor, and difficulty clearing secretions develop 10-40 days after extubation. Narrowing of the tracheal air shadow is seen on lateral x-rays of the neck. Xeroradiograms, tomograms, and contrast studies may help. Laryngoscopy and bronchoscopy differentiate tracheal stenosis from other (laryngeal or pharyngeal) causes of obstruction. Pulmonary function studies are consistent with upper airway obstruction. Late onset of dyspnea and stridor may be confused with asthma.

Tracheal stenosis due to endotracheal and tracheostomy tubes is preventable. Tracheal tubes with cuffs designed to minimize pressure necrosis (foam cuffs, large volume cuffs, and others) are available. Pressure in the cuff should be minimized, using just enough to produce a seal or even allow a small leak. The tube should remain in place with the cuff inflated for the least time possible.

Thin stenotic webs can be stretched with dilators or by passing increasingly larger bronchoscopes. Unfortunately, symptomatic stenosis often does not respond and surgical resection with end-to-end anastomosis is required. If the distal trachea is mobilized and the larynx is lowered by division of the suprahyoid muscles, as much as 3 cm of trachea can be resected and repaired primarily. The results are good.

VI. NEOPLASMS

A. BENIGN NEOPLASMS OF THE ORAL CAVITY

1. Warts, verrucae, and papillomas form folded ridges of epithelium over a scant connective tissue and vascular stalk. They are usually solitary and either sessile or pedunculated. They are excised under local or topical anesthesia.

2. Leukoplakia is a premalignant lesion that is common in heavy smokers. Whitish plaques appear on the oral mucosa; thickened, fissured areas are more suspicious of malignancy than thin, soft, smooth patches.

Correction of sources of chronic irritation (jagged teeth, ill-fitting dentures and tobacco) may reverse the leukoplakic process. Small patches may be excised completely. Larger areas require close observation and multiple biopsies at frequent intervals to detect malignancy.

3. Hemangiomas are purplish and **lymphangiomas** are pale. Either may be capillary, cavernous, or mixed. The diagnosis is made by inspection and palpation, **not** by biopsy. If there is no functional disability, observation is preferred because those tumors may resolve spontaneously. Surgical excision can be done if there is a good chance of total excision with safety. Sclerosing agents (sodium morrhuate) can be used in small amounts.

4. Median rhomboid glossitis is not a neoplasm but it resembles one. It is a congenital developmental defect caused by improper fusion of the anterior two-thirds and the posterior third of the tongue. Biopsy is unnecessary and no treatment is required.

5. Torus palatinus also is not a neoplasm; it is a mucosa-covered exostosis in the midline of the hard palate. It is usually asymptomatic and needs no treatment unless it interferes with the fitting of an upper denture. The overlying mucosa can be elevated and the bony protrusion excised with a chisel and rongeur or by dental burr. The overlying mucosa may be traumatized by hot or rough food producing a painful ulcer that might be mistaken for neoplasm. The ulcer usually heals in 7–10 days.

B. SQUAMOUS CELL CARCINOMA accounts for 95% of malignancies of the oral cavity; adenocarcinoma, melanoma, and sarcomas comprise the remainder.

1. Diagnosis   Pain is the usual presenting symptom. Advanced lesions cause bleeding, airway obstruction, and interference with swallowing and speech. Typically the cancer is an indurated ulcer, often best appreciated on bimanual palpation. The presence of suspicious nodes in the neck should be noted. Biopsy is mandatory to make the diagnosis. Bony involvement should be determined by x-rays of the mandible, palate, and sinuses. Distant metastases are sought by obtaining chest x-ray and other x-rays and isotope scans as appropriate.

The differential diagnosis includes chronic granulomatous diseases, trauma, benign neoplasms, and necrotizing angiitis (Wegener's granuloma).

2. Treatment   Oral cancer should be managed by a team of specialists including a surgeon, radiation therapist, and chemotherapist. Generally, treatment depends on the size and location of the tumor, the presence of invasion into bone, and the presence of regional or distant metastases.

Small tumors of the **uvula** can be excised completely. **Soft palate** tumors are excised or treated by radiation to the primary and its lymph drainage in the retropharynx and neck. **Small buccal mucosal** tumors are excised or irradiated;

larger lesions may require both. Radical neck dissection for cervical lymph node metastasis is done if the primary tumor is controlled. Extensive loss of tissue may require immediate or delayed plastic repair with pedicle grafts.

Floor of mouth cancer may involve part of the tongue or mandible. Intraoral excision or radiation therapy is used for small tumors. Larger tumors require removal by an external approach. If the tumor involves the periosteum or bone of the mandible, a portion of the mandible must be excised with the tumor. This can be a full thickness segment of the mandible or a marginal resection of the inner plate of bone. Radical neck dissection should be done if there are cervical metastases or if the primary tumor is extensive. The neck dissection can be done in continuity with removal of the primary tumor and segment of mandible (combined or composite resection).

The management of **tongue cancer** varies with its size and location. Small tumors of the tip can be treated by wedge excision. Cancer of the mobile anterior two-thirds of the tongue must be widely excised. Tumors measuring 1-1.5 cm can be excised by hemiglossectomy. Larger tumors require radical neck dissection. Tumors of the posterior third of the tongue have a poorer prognosis. Total or partial glossectomy with radical neck dissection and/or radiation therapy have been used for cancer at this site. If cervical lymph node metastases appear after radiation therapy has controlled the primary lesion, neck dissection should be done. Some specialists prefer radiation therapy (intraoral, external, and/or interstitial) for all tumors of the tongue.

3. Prognosis Small tumors (under 1.5-2 cm in diameter) without cervical metastasis have a 70-80% 5-year survival rate. Larger tumors have correspondingly poorer outlooks.

C. BENIGN NEOPLASMS OF NOSE AND SINUSES

1. Papilloma is common in the skin of the nasal vestibule and is easily excised. Squamous papillomas arising in the nasal chamber or paranasal sinuses present greater problems (inverting papilloma). They do not metastasize but can invade and erode vital structures locally causing proptosis, diplopia, blindness, meningitis, and death.

Nasal obstruction (usually unilateral) and the presence of an irregular, meaty polypoid mass filling the nasal chamber lead to the diagnosis. Papillomas may be mistaken for inflammatory or allergic nasal polyps or carcinoma. X-rays show involvement, and tomography demonstrates extension into bone.

Intranasal excision is inadequate treatment for these lesions. Lateral rhinotomy with complete removal of the papilloma is necessary to prevent extension and recurrence. Often the nasal sinuses, the lateral nasal wall, and at times the orbital contents must be removed. Growth through the cribriform plate or extension into the pterygomaxillary fossa are causes of failure. Radiation therapy has been used postoperatively and for recurrence with indifferent success.

2. Osteomas occur chiefly in the frontal and ethmoid sinuses. They are usually asymptomatic incidental findings on x-rays. Obstruction of the nasofrontal duct may lead to stasis and infection, and extension into the orbit may produce diplopia and proptosis. No treatment is necessary if asymptomatic. Excision is by external frontoethmoid sinusotomy.

3. Ossifying fibroma is a fibrous tumor containing bony spicules in varying amounts. They most commonly arise in the maxillary sinus and upper jaw, grow slowly, and produce symptoms by encroachment on neighboring structures. The treatment is surgical excision which must be extensive if the palate and orbit are involved.

4. Nasal polyps are nonneoplastic lesions, usually bilateral, and usually associated with allergies. The polyps are smooth, pale, and boggy in appearance. Intranasal excision followed by control of associated allergy and infection is the preferred treatment. More extensive surgical procedures are required sometimes.

D. MALIGNANT NEOPLASMS OF NOSE AND SINUSES   Squamous cell carcinoma is the most common malignancy in the nose and paranasal sinuses; papillary carcinoma, sarcoma, and lymphoma also occur.

Nasal obstruction, epistaxis, postnasal drainage, and pain in the forehead, face, or teeth are the symptoms. A meaty friable nasal mass, swelling of the cheek, signs of orbital invasion, and cranial nerve paresthesia and hypesthesia are seen. Bony involvement is shown on x-rays. Infection, foreign body, and benign neoplasms must be differentiated.

Radical excision is the treatment of choice. Unresectable lesions are managed by a drainage procedure and radiation therapy. Radical neck dissection is added if cervical nodes become involved in otherwise favorable cases.

The five year survival rate is about 50%.

E. BENIGN NEOPLASMS OF THE JAW

1. Adamantinoma (ameloblastoma) is a tumor of the enamel organ epithelium of a tooth. It occurs more often in the mandible and grows slowly causing a painless swelling of the bone. Palpation sometimes produces a crackling sensation in the thinned cortex of the bone. X-rays often show cystic features of the tumor. Biopsy makes the diagnosis. Small tumors can be excised. Large tumors may require extensive resection of the mandible with reconstruction.

2. Giant cell tumors of the mandible and maxilla are similar to giant cell tumors of bone elsewhere in the body. Although usually benign, malignant varieties occur. It is histologically indistinguishable from the brown tumor of hyperparathyroidism. Treatment is by excision.

F. PRIMARY MALIGNANT tumors are rare in the jaw.

G. BENIGN NEOPLASMS OF THE NASOPHARYNX

1. Juvenile fibroma (juvenile nasopharyngeal angiofibroma) occurs most often in adolescent males. They arise in or near the vault of the nasopharynx and are attached by either a stalk or a sessile base and can reach considerable size. Histologically the tumor is composed of a vascular connective tissue.

Juvenile fibroma causes nasal obstruction (unilateral or bilateral), epistaxis, headache, otalgia, and deafness. Bleeding can be severe. A friable, bleeding mass is visible intranasally or with indirect mirror examination. Serous otitis media occurs with auditory tube obstruction. X-ray shows a soft tissue mass in the nasopharynx, and tomography may show extension into maxillary sinus, sphenoid sinus and pterygomaxillary space. Biopsy should not be done unless complete hospital surgical facilities are available.

Surgical excision is the treatment of choice. Hemorrhage during operation is often severe and abundant quantities of whole blood must be available. Preliminary radiation (external or interstitial), estrogen therapy, cryosurgery, and ligation or embolization of the internal maxillary artery have been tried to decrease operative blood loss.

Recurrence results from incomplete excision. Improved surgical approaches have decreased the incidence of recurrence. Spontaneous involution usually occurs after age 25.

H. MALIGNANT NEOPLASMS OF THE NASOPHARYNX

1. Squamous cell carcinoma (transitional cell carcinoma, lymphoepithelioma) commonly arises in Rosenmuller's fossa. Histologically the cells may be so anaplastic as to make it difficult to determine their type, and lymphoid tissue is abundant. It is a common disease in Chinese people.

Symptoms are nasal obstruction, epistaxis, cervical mass, hearing loss, and visual disturbances. Mirror examination shows a friable mass. One half of patients have a palpable cervical mass at first examination. Any of the cranial nerves can be involved. X-ray may show erosion of the bone in the base of the skull. Intracranial extension can occur through the foramina of the base of the skull without any erosion of bone or cranial nerve involvement. CT scanning is very helpful to determine the size of the tumor. Complications are intracranial extension and cervical and distant metastasis as well as hemorrhage.

External radiation therapy is the treatment of choice for the primary tumor and for cervical metastasis. Radical neck dissection is done infrequently because it does not remove the first level of lymph node metastasis (retropharyngeal nodes).

There is about a 25% five-year survival rate. Absence of cranial nerve involvement and cervical adenopathy improves the outlook.

2. Squamous cell carcinoma of the tonsil causes a sticking sensation in the throat, pain, otalgia, interference with swallowing, and trismus. A foul, ulcerated mass in the tonsil often spreads to pillars, tongue, and palate. Cervical nodes may be involved. Lymphomas and granulomas must be distinguished.

Radiation therapy is preferred by many, sometimes followed by radical neck dissection. Radical surgical excision is used sometimes.

Five-year survival rates are 25% with cervical node involvement and 60% if these nodes are negative.

I. BENIGN NEOPLASMS OF THE LARYNX AND HYPOPHARYNX Polyps, papillomas, vocal nodules, and leukoplakia on the vocal cords produce hoarseness. Mucosal cysts in the vallecula are usually asymptomatic. Fibroma, neurofibroma (neurilemmoma), and lipoma in the hypopharyngeal wall can cause dysphagia. The diagnosis is made by indirect mirror examination or by direct laryngoscopy and biopsy. Small tumors are treated by local excision, but large tumors may require external laryngotomy for removal.

J. MALIGNANT NEOPLASMS OF THE LARYNX AND HYPOPHARYNX
Nearly all laryngeal malignancies are squamous cell carcinomas. About 60% arise on the vocal cords and the others occur in the laryngeal ventricles, false cords, aryepiglottic folds, epiglottis, arytenoid, and subglottic areas. Hypopharyngeal cancer arises in the pyriform sinuses, pharyngeal walls, and postcricoid area.

1. Diagnosis
a. Symptoms Hoarseness is the chief early symptom of vocal cord tumors. Minor throat discomfort, sometimes referred to the ear, or a mild cough may be the only early manifestations. Voice change, stridor, and dyspnea occur later with enlargement in the larynx.

b. Signs Fullness beneath the mucosa, a mass, or ulceration are seen. Biopsy should be done. Cervical metastases may be palpable.

c. X-rays Laryngograms, tomograms, and xeroradiograms help determine size and extent of tumors, especially in the ventricle and subglottic areas which are difficult to see.

2. Differential diagnosis Chronic laryngitis, leukoplakia, tuberculosis, syphillis, contact ulcer, and granuloma are differentiated by biopsy and specific tests for these diseases.

3. Complications Airway obstruction, hemorrhage, dysphagia, and effects of distant metastasis.

4. Treatment Very small (2 mm) **vocal cord tumors** can be removed endoscopically with a forceps and electrocoagulation of the base. Tumors of the middle third of the vocal cord (Stage I) can be treated by external radiation therapy or by thyrotomy and excision of the entire vocal cord (laryngofissure). Larger lesions of the vocal cord extending to the anterior commissure or the arytenoid cartilage (Stage II) or beyond (Stage III) need more extensive hemilaryngectomy or wide-field laryngectomy. True vocal cord tumors require radical neck dissection in continuity if there are palpable cervical nodes or if the primary lesion has extended to supraglottic or infraglottic structures.

Many noncordal carcinomas require total laryngectomy with or without radical neck dissection. Conservative surgical procedures are sufficient for some supraglottic and hypopharyngeal tumors. Radiation therapy alone or combined with radical surgery is used in selected cases.

K. BENIGN NEOPLASMS OF THE SALIVARY GLANDS Most neoplasms of the salivary glands are benign.

1. Benign mixed tumor (pleomorphic adenoma) is the most common benign lesion. The parotid gland is the usual site. The tumor causes slowly progressive painless swelling, and a firm nontender mass is the only finding. Biopsy should **not** be done to avoid seeding tumor into uninvolved tissue. The differential diagnosis includes sialolithiasis and sialadenitis which are usually evident because of diffuse and fluctuating enlargement of the gland; x-ray rules out sialolithiasis and, if necessary, a retrograde sialogram demonstrates sialadenitis. Preauricular lymph nodes are more mobile than parotid tumors; hyperplastic nodes within the gland usually become smaller with time. Malignant salivary tumors grow faster, are tender, and may cause paresis of the facial nerve.

Benign mixed tumor of the superficial lobe of the parotid gland should be treated by superficial lobectomy with preservation of the facial nerve; local excision or enucleation gives rise to recurrence because the tumor sends projections through the capsule. Lesions arising in the deep lobe are more difficult to remove without injury to the facial nerve, but every attempt should be made to do so. Mixed tumors of the submaxillary gland are managed by total excision of the gland with care to preserve the marginal mandibular branch of the facial nerve, the lingual, and the hypoglossal nerves.

Recurrence is infrequent after wide excision.

2. Papillary cystadenoma lymphomatosum (Warthin's tumor) occurs in the parotid gland and is bilateral in 10% of patients. They cause painless enlargement, often in the inferior pole of the superficial lobe. Lobectomy with preservation of the facial nerve is the treatment.

L. MALIGNANT TUMORS OF THE SALIVARY GLANDS may be clinically indistinguishable from benign tumors presenting as a firm mass in the gland. Rapid growth, pain, tenderness, and facial nerve involvement suggest malignancy. Definitive diagnosis depends on microscopic examination of the excised tumor specimen. Biopsy is indicated only in rare salivary gland tumors that are inoperable and highly suspicious of malignancy.

1. Squamous cell carcinoma of ductal origin in the salivary gland spreads rapidly and has a poor prognosis. Wide surgical excision with sacrifice of the facial nerve and radical neck dissection is usually necessary. Radiation therapy is an adjunct to surgery in some cases and is used alone in others.

2. Adenoid cystic carcinomas (cylindroma) occur in the major or minor salivary glands of young adults. They grow slowly and spread by direct extension, along nerve sheaths, to regional nodes, and via the blood stream. Wide excision with sacrifice of involved branches of the facial nerve and preservation of uninvolved branches followed by radiation therapy is the treatment of choice. The most unusual feature of this tumor is its tendency to recur locally or distantly 10-15 years or more after primary treatment.

3. Most **mucoepidermoid tumors** are benign but some are malignant. Since the benign or malignant nature of the tumor cannot be identified histologically it must be determined by the clinical course. A capsule is frequently very thin or absent and the tumor is adherent to surrounding structures. It is excised widely with preservation of the facial nerve if possible. If lymph node metastases are found by frozen section at the time of operation, it is obviously malignant, and sacrifice of the facial nerve and radical neck dissection are given greater consideration. Postoperative radiation therapy has been recommended but this tumor is often not radiosensitive.

M. NEOPLASMS OF BLOOD VESSELS

1. Chemodectoma (carotid body tumor) is a rare, slowly growing tumor arising in paraganglionic tissue at the carotid bifurcation. A mass in the neck is the only early symptom; pain and dysphagia occur later. The mass is fixed to the carotid bifurcation, and arteriography shows a vascular soft tissue lesion at this site.

Small tumors are excised easily; larger ones may require resection and reconstruction of the carotid artery. The prognosis is good.

2. Glomus jugulare arises from the jugular bulb and extends upward into the middle ear where it can be seen as a pink mass behind the tympanic membrane. Tinnitus and weakness of cranial nerves that exit through the jugular foramen are the symptoms. Arteriography and jugular venography are needed for thorough evaluation. Total excision is difficult, and postoperative radiation therapy may be helpful.

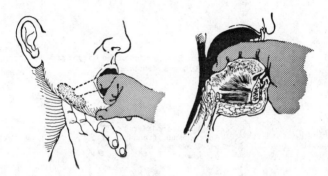

Manual Palpation of the Structures of the Floor of the Mouth

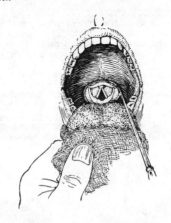

**Indirect Mirror Examination of the Larynx and
Adjacent Structures**

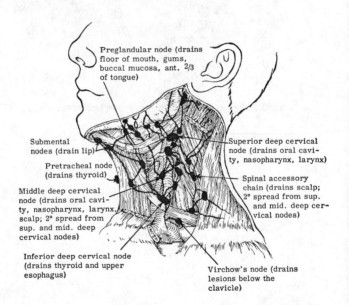

Preglandular node (drains
floor of mouth, gums,
buccal mucosa, ant. 2/3
of tongue)

Submental
nodes (drain lip)

Pretracheal node
(drains thyroid)

Middle deep cervical
node (drains oral cavi-
ty, nasopharynx, larynx,
scalp; 2° spread from
sup. and mid. deep
cervical nodes)

Superior deep cervical
node (drains oral cavi-
ty, nasopharynx, larynx)

Spinal accessory
chain (drains scalp;
2° spread from sup.
and mid. deep cer-
vical nodes)

Inferior deep cervical node
(drains thyroid and upper
esophagus)

Virchow's node (drains
lesions below the
clavicle)

Lymphatic Drainage in the Neck (Left Lateral View)
(Modified after Richards)

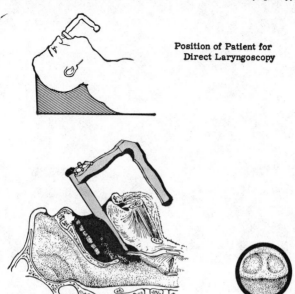

Position of Patient for Direct Laryngoscopy

Standard Distal Lighting Laryngoscope Being Introduced. Tip of laryngoscope in vallecula. At right, anterior surface of epiglottis and vallecula as seen with the laryngoscope in the position shown at left.

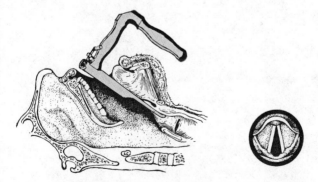

Tip of Laryngoscope Within Larynx. At right, direct view within larynx as seen with the laryngoscope in the position shown at left.

7

BREAST

Muriel Steele, MD

I. EVALUATION OF BREAST DISEASE

A. HISTORY (1) *Lump or mass:* when detected, how detected, change in size of lump with menstrual cycle. (2) *Pain:* in a lump or elsewhere in breasts; does pain vary with the menstrual cycle? (3) *Nipple bleeding or discharge:* unilateral or bilateral, when first noted, volume and character of discharge. (4) *Previous breast masses,* biopsies, etc. (5) *Menstrual history:* menarche, menopause (spontaneous or surgical), last menstrual period, anticipated next menses. (6) *Obstetrical history:* parity, date of last delivery, pregnant now? (7) *Exogenous hormones* (birth control or other). (8) *Family history* of breast disease, particularly on the maternal side. (9) *Systemic symptoms:* bone pain, jaundice, weight loss, lethargy, etc.

B. EXAMINATION Breast examination by a physician or surgeon should be performed annually in all women over age 30 and in younger women who have breast disease or who have risk factors for breast cancer. Women should be instructed in the technic of monthly self-examination.

1. Examination by the physician or surgeon

a. Inspection (1) The patient disrobes to the waist and sits erect. (Fig 7-1a). (2) Observe: size, symmetry, deformity, scars, dimpling, ulceration, skin discoloration, retraction or inversion of the nipples (ask the patient if this is a recent change). (3) Have the patient raise her arms (Fig. 7-1b): look for fixation or dimpling of the skin or change in relative position of the nipples. (4) Have the patient place hands on hips and press inward to contract the pectoralis muscles (Fig. 7-1c): look for fixation, dimpling, asymmetric movement of the breasts.

b. Palpation (1) With the patient sitting, palpate the axillary and supraclavicular areas (Fig. 7-1d and e). (2) With the patient supine, palpate the breast with her arm at her side and then with the arm abducted (Fig. 7-1f).

c. Self-examination Inspection is performed while standing in front of a mirror, and palpation of breasts and axillae is done in the supine position. Patients should be told that a ridge of thickened tissue along the inferior edge of both breasts is a normal finding. Prominent ribs or costochondral junctions may appear to patients as breast masses, but palpation of the breast with a circular motion against the chest wall will obviate this mistake. Any abnormal finding should be confirmed by a physician.

C. LABORATORY TESTS Routine laboratory tests are of little value in the evaluation of breast disease, except in patients with advanced cancer (See Section III).

D. X-RAYS

1. Mammography by various technics is helpful if no mass is palpable in a patient at high risk for cancer, if the breasts are large, if symptoms are unexplained by the physical findings, or if there are multiple masses which are difficult to evaluate clinically.

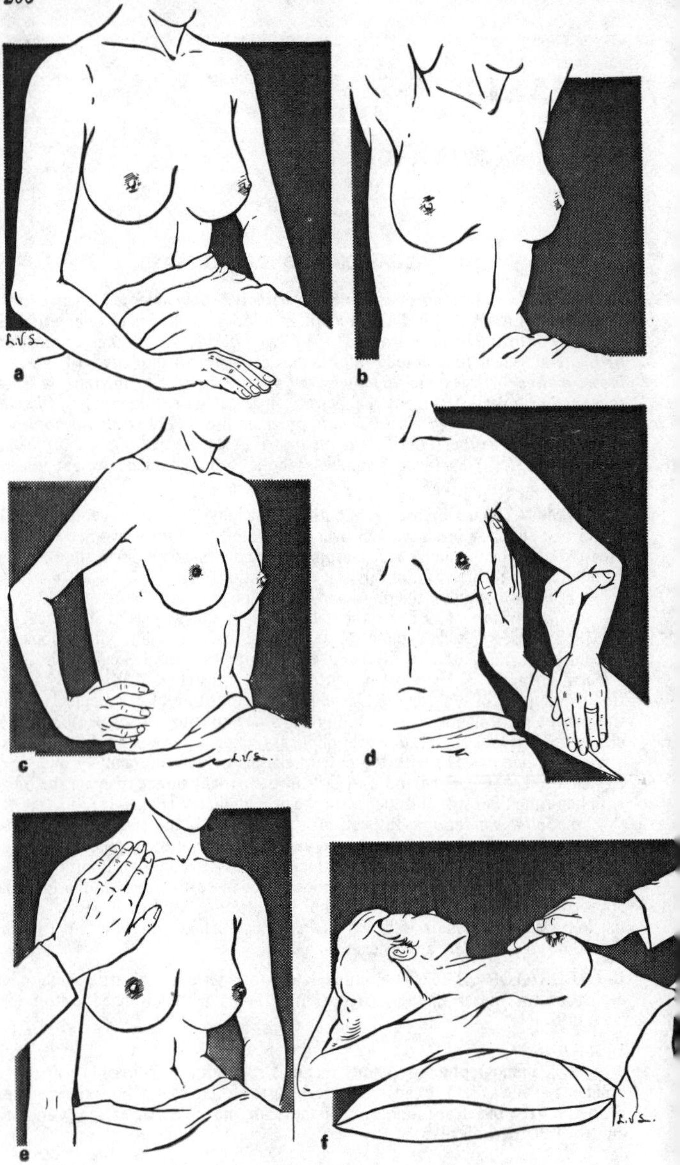

Fig. 7-1. Inspection of breasts

2. Sonography may help differentiate a cyst from a solid mass.

3. Radiographic study of a duct is obtained by instillation of contrast medium through the duct orifice in the nipple. This is a highly specialized technic.

E. SPECIAL PROCEDURES

1. Breast secretions can be studied for cytologic evidence of malignancy.

2. Needle aspiration A cystic mass is immobilized with one hand or by an assistant. The skin is painted with tincture of iodine, and a wheal is raised with local anesthetic. An 18 or 20 gauge needle attached to a small syringe is inserted through the wheal into the cyst, and the contents are aspirated. Papanicolau smears of the fluid can be obtained.

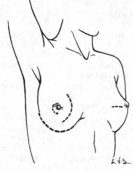

Fig. 7-2. Incisions for biopsy and for removal of benign tumors

3. Excisional biopsy Small solid masses that are clinically benign can be excised under local anesthetic as an outpatient procedure. Excision should be done under general anesthesia if the lesion is large, if it is probably malignant, or if the patient cannot tolerate a procedure under local anesthesia. Circumareolar and para-areolar incisions give the best cosmetic results (Fig. 7-2).

4. Needle biopsy Percutaneous needle biopsy of clinically malignant lesions can be done under local anesthesia.

5. Incisional biopsy Large, clinically malignant lesions can be biopsied by removing a wedge of tissue from the mass. This procedure is done under general anesthesia, a frozen section is obtained, and definitive operation is performed immediately.

II. BENIGN DISEASES OF THE FEMALE BREAST

Although most diagnostic and therapeutic efforts are aimed at detecting and treating cancer, the majority of breast disease is benign. About 25% of women have some disorder of the breasts, while only 7% of women develop breast cancer.

A. MAMMARY DYSPLASIA sometimes called 'chronic cystic mastitis', is the most common disease of the breast. It occurs most frequently in the 25–45 age group and is rarely seen in postmenopausal women who are not on exogenous estrogen therapy. The pathologic process is the formation of microscopic or gross cysts in the terminal ducts and acini.

1. Diagnosis

a. Symptoms (1) Pain or discomfort in the breasts occurring or worsening just before the menses. (2) One or more painful masses which fluctuate in size and sensitivity during the menstrual cycle. Masses may disappear and reappear at the same or new sites. (3) Asymptomatic lump(s) sometimes.

b. Signs (1) Multiple masses, thickened areas, and nodularity bilaterally, most marked in the upper outer quadrants. (2) Masses are usually tender. (3) Lesions change in number, size, and tenderness during the menstrual cycle. Examination should be repeated at different phases of the menstrual cycle or through several menstrual cycles.

c. X-rays Indications for mammography are listed in Section I.D.1.

2. Treatment

a. If all lumpy areas respond cyclically, one is reassured that the disease is mammary dysplasia. The following measures are suggested: (1) A well-supportive brassiere worn day and night. (2) Discontinuance of birth control pills. (3) Diuretics given premenstrually in severe cases. (4) Self-examination is performed monthly (just after menses), and the woman is advised to report changes or new lumps. (5) The patient is examined by a physician or surgeon every 3 months initially and then every 6 months for life.

b. A dominant mass, a very painful mass, or one which does not respond cyclically should be aspirated. Straw-colored, green, brown, or black fluid is obtained; this material may be submitted for cytologic examination. If the mass disappears completely after aspiration and does not recur on repeated examination over several weeks, no further special treatment is necessary.

c. If the lesion contains no fluid, if it fails to disappear completely, or if it recurs, it should be excised.

d. Sclerosing adenosis is a type of mammary dysplasia which forms a firm mass with indistinct borders. Excisional biopsy is required because this disease is impossible to differentiate from cancer on clinical or radiographic grounds.

3. Prognosis The disease subsides after menopause. It is uncertain whether the incidence of breast cancer is increased in patients with mammary dysplasia, but the development of cancer is more difficult to detect in dysplastic breasts and vigilance is required.

B. FIBROADENOMA is the second most common benign lesion. It occurs between 15 and 30 years of age and even earlier in black women. Fibroadenomas are rare after the menopause. These lesions grow rapidly during pregnancy.

1. Diagnosis Fibroadenoma usually is asymptomatic and is discovered accidentally. Fibroadenomas are multiple in 10-15% of cases. The tumor is firm, rubbery, nontender, spherical, discrete, and 'slippable' (so easily movable that it slips away from the examining fingers).

2. Treatment Excisional biopsy is recommended because fibroadenomas tend to enlarge and histologic proof of benignancy should be obtained. Excision can be done under local anesthesia unless the mass is very large (> 3 cm).

C. INTRADUCTAL PAPILLOMA AND NIPPLE DISCHARGE Intraductal papilloma is the most common cause of nipple discharge. The tumor arises within the ducts, usually under or near the areola. It is too small and too soft to be palpable, but it obstructs the duct and causes it to fill with serous, brown, green, or bloody fluid which is expelled at intervals. The involved duct can be localized by fingertip pressure at successive points around the areola, observing for discharge from a single duct orifice. If the lesion cannot be localized at the first visit, reexamine the patient at intervals. Treatment is by careful excision of the involved duct and adjacent breast tissue up to the nipple.

Other causes of nipple discharge include carcinoma, mammary dysplasia (see Section A), and duct ectasia (see Section D). The character of the discharge gives no clue to the cause. Carcinoma responsible for nipple discharge should be palpable beneath or close to the areola. Mammography and cytology on the fluid may help in doubtful cases. If nipple discharge persists, the breast should be explored even though no mass is palpable.

D. MAMMARY DUCT ECTASIA This uncommon lesion occurs in women over age 40. Inspissation of lipid debris causes dilatation of the ducts. The ducts rupture, fluid escapes into the surrounding tissues, and inflammation occurs (hence the other term for this disease, 'plasma cell mastitis'). The sterile inflammatory process may become secondarily infected and form abscesses.

This lesion is benign, but it can mimic cancer because retraction of the skin or nipple is a consequence of the inflammation, and usually a mass is palpable. The history of pain and erythema before retraction developed is typical of duct ectasia, but with the findings of a mass and retraction, biopsy is necessary to exclude the presence of cancer.

E. FAT NECROSIS is presumably due to trauma, although many patients do not recall any injury. The lesion is a hard irregular mass, often with retraction of the overlying skin, and it may be indistinguishable from carcinoma. Ecchymosis and tenderness are differentiating features if present. Biopsy is usually necessary to be certain the lesion is benign.

F. BREAST ABSCESSES occur in 3 different circumstances:

1. Lactating breast Abscesses most commonly arise in lactating breasts. Erythema, pain, and induration may resolve if nursing is discontinued and antibiotics are administered. At a later stage, with frank abscess formation, incision and drainage is required. The operation should be done under general anesthesia, and all loculations in the abscess should be broken up.

2. Nonlactating breast Young and middle-aged women may develop subareolar or periareolar abscesses which tend to recur after drainage. The involved ducts and the scarred tissue should be excised during a quiescent interval.

3. Mammary duct ectasia This lesion, discussed above (Section D), is the least common cause of breast abscess.

G. MISCELLANEOUS BENIGN CONDITIONS

1. Subcutaneous phlebitis (Mondor's disease) Spontaneous inflammation in subcutaneous veins occurs along the anterior axillary fold and extends downward onto the lateral aspect of the breast. The lesion is very painful and is treated by warm compresses and analgesics. The overlying skin may retract, raising the suspicion of carcinoma, but the history and the long linear skin retraction are typical of phlebitis.

2. Costochondritis (Tietze's syndrome) Pain and tenderness over the third or fourth costochondral junction may be thought by the patient to represent breast disease. No treatment is necessary; the process resolves after several weeks.

III. CARCINOMA OF THE FEMALE BREAST

Cancer of the breast affects about 70 women per 100,000 annually, and the incidence appears to be rising. Breast cancer is the leading cause of death from cancer in women, and it causes more deaths than any other disease or injury in women ages 40–44. The 5-year survival rate has increased, but the overall mortality rate in women with this disease has not changed during the last 25 years.

The major risk factors which make it more likely that breast cancer will develop are carcinoma in the opposite breast and breast cancer in siblings, mother, or maternal female relatives. Minor risk factors include low parity and early menarche. The use of rauwolfia compounds appears to increase the incidence; the use of birth control pills has not been found to do so.

A. DIAGNOSIS

1. Symptoms A painless lump in the breast. Nipple discharge is uncommon but may be the only symptom. Sometimes erythema, hardness, enlargement, shrinkage, retraction, or asymmetry of one breast. Symptoms of metastatic disease.

2. Signs A hard, nontender, minimally mobile mass with indistinct borders. Skin or nipple retraction. Nipple discharge (infrequently). Locally advanced carcinoma: edema, erythema, or ulceration of the skin, fixation to the chest wall, enlargement or shrinkage of the breast. Axillary and/or supraclavicular lymphadenopathy. Signs of metastatic disease (e.g., hepatomegaly, bone tenderness).

3. Laboratory tests There are no abnormalities in localized disease. Elevated serum alkaline phosphate may reflect hepatic metastases. Hypercalcemia may occur with advanced malignancy.

4. X-ray findings Chest x-ray may show metastases. Mammography is most useful in patients with equivocal lesions, in patients with symptoms (e.g., nipple discharge) not explained by physical findings, to survey the opposite breast when cancer is diagnosed (about 10% have synchronous or metachronous cancer in the contralateral breast), and in patients at high risk (1 major or 2 minor risk factors). A mammogram may detect cancers that are too small to palpate. A benign mammographic appearance is not a reason to avoid biopsy of a dominant mass; false-negatives occur on mammography.

Skeletal x-rays are not obtained unless the patient has bone symptoms, because these x-rays are less sensitive than the bone scan in detecting metastases.

5. Special tests Biopsy the breast mass (see below). A radioisotope bone scan is recommended routinely; suspicious areas should be studied by x-ray and possibly biopsy. Liver scan is performed if metastases are suspected on clinical or chemical grounds. Brain scan is done if there is a recent history of headaches or changes in mentation. Assay for estrogen receptors in the cancer obtained by biopsy mastectomy.

B. DIFFERENTIAL DIAGNOSIS hinges on the results of biopsy. The clinical diagnosis of cancer is accurate in only 80-90% of cases. Any dominant mass, skin or nipple retraction, or suspicious mammographic lesion must be biopsied. The surgeon must decide whether to do the biopsy under local or general anesthesia; the metastatic workup is completed before biopsy under general anesthesia because mastectomy is usually done at the same operation if the lesion is malignant on frozen section.

Small lesions can be excised under local anesthesia in outpatients; there is no evidence that delay of a few days between biopsy and mastectomy adversely affects outcome. Large lesions can be biopsied by percutaneous needle in outpatients; about 10% of cancers are false-negative by this test, so open biopsy is required if the needle biopsy is benign.

Suspicious mammographic lesions that are not palpable can be localized with a needle positioned by the mammographer immediately before biopsy under general anesthesia. A drop of methylene blue is injected, the needle withdrawn, and the entire stained area is excised with a wide margin. Mammograms are then obtained on the specimen to prove the suspicious area has been excised; further treatment depends on results of the frozen section.

C. CLINICAL STAGING Several clinical staging systems are used to evaluate the extent of disease and to help determine treatment. Table 7-1 shows the International and the American Systems.

D. SPECIAL FORMS OF BREAST CANCER Breast cancers are a variety of histologic types, the most common of which is infiltrating ductal carcinoma. This lesion and most of the others (infiltrating adenocarcinoma, medullary carcinoma, invasive lobular carcinoma) share similar biologic characteristics and are treated as outlined in the next section. Lobular carcinoma-in-situ is an exception; it rarely metastasizes, is bilateral in 20-30% of cases, and is treated by wide local or quadrant excision. The two types of cancer listed below are uncommon clinical forms.

Table 7-1. Clinical staging of cancer of the breast

Stage	International System[1]	American System[2]
I	0 No distant metastases. 1 Tumor of 5 cm. or less. 2 Skin fixation absent or incomplete. 3 Nipple may be retracted, or Paget's disease may be present. 4 Pectoral muscle or chest wall fixation absent. 5 No ipsilateral axillary nodes palpable.	0 No distant metastases. 1 Tumor of any size. 2 Skin not involved or involved locally with Paget's disease. 3 Skin attachment (dimpling) or nipple retraction. 4 No pectoral muscle or chest wall attachment. 5 No clinically palpable axillary lymph nodes (no metastases suspected).
II	0-4 As above. 5 Ipsilateral axillary nodes palpable but movable.	0-4 As above. 5 Clinically palpable axillary lymph nodes that are not fixed (metastases suspected).
III	0 As above. 1 Tumor more than 5 cm. in diameter or 2 Skin fixation complete, or skin involvement wide of tumor or 3 Peau d'orange present in tumor area or wide of tumor or 4 Pectoral muscle fixation complete or incomplete, or chest wall fixation or 5 Ipsilateral axillary nodes fixed or 6 Ipsilateral supraclavicular or infraclavicular nodes movable or fixed or 7 Arm edema.	0 As above. 1 Tumor of any size. 2 Skin infiltration or ulceration or 3 Peau d'orange or skin edema or 4 Pectoral muscle or chest wall attachment or 5 Clinically palpable ipsilateral axillary nodes fixed to one another or to other structures (metastases suspected) or 6 Clinically palpable ipsilateral infraclavicular lymph nodes fixed to one another or to other structures (metastases suspected).
IV	Distant metastases, regardless of the condition of the primary tumor and regional lymph nodes.	Clinical, radiographic evidence of metastases except those to ipsilateral axillary or infraclavicular nodes.

[1] Committee on Clinical Stage Classification and Applied Statistics, Malignant Tumors of the Breast, 1960-1964. International Union Against Cancer, Paris, 1960.
[2] American Joint Committee on Cancer Staging and End Results Reporting: Clinical Staging System for Cancer of the Breast. American College of Surgeons, 1962.

1. Paget's disease is intraductal carcinoma which causes crusting, erosion, or ulceration of the nipple. The significance of this finding is often underestimated by the patient or the physician because a mass usually is not palpable and a dermatologic disorder is suspected. The correct diagnosis is established by biopsy of the nipple. Paget's disease metastasizes to regional lymph nodes and should be treated like other carcinomas of the breast.

2. Inflammatory carcinoma This is the most malignant form of breast carcinoma and may be caused by a variety of histologic types. Invasion of subdermal lymphatics results in edema, erythema, and warmth which extends rapidly to involve a third or more of the breast. The edematous skin appears pitted like an orange peel (peau d'orange). The cancer metastasizes rapidly and widely and is surgically incurable. Needle biopsy or a small incisional biopsy confirms the diagnosis. Radiation therapy is the palliative treatment of choice; radical operations have no place in this disease.

3. Cystosarcoma phyllodes This lesion is a highly cellular, rapidly growing variant of fibroadenoma. It rarely metastasizes, but it recurs locally after inadequate excision. Treatment is by excision with a wide margin of surrounding tissue.

E. CURATIVE TREATMENT Cure is the objective in patients with Stage I or II disease and in selected patients with Stage III lesions (Table 7-1). The selection of a therapeutic method is an emotionally charged issue for which supporting data are incomplete.

1. Surgical

a. Standard radical mastectomy involves en bloc excision of the breast, pectoral muscles, and axillary lymph nodes, sometimes with a skin graft to cover the defect. This operation was the generally accepted treatment of choice until about 15 years ago and is still preferred by some surgeons. For lesions which lie close to the pectoral fascia, radical mastectomy is the only surgical means of encompassing the tumor.

b. Modified radical mastectomy is the same operation except that the pectoralis muscles are preserved. This procedure, especially if done through a transverse incision, gives better cosmetic results and arm function and may be as effective as radical mastectomy in achieving cure. Many centers have adopted this type of mastectomy as the treatment of choice.

c. Other procedures have few advocates at present.

Extended radical mastectomy involves removal of the internal mammary lymph nodes in addition to standard radical mastectomy. Survival is not greatly increased by this procedure.

Simple mastectomy is removal of just the breast, leaving the pectoralis muscles and the axillary nodes. The axillary nodes are involved histologically in 30% of patients with clinically negative nodes, so this procedure is seldom the only therapeutic measure if cure is the objective.

Local excision or 'lumpectomy' effectively removes small primary cancers but does not remove axillary metastases or foci of synchronous cancer in the same breast.

d. Complications of mastectomy Wound seromas, edema of the arm, and stiffness of the shoulder are complications of mastectomy. Edema of minor extent can result from excision of lymphatic channels in the axilla, but significant edema usually is the consequence of postoperative wound infection or later infection in the hand or arm. The patient must always avoid breaks in the skin or injections in the ipsilateral hand or arm after mastectomy. Elevation and elastic support are required for established chronic edema.

Exercises to prevent stiffness of the shoulder should begin as soon as the skin flaps are adherent to the chest wall.

The psychological trauma of mastectomy is managed by preoperative and postoperative counseling. The American Cancer Society has a program called

'Reach for Recovery' in which volunteer mastectomy patients give emotional support to recently operated patients.

   e. Reconstructive procedures after mastectomy Many women are rehabilitated by a well-fitting prosthesis, but others express interest in surgical reconstruction of the breast. A subcutaneous silastic implant can be considered after local control of cancer is personably assured. An areola can be fashioned from labial tissue.

   2. Radiation therapy with or without simple mastectomy, is another therapeutic option, particularly for advanced lesions (Stage III) that radical operations are unlikely to cure.

   3. Adjuvant therapy after curative surgery

   a. Radiation therapy Preoperative or postoperative radiation therapy has the goal of reducing local recurrence in the chest wall and sterilizing the supraclavicular and internal mammary lymph nodes. Carcinomas arising in the inner quadrants have a high incidence of metastases to the internal mammary nodes, and these patients are candidates for radiation therapy. Other indications are tumor at the surgical margins, numerous involved axillary lymph nodes, or tumor widely disseminated in the breast. Preoperative irradiation is used for selected cases of locally advanced disease.

   b. Chemotherapy C-M-F (cytoxan-methotrexate-5-fluorouracil) is a promising adunct. It is given at intervals for a year in patients with 4 or more positive axillary lymph nodes. L-PAM (L-phenylalanine mustard) is probably less effective in prolonging the disease-free interval. It is too early to tell whether C-M-F will improve long-term survival.

F. PALLIATIVE TREATMENT is given to patients with distant metastases, Stage III patients who are unsuitable for curative procedures, and patients whose disease recurs after curative treatment. Treatment is directed at local control of the primary tumor and systemic control of distant metastases. Management decisions require the combined efforts of surgeons, radiation oncologists, and medical oncologists.

   1. Local control is obtained by local excision, simple mastectomy, or radiation therapy.

   2. Localized metastases, such as symptomatic bone lesions, are treated by irradiation.

   3. Chemotherapy C-M-F, with or without prednisone, is the chemotherapeutic regimen of choice without respect to menopausal status. Approximately 65% of patients respond favorably. When treatment fails after initial response, a combination of cytoxan and adriamycin can be tried. These regimens may change with more experience or as new drugs appear.

   4. Hormonal therapy Samples of the primary or metastatic tumor should be assayed for estrogen receptors. Preliminary evidence suggests that cancers with a high level of estrogen receptors are more responsive to hormonal manipulation.

   a. Oophorectomy is recommended in premenopausal patients with disseminated disease.

   b. Exogenous *estrogen* therapy may benefit late postmenopausal patients. One program is diethylstilbestrol 5 mg orally t.i.d.

   c. Androgen therapy may be helpful in premenopausal women with osseous metastases; androgens usually are given after oophorectomy.

   d. Corticosteroids are indicated for tumors which do not respond to other endocrine therapy.

   e. Hypophysectomy or *adrenalectomy* achieves regression in about 30% of patients, especially if the tumor responded previously to oophorectomy or administration of hormones.

G. PROGNOSIS The patient should be examined every 3-4 months for 3 years and every 6 months thereafter for life. Most recurrences appear within 3 years, but extremely long intervals between initial treatment and recurrence are not unusual. The opposite breast should be carefully examined in these follow-up visits.

The 5-year survival rates for different stages are shown in Table 7-2.

Table 7-2. Five-year survival rates according
to stage of breast cancer

Stage	International System	American System
I	80%	75%
II	70%	65%
III	50%	45%
IV	None	None

IV. LESIONS OF THE MALE BREAST

A. GYNECOMASTIA   A tender discoid enlargement beneath the areola, usually bilateral, is common in adolescence. It subsides within a year in most cases.

Men age 50–70 also develop gynecomastia characterized by a tender central mass. Bilateral enlargement may be idiopathic, but diseases such as hepatic cirrhosis, testicular or adrenal cortical tumors, hyperthyroidism can be responsible. The use of reserpine and marijuana is said to cause gynecomastia. The idiopathic variety often subsides spontaneously. Biopsy is necessary if breast cancer is a possibility, but otherwise the only indication for excision is cosmetic.

B. CARCINOMA   Breast cancer is rare in men. It usually occurs after age 50, it tends to metastasize early, and the prognosis is worse than for the female patient.

The clinical findings are a painless lump, with retraction and sometimes ulceration or nipple discharge. On examination the mass is firm, nontender, has indistinct borders, and frequently is fixed to skin or underlying fascia.

1. Curative treatment   Mastectomy and axillary node dissection are performed on patients selected for operation by the same criteria as for the female patient.

2. Palliative treatment   Castration is the most successful palliative treatment at present. Radiation therapy is given to localized metastases. The role of hormonal therapy and chemotherapy is as yet unclear because clinical experience is limited.

8

PULMONARY SYSTEM

Arthur N. Thomas, MD

I. GENERAL PRINCIPLES

A. DIAGNOSTIC AND THERAPEUTIC PROCEDURES

1. Thoracentesis

a. Preparation of the patient The site of the tap is selected by x-ray, fluoroscopy, or physical examination. When there is a large basilar effusion or total hydrothorax, the best site of aspiration is usually the seventh or eighth interspace in the posterior axillary line. The patient is placed in a comfortable sitting position, leaning slightly forward on a padded stand or supported by an attendant. Premedication with a barbiturate or narcotic is optional. The skin of the chest wall is prepared with antiseptic, and draped.

b. Technic of the tap (Fig. 8-1) (Aseptic technic must be used throughout.) The entire thickness of the chest wall, including the parietal pleura, is infiltrated with 5–10 ml of 1% lidocaine through a #22 gauge needle. Thoracentesis is virtually painless if this is properly done. A short-bevel needle (7.5–10 cm long, 18–13 gauge) is attached by a 3-way stopcock to a 20–50 ml syringe. A needle through which is passed a plastic catheter (Intracath) is an alternative. With firm, steady pressure the needle is advanced into the pleural space. In order to avoid injury to the intercostal nerve and vessels, pass the needle through the chest wall at the lower margin of the intercostal space (except when making a tap on the anterior chest wall, in which case the needle is passed through the center of the interspace). A clamp may be placed on the needle to steady it at the chest wall. Care is taken during aspiration to prevent air from entering the chest.

c. Volume of fluid removed The amount of fluid removed at one sitting depends upon circumstances. A total of 2000 ml can often be gradually evacuated at one sitting from a large effusion. If the patient complains of a feeling of tightness in the chest, cough, palpitation, fatigue, faintness, or other untoward symptoms, slow the rate of aspiration or discontinue until another occasion.

d. Laboratory examination of pleural fluid may include one or more of the following: total volume, odor, color, turbidity, viscosity, coagulability, specific gravity; smear for Gram's and acid-fast stains; total and differential blood cell count; aerobic, anaerobic, and acid-fast cultures; cytologic study for neoplastic cells; histologic study of sediment from a centrifuged specimen.

2. Tube thoracostomy
Closed drainage of the pleural space is obtained by tube thoracostomy. Chest tubes (one or two) are used routinely after thoracotomy, and they are required in the management of traumatic or spontaneous pneumothorax, hemothorax, or recurrent pleural effusions.

The older technic of tube thoracostomy by passing the tube through a trocar is seldom used now. It is safer to insert the tube through an opening made in

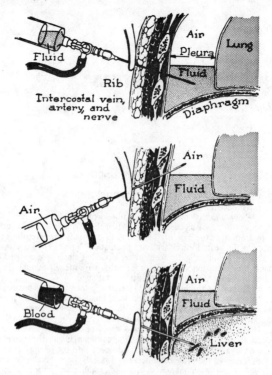

Fig. 8-1. Thoracentesis. *Top:* A successful tap with fluid obtained. Note the position of the needle with relation to the intercostal bundle, and the use of the clamp to steady the needle at skin level. *Center:* Air is obtained as the needle is shifted upward. *Bottom:* A bloody tap results from an excessively low position of the needle with puncture of the liver.

the chest wall with a hemostat after incision of the skin with a scalpel. This method allows insertion of a finger into the pleural space to be certain that the pleural cavity, not the abdomen, has been entered, and also to ensure that adhesions of the lung to the pleura will not result in damage to the lung when the tube is inserted.

The tube should be clamped during insertion and immediately connected to waterseal drainage after it is secured to the chest wall with a suture. Care of chest tubes is described under Postoperative Care in this section.

3. **Bronchoscopy** Fiberoptic bronchoscopes are superior to the older, rigid metal instruments. Bronchoscopy requires only topical anesthesia and is easily performed. Bronchoscopy should be done for the diagnosis of tracheobronchial lesions; biopsies, brushings, and washings for cytology can be obtained.

4. Mediastinoscopy This procedure is performed by passing a short endoscope into the upper mediastinum through a small transverse incision just above the suprasternal notch, under general anesthesia. Biopsy of mediastinal nodes and masses is possible as far down as the carina and upper main-stem bronchi. When nodes are not palpable in the supraclavicular areas, mediastinoscopy offers a better chance of yielding a positive histologic diagnosis than scalene node biopsy in patients with thoracic disease.

5. Scalene node biopsy The anterior scalene and paratracheal nodes may be excised for diagnostic purposes if they are enlarged. Mediastinoscopy has replaced routine biopsy of clinically uninvolved scalene nodes.

6. Open lung biopsy through a limited thoracotomy is indicated to obtain a wedge of lung tissue for pathology and culture. It is used in selected patients with pulmonary infiltrates requiring definitive diagnosis as a guide to specific treatment (e.g., a patient with lymphoma receiving intensive chemotherapy in whom pulmonary infiltrate may be either a neoplasm or an infection).

7. Percutaneous aspiration and biopsy Tumors and abscesses located near the chest wall can be biopsied or aspirated percutaneously under radiographic control. The possibility of spreading tumor or infection should be considered in the decision to use this diagnostic test.

B. PREOPERATIVE AND POSTOPERATIVE CARE

1. Preoperative evaluation It is necessary to evaluate patients for their ability to withstand thoracotomy, particularly if pulmonary resection is planned. Tests of pulmonary function and preparation of patients with chronic respiratory disease are discussed in Chapter 2.

2. Postoperative care The immediate objective of management after thoracic surgery or trauma is complete expansion and normal function of the lung without residual air or fluid in the chest.

a. Position and ambulation

(1) The patient should be placed in a semi-sitting position as soon as tolerated; this makes breathing and coughing more efficient.

(2) Pneumonectomy patients should lie alternately on the back and on the operated side; if such a patient is placed on his normal side, severe respiratory embarrassment may result.

(3) Ambulation should be started as soon as possible (usually on the day following operation). Breathing exercises and other exercises to mobilize the shoulder girdle and thoracic cage should be taught preoperatively and encouraged throughout the convalescent period.

b. Prevention of atelectasis See Chapter 2.

c. Pain relief The dosage of narcotics given to thoracic patients should be individualized. Pain relief sufficient to make coughing bearable is essential, but depression of respirations and cough reflex must be minimized. Barbiturates can often be used for sedation to reduce the need for narcotics. Blocking of the intercostal nerves with marcaine can be used intraoperatively or after operation or injury. Several spaces above and below the operative wound or site of injury are injected.

d. Ventilatory assistance See Chapter 2.

e. Management of chest tubes One or more chest tubes for postoperative drainage of fluid and air are usually placed at thoracotomy through the intercostal spaces. (Tubes are rarely used when a pneumonectomy has been performed.) Continuous functioning of these tubes is essential to ensure full lung expansion and obliteration of the pleural space. The tubes must be inspected every few hours, must not be blocked for long periods, and must never be opened to the air. Tubes should be attached at the operating table to gentle suction with a waterseal incorporated into the system. Modern versions of the 3-bottle suction are available in disposable plastic form.

When an air leak from the lung is present, sufficient suction should be applied to the chest catheter so that bubbles appear in the waterseal bottle on expiration or cough but not on inspiration. The amount of suction usually required is 15-25 cm of water. Strong suction (up to 40 cm of water or more) to 'pull out' the lung to the chest wall and seal the leak may occasionally be successful. Chest tubes are removed when they have been blocked for 24 hours.

Alveolar air leaks may continue for days and occasionally weeks after segmental resection or lobectomy. These usually seal if tube drainage and suction are maintained. If an undrained air space of significant size persists, a tube should be placed in it for closed drainage. Small, uninfected air pockets usually resorb completely without drainage.

C. COMPLICATIONS

1. Atelectasis and pneumonia   See Chapter 2.

2. Chest fluid and empyema   Fluid or blood occasionally accumulates in the chest in spite of tube drainage. Small amounts of uninfected fluid and blood will resorb without incident. Fluid of sufficient volume to be apparent on x-ray should usually be removed as completely as possible by thoracentesis, and culture should be obtained. If the fluid is infected (empyema), complete evacuation by repeated thoracenteses or by tube thoracostomy is indicated. Until sensitivity tests can be completed, a systemic antibiotic is administered empirically, then altered as necessary when sensitivity studies are known.

Complete removal of air and fluid from the chest and full expansion of the lung postoperatively are the most important means of preventing empyema.

3. Bronchopleural fistula (an air leak from a bronchus into the pleural space) may or may not be associated with an empyema. The fistula usually opens within the first 1-2 weeks after pulmonary resection. Many will close with prolonged tube drainage; others require open drainage by rib resection. When simpler measures fail, suture of the fistula with buttressing by pedicle graft is necessary.

II. TRAUMA

A. RIB FRACTURES   Direct violence is the usual cause of rib fractures, but pathologic fractures may occur with minimal force at sites of metastatic malignancy or bone disease. **Flail chest** is movement in and out with respiration of a segment of chest wall isolated by multiple rib fractures. Ventilation is severely impaired in these patients.

1. Symptoms and signs   Pain, sharply localized to the fracture site and aggravated by breathing and other motions of the rib cage, is typical. Limitation of respiratory motion on the injured side is often present. Tenderness and sometimes crepitation at the fracture site. Severe injury may be complicated by subcutaneous emphysema, pneumothorax, and hemothorax.

These findings are diagnostic of rib fracture even if chest x-rays with detailed views of the ribs do not demonstrate the fracture.

Fractured ribs over the spleen or liver should raise the question of associated injuries of those structures. Fracture of the first or second ribs denotes severe trauma; the possibility of associated major vascular injury should be considered and ruled out by angiography.

2. Complications   Atelectasis and pneumonitis frequently follow rib fractures in elderly persons. Respiratory failure develops in patients with flail chest.

3. Treatment

a. All patients with flail chest, young patients with multiple rib fractures, and elderly patients with any rib fractures must be hospitalized.

b. The pain of uncomplicated rib fracture is best controlled by analgesics or intercostal nerve block. In minor fractures, placement of a wide band of self-retaining web belting around the lower thorax reduces chest motion and pain. Multiple fractures with slight hypermobility of a segment of chest wall are an indication for localized strapping over the mobile segment to control pain and slight paradoxical motion.

   c. Severe thoracic trauma with multiple fractures and flail chest require immediate intubation with a cuffed endotracheal tube. Several weeks of positive pressure ventilation may be necessary before the chest wall becomes stabilized. Tracheostomy is done if chest wall stabilization has not occurred after 2 or 3 weeks. A tracheostomy tube with a low pressure cuff controlled by a pilot balloon is preferred. Intensive pulmonary care is required (see Chapter 2). Operative stabilization of the flail segment is required occasionally.

B. FRACTURE OF THE STERNUM is caused by severe direct trauma, as in steering wheel injury. Multiple rib fractures and other injuries are usually also present. Contusion of the heart is not uncommon. Severe precordial pain and dyspnea are the chief symptoms. Crepitus and deformity of the sternum may be noted.

   In most cases, the only treatment required is rest in the sitting position, pain relief with narcotics, and intercostal nerve block for associated rib fractures. If the chest wall is excessively mobile, internal stabilization by controlled mechanical ventilation is the usual treatment. This must be continued for days or weeks until the chest wall is stabilized. When there is severe chest wall deformity, operative fixation is indicated.

C. HEMOTHORAX   Bleeding from the pulmonary parenchyma tends to be self-limited. Continued bleeding usually originates in the chest wall, diaphragm, mediastinum, or hilus. Several liters of blood may accumulate in the thorax. In 75% of patients, the blood remains fluid.

   1. Symptoms and signs depend upon the extent of the hemothorax and the associated injuries. If large collections of blood are present, shock and physical signs of chest fluid are seen.

   2. Treatment is directed toward immediate replacement of blood loss and closed drainage by tube thoracostomy. Other general supportive measures are also instituted. If marked hemorrhage continues or recurs (as indicated by reappearance of shock or continued loss of 100-200 ml or more of blood every hour through the thoracostomy tube), operation should be considered. Most such persistent bleeding is from the intercostal vessels. Only 10-20% of patients require operation.

   When hemopneumothorax is present, the early placement of large bore chest tubes through both the upper anterior and the lower posterolateral chest wall may be necessary to achieve complete evacuation of air and blood and full lung expansion. The intrathoracic condition is monitored by hemodynamic events. Some patients require special studies such as arteriography for definitive diagnosis.

D. TRAUMATIC PNEUMOTHORAX   Pneumothorax may be caused by an open 'sucking' wound in the chest wall or, more commonly, an air leak in an injured lung. It can also be caused by injury to major airways or the esophagus.

   1. Sucking wounds of the thorax   These must be closed immediately with a bulky occlusive dressing of petrolatum gauze held in place by adhesive or a bandage encircling the chest. Open pneumothorax causes marked to-and-fro shifting of the mediastinum during respiration ('mediastinal flutter') which must be promptly controlled to prevent respiratory and circulatory failure. Surgical closure of the wound in the chest wall is carried out as soon as the patient's condition permits. Meanwhile, air is evacuated from the chest as described below.

   2. Closed pneumothorax is caused by air leak from the lung, tracheobronchial tree or esophagus. It may result either from a penetrating chest wound or blunt injury.

a. Simple pneumothorax Pneumothorax accompanies many blunt and penetrating chest injuries and is often associated with hemothorax. When lung collapse is no more than about 10%, special treatment is not necessary. If there is lung collapse of more than 25% initially, or if pneumothorax recurs after thoracentesis, tube thoracostomy with placement of a catheter in the anterior upper chest through the second or third interspace is indicated. A tube through a lower interspace is also required for associated hemothorax. Gentle suction (15-25 cm of water) is applied for 3-5 days or until blocking of the catheter indicates that expansion is complete and the lung adherent.

b. Tension pneumothorax See page 229.

E. SUBCUTANEOUS AND MEDIASTINAL EMPHYSEMA Rib fractures, chest wounds, traumatic rupture of the trachea or a major bronchus, spontaneous pneumothorax, and pulmonary resection are occasionally followed by subcutaneous emphysema. In advanced cases, emphysema extends from head to foot and produces an alarming degree of swelling and crepitation, especially of the head, neck, and scrotum. Air in the tissues causes little harm and, as a rule, requires no treatment.

Attention should be directed toward correction of the underlying cause. Pneumothorax should be controlled by tube thoracostomy, and irritating, useless cough should be minimized. Major air leaks in the lung or tracheobronchial tree may require surgical repair (see below).

Marked emphysema of the mediastinum will on rare occasions produce sufficient tension to threaten life. If dyspnea, cyanosis, tachycardia, and shock progress in spite of other measures, tracheostomy or cervical mediastinotomy is indicated. Tracheostomy serves to control respirations, remove secretions, and reduce intratracheal pressure during coughing. Mediastinotomy (under local anesthesia) consists of blunt dissection into the superior mediastinum through a transverse incision in the suprasternal notch to permit the egress of air. The possibility of an esophageal injury should be considered.

F. TRAUMATIC RUPTURE OF THE TRACHEA OR BRONCHI Severe crushing trauma to the chest may cause injury to the trachea or major bronchi. Bronchial rupture, usually within 1-2 cm of the carina, occurs about four times as often as tracheal tear. Tracheobronchial injuries are often overlooked.

1. Symptoms and signs include dyspnea, subcutaneous emphysema, cyanosis, pain, hemoptysis, shock, cough, pneumothorax, extensive atelectasis, and hemothorax. Chest films and bronchoscopy are indicated. The diagnosis may be overlooked until weeks or months after the injury. X-rays then usually show complete atelectasis of the involved portion of lung.

2. Treatment is by suture of the tear if the patient's other injuries do not contraindicate thoracotomy. Emergency operation is usually required to relieve airway obstruction or to correct uncontrollable air leak, tracheobronchial hemorrhage, or rapidly advancing mediastinal emphysema. Chronic stricture with obstruction due to delayed treatment requires bronchoplastic operation. The distal lung, although collapsed, is often functional when reexpanded; pulmonary resection should therefore be reserved for cases with irreversible damage.

G. PULMONARY CONTUSION Contusion of the lung results from blunt or penetrating trauma. Rupture of alveoli, extravasation of blood, and transudation of fluid into the injured area lead to airway obstruction and atelectasis. Copious bloody secretions, chest pain, and evidence of respiratory distress develop 12-24 hours after the injury. X-rays show opacification of variable amounts of the parenchyma. Intensive pulmonary care is required.

H. PULMONARY LACERATION Laceration of the lung is usually caused by penetrating injury. Pneumothorax and hemothorax are treated as outlined above.

These measures usually succeed in expanding the lung out to the pleural surface where it adheres and the laceration heals.

III. TRACHEOBRONCHIAL FOREIGN BODY

Infants, children, and intoxicated, anesthetized, and unconscious individuals are most likely to aspirate foreign bodies. Coughing, choking, and cyanosis may occur immediately after inhalation but often subside for a variable period. Depending upon the size, nature, and site of lodgement of the foreign body, later findings may include cough, wheezing, atelectasis, or pulmonary infection. Unless the foreign body is radiopaque, x-ray evidences are indirect: obstructive emphysema, atelectasis, or pneumonitis. Intermittent findings of this nature, especially in children, are highly suggestive of foreign body. Bronchoscopy should be performed and removal of the foreign body attempted. If successful, inflammatory reactions usually subside promptly; if unsuccessful, thoracotomy and bronchotomy or resection are necessary. Foreign bodies in the tracheobronchial tree should always be removed, since prolonged retention usually leads to bronchiectasis or abscess formation requiring pulmonary resection.

IV. DISEASES OF THE CHEST WALL

PECTUS EXACAVATUM (Funnel Breast) is a congenital, hereditary malformation characterized by depression of the sternum below the gladiomanubrial junction with symmetric inward bending of the costal cartilages. As the infant develops, kyphoscoliosis may also occur. Severe degrees of funnel breast very rarely embarrass pulmonary and cardiac function. As a rule, the only disturbance is cosmetic. Operative treatment may be indicated for either reason. The preferred operation consists of resection of all the deformed costal cartilages with extensive mobilization of the sternum to allow its elevation to a normal position. Lesser procedures fail. The best results are obtained between the ages of 4 and 8. Successful surgery significantly improves appearance but often will not correct the deformity completely.

V. DISEASES OF THE PLEURA

A. SYMPTOMS AND SIGNS **Pleuritic pain** is chest pain associated with inspiration and expiration. Pleuritic pain arises in the parietal pleura or diaphragm; the visceral pleura contains no pain fibers. Respiratory excursion may be limited on the affected side. Acute inflammation is associated with tenderness in the intercostal spaces. A friction rub may be audible. If pleural effusion develops, pleuritic pain and the friction rub lessen, tactile fremitus to the spoken voice diminishes, and there is dullness to percussion. Breath sounds may be exaggerated or bronchial in the area of effusion.

B. PLEURAL EFFUSION is endogenous fluid in the pleural space. **Hydrothorax** refers to a serous effusion, either a transudate or an exudate. **Pyothorax** is synonymous with **empyema** and is discussed below. **Hemothorax** refers to blood in the pleural space, and **chylothorax** is the accumulation of chyle.

Pleural effusions may result from diseases of the mediastinum, lungs, or chest wall. Thoracentesis should be performed to obtain fluid for examination. The differential diagnosis is listed in Table 8-1. Transudates occur in congestive heart failure, renal disease, and cirrhosis; the specific gravity is less than 1.016 and the protein content is <3 gm/100 ml. Exudates have a higher specific gravity and protein content.

Table 8-1. Differential diagnosis of pleural effusions.*

	Tuberculosis	Malignancy	Congestive failure	Pneumonia and other non-tuberculous infections	Rheumatoid arthritis and collagen disease	Pulmonary embolism
Clinical context	Younger patient with history of exposure to tuberculosis	Older patient in poor general health	Presence of congestive failure	Presence of respiratory infection	History of joint involvement; subcutaneous nodules	Postoperative, immobilized, or venous disease
Gross appearance	Usually serous; often sanguineous	Often sanguineous	Serous	Serous	Turbid or yellow-green	Often sanguineous
Microscopic examination	May be positive for acid-fast bacilli; cholesterol crystals	Cytology positive in 50%		May be positive for bacilli		
Cell count	Few have > 10,000 erythrocytes; most have > 1000 leukocytes, mostly lymphocytes	Two-thirds bloody; 40% > 1000 leukocytes, mostly lymphocytes	Few have > 10,000 erythrocytes or > 1000 leukocytes	Polymorphonuclears predominate	Lymphocytes predominate	Erythrocytes predominate
Culture	Many have positive pleural effusion; few have positive sputum or gastric washings			May be positive		

	Most > 1.016	Most > 1.016	Most < 1.016	> 1.016	> 1.016	> 1.016
Specific gravity	Most > 1.016	Most > 1.016	Most < 1.016	> 1.016	> 1.016	> 1.016
Protein	90% 3 gm/100 ml or more	90% 3 gm/100 ml or more	75% < 3 gm/100 ml	3 gm/100 ml or more	3 gm/100 ml or more	3 gm/100 ml or more
Sugar	60% < 60 mg/100 ml	Rarely < 60 mg/100 ml		Occasionally 60 mg/100 ml	5-17 mg/100 ml (rheumatoid arthritis)	
Other	No mesothelial cells on cytology. Tuberculin test usually positive. Pleural biopsy positive	If hemorrhagic fluid, 65% will be due to tumor; tends to recur after removal	Right-sided in 55-70%	Associated with infiltrate on x-ray	Rapid clotting time; LE cell or rheumatoid factor may be present	Source of emboli may be noted

Other exudates: (Sp gr > 1.016.)

Fungal infection: Exposure in endemic area. Serous fluid. Microscopy and culture may be positive for fungi. Protein 3 gm/100 ml or more. Skin and serologic tests may be helpful.

Trauma: Serosanguineous fluid. Protein 3gm/100 ml or more.

Chylothorax: History of injury or cancer. Chylous fluid with no protein but with fat droplets.

*Modified from: Therapy of pleural effusion: A statement by the Committee on Therapy of the American Thoracic Society. *Am Rev Respir Dis* 97:479, 1968.

C. MALIGNANT PLEURAL EFFUSION Primary or metastatic malignancy of the lung or pleura can cause pleural effusions. The diagnosis is made by cytologic examination of pleural fluid and/or by pleural biopsy. Treatment is directed at expansion of the lung and adherence of the visceral and parietal surfaces to prevent recurrent effusion. Tube thoracostomy with drainage for 5-7 days may be effective. A sclerosing solution is instilled into the pleural space in some cases. The prognosis is poor.

D. EMPYEMA is a suppurative pleural exudate. The pleural space becomes involved by (1) direct spread from pneumonic focus, (2) lymphatic spread, (3) contamination as a result of operation or trauma, (4) extension from below the diapragm, (5) hematogenous infection, or (6) ruptured thoracic viscus.

Causative organisms include pneumococci, streptococci, staphylococci, bacteroides, tubercle bacilli, E. coli, Proteus vulgaris, and fungi.

1. Acute empyema

a. Diagnosis The diagnosis of acute empyema is seldom difficult. A predisposing condition is usually apparent. Findings related primarily to the empyema consist of chest pain, cough, malaise, fever, and leukocytosis. Large acute effusions may be associated with considerable toxicity and dyspnea. Physical examination discloses signs of pleural fluid; more accurate localization is provided by chest films. If air is seen in the empyema cavity on x-ray, it can be assumed that a bronchopleural fistula has developed. Thoracentesis is done promptly in order to obtain material for smears, cultures, and antibiotic sensitivity studies.

b. Treatment The principles of treatment in empyema are early evacuation of all fluid and purulent exudate in order to achieve complete lung expansion, and eradication of the infecting organism by adequate drainage, antibiotic therapy, and supportive measures.

  (1) *Antibiotic therapy* Systemic antibiotic therapy is based on sensitivity studies.
  (2) *Thoracentesis* The empyema cavity is evacuated completely by thoracentesis each day until less than 50 ml can be aspirated on successive days.
  (3) *Tube thoracostomy* If the exudate is thick or large in volume, adequate chest tube drainage should be provided.
      Only closed methods of pleural drainage (thoracentesis and tube thoracostomy) should be used until the lung is firmly adherent to the chest wall around the empyema cavity. If open drainage is established before this occurs, total collapse of the lung may result.

c. Prognosis Postpneumonic empyema usually subsides promptly when treatment is begun early. Empyema of other etiology is often more complicated and the prognosis less satisfactory. When closed methods of management fail, treatment must be along the lines described below for chronic empyema.

2. Chronic empyema As an empyema becomes chronic, the pleura thickens and adheres firmly around the encapsulated exudate. There may be a history of recent acute empyema, or chronic empyema may exist for years in a latent or intermittently symptomatic state.

Empyemas become chronic for the following reasons: (1) delay in diagnosis or inadequate treatment of the acute stage; (2) bronchopleural fistula; (3) specific infection, such as tuberculosis or actinomycosis; (4) retained foreign body, (5) osteomyelitis of a rib, (6) disease of the lung preventing expansion, and (7) underlying malignant neoplasm.

a. Diagnosis Cough and recurrent fever are usually the principal complaints. When some form of suppurative lung disease is associated with the empyema, the cough is usually productive of frankly purulent and sometimes foul-smelling sputum. Chest pain, clubbing of the fingers, chronic malaise, dyspnea, anorexia, and weight loss may occur. Draining sinuses are occasionally present.

Physical examination discloses signs of chest fluid or thickened pleura. Respiratory excursions are usually limited on the affected side, and there may be contraction of the thoracic cage. These changes are usually readily apparent on x-ray.

Thoracentesis is performed to obtain material for examination of smears and cultures for pyogenic and acid-fast organisms.

b. Treatment Anemia, malnutrition, and debility due to chronic sepsis should be corrected. Systemic antibiotic therapy is usually indicated as an adjunct to drainage or other local treatment.

(1) *Drainage* It is usually impossible to evacuate a chronic empyema cavity adequately by needle aspiration. If the exudate is relatively thin and the pleura not markedly thickened, closed drainage by tube thoracostomy may be effective.

Chronic empyema frequently requires open drainage. This is accomplished by resection under local or general anesthesia of a small segment of rib over the lower portion of the cavity. A generous biopsy of the wall of the empyema cavity should be obtained as it is opened. A large tube is inserted and is shortened gradually as the cavity slowly heals, which may require many weeks or even months. Irrigations are unnecessary if adequate drainage is maintained. The rate of healing may be determined by filling the cavity at weekly intervals with saline.

Large cavities (e.g., postpneumonectomy empyema), especially if associated with bronchopleural fistula, are well managed by the Eloesser flap method of providing continuous open drainage.

A well-drained and stabilized residual cavity—such as a postpneumonectomy empyema space—may occasionally be sterilized and closed after instillation of neomycin, 250 mg/100 ml of saline solution.

(2) *Decortication* Patients in whom infection has been controlled by chemotherapy or drainage may be suitable candidates for decortication, in which thickened pleura is excised in order to permit full expansion of the lung. Expansion is carefully maintained postoperatively by closed tube drainage. Decortication combined with pulmonary resection is the treatment of choice in selected cases of bronchopleural fistula, bronchiectasis, lung abscess, and other disorders in which the underlying lung is severely damaged.

c. Tuberculous empyema The management of tuberculous empyema, much less common since the advent of the antituberculosis drugs, is always complex. Bronchopleural fistula and secondary infection are frequently present. The proper timing and selection of therapeutic procedures requires experience and judgment. Consideration must be given to the systemic reaction of the patient, the extent of the tuberculosis, and the response to specific chemotherapy.

Tuberculous empyema (without secondary infection) may respond to general supportive measures, antituberculosis chemotherapy, and closed drainage by repeated thoracentesis or tube thoracostomy. The chest tube is usually placed in the anterior axillary line. Closed drainage is always used in order to minimize secondary pyogenic infection.

Mixed infections of the pleura, usually associated with bronchopleural fistula, may occasionally respond to intensive treatment along the same lines combined with penicillin or other antibiotic agent. In these cases decortication, with or without resection, is more often required.

E. NEOPLASMS OF THE PLEURA Primary tumors of the pleura are very rare and are difficult to distinguish from malignancies arising in the lung, diaphragm, or elsewhere. The most frequent pleural neoplasm is the mesothelioma, which tends to spread diffusely in the pleural space. Mesothelioma is more common in persons with a history of exposure to asbestos (magnesium silicate) dust. It occurs most commonly in men between 40 and 50. The chief complaint is usually pleural pain but large size may be obtained without any symptoms. Additional symptoms may include malaise, weakness, cough, dyspnea, weight loss, and fever. The physical and radiologic signs are those of pleural fluid and thickening. Plaques of calcium in the pleura are helpful in suggesting the diagnosis of pleural malignancy. Fluid tends to reaccumulate rapidly after thoracenteses. The diagnosis is established by cytologic study of the pleural fluid or by pleural biopsy. Although pleuropneumonectomy has been carried out in some cases, no treatment is curative. Radiotherapy or cancer chemotherapy may have a transient palliative effect.

VI. DISEASES OF THE LUNG

A. LUNG ABSCESS The causes of pyogenic lung abscess are (1) necrotizing pneumonia, (2) aspiration of infected material or a foreign body, (3) septic embolus or infection of a pulmonary infarct, (4) bronchial obstruction by tumor, (5) infection of a cyst or bulla, (6) extension of bronchiectasis into the parenchyma, (7) penetrating chest wounds, and (8) transdiaphragmatic extension of infection, e.g., from a subphrenic or amebic abscess. When a lung abscess develops in childhood, suspect a foreign body. In the older age group, consider the possibility of bronchial obstruction by cancer.

1. Diagnosis

a. Symptoms A history of alcoholism or intravenous drug abuse is often present. There may be a latent period of several days or weeks during which only malaise and fever are noted. Cough, pleuritic pain, chills, and fever occur as the process develops. Within a few days the patient may suddenly cough up a large amount of very foul, purulent sputum, usually blood streaked or frankly bloody. Copious, malodorous sputum associated with the debility of long-standing infection is typical of chronic abscess.

b. Signs vary with the size, position, and contents of the cavity and with the local pulmonary reaction. Clubbing of the fingers sometimes develops rapidly.

c. Laboratory tests Leukocytosis and anemia are usually consistent with severe infection. Sputum shows infection and may disclose the cause, e.g., tuberculosis or neoplasm.

d. X-rays Early films often show only an area of consolidation; cavitation with fluid level and surrounding pneumonitis is seen later. Tomography is useful to reveal the location, extent, and early evidence of cavitation. Bronchography is helpful in chronic cases to delineate local complications such as multiple abscesses and bronchiectasis.

e. Bronchoscopy is usually indicated to rule out an obstructing bronchial lesion such as carcinoma or foreign body.

2. Complications include brain abscess, massive hemoptysis, amyloidosis, and pyopneumothorax. Rupture of the abscess into the pleural space may produce tension pneumothorax. There is a sudden onset of pleural pain, dyspnea, and shock. This is a grave surgical emergency requiring immediate tube thoracostomy.

3. Medical treatment

a. Antibiotics In acute abscess, treat intensively with an antibiotic to minimize lung destruction while sensitivity tests are being done on sputum. Over 90% of acute lung abscesses respond favorably to intensive antibiotic therapy. The response in chronic abscess is less satisfactory, but antibiotics usually reduce the pulmonary infection to a significant degree.

b. Postural drainage.

c. Bronchoscopic aspiration to promote drainage in selected cases.

d. High-protein, high-caloric diet with supplementary vitamins. Correct anemia by transfusion if necessary.

4. Surgical treatment

a. Acute abscess Medical measures should be given a thorough trial before surgery is considered. Evidence of satisfactory progress includes decrease in cough, sputum, fever, and toxicity, and radiologic evidence of diminishing pulmonary infiltration and cavitation. If improvement has not occurred or if progress is arrested after 3-6 weeks, surgical treatment may be warranted. The condition of the patient may make resection unwise, and drainage through the bed of a resected rib is all that is needed.

b. Chronic abscess Chronic abscess which is unresponsive to medical management requires resection of the involved segment or lobe. Preoperatively, infection should be vigorously treated by antibiotics, postural drainage, and general supportive therapy. Bronchoscopy should be performed and, in some cases, the bronchial tree in the region of the abscess should be mapped by bronchography. These two examinations are done to explore the possibility of foreign body or neoplasm.

B. BRONCHIECTASIS is a disorder characterized by tubular or saccular dilatation and chronic infection of the distal bronchial tree. Most cases are secondary to focal pneumonitis occurring in childhood during an attack of pertussis, measles, scarlet fever, or other infection. Obstruction of the bronchi by foreign body is an occasional cause. The basal segments of the lower lobes, the lingula, and the right middle lobe are the usual sites of bronchiectasis.

1. Diagnosis

a. Symptoms and signs Chronic cough productive of much purulent sputum, more marked on arising in the morning. Recurrent attacks of pulmonary infection, often dating back to childhood, with fever, malaise, and increased cough and sputum, are also characteristic. Hemoptysis occurs at some time in about half of cases and may be severe.

Coarse moist rales are audible over the involved segments. Bronchial breathing and other chest findings are related to the extent of parenchymal involvement. Clubbing occurs in severe cases.

b. Laboratory tests Bacteriologic studies of the sputum always reveal mixed infection, usually predominantly streptococci and staphylococci. Antibiotic sensitivity tests should be done. Acid-fast infection should be ruled out.

c. X-rays Plain films of the chest usually show increased bronchial markings and a variable degree of peribronchial infiltration, but changes may be minimal or absent. Bronchograms should be performed on all suspected cases. Avoid bronchography during acute episodes of infection and in patients sensitive to iodine.

d. Bronchoscopy should be performed.

2. Treatment Postural drainage, antibiotics, and treatment of underlying conditions (e.g., sinusitis) are important. Bronchodilators and expectorants may assist in clearing secretions. Good nutrition and ample rest are essential.

Pulmonary resection is performed in rare patients who have disease limited to one lobe and who do not respond to medical therapy.

C. TUBERCULOSIS Early tuberculosis is usually asymptomatic, and the disease is detected on routine chest x-ray. Characteristic symptoms of advanced disease include cough, weight loss, night sweats, hemoptysis, and pleuritic pain.

The skin test with intermediate strength PPD is positive (more than 10 mm of induration after 48-72 hours) in over 90% of patients with active disease. Culture of sputum, gastric aspirate, pleural fluid, and pleural or lung biopsies prove the diagnosis.

Antituberculous chemotherapy is effective in most cases (see Chapter 4). Surgical treatment is indicated for patients with an uncertain diagnosis, failure to respond to chemotherapy, destroyed lung, bronchopleural fisutla, and tuberculous bronchiectasis. Pulmonary resection is the surgical method of choice, but lesser procedures (e.g., decortication) are useful sometimes. The operative mortality rate for resection is 1-10%, depending upon the extent of the procedure.

D. FUNGAL AND PARASITIC INFESTATIONS

1. Histoplasmosis is a systemic infection caused by the fungus Histoplasma capsulatum and is usually manifested by a benign transient pneumonia. The organism is world-wide in distribution, but it is particularly prevalent in central United States, Mexico, Central and South America, northern Europe, and Australia. Histoplasmosis in its chronic form may be associated with nodular pulmonary densities, apical cavities, bronchiectasis, empyema, or pneumothorax. Disseminated histoplasmosis is frequently fatal and fortunately rare.

The diagnosis is based on x-ray findings, serologic and skin tests, and on cultures of sputum, exudates, or tissues. The clinical picture resembles chronic tuberculosis, from which it may be differentiated by positive cultures and skin tests for histoplasmosis, and negative cultures and skin tests for tuberculosis. The differentiation is sometimes made difficult by the fact that many patients have both diseases.

Medical treatment consists of amphotericin B. Surgical excision is performed for diagnosis in patients with solitary pulmonary nodules or for treatment of large cavitary lesions.

2. Coccidioidomycosis This disease, also known as valley fever, is caused by Coccidiodes immitis, which is endemic in certain regions of the southwest United States, Mexico, and Central and South America. The highly infectious organisms (arthrospores) are carried on wind-borne dust and inhaled. Even very brief exposure may produce the disease, and persons traveling through endemic areas may be infected.

About 60% of infections occur without symptoms and are detected only by the conversion of the coccidioidin skin reaction from negative to positive. Clinical manifestations in overt cases usually suggest a respiratory infection and include fever, cough, erythema nodosum, and pleuritic pain. X-ray of the lungs during the primary disease, which may last a few weeks, shows patchy soft infiltration; as this clears, residual nodules or thin-walled cavities with little surrounding infiltration may persist. In the acute stage, the organisms may be found in sputum cultures. The coccidioidin skin test usually becomes positive after 10-14 days and remains positive for years.

The primary infection progresses to the granulomatous stage in 0.2% of cases.

Treatment is with amphotericin B. Surgical excision of a nodule or resection of an involved lobe is needed occasionally.

3. Echinococcus (hydatid) cyst of the lung is the larval stage of the dog tapeworm, Echinococcus granulosus. Human infection occurs from ingestion of material contaminated with dog feces containing tapeworm eggs, which hatch in the intestine; the larval embryos then penetrate the bowel wall and disseminate via the blood stream. The larvae may come to rest and develop into hydatid cysts in any part of the body, but the liver (70%) (see Chapter 10) and lungs (20%) are most commonly affected.

Hydatid cyst of the lung may be asymptomatic but usually causes productive cough, minor hemoptysis, chest pain, and fever by local pressure or by rupture with secondary infection. X-ray shows a sharply defined round or oval density in the lung field. A small crescent of air is sometimes seen between the cyst and the surrounding lung and is pathognomonic. A ruptured, infected cyst has the appearance of a lung abscess. Hydatid cysts are usually solitary, but may be multiple. They grow slowly and occasionally reach 15 cm or more in diameter. They are most commonly confused with neoplasm or lung abscess.

All hydatid cysts should be removed surgically if the patient's general condition permits. The mortality rate is quite low in uncomplicated cysts.

E. SPONTANEOUS PNEUMOTHORAX is usually caused by the rupture of a small emphysematous bleb. It occurs most frequently in healthy young adult males. Occasionally there is a history of recurrent pneumothorax. Onset is usually acute and characterized by severe chest pain, cough, and dyspnea. Physical signs are proportional to the extent of pneumothorax and consist of hyperresonance and diminished to absent breath sounds on the involved side. Diagnosis is confirmed by chest film.

1. Treatment

a. A small pneumothorax (less than 25% collapse) will absorb completely within a few weeks unless the air leak in the lung continues. The patient need not be at bed rest during this period, but his activities should be limited. It may be elected to allow the air to absorb spontaneously or to obtain more rapid expansion by aspiration with a needle or small plastic catheter (Intracath), usually through the second interspace anteriorly.

b. Large pneumothorax (greater than 25% collapse) should be treated by tube thoracostomy to expand the lung rapidly and thereby reduce morbidity. Constant suction (-25 cm of water) is applied to the tube and immediate expansion of the lung will usually occur. Suction is continued until lung expansion is shown on x-ray and the tube or catheter is blocked by the lung. Waterseal drainage is then provided for another 24 hours; at the end of this time, if x-ray shows full expansion, the tube or catheter is removed. The entire process of expansion usually requires only 3-5 days.

c. Recurrent pneumothorax, either ipsilateral or contralateral, occurs in approximately 20% of cases. If two or more episodes have occurred on one side, thoracotomy should be considered to excise blebs and create a pleural symphysis, preferably by pleural abrasion. Thoracotomy is also occasionally necessary to control pneumothorax associated with bleeding or persistent air leak.

2. Tension pneumothorax occasionally develops as a result of a check-valve type of leak in the lungs. Complete collapse of the lung occurs rapidly, and the mediastinal structures are shifted to the opposite side as intrathoracic tension rises. When positive pressure rises above 15-20 cm of water, venous return to the heart is impeded and circulatory collapse results. Physical signs include marked dyspnea, cyanosis, shift of the trachea and the apical impulse of the heart to the opposite side, and tympany to percussion and absent breath sounds on the involved side. It may be necessary to begin treatment promptly without waiting for x-rays of the chest.

When tension pneumothorax occurs, a needle should be inserted into the chest through the second or third interspace anteriorly. Air will rush out under pressure and relieve the tension. The needle should then be aspirated with a syringe or connected by a tubing to waterseal drainage until a tube thoracostomy can be done. Treatment thereafter is the same as for spontaneous pneumothorax. Persistent air leak or recurrent pneumothorax is an indication for thoracotomy.

F. BENIGN NEOPLASMS OF THE LUNG

1. Hamartomas are the most common benign pulmonary neoplasms. They are embryologic remnants consisting largely of cartilage containing variable quantities of epithelial, adipose, or muscular tissue. Calcification may be present. Hamartomas are twice as common in men. They are usually small and located in the periphery of the lung. Wedge excision is performed for diagnosis; the prognosis is excellent.

2. Other benign tumors are rare and include fibrous mesotheliomas, lipomas, leiomyomas, etc.

G. PRIMARY CARCINOMA OF THE LUNG is the most common cause of death from cancer in men. The incidence in women is increasing. The peak incidence is between age 50 and 70. Cigarette smoking is the most important causative factor; asbestos and other industrial materials are etiologic also.

1. Pathologic types

a. Epidermoid (squamous cell) carcinomas comprise 45% of lung tumors. About one-third arise in the periphery and two-thirds near the hilus.

b. Oat cell carcinomas are highly malignant. They may secrete endocrine hormones. About 35% of malignant lung tumors are of this type; most (80%) arise centrally.

c. Adenocarcinomas begin in the periphery in 75% and centrally in 25%. They make up 15% of primary lung cancers. They are less malignant than oat cell and more malignant than epidermoid cancers.

d. Undifferentiated large cell carcinomas are less malignant than oat cell cancers. About 3–5% of tumors fit into this category.

e. Bronchial adenomas are low-grade malignant tumors; about 15% metastasize. *Bronchial carcinoid* is the most common type (85%) and they occur twice as often in women as in men. The majority arise in the main stem or lobar bronchi.

f. Papillary carcinomas and sarcomas are rare.

2. Diagnosis

a. Symptoms and signs

About 10–20% are asymptomatic when diagnosed by routine chest x-ray or sputum cytology.

Cough, hemoptysis, chest pain, dyspnea.

Pneumonia, localized wheeze, or atelectasis due to bronchial obstruction.

Pleuritic pain and pleural effusion. The effusion is serous if due to lymphatic obstruction, and it is bloody if tumor involves the pleura directly.

Mediastinal spread may cause hoarseness from involvement of the left recurrent laryngeal nerve; phrenic nerve involvement leading to diaphragmatic paralysis; superior vena caval obstruction.

Pancoast's syndrome is a consequence of a tumor in the superior pulmonary sulcus. It consists of pain, weakness of the arm, and **Horner's syndrome** (ptosis, miosis, enophthalmos, and decreased sweating on the involved side).

Lung cancer spreads via lymphatics to hilar, paratracheal, supraclavicular, and abdominal nodes. Hematogenous metastases commonly affect brain, liver, adrenals, and bones.

A large variety of extrathoracic manifestations occur even in the absence of metastases: endocrine and metabolic disorders; vascular and hematologic effects (e.g., thrombophlebitis); connective tissue disorders (e.g., dermatomyositis); and neuromyopathies.

b. Laboratory tests Sputum cytology is positive in 30–60% of cases, more if repeated specimens are examined. Postbronchoscopy sputums are especially valuable.

c. X-rays Chest films may show a mass in the periphery or in the hilum. Signs of extension may be present. Tomograms may reveal multiple lesions.

d. Special tests Bronchoscopy, mediastinoscopy, thoracentesis, percutaneous biopsy, angiography, bone x-rays, and other tests are directed at confirming the diagnosis of lung cancer and assessing its resectability.

3. Treatment

a. Two-thirds of patients are incurable when the diagnosis is made. Signs of incurability include: metastases outside the thorax; metastases to paratracheal nodes or contralateral hilar nodes; malignant pleural effusion; recurrent laryngeal or phrenic nerve paralysis; superior vena cava syndrome; involvement of the main pulmonary artery.

b. Features which do not categorically indicate incurability, but which carry an unfavorable prognosis, include; involvement of the chest wall; Pancoast's syndrome; tumor visible bronchoscopically; oat cell tumor.

c. The patient's medical condition, especially pulmonary function, may contraindicate surgery.

d. Patients who are likely to be curable should undergo thoracotomy. About 5-10% of patients are found to be incurable at operation despite thorough preoperative evaluation. The remainder are treated by pulmonary resection (lobectomy if possible, bilobectomy or pneumonectomy if necessary).

e. Radiation therapy is used for palliation or occasionally as a preoperative adjunct (e.g., in Pancoast's syndrome).

4. Prognosis 95% of patients are dead within 2 years if surgery is not done. The operative mortality rate depends upon age, general condition, and extent of resection; about 5% of patients age 40-60 die after major pulmonary resection.

The 5-year survival rate is about 35% after lobectomy and 25% after pneumonectomy. Since two-thirds of patients are not candidates for operation, the overall survival rate from lung cancer is 5-10%. However, asymptomatic patients who are operated on solely on the basis of an abnormal x-ray have a 5-year survival rate of 40-50%. This illustrates the importance of routine chest x-rays. The prognosis is less favorable if lymph node involvement or blood vessel invasion has occurred. Epidermoid carcinoma is generally considered to have a better prognosis than the other cell types.

H. METASTATIC TUMORS Solitary metastases to the lungs from primary cancers elsewhere may be treated by surgical resection in certain cases. The primary tumor must be controlled, and no metastases must be present in other sites. Tomograms of both lungs should be done to exclude multiple metastases. The longer the interval from control of the primary to the appearance of the pulmonary metastasis, the better the prognosis. It is important to bear in mind that a pulmonary lesion may be primary instead of metastatic in a patient with a history of cancer elsewhere.

The 5-year survival rate after resection of solitary pulmonary metastases is 35% if the tumor is a carcinoma and 20% if it is a sarcoma.

I. SOLITARY PULMONARY NODULES (coin lesions) are peripheral, discrete lesions that usually appear on routine x-rays in asymptomatic patients. The lesion may be granulomatous or neoplastic. Overall, about 5-10% of these lesions are malignant.

Smoking, cough, hemoptysis, weight loss, and hypertrophic osteoarthropathy are suggestions of malignancy. Granulomatous disease is unlikely if skin tests are negative. Sputum cytology proves the diagnosis of malignancy in only 5-20% of cases. Concentric or laminated calcification and documented absence of growth for 1 year are strong radiographic indications of benignity.

Patients in whom malignancy cannot be excluded should be managed by surgical excision for diagnosis and treatment. The 5-year survival rate for removal of malignant coin lesions is as high as 90%, and the operative mortality rate is only 1%.

VII. MEDIASTINAL MASSES

Mediastinal masses consist chiefly of a variety of neoplasms and cysts which tend to occur in characteristic sites (Table 8-2).

A. DIAGNOSIS About half of mediastinal tumors are discovered on routine chest x-ray, and the majority of these are asymptomatic. Specific symptoms and signs depend upon the size, location, and nature of the tumor. Cough, chest pain, and dyspnea are among the commonest complaints. Physical signs are frequently absent or minimal. The following are of particular interest when present: cervical or generalized lymphadenopathy; venous congestion in the head, neck, and upper extremities (superior vena caval obstruction); hoarseness (recurrent nerve palsy); Horner's syndrome (involvement of the cervical sympathetic nerves); and elevation of the diaphragm (phrenic nerve paralysis). Nerve damage is usually caused by inoperable malignant invasion. When a malignant mediastinal tumor is suspected, a careful search should be made for evidence of primary or metastatic neoplasm outside the mediastinum.

Laboratory tests include chest films, tomography, and, if a vascular lesion is suspected, angiography. Blood and bone marrow studies for blood dyscrasias

Table 8-2. Distribution of tumors and other mass lesions in the mediastinum

All parts of mediastinum	
Lymph node lesions	
Bronchogenic cysts	
Middle mediastinum	
Teratoma	
Thymoma	
Parathyroid adenoma	
Aneurysms	**Posterior mediastinum**
Lipoma	Neurogenic tumors
Myxoma	Pheochromocytoma
Goiter	Aneurysms
	Enterogenous cysts
Anterior mediastinum	Spinal lesions
Teratoma	Hiatus hernia
Lymphangiomas	
Angiomas	
Pericardial cysts	
Esophageal lesions	

Reproduced with permission from Dunphy JE, Way LW (Eds.): *Current Surgical Diagnosis & Treatment,* 3rd Ed. Lange 1977

are indicated if a lymphoma is suspected. Sputum smears, cultures, and cytologic studies may be indicated. Thyroid scan is diagnostic in substernal goiter. Bronchoscopy and esophagoscopy are useful in some cases. Mediastinoscopy should not be done in potentially curable cases. Direct needle biopsy of the mediastinal mass by percutaneous needle or limited anterior thoracotomy may occasionally be feasible in order to establish the diagnosis in an accessible but obviously inoperable tumor.

B. TREATMENT The majority of mediastinal enlargements requires thoracotomy or median sternotomy for positive diagnosis and definitive treatment. In most cases nothing is to be gained by delay of exploration when an operable lesion cannot be ruled out. Even benign, asymptomatic lesions should rarely be treated expectantly. Sooner or later, because of their critical location, they usually cause serious difficulty as a result of pressure, infection, or rupture.

C. CHARACTERISTIC FEATURES OF COMMON MEDIASTINAL TUMORS
1. Mediastinal goiter In 50% of cases the disease is asymptomatic and is detected by routine chest films; in the remainder, symptoms include dyspnea, cough, pain, and dysphagia. The cervical portion of the thyroid is usually, but not always, enlarged and palpable. The substernal thyroid is readily demonstrated by x-ray. Some degree of tracheal (and possibly esophageal) deviation and compression is typically present. The rounded, homogeneous density in the mediastinum

is continuous above with the cervical shadow, and on fluoroscopy the mass is usually seen to move upward with swallowing. If functioning thyroid tissue is present in a mediastinal goiter, the diagnosis can be confirmed by thyroid scan. Superior mediastinal enlargements should be examined by radioisotope scanning unless thyroid origin can be ruled out. Mediastinal goiters should be approached through the usual thyroidectomy incision except in the rare instance (e.g., posterior mediastinal goiter) where a combined thoracic and cervical approach may be required.

2. Bronchogenic and enterogenous cysts These cysts represent embryological remnants of the respiratory and alimentary tracts, respectively. Bronchogenic cysts are lined with respiratory epithelium, and may contain smooth muscle and cartilage in the wall. They are most often found in the parahilar or right paratracheal regions. Enterogenous cysts are usually closely associated with the esophagus or are actually intramural, and are lined by squamous, gastric, or intestinal epithelium. They are sometimes referred to as alimentary tract duplications.

Bronchogenic cysts usually become symptomatic only in adult life, if at all, whereas 75% of enterogenous cysts are diagnosed in the first year of life because of such serious complications as peptic ulceration, perforation into a bronchus or pleural cavity, or hemorrhage. The symptoms of both types of cysts depend primarily on their size and location and on the presence or absence of infection. Chest pain, cough, wheezing, and slight dysphagia are the commonest complaints. By x-ray, bronchogenic cysts are ovoid, smooth in outline, and homogeneous in density except when a bronchial fistula exists, in which case an air-fluid level can be seen. They are usually located near the midline and, because of their close relation to the trachea, bronchi, and esophagus, may be seen on fluoroscopy to move up and down with respiration or swallowing.

The treatment of these cysts is surgical removal.

3. Thymoma The histological differentiation of benign from malignant variants of thymoma is difficult or impossible. About one-fourth of these lesions break through their capsule and invade locally or implant on neighboring surfaces, and in this sense they are 'malignant'; lymphogenous or hematogenous metastases are quite rare. Roentgenologically, the tumor is usually round or oval and sharply delineated from the surrounding tissues. Its typical location is anterior to the aortic arch and the base of the heart.

Thymoma occurs in about 15% of patients with myasthenia gravis, and about 75% of patients with thymoma have myasthenia gravis. In young women, the removal of a non-neoplastic thymus gland is said to be associated with an increased remission rate in myasthenia gravis. Thymomas should be removed since one-fourth of these tumors are locally invasive.

4. Teratomas may occur at any age but are most frequently seen in persons between 20 and 40. About one-third are asymptomatic; the remainder cause cough, chest pain, dyspnea, or other pressure symptoms. About one-third are malignant. Dermoid cyst is a type of benign, unilocular teratoma containing sebaceous material and hair and lined by stratified squamous epithelium and dermal appendages.

Teratomas are homogeneous, discrete, round, and smooth, unless local invasion has occurred.

Treatment is by excision, which is curative in benign lesions. The prognosis of malignant teratoma is very poor; most patients die within 1 year after diagnosis.

5. Lymphoma This is the most frequent cause of a mediastinal mass. The most common symptoms are cough, pain, dyspnea, wheezing, hoarseness, weight loss, fatigue, and fever. Peripheral lymphadenopathy or splenomegaly may be present. The mediastinal tumor consists of involved lymph nodes, usually in the anterior or middle mediastinum. Surgical excision, radiation therapy, and chemotherapy are used individually or in combination, depending upon the type and stage of the disease.

6. Neurogenic tumors These are the most frequent primary mediastinal neoplasms. Nearly all neurogenic tumors of the mediastinum arise from the intercostal nerves or the paravertebral sympathetic trunks and are therefore usually found in the posterior mediastinum. 10% are malignant, and malignancy is more common in children.

Neurogenic tumors are usually asymptomatic. Chest x-rays characteristically show a round, homogeneous mass with distinct borders in the posterior mediastinum. Rib or vertebral erosion may occur, and widening of the intervertebral foramen may be present in the 'hourglass' or 'dumbbell' lesions.

Treatment is by excision. It is important to perform myelography preoperatively if intraspinal extension is suspected because the surgical approach is different in these cases.

9

HEART & GREAT VESSELS

Daniel J. Ullyot, MD

Surgical management of lesions of the heart and great vessels requires application of general surgical principles, a knowledge of special diagnostic technics (e.g., electrocardiography, echocardiography, cardiac catheterization, and cineangiocardiography), and familiarity with the technology of extracorporeal circulation.

The ability to assess the patient's circulatory status is essential. This requires systematic evaluation of cerebral function (state of consciousness), respiratory function (dyspnea and auscultatory findings), renal function (urine output), peripheral perfusion (presence of peripheral pulses, vasoconstriction as manifested by cool clammy skin), and the various hemodynamic indices (venous pressure, cardiac output, AV O_2 difference). These observations must be integrated to accurately appreciate the adequacy of circulation in providing for tissue needs.

Extracorporeal circulation provides a flow of oxygenated blood to the body during cardiac operations. Venous blood returning to the heart is diverted to a reservoir through tubes placed into the vena cavae through the right atrium. The blood is artificially oxygenated and returned to the arterial system through a tube placed into the ascending aorta or the femoral artery. Heparin must be given to prevent clotting which occurs when blood contacts artificial surfaces. The heparin effect is later neutralized with protamine sulfate after cardiac function is reestablished, and the arterial and venous cannulae are removed. Artificial circulation with present bubble oxygenator apparatus can be maintained up to 6 hours with survival in most patients. Perfusion times greater than 3 hours, however, are usually associated with impaired hemostasis, pulmonary damage, and general cellular dysfunction.

I. TRAUMA

A. PENETRATING INJURY OF THE HEART implies direct mechanical damage to cardiac tissues by a foreign body, usually a knife, ice pick, or bullet; and includes lacerations of the pericardium. The result is bleeding which produces circulatory embarrassment either by cardiac tamponade or by blood loss into the pleural space. There may be direct injury to major coronary arteries producing myocardial infarction, to valves causing valvular insufficiency, or to the atrial or ventricular septae producing intracardiac shunts.

1. Diagnosis

a. Symptoms Pain in the region of the wound. Dyspnea, lightheadedness, altered consciousness.

b. Signs Hypotension, peripheral vasoconstriction and cyanosis, distended neck veins, pulsus paradoxicus (see Section B), and oliguria.

c. Laboratory tests Usually normal but often not obtained because of the patient's critical condition.

d. X-rays   Chest film may show a widened mediastinal shadow and/or a pleural fluid collection.

e. Special tests   ECG is usually not helpful. After initial surgical management, cardiac catheterization may show valvular injury or an intracardiac shunt.

2. Differential diagnosis   Injury to adjacent structures such as the great vessels, lung, or esophagus must be considered.

3. Complications   Untreated lesions are usually rapidly fatal. Brain, kidney, and other organs may sustain irreversible damage secondary to shock during the interval between wounding and surgical treatment.

4. Treatment

a. Placement of intravenous lines for fluid replacement.

b. Pericardiocentesis is a temporizing measure applied only in stable patients to confirm the presence of blood in the pericardium. This maneuver may temporarily improve cardiac function.

c. Definitive therapy consists of thoracotomy through a left anterolateral incision through the 4th interspace. This may need to be done in the emergency room if tamponade is severe. The pericardium is opened longitudinally anterior to the left phrenic nerve. Blood is aspirated from the pericardium and bleeding is controlled by finger pressure over the bleeding point. The laceration is controlled by simple sutures. The pericardium is closed loosely to prevent cardiac herniation. The chest is drained with a thoracostomy tube connected to underwater-seal drainage. Blood loss through chest tubes, urine output, arterial and venous pressures, and electrocardiogram are monitored postoperatively.

5. Prognosis depends upon the extent of injury and the duration of shock. The majority of patients will show electrocardiographic abnormalities (40% have ventricular ectopy). 90% of survivors will regain full functional capacity as confirmed by exercise testing. However, 40% will not return to work, presumably because of posttraumatic neurosis.

B. BLUNT INJURY OF THE HEART   Blunt trauma to the heart often results from a steering wheel injury or other direct blow to the anterior chest. The heart may be contused or lacerated.

1. Diagnosis

a. Symptoms   Anterior chest pain, feeling of oppression, dyspnea, altered state of consciousness.

b. Signs   Hypotension, peripheral vasoconstriction, distended neck veins. Pulsus paradoxicus is an important finding. With the patient in the supine position and breathing normally, the blood pressure cuff is inflated and the reading at which the Korotkoff sounds are heard only in expiration is noted. As the cuff is further deflated, the point at which the Korotkoff sounds are heard throughout the respiratory cycle is recorded. Under normal conditions, the difference between the two readings is 10 mm Hg. If the discrepancy is wider than this, cardiac tamponade is probably present.

c. X-rays   Chest x-rays may show a widened mediastinal shadow, fractured ribs, or (rarely) a fractured sternum.

d. Special tests   The electrocardiogram is generally not diagnostic, but a variety of abnormalities may be found, including ventricular ectopy, ST segment elevation, or T-wave inversion. Echocardiography may show pericardial fluid accumulation.

2. Differential diagnosis   Myocardial infarction; associated injuries such as pneumothorax, esophageal injury, or injury to the great vessels.

3. Complications   Myocardial dysfunction secondary to extensive myocardial contusion, cardiac tamponade, and organ damage as a consequence of shock.

4. Treatment

a. Medical   Patients showing no evidence of circulatory compromise may be observed.

b. Surgical A diagnostic pericardiocentesis is performed. This is done with a long number 16 needle attached to the indifferent lead of an electrocardiogram machine. A current of injury (ST segment elevation) indicates when the needle is in contact with the myocardium. If blood is aspirated from the pericardial space or if the patient is in shock despite adequate blood volume, pericardial exploration is undertaken through an incision in the anterior left 4th interspace.

5. Prognosis depends upon the extent of myocardial contusion and the extent of associated injuries (e.g., pulmonary contusion and pulmonary laceration).

C. PENETRATING WOUNDS OF THE GREAT VESSELS

Penetrating trauma to the chest may result in laceration of the thoracic aorta or the brachiocephalic vessels with bleeding into the thoracic cavity, mediastinum, or pericardium. The manifestations of bleeding are hypovolemia or, if the aorta within the pericardial sac is disrupted, cardiac tamponade.

1. Diagnosis

a. Symptoms Pain, feeling of lightheadedness, or dyspnea.

b. Signs If bleeding is into the pericardial space, neck vein distention, pulsus paradoxicus, diminished heart sounds, hypotension, and peripheral cyanosis. If bleeding is into the pleural space or mediastinum, the patient is usually in shock. Disruption of a brachiocephalic branch (e.g., the left subclavian), may result in blood pressure differences in the two upper extremities.

c. X-rays Chest film may disclose mediastinal widening, an enlarged cardiac silhouette, or pleural fluid.

d. Special tests Aortogram may disclose great vessel laceration.

2. Differential diagnosis Penetrating trauma to the heart or injury to adjacent viscera such as lung or esophagus.

3. Complications Exsanguination, or damage to brain or kidneys due to shock.

4. Treatment If cardiac tamponade is suspected, pericardiocentesis is performed; if blood is aspirated, pericardial exploration is undertaken through an anterior left 4th interspace incision. If pleural effusion is present, tube thoracostomy is performed. If bleeding is persistent following chest tube insertion, thoracotomy is undertaken to repair the lacerated great vessel. If great vessel injury is suspected and the patient is stable, an arteriogram is useful in localizing the point of laceration.

5. Prognosis depends on the duration of shock and the extent of injury.

D. BLUNT TRAUMA TO THE GREAT VESSELS

Blunt trauma to the thoracic aorta is commonly seen after steering wheel injury to the chest. The most common injury is laceration or complete transection of the descending thoracic aorta just distal to the left subclavian artery. Partial or total disruption at this level must be suspected whenever major blunt chest trauma is encountered, especially when a widened mediastinal shadow is evident on chest film. Aortography should be performed in all cases of major blunt trauma to the chest, regardless of whether the mediastinum is widened on chest film.

1. Diagnosis

a. Symptoms Chest pain, shortness of breath, pleuritic pain, lightheadedness.

b. Signs Broken ribs or, rarely, a fractured sternum.

c. X-rays Chest film may show a widened mediastinal silhouette or a pleural fluid collection.

d. Special tests Aortography may show extravasation of contrast at the point of injury, usually just distal to the left subclavian artery.

2. Differential diagnosis Injury to other thoracic viscera such as heart, lung, esophagus, or diaphragm.

3. Complications Organ damage due to hypovolemic shock is related to the severity and duration of shock. Trauma to the great vessels may result in an aneurysm of the thoracic aorta or (rarely) a false aneurysm.

4. Treatment If disruption of the aorta is diagnosed, prompt operation must be done. The descending thoracic aorta is approached through a left posterolateral thoracotomy. When multiple trauma is present, it is desirable to avoid the use of systemic heparinization and cardiopulmonary bypass. Transection of the thoracic aorta distal to the left subclavian artery is best managed using a heparin-bonded shunt which is inserted into the ascending aorta and connected either to the descending thoracic aorta or to the left femoral artery. Placement of the shunt allows aortic clamping without proximal hypertension or distal hypotension while repair is effected. Repair consists of either suture control of the laceration or resection of the disrupted portion and replacement with a tube graft.

5. Prognosis depends on the duration of shock. One of the rare but important complications of repair is paraplegia. This complication may occur even with the use of a shunt.

II. THORACIC AORTA

A. ANEURYSM An aneurysm of the thoracic aorta is a local bulge which, if untreated, may continue to enlarge and ultimately rupture. Aneurysms may be fusiform (enlargement of the entire or a major portion of the circumference) or sacular (localized protrusion from a small part of the aortic wall). Aneurysms may involve the ascending aorta, the descending aorta, or the transverse thoracic aorta. The cause is usually atherosclerosis; other causes are lues, previous dissection, trauma, and cystic medial necrosis.

1. Diagnosis

a. Symptoms The lesion may be asymptomatic, an incidental finding on routine chest film. If the aneurysm involves the ascending aorta, there may be associated aortic valvular insufficiency and symptoms of congestive heart failure. Aneurysms of the transverse aorta may cause a hoarseness secondary to pressure on the recurrent laryngeal. Aneurysms of the descending thoracic aorta may present back-pain secondary to spinal erosion, or dyspnea related to phrenic nerve involvement and lung compression.

b. Signs Usually none unless aortic valvular insufficiency, vocal cord paralysis, or phrenic nerve involvement is present.

c. Laboratory tests Positive serology in cases of luetic aortitis.

d. X-rays Chest film shows mediastinal widening. The left anterior oblique view is particularly useful.

e. Special tests Aortography may be useful in delineating the extent of the aneurysm. Commonly, however, atherosclerotic debris gives a relatively normal appearance to the aortic lumen.

2. Differential diagnosis Primary aortic valvular insufficiency.

3. Complications The major complication is rupture with exsanguinating hemorrhage. Approximately 50% of patients with thoracic aneurysm die as a result of rupture within a few years following diagnosis. Other complications include paraplegia due to impaired blood supply to the spinal cord (descending aorta), and the development of aortic valvular insufficiency (ascending aorta).

4. Treatment Indications for surgery are rupture, documentation of progressive enlargement on serial chest films, pain suggestive of enlargement or erosion, and symptomatic aortic valvular insufficiency.

a. Ascending aorta Exposed through a median sternotomy incision and excised using cardiopulmonary bypass. The aneurysmal segment is replaced with a prosthetic graft. Aortic valve replacement or reimplantation of the coronary ostia may be required.

b. Descending aorta   Exposed through a left thoracotomy. During the period of aortic clamping, partial cardiopulmonary bypass is employed from femoral vein (or left atrium) to femoral artery. Alternatively, a heparin-bonded shunt may be used between the ascending aorta and the descending aorta or the left femoral artery. In experienced hands it may be possible to simply cross-clamp the aorta and control proximal hypertension with agents such as sodium nitroprusside. The most serious complication of descending thoracic aneurys-mectomy is paraplegia, occurring in 5–15% of cases.

c. Transverse aorta   Exposed through a bilateral 4th interspace anterior thoracotomy incision with sternal transection. These aneurysms are a formidable challenge. The intraoperative complications are cerebral damage, myocardial damage, and hemorrhage. It is possible to replace the transverse aorta using a complex cardiopulmonary bypass arrangement with selective perfusion of the brachiocephalic vessels, the femoral artery, and the coronary arteries. Recently, cardiopulmonary bypass with profound systemic hypothermia and circulatory arrest during the time of cross-clamping of the brachiocephalic vessels has been used.

5. Prognosis is determined by size and location of the aneurysm, the surgeon's skill and experience, and associated conditions such as coronary artery disease or pulmonary disease.

B. AORTIC DISSECTION   Acute dissection of the thoracic aorta is a condition in which blood creates a false channel in the wall of the aorta by breaking through the intima and finding a pathway in the medial layer. This results in aneurysmal dilatation of the outer wall of the aorta. The outcome of progressive dissection is rupture and exsanguination, or occlusion of the normal lumen with obstruction of blood flow to major branches. Dissections occur in patients with hypertension and in Marfan's disease; cystic medial necrosis, a weakness in the medial layer of the aorta, is common to both conditions.

Acute dissections may be of 3 types:

Type I   Entry point in the ascending aorta with the dissection plane progressing distally to involve the transverse aorta, descending thoracic aorta, and commonly into the abdominal aorta.

Type II   Entry point in the ascending aorta with a dissection plane which stops at the level of the transverse arch.

Type III   Entry point distal to the left subclavian artery with the dissection plane progressing distally down the thoracic aorta, usually to involve the abdominal aorta.

1. Diagnosis

a. Symptoms   Excruciating chest and back pain, sometimes indistinguishable from that of myocardial infarction. The pain is frequently more severe and more posterior than that associated with myocardial infarction.

b. Signs   The patient is commonly hypertensive. There may be a disparity in pulse or blood pressure findings in the extremities or in the carotid arteries. If dissection has progressed to involve the femoral arteries, a double pulsation may be palpated.

c. Laboratory tests   ECG is not diagnostic of acute myocardial infarction or angina pectoris.

d. X-rays   Chest x-rays may show widening of the mediastinal silhouette. In cases where rupture has occurred, pleural effusion may be evident.

e. Special tests   A thoracic aortogram is mandatory in all cases of suspected dissection. The important distinction is between a dissection arising in the ascending aorta (Type I or II) and one which begins beyond the origin of the left subclavian artery (Type III).

2. Differential diagnosis   Myocardial infarction, atherosclerotic thoracic aneurysm. If a patient has occlusion of a major aortic branch, embolus must be considered as a possible cause.

3. Complications   Rupture of the thoracic aorta and death by exsanguination occurs in approximately 80% of patients within 48 hours of the onset of symptoms.

Ischemia and infarction of organs whose blood supply is compromised by the dissection; stroke, paraplegia, intestinal infarction, renal infarction, or loss of an extremity are examples of these complications.

Type I and Type II dissections may perforate at the root of the aorta into the pericardial space and cause death by cardiac tamponade.

Obstruction of coronary blood flow or aortic valvular insufficiency may be secondary to dissection involving the aortic root.

4. Treatment

a. Initial treatment is medical   Hypertension is controlled by IV antihypertensive agents such as sodium nitroprusside. The arterial pressure, state of consciousness, and urine output are carefully monitored while blood pressure is lowered. The use of Beta blocking agents such as propranolol to diminish the systolic thrust has been advocated. When blood pressure is controlled, an arteriogram is obtained to determine the nature of the dissection and to opacify major arterial branches.

b. Surgical   If Type I or Type II dissection is identified, operation is undertaken urgently because of the tendency for rupture to occur at the junction of the ascending aorta and the myocardium resulting in hemopericardium and death. Exposure is through a median sternotomy incision. Vena cavae to femoral artery cardiopulmonary bypass is established. The ascending aorta is resected and replaced with a tube graft. The layers of the aorta at the distal anastomosis are sutured together insuring that flow will be through the true lumen. If dissection has produced aortic valvular insufficiency, the valve cusps are resuspended to restore valvular competence. In the unusual event that the coronary arteries are involved in the dissection, implantation of the coronary ostia into the graft or coronary artery bypass may be required.

If the dissection is Type III, either continued medical or surgical therapy may be applied with similar results. Operation is indicated for rupture, impending rupture, failure to control blood pressure without complications such as oliguria or myocardial ischemia, and occlusion of major vessels. Surgical management consists of exposure through a left thoracotomy, excision of the proximal descending aorta, and replacement with a tube graft using partial cardiopulmonary bypass (femoral vein or left atrium to femoral artery bypass). An important complication of Type III dissection is the possibility of paraplegia due to compromise of blood supply to the spinal cord. Care is taken to maintain blood flow below the distal clamp so that renal perfusion and segmental blood supply to the spinal cord are preserved.

The purpose of operation for any type of dissection is to replace the segment of aorta where blood has entered the false channel and to reapproximate the layers of the aorta at the distal suture line. This forces blood to enter the true lumen of the aorta, thereby decompressing the false channel and restoring blood flow through the natural pathway.

Because of friability of tissues, bleeding is often a problem in repair of acute dissection.

5. Prognosis   The operative mortality rate is in the range of 10-20%. If medical therapy is continued and progression of the acute dissection appears to be halted, patients must be followed closely with careful attention to control of blood pressure. These patients frequently develop chronic aneurysm of the aorta with progressive enlargement requiring surgical correction.

III. PERICARDIUM

A. PERICARDITIS is an inflammation of the parietal and visceral layers of pericardium and the outer myocardium. It may occur as an isolated process or as a local manifestation of systemic disease. The most common variety is idiopathic—probably viral—occurring in young adults and having a generally favorable prognosis. Other causes are acute myocardial infarction, tuberculosis, direct bacterial contamination, rheumatic fever, postpericardiotomy syndrome, and uremia. Complications of pericarditis such as cardiac tamponade and fibrous constriction may require operative management.

1. Diagnosis

a. Symptoms Precordial pain or discomfort, malaise, occasionally pleuritic pain.

b. Signs Fever, pericardial friction rub. If pericardial effusion is present, heart sounds are diminished, and there is evidence of cardiac tamponade.

c. Laboratory studies Elevated erythrocyte sedimentation rate. Leukocytosis. The electrocardiogram characteristically shows ST segment elevation without reciprocal depression.

d. X-rays Chest film is usually normal. If pericardial effusion is present, a globular cardiac silhouette may be seen.

e. Special tests The presence and nature of pericardial fluid can be demonstrated by radioisotope scanning, echocardiography, pericardiocentesis, and, less commonly, angiocardiography using CO_2 or iodinated contrast material. The specific etiologic diagnosis may require open pericardial biopsy.

2. Differential diagnosis Angina pectoris (particularly the Prinzmetal type), acute myocardial infarction, pleuritis, spontaneous pneumothorax, pulmonary embolism, aortic dissection, and mediastinal emphysema. Acute pericarditis may simulate peritonitis, especially in children.

3. Complications

a. Cardiac tamponade Rapid development of pericardial effusion may interfere with diastolic filling and result in diminished cardiac output and circulatory failure. Experimental evidence shows that increased pericardial pressure may interfere directly with coronary blood flow.

Heart tones are diminished. The neck veins are distended and distend even more on inspiration (Kussmaul's signs). The paradoxical pulse is accentuated. If peripheral signs of circulatory failure are present, prompt treatment must be undertaken. Early pericardiocentesis is indicated, especially when there is evidence of diminished cardiac output.

b. Constrictive pericarditis Patients with chronic constrictive pericarditis typically have congestive heart failure, hepatomegaly, ascites, and peripheral edema. The neck veins are distended. Kussmaul's sign is commonly present. An accentuated paradoxical pulse is present in about 30% of cases. The heart sounds are quiet and the apical impulse is usually absent. A pericardial knock may be heard corresponding to fast ventricular filling in early diastole.

Low QRS voltage may be seen on the ECG. Pericardial calcification is present on x-ray in 40-50% of patients but is not diagnostic of constriction. Cardiac catheterization may show characteristic early, rapid elevation of diastolic pressure and high end-diastolic pressure in both ventricles. In some instances, open pericardial biopsy is required to distinguish between chronic constrictive pericarditis and cardiomyopathy.

4. Treatment

a. Medical Medical treatment of acute pericarditis consists of bed rest, salicylate analgesics for pain, and therapy directed against specific etiologic factors. Occasionally, corticosteroids are employed in idiopathic acute pericarditis, but relapse on withdrawal of therapy is common.

The results of therapy depend upon the cause. Relapsing acute pericarditis may develop in as many as 10% of patients treated for acute idiopathic pericarditis.

b. Surgical   Surgical management includes pericardiocentesis for cardiac tamponade, open pericardial drainage for acute suppurative pericarditis, and pericardiectomy for chronic constrictive pericarditis, recurrent cardiac tamponade, and in some patients with relapsing acute pericarditis. Pericardiectomy through a median sternotomy or left thoracotomy incision consists of removing the pericardium anterior to both phrenic nerves and posterior to the left phrenic nerve. An adequate epicardiectomy as well as pericardiectomy over both ventricles must be accomplished to relieve chronic constriction.

5. Prognosis   Approximately 75% of surviving patients experience long-term benefit from pericardiectomy for chronic constrictive pericarditis. The procedure has an operative mortality rate of about 10%. Results seem to be related to the extent of associated myocardial fibrosis and atrophy and to the completeness of pericardiectomy. Some hemodynamic improvement is seen immediately after pericardiectomy, and normal intracardiac pressures are usually found on studies performed several months later. When the development of chronic constrictive pericarditis can be anticipated (e.g., in tuberculous pericarditis with delayed medical treatment), early pericardiectomy is encouraged before dense fibrosis and myocardial atrophy occur.

IV. HEART BLOCK

Cardiac conduction disturbances include defective impulse formation (Sinoatrial node dysfunction, sick sinus syndrome) and delay or interruption of impulse propagation (heart block). Symptoms are due to low cardiac output secondary to bradycardia, asystole, or escape tachyarrhythmias. The most common cause of heart block is idiopathic degeneration of the specialized conductive tissue of the heart. Other causes are myocardial infarction or ischemia secondary to coronary atherosclerosis, cardiomyopathy, drug effects, operative injury, and congenital defects.

1. Diagnosis

a. Symptoms   Lightheadedness, loss of consciousness, weakness, shortness of breath, easy fatiguability.

b. Signs   Bradycardia, obtundation, and, less commonly, evidence of congestive heart failure.

c. Laboratory tests   Serum electrolytes should be checked. Occasionally patients on digitalis will develop heart block in conjunction with hypokalemia.

d. X-rays   Usually noncontributory unless a previous permanent pacemaker has been placed, in which case pacemaker dysfunction should be suspected.

e. Special tests   The electrocardiogram may show sinus bradycardia, tachycardia-bradycardia syndrome, atrial fibrillation or flutter with slow ventricular response, junctional bradycardia, second or third degree A-V block, and bifascicular or trifascicular block.

2. Differential diagnosis   Abnormal bradycardia must be distinguished from the resting bradycardia often seen in trained athletes. Episodes of syncope or lightheadedness due to heart block must be differentiated from basilar artery insufficiency, convulsive disorder, transient cerebral ischemic attacks associated with extracranial cerebrovascular disease, and syncope associated with aortic stenosis.

3. Complications   Sudden death due to low cardiac output or escape ventricular tachyarrhythmias. Before pacemakers became available, the 1-year mortality was as high as 50% in patients with complete heart block.

4. Treatment

a. Medical Temporary bradycardia associated with acute myocardial infarction or with certain drugs may be treated by correction of electrolyte imbalance, the administration of Atropine, or in some instances the use of chronotropic agents such as isoproterenol.

b. Surgical Conditions producing symptomatic bradycardia which may be reversible over a period of days or a few weeks may be treated with a temporary transvenous pacemaker. Transient intraoperative damage to the conduction system may be treated with temporary myocardial pacemaker wires which are usually removed within 10 days after surgery.

Stable causes of symptomatic conduction disturbances are treated by implantation of a permanent pacemaker. Permanent pacemaker electrodes are of two types: myocardial wires placed directly on the left ventricle; and transvenous electrodes wedged in the right ventricular endocardium under fluoroscopic control. Transvenous insertion is generally preferred because it does not require exposure of the heart, and it can be performed under local anesthesia. Electrodes are connected to an implantable demand (asynchronous) pacemaker generator which is buried in the subcutaneous tissues of the chest wall or abdominal wall.

5. Prognosis Permanent pacemaker implantation can be done with very low operative risk even in elderly patients and results in good palliation of symptoms and prolongation of life. Present battery-powered pacemaker generators must be replaced every 4–7 years. The incidence of displacement of transvenous electrodes is about 5% in experienced hands, and it usually occurs within 48 hours of insertion. Complications such as electrode fracture, pacemaker extrusion, infection, ventricular perforation, external interference with pacemaker function, and premature electronic failure are rare.

V. ISCHEMIC HEART DISEASE

A. CORONARY ATHEROSCLEROSIS may result in narrowing of the coronary arteries causing myocardial ischemia and necrosis. The cause of coronary atherosclerosis is unknown. Epidemiologic studies have identified the following risk factors to be associated with atherosclerosis: hypercholesterolemia, hypertension, cigarette smoking, maleness, and a family history of coronary artery disease. Patients with diabetes mellitus have a greater extent of coronary atherosclerosis than in nondiabetic populations matched for age and sex. The clinical manifestations of ischemic heart disease are angina pectoris, sudden death, acute myocardial infarction, and ventricular arrhythmias.

1. Diagnosis

a. Symptoms Chest pain. Shortness of breath, dyspnea, and easy fatiguability may be present.

b. Signs A third heart sound may be present during either ischemia or infarction. Xanthelasma, premature arcus senilis, or tendon xanthomata may indicate hypercholesterolemic states. Hypertension may be present.

c. Laboratory tests Hypercholesterolemia may be present.

d. X-rays The chest x-ray is usually normal unless ischemic cardiomyopathy is present; in this case, the heart may be enlarged.

e. Special tests

(1) *ECG:* The resting electrocardiogram may show evidence of previous myocardial damage in the form of Q waves. ST segment depression during episodes of chest pain suggest myocardial ischemia. Persistently inverted T-waves may indicate subendocardial myocardial infarction. The presence of elevated ST segments during chest pain at rest, but reverting to normal, suggest variant or Prinzmetal angina. ST segment elevation and the presence of new Q waves are typical of acute myocardial infarction.

(2) *Exercise ECG:* This test in patients with stable angina pectoris may disclose ST segment depression suggesting ischemia. If the ST segment is down-sloping during provocative testing, significant coronary artery disease is likely. If ST segments are depressed 2 mm or more, high-grade coronary artery obstruction may be anticipated.

(3) *Myocardial scintigraphy* using thalium may show a filling defect associated with exercise and not present at rest; this finding reflects myocardial ischemia.

(4) *Coronary arteriography* documents obstructive lesions. Angiography will demonstrate vessels 100 microns in diameter or larger. A 50% obstruction on the coronary arteriogram is equivalent to 75% obstruction of the cross-sectional area, a hemodynamically significant lesion.

(5) *Left ventriculography* is the most sensitive determinant of left ventricular function in patients with ischemic heart disease.

2. Differential diagnosis Other causes of chest pain such as pericarditis, dissection of the thoracic aorta, pleuritic pain, and esophagitis must be considered.

3. Complications of ischemia are ventricular arrhythmias, myocardial infarction and death. Complications of acute myocardial infarction include ventricular arrhythmias, low cardiac output due to extensive muscle destruction, perforation of the ventricular septum, acute mitral insufficiency, and myocardial rupture.

4. Treatment

a. Medical Angina pectoris may be treated with nitrites (e.g., nitroglycerin or isosorbide dinitrate) and beta-blocking agents (e.g., propranolol). Attention is paid to coronary risk factors such as treatment of hypertension, proscription of smoking, weight-loss to attain ideal weight, and low fat, low cholesterol diet.

b. Surgical treatment is described in the following 2 sections.

B. CORONARY ARTERY BYPASS

1. Indications for bypass Patients who meet the following criteria are candidates for coronary artery bypass: (a) Disabling angina pectoris despite medical therapy. (b) Documentation of myocardial ischemia by either electrocardiography or myocardial scintigraphy. (c) Preserved left ventricular function. (d) Angiographically confirmed obstruction of 1 or more major coronary vessels with distal segments favorable for anastomosis.

2. Contraindications to bypass Relative contraindications to operation include: (a) Poor left ventricular function (ejection fraction less than 0.3). (b) Diffuse, distal coronary disease. (c) Recent transmural myocardial infarction.

3. Technic

a. Saphenous vein is the conduit most commonly used for coronary artery bypass. One end of the vein graft is anastomosed to the side of the ascending aorta, and the other end of the vein is anastomosed to the side of the diseased coronary artery, distal to the obstructing atheroma. From 1 to 4 diseased coronary arteries are usually bypassed in an individual patient.

b. Other conduits include the internal mammary artery and (rarely) the antecubital or cephalic veins. Direct anastomosis of the distal end of the internal mammary artery to one of the coronary arteries has a better patency rate (about 95% at 1 year) than saphenous vein grafts; but often other considerations favor use of saphenous vein.

4. Prognosis Operative mortality is 3% or less in experienced hands. The major complication is perioperative myocardial infarction; this occurs in 2-6% of cases. 65-70% of patients are asymptomatic during follow-up for a mean of 1-3 years and another 20% experience improvement in symptoms. Randomized studies show improved survival over medical management in patients with left main coronary artery obstruction, a subgroup of patients making up about 15% of most surgical series. The impact of coronary artery bypass on the rate of eventual myocardial infarction is unknown. Vein graft patency rate is approximately 70-85% at 1 year. There is a further 5% closure rate in grafts between the first and the third year. Patency of saphenous vein grafts has been documented up to 7 years postoperatively.

C. LEFT VENTRICULAR ANEURYSMECTOMY Left ventricular aneurysm is defined as a localized protrusion of the left ventricular wall beyond the normal outer and cavitary contours. It occurs in approximately 4% of cases of acute myocardial infarction by autopsy criteria. By cineangiographic criteria, the incidence is about 20%. The majority of aneurysms involve the anteroseptal portion of the left ventricle. Over 50% contain mural thrombus.

    1. Diagnosis The manifestations are abnormal precordial pulsation sustained throughout ventricular systole, ECG evidence of myocardial infarction with persistent ST segment elevation, localized left ventricular bulge seen on chest film or fluoroscopy, and demonstration of localized protrusion on left ventriculogram.

    The primary clinical manifestation is left ventricular failure, which is related to the extent of myocardial damage and to the degree of impairment of the efficiency of left ventricular contraction.

    2. Complications Less than 20% of unoperated patients live 5 years. Death occurs from left ventricular failure or recurrent myocardial infarction. Rupture is rare. Other clinical sequelae include angina pectoris, ventricular tachyarrhythmias, and systemic emboli from mural thrombi.

    3. Treatment Indications for surgery are intractable congestive heart failure, disabling angina pectoris, recurrent ventricular tachyarrhythmia, and (rarely) systemic emboli.

    The principal contraindication to surgery is generalized myocardial dysfunction.

    Left ventriculography is necessary to localize the aneurysm and to evaluate residual myocardial function.

    Selective coronary angiography is done to assess the coronary circulation for possible concomitant bypass grafting.

    Surgical treatment consists of excision of the aneurysm combined with coronary artery bypass when appropriate.

    4. Prognosis Operative mortality rate varies from 7-20%. Improvement in symptoms of congestive heart failure is seen in about 80% of surviving patients. Objective improvement in left ventricular function can be shown in two-thirds of patients studied postoperatively. 90% of patients with angina pectoris experience good to excellent palliation. Improvement in survival is striking. In the largest surgical series reported, 76% of patients were alive 4 years postoperatively. Ventricular aneurysmectomy combined with coronary artery bypass has been shown to result in better long-term survival than aneurysmectomy alone, and the operative mortality rate does not seem to be adversely affected by this combination of procedures.

VI. VALVULAR HEART DISEASE

Acquired valvular heart disease is limited to the aortic, mitral, and occasionally tricuspid valves. The pulmonic valve is rarely affected. The pathologic process may narrow the valve opening (stenosis), render the valve incompetent (insufficiency, regurgitation), or produce both stenosis and insufficiency.

    The New York Heart Association Classification is useful in describing the status of patients with valvular heart disease. Clinical Class I refers to patients who are symptomatic only with heavy exertion. Class II patients are symptomatic on moderate exertion, Class III patients are symptomatic on mild exertion, and Class IV patients are symptomatic at rest.

Except for mitral stenosis and tricuspid insufficiency, surgical treatment of acquired valvular disease requires valve replacement. Prosthetic valves most commonly used are the ball and cage (Starr Edwards, Cutter-Smeloff), the pivoting disk (Bjork-Shiley, Lillehei-Kastor), and the porcine bioprosthesis, a pig aortic valve mounted on a flexible stent (Hancock, Carpentier Edwards). Mechanical valves have the advantage of proven durability over a 10-year follow-up period. Porcine heterograft valve appears to be free of thromboembolic complications and obviates the need for chronic anticoagulation.

The hospital mortality for elective valve replacement is 5-10%. Most deaths are due to low cardiac output. Late mortality is 3.5% per year and is due to thromboembolism, bleeding complications of anticoagulation, myocardial failure, associated coronary artery disease, prosthetic infection, sudden death, and (rarely) mechanical valve dysfunction. Most patients improve symptomatically and enjoy prolonged survival following valve replacement.

A. AORTIC STENOSIS The most common cause of aortic stenosis is congenital malformation of the valve with progressive thickening and calcification. The mean age of onset of symptoms is 52 years, suggesting that a long latent period is necessary for a congenitally deformed valve to become critically narrowed.

1. Diagnosis

a. Symptoms Shortness of breath, easy fatiguability, syncopal episodes, angina pectoris.

b. Signs Systolic ejection murmur, best heard over the second intercostal space to the right of the sternum; murmur radiating to the neck; prominent left ventricular impulse.

c. X-ray Chest x-ray shows left ventricular prominence and enlargement of the ascending aorta due to poststenotic dilatation.

d. Special tests ECG shows left ventricular hypertrophy or strain. Cardiac catheterization reveals elevated left ventricular pressure with a gradient across the aortic valve.

2. Differential diagnosis Idiopathic, hypertrophic, subaortic stenosis. Patients with angina pectoris must have coronary angiography to exclude associated coronary artery disease. Patients with syncope must have other causes of syncope investigated (e.g., heart block, extracranial cerebrovascular disease, or convulsive disorder).

3. Natural history Symptomatic patients with aortic stenosis have a mortality rate of about 80% within 2 years following diagnosis.

4. Treatment

a. Medical Patients with suspected aortic stenosis should not receive digitalis or other medical management because this tends to mask progression of disease.

b. Surgical Symptomatic patients with pressure gradients of 50 mm Hg or greater, or a calculated valve area less than 1 cm^2, should undergo valve replacement.

5. Prognosis Patients undergoing successful valve replacement usually improve by one or two clinical classes (New York Heart Association Classification) and enjoy a 5-year survival approximating 75%.

B. AORTIC INSUFFICIENCY Rheumatic valvulitis is the most common cause of aortic insufficiency. Acute bacterial endocarditis and luetic aortitis are other causes.

1. Diagnosis

a. Symptoms Fatiguability, shortness of breath, chest pain (less common).

b. Signs Prominent left ventricular impulse, a diastolic murmur best heard along the left sternal border with the patient sitting forward, prominent peripheral pulses, widened pulse pressure, low diastolic pressure.

c. X-rays Chest x-ray shows prominent left ventricle and enlargement of the ascending aorta.

d. Special tests ECG shows left ventricular hypertrophy or strain. Echocardiogram may show early closure of the septal leaflet of the mitral valve. Cardiac catheterization may reveal an elevated left ventricular end diastolic pressure. Cineangiocardiography demonstrates aortic incompetence when dye is injected into the aortic root. Coronary arteriography is necessary to rule out associated coronary artery disease, especially if the patient has angina pectoris.

2. Differential diagnosis Elevated pulse pressure can be seen in patients with peripheral AV shunts.

3. Natural history Patients with aortic regurgitation develop compensatory left ventricular dilatation, hypertrophy, fibrosis, and ultimately failure. Patients may be asymptomatic for many years with mild aortic insufficiency. Operative mortality increases and late results are less satisfactory when the condition is of long standing and ventricular fibrosis has occurred.

4. Treatment

a. Medical Patients with aortic insufficiency should not be treated with digitalis because this masks clinical evidence of progression and may prejudice surgical results. In acute aortic insufficiency, such as seen in cusp perforation following bacterial endocarditis, afterload reducing agents (e.g., sodium nitroprusside) relieve left ventricular work while the patient is being prepared for surgery.

b. Surgical Aortic valve replacement is recommended for symptomatic patients in Class III or IV and for less symptomatic patients who have evidence of progressive cardiac enlargement on chest x-ray, progressive LV strain on ECG, or elevated resting left ventricular end diastolic pressure.

5. Prognosis Results depend upon the state of the left ventricular muscle at the time of operation, and on the effectiveness of myocardial protection during the procedure. Operative survivors usually improve symptomatically and have longer survival than unoperated patients.

C. MITRAL STENOSIS is the result of rheumatic carditis. The rheumatic process results in fusion of the valve commissures, thickening, fibrosis, and calcification of the leaflets, and thickening and shortening of the chordae tendineae and papillary muscles.

1. Diagnosis

a. Symptoms Shortness of breath, nocturnal dyspnea, hemoptysis, and in long-standing cases, abdominal swelling and ankle swelling.

b. Signs Mid-diastolic murmur, best heard at the cardiac apex. The murmur is elicited with the bell of the stethoscope with the patient leaning on the left side. There is often an accentuated pulmonic second sound, secondary to pulmonary hypertension. Pulmonary congestion may be present on auscultation of the lungs. In severe cases, hepatomegaly, ascites, and peripheral edema are noted.

c. X-rays Cardiomegaly due to enlargement of left atrium, right ventricle and right atrium. In the anterioposterior projection, there is often a double shadow produced by the superimposition of the dilated left atrium and dilated right atrium. The left main stem bronchus is displaced upward by the enlarged left atrium. 'Kerley B lines,' representing enlarged pulmonary lymphatics, may be seen in the peripheral lung fields.

d. Special tests ECG frequently shows atrial fibrillation. Echocardiogram may demonstrate thickening of the mitral valve. Cardiac catheterization shows elevated pulmonary capillary wedge pressure, pulmonary hypertension, and a gradient across the mitral valve (between the pulmonary wedge and the left ventricular end diastolic pressures).

2. Differential diagnosis Left atrial myxoma should be considered, particularly when symptoms are episodic or positional in nature.

3. Natural history   There is a latent period of 1 or more decades between the episode of rheumatic carditis, which usually occurs in childhood, and the onset of symptoms of mitral stenosis. The onset of atrial fibrillation commonly produces symptoms or an increase in preexisting symptoms and may lead to the development of left atrial thrombus and subsequent systemic emboli.

4. Treatment

a. Medical   Digitalis and diuretics for symptoms of congestive heart failure. Coumadin for patients in chronic atrial fibrillation.

b. Surgical   Patients in Class III or IV are surgical candidates. Open mitral commissurotomy is preferred to valve replacement and is attempted in most cases of pure mitral stenosis. Valve replacement is performed if commissurotomy cannot be done satisfactorily; for example, when the valve is extensively calcified or if mitral regurgitation is present.

5. Prognosis   The operative mortality is 5-8%. Patients improve symptomatically after operation, with a consistent fall in left atrial pressure and in pulmonary vascular resistance. Those in chronic atrial fibrillation and those requiring valve replacement should be anticoagulated to prevent systemic embolism. Restenosis of a severity requiring valve replacement occurs in approximately 10% of patients at 5 years and 40% at 10 years after open mitral commissurotomy.

D. MITRAL REGURGITATION   Causes of mitral regurgitation include rheumatic valve disease (often a mixed lesion with both stenosis and regurgitation), bacterial endocarditis, and the so-called 'floppy valve syndrome,' a condition in which the valve leaflets and the chordae tendineae are elongated. Mitral valve insufficiency also occurs in ischemic heart disease as a result of extensive inferior wall infarction or papillary muscle dysfunction or rupture. Acute mitral insufficiency as a complication of myocardial infarction is associated with a high mortality, and the risk of operation is correspondingly high.

1. Diagnosis

a. Symptoms   Dyspnea, easy fatiguability.

b. Signs   In the acute syndrome, low cardiac output, severe congestive heart failure, and cardiogenic shock. Apical pansystolic murmur, evidence of pulmonary congestion, accentuated pulmonic second sound, left ventricular enlargement.

c. X-rays   Cardiomegaly with left ventricular enlargement as well as left atrial enlargement.

d. Special tests   Left ventricular hypertrophy on ECG. Echocardiogram may disclose abnormal mitral valve motion. Right heart catheterization shows an elevated mean pulmonary capillary wedge pressure with a prominent V wave. This can be done at the bedside in cases of acute mitral insufficiency, and can be used to differentiate from ruptured ventricular septum complicating acute myocardial infarction. Left ventriculography will confirm regurgitation. In cases related to ischemic heart disease, concomitant coronary arteriography should be done. If the patient is in cardiogenic shock, an intra-aortic balloon counterpulsation device should be inserted prior to cardiac catheterization.

2. Differential diagnosis   Left atrial myxoma should be considered as a cause of mitral insufficiency.

3. Natural history   Chronic mitral insufficiency is often well-tolerated for many years.

4. Treatment

a. Medical   Patients with acute mitral insufficiency complicating acute myocardial infarction should, if possible, be treated medically with afterload-reducing agents, diuretics, and in some cases inotropic agents in an attempt to stabilize the patient while the myocardial infarction heals. The operative mortality is high in the immediate post-infarction period, and the surgical risk is greatly improved if operation can be delayed 4-6 weeks.

Chronic mitral insufficiency is treated with digitalis and diuretics.

b. Surgical   Patients with mitral insufficiency complicating myocardial infarction with cardiogenic shock refractory to medical management are candidates for urgent mitral valve replacement. Operative mortality is 20% or more in this context. Patients with chronic mitral insufficiency who are in Class III or IV should be considered for mitral valve replacement. The operative mortality is 10-20% in this group.

5. Prognosis   In cases of mitral insufficiency complicating ischemic heart disease, the prognosis is related to the degree of left ventricular dysfunction and the extent of coronary artery disease. In chronic mitral insufficiency, symptomatic improvement with consistent lowering of pulmonary vascular resistance can be anticipated. Late prognosis is related to the degree of left ventricular dysfunction present prior to surgery and the extent of perioperative myocardial damage.

E. TRICUSPID VALVE DISEASE   Primary tricuspid stenosis is a rare complication of rheumatic fever. Tricuspid insufficiency is usually a consequence of mitral valve disease with right ventricular enlargement and dilatation of the tricuspid valve annulus. Infection of the tricuspid valve, particularly in drug addicts, may cause tricuspid insufficiency that requires surgical treatment.

1. Diagnosis

a. Symptoms   Easy fatiguability, swelling of the abdomen and extremities.

b. Signs   A holosystolic murmur best heard over the right sternal border, V wave present in the neck, pulsatile liver, ascites, peripheral edema.

c. X-rays   Enlargement of right ventricle and right atrium.

d. Special tests   ECG may show right ventricular enlargement and right atrial enlargement. Cardiac catheterization may show a prominent V wave in the right atrium.

2. Differential diagnosis   Tricuspid insufficiency may be difficult to diagnose in the presence of mitral insufficiency because of the similarity of the auscultatory findings.

3. Natural history   Untreated tricuspid insufficiency leads to hepatic dysfunction (abdominal pain, ascites and bleeding diathesis), low cardiac output, and in far advanced cases, intestinal malabsorption.

4. Treatment

a. Medical   Diuretics and digitalis.

b. Surgical   The best assessment of tricuspid insufficiency is by palpation of the regurgitant jet with a finger inserted into the right atrium at the time of mitral valve surgery. Surgical management consists of annuloplasty to reduce the circumference of the tricuspid valve ring. Tricuspid valve replacement may be performed instead of annuloplasty.

In patients with tricuspid valve infection (e.g., drug addicts without associated pulmonary hypertension), excision of the tricuspid valve without valve replacement may be preferable because the infection is more readily controlled thereafter.

5. Prognosis   Results depend upon left ventricular function and the relief of associated mitral and aortic valve dysfunction.

VII. CONGENITAL HEART DISEASE

Congenital heart disease includes a wide variety of developmental defects which give rise to a correspondingly wide spectrum of circulatory dysfunction. Approximately 9 newborns out of every 1000 have some type of congenital heart lesion. The cause is unknown in most cases. Maternal rubella has been associated with approximately 1% of all congenital heart lesions, the most common abnormalities being patent ductus arteriosus and peripheral pulmonary stenosis. Persistent atrioventricular canal is commonly associated with Down's syndrome.

It is important for the clinician to understand the structural derangements and the pathophysiology. In order of decreasing frequency, some of the congenital heart defects are ventricular septal defect, atrial septal defect, pulmonic stenosis, patent ductus arteriosus, aortic stenosis, tetralogy of Fallot, coarctation of the aorta, transposition of the great arteries, and miscellaneous others. The more common defects are discussed below and are classified into those which produce significant right to left shunting (cyanotic) and those which do not (acyanotic).

Acyanotic Defects

A. VENTRICULAR SEPTAL DEFECT   Symptoms are related to the size of the ventricular defect and to pulmonary vascular resistance. The intensity of the heart murmur is poorly correlated with symptoms. Small defects may produce loud murmurs.

1. Diagnosis

a. Symptoms   Failure to thrive, poor feeding patterns, and congestive heart failure in infants. Frequent colds and upper respiratory problems in older children.

b. Signs   Harsh systolic murmur best heard at the left sternal border. Loud S_2 with an apical diastolic flow murmur. Biventricular enlargement with large defects.

c. X-rays   Biventricular enlargement and evidence of pulmonary congestion on chest film.

d. Special tests   Cardiac catheterization shows an increase in oxygen saturation at the right ventricular level. Pulmonary vascular resistance may or may not be elevated.

2. Differential diagnosis   Must be differentiated from lesions producing left to right shunt, such as atrial septal defect. In infancy, ventricular septal defect must be distinguished from aortic or pulmonic stenosis which produce similar murmurs.

3. Complications   Pulmonary vascular disease will develop in approximately 50% of children with large defects. Other sequelae include episodes of heart failure and respiratory distress in infants. Bacterial endocarditis and repeated respiratory infections occur in children. Some patients with large ventricular septal defects develop infundibular stenosis with reduction of pulmonary blood flow.

4. Treatment

a. Medical   Between 25% and 40% of ventricular defects become smaller with age, and many of these close spontaneously. If pulmonary vascular resistance is low as shown by cardiac catheterization, and if medical therapy is effective in controlling symptoms, patients may be followed.

b. Surgical   Infants who do not respond to medical management should have closure of the defect using cardiopulmonary bypass. Closure of the defect requires a prosthetic patch. Some infants may be managed with banding of the pulmonary artery, particularly those with muscular defects. Children with evidence of increasing pulmonary vascular resistance and those failing to respond to medical management are treated surgically.

5. Prognosis   The operative mortality rate is approximately 5%. Operative mortality is considerably increased in the presence of pulmonary vascular disease. About 1% of patients develop complete heart block after surgical repair.

Patients without pulmonary vascular disease experience symptomatic improvement, reduction of heart size, and improvement in growth pattern with surgical management. Moderately increased pulmonary vascular resistance usually falls after surgery.

B. ATRIAL SEPTAL DEFECT includes secundum defect (most common), sinus venosus defect, ostium primum defect, and partial anomalous pulmonary venous return. These lesions are associated with left to right shunting which is in proportion to the size of the atrial defect and the relative compliance of the left and right ventricles. With large septal defects, the mean pressure in the 2 atrial chambers is equal. During diastole, blood flows preferentially into the more compliant right ventricle causing an increased stroke output into the pulmonary circulation and an increased pulmonary to systemic flow ratio.

1. Diagnosis

a. Symptoms   The patient is usually asymptomatic. Occasionally children develop easy fatiguability or some retardation of growth.

b. Signs   Prominent right ventricular impulse, fixed splitting of the second heart sound, diastolic flow murmur across the tricuspid valve, and systolic flow murmur across the pulmonic valve.

c. X-rays   Right ventricular enlargement on lateral chest film and prominent vasculature suggesting excessive pulmonary circulation.

d. Special tests   Cardiac catheterization discloses increased oxygen saturation in the right atrial chamber.

2. Differential diagnosis   Patent foramen ovale and other lesions producing left to right shunting (e.g., a small ventricular septal defect) must be differentiated. The ostium primum defect is distinguished from an ostium secundum defect by the presence of superior axis on the ECG, a 'goose neck' deformity on the left ventricular angiogram, mitral insufficiency, and occasionally shunts from left ventricle to right ventricle or from left ventricle to right atrium.

Congestive heart failure secondary to atrial septal defect suggests the presence of other lesions such as patent ductus arteriosus.

3. Complications   Most patients are asymptomatic. Complications of atrial septal defect include bacterial endocarditis and the development of pulmonary hypertension and right ventricular failure later in life. Life expectancy is shortened to the fifth or sixth decade in patients with this lesion.

4. Treatment   Patients with 2:1 systemic to pulmonary flow ratio should undergo surgical correction in childhood, usually between the ages of 5 and 7.

Ostium secundum defects are closed with a patch of prosthetic material or pericardium.

Sinus venosus defects are corrected with a prosthetic patch. Some of these patients benefit from enlargement of the atriotomy so that superior vena caval obstruction does not occur.

Ostium primum defects are closed with a patch. If significant mitral insufficiency is present due to a cleft mitral valve, an attempt is made to close the cleft with interrupted sutures.

Partial anomalous pulmonary venous return is treated with a patch to divert pulmonary blood flow into the left atrium.

5. Prognosis   Operative mortality is less than 1% for ostium secundum defects and in the range of 3–4% for ostium primum. The prognosis is excellent after successful repair, and patients can anticipate full activity with normal life expectancy.

C. PULMONIC STENOSIS with intact ventricular septum is a common congenital anomaly. The abnormality responsible for pulmonic stenosis varies greatly. In the mildest form, there are 3 leaflets with commissural fusion. There is often considerable poststenotic dilatation of the pulmonary artery. Hypertrophy of the infundibular muscle involving the crista supraventricularis and its parietal and septal bands is commonly present, and this may contribute to right ventricular outflow obstruction. In the more severe forms, the pulmonary valve annulus is small and the valve leaflets are thickened and immobile without separation into distinct cusps. Primary infundibular stenosis is very rare in the absence of severe valvular stenosis or ventricular septal defect.

1. Diagnosis

a. Symptoms Infants with severe valvular stenosis are often cyanotic due to right to left shunting through a patent foramen ovale. The majority of patients with severe pulmonic stenosis develop heart failure and low cardiac output in the first 3 months of life. Most children with mild or moderate pulmonic stenosis and an intact ventricular septum have no symptoms and develop normally. Some complain of fatigue and dyspnea. Children with severe pulmonic stenosis have anginal chest pain, dizziness, and episodic dyspnea. They may have poor feeding habits, lethargy, and hypoxic spells. Sudden death may occur.

b. Signs Cyanosis and right heart failure in infants. High-pitched systolic ejection murmur best heard in the second left intercostal space. Increased right ventricular impulse.

c. X-rays Chest x-ray shows enlargement of the right ventricle, reduced pulmonary vascular markings, and dilatation of the main pulmonary artery.

d. Special tests ECG shows right atrial and right ventricular hypertrophy. Cardiac catheterization demonstrates elevated right ventricular pressure with a gradient across the pulmonary outflow tract. Angiography is done to rule out associated lesions.

2. Differential diagnosis Aortic stenosis, small ventricular septal defect, tetralogy of Fallot.

3. Complications Death, particularly in the first 3 months of life.

4. Treatment Infants with severe right ventricular failure or hypoxic spells require emergency surgical intervention. The patient is placed on cardiopulmonary bypass, the pulmonary artery opened, and the pulmonary valve commissures are incised to the annulus. In severe forms of pulmonic stenosis with annular atresia, the annulus is opened and a pericardial patch is placed across the right ventricular outflow tract. Children with a gradient of 45-50 mm Hg are candidates for surgery.

5. Prognosis Many infants operated on in the first weeks of life have recurrent pulmonary stenosis and require a second procedure later. Older children do not tend to have recurrence of stenosis and show regression of right ventricular hypertrophy.

D. PATENT DUCTUS ARTERIOSUS (PDA)

In fetal life approximately 50% of the cardiac output is diverted away from the pulmonary circulation into the descending aorta via the ductus arteriosus. At birth the ductus arteriosus is as large as the descending thoracic aorta, approximately 10 mm in diameter. Permanent spontaneous closure of the ductus is usually complete within 5-7 days in most infants, but it may not occur for up to 21 days. In some patients with atresia of the aortic arch or preductal coarctation, blood flow through the ductus is mandatory for perfusion of the lower body. The pathophysiology of uncomplicated patent ductus arteriosus is increased pulmonary blood flow with resultant pulmonary congestion and left ventricular overload. Patent ductus arteriosus is commonly associated with maternal rubella.

1. Diagnosis

a. Symptoms Poor feeding, respiratory distress and frequent respiratory infections in infants. In older children and adults, the abnormality is usually asymptomatic although in some it may lead to the development of congestive heart failure.

b. Signs A continuous murmur over the pulmonic area, also heard over the back, a loud S_2, and widened pulse pressure with prominent peripheral pulses.

c. X-rays Chest film may show increased pulmonary vascularity and enlargement of the left ventricle. In infants, pulmonary infiltrates may be seen.

d. Special tests ECG is often normal but may show left atrial or left ventricular or combined ventricular hypertrophy. Cardiac catheterization discloses increased oxygen saturation in the pulmonary artery and increased pulmonary artery pressure in neonates. Angiography demonstrates the lesion when contrast is injected into the aorta distal to the subclavian artery. In premature infants, the clinical diagnosis can be confirmed by echocardiography.

2. Differential diagnosis Aortopulmonary window cannot be distinguished by oxygen saturation or pressure measurements alone. Angiography is required to demonstrate the communication at this level. Patent ductus arteriosus must be distinguished from other lesions which are associated with a wide pulse pressure such as truncus arteriosus communis, systemic AV fistula, aortic insufficiency with or without a ventricular septal defect, sinus of Valsalva defects, and coronary AV fistula.

3. Natural history Patent ductus arteriosus is common in premature infants, and it occurs in association with idiopathic respiratory distress syndrome. Approximately 10% of patients with large shunts may develop pulmonary vascular disease in childhood or early adult life. The remainder of patients are at risk for bacterial endocarditis at the site of the ductus arteriosus. Later in adulthood, patients may develop left heart failure secondary to volume overload.

4. Treatment

a. Medical Premature infants with respiratory distress syndrome and patent ductus arteriosus are managed with digitalis, diuretics, blood replacement to maintain an adequate hematocrit, and positive pressure ventilation. If the patient improves on this regimen the ductus will often close spontaneously within several weeks. If symptoms do not improve, catheterization is undertaken to confirm the presence of a ductus with a large shunt and surgery is recommended. Presently there is interest in the administration of indomethacin as a pharmacologic means of stimulating ductal closure in premature infants.

b. Surgical Simple ligation is probably preferable to division of the PDA in children. Operation is contraindicated in patients with large patent ductus arteriosus with increased pulmonary vascular resistance and right-to-left shunting.

5. Prognosis The operative mortality rate is less than 1% in uncomplicated cases. Successful ligation or division totally corrects the abnormality.

E. AORTIC STENOSIS The term 'aortic stenosis' is used to indicate any of the obstructive lesions of the left ventricular outflow tract which include valvular stenosis, discrete subvalvular stenosis, diffuse subvalvular stenosis (idiopathic hypertrophic subaortic stenosis), and supravalvular stenosis. The most common of these is valvular stenosis; it is 4 times as common in males as in females.

In valvular aortic stenosis the valve is often bicuspid, the commissures are frequently fused, and the orifice of the valve is somewhat eccentric. In severe forms, the annulus is narrow, and the aortic valve consists of 3 thickened, poorly formed adherent cusps. Subvalvular aortic stenosis usually occurs 1-2 cm proximal to the aortic valve annulus and is a discrete fibrous ring or membrane. Idiopathic hypertrophic subaortic stenosis is a form of cardiomyopathy with generalized myocardial thickening most prominent in the region of the septum causing left ventricular outflow obstruction. Supravalvular aortic stenosis is the least common form and consists of a constriction or diffuse hypoplasia of the ascending aorta.

1. Diagnosis

a. Symptoms Heart failure in infants. Usually asymptomatic in children. Angina and syncope indicate severe obstruction.

b. Signs Harsh systolic murmur and thrill along the right upper sternal border, systolic ejection click.

c. X-rays The heart size usually appears normal. The ascending aorta may be dilated (poststenotic dilatation). In infants the chest x-ray shows cardiac enlargement and pulmonary congestion.

d. Special tests All patients suspected of having aortic stenosis should undergo cardiac catheterization and angiography. The left ventricular pressure is elevated, and a pressure difference is recorded across the aortic outflow tract. Angiography is helpful in planning the operation by differentiating among the various types of aortic stenosis.

2. Differential diagnosis In newborns where there may be difficulty in detecting cyanosis, one must consider total anomalous pulmonary venous return or double outlet right ventricle.

3. Complications Congestive heart failure and death in infancy. Thickening, fibrosis, and calcification of the valve with progressive stenosis later in life. Sudden death. The development of aortic regurgitation or bacterial endocarditis.

4. Treatment

a. Medical In infancy, congestive heart failure is treated with digitalis and diuretics. If there is not prompt improvement, surgical therapy is undertaken.

b. Surgical The various defects are treated by incising the valve commissures, resecting the subvalvular membrane, cutting a channel through the hypertrophic septal muscle, or patching the supravalvular stenosis.

5. Prognosis The operative mortality rate is high in infancy, often because of associated endocardial fibroelastosis. In older children, elective valvulotomy has a 5% operative mortality. Most symptomatic patients improve after operation. About 40% of children who have aortic valvulotomy have postoperative aortic regurgitation.

Within 10 years after aortic valvulotomy, approximately 25% of patients develop significant restenosis and require reoperation. Most patients who undergo aortic valvulotomy in infancy or childhood will need aortic valve replacement during adult life.

F. COARCTATION OF THE AORTA Narrowing of the thoracic aorta in the region of the ligamentum arteriosum is a common congenital defect producing proximal hypertension and left ventricular overload. Blood flow to the lower extremities is usually normal, although the pulse pressure below the coarctation is decreased. The aortic constriction is usually well-localized and is produced by both external narrowing and an intraluminal diaphragm. The majority of patients are asymptomatic during infancy. However, when the lesion is severe and heart failure develops in infancy, emergency surgery is required. There are often associated lesions such as bicuspid aortic valve and ventricular septal defect.

1. Diagnosis

a. Symptoms Infants may develop severe heart failure. Children are usually asymptomatic.

b. Signs Absent or weak femoral pulses. Proximal hypertension. Harsh systolic murmur heard over the back. Prominent pulsations on palpation of the latissimus dorsi.

c. X-rays Left ventricular enlargement, rib notching in children, aortic bulging proximal and distal to the coarcted segment producing a '3 sign' on the plain chest film or a 'reversed 3 sign' on the barium esophagram. Cardiac enlargement and congested peripheral lung fields in infants.

d. Special tests A pressure difference across the coarcted segment is shown by retrograde catheterization of the aorta. Cardiac catheterization may disclose associated intracardiac lesions. Angiography demonstrates the length of the coarcted segment.

2. Differential diagnosis In infants, other diseases causing heart failure (e.g., aortic stenosis, interrupted aortic arch, hypoplastic left heart, and fibro-elastosis) should be considered.

3. Complications Death due to congestive heart failure, cerebral hemorrhage, cerebral thrombosis, ruptured intercostal arterial aneurysms, and bacterial infection of the coarcted segment.

4. Treatment

a. Medical Digoxin, diuretics, morphine, and oxygen for all infants in severe heart failure associated with coarctation. If the infant improves within a few hours, operation can be postponed. Infants who do not improve should be operated on promptly.

b. Surgical In infants, urgent operation with ligation of the ductus arteriosus, resection of the coarcted segment with end-to-end anastomosis, or incision and subclavian patch angioplasty. In children and adults, repair may be done by widening the coarcted segment with a prosthetic patch, resection with end-to-end anastomosis, or replacement with a prosthetic graft.

5. Prognosis The operative mortality rate in infants is 15-25%. It is very low in older children and rises again in later adult life. Necrotizing arteritis of the mesenteric vessels may develop postoperatively leading to intestinal ischemia and gangrene. Postoperative hypertension should be treated with antihypertensive agents to prevent this complication. Paraplegia is a rare complication occurring in approximately 0.4% of patients.

Hypertension may persist after coarctation repair and does not correlate well with the adequacy of anatomic relief of obstruction. In general, the earlier the repair is effected, the better the chance of relief of hypertension. Restenosis is seen only in patients operated on in infancy and is probably due to a failure of the repaired segment to grow rather than an actual restenosis.

Cyanotic Defects

A. TETRALOGY OF FALLOT is characterized by right ventricular outflow obstruction, ventricular septal defect, right ventricular hypertrophy, and dextro-position of the aorta. The features which are important from a surgical standpoint are ventricular septal defect and RV outflow obstruction. The ventricular septal defect is usually large and involves the area of the membranous septum close to the crista supraventricularis. Right ventricular outflow obstruction is due to a combination of valvular stenosis and infundibular stenosis.

1. Diagnosis

a. Symptoms Hypoxic spells and squatting.

b. Signs Clubbing, cyanosis, prominent right ventricular impulse, absent S_2, a loud ejection murmur in the third left intercostal space, and softening or disappearance of the systolic murmur during cyanotic spells.

c. Laboratory tests Secondary polycythemia. Red-cell indices may show iron deficiency anemia.

d. X-rays Chest film shows the classical boot-shaped heart without cardiomegaly. A right-sided aortic arch is present in about 25% of patients.

e. Special tests Cardiac catheterization shows right to left shunting at the ventricular level and equalization of right and left ventricular pressures. Angiography discloses characteristic right ventricular and pulmonary artery anatomy.

2. Differential diagnosis In infancy, severe forms of tetralogy of Fallot are difficult to distinguish from other cyanotic abnormalities such as transposition of the great vessels with pulmonic stenosis and ventricular septal defect; pulmonic stenosis with a patent foramen ovale; double outlet right ventricle; and tricuspid atresia. In older children, tetralogy of Fallot can usually be diagnosed accurately on clinical findings.

3. Natural history Most patients with tetralogy of Fallot do not live past age 20, and the average age of death is 12 years in patients who survive infancy. Infants with severe right ventricular outflow obstruction often die during hypoxic spells. Other causes of death include cerebral venous thrombosis secondary to polycythemia, bacterial endocarditis, and cerebral abscess resulting from bacteria crossing the ventricular septal defect. Some patients develop a large bronchial arterial circulation which provides sufficient pulmonary blood flow to sustain life.

4. Treatment

a. Medical In infants, supportive measures such as correcting acidemia and hypoglycemia and maintaining body temperature are given while the diagnosis is established. Anemia is treated with iron. Orally administered propranolol has been effective in relieving or reducing the frequency of hypoxic spells.

b. Surgical Definitive surgical correction is directed at reconstruction of the right ventricular outflow tract and closure of the ventricular septal defect, but many surgeons prefer a palliative procedure in the first year of life. The most common of these is the Blalock-Taussig shunt in which the subclavian artery is anastomosed to the ipsilateral pulmonary artery to improve pulmonary blood flow. Patients so managed undergo operation to close the shunt and correct the defects between the ages of 3 and 5.

There is increasing enthusiasm for early correction of tetralogy of Fallot. The advantage of this approach is that right ventricular fibrosis and hypertrophy are minimal, and outflow stenosis can be more easily managed. Early correction may promote better growth of the pulmonary annulus. If, however, the pulmonary annulus is badly deformed, early operation necessitates division of the annulus and reconstruction of the right ventricular outflow tract with a pericardial patch.

The ventricular septal defect is closed with a patch. Careful attention is paid to suture placement in the area of the atrioventricular conduction bundle. When pulmonary atresia is present, a valve conduit is placed between the right ventricle and the pulmonary artery.

5. Prognosis
Operative mortality in tetralogy of Fallot is approximately 5-7%. Physiologic success is related to the size of the pulmonary annulus as compared with that of the aorta; the greater the discrepancy in size, the higher the operative risk.

A major problem following surgical correction is cardiac arrhythmias. Complete heart block occurs in about 1% of cases, and right bundle branch block is common.

B. TRANSPOSITION OF THE GREAT VESSELS is an abnormality in which the aorta arises from the morphologic right ventricle and the pulmonary artery from the morphologic left ventricle. Survival depends upon the presence of associated defects (e.g., patent ductus arteriosus, atrial septal defect, or ventricular septal defect) which permit mixing between the two independent circulations. Nearly half of the patients with transposition have a ventricular septal defect.

1. Diagnosis

a. Symptoms Hypoxic spells occasionally.

b. Signs Cyanosis is evident soon after birth. Heart failure is often present.

c. Laboratory tests Polycythemia, arterial desaturation.

d. X-ray On chest x-ray the supracardiac shadow is narrow because the aorta and the pulmonary artery are superimposed. The pulmonary artery arises posterior to the aorta.

e. Special tests Cardiac catheterization discloses systemic pressure in the right ventricle. There is inability to enter the pulmonary artery from a systemic vein except when a ventricular septal defect is present. Cineangiography shows the aorta located anterior to the pulmonary artery and filling from the right ventricle. The left ventricle is posterior.

2. Natural history Without treatment 50% of newborns with transposition die by the age of 1 month and 90% die within the first year of life. Patients with ventricular septal defects and mild to moderate pulmonary stenosis have the best prognosis. Patients with an intact ventricular septum have the worst prognosis. The combination of heart failure and hypoxia is the most common cause of death.

3. Treatment

a. Medical Balloon septostomy (rupture of the atrial septum at the time of cardiac catheterization) during the first days or weeks of life promotes mixing between the 2 atrial chambers and results in physiologic improvement in all patients.

b. Surgical A decision to perform corrective surgery is based upon the degree of cyanosis and the growth rate. If cyanosis is progressive or if growth is not adequate, operation is mandatory irrespective of age.

Patients are operated on using either standard cardiopulmonary bypass or surface cooling and profound hypothermia. An atrial baffle of pericardium is constructed, which directs venous blood across the atrial septum to the morphologic left ventricle (Mustard's operation). This results in oxygenation of venous blood and correction of cyanosis, and it leaves the right ventricle as the systemic ventricle. Since the right ventricle is required to provide systemic output, competence of the tricuspid valve is of major importance. Associated defects such as ventricular septal defect or pulmonic stenosis are repaired at the same time as construction of the atrial baffle.

4. Prognosis The operative mortality rate is 5-10%. Approximately 50% of patients have supraventricular arrhythmias following Mustard's operation. Late postoperative complications include obstruction of the vena cavae and pulmonary venous hypertension. Survivors are dramatically improved. Long-term results are not known.

VIII. TUMORS OF THE HEART AND PERICARDIUM

Tumors of the heart and pericardium are rare. In large series of autopsies, the incidence is 0.25% or less. Formerly, these tumors were of interest only to pathologists, but with the development of cardiac surgical technics, successful removal, especially of pedunculated intracardiac tumors, is a subject of practical clinical concern. Tumors of the heart and pericardium may be metastatic or primary.

A. METASTATIC TUMORS are 10-40 times more frequent than primary tumors. Metastases to the heart and pericardium may occur by hematogenous spread, lymphatic spread, or by direct invasion. Almost any malignant neoplasm can metastasize to the heart and pericardium; the most common are cancers of the lung or breast, lymphoma, and melanoma.

Cardiac symptoms and signs secondary to metastatic disease are usually late manifestations of the primary tumor. A common consequence of metastasis to this site is hemorrhagic pericardial effusion and cardiac tamponade. The diagnosis is confirmed by cytologic study of the pericardial fluid.

B. PRIMARY TUMORS

1. Mesothelioma is the most common primary tumor of **pericardium.** Obliteration of the pericardial cavity by the diffuse form of the tumor may simulate constrictive pericarditis; this form of mesothelioma is always malignant. The solitary form may be benign or malignant.

2. Sarcomas are the most common primary malignant tumor of the

heart. Metastases occur in approximately 80% of cases and usually involve the lung and mediastinum. These tumors may grow as exophytic masses and they commonly involve the pericardium, producing bloody pericardial effusion. They may grow intramurally causing heart block or myocardial failure. The differential diagnosis includes other causes of bloody pericardial effusion and myocardiopathy.

70% of primary tumors of the heart are benign and one half of these are myxomas.

C. MYXOMA Cardiac myxoma is a solid tumor arising from the endocardial surface as a gelatinous, bulky mass which may be lobulated or smooth. 95% of these tumors occur in the atria, the left atrial site being 3 or 4 times more frequent than the right. Left atrial myxoma usually originates from the atrial septum in the region of the fossa ovalis. Two-thirds of myxomas occur between 30 and 60 years of age; they are not seen in infants.

1. Diagnosis

a. Symptoms Dyspnea, fever, syncope, or peripheral embolization.

b. Signs Left atrial myxoma may simulate mitral stenosis with a characteristic murmur and physical findings of pulmonary congestion. Embolization of myxomatous material or blood clot arising from the tumor is common, and sudden death from coronary embolus may occur.

c. Laboratory tests Anemia, increased erythrocyte sedimentation rate, polycythemia.

d. X-rays Usually normal, although in long-standing cases left atrial enlargement may be present.

e. Special tests ECG findings are inconsistent and nondiagnostic. Echocardiography may disclose the presence of a left atrial mass which is difficult to distinguish from atrial clot. Cardiac angiography may reveal a space-occupying lesion which may move during the cardiac cycle. Depending on the length of the stalk and the size of the tumor, a ball valve mechanism with to-and-fro motion across the valve may be evident. Coronary angiography may delineate the vasculature of the tumor.

2. Differential diagnosis Mitral stenosis in the case of left atrial myxoma, thromboembolic disease producing pulmonary infarction in the case of right atrial myxoma, bacterial endocarditis (anemia, elevated erythrocyte sedimentation rate, peripheral embolization), Ebstein's anomaly in cases of right atrial myxoma, carcinoid syndrome, collagen diseases producing Raynaud's phenomenon, and atrial thrombus.

3. Natural history Cardiac myxomas grow slowly and have little potential for local invasiveness. Damaging or fatal systemic embolization may occur. Chronic congestive heart failure may result from obstruction of the mitral or tricuspid valves.

4. Treatment These tumors lend themselves to surgical excision. They are noninvasive and commonly arise from a stalk with a relatively small base. Care should be taken to excise as much of the base of the tumor as possible because of the tendency for recurrence following inadequate excision. When the tumor arises from the fissa ovalis of the atrial septum, a generous portion of the atrial septum is excised and the defect repaired with pericardium or prosthetic material. Cardioplegia is induced prior to atriotomy to prevent embolization of air or tumor.

5. Prognosis Cure is the rule, although local recurrence has been reported when excision was inadequate.

IX. CARDIAC TRANSPLANTATION

Clinical cardiac transplantation was begun in 1968 and continues to be performed in a few centers which have a research interest in this form of management. Patients with end-stage myocardial insufficiency may be candidates for this procedure, provided they meet certain criteria such as relatively young age and absence of other diseases. The survival rate after transplantation has improved with increasing clinical experience. At present, approximately 50% are alive at 1 year, and 25% at 5 years. These statistics compare favorably with the survival of patients designated as transplant candidates who die before a donor becomes available; all of these patients are dead within 1 year.

Early operative mortality is secondary to acute allograft rejection and infection. Immunosuppressive therapy consists of azathioprine which is begun preoperatively and continued indefinitely at the highest dose compatible with adequate marrow function. Corticosteroid therapy is begun intraoperatively and continued indefinitely at the lowest dose compatible with satisfactory allograft function. Intramuscular rabbit anti-human thymocyte globulin (RATG) is begun immediately after the operation and continued for the first 10 postoperative days.

Episodes of acute graft rejection are diagnosed by ECG and auscultatory findings and confirmed by endomyocardial biopsy. Decrease in the QRS voltage, the appearance of arrhythmias (usually atrial in origin), and the appearance of an S-3 gallop constitute presumptive evidence of graft rejection and require endomyocardial biopsy for confirmation. Therapy for rejection episodes includes increasing the dosage of steroid and beginning the administration of Actinomycin D, heparin, and occasionally RATG.

The major determinant of long-term survival is the development of accelerated coronary atherosclerosis in the transplanted heart. It is speculated that immune injury to the coronary vascular intima results in sloughing of the endothelial lining, exposing a thrombogenic surface which in turn produces platelet aggregation, organization, and lipid infiltration. Accordingly, chronic anticoagulation with coumadin as well as a regimen to lower serum cholesterol is maintained. When this regimen is carefully followed, accelerated atherosclerosis is controlled and long-term survival is increased. Some patients have survived cardiac retransplantation for intractable rejection or late development of coronary atherosclerosis.

Current clinical results suggest that cardiac transplantation may offer a useful means of management for selected patients with end-stage myocardial insufficiency.

10

ALIMENTARY TRACT

Theodore R. Schrock, MD

I. TRAUMA: GENERAL PRINCIPLES

Penetrating wounds made by missiles and knives may injure any structure in the abdomen. Blunt trauma is likely to damage solid organs (spleen, liver, pancreas, kidneys), although a distended hollow viscus (bladder, intestine) may be ruptured by a direct blow, and deceleration forces may avulse organs (liver, bladder, intestine) from their attachments.

A. DIAGNOSIS
1. History Obtain information about the injury, if possible, from the patient, relatives, ambulance attendant, police, or witnesses as resuscitation is begun.

2. Findings

a. Penetrating wounds may not be obvious. Do not overlook wounds of entry or exit in the flanks or posteriorly. Penetrating wounds of the thorax below the nipples are injuries of the chest and abdomen until proved otherwise.

b. Blunt trauma to the abdomen typically causes pain, distention, tenderness, and muscular rigidity from leakage of blood or intestinal contents. These signs may not appear for 12 hours or more, so repeated observation is necessary in some cases. Pain from visceral injury may be difficult to distinguish from muscular or skeletal pain, and there may be no objective findings despite extensive visceral damage.

Fractures of the lower ribs are common accompaniments of splenic and hepatic injuries.

Digital rectal examination may reveal blood in the stool.

3. Laboratory tests Hematocrit, leukocyte count, and urinalysis are obtained routinely, and other tests are ordered as necessary. Serum and urine amylase values reflect pancreatic injury.

4. X-rays

a. Plain x-rays of the abdomen may reveal free intraperitoneal air, obliteration of the psoas shadow, and other findings, most of them nonspecific. Fractures of transverse processes indicate severe trauma and should alert one to the possibility of extensive visceral injury.

b. Chest x-ray may disclose rib fractures, hemothorax, pneumothorax, or other evidence of thoracic injury.

c. The patient with blunt trauma often requires x-rays of skull, pelvis, and extremities.

d. Contrast studies of the urinary tract are necessary if hematuria is present.

e. Contrast x-rays of the upper or lower GI tract are helpful in selected cases.

f. Angiography may resolve questions about injury to the spleen, liver, or pancreas. In actual practice, abdominal angiography is seldom done.

5. Special tests *Peritoneal lavage* is useful to detect intraabdominal bleeding after blunt trauma if the diagnosis is unclear from physical and radiographic signs. The test should not be used in combative or uncooperative patients or in those with previous abdominal operations. **The bladder must be empty.**

With the patient supine, prepare the skin of the lower abdomen with tincture of iodine and infiltrate local anesthetic at a point in the midline, midway between the umbilicus and the pubis. A small incision is made in the skin and a peritoneal dialysis catheter is inserted into the peritoneal cavity. It helps if the patient tenses the abdominal musculature by raising the head. The operator must use both hands on the catheter to avoid plunging uncontrolledly into the abdomen. The stylet is withdrawn and the catheter is gently inserted into the pelvis toward the hollow of the sacrum.

Blood flowing through the catheter spontaneously is a positive result, but this is unusual. Instill 1000 ml of normal saline into the peritoneal cavity, then allow the fluid to return by gravity. Intraabdominal bleeding is indicated by a red color (like rosé wine) or a hematocrit of 1% or more in the returned fluid. Clear or only slightly blood-tinged fluid is a negative result.

B. TREATMENT

1. Emergency treatment of injured patients and the management of shock are discussed in Chapter 1.

2. IV antibiotics are begun in patients with penetrating injuries and in patients with blunt trauma if intestinal injury is suspected.

3. Penetrating wounds are indications for exploratory laparotomy if the peritoneum has been entered. Apparently-superficial knife wounds are explored under local anesthesia; if the posterior rectus sheath has not been penetrated, laparotomy is unnecessary.

4. Patients with blunt trauma who have obvious blood loss, circulatory instability, or other signs of abdominal injury require operation. Repeated examination may be necessary in some cases. **Note:** If a patient is in shock and has no source of blood loss externally or in the thorax, one must assume that abdominal bleeding is present and laparotomy must be undertaken.

5. Laparotomy

a. Control of bleeding is the first priority. Packs may stop bleeding in one area while another, more major, bleeding site is attended to.

b. Further contamination by intestinal contents should be prevented by isolating perforated intestine between clamps as soon as possible after massive bleeding is controlled.

c. Thorough exploration is then carried out, with special care to identify all intestinal perforations in patients with penetrating wounds. Victims of blunt trauma require careful inspection of the pancreas and duodenum.

d. Retroperitoneal hematomas that are not expanding or pulsating should not be opened.

e. Specific injuries are treated (see sections on individual organs in this chapter).

f. The peritoneal cavity is irrigated copiously with saline solution before closure.

g. The skin and subcutaneous fat are left open if fecal contamination was found; delayed primary closure can be attempted 4-5 days later.

II. ACUTE ABDOMEN

Most severe abdominal pain which lasts 6 hours or longer in a previously well patient is caused by a surgical condition. Every effort should be made to **diagnose the problem early** by taking a careful history and performing a thorough physical examination. Laboratory tests and x-rays are supplementary.

A. HISTORY

1. Age of the patient has obvious importance in determining the probable cause of an acute abdominal problem.

2. Pain is the cardinal symptom of the acute abdomen. Note the following:

a. Time and mode of onset (explosive, rapid, gradual). Note the relationship of onset to the last meal.

b. Character (dull, burning, cramping).

c. Severity (excruciating, severe, moderate, mild).

d. Constancy (steady, intermittent).

e. Location at onset.

f. Shift (subsides in one area and reappears in another) or *radiation* (remains in original site but extends to involve adjacent areas supplied by the same somatic nerves).

g. Effect of *respiration, movement, position* (erect, supine, lateral decubitus, hips flexed), *eating, defecation,* and *micturition.*

3. Vomiting Anorexia, nausea, and vomiting are gradations of the same mechanism. These symptoms result from irritation of the peritoneum, obstruction of a muscular tube, or absorption of toxic substances. Note these characteristics:

a. Time of onset If vomiting *preceded* abdominal pain, a surgical cause is unlikely.

b. Frequency and persistence.

c. Character Note especially if the appearance of the vomitus changes with repeated episodes. Patients may continue to retch (dry heaves) after the stomach is emptied. Hematemesis should be noted.

4. Defecation

a. Diarrhea (frequency, consistency, character, continence, hematochezia).

b. Constipation is infrequent bowel movements and *obstipation* is absence of bowel movements. Failure to pass any stool or flatus for 24 hours is indicative of intestinal obstruction.

5. Fever Note the time of appearance of fever, and note especially if shaking chills (rigors) occurred. Chills are a symptom of bacteremia (or viremia) and are most typical of infection in the urinary, biliary, or portal venous systems.

6. Past history

a. Previous abdominal disease and operations.

b. Systemic diseases and diseases of other organ systems.

c. Recent trauma, even if it seemed trivial at the time.

d. Menstrual history: last menstrual period, use of oral contraceptives.

B. PHYSICAL EXAMINATION

1. General appearance

a. Facial expression Flushed, pale, flaring nostrils.

b. Position and activity in bed Lying quietly, restless, writhing, hips and knees flexed.

2. Vital signs Fever, pulse rate, respiratory rate.

3. Chest Look for signs of pneumonitis.

4. Abdomen The following sequence elicits maximal information with minimal discomfort to the patient.

a. Inspection Scars, contour (scaphoid, distended), visible peristalsis.

b. Hernia orifices Inguinal, femoral, umbilical, incisional (if any).

c. Cough tenderness Ask the patient to cough and then point to the painful spot. Cough tenderness is a sign of peritoneal irritation; it may also be found with tenderness in the muscles of the abdominal wall. The examiner learns the location and the degree of localization of peritoneal irritation by this simple maneuver.

d. Palpation

(1) Muscle spasm: *Gently* place the flat of the hand over the abdomen and depress it slightly. True muscle spasm persists as the patient takes a deep inspiration; if guarding is voluntary, the muscle relaxes during inspiration. Muscle spasm indicates peritoneal irritation.

(2) One-finger palpation: Begin away from the point of cough tenderness and systematically examine the abdomen by *gently* probing with one index finger. If properly performed, this step is not painful and it localizes the peritoneal irritation. *Direct tenderness* is sensed beneath the examining finger; *referred tenderness* is felt in some other area.

(3) Deep palpation should not be performed in an area that is tender to one-finger palpation. A mass is the chief abnormality detected by deep palpation.

(4) Rebound tenderness is elicited by pressing gradually on the abdominal wall and releasing the pressure suddenly. Tenderness sensed in that area on release of pressure is *rebound tenderness;* pain felt elsewhere is *referred rebound tenderness.*

> **Note:** Testing for rebound tenderness elicits no information that cannot be obtained by gentler methods (cough and one-finger palpation); it may also be misleading, since many patients have 'rebound' without peritoneal irritation.

(5) Tenderness should be sought in the costovertebral angles.

e. Percussion of the mid and lower abdomen is just another means of detecting peritoneal irritation and usually is unnecessary. Percussion over the liver may reveal absence of dullness, a sign of free intraperitoneal air. Percussion may identify free fluid in the abdomen, but this finding usually is of little diagnostic value.

f. Auscultation is useful mainly in the diagnosis of intestinal obstruction in which peristaltic rushes and high-pitched tinkles are audible. In other acute abdominal conditions, peristalsis varies from absent to hyperactive. It is clearly an error to assume that active bowel sounds exclude the possibility of peritonitis.

g. Other signs

(1) *Iliopsoas sign* There are two methods of eliciting this sign of inflammation in or adjacent to the iliopsoas muscle. (a) With the patient supine, the patient actively flexes the hip and knee against the resistance of the examiner's hand. (b) Have the patient lie on the side opposite the area of abdominal pain. With the hip and knee straight, the examiner passively extends the thigh on the affected side.

(2) *Obturator sign* With the patient supine, flex the hip and knee and rotate the hip internally and externally. Inflammation adjacent to the obturator internus muscle is indicated by pain on this movement.

(3) *Murphy's sign* Inspiratory arrest during a deep breath as the examiner palpates the right upper quadrant. Classically, this sign is elicited when an acutely inflamed gall bladder comes into contact with examining fingers.

h. Pelvic and rectal examination These examinations are just as important as the abdominal examination. Tenderness of the pelvic peritoneum is elicited rectally or vaginally. Masses, rectal bleeding, and cervical discharge may be detected also.

C LABORATORY TESTS

1. Blood

a. Hematocrit may reflect bleeding or dehydration.

b. Leukocyte count and differential are useful if they are abnormal, but normal leukocyte profiles do not exclude a surgical condition.

c. Amylase may be elevated in many conditions other than pancreatitis, including perforated viscus, intestinal obstruction, and intestinal ischemia.

d. Serum electrolytes, creatinine, bilirubin, etc. are helpful in ill patients.

2. Urine should be examined for specific gravity, glucose, albumin, blood, leukocytes, casts, and bacteria.

3. Peritoneal fluid Paracentesis or peritoneal lavage (described in Section I of this Chapter) is helpful in some cases, especially in patients with such severe associated disease that exploratory operation would be hazardous. Examine the fluid for blood and bacterial content; amylase may be determined on the specimen also.

D. X-RAYS If perforation or obstruction is suspected, insert a nasogastric tube **before** sending the patient for x-rays.

1. Plain x-rays of the chest and abdomen are essential in most patients with acute abdominal disease. Abdominal films should be obtained in the supine and erect (or decubitus) positions. Look for gas pattern, masses, free air, obliteration of the properitoneal fat line or the outlines of the psoas muscles, liver and kidney shadows, and air in the biliary tree.

2. Intravenous urography is obtained if disease of the urinary tract is likely.

3. Studies of the upper or lower GI tract with water-soluble media may diagnose intestinal obstruction or perforation. Barium should be used only when perforation is clearly absent.

4. Intravenous cholangiography is sometimes performed.

5. Angiography diagnoses sites of intestinal bleeding and rupture of solid viscera.

6. Ultrasound is useful in some cases (e.g., to detect gallstones, pancreatic masses, pelvic masses).

7. The role of **CT scans** in the diagnosis of the acute abdomen has not been established.

E. SPECIAL TESTS One special test that may prove useful is diagnostic laparoscopy or peritoneoscopy. At present, it is performed most often in patients with suspected gynecologic disease.

F. DIAGNOSIS BY GROUPING OF SYMPTOMS AND SIGNS Possible causes of an acute abdominal illness can be estimated from the grouping of symptoms and signs.

1. Abdominal pain alone

a. The early stages of many conditions fall into this category, and only with repeated evaluation do other symptoms and signs appear.

b. Central, severe abdominal pain with no other abnormalities is seen in early appendicitis, intestinal obstruction, gastroenteritis, and pancreatitis.

c. Biliary colic and renal colic have characteristic distributions in most cases.

2. Severe central pain with shock Consider pancreatitis, intestinal ischemia, and intraabdominal bleeding (e.g., ruptured ectopic pregnancy, ruptured aneurysm).

3. Pain with vomiting and distention but no rigidity Small bowel obstruction.

4. Pain with obstipation and distention Colonic obstruction.

5. Severe pain with collapse and generalized rigidity Perforated ulcer or other perforated viscus.

6. Pain, tenderness, and rigidity

a. Right upper quadrant Cholecystitis, perforated ulcer, inflammation of a high-lying appendix.

b. Left upper quadrant Ruptured spleen, perforated ulcer, and various uncommon diseases.

c. Left lower quadrant Diverticulitis, perforated colonic cancer, pelvic peritonitis.

   d. Right lower quadrant   Appendicitis, perforated ulcer, gastroenteritis, Meckel's diverticulitis, cholecystitis (low-lying gallbladder), gynecologic diseases.

G. CONDITIONS WHICH MIMIC THE ACUTE ABDOMEN   In addition to many nonsurgical abdominal causes of abdominal pain, extraabdominal and systemic diseases can simulate the acute abdomen.
   1. Pulmonary diseases (pneumonia, pleurisy) that irritate the diaphragm may cause upper abdominal pain.
   2. Myocardial infarction often is associated with epigastric pain, but objective findings of tenderness and spasm are absent.
   3. Porphyria may cause severe abdominal pain. Porphobilinogen is found in the urine.
   4. Lesions of the spine and hip result in radicular pain or lower abdominal pain. Hyperesthesia of the skin and a dermatomal distribution are typical of radicular pain.

H. TREATMENT
   1. If the diagnosis is uncertain, reevaluate the patient frequently and attempt to make a diagnosis as soon as possible. The patient should be NPO; IV fluids are given, and nasogastric suction is often advisable.
   2. Narcotic analgesics should be given. Seldom do analgesics mask the objective findings of surgical disease.
   3. Antibiotics are not administered until a decision is made about the need for operation.
   4. The most important decision is whether the acute abdomen is 'surgical'; if so, operation should be performed as soon as the patient is prepared by correction of fluid and electrolyte imbalances. Most patients with localized peritoneal irritation and muscular rigidity, and essentially all patients with generalized peritonitis, septicemia, or hemodynamic instability should have exploratory laparotomy. A precise preoperative diagnosis of the condition causing the acute abdomen is a worthy objective, and it certainly helps the surgeon plan the placement of the incision, but it is less critical than the recognition that some form of surgical disease is in progress and must be treated by operation.

III. PERITONITIS AND ABDOMINAL ABSCESS

Peritonitis is inflammation of the peritoneum, a thin endothelial layer with a rich vascular and lymphatic supply. Abdominal abscess is one consequence of peritonitis.

A. ACUTE PERITONITIS
   1. Bacterial causes   The peritoneum is normally resistant to infection by small inocula of common bacteria; continuous contamination, virulent bacteria, diminished host resistance, and the presence of ascites, foreign bodies or active digestive enzymes are additive factors that increase the likelihood of peritonitis from bacterial contamination.
   a. Primary bacterial peritonitis is the result of hematogenous bacterial contamination of the peritoneal cavity. Streptococci and pneumococci are the usual organisms. The condition occurs mainly in patients with ascites.
   b. Secondary bacterial peritonitis follows acute infections or perforations of the gastrointestinal or genitourinary tracts. It is much more common than the primary form.
   2. Chemical causes
   a. Gastric and pancreatic juice are severely irritating to the peritoneum and may cause shock within a very short time. Eventually, secondary bacterial peritonitis is superimposed on the chemical irritation.

b. Bile, in the absence of bacteria and pancreatic juice, causes little peritoneal reaction. The addition of bacteria and/or pancreatic enzymes results in severe peritonitis.

c. Blood is a mild irritant in the peritoneal cavity. Bacteria or particulate matter make blood more likely to cause inflammation.

d. Urine is only mildly irritating by itself, but urine mixed with bacteria causes a severe form of peritonitis.

3. Diagnosis The clinical picture depends upon the cause of peritonitis, the extent of inflammation, and the interval after onset. Peritonitis may be **localized, diffuse, or generalized.** The following comments apply to chemical peritonitis and secondary bacterial peritonitis.

a. Symptoms

(1) Acute abdominal pain is a characteristic symptom. Pain is sudden, severe, and generalized in patients with chemical peritonitis due to a perforated viscus (e.g., perforated ulcer). In other conditions (e.g., appendicitis), pain is caused by the underlying disease initially, and it becomes more diffuse as peritonitis spreads gradually from the focus of infection. In these cases, peritonitis extends slowly from localized to diffuse to generalized, and if the host defenses contain the infection, peritonitis does not progress to the generalized stage.

(2) Nausea and vomiting are usually present.

(3) Sudden collapse may occur at the onset of chemical peritonitis.

b. Signs

(1) Shock (neurogenic, hypovolemic, or septic) is present in many patients with generalized peritonitis.

(2) Fever is routinely noted with advanced peritonitis, although it may be deceptively mild or even absent in elderly patients.

(3) Abdominal distention becomes more marked with the passage of time.

(4) Abdominal tenderness and rigidity are localized, diffuse, or generalized, depending upon the extent of peritoneal irritation.

(5) The abdomen classically is silent with generalized peritonitis, although bowel sounds are audible in areas remote from localized peritonitis.

c. Laboratory tests Leukocytosis, elevated hematocrit (hemoconcentration), and metabolic acidosis are found with peritonitis. Tests reflect respiratory, hepatic, and renal failure in advanced untreated peritonitis.

d. X-rays Ileus is a nonspecific finding in peritonitis; both small and large bowel are dilated. Free air may be noted in cases of perforated viscus. More specific signs of the underlying cause of peritonitis may be present.

e. Special tests Paracentesis or peritoneal lavage (see Section I) may be useful in doubtful cases.

4. Differential diagnosis The surgeon's task is to differentiate peritonitis from diseases that mimic it and to distinguish between surgical and nonsurgical causes of true peritonitis. Acute edematous pancreatitis, salpingitis, and gastroenteritis are among the diseases that do not require operation ordinarily. The differential diagnosis of peritonitis, therefore, is essentially the differential diagnosis of the acute abdomen. (See Section II and specific disease entities in other sections.)

5. Complications Death may result from hypovolemia in patients with chemical peritonitis and from overwhelming sepsis in patients with bacterial peritonitis. Multiple organ failure (pulmonary, cardiac, hepatic, and renal) precede death by hours to days.

Late complications include abdominal abscess (see below) and adhesions that may cause intestinal obstruction at some future date.

6. Treatment

a. Primary peritonitis is treated with antibiotics if the diagnosis is established with certainty.

b. Treatment of secondary peritonitis is directed toward the underlying cause and requires operation in most cases.

(1) Treat shock (see Chapter 1) and correct fluid and electrolyte derangements (Chapter 2).

(2) Broad spectrum antibiotics are begun empirically and modified later as culture reports become available. The choice of antibiotics depends upon the suspected origin of peritonitis (see Chapter 4).

(3) Treat associated diseases and the systemic consequences of peritonitis (e.g., respiratory or renal insufficiency).

(4) Operation (a) Correct the inciting disease. (b) Aspirate peritoneal fluid and irrigate copiously with saline solution. Irrigation with antibiotics or antiseptics (e.g., povidone-iodine) is controversial. Note: If peritonitis is localized, it is best not to irrigate the general peritoneal cavity lest bacteria be spread in the process. (c) Drainage of the general peritoneal cavity is not recommended. Drains become isolated from the area they are supposed to drain within a few hours, they interfere with peritoneal defenses, and they may erode into viscera. Drains are beneficial in localized abscesses or if there is a source of continuing contamination.

(5) Postoperative care is essentially the care of a critically ill patient. Antibiotics should be continued and changed as necessary. The surgeon should be vigilant to detect abscess formation. The semi-sitting (semi-Fowler) position may permit residual or newly formed pus to collect in the pelvis by gravity, but the value of this position is probably not as great as once thought.

7. Prognosis depends upon age, associated diseases, the cause of peritonitis, and the promptness and effectiveness of surgical treatment.

B. CHRONIC PERITONITIS

1. Chylous ascites

a. Congenital chylous ascites is due to abnormal communication of intestinal lymphatics with the peritoneal cavity. In some patients, chyle refluxes into the lower extremities as well. Surgical ligation and division of the abnormal lymphatic communications may be effective.

b. Acquired chylous ascites may be due to obstruction of major lymphatics (e.g., the thoracic duct) by tumor, disruption by surgical dissection, or idiopathic. Most cases resolve spontaneously, although malignant obstructions persist until death from the tumor.

2. Tuberculous peritonitis may be primary or the result of spread from a focus in the lungs, intestine, or genital tract.

a. Diagnosis Weakness, night sweats, weight loss, and abdominal distention are present for weeks to months. Ascites, masses, and a 'doughy' feel to the abdomen may be noted. Peritoneal fluid has a high protein (>3 gm/100 ml) and lymphocyte content; tubercle bacilli are identified by culture. Biopsy of the peritoneum percutaneously or by laparoscopy shows typical tuberculous granulomas and yields a diagnosis long before culture results are available.

b. Treatment Antituberculosis chemotherapy is effective (see Chapter 4).

3. Talc and starch peritonitis Chronic granulomatous peritonitis may result from powders on surgical gloves. Talc is no longer used, but starch powder apparently can have a similar effect. The disease is prevented by washing gloves thoroughly before placing the hands in the peritoneal cavity.

Severe abdominal pain, fever, and signs of peritonitis develop about 2 weeks after operation. Reoperation should be avoided if other causes of peritonitis can be excluded. Corticosteroids may be beneficial.

C. ABDOMINAL ABSCESS

Abdominal abscesses are common sequelae of bacterial peritonitis. Persistent fever, anorexia, malaise, and leukocytosis are typical. Other symptoms and signs and the treatment depend upon the location of the abscess. Common sites are shown in Fig. 10-1.

1. Subphrenic abscess An abscess may form in any of the subphrenic spaces. There are three spaces on either side of the midline. On the right, the spaces are superior to the liver, inferior to the liver, and subhepatic. On the left, one space is anterior to the liver, one is anterior to the lesser sac, and another is the lesser sac itself.

a. Diagnosis The difficulty of diagnosing subphrenic abscess is expressed in the adage 'pus somewhere, pus nowhere, pus under the diaphragm'.

(1) *Symptoms and signs* (a) Spiking fever that is not explained by infection elsewhere. (b) Anorexia and malaise. (c) Pain and tenderness over the lower thorax, flank, or upper abdomen in some cases. (d) Pleural effusion and limitation of diaphragmatic excursion.

(2) *X-rays* Films of the upper abdomen and chest may show pleural effusion, stippled gas beneath the diaphragm, and an elevated and immobile diaphragm on the affected side. Fluoroscopy may demonstrate diaphragmatic fixation.

(3) *Special tests* (a) Ultrasound is not as useful in demonstrating abscesses in the subphrenic spaces as it is for abscesses lower in the abdomen. (b) CT scan is relatively new, and its role in the diagnosis of subphrenic abscess is not established; potentially, it could prove very helpful. (c) Gallium scan identifies inflammation, but it is not specific for abscess. False-positive results are due to uptake of gallium by stool in the colon, tumor, and phlegmon. (d) Thoracentesis proves that the pleural effusion is sterile and increases the likelihood that a subphrenic abscess, rather than a primary pulmonary problem, is responsible for the effusion.

b. Treatment Antibiotic therapy alone may resolve subphrenic cellulitis (phlegmon), but once a true abscess containing pus has formed, surgical drainage is required.

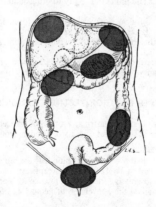

Fig. 10-1. Common locations of peritoneal abscess formation (Reproduced with permission from Dunphy JE, Way LW (Eds.) *Current Surgical Diagnosis & Treatment*, 3rd Ed. Lange 1977)

Solitary abscesses are best drained extraperitoneally (through a subcostal incision) or extrapleurally (through the bed of the resected 12th rib posteriorly: Ochsner approach).

If the surgeon cannot be certain that a subphrenic abscess is solitary, the abscess(es) should be drained transperitoneally.

Drains placed into the abscess should be withdrawn slowly as the cavity shrinks.

c. Prognosis is excellent if the abscess is well-drained. Some abscesses, particularly those in the lesser sac, are difficult to drain adequately, and repeated operations may be necessary.

2. Pelvic abscess

a. Diagnosis   Pelvic abscess is more easily diagnosed than subphrenic abscess in most cases. Symptoms are fever, pelvic discomfort, rectal pressure, diarrhea, and urinary symptoms.

A tender, boggy or indurated mass is palpable anterior to the rectum. In women, the abscess may bulge into the vagina from the pouch of Douglas.

b. Treatment   Antibiotics should be given to help contain the infection; pelvic cellulitis may resolve with antibiotics alone.

Mature abscesses are drained into the rectum or vagina. The classic indication of a maturing abscess is downward descent of the mass, often with gaping and incontinence of the anus. Drains are removed from the abscess in a few days.

c. Prognosis   Recovery is rapid and complete in most patients.

3. Other abdominal abscesses   Abscesses often form in the lateral gutters, between loops of small bowel, or beneath an abdominal incision.

a. Diagnosis   Symptoms include fever, malaise, and pain.

Repeated, careful one-finger palpation may disclose tenderness over an abscess as it develops, and a mass becomes palpable in many cases.

Plain x-rays may reveal collections of gas and fluid outside the bowel or displacement of dilated intestinal loops.

Ultrasound and gallium scan are useful tests. A recent incision is a relative barrier to sound waves and limits the ability of ultrasound to detect abscesses beneath a wound.

b. Treatment   Surgical drainage is best performed after the abscess is localized so that the general peritoneal cavity is not contaminated during the procedure. In the critically ill patient, however, operation may be necessary despite the lack of localizing information.

c. Prognosis depends upon the patient's age and general condition, the location and multiplicity of abscesses, and the adequacy of surgical drainage.

IV. UPPER GASTROINTESTINAL HEMORRHAGE

Duodenal ulcer, gastric ulcer, gastritis, esophageal varices, and Mallory-Weiss syndrome account for 95% of cases of massive bleeding from the upper GI tract.

A. MANIFESTATIONS

1. Hematemesis is the vomiting of blood. If the blood is red, the source is proximal to the ligament of Treitz with few exceptions.

2. Coffee-ground emesis reflects the presence of blood in the stomach for a sufficient time to allow the conversion of hemoglobin to methemoglobin by gastric acid.

3. Melena is the passage of black stools. Blood must remain in the gut several hours for it to change color, so most patients with melena are bleeding from the upper GI tract.

4. Hematochezia is the passage of bright red blood per rectum. This too may originate in the upper tract. Management is discussed in Section V.

B. DIAGNOSIS AND TREATMENT The amount of blood loss and the rate of bleeding determine the urgency of the diagnostic and therapeutic efforts. Hematemesis always implies the threat of exsanguination and requires immediate action. Coffee-ground emesis and melena (especially if present for several days) may be evaluated more leisurely. Hematochezia is discussed in Section V. The following comments apply to massive bleeding.

1. Question the patient about known upper GI disease or symptoms that may suggest the cause of bleeding.

2. Physical examination may reveal stigmata of cirrhosis and portal hypertension, but bleeding cannot be assumed to be variceal since about 50% of cirrhotics with acute upper GI hemorrhage are bleeding from peptic ulcer or gastritis.

3. Resuscitation with IV fluids is begun immediately, and transfusions are given as necessary. Avoid inadequate transfusion; hypotension is a poor way to stop bleeding, and it leads to pulmonary and renal failure.

4. Pass a large Ewald (32–36F) tube through the mouth into the stomach and lavage the stomach with iced saline to evacuate liquid and clotted blood. The Ewald tube can be removed and a nasogastric tube inserted after bleeding stops. Remember that patients may bleed from a duodenal ulcer without reflux of blood into the stomach; the gastric aspirate in such patients contains no blood.

5. Measure prothrombin time, serum creatinine, hematocrit, albumin, and liver function.

6. If the patient is stable, fiberoptic endoscopy should be done to determine the bleeding site. Upper GI x-rays also detect lesions, but they do not determine if a lesion is bleeding. X-rays should be done if doubt remains about the bleeding site after endoscopy.

7. Angiography is useful to diagnose bleeding sites if endoscopy fails (e.g., bleeding distal to the ligament of Treitz). Angiography with infusion of vasoconstricting agents is used therapeutically in selected patients who are prohibitive operative risks (e.g., jaundiced cirrhotic patients who are bleeding from gastritis).

8. Bleeding may stop with iced saline lavage. Subsequent management is directed at the specific cause of the bleeding episode. The nasogastric tube is removed as soon as it is certain that bleeding has ceased.

9. If bleeding persists, continued nasogastric suction, careful monitoring of vital signs, and serial hematocrits are guides to the rate of bleeding and help determine the course of action.

10. Operation to control bleeding is advisable if a patient requires more than 4 units of blood to achieve hemodynamic stability initially, or if more than 1 unit of blood is required every 8 hours thereafter. These are general rules, and exceptions must be made. It is essential to operate before the systemic effects (especially pulmonary and renal) of prolonged hypotension and multiple transfusions occur. Elderly patients tolerate massive hemorrhage poorly and should be operated on earlier rather than later compared with younger patients. Early operation also is indicated if compatible blood is not available for transfusion or if the patient refuses transfusions.

11. Management of specific causes of upper GI hemorrhage is discussed in appropriate sections in this chapter.

V. LOWER GASTROINTESTINAL HEMORRHAGE

Massive bleeding per rectum can arise from lesions at any level in the gastrointestinal tract. The lower tract (distal small bowel, colon, and anorectum) is the probable source of dark red to bright red blood (**hematochezia**), but it is important to keep in mind that the color of evacuated blood is a function of the length of time it resided in the bowel, and bright red blood can originate at any level. If the patient is not in shock, bright red blood is likely to be coming from the lower tract.

Colonic lesions that give rise to massive hemorrhage include vascular ectasias or malformations, diverticula, ulcerative colitis, ischemic colitis, and solitary ulcer. Neoplasms rarely cause exsanguinating hemorrhage. Massive bleeding originates with equal frequency in the right colon and the left colon.

Diagnostic and therapeutic maneuvers are performed simultaneously.

1. Resuscitation with IV fluid and whole blood takes first priority.

2. Anoscopy and sigmoidoscopy are mandatory. Bleeding hemorrhoids, ulcerative colitis, or ischemia may be detected.

3. A nasogastric tube should be inserted. Some patients with duodenal ulcers do not reflux blood back into the stomach, and **gastroduodenoscopy** should be considered.

4. If bleeding stops spontaneously shortly after admission to the hospital (75% of patients), a barium enema is performed after the colon is cleansed. Fiberoptic colonoscopy and abdominal angiography are alternatives, or they may be done in addition to barium enema. If the bleeding site is not found and bleeding does not recur, nothing further should be done.

5. If bleeding continues, abdominal angiography should be obtained. The bleeding site is found in 60-80% of patients. If the bleeding site is identified, a vasoconstrictor (epinephrine or vasopressin) is infused into the artery supplying the bleeding point. This method is successful in about 75% of patients and if bleeding does not recur, operation is not required in most cases. Elective operation after preparation of the colon is advisable in some instances.

6. If bleeding is extremely rapid, if angiography cannot be obtained or is unsuccessful, or if bleeding recurs, operation should be done. The affected portion of colon should be resected if the bleeding site is known. Patients who are bleeding from an undetermined site require operative examination of the upper tract, small bowel, and colon. In many cases, total abdominal colectomy with ileorectal anastomosis is the only recourse for colonic bleeding of unknown origin. The operative mortality rate is about 10% in this situation.

VI. INTESTINAL OBSTRUCTION*

Mechanical obstruction of the intestine refers to complete or partial physical blockage of the lumen. **Simple obstruction** implies one obstructing point; obstruction at two or more points is a **closed loop.** The intestine is viable in **nonstrangulating obstruction** and necrotic (due to impaired blood supply) in **strangulation obstruction.** Strangulation may result from high intraluminal pressure as the bowel distends with gas and fluid. More often, however, strangulation occurs when the obstructing mechanism occludes the mesenteric blood supply as well as the lumen; thus, strangulation is more likely in closed loop than in simple obstruction.

About 85% of mechanical obstructions occur in the small intestine and 15% in the large intestine. The causes of obstruction in the western world are listed in Table 10-1; the relative incidence of these causes is very different in developing countries. Miscellaneous causes of small bowel obstruction include intussusception, internal hernia, volvulus, foreign body, gallstone, inflammatory bowel disease, and stricture from ischemia or radiation injury. Diverticulitis seldom obstructs the colon completely; volvulus is the second most common cause of complete colonic obstruction. Miscellaneous causes of large bowel obstruction include inflammatory bowel disease, benign tumors, ischemic stricture, and fecal impaction.

---

*Obstruction in infants and children is discussed in Chapter 18.

A. OBSTRUCTION OF THE SMALL INTESTINE

1. Diagnosis

a. Symptoms

(1) Cramping abdominal *pain* with a crescendo-decrescendo pattern, recurring every few minutes, is typical. Obstruction of the proximal intestine causes variable kinds of upper abdominal discomfort rather than cramps. Continuous pain suggests strangulation.

(2) *Vomiting* occurs minutes to hours after the onset of pain, depending on how distal the obstruction is. Vomitus becomes feculent due to bacterial overgrowth, especially with distal obstruction. Blood in the vomitus indicates strangulation or an associated lesion.

(3) *Obstipation* is a feature of complete obstruction, although gas and feces in the colon can be expelled after the obstruction begins.

b. Signs

(1) Vital signs are normal, or they reflect dehydration. Shock or high fever suggests strangulation.

(2) Abdominal distention is minimal in proximal obstruction and marked in distal obstruction. Mild tenderness is common; severe tenderness warns of strangulation. Peristaltic rushes and high-pitched tinkles are audible coincident with cramps.

(3) A tender, incarcerated external hernia (inguinal, femoral, umbilical, incisional) should be sought; femoral hernias are difficult to find in obese patients.

c. Laboratory tests Results of blood chemistries depend upon the degree of dehydration. Leukocytosis may indicate strangulation, but the leukocyte count can be normal even in patients with necrotic bowel. Urinalysis reflects dehydration.

d. X-ray findings Plain abdominal films in the supine and erect (or lateral decubitus) positions show dilated small bowel loops with gas-fluid levels in a ladder-like pattern. This picture is absent in proximal obstruction. The colon typically contains no gas. Gas in the intestinal wall is a late sign of strangulation.

Oral contrast medium establishes the diagnosis of obstruction in equivocal cases.

2. Differential diagnosis

a. Small vs. large bowel obstruction is discussed in the following section.

b. Paralytic (adynamic) ileus follows abdominal surgery (see Chapter 2), or it is associated with peritonitis, trauma to the abdomen or back, etc. The inciting cause, such as appendicitis or pancreatitis, should be evident. Ileus causes constant mild pain and abdominal distention. Plain films show gas in both the small intestine and colon. Contrast x-rays help in doubtful cases.

3. Complications Strangulation is the cause of most deaths from intestinal obstruction. The luminal contents are a lethal mixture of bacteria, bacterial products, necrotic tissue, and blood. The strangulated bowel may perforate, releasing this material into the peritoneal cavity; even if the bowel does not perforate, bacteria may transude through the permeable bowel or enter the circulation via lymphatics and cause septic shock.

4. Treatment With few exceptions, complete obstruction of the small intestine is treated by operation because of the risk of strangulation. No symptom, sign, or laboratory test excludes the possibility of strangulation with certainty.

a. Preoperative preparation

(1) A *nasogastric tube* should be inserted to relieve vomiting and to avoid further distention of the bowel by swallowed air. A long intestinal tube has no advantage if prompt operation is planned.

(2) *Fluid and electrolyte resuscitation* is crucial. Huge amounts of isotonic fluid are lost into the bowel lumen, intestinal wall, peritoneal cavity, and by vomiting. Hypovolemia is the cause of death in nonstrangulating ob-

Table 10-1. Causes of mechanical intestinal obstruction in adults

Site of obstruction	Cause	Relative incidence (%)
Small intestine	Adhesions	60
	External hernia	20
	Neoplasm	10
	Miscellaneous	10
Large intestine	Carcinoma of colon	65
	Diverticulitis	20
	Volvulus	5
	Miscellaneous	10

struction. It may take several hours to replace these losses and correct the acid-base imbalances before operation.

(3) *Antibiotics* are advisable. They are essential in strangulation, and strangulation is always a possibility until operation proves otherwise.

b. Operation is begun when the patient has been rehydrated and vital organs are functioning properly.

If a groin hernia is the cause of obstruction, the incision is made over that area. Otherwise, a generous abdominal incision should be made.

Operative details depend on the cause of obstruction. Adhesive bands are lysed or the obstructing lesion is removed. Strangulated bowel is resected.

5. Prognosis Nonstrangulating obstruction has a mortality rate of about 5%; most deaths are in the elderly. Strangulation obstruction has a mortality rate of 8% if operation is performed within 36 hours after the onset of symptoms and 25% if operation is delayed beyond 36 hours.

B. OBSTRUCTION OF THE LARGE INTESTINE In 10-20% of patients, the ileocecal valve is incompetent, and pressure proximal to an obstructing lesion in the colon is relieved by reflux into the ileum. In most patients, however, a closed loop is formed between the obstructing point and the ileocecal valve, and perforation of the cecum may result from progressive distention with impairment of blood flow in the cecal wall.

1. Diagnosis

a. Symptoms Cramping *pain* develops insidiously in the hypogastrium, left lower quadrant, or diffusely in the abdomen. Severe, continuous pain suggests strangulation. Loud borborygmi are common.

Obstipation is a universal feature if obstruction is complete.

Vomiting occurs late or not at all.

b. Signs The abdomen is markedly distended and tympanitic; tenderness may overlie the distended colon; diffuse severe tenderness and rigidity indicate perforation. Gross or occult blood may be present in the stool. Sigmoidoscopy is mandatory; the obstructing lesion may be seen.

c. X-ray findings Plain films show a distended colon outlining the peritoneal cavity like a 'picture frame'. The small bowel is dilated also if the ileocecal valve is incompetent.

Contrast enema (water-soluble medium is safer than barium) is performed unless strangulation is suspected; the examination should stop when the lesion is seen. Oral barium is contraindicated because it will impact in the colon proximal to the obstruction.

2. Differential diagnosis

a. Small versus large bowel obstruction Large bowel obstruction is slower in onset, the pain is less severe, and vomiting is not always present. X-ray usually differentiates the two conditions.

b. Pseudo-obstruction is colonic distention in the absence of a mechanical block. It is associated with systemic illnesses. Distention without pain is the first symptom. Contrast enema excludes a mechanical problem; the colon should not be overfilled lest perforation occur. Decompressive cecostomy may be necessary.

c. Paralytic ileus (see section on small bowel obstruction).

3. Complications Gangrene and perforation of the cecum is a threat if the cecum is 10 cm or more in diameter.

4. Treatment Decompression of the obstructed colon to avoid perforation is the most important goal; resection of the obstructing lesion usually is required eventually but has secondary importance in the emergency situation.

a. Preoperative preparation requires the same measures described for small bowel obstruction; fluid and electrolyte deficits usually are less severe.

b. Operation consists of decompressing cecostomy or diverting transverse colostomy in most cases. Obstructing cecal lesions are resected. Obstructing cancers of the left colon may be resected in good risk patients.

c. Postoperative care is directed toward preparation of the patient for elective resection if the obstructing lesion is not removed initially.

5. Prognosis Overall mortality rates of 15-30% are common. Cecal perforation is the most important preventable cause of death.

C. VOLVULUS OF THE LARGE INTESTINE
Volvulus is rotation of the bowel (usually the cecum or the sigmoid colon) on its mesocolon, causing obstruction of the lumen and compromise of the circulation simultaneously.

1. Cecal volvulus results from incomplete embryologic fixation of the ascending colon.

Because the cecum and the terminal ileum rotate together, the symptoms include those of small bowel obstruction. Pain in the right abdomen is severe and cramping initially, and then it becomes continuous. Vomiting and obstipation follow. The abdomen is distended.

The x-ray picture is characteristic, with a dilated cecum in the left upper quadrant.

Operation is mandatory as soon as the patient is prepared. The right colon is resected if it is strangulated; resection should also be performed if viable bowel is found in a good risk patient. If the patient's condition is precarious and the bowel is viable, the volvulus is untwisted and cecostomy is done.

The mortality rate is 30%; death is the consequence of delayed recognition and treatment.

2. Sigmoid volvulus results from elongation of the sigmoid in elderly, bedridden, or mentally ill patients.

Pain is cramping. Obstipation occurs immediately.

Plain films show a huge distended loop rising out of the pelvis into the right upper quadrant. Barium enema findings are pathognomonic.

Unless strangulation is suspected, the first episode is treated by passing a soft rubber tube through a sigmoidoscope into the twisted loop. The patient is placed in the knee-chest position. A size 30 F tube 60 cm long is lubricated well; if the mucosa has good color at the point of torsion, the tube is gently slid upward until decompression occurs. The tube is sutured to the perional skin, irrigated, and removed after several days. Resection of the sigmoid is advisable for recurrent episodes, but preliminary deflation with a rectal tube permits resection to be done electively.

The mortality rate is 25% for the first episode. Death is due to perforation (50% mortality) or associated disease in these elderly people.

VII. ACUTE INTESTINAL ISCHEMIA*

Acute intestinal ischemia may result from **arterial** occlusion (thrombosis or embolus), **venous** occlusion (thrombosis), or **nonocclusive** mechanisms (splanchnic hypoperfusion).

The consequences of ischemia vary with the vessel involved, adequacy of collateral, and other factors. The mucosa becomes ischemic first and may ulcerate, slough, and bleed. Severe ischemia leads to full thickness infarction of the gut. The clinical course depends upon many variables and may range from mild to fulminating. Most patients are elderly.

A. DIAGNOSIS
1. Symptoms   Severe, poorly localized abdominal pain is the hallmark of intestinal ischemia. It may not respond to analgesics and is worse with movement.

Vomiting, diarrhea (commonly bloody, especially if the colon is involved), or even constipation may occur.

History may reveal an underlying cause, e.g., cardiac arrhythmia, sepsis, hypercoagulable state, oral contraceptives, malignancy, portal hypertension, trauma, or intestinal angina.

2. Signs   *Pain out of proportion to the objective findings* is typical of intestinal ischemia. There may be no abdominal abnormalities initially.

Shock, fever, abdominal tenderness, distention, and peritonitis are late findings.

Sigmoidoscopy may disclose ischemia of the rectum (uncommon) or blood coming from above.

An underlying cause of ischemia may be evident on examination (e.g., hypoperfusion in cardiogenic shock).

3. Laboratory tests   Gastric contents and stool should be examined for blood.

Leukocytosis often is striking and hyperamylasemia is present in many cases.

Other tests reflect the severity of hemoconcentration, fluid and electrolyte losses, and acid-base imbalance.

Hematologic studies (e.g., prothrombin time, partial thromboplastin time, antithrombin III assay, etc.) may reveal hypercoagulation in patients with no apparent cause for mesenteric venous occlusion.

4. X-rays   Plain abdominal x-rays are nonspecific at first: diffuse distention of small bowel and/or colon, blunt plicae, thickened bowel wall, and small bowel loops that remain unchanged over several hours are suggestive. Late findings are diagnostic of intestinal necrosis: intramural gas and gas in the portal venous system

Contrast x-rays reveal 'thumbprinting' and either slow or rapid motility. These findings are most often limited to the left colon in cases of colonic ischemia.

The role of selective mesenteric arteriography is uncertain. The arteriogram may reveal major arterial occlusion, or it may be entirely normal despite extensive infarction. Arteriography is not obtained routinely because a normal study does not exclude intestinal ischemia.

5. Special tests   Paracentesis returns bloody fluid, but this test is positive only in the late stages as a rule.

Fiberoptic colonoscopy reveals colonic ischemia, but it should be reserved for subacute cases because of the risk of perforation.

B. DIFFERENTIAL DIAGNOSIS   Acute pancreatitis is associated with a high serum amylase, but ischemic intestine may also result in hyperamylasemia. It

---

*Chronic intestinal ischemia is discussed in Chapter 13.

may be impossible to differentiate the two conditions without exploring the abdomen.

Strangulation obstruction is difficult to differentiate from ischemia; both conditions require operation.

Ischemic colon may be confused with diverticulitis, ulcerative colitis, Crohn's disease, and carcinoma. Crohn's disease is the most difficult to differentiate, but ischemia usually has a more rapid onset and bleeding is more prominent than in granulomatous colitis.

C. COMPLICATIONS Gangrene of the bowel wall leads to perforation and a high mortality rate.

Massive bleeding from extensive mucosal ulceration can cause hypovolemic shock.

D. TREATMENT Mild ischemia may be treated expectantly with IV fluids and antibiotics. The problem is to determine which cases of ischemia are mild, and it is better to operate if there is any doubt.

Nonocclusive ischemia is treated first by correcting the precipitating cause (e.g., congestive heart failure). Operation is usually required, however, to exclude other diseases and to resect infarcted bowel. The infarction may be patchy or diffuse.

Severe ischemia requires prompt operation to resect infarcted bowel. Embolectomy or arterial reconstruction may relieve the arterial occlusion in some cases. Venous thrombosis is managed by resection of gangrenous intestine.

Postoperative care involves close attention to maintenance of tissue perfusion by well-oxygenated blood. Anticoagulants are recommended for venous thrombosis, and antiplatelet-aggregating drugs are used by some surgeons for arterial thrombosis. A 'second look' operation is performed 6–12 hours after the initial procedure to assess viability of remaining bowel in many cases.

E. PROGNOSIS Acute intestinal ischemia is fatal in 70% of patients; severe associated diseases, delay in diagnosis, and extensive infarction are factors responsible for death.

VIII. ESOPHAGUS

A. PERFORATION Most esophageal perforations occur during diagnostic or therapeutic instrumentation (esophagoscopy or esophageal dilatation). Perforation from external penetrating trauma is uncommon, and esophageal injury from blunt trauma is rare. The esophagus may perforate spontaneously during vomiting, or perforation may result from ingestion of a foreign body; these two mechanisms are discussed in subsequent sections.

1. Instrumental perforation The esophagus is most susceptible to perforation just above sites of narrowing. The normal esophagus is narrowed at the cricopharyngeal area, in its midportion where it is compressed by the aortic arch and the left mainstem bronchus, and at the diaphragmatic hiatus. Pathologic narrowing may occur at any level. Injury is prevented by skillful, gentle technic; the instrument should never be forced blindly.

a. Diagnosis The manifestations depend upon the level of perforation, the extent of perforation, and the interval after perforation.

(1) *Symptoms and signs* History of instrumentation. Pain on swallowing. Fever. Hypotension; shock may occur early after perforation of the thoracic esophagus. Pain, tenderness, and crepitus in the neck with perforation of the cervical esophagus. Pain in the chest, dyspnea, and pleural effusion with thoracic perforation; tenderness and crepitus in the neck may be minimal or absent. Pneumomediastinum may be reflected in the auscultatory finding of a 'mediastinal crunch' (Hamman's sign).

(2) *Laboratory tests* Leukocytosis usually develops.

(3) *X-rays* Depending upon the site of perforation, chest x-ray and films of the neck may show air in the soft tissues, air and fluid behind the cervical esophagus, mediastinal widening and emphysema, pneumothorax, and pleural effusion. Swallowing of water-soluble contrast media demonstrates the site of perforation.

b. Complications Virulent bacteria from the oropharynx cause rapidly progressive infection in the neck, mediastinum, or pleural space. These infections are fatal if untreated.

c. Treatment Antibiotics should be started immediately.

Operation to suture the perforation and establish external drainage is required in nearly all cases. The esophagus lacks a serosa and does not heal as well after suturing as other parts of the GI tract.

Expectant management, with nasogastric suction and antibiotics, is acceptable for small perforations with leakage confined to the mediastinum.

d. Prognosis Perforation of the thoracic esophagus has a worse prognosis than cervical injuries, but most patients recover if they are treated promptly.

2. External trauma The manifestations of perforation from external penetrating trauma are identical with those of instrumental perforation. Treatment is by surgical repair in early cases. If more than 24 hours have elapsed before the injury is recognized, drainage alone or special technics of repair may be required. Infection is the main determinant of prognosis.

B. EMETOGENIC INJURIES The esophagus (and/or the stomach) may be injured by violent vomiting. The esophageal wall may be perforated or torn only partially.

1. Perforation Postemetic perforation of the esophagus (Boerhaave's syndrome) follows violent retching, often the consequence of an alcoholic binge. The most frequent site of perforation is the left posterior part of the distal esophagus. Men are more commonly affected than women.

a. Diagnosis History of alcoholic binge or excessive eating. Violent retching. Sudden, severe pain in the lower chest and upper abdomen followed rapidly by shock. There may be crepitus in the neck, a rigid abdomen, and/or a mediastinal crunch. Pneumothorax, usually on the left. Esophagram demonstrates the site of rupture.

b. Differential diagnosis Myocardial infarction, pulmonary embolus, perforated peptic ulcer, and pancreatitis are excluded by radiographic proof of esophageal perforation.

c. Treatment

(1) *Early* (within 12 hours of perforation): antibiotics and surgical repair.

(2) *Late* (more than 12 hours after perforation): antibiotics and tube thoracostomy to establish drainage. Cervical esophagostomy and tube gastrostomy should be considered. This treatment leaves an esophagocutaneous fistula that may close spontaneously or can be repaired later.

d. Prognosis About 70% of surgically treated patients survive. The diagnosis is often overlooked, however, and the mortality rate in these patients is nearly 100%.

2. Mallory-Weiss syndrome is a longitudinal tear at the esophagogastric junction as a result of vomiting. The laceration extends through the mucosa and submucosa. Approximately 75% are on the gastric side, and 5% are on the esophageal side of the esophagogastric junction; 20% cross the junction. About 25% have multiple tears. Nearly all patients have an associated hiatal hernia. Mallory-Weiss syndrome accounts for about 10% of cases of acute upper GI hemorrhage.

a. Diagnosis Vigorous vomiting of food or nonproductive retching, *followed by* hematemesis. *Endoscopy* identifies the laceration(s) and excludes other causes of bleeding.

b. Treatment   Initial management of upper GI hemorrhage is described in Section IV above.

About 90% of patients with Mallory-Weiss lesions stop bleeding with gastric lavage. IV Vasopressin may be useful. The remainder require operation to suture the laceration. The esophagogastric junction should be examined through a high gastrotomy; multiple tears should be sought. The prognosis is excellent after surgical treatment.

C. FOREIGN BODIES   Children and mentally disturbed adults often ingest foreign bodies. Large chunks of meat are swallowed by edentulous patients. Depending on its size, the object may pass into the stomach or become lodged at sites of anatomic or pathologic narrowing.

1. Diagnosis

a. Symptoms and signs   History of ingesting a foreign body or swallowing a bolus of meat. Pain in the mediastinum or neck. Dysphagia may be mild or severe. Dyspnea in some cases.

b. X-rays   Opaque objects are visible on plain chest x-rays. Esophagram detects most objects.

c. Special tests   Esophagoscopy is diagnostic and therapeutic.

2. Complications   Infection above the impacted object, perforation, and erosion into adjacent blood vessels or the tracheobronchial tree.

3. Treatment   Esophagoscopy safely removes most objects.

Proteolytic enzymes (e.g., commercially available meat tenderizers) may disimpact meat, but the esophageal wall has been injured by such treatment.

Surgical extraction through an esophagotomy is rarely required.

D. CORROSIVE ESOPHAGITIS   Ingestion of strong acid or alkali produces chemical burns of the pharynx, esophagus, and stomach.

1. Diagnosis

a. Symptoms and signs   History of ingestion of acid or alkali (determine the chemical nature of the substance). Fever and shock in severe cases. Respiratory distress if the airway is obstructed by edema or if some of the caustic material was aspirated. Severe burning pain from mouth to stomach; accentuated by swallowing. Edema and mucosal destruction of lips, tongue, pharynx, and (in some cases) larynx **(the absence of these findings does not exclude esophageal injury)**. Signs of esophageal or gastric perforation may be noted.

b. Special tests   Esophagoscopy determines the extent of injury; some patients have oropharyngeal burns only, and others have extensive damage to the esophagus and stomach. Direct laryngoscopy to assess the degree of damage to the larynx.

2. Complications   Bleeding and perforation are early complications. Late sequelae include tracheoesophageal fistula and stricture.

3. Treatment

a. Immediate measures

(1) Do **not** induce vomiting and do **not** perform gastric lavage.

(2) Establish and maintain the airway.

(3) Lavage the mouth and have the patient swallow milk, water, or **dilute** acid or alkali to neutralize the caustic substance. This procedure is probably ineffective if instituted more than a few minutes after ingestion.

(4) Broad-spectrum antibiotics should be started immediately.

(5) Esophagoscopy should be performed under general anesthesia within 12 hours of ingestion if possible, within 48 hours at the latest. Endoscopy is contraindicated in patients with severe respiratory distress or suspected perforation. The proximal point of esophageal injury should be noted and the esophagoscope advanced no farther. The depth of the mucosal burn should be characterized as superficial or deep.

(6) Corticosteroids are begun immediately if an esophageal burn has been

proved. In children age 1-4 years, give prednisone 60 mg/day in divided doses for 4 days, 40 mg/day for the next 4 days, then 20 mg/day until the esophagus is healed (about 3 weeks).

(7) For burns by acids, give bismuth subcarbonate 2 gm/day.

   b. Subsequent measures

(1) Steroids should be tapered and discontinued after 3 weeks.

(2) Bougienage has been advocated in patients who are developing stenosis. The value of this procedure has not been proved.

(3) If a severe stricture develops, the esophagus must be replaced by stomach or colon.

   4. Prognosis   Up to 70% of patients with oropharyngeal burns have no esophageal involvement. Superficial esophageal burns usually heal without residual stricture. Deep burns progress to stricture formation in nearly every case despite the treatment outlined.

E. HIATAL HERNIA AND REFLUX ESOPHAGITIS   Hiatal hernia is displacement of the stomach through the esophageal hiatus into the mediastinum. There are two types of hiatal hernia; sliding (type I) and paraesophageal (type II).

   1. Sliding hiatal hernia and reflux esophagitis   About 95% of hiatal hernias are of the sliding variety in which the esophagogastric junction and the proximal stomach are displaced upward into the mediastinum. Obesity and loss of strength of the fascial attachments are probably responsible.

   The clinical manifestations of sliding hiatal hernia are not caused by the hernia itself but by the **gastroesophageal reflux** which frequently accompanies it. Sliding hiatal hernia does not strangulate. Reflux normally is prevented by an intraabdominal segment of esophagus and by the gastroesophageal (lower esophageal) sphincter; the relative importance of these two mechanisms is a subject of debate. In about half of patients with sliding hiatal hernia, the barrier to reflux is impaired. Reflux may occur also in the absence of any demonstrable hiatal hernia, presumably because the sphincter is weak in these individuals.

   In the diagnosis and treatment of these patients it is important to bear in mind that gastroesophageal reflux, not a hiatal hernia, is the clinically significant finding. Persistent gastroesophageal reflux leads to **reflux esophagitis,** and continued esophagitis may result in **esophageal stricture.**

   a. Diagnosis

(1) *Symptoms*   Hiatal hernia alone is asymptomatic. Gastroesophageal reflux typically causes retrosternal burning pain (heartburn) which is exacerbated by gravity (e.g., lying supine) or by increasing pressure in the abdomen (e.g., lifting, straining). Regurgitation of sour or bitter fluid into the mouth is a common symptom of reflux. Nocturnal cough and repeated episodes of pneumonia may result from aspiration of regurgitated gastric contents. Dysphagia may be due to edema or to formation of a fibrous stricture. Bleeding is a symptom of esophagitis; it is seldom massive.

(2) *Signs*   None.

(3) *X-rays*   Chest x-rays may show a gas-fluid shadow in the mediastinum. Esophagram may demonstrate a hiatal hernia, and cine-esophagography or fluoroscopy may document the presence of gastroesophageal reflux; strictures are evident on these studies also.

(4) *Special tests*   Esophagoscopy and biopsy reveals the presence and degree of esophagitis, although the findings are not completely reliable; endoscopy rules out other esophageal or gastric lesions. Esophageal motility studies measure the strength of the gastroesophageal sphincter and exclude motility disorders as a cause. Monitoring of pH in the distal esophagus is the most reliable method of detecting gastroesophageal reflux; an acid reflux test, in which 0.1 N HCl is instilled into the stomach and the patient is instructed to execute certain maneuvers (e.g., Valsalva, cough) is diagnostic of abnormal reflux if the esophageal pH is 4 or less in three or more of the specified

maneuvers. The Bernstein test determines whether the patient's symptoms are due to esophagitis; 0.1 N HCl instilled into the distal esophagus reproduces the patient's pain if esophagitis is responsible for it.

b. Differential diagnosis   Myocardial ischemia, peptic ulcer, and cholelithiasis are just a few of the other diseases that can be confused with gastroesophageal reflux.

c. Complications   Esophagitis, sometimes progressing to stricture formation, is the most common complication of gastroesophageal reflux. Pulmonary complications from repeated aspiration also occur. Esophageal carcinoma is an occasional late development.

d. Medical treatment   Asymptomatic sliding hiatal hernia requires no treatment.

Antacids are the mainstay of medical treatment of reflux.

Bethanechol is a new and useful drug for prevention of reflux in some patients.

The head of the bed should be elevated about 15 cm on wooden blocks to prevent nocturnal reflux.

Patients should not lie down after meals and should not eat before bedtime.

Strictures of a mild degree can be treated by periodic dilatations in addition to the regimen described above.

e. Surgical treatment   Surgical repair is indicated for refractory esophagitis, stricture, and recurrent pneumonia. Operation is performed through the abdomen or through the thorax depending upon the patient's obesity, previous operations, associated diseases, and the surgeon's preference.

Three procedures are popular currently: **Hill** (posterior gastropexy), **Nissen** fundoplication (360° fundic wrap around the distal esophagus), and **Belsey Mark IV** (270° fundic wrap). These procedures are empirically effective in preventing gastroesophageal reflux, but the reasons for their success is incompletely understood. Restoration of a 4 cm segment of intraabdominal esophagus and some means of securing the esophagogastric junction to prevent herniation again seem to be important factors. Creation of a flap valve at the gastroesophageal junction is accomplished by all three operations, and this may be important also.

An acid-reducing procedure should not be added to the antireflux operation unless the patient has associated gastric or duodenal ulcer. Strictures may respond to an antireflux procedure and esophageal dilatation during and after operation; severe strictures require esophageal resection and replacement.

f. Prognosis   Most patients with gastroesophageal reflux respond to medical therapy. Surgical repairs of the three types mentioned are successful in about 90% of patients, a great improvement over older and less effective surgical methods.

2. Paraesophageal hiatal hernia   In this type of hiatal hernia, the esophagogastric junction remains in the normal position, and the fundus of the stomach herniates through the hiatus to the left of the esophagus. With time, increasing amounts of stomach are included in the hernia.

Reflux is uncommon in paraesophageal hiatal hernia, and the clinical manifestations are due to obstruction of the herniated stomach. Eructation and postprandial pain in the lower chest are typical symptoms. If untreated, the herniated stomach may ulcerate, bleed, or strangulate.

The diagnosis often is unsuspected in a patient with nonspecific complaints. Chest x-ray shows a gas-fluid level in the mediastinum, and esophagram establishes the diagnosis.

Unlike sliding hiatal hernia, paraesophageal hiatal hernia should be repaired surgically in nearly every instance.

F. MOTILITY DISORDERS

1. Achalasia is a motility disorder in which primary peristalsis is deficient, and the gastroesophageal sphincter fails to relax with swallowing. The circular muscle of the distal esophagus is thickened, and the esophagus dilates progressively above this point. The ganglion cells of Auerbach's plexuses in the esophagus are absent in many of these patients, but the cause is unknown.

a. Diagnosis

(1) *Symptoms and signs*   **Dysphagia** is the most common symptom. Pain is not prominent, and weight loss is not severe. Regurgitation and aspiration occur when the patient is recumbent. **Vigorous achalasia** is a variant of this disease characterized by chest pain due to muscular esophageal spasms.

(2) *X-rays*   Esophagrams show dilatation above a narrow distal esophagus. Barium does not empty readily into the stomach. Peristalsis is abnormal. In advanced cases, the esophagus is markedly dilated and tortuous ('sigmoid esophagus').

(3) *Special tests*   Esophagoscopy excludes organic obstruction; the instrument advances into the stomach with minimal force despite the narrowing. Motility studies reveal the following: peristalsis in the esophagus is uncoordinated, and primary peristalsis is absent; the gastroesophageal sphincter has above normal resting pressure and does not relax completely when the patient swallows; Bethanecol given subcutaneously causes strong contraction of the distal esophagus because it is autonomically denervated.

b. Differential diagnosis

Carcinoma is excluded by esophagoscopy, biopsy, and cytology. Benign stricture from reflux esophagitis is not associated with as marked proximal dilatation, and peristalsis is normal in the body of the esophagus. Scleroderma is associated with gastroesophageal reflux in the early stages, but when esophagitis progresses to stricture, the radiographic findings resemble those of achalasia with a dilated body and narrow distal segment; scleroderma is distinguished by the persistence of peristalsis in the upper third of the esophagus and by the lack of response to Bethanecol. Chagas' disease, caused by Trypanosoma cruzi, may destroy ganglion cells and produce a condition identical with achalasia. Diffuse spasm is discussed below.

c. Complications

Progressive esophageal dilatation and repeated aspiration. Carcinoma occasionally is associated with achalasia, but the etiologic relationship has not been proved. Malnutrition is rarely marked.

d. Medical treatment

Patients with early achalasia, before the esophagus becomes tortuous, are readily treated by pneumatic dilatation. A special balloon is positioned through the narrow distal segment and inflated sufficiently to partially disrupt the hypertrophied muscle.

e. Surgical treatment

Longitudinal esophageal myotomy (Heller procedure) is the surgical method of choice. It is usually performed through the left chest, but it can be accomplished through the abdomen. Gastroesophageal reflux is avoided by limiting the distal extent of the myotomy.

f. Prognosis

85% of patients are relieved by one or more pneumatic dilatations. Excellent results are obtained in 90% of surgically treated patients; incomplete myotomy and gastroesophageal reflux are the two chief sources of poor results.

2. Cricopharyngeal achalasia   In this condition, the cricopharyngeal sphincter does not relax completely, and dysphagia results. The diagnosis is made by esophagram, endoscopy, and motility studies. Treatment is by cricopharyngeal myotomy. Results of operation are excellent.

3. Diffuse esophageal spasm is associated with intermittent retrosternal pain and dysphagia. The esophagram shows segmental spasms that may take a 'corkscrew' configuration. The esophagus is not dilated. Motility studies demonstrate disorganized peristalsis, usually involving only the lower half or third of the esophagus. There may be a response to Bethanecol.

Patients may benefit from long acting nitrates (e.g., Isordil). A long esophageal myotomy gives lasting relief in 70-80% of cases.

G. DIVERTICULA Most esophageal diverticula are of the **pulsion** variety; they are protrusions of mucosa and submucosa through defects in the muscle layers. They are usually manifestations of abnormal motility. **Traction** diverticula are a different sort of problem (see below).

1. Pharyngoesophàgeal (Zenker's) diverticulum Pressures generated by swallowing may cause a diverticulum to form above the cricopharyngeal sphincter. The diverticulum arises posteriorly in the midline and projects laterally, usually to the left. Most patients are men over age 60.

Dysphagia, regurgitation of undigested food, and halitosis are typical symptoms. Esophagram reveals the diverticulum and thus excludes other causes of cervical dysphagia.

Repeated aspiration pneumonitis is the most common complication. The diverticulum may ulcerate, perforate, or fistulize.

Excision of the diverticulum, with or without cricopharyngeal myotomy, is the treatment of choice. Results are excellent.

2. Epiphrenic diverticulum Diverticula form in the distal esophagus in some patients with motility disorders, particularly diffuse esophageal spasm. Dysphagia, pain, and regurgitation are symptoms. The diagnosis is made by x-ray studies. The diverticulum may become inflamed, ulcerate, and bleed.

Surgical excision in combination with esophageal myotomy is successful in 80% or more of cases and is indicated for severe symptoms.

3. Traction diverticulum Inflammation of mediastinal lymph nodes (e.g., in tuberculosis) may pull the wall of the adjacent esophagus outward as the nodes heal with contraction and fibrosis. This forms a traction diverticulum, a conical projection of the entire wall, usually directed anteriorly.

The lesion is most often asymptomatic. Dysphagia results if the diverticulum becomes inflamed. Surgical excision is warranted in very few patients.

H. NEOPLASMS

1. Benign

   a. Leiomyoma is the most common benign esophageal neoplasm. The tumor is intramural. Small leiomyomas are asymptomatic; larger ones cause dysphagia, and the mucosa may ulcerate and bleed. The radiographic appearance is distinctive: a smooth, rounded mass compressing the lumen. Symptomatic leiomyomas should be excised.

   b. Benign neoplasms may arise from other tissue elements: lipomas, fibromas, etc. These lesions also cause symptoms by compressing the lumen.

   c. Congenital cysts or reduplications are most common in the distal esophagus. They may require excision.

2. Malignant Squamous cell carcinoma of the esophagus is most common in men 50-60 years of age. Nearly half arise in the distal third of the esophagus, about 35% in the middle third, and the remainder in the upper third. They spread by lymphatics, vascular invasion, and direct extension.

   a. Diagnosis

   (1) *Symptoms and signs* Progressive dysphagia is the typical symptom. Weight loss and anemia are present.

   (2) *X-rays* Esophagram reveals an irregular mass narrowing the esophagus. Proximal dilatation is not marked.

   (3) *Special tests* Esophagoscopy with biopsy or brushings usually is diagnostic. Cytologic examination of esophageal washings is conclusive if the tumor cannot be biopsied directly. Bronchoscopy is advisable for mid or upper esophageal lesions, since involvement of the tracheobronchial tree is common.

   b. Differential diagnosis Benign strictures and neoplasms are distinguishable by radiographic and endoscopic studies, and most importantly by biopsy.

   c. Complications Obstruction of the esophagus is inevitable unless the patient dies earlier of some other complication. Extension of the lesion may lead to tracheoesophageal fistula or massive hemorrhage from major mediastinal vessels.

d. Treatment Radiation therapy is used alone or as a preoperative adjuvant for lesions in the middle or upper third.

Esophagectomy (or esophagogastrectomy) is often done primarily for distal lesions 'or following preoperative radiation of higher lesions. The esophagus is replaced by bringing the stomach up into the chest, or colon may be used if the stomach is insufficiently long to bridge the gap. These patients are invariably malnourished, and they benefit from a course of preoperative parenteral nutrition.

An intraluminal plastic (Celestin) tube can be placed through the obstructing lesion to permit swallowing in unresectable patients. A laparotomy is required to dilate the esophagus and insert the tube.

e. Prognosis Only about one-third of esophageal carcinomas are resectable when diagnosed. About 95% of patients die of the disease within 3 years.

IX. STOMACH AND DUODENUM

A. TRAUMA
1. Stomach Penetrating injuries of the stomach are managed relatively easily by simple suture. Results are excellent.
2. Duodenum
a. Minor lacerations or perforations from blunt or penetrating trauma are treated by suture. Leakage from duodenal closures is fairly common. An onlay serosal patch (suturing a loop of jejunum against the duodenal suture line) is a useful device to minimize the chances of leakage.
b. Major lacerations and disruptions are sutured or resected. For major injuries, especially if the pancreas is also injured, the duodenum should be defunctionalized by a tube duodenostomy, antrectomy, and Roux-en-Y gastrojejunostomy.

B. PEPTIC ULCER The combined effects of acid and peptic enzymes in gastric juice may produce ulceration of the gastric or duodenal mucosa.
Duodenal ulcer is most common in men 20-40 years of age. Gastric ulcer affects a group about 10 years older. The incidence of this disease is declining for unknown reasons; currently about 5% of adults in the USA have active peptic ulcers.
1. Cause
a. Duodenal ulcer Patients with duodenal ulcer typically have increased gastric acid secretion, both basally and in response to stimulation. They have an increased parietal cell mass and a greater and more sustained drive to secrete acid. The fundamental cause of these abnormalities is unknown. Most duodenal ulcers are located in the duodenal bulb.
b. Gastric ulcer Patients with gastric ulcer fall into two groups. (1) Gastric ulcer in association with duodenal ulcer is similar physiologically to duodenal ulcer alone. These patients are hypersecretors, and the ulcer is prepyloric. (2) Gastric ulcer in the absence of a history of duodenal ulcer is located in the antral mucosa within 2 cm of the junction with the parietal cell mucosa. 95% are on the lesser curvature. These patients have low or normal acid secretion. Damage to the antral mucosa by reflux of duodenal juice, ingestion of salicylates, or other mechanisms is at least partially responsible for making the mucosa vulnerable to acid-peptic digestion.
2. Diagnosis
a. Symptoms and signs There are minor differences in the typical symptoms of gastric and duodenal ulcer, but these differences are not reliable enough to allow a definite diagnosis based on history alone.

Pain in the epigastrium, relieved by food or antacids, often awakening the patient at night; paradoxically, some patients with ulcers have no pain at all. Nausea and vomiting are variable. Epigastric tenderness may be present. Symptoms tend to exacerbate and remit in cycles of a few months or a few years.

b. Laboratory tests Anemia and occult blood in the stool may be noted.

Serum calcium determination should be obtained, since patients with hyperparathyroidism are prone to develop duodenal ulcer.

Gastric analysis is not essential in duodenal ulcer, but it should be performed for refractory ulcer, recurrent ulcer, or suspected Zollinger-Ellison syndrome. Basal and maximal acid output are normal or elevated in duodenal ulcer. In gastric ulcer patients, **achlorhydria** after stimulation with Histalog or pentagastrin is presumptive evidence of a **malignant** ulcer.

Serum gastrin levels are normal in conventional peptic ulcer disease and elevated in Zollinger-Ellison syndrome.

c. X-rays Barium study of the stomach and duodenum may show a gastric or duodenal ulcer crater or deformity of the duodenum. X-rays are about 90% reliable in diagnosing an active ulcer, and they have about the same degree of accuracy in distinguishing benign from malignant gastric ulcers.

d. Special tests Gastroduodenoscopy is important for examination and biopsy of gastric ulcers; duodenal ulcers do not require endoscopy unless the diagnosis is uncertain, the patient is bleeding, or the ulcer is recurrent. Gastric cytology is useful in the evaluation of gastric ulcers.

3. Differential diagnosis Nearly any other upper abdominal disease can mimic peptic ulcer; cholelithiasis, reflux esophagitis, pancreatitis, and functional complaints are among the conditions to be considered.

4. Complications

a. Hemorrhage (see Section IV of this Chapter).

b. Perforation Ulceration completely through the gastric or duodenal wall results in perforation into the peritoneal cavity if the ulcer is anterior. Posterior gastric ulcers may perforate into the lesser sac; posterior duodenal ulcers may penetrate into the pancreas but do not, as a rule, perforate freely.

Perforation causes sudden, severe abdominal pain which rapidly becomes generalized as corrosive gastric juice spreads throughout the peritoneal cavity. Eventually, bacterial peritonitis is superimposed on the initial chemical peritonitis.

Examination discloses a rigid abdomen in a patient who moves cautiously and breathes shallowly. Liver dullness may be absent, and bowel sounds are quiet. The patient may be in shock.

Leukocytosis, elevated amylase, and hemoconcentration are noted. Free abdominal air is present on x-ray in 80-90% of patients. Water-soluble contrast medium given orally or through a nasogastric tube may be used to demonstrate perforation if the diagnosis is uncertain; small perforations may seal quickly, and the x-ray will not show perforation in these patients.

c. Pyloric obstruction The pylorus may be obstructed by edema (potentially reversible) or fibrosis (irreversible). Vomiting of food containing no bile develops progressively. Examination may reveal a succussion splash. Metabolic alkalosis and dehydration are found by laboratory tests.

A saline load test helps determine the completeness of obstruction; 700 ml of saline are instilled through the nasogastric tube, the tube is plugged, and the residual volume is aspirated 30 minutes later; a residual of more than 350 ml is diagnostic of obstruction. X-rays are definitive.

5. Treatment of uncomplicated peptic ulcer is medical; operation is performed for complications or intractability.

a. Medical

(1) *Diet, drugs, and habits* Smoking, alcohol, and xanthines (coffee, tea, cola beverages, and chocolate) should be avoided as should all known ulcerogen-

ic drugs (corticosteroids, salicylates). Diet otherwise need not be restricted. 'Bland' diets offer no advantages over ordinary foods.

(2) *Antacids* The choice of antacids depends upon taste, cost, the need to avoid exacerbation of associated diseases (e.g., by giving antacids rich in sodium to cardiac patients), side-effects (e.g., diarrhea), etc. One effective type of antacid is a combination of aluminum hydroxide and magnesium hydroxide. In general, antacids should be given 1 and 3 hours after each meal. Liquids are preferable to tablets.

(3) *H_2-receptor antagonists* Cimetidine has been approved in the USA for the short-term treatment of duodenal ulcer. In other countries, it is also used for chronic therapy of duodenal and gastric ulcer. It is a useful agent in patients with Zollinger-Ellison syndrome. The long-term effectiveness and safety of cimetidine have not been determined. The usual dosage is 300 mg 4 times a day. It is also available as a parenteral preparation.

(4) The value of anticholinergics has not been proved.

(5) Hospitalization probably increases the healing rate.

(6) Irradiation of the stomach with 1600-2000 rads over 10 days depresses gastric secretion by 50% and helps ulcers heal. Recovery of acid secretion, and recurrence of ulcer, limits application of this modality to elderly or debilitated patients who respond poorly to other medical treatment.

b. Surgical Complications (hemorrhage, perforation, and obstruction) are indications for operation. Intractability is difficult to define and is a highly subjective indication for operation in patients with duodenal ulcer. Gastric ulcer requires operation if it does not heal in 2-3 months because such an ulcer may be malignant.

Several technics are currently used for surgical treatment of peptic ulcer.

(1) *Vagotomy* There are three types of vagotomy: Truncal vagotomy with a drainage procedure (pyloroplasty or gastrojejunostomy). Selective (gastric) vagotomy with a drainage procedure. Proximal gastric (parietal cell, highly selective) vagotomy, usually without a drainage procedure.

(2) *Vagotomy and antrectomy,* with gastroduodenostomy (Billroth I) or gastrojejunostomy (Billroth II). Antrectomy is a 40-50% distal gastrectomy.

(3) *Subtotal gastrectomy (Billroth I or II)* 'Subtotal' refers to 65-75% resection of the distal stomach.

(4) *Antrectomy* alone is useful for gastric ulcer.

Selection of the operative method is largely a matter of the surgeon's preference and the operative findings. The following comments are generally accurate: (a) Operative mortality is lower after vagotomy than after gastric resection (antrectomy or subtotal); among the vagotomies, proximal gastric vagotomy has the lowest mortality rate. (b) Recurrent ulcer is more frequent after any type of vagotomy than after vagotomy and antrectomy or subtotal gastrectomy. (c) The incidence of postoperative sequelae (see below) is about the same after any of these procedures except proximal gastric vagotomy; this operation has a lower incidence of sequelae.

Ulcers may persist or recur at the same or new sites because of: (a) Inadequate operation—this may reflect a technical or anatomic problem (e.g., incomplete vagotomy), or more often, it means simply that the operation achieved insufficient acid reduction to control the individual patient's ulcer diathesis. (b) Retained (excluded) antrum. (c) Inadequate drainage of the stomach. (d) Loss of alkaline fluid to neutralize acid at the anastomosis. (e) Zollinger-Ellison syndrome.

The so-called **postgastrectomy syndromes** are a heterogeneous group of unpleasant consequences of gastric surgery.

(1) *Dumping syndrome* Cardiovascular symptoms (sweating, palpitations, desire to lie down) and intestinal symptoms (nausea, cramps, diarrhea) are noted postprandially. Dumping seems to be limited to operations which destroy or bypass the pylorus.

(2) *Diarrhea* 'Postvagotomy diarrhea' is probably the result of intestinal denervation and precipitous gastric emptying.

(3) *Alkaline gastritis* Reflux of duodenal juices into the stomach produces gastritis, pain, and bilious vomiting in some patients after gastrectomy or a drainage procedure.

(4) *Malabsorption* Steatorrhea occurs to a mild degree after gastrectomy. Blind loop syndrome (bacterial overgrowth in the afferent limb of a Billroth II reconstruction) may lead to severe malabsorption.

(5) *Anemia* Iron deficiency or vitamin B_{12} deficiency may produce anemia after gastric surgery.

c. Treatment of complications

(1) *Hemorrhage* (see also Section IV of this Chapter). Emergency operation is required if bleeding peptic ulcer does not respond to ice-water lavage, or if bleeding recurs after transient cessation. Duodenal ulcer is usually treated by truncal vagotomy, pyloroplasty, and suture of the bleeding vessel in the ulcer crater. Gastric ulcer is managed in the same way or by gastrectomy.

(2) *Perforation* Operation is undertaken as soon as the patient is resuscitated. (a) Acute duodenal ulcers (less than a 3-month history before perforation) are simply sutured. (b) Chronic duodenal ulcers (greater than a 3-month history) are best treated by suture and a definitive acid-reducing procedure (e.g., vagotomy). (c) Gastric ulcers can be locally excised (to exclude cancer) and the defect sutured, or an antrectomy can be performed.

(3) *Pyloric obstruction* is treated initially with nasogastric suction. A saline load-test is performed after 72 hours to assess the degree of obstruction, and if obstruction persists, operation is indicated. Vagotomy and drainage or a gastrectomy are suitable procedures.

C. ZOLLINGER-ELLISON SYNDROME

(ZE) is peptic ulcer disease caused by excessive production of gastrin by a pancreatic islet cell carcinoma (60%), pancreatic adenoma (25%), multiple pancreatic adenomas or hyperplasia (10%), or a duodenal adenoma (5%). The gastrin-producing tumor is called a gastrinoma. Multiple endocrine adenomatosis (MEA-I) is present in about 30% of patients.

1. Diagnosis

a. Symptoms and signs Symptoms and signs of peptic ulcer. Diarrhea from massive outpouring of gastric acid. Complications (bleeding, perforation, obstruction) are frequent. Recurrent ulcer after acid-reducing surgery.

b. Laboratory tests Gastric analysis shows basal hypersecretion (>15 mEq H+/hour) and little increase in acid secretion with stimulation by pentagastrin or Histalog. The BAO/MAO ratio is greater than 0.6 in most cases.

Serum gastrin levels are elevated. The diagnosis of ZE is secured in patients with borderline values by IV infusion of calcium or secretin which stimulates release of gastrin and raises serum levels into the clearly abnormal range.

Serum Ca^{++} is elevated in patients with hyperparathyroidism (a component of MEA-I).

c. X-rays Upper GI series demonstrates ulcer(s) in the stomach, duodenum, and/or the jejunum. The gastric folds are prominent, and liquid is present in the stomach even in fasting patients. The duodenal and jejunal mucosa may be edematous.

Angiography may show the tumor.

2. Treatment

a. Medical Antacids alone are inadequate treatment. Cimetidine is effective in most patients, at least over the short term. Long-term results are unknown.

b. Surgical Total gastrectomy cures the ulcer disease and is well-tolerated by these patients; it is the surgical treatment of choice in most cases. Removal of the tumor is possible in only one-third of patients (those with solitary adenomas, especially in the duodenum).

3. Prognosis   Most patients, even those with malignant gastrinomas, lead a normal life after total gastrectomy. Some of the malignant tumors behave like typical cancers and cause death from metastases.

D. STRESS ULCER   Acute ulceration of the stomach and/or the duodenum develops in some severely ill patients. Ulcers occurring in burned patients are termed **Curling's ulcers.** Ulcers in association with CNS lesions are termed **Cushing's ulcers.** The majority of patients are not in these two categories; they have had extensive trauma or major surgical procedures, often complicated by shock and sepsis, and the ulceration results from a combination of mucosal ischemia and acid hypersecretion.

Gastritis induced by alcohol or salicylates is a related condition in which the gastric mucosa is damaged by the pharmacologic agent.

1. Diagnosis   Hemorrhage is the most common mode of presentation. Perforation is the first manifestation in some cases. Diagnostic evaluation of upper GI hemorrhage is discussed in Section IV of this chapter.

2. Prevention   Antacids by constant instillation through a nasogastric tube or hourly by mouth should be a routine measure in severely ill patients. Gastric pH should be maintained at greater than 4. Cimetidine given orally or IV is a promising method of prevention also.

3. Treatment

a. Medical   (1) Gastric lavage with iced saline may stop the bleeding. (2) Selective abdominal angiography with infusion of a vasoconstricting agent (vasopressin or epinephrine) into the left gastric artery is worth a trial in critically ill patients.

b. Surgical   Operation is necessary if bleeding is not controlled medically. Vagotomy, pyloroplasty, and suture of bleeding sites carries a high risk of recurrent bleeding (40%). If the patient's condition allows it, vagotomy and subtotal gastrectomy is probably more effective. Total gastrectomy is indicated in rare instances.

4. Prognosis   Stress ulcer is a grave complication, and the emphasis should be on prevention.

E. GASTRIC NEOPLASMS

1. Adenocarcinoma of the stomach is declining in frequency in western countries, but it remains a common disease in Japan.

Cancer arises in the pyloric area in about two-thirds of cases. Morphologically, gastric carcinoma may be ulcerating, polypoid, superficial spreading, linitis plastica, or so advanced that it cannot be classified into one of the other four groups.

a. Diagnosis

(1) *Symptoms*   Vague postprandial discomfort. Anorexia and weight loss. Vomiting. Chronic bleeding (vomiting of small amounts of blood; melena).

(2) *Signs*   Epigastric mass in 25%. Hepatomegaly in 10%. Evidence of metastases: Virchow node in the neck, Blumer shelf on rectal examination, enlarged ovaries (Krukenberg tumors). Gross or occult blood in the stool.

(3) *Laboratory tests*   Anemia is common. Elevated CEA reflects large tumor bulk.

(4) *X-rays*   Most gastric cancers are visible on upper GI series. Benign ulcers may be difficult to distinguish from malignant ones.

(5) *Special tests*   (a) Gastric analysis reveals achlorhydria basally and after stimulation in one-fourth of cases. The presence of small amounts of acid, therefore, does not preclude the possibility of cancer. (b) Gastroscopy with biopsy or brushings usually proves the diagnosis. (c) Gastric lavage to obtain cytologic material is accurate in 90% of cases.

b. Differential diagnosis Benign ulcers must be differentiated from malignant ulcers. Other gastric malignancies (lymphoma, leiomyosarcoma) are discussed below. Rarely, cancer arising in the pancreas or colon invades the stomach and mimics a primary gastric lesion.

c. Treatment

(1) *Surgical* (a) Malnutrition should be treated by parenteral feeding before operation. (b) Resection of the stomach, omentum, and regional lymph nodes is performed for cure if there is no distant spread or unresectable local extension. Subtotal gastrectomy is sufficient for distal tumors. Total gastrectomy is required if lesser resection does not encompass the tumor. Esophagogastrectomy is performed for tumors arising in the proximal stomach. (c) Palliative resection is preferable to gastrojejunostomy for incurable distal cancers.

(2) *Chemotherapy* Combination chemotherapy is reserved for unresectable or recurrent disease.

d. Prognosis The overall 5-year survival rate is about 10%. Resected cancers without lymph node metastases are cured in one-half or more of cases; with lymph node involvement, the survival rate after curative resection falls to about 35%.

2. Polyps Adenomatous polyps often occur in association with adenocarcinoma, and some gastric polyps are themselves malignant. Achlorhydria is found in most patients with polyps. Anemia from chronic bleeding or from vitamin B_{12} deficiency may be noted. Gastric cytology should be obtained.

One or a few pedunculated polyps can be excised through the gastroscope. A polyp greater than 2 cm in diameter is an indication for laparotomy if it cannot be excised through the gastroscope. Partial gastrectomy should be done for multiple polyps confined to one part of the stomach, and total gastrectomy is performed in rare instances of diffuse polyposis.

3. Leiomyoma and leiomyosarcoma

a. Leiomyoma of the stomach may bleed and should be excised surgically.

b. Leiomyosarcoma often ulcerates centrally and bleeds. These tumors may reach a large size. Gastrectomy is required. The 5-year survival rate is 50%.

4. Lymphomas Symptoms of gastric lymphoma are the same as those of adenocarcinoma. Half of gastric lymphomas are palpable in the epigastrium. Upper GI series, endoscopy, biopsy, and cytology should lead to the diagnosis. Treatment is by resection followed by radiation therapy and sometimes chemotherapy. The prognosis is relatively good; about 50% of patients survive 5 years.

F. DUODENAL LESIONS

1. Diverticula Acquired false diverticula of the duodenum are common. They usually occur on the medial wall of the duodenum near the ampulla of Vater. Most diverticula are asymptomatic. Bleeding, perforation, obstruction of the bile duct, and acute pancreatitis are rare complications. Symptomatic diverticula should be excised.

2. Neoplasms

a. Benign Gastrinomas, Brunner's gland adenomas, leiomyomas, carcinoids, and pancreatic rests may occur in the duodenum.

b. Malignant Adenocarcinoma of the duodenum is rare. It may arise near the bile duct and cause obstructive jaundice. Malignancies arising in other tissue elements (e.g., leiomyosarcoma) are very rare.

3. Superior mesenteric artery syndrome Compression of the third portion of the duodenum by the superior mesenteric artery may cause obstruction in patients who have lost a great deal of weight from illness or injury. Assuming the prone position after eating may allow the artery to fall away from the duodenum, and the condition improves as weight is gained.

The existence of this syndrome in adults who have not lost weight is questionable. Most patients who were believed previously to have this condition have scleroderma or some other cause of abnormal duodenal motility. Operation is rarely required.

X. SMALL INTESTINE (JEJUNUM AND ILEUM)*

A. TRAUMA   Penetrating injuries from knives and low velocity missiles are simply sutured. High velocity missiles and blunt trauma cause extensive damage to the bowel wall and the mesentery; these injuries usually require resection with end-to-end anastomosis.

B. FISTULAS   Most external fistulas of the small bowel are complications of surgical procedures.

1. Diagnosis

a. Symptoms and signs   Postoperative fever and abdominal pain. Leakage of intestinal contents through the abdominal incision. Persistent sepsis if abscess drainage is incomplete. Excoriation of the skin by intestinal juices. Fluid and electrolyte losses, most marked with proximal fistulas. Rapid weight loss.

b. Laboratory tests   Studies reflect the presence of sepsis and the degree of dehydration and malnutrition.

c. X-rays   Plain abdominal films may show intestinal obstruction or suggest the presence of abscess. Contrast given orally, by enema, or through the fistula (fistulogram) delineates the anatomy.

d. Special tests   If the presence of a fistula is uncertain, charcoal tablets or methylene blue given orally may be diagnostic.

2. Complications   Death in the early stages is the result of hypovolemia and sepsis. Late death is due to malnutrition and sepsis.

3. Treatment   An orderly treatment program should follow this sequence:

a. Fluids and electrolytes   In addition to the usual measures for resuscitation of profoundly depleted patients (see Chapters 1 and 2), losses from the fistula should be collected and the volume and electrolyte content measured at least daily.

b. Control of fistula drainage is necessary to minimize excoriation of the skin. Stoma appliances and catheters are useful methods.

c. Treatment of sepsis   Abscesses should be sought and drained when discovered. Antibiotics are not a substitute for drainage of localized abscesses.

e. Nutrition   Oral intake should be avoided initially; a nasogastric tube may be required. Parenteral nutrition is begun when the patient is stable hemodynamically. As soon as possible, alimentary feedings should be instituted, either orally or through the fistula. The goal is 3000 calories or more per day.

f. Operation   Many fistulas close spontaneously. Causes of failure to close include distal obstruction, neoplasm or foreign body at the fistula site, and extensive disruption of the bowel wall. Operation is required in these cases and usually consists of resection with anastomosis.

4. Prognosis   About 80% of patients survive. Sepsis and untreatable underlying diseases (e.g., malignancy, radiation damage) are the chief causes of death.

C. BLIND LOOP SYNDROME is a form of malabsorption caused by bacterial proliferation in stagnant intestinal contents in a variety of situations, including blind (poor emptying) loops. The syndrome consists of steatorrhea, diarrhea, macrocytic (vitamin B_{12} deficiency) anemia, hypocalcemia, and malnutrition.

Standard laboratory tests show high fecal fat content, abnormal absorption of vitamin B_{12} (Schilling test), and normal or low D-xylose absorption. More than 10^5 bacteria/ml in upper intestinal aspirates is evidence of bacterial

*Obstruction is discussed in Section VI. Regional enteritis (Crohn's disease) is discussed in Section XI. Intestinal stomas are covered in Section XI. Ischemia is covered in Section VII.

overgrowth in the region sampled. the $^{14}CO_2$ breath test helps make the diagnosis of blind loop syndrome.

Oral broad-spectrum antibiotics improve the results of laboratory tests and relieve symptoms, at least temporarily. Surgical treatment of the underlying disorder is required in many cases.

D. SHORT BOWEL SYNDROME Extensive resection of the small intestine produces a group of deficiencies from loss of absorptive surface. Severity of the syndrome depends on the length of gut removed, the site of resection, the underlying disease, and other factors. Loss of ileum is poorly tolerated because transport of bile salts, vitamin B_{12}, and cholesterol is limited to this area; if jejunum is resected, the ileum is able to compensate.

   1. Clinical course and treatment
   a. Stage 1   Huge fluid and electrolyte losses from diarrhea require careful replacement therapy. No food should be given orally; IV feeding is required. Codeine helps control the diarrhea. This stage lasts from 1-3 months.
   b. Stage 2   Parenteral nutrition continues as isotonic fluids are begun orally after stool volume diminishes to 2500 ml/day. Hypertonic oral fluids exacerbate diarrhea, but dilute elemental diets may be helpful. Foods are added to the diet by trial and error; fat is poorly absorbed after ileal resection because the pool of bile salts shrinks. Dairy products are avoided because lactase deficiency is common in short bowel syndrome. Antacids should be given for the gastric hypersecretion that often complicates this condition.
   c. Stage 3   Complete dependence on oral intake is expected eventually if the intestinal remnant is sufficiently long; 6 months to 2 years may be necessary for full adaptation. After ileal resection, patients need injections of vitamin B_{12} (1000 μg IM every 2-3 months) for life. Other vitamin deficiencies should be prevented. Enteric hyperoxaluria, causing urinary tract stones, is prevented by a low oxalate, low fat diet plus oral calcium, aluminum or cholestyramine (4 gm 3-4 times a day). Blind loop syndrome requires treatment if it appears. Surgical procedures such as reversed intestinal segments are seldom helpful. Patients who are unable to maintain nutrition orally are candidates for chronic parenteral nutrition on an outpatient basis.

E. BYPASS FOR OBESITY Morbid obese patients (those weighing more than 45 kg over the ideal) are considered for jejunoileal bypass. Gastric bypass, a reversible exclusion of most of the stomach, is another alternative.

Jejunoileal bypass creates a short bowel syndrome; usually, all but 14 inches (35 cm) of jejunum and 4 inches (10 cm) of ileum are excluded from the intestinal stream. Weight loss is rapid for 6 months and then slows as the bowel adapts.

Severe complications include fatty liver, arthritis, and oxalate urinary tract calculi. Management after bypass requires detailed attention to fluid and electrolyte balance, vitamin and mineral deficiencies, and prevention of protein malnutrition as in other forms of short bowel syndrome. Intestinal bypass is also done experimentally for some types of hyperlipidemia.

F. DIVERTICULA
   1. Meckel's diverticulum is a congenital anomaly due to persistence of the omphalomesenteric duct. It is a true diverticulum and is located within 100 cm of the ileocecal valve. About half of them contain heterotopic gastric, pancreatic, or other alimentary tissue. Only 4% become symptomatic, usually in childhood, and nearly always before age 30.
   a. Manifestations   Lower gastrointestinal bleeding results from erosion by heterotopic gastric tissue in early childhood. Meckel's diverticulitis resembles appendicitis in its pathogenesis, symptoms, and signs; perforation is common. Intestinal obstruction is caused by intussusception, entrapment of bowel beneath a mesodiverticular band, or other mechanisms.

b. Treatment Demonstration of the diverticulum by x-rays or ^{99m}Tc sodium pertechnetate is unreliable. Laparotomy is required to identify and remove the diverticulum. About 6% of patients with symptomatic Meckel's diverticula die of the disease due to delayed recognition and treatment.

2. Acquired diverticula are uncommon false diverticula, most often found in the jejunum. They cause bleeding, diverticulitis, or blind loop syndrome. Barium x-rays demonstrate the diverticula which are treated by resection of the involved segment.

G. RADIATION ENTEROPATHY Radiation therapy for abdominal or pelvic malignancy injures the proliferating intestinal epithelium transiently. If large doses of irradiation are given, the intestinal blood vessels are gradually obliterated and the intestine becomes ischemic. Symptoms may begin months to years after radiation and consist of obstruction due to stricture, bleeding from ulcerated mucosa, or necrosis with perforation and formation of abscesses and fistulas. Surgical treatment is required for these complications. The operative mortality rate is high (10–15%); the long-term outlook depends upon the presence of residual malignancy and the extent of the radiation injuries.

H. TUMORS The jejunum and ileum give rise to 1–5% of all tumors of the alimentary tract. Only 10% become symptomatic, and most of the symptomatic ones are malignant despite the fact that benign tumors outnumber malignant ones by 10 to 1. Bleeding and obstruction are the usual symptoms.

1. Benign tumors include leiomyomas, lipomas, neurofibromas, etc. **Polyps** may be adenomatous or villous, but more often they are hamartomas. Hamartomas are multiple in 50% of cases, and 10% of these patients have a familial disorder, **Peutz–Jeghers** syndrome (intestinal polyposis and mucocutaneous pigmentation). These polyps have no malignant potential; symptomatic ones are removed by operation. Polyps occur in the small intestine in **Gardner's syndrome** also.

2. Malignant tumors

a. Adenocarcinoma, usually of the jejunum, is rare in the small bowel; it is seldom diagnosed preoperatively and usually is fatal.

b. Lymphoma arises in the terminal ileum and causes obstruction, fever, and malabsorption. Segmental resection is the preferred treatment.

c. Leiomyosarcoma ulcerates centrally and bleeds.

d. Carcinoid tumor of the ileum grows slowly, but 80% of tumors greater than 2 cm in diameter have metastasized at the time of operation. **Carcinoid syndrome** (cutaneous flushing, diarrhea, bronchoconstriction, and right-sided cardiac valvular disease) is due to vasoactive substances released by hepatic metastases or by primary ovarian or bronchial carcinoids; it may be the first symptom. Urinary levels of 5-hydroxyindoleacetic acid are elevated in some patients if serotonin is one of the substances released. Primary small bowel carcinoids are resected; hepatic metastases are treated medically. The 5-year survival rate is 70% for small bowel carcinoids; only 20% of those with liver metastases live 5 years.

e. Metastases to the small bowel are common in malignant melanoma, breast cancer, etc. Occasionally operation to relieve symptoms of obstruction or bleeding is worthwhile.

XI. LARGE INTESTINE*

A. GENERAL PRINCIPLES

1. Diagnostic evaluation In addition to a complete history and thorough physical examination, the following procedures should be performed:

a. Mandatory Digital rectal examination. Examination of stool for gross

---

*Obstruction is covered in Section VI. Ischemia is covered in Section VII. Bleeding is covered in Section V. Anorectum is covered in Section XII.

or occult blood. Anoscopy. Proctosigmoidoscopy. Plain abdominal x-rays. Barium enema (contraindicated if perforation suspected).

b. Very useful Air-contrast barium enema (pneumocolon). Fiberoptic colonoscopy.

c. Useful in selected patients Examination of stool for ova, parasites, and enteric pathogens. Intravenous urography. Mesenteric arteriography. Abdominal ultrasound.

2. Preoperative preparation

a. Bowel preparation Elective operations on the large intestine require mechanical evacuation of feces. Antibiotic suppression of fecal bacteria is also recommended. One method of preparation is listed here; the regimen must be modified if the colon is obstructed or if the patient has inflammatory bowel disease.

(1) Clear liquid diet on day 1 and 2.

(2) Magnesium citrate (12 ounce bottle) orally at 1 pm on day 1 and 2.

(3) Saline enemas at bedtime on day 1; no enemas on day 2.

(4) Neomycin (1 gm) and erythromycin base (1 gm) orally at 1 pm, 2 pm, and 11 pm on day 2.

(5) Operation on day 3.

b. Elderly patients require IV fluids to replace losses from laxatives and enemas.

c. After induction of anesthesia, a Foley catheter and a nasogastric tube are inserted.

3. Postoperative care

a. The nasogastric tube is removed on the first postoperative day in most cases; longer intubation does not prevent anastomotic leakage.

b. Oral fluids and then food are begun when flatus is passed per rectum or per intestinal stoma, usually 2-5 days after operation. Laxatives and enemas are absolutely contraindicated if a colonic anastomosis has been done.

4. Complications

a. Important complications to look for are wound infection, intraabdominal abscess, and anastomotic leakage.

b. Anastomotic leakage (dehiscence) is suggested when a previously afebrile patient suddenly develops a high fever and abdominal pain and tenderness. In some cases, a water-soluble contrast enema to confirm the diagnosis is useful; it must be done cautiously with low pressure to avoid creating a leak. Systemic antibiotics are sufficient treatment for small localized leaks; operation to exteriorize the anastomosis or divert the fecal stream is necessary in large leaks associated with diffuse or generalized peritonitis.

B. TRAUMA

1. Preoperative preparation IV antibiotics are begun preoperatively when colonic injury is suspected.

2. Operation Surgical treatment depends upon the portion of bowel injured, size of the colonic wound, associated damage to the mesocolon, fecal contamination, shock, and other injuries. These principles generally apply:

a. Right colon Small perforations are sutured primarily. Large wounds require right colectomy, usually with immediate anastomosis.

b. Left colon Primary suture is prone to dehiscence. Small wounds are exteriorized as a colostomy, and large injuries are resected and the ends of the bowel fashioned as a colostomy and a mucous fistula. Anastomosis is done later.

c. Intraperitoneal rectum Diverting sigmoid colostomy, suture of the perforation, and intraoperative irrigation of the rectum to cleanse it of feces is the treatment of choice. The colostomy is taken down a few weeks later.

C. CARCINOMA
Adenocarcinoma of the colon or rectum is the most common visceral malignancy that affects both sexes in western countries. Other large bow-

el malignancies comprise no more than 5% of the total. Adenocarcinoma reaches a peak incidence between the ages of 60 and 75. These tumors spread by direct extension, hematogenous metastases, lymphatic metastases to regional nodes, gravitational metastases (seeding from tumor on the serosal surface), and perineural invasion. Multiple synchronous cancers occur in 5% of patients.

1. Diagnosis

a. Symptoms depend upon the location and the size of the tumor and the presence of complications. Cancer of the colon or rectum remains asymptomatic for a long period. Routine screening procedures (digital rectal examination, stool for occult blood, and, in patients over 50, routine annual sigmoidoscopy) are methods of detecting asymptomatic cancers.

(1) *Right colon* Fatiguability and weakness due to chronic anemia, vague abdominal discomfort, and weight loss.

(2) *Left colon* Change in bowel habits (alternating constipation and diarrhea), colicky abdominal pain, and gross blood and/or mucus in the stool.

(3) *Rectum* Blood and mucus in the stool, change in bowel habits, and tenesmus.

b. Signs The tumor may be palpable abdominally; this is more often true in cancer of the right colon. Occult or gross blood in the stool. Digital rectal and sigmoidoscopic examinations reveal one-half to two-thirds of cancers of the large bowel; biopsy should be obtained. Metastases to supraclavicular and groin nodes, umbilicus, and liver should be sought.

c. Laboratory tests Iron-deficiency anemia is common, especially with right-sided lesions.

Liver function tests (e.g., elevated alkaline phosphatase) may suggest that hepatic metastases are present.

Carcinoembryonic antigen (CEA) is elevated in large tumors but is normal in more than half of patients with tumors confined to the bowel wall. A base-line value should be obtained.

d. X-rays Barium enema usually demonstrates the tumor and should be obtained to identify synchronous lesions even when a distal tumor is palpable or is visible through the sigmoidoscope.

Air-contrast enema may clarify equivocal lesions.

Chest-x-ray should be obtained.

Intravenous urography often is done to ascertain the number and position of the kidneys and ureters preoperatively; this is most important before operating on rectal cancer.

e. Special tests Fiberoptic colonoscopy with biopsy is useful to confirm the diagnosis, it also excludes synchronous polyps and cancers more accurately than the barium enema.

Hepatic scan is not an essential routine study because the primary tumor should be resected in most cases even if hepatic metastases are present.

2. Differential diagnosis Symptoms may be mistakenly attributed to benign gastrointestinal disorders, functional problems, primary hematologic diseases, etc.

Symptoms may be ascribed erroneously to benign anorectal disease (e.g., hemorrhoids).

Benign colonic diseases, including diverticular disease, granulomatous colitis, amebiasis, and ischemic colitis, are ruled out by colonoscopic biopsy of the cancer if the radiographic appearance is equivocal.

3. Complications

a. Obstruction is most common in the left colon because the lumen is smaller in that location. Treatment is discussed in Section VI.

b. Perforation can occur into the general peritoneal cavity, or it can form a localized abscess or fistula. Treatment is by resection.

c. Bleeding from cancer is rarely massive.

d. Spread to adjacent organs (bladder, small bowel, uterus, vagina, prostate, spleen, pancreas, etc.) is treated by removing the involved organ or a part of it.

4. Treatment

a. Cancer of the **colon** is resected together with the regional lymphatic drainage of the affected part. Primary anastomosis is usually done. Distant metastases do not contraindicate resection of the primary tumor. Postoperative adjuvant chemotherapy is an experimental approach.

b. Cancer of the **rectum** is resected with primary anastomosis if possible; for lesions situated very low in the rectum, abdominoperineal resection with permanent colostomy is required. Fulguration (electrocoagulation) and focal radiation therapy are not definitive therapy for invasive cancer at present. Postoperative adjuvant radiation therapy and/or chemotherapy is experimental.

5. Prognosis The operative mortality rate is 2-4%. 5-year survival rates after resection depend on the stage of the lesion:

Dukes A (limited to bowel wall): 90%
Dukes B (through entire wall): 65%
Dukes C (lymph nodes positive): 30%
Dukes D (distant metastases or unresectable local spread): 5%

Long-term follow-up is essential to detect recurrence and metachronous lesions. Sigmoidoscopy and examination of stool for occult blood should be done every 3-6 months for 2 years, annually thereafter; barium enema is done annually for 3 years, every 2 years thereafter. Fiberoptic colonoscopy is usually reserved for patients with abnormal findings on the other tests. Serial CEA values are used increasingly to detect recurrence; if the CEA level is normal after curative resection, a sustained rise subsequently is presumptive evidence of recurrence.

D. POLYPS are lesions that project into the lumen. They are a variety of tumors histologically, including adenomatous polyps, villous (papillary) adenomas, a mixture of the two (villoglandular polyps), carcinoma, and many others. About 5% of adenomatous polyps and 30% of villous adenomas become malignant; most cancers of the colon and rectum probably arise from previously benign neoplasms. The implications of the presence of a polyp are that it may be malignant now, it may become malignant in the future, and until the polyp is removed, we do not know what it is histologically.

1. Diagnosis

a. Symptoms Many polyps are asymptomatic. Rectal bleeding is the most common symptom; bleeding is rarely massive. Altered bowel habits, mucus in the stool, and tenesmus are noted in some patients with large polyps, especially in the rectum.

b. Signs Colonic polyps are not evident on physical examination; polyps in the lower rectum are palpable. Villous adenoma in the rectum is a soft, velvety mass. Sigmoidoscopy reveals many of these lesions.

Stigmata of familial polyposis syndromes may be present (see below).

c. X-rays Barium enema or pneumocolon shows about 70% of polyps, including nearly all the large ones.

d. Special tests Fiberoptic colonoscopy is the most accurate method of detecting polyps.

2. Differential diagnosis Artifacts on the barium enema include bits of stool and air bubbles. Colonoscopy resolves these questions.

3. Treatment Pedunculated or small sessile polyps within reach of the sigmoidoscope are removed with an electrocautery snare passed through the instrument. Tiny lesions are biopsied or destroyed by fulguration. Large sessile lesions in the rectum are surgically excised; radical operation is done only if the histologic sections show invasive malignancy.

Pedunculated polyps in the colon are removed with the fiberoptic colonoscope. If invasive cancer is found in the specimen, the segment of colon may need to be resected, but this decision requires careful consideration.

Multiple polyps in the colon and large sessile lesions may require resection of all or part of the colon.

4. Prognosis Villous adenomas recur in about 15% of patients, and new polyps may develop. Patients should be followed with periodic examinations as for cancer of the colon.

5. Familial polyposis syndromes

a. Familial polyposis is an autosomal dominant disease in which multiple adenomatous polyps are scattered throughout the colon and rectum. Malignancy develops before age 40 in nearly all untreated patients. Rectal polyps often regress after abdominal colectomy with ileorectal anastomosis, and that procedure is preferable initially in the majority of patients. Polyps which remain in the rectum after 6 months, and those which arise later are fulgurated. The rectum should be removed if large crops of new polyps suddenly appear.

b. Gardner's syndrome is a variant of familial polyposis with the same malignant potential. Polyps also can occur in the small bowel in this disease. Other features of the syndrome include desmoid tumors, osteomas of the skull or mandible, and sebaceous cysts.

c. Peutz-Jeghers' syndrome consists of mucocutaneous pigmentation of the lips, gums, and axillae, and polyps throughout the GI tract. The polyps are hamartomas and have no malignant potential.

E. DIVERTICULAR DISEASE True diverticula of the colon (containing all layers of the bowel wall) are rare; false diverticula are acquired herniations of mucosa and submucosa through the muscular coats. The prevalence increases from 10% at age 40 to 65% at age 80. Diverticula result from high pressures in the colon, perhaps as a consequence of firm, tenacious stools in people who consume fiber-deficient diets. Diverticula are present in the sigmoid colon in 95% of those affected, with or without involvement of the more proximal colon.

1. Diverticulosis refers to the presence of diverticula.

a. Diagnosis

(1) *Symptoms and signs* Most patients with diverticulosis are asymptomatic. Some patients develop cramping, lower abdominal pain and constipation, diarrhea, or both; these symptoms are caused by spastic contractions of the thickened muscle, and the diverticula themselves are merely coincidental. A mildly tender tubular structure (sigmoid colon) is sometimes palpable in the left lower quadrant in patients with pain. There are no systemic symptoms or signs of infection.

(2) *X-rays* Barium enema shows diverticula. In patients with pain, x-rays may reveal segmental spasm which gives a 'sawtooth' appearance to the colon.

b. Differential diagnosis Diverticulosis with pain from muscular spasm may be difficult to distinguish from diverticulitis. The absence of systemic signs of infection (fever, leukocytosis), and the relatively rapid subsidence of pain, exclude diverticulitis in most cases.

c. Complications Diverticula bleed (see Section V) or perforate (see Diverticulitis below) in approximately 15% of patients.

d. Treatment Asymptomatic patients require no treatment. Patients with painful diverticular disease without diverticulitis may benefit from a high-bulk diet. Unprocessed bran (20 gm/day added to food) or hemicellulose (5 gm in a glass of water twice a day) are methods of increasing fiber in the diet.

Surgical treatment is not indicated in the absence of complications.

2. Diverticulitis is more accurately termed 'peridiverticulitis'; it results from perforation of a diverticulum which causes infection in the adjacent tissues, or, occasionally, in the entire peritoneal cavity. The sigmoid colon is nearly always the site of perforation.

a. Diagnosis

(1) *Symptoms and signs* Mild to severe, steady, aching or cramping pain develops abruptly in the left lower quadrant. Constipation, diarrhea, abdominal distention, nausea, and vomiting depend upon the extent and severity of the inflammation. Dysuria is noted if inflammation is adjacent to the bladder. Physical examination shows fever, abdominal distention, tenderness, and sometimes a mass in the left lower quadrant. Tenderness on rectal examination and gross or occult blood in the stools are common. Sigmoidoscopy shows erythema, edema, spasm, and angulation at the rectosigmoid. Perforation into the free peritoneal cavity produces symptoms and signs of generalized peritonitis. In some patients, the acute attack is insidious and patients first seek medical care for a complication such as colovesical fistula or large bowel obstruction.

(2) *Laboratory test* Leukocytosis.

(3) *X-rays* Plain abdominal films may show ileus, colonic obstruction, or abdominal mass; free air is present rarely. Barium enema is contraindicated for the first week to avoid leakage of barium into the peritoneal cavity through the perforation; a water-soluble study may be obtained if there is doubt about the diagnosis; contrast enema x-rays show a sinus tract, fistula, intramural abscess, or compression by an extrinsic mass. Intravenous urography may reveal compression or distortion of the ureters or bladder.

b. Differential diagnosis Many other acute abdominal diseases can produce the same picture; appendicitis, colonic ischemia, Crohn's disease, and perforated carcinoma are the most difficult to distinguish. Colonoscopy may help differentiate these diseases in the chronic phase.

c. Complications

(1) *Abscess* may form in the colonic wall, in the mesocolon, or in the paracolic tissues.

(2) *Fistula* results from erosion of an abscess into a hollow viscus such as the bladder, vagina, or small bowel. Colovesical fistula causes dysuria, fecaluria, and pneumaturia (passage of gas in the urine).

(3) *Colonic obstruction* is usually partial.

(4) *Massive bleeding* rarely is a complication of diverticulitis; bleeding diverticula usually have not perforated.

d. Medical treatment Acutely ill patients should be hospitalized. Nothing is allowed by mouth; nasogastric suction is instituted if the abdomen is distended. IV fluid and electrolyte therapy is important. Meperidine is preferable to morphine for analgesia because morphine causes muscular spasm in the colon. Broad-spectrum antibiotics are given IV.

If the patient does not improve on this treatment, operation is performed.

e. Surgical treatment Free perforation with generalized peritonitis requires resection or exteriorization of the perforation; primary anastomosis is not attempted.

Fistulas and very small abscesses are treated by one-stage resection with anastomosis.

Small to medium abscesses are removed together with the diseased sigmoid; temporary end colostomy and Hartmann (oversew of the rectal stump) are performed, and anastomosis is done a few weeks later.

Large abscesses are drained through a stab wound in the left lower quadrant, and the fecal stream is diverted by a transverse colostomy. Later, the sigmoid is resected and anastomosis is performed; finally, the colostomy is taken down. This approach requires three operations.

Obstruction without a large abscess is treated by cecostomy or transverse colostomy initially in some cases and by immediate resection in others.

f. Prognosis The mortality rate for the first attack of diverticulitis is 4%. About 25% of hospitalized patients require operation for the first attack. Elective interval resection of the sigmoid colon, after the first attack subsides, is indicated in young patients (under age 50) or if symptoms persist or recur. Recurrent diverticulitis after colonic resection is rare.

F. INFLAMMATORY DISEASE OF THE BOWEL Ulcerative colitis and Crohn's disease (regional enteritis, granulomatous colitis) are idiopathic inflammatory diseases that affect the small bowel, large intestine, or both. About 10% of patients have features of both diseases and cannot be labelled as one or the other. Comparison of the two diseases is shown in Table 10-2.

1. Ulcerative colitis

a. Diagnosis

(1) *Symptoms and signs* (a) Onset between 15 and 30 years of age usually; it can appear earlier or later. (b) Onset may be fulminating or insidious. Typical symptoms are frequent watery stools mixed with pus, blood, and mucus. Rectal urgency is common. Cramping abdominal pain, vomiting, fever, weight loss, and dehydration are variable. (c) Abdominal distention and tenderness in serious cases. Superficial anal fissures and gritty rectal mucosa on rectal examination; blood, pus, or mucus are seen on the examining finger. (d) Sigmoidoscopy is essential; enemas are not given beforehand. The rectum is involved in nearly all cases. The rectal mucosa is granular, dull, erythematous and friable (bleeds when wiped with a swab). The submucosal vascular pattern is obliterated. Gross large ulcers are rare. Mucosal involvement is confluent.

(2) *Laboratory tests* Anemia and leukocytosis are typical. Severe illness results in derangements of fluid and electrolyte balance, hypoalbuminemia, etc.

(3) *X-rays* Barium enema should not be performed in acutely ill patients and should not be preceded by vigorous catharsis. In acute colitis, the mucosa is serrated. In chronic disease, haustrations are effaced and the colon is shortened and narrowed. Strictures raise the suspicion of malignancy.

(4) *Special tests* Fiberoptic colonoscopy should not be done in fulminating disease. It is helpful in chronic disease to detect cancer or to assess extent of involvement or response to treatment. Occasionally it makes the diagnosis when other tests fail.

b. Differential diagnosis
Crohn's disease (see Table 10-2). Bacillary dysentery or parasitic disease (amebiasis, schistosomiasis) are excluded by bacterial culture and examination of stools for ova and parasites. Ischemic colitis has a segmental distribution.

c. Complications

(1) Systemic or *extracolonic manifestations* occur as part of the disease. They include: hepatobiliary lesions (steatosis, pericholangitis, gallstones, bile duct carcinoma); skin and mucous membrane lesions (erythema nodosum, pyoderma gangrenosum, aphthous stomatitis); bone and joint lesions (arthralgia, arthritis, ankylosing spondylitis); uveitis; delayed growth and maturation in children.

(2) *Acute colonic dilatation* (toxic megacolon) occurs in 3-5% of cases. Patients are seriously ill (toxic), and plain abdominal films show dilatation of the transverse colon to greater than 6 cm diameter. Perforation is a risk.

(3) *Perforation* occurs with or without preceding acute dilatation and is often lethal. The appearance of this complication is masked by corticosteroids.

(4) *Massive hemorrhage* is uncommon but life-threatening.

(5) *Carcinoma* of the colon has a greatly increased incidence after the disease has been present for 10 years or longer.

d. Medical treatment

(1) *Mild attacks* often respond to outpatient management, including reduced physical activity, milk-free diet, and oral sulfonamides (salicylazosulfapyridine 2-8 gm/day or sulfisoxazole 2 gm/day). If response is not prompt,

Table 10-2. Comparison of ulcerative colitis and Crohn's disease

	Ulcerative colitis	Crohn's disease
Symptoms and signs		
Diarrhea	Severe	Less severe
Rectal bleeding	Typical	Uncommon
Anal lesions	Occasional	Frequent, complex
X-ray findings		
	Colon only	Colon and/or small bowel
	Confluent, concentric	Skip areas, eccentric
	Serrations, pseudopolyps	Longitudinal ulcers, 'cobblestoning'
	Internal fistulas very rare	Internal fistulas common
Complications		
Toxic dilatation	3–20%	Less common
Carcinoma	Greatly increased incidence	Increased incidence
Systemic	Common	Common
Massive hemorrhage	Uncommon	Rare
Morphology		
Gross	Confluent	Skip areas
	Rectum involved	Rectum often spared
	Thin mesentery	Thickened mesentery
	Diffuse superficial ulceration	Deep longitudinal ulcers or transverse fissures
	Bowel wall thin	Bowel wall greatly thickened
	Pseudopolyps common	Pseudopolyps uncommon
Microscopic	Inflammation limited to mucosa and submucosa	Transmural inflammation with submucosal fibrosis
	Crypt abscesses common	Crypt abscesses uncommon
	Granulomas rare	Granulomas frequent
Prognosis		
	Exacerbations, remissions	Indolent, progressive
	Good response to medical treatment	Poor response to medical treatment
	Seldom recurs after proctocolectomy with ileostomy	Often recurs after resection of involved bowel

topical hydrocortisone should be self-administered as a retention enema at bedtime. Mix 1.6 gm of hydrocortisone hemisuccinate in 1 liter of vegetable oil; 60 ml (approx 100 mg) of the mixture are instilled into the rectum with a bulb syringe with the patient lying on his left side and the buttocks elevated on a pillow. Hydrocortisone suppositories are an alternative for disease limited to the rectum.

(2) *Severe attacks* require hospitalization. Nothing is given by mouth, and nasogastric suction may be needed. Careful attention to fluid and electrolyte balance (especially hypokalemia) is essential; transfusions may be necessary. IV broad-spectrum antibiotics are given. Corticosteroids are administered IV as hydrocortisone (100–300 mg/day) or corticotropin (ACTH, 20–40 units dripped per 8 hours). Parenteral nutrition is required if the disease does not respond promptly. Oral food and medications (corticosteroids and antibacterials) are resumed as symptoms subside.

(3) *Maintenance* on sulfonamides (2 gm/day orally) reduces relapse rates. Topical hydrocortisone (by enema) or oral prednisone (20–40 mg/day) may be helpful; long-term maintenance on high-dose steroids causes complications and should be avoided.

e. Surgical treatment

(1) *Emergency* colectomy or proctocolectomy is required for severe attacks or complications (hemorrhage, toxic dilatation) that do not respond promptly to medical management.

(2) *Elective* operation, usually proctocolectomy with ileostomy, is indicated for chronic continuous symptoms, frequent exacerbations, or to prevent cancer in long-standing disease.

f. Prognosis The first attack has a mortality rate of 4–15%; nearly all of these deaths occur in the course of a fulminating attack. About 80% of patients have a second attack within 1 year. Approximately 15% undergo colectomy at some time. The mortality rate is about 2% for elective operations and 5–10% for emergency colectomy. Impotence occurs in 15% of men after proctectomy; most of those affected are over 50 years of age.

2. Crohn's disease

a. Diagnosis

(1) *Symptoms and signs* (1) The peak incidence is between 15 and 20 years of age. (b) Continuous or episodic diarrhea occurs in 90% of patients. (c) Blood in the stools is unusual if only the small bowel is diseased; more common with colonic involvement. (d) Postprandial cramping midabdominal pain, weight loss, fever, and anemia. (e) Large and complex anal lesions (abscess, fistula, fissure), may precede the appearance of intestinal symptoms. (f) A mass is palpable in the right lower quadrant in some patients. (g) Sigmoidoscopy shows a normal rectum in 50% of cases. Diseased mucosa is patchy, with gross irregular ulcerations separated by edematous or even normal-appearing mucosa.

(2) *X-rays* (a) The involvement is limited to the distal small bowel in 30%, large bowel in 30%, and both distal ileum and colon in 40%. Barium enema and small bowel contrast studies are required. (b) Thickened, strictured bowel wall with deep, undermining longitudinal ulcers, transverse fissures which look like spicules, and cobblestoning are characteristic. Skip lesions with normal intervening bowel, abscesses, and internal fistulas are important findings.

b. Differential diagnosis Ulcerative colitis (see Table 10-2), tuberculous enteritis, lymphoma, and intestinal ischemia need to be differentiated.

c. Complications Extraintestinal manifestations are the same as in ulcerative colitis. Acute colonic dilatation can occur. Abscesses and internal fistulas are present routinely. Carcinoma of the colon or small bowel is associated with chronic Crohn's disease.

d. Medical treatment The initial treatment in most cases is medical, and the regimen is the same as for ulcerative colitis. Total parenteral nutrition is a useful adjunct.

e. Surgical treatment Operation is required for complications of the disease. Involved intestine is resected, with anastomosis if possible; the rectum can be preserved in many cases.

f. Prognosis Crohn's disease is an indolent disease which responds to medical therapy less well than does ulcerative colitis. The recurrence rate after surgical resection is about 50%.

G. INTESTINAL STOMAS An intestinal stoma is a temporary or permanent opening of the bowel onto the surface of the abdomen. Ileostomy and colostomy are the most common types.

1. Ileostomy Permanent ileostomy is required when proctocolectomy is performed for familial polyposis or inflammatory bowel disease. It is usually placed in the right lower quadrant and projects about 3 cm above the skin level to permit adherence of an appliance. Small amounts of liquid and gas are expelled intermittently, and the appliance must be worn constantly. Patients lead normal lives in every other way. Problems and complications include the following:

a. Dehydration and electrolyte depletion if the patient does not take sufficient salt and water to replace the fixed losses that are a consequence of removing the colon. Ileostomates should take fluids in large quantities and should salt their food liberally. They should not get into a position (e.g., hiking in the desert) where water is unavailable. Viral gastroenteritis, with vomiting and large losses through the ileostomy, requires aggressive treatment, even hospitalization in some cases.

b. Ileostomy dysfunction is profuse watery discharge from the ileostomy due to obstruction. A minor surgical procedure to release the subcutaneous cicatrix may be necessary.

c. Stenosis due to circumferential scarring should be revised.

d. Retraction of the stoma causes leakage beneath the appliance.

e. Prolapse is usually preventable by good operative technic.

f. Periileostomy fistula results from an ill-fitting appliance or recurrent inflammatory disease.

g. Skin irritation is common and is due to leakage and soiling of the skin. An *enterostomal therapist* is trained to treat this and many other problems with stomas.

h. Odor is minimal with modern appliances.

i. Uric acid urinary tract calculi probably result from chronic dehydration.

2. Continent ileostomy   This is a new technic in which a reservoir is constructed within the abdomen, and a valve is made of intestine to prevent leakage from the reservoir. Gas and fluid are emptied by inserting a catheter into the stoma several times a day; an appliance is unnecessary.

3. Colostomy   Temporary colostomies are made to decompress the colon and/or divert the fecal stream; permanent colostomy is required when the rectum is removed, usually for carcinoma. The permanent type is an **end colostomy** and is made by bringing the end of the colon out to the skin. A temporary colostomy may be an end colostomy or a **loop colostomy**; (an opening is made in the side of a loop of colon at the skin level).

A permanent sigmoid colostomy expels stool once or twice a day. An appliance is not required, but many patients wear a light plastic pouch for reassurance. Many surgeons instruct patients to irrigate end-colostomies by carefully inserting a lubricated catheter and instilling water, 500 ml at a time, by gravity flow from a reservoir held at shoulder height. Irrigations should not begin until at least 1 week after operation. Most patients are able to eat the same foods that they enjoyed before. Colostomies do not require dilatation.

Many of the same complications occur with colostomy as with ileostomy, e.g., stenosis and prolapse. Paracolostomy hernia is common in these generally elderly patients with weak tissues.

XII. ANORECTUM*

A. EXAMINATION   The following sequence should be followed in the physical examination of patients with anorectal complaints. Occasionally, a step may be deferred (e.g., if a painful lesion is present), but all maneuvers should be completed eventually.

1. Preparation

a. Rapport is important; the examiner must describe the expected sensations before they appear.

---

*Pilonidal sinus and hidradenitis suppurativa are discussed in Chapter **4**.

b. The inverted (knee-chest, prone jackknife) position requires a special examining table; the left lateral decubitus (Sims') position is also satisfactory.

c. Good lighting, an assistant, and conveniently arranged instruments are essential.

2. Inspection

a. The buttocks are retracted with the fingers of both hands, and the perineum is inspected.

b. The anal orifice is gently everted by lateral retraction on each side of the anus.

3. Palpation

a. The perineal and perianal tissues are gently palpated to search for a mass, induration, or tenderness.

b. The lubricated index finger is placed at the anal orifice and gently inserted, and digital examination of the anorectum is accomplished.

4. Anoscopy

a. A tubular metal or plastic anoscope (proctoscope) is lubricated and gently inserted, aiming toward the umbilicus. After the sphincteric ring is passed, the tip of the instrument is directed posteriorly to negotiate the anorectal angle.

b. The obturator is removed and the lower rectum and anal canal are inspected.

5. Sigmoidoscopy

a. Sigmoidoscopy is done without prior laxatives or enemas.

b. The rigid metal instrument is lubricated and inserted, changing the direction after the sphincters are passed as with anoscopy.

c. The obturator is removed and the instrument is advanced, following the lumen under direct vision.

d. At the rectosigmoid junction, about 12-15 cm from the anal verge, the lumen bends sharply forward and to the left. Anterior pressure with the tip of the instrument usually straightens this turn, and the sigmoid colon is entered.

e. The bowel is examined by sweeping the tip circumferentially as the instrument is withdrawn. Care must be taken to flatten out the rectal valves, two on the left and one on the right, because lesions may be hidden above them.

B. TRAUMA Perforation of the intraperitoneal rectum is managed as described in the section on Large Intestine. Perforating injuries of the extraperitoneal rectum caused by sharp trauma are diagnosed by anoscopy and sigmoidoscopy. Blood is present in the lumen, and the perforation can be seen in most cases. If there is doubt, a water-soluble contrast medium can be instilled and x-rays obtained. Injury of associated structures, especially the urinary tract, should be sought.

Patients should be placed on IV broad-spectrum antibiotics. Operative treatment consists of: diverting sigmoid colostomy; irrigation of the rectum to cleanse it of feces; and drainage of the area of perforation, usually by presacral sump or penrose drains. No attempt should be made to suture perforation. The colostomy is taken down after the rectal wound heals. Wounds that disrupt the sphincters extensively are managed in the same way, deferring definitive repair until conditions improve. Occasionally, the sphincters can be repaired primarily.

C. RECTAL PROLAPSE Partial rectal prolapse is protrusion of the rectal mucosa through the anus; true or complete prolapse (procidentia) is prolapse of the entire thickness of the rectum. Both types of prolapse are more common in women; procidentia occurs in children, but in adults it increases in frequency with advancing age. Laxity of the pelvic musculature from aging or neurologic disease is responsible for most cases of prolapse in adults. In children, straightness of the anorectal junction is responsible; it is corrected with growth and development.

1. Diagnosis

a. Symptoms A mass protrudes from the anus during defecation. Initially it reduces spontaneously, but eventually it protrudes with standing and is difficult to reduce. Blood and mucus from the exposed mucosa is common. Partial or complete incontinence is typical in adults with chronic prolapse.

b. Signs Examine the patient in the squatting position and in the prone-jackknife or lateral decubitus position.

Mucosal prolapse (partial prolapse) is a symmetrical protrusion 2-4 cm long with radial folds. Palpation between finger and thumb reveals two layers of mucosa. The sphincters often are lax.

Procidentia (complete prolapse) is an asymmetrical projection up to 12 cm long with concentric folds. The lumen points posteriorly due to the presence of small bowel and omentum in a hernia sac on the anterior wall; this large mass of tissue anteriorly is palpable. The anal orifice may gape widely even with the prolapse reduced, and the patient may be unable to contract the sphincter muscles.

2. Differential diagnosis Prolapsing hemorrhoids and polyps are easily differentiated.

3. Complications Chronic procidentia impairs the sphincters so that incontinence may be a problem even if the prolapse is repaired.

4. Treatment Prolapse in children is treated by correction of constipation, instruction not to strain, defecation in a recumbent position, and strapping the buttocks together between bowel movements.

Mucosal prolapse is treated by fixation of the sliding mucosa by submucosal injections of sclerosing solution (e.g., 5% phenol in oil). Excision of the prolapsing mucosa is also successful.

Procidentia in adults is treated by surgical repair. Transabdominal fixation of the rectum to the sacrum (posterior proctopexy) is the most popular technic. Encircling the anus with a suture (Thiersch wire) is reserved for aged or debilitated patients.

5. Prognosis Prolapse in children usually is self-correcting. Partial prolapse in adults responds well to treatment. Surgical repair of complete prolapse is successful in most cases, but residual incontinence due to chronic stretching of the sphincters is difficult to treat, especially in elderly patients.

D. HEMORRHOIDS, or piles, are enlarged vascular cushions in the lower rectum and anal canal. They are not simply varicose veins. **Internal hemorrhoids** arise above the pectinate line; **external hemorrhoids** arise below the pectinate line. Many patients have **mixed** (intero-external) hemorrhoids.

1. Diagnosis

a. Symptoms

(1) *Bleeding* with defecation is a cardinal symptom. Typically, bright red blood is noted on the toilet tissue, on the stool, or in the water of the toilet bowl. Blood may drip from the anus for a few moments after defecation.

(2) *Prolapse* of a mass with defecation is the second cardinal symptom. The mass slips back spontaneously after defecation at first, but later it must be reduced manually, and eventually it may become irreducible.

(3) *Mucoid discharge* is noted by some patients with prolapsing hemorrhoids.

(4) Difficulty with hygiene is common when there are large external components.

(5) Pain is not a symptom of internal hemorrhoids, except when they prolapse and thrombose. Pain is nearly always due to another associated condition.

b. Signs

(1) External hemorrhoids are visible beneath the perianal skin or anoderm.

(2) Internal hemorrhoids are found by inspection if they prolapse. The three primary locations of internal hemorrhoids are left lateral, right anterior, and right posterior.

(3) Internal hemorrhoids usually are not palpable in the anal canal. Anoscopy is required to diagnose nonprolapsing internal hemorrhoids.

2. Differential diagnosis   Other causes of rectal bleeding (e.g., carcinoma) must be ruled out by sigmoidoscopy, barium enema, and sometimes fiberoptic colonoscopy.

3. Complications   Anemia from chronic bleeding is uncommon and acute massive hemorrhage is rare. Prolapsed hemorrhoids may thrombose, become inflamed, and cause severe pain.

4. Treatment

a. General measures   A high-residue diet minimizes straining at stool. Patients should avoid sitting on the toilet for prolonged periods. Prolapse should be reduced. Topical ointments and suppositories have little value.

b. Surgical treatment

(1) *Injection* of sclerosing solutions (e.g., 5% phenol in oil) into the submucosal tissue at the upper pole of each hemorrhoid is effective for small bleeding internal hemorrhoids.

(2) *Ligation* with rubber bands using a special instrument causes slough of the hemorrhoid and tethers the mucosa within the anal canal to prevent prolapse. Care must be taken to place the bands in an insensitive area at least 0.5 cm above the pectinate line.

(3) *Cryosurgery* is destruction of hemorrhoids by freezing. The method has few proponents at present.

(4) *Manual dilatation of the anus* is a vigorous stretching of the anus under general anesthesia. The method is successful in 85% of patients, although the reason for resolution of hemorrhoids after dilatation is unknown. Patients over age 60 are not candidates for this procedure because of the risk of incontinence.

(5) *Hemorrhoidectomy* is used mainly for large prolapsing hemorrhoids where the skin-covered external components are a source of difficulty.

c. Acutely prolapsed, inflamed, thrombosed hemorrhoids can be treated by bed rest, ice packs, analgesics, and bulk laxatives. Manual dilatation or emergency hemorrhoidectomy may speed recovery.

5. Prognosis   Most methods of treatment are successful in controlling bleeding, although repeated injections or ligations may be required at intervals over the years. Manual dilatation and hemorrhoidectomy appear to be more permanently effective.

E. THROMBOSED EXTERNAL HEMORRHOID   An external hemorrhoid may thrombose acutely as a result of vigorous exercise, straining to defecate, or unknown causes. A severely painful mass appears suddenly at the anus; pain is aggravated by sitting, walking, and defecation, and it begins to subside in a few days. Bleeding is noted if the thrombosed hemorrhoid ulcerates and extrudes the clot.

On examination, one or more bluish, tender, spherical masses varying from a few millimeters to several centimeters in diameter are seen at the anal verge. Anoderm covers the upper portion of the mass, thus distinguishing it from a prolapsed internal hemorrhoid which has pink rectal mucosa on the upper portion.

These lesions subside spontaneously, but severe pain is relieved and recovery hastened by excising the mass under local anesthesia. Alternatively, the mass can be incised and the clot extracted from the thrombosed veins with a hemostat. The incision should not be sutured.

F. FISSURE   Anal fissure (fissure-in-ano) is a tear in the anoderm. More than 90% occur in the posterior midline, and the remainder are in the anterior midline.

1. Diagnosis   Pain with defecation is the typical symptom. In some patients, a different type of pain that begins an hour or so after defecation is present also. A few spots of blood may be noted on the toilet tissue.

An **acute fissure** is visible as a tear in the anoderm when the anus is gently everted. **Chronic fissure** has the white transverse fibers of the internal sphincter exposed in its base. A **sentinel tag** or pile (a swollen tag of skin at the anal verge) and a **hypertrophied papilla** at the upper end of the fissure complete the triad of chronic fissure.

Fissures located off the midline suggest that inflammatory bowel disease, carcinoma, venereal disease, or immunologic deficiency may underlie the problem.

2. Treatment

a. Acute fissures usually heal in 2–3 weeks with bulk laxatives, analgesics, and sitz baths. Acute fissures can be painted with 50% phenol in oil to interrupt the cycle of pain-spasm-pain until healing occurs.

b. Chronic fissures that do not respond to simple measures may be treated surgically. Lateral subcutaneous sphincterotomy is the method of choice. It can be performed under local or general anesthesia and is successful in 97% of patients.

G. ABSCESS   An abscess can develop in any of the tissue spaces adjacent to the anorectum. Anorectal abscess is believed to begin as infection in an anal crypt which then spreads along tissue planes. Abscesses are named according to their location in the anatomic spaces, e.g., **perianal** (beneath the anoderm or perianal skin); **ischiorectal** (in the ischiorectal fossa); **intermuscular** (between the internal and external sphincters); and others.

1. Diagnosis   Throbbing, constant pain made worse by sitting or walking is typical of superficial abscesses. Deeper abscesses may cause pain high in the rectum or in the lower abdomen. Fever is common.

An indurated, tender mass is visible and palpable externally or by digital rectal examination. Often, fluctuance cannot be appreciated in the mass although it is filled with pus.

2. Complications   Abscesses may extend along tissue planes to adjacent areas, e.g., the scrotum or lower abdominal wall.

3. Treatment   There is no medical treatment for anorectal abscess. Prompt surgical drainage must be done when the diagnosis is made. It is incorrect to assume that a mass contains no pus because it is not fluctuant; these lesions are ready to drain when first seen. Patients with immunologic deficiency or hematologic malignancy are exceptions to this rule.

Small superficial abscesses may be drained under local anesthesia; larger ones require a general anesthetic. Care must be taken to avoid cutting the sphincters; an incision parallel to the anus is safe in this regard.

4. Prognosis   About two-thirds of anorectal abscesses heal with formation of an anorectal fistula. Abscesses in immune-deficient patients can be lethal.

H. FISTULA   An anorectal fistula (fistula-in-ano) is a hollow tract filled with granulation tissue. It has an opening (primary or internal) inside the anal canal and one or more orifices (secondary or external) in the perianal skin. An anorectal **sinus** has only one opening and is blind at the other end.

Because most fistulas begin with infection in a crypt as described for anorectal abscesses, most primary openings are at the pectinate line. Fistulas from Crohn's disease, carcinoma, lymphopathia venereum, etc. may be bizarre and complex.

Secondary openings appearing anterior to a transverse line through the center of the anus arise from primary openings which are located radially in the anal canal. If the secondary orifice is posterior to this imaginary line, the primary opening is in the posterior midline. This useful general guide is the Goodsall-Salmon rule.

1. Diagnosis

a. Symptoms   There may be a history of abscess which drained spontaneously or was drained surgically. Drainage of pus, blood, mucus, and occasionally stool is the chief complaint; drainage is intermittent if the fistula seals and reopens.

b. Signs Secondary openings are raised, reddish papules; a drop of pus can be expressed if the fistula is patent. The tract is palpated as an indurated cord extending toward the anus.

Anoscopy reveals the primary opening, and a hooked probe can be inserted into it; probing the tract from the secondary orifice is helpful sometimes.

The relationship of the fistula to the puborectalis sling is important.

Sigmoidoscopy is done to rule out other rectal diseases. Barium enema is indicated in patients with unusual fistulas or a history suggesting inflammatory bowel disease.

2. Differential diagnosis Hidradenitis suppurativa and pilonidal sinus (see Chapter 4) are easily distinguished because there is no communication with the anal canal in these conditions. Presacral teratoma may be difficult to differentiate.

3. Complications Recurrent abscess, systemic infection, and carcinoma (rare).

4. Treatment Surgical **fistulotomy** is the treatment of choice because established fistulas do not heal. The procedure requires general or regional anesthesia; all tracts must be identified and exposed. Great care must be taken to avoid division of the puborectalis muscle because incontinence invariably results; fortunately, fistulas which extend above the level of the puborectalis are rare, and they require management by a specialist. Fistulotomy should not be performed in the presence of active Crohn's disease.

5. Prognosis Recurrent fistula after surgical treatment is due to an overlooked primary opening, inadequate exposure of the tracts, failure to care for the wound to ensure healing from the base outward, or underlying intestinal disease.

I. PRURITUS ANI Itching of the perianal skin is a symptom, not a diagnosis.

1. Causes

a. Anorectal diseases (fistulas, condylomata acuminata, neoplasms, etc.).

b. Dermatologic diseases (e.g., psoriasis, atopic eczema).

c. Contact dermatitis from ointments, deodorants, soaps, etc.

d. Infections (fungal, bacterial).

e. Parasitic infestations (enterobius vermicularis, scabies, pediculosis).

f. Oral antibiotics, especially tetracyclines; the mechanism may be the frequent, loose, irritating stools resulting from oral antibiotics.

g. Systemic diseases (diabetes, liver disease).

h. Hygiene Poor hygiene or excessively vigorous rubbing and cleansing with irritant soaps.

i. Warmth and moisture Tight clothing, obesity, hot climate, exercise.

j. Psychogenic.

k. Idiopathic Some of these patients probably have pruritus from irritant stools which have an alkaline pH and contain active digestive enzymes.

2. Diagnosis

a. Symptoms Pruritus is worse at night regardless of the cause; it may spread to involve the entire perineum and the vulva or scrotum. Relationships of pruritus to foods (peppers, citrus fruits) and beverages (coffee, milk, alcohol) should be ascertained. Inquire about bowel habits, hygienic practices, topical medications, oral antibiotics, types of clothing, pruritus elsewhere, etc.

b. Signs The perianal skin may be completely normal, or it may be erythematous, lichenified, moist, and macerated. Dermatologic disease (especially psoriasis) may be evident. Anorectal disease is sought by anoscopy.

c. Laboratory tests Candidiasis is diagnosed by mixing scrapings with 10% KOH, warming the preparation, and examining it microscopically. Since fungi grow secondarily on moist surfaces, it is difficult to prove that fungi are the primary problem.

Scabies and pediculosis are diagnosed by identifying the parasites or nits.

Enterobius is identified by finding eggs on the perianal skin. The patient should place transparent adhesive tape against the skin on awakening in the morning and then affix the tape to a glass slide.

3. Treatment

a. Specific treatment is used for systemic, dermatologic, malignant, anorectal, fungal, or parasitic disease.

b. Nonspecific treatment

(1) Stop all current antibiotics and topical medications.

(2) Modify diet if certain foods or beverages are contributory.

(3) Tight underclothing and heavy bedclothing should be avoided.

(4) Cleansing after defecation is best accomplished by moist cotton followed by gentle swabbing with soft cloth impregnated with glycerin and witch hazel (Tuck's pads).

(5) Protective ointment (e.g., petrolatum jelly) or nonmedicated talcum powder is used to combat moisture.

(6) If stools are loose, prescribe a bulk agent (e.g., unprocessed bran 3 tablespoons in food daily) and discontinue all laxatives.

(7) Alkaline irritant stools are treated empirically by oral administration of Lactobacillus acidophilus to promote the growth of acidic flora in the colon.

(8) Refractory patients benefit from 1% hydrocortisone cream applied sparingly 4 times daily.

4. Prognosis Most patients respond to treatment, but a few seem refractory to all therapy.

J. VENEREAL DISEASES

1. Condylomata acuminata are caused by a virus. They are found on the perianal skin of patients who have no anal sexual contact, but inoculation of the virus into the anal canal probably requires anal intercourse or instrumentation.

Condylomata are small warts initially, but they gradually enlarge to form confluent exophytic masses in some patients. Bleeding, pruritus, and difficulty with hygiene are the main symptoms.

Small external warts are painted with 25% podophyllin in tincture of benzoin. Apply podophyllin only to the warts and have the patient bathe within a few hours to avoid ulcerating normal skin.

Warts within the anal canal and large external warts are best excised or fulgurated under local anesthesia (or general anesthesia if they are extensive).

Recurrence is the rule, and patients must be followed closely for months after the last known sexual contact.

2. Gonorrhea Rectal gonorrhea causes inflammation of the rectal mucosa, sparing the anoderm. Pain, diarrhea, bleeding, and purulent discharge are the symptoms. Anoscopy shows friable ulcerated mucosa, and thick pus often exudes from the crypts.

Obtain cultures to confirm the diagnosis. Cervical gonorrhea and syphilis must be investigated also.

a. Treatment

(1) Aqueous procaine penicillin G. 4.8 million units IM (2.4 million units in each buttock) 1 hour after probenecid 1 gm orally.

(2) Alternative: Ampicillin 3.5 gm orally and probenecid 1 gm orally at the same time.

(3) **Never** treat gonorrhea with benzathine penicillin G.

(4) Penicillin-resistant gonorrhea requires treatment with drugs selected on the basis of sensitivity testing.

b. Follow-up Obtain a rectal specimen for culture 7 days after completion of treatment.

3. Syphilis Primary anorectal syphilis is an ulcer which resembles an anal fissure; the lesion heals in 3–4 weeks. Secondary lesions are multiple plaques with a wet odorous discharge. The diagnosis is made by darkfield examination and serologic tests.

Benzathine penicillin G is the drug of choice. For primary or secondary syphilis, give 1.2 million units IM in each buttock (total 2.4 million units).

4. Other Lymphopathia venereum, chancroid, granuloma inguinale, and herpes simplex are other anorectal venereal diseases.

K. MALIGNANT TUMORS OF THE ANUS Epidermoid carcinomas are the most common anal malignancies. Melanoma, mucinous adenocarcinoma, Bowen's disease, and Paget's disease are other malignant lesions that can arise in the anal canal or on the perianal skin. The following comments apply to epidermoid cancer.

1. Diagnosis Bleeding, pruritus, pain, drainage, and a mass are the usual symptoms that bring a patient to the physician complaining of 'hemorrhoids'.

The tumor is visible and/or palpable. Its size, location, and depth of invasion should be noted. Biopsy confirms the diagnosis.

Anal cancer can metastasize to lymph nodes in the groins as well as to the retrorectal nodes and by the hematogenous route to liver, lungs, etc.

2. Treatment Small noninvasive lesions can be excised locally or treated by irradiation. Lesions that invade the sphincters, and those arising at the pectinate line, require abdominoperineal resection. Inguinal metastases are treated by lymph node excision or irradiation.

3. Prognosis The 5-year survival rate is about 60% after surgical treatment of invasive epidermoid cancer.

XIII. APPENDIX

A. ACUTE APPENDICITIS is the most common abdominal surgical emergency in western countries. The incidence is highest in young adults, but any age may be affected. Appendicitis results from obstruction of the lumen by a fecalith, foreign body, tumor, or parasites. The mucosa secretes fluid behind the obstruction, the intraluminal pressure rises, the mucosa becomes hypoxic and ulcerates, and bacteria invade into the wall. The appendix is viable and intact in **simple appendicitis; gangrenous appendicitis** implies necrosis of the wall, and **perforated appendicitis** refers to gross disruption. Gangrene and perforation are likely to occur after 24–36 hours.

1. Diagnosis
   a. Symptoms
   (1) Pain in the epigastrium, periumbilical area, generalized in the abdomen, or in the right lower quadrant is the first symptom. This pain is vague, mild to moderate in severity, and sometimes colicky. It subsides gradually after about 4 hours and then **shifts** to the right lower quadrant where it is a steady, progressively severe ache made worse by movement.
   (2) Anorexia, nausea, or vomiting follows the onset of pain by a few hours.
   (3) Other symptoms include low-grade fever and constipation.
   (4) Infants with appendicitis are lethargic, irritable and anorexic.
   (5) In the elderly, symptoms are less marked than in younger adults.
   b. Signs
   (1) Localized tenderness in the right lower quadrant is the most important finding. Tenderness may be found in the right flank if the appendix is retrocecal. Tenderness to rectal or vaginal examination is detected in pelvic appendicitis. If the appendix is bizarrely situated, tenderness is localized to other sites.

(2) Other signs include fever (<38°C), muscular rigidity, rebound tenderness, referred tenderness, and positive psoas and obturator signs.

(3) Infants may require sedation; localized tenderness is present. In the elderly, tenderness may be deceptively mild. In pregnant women, tenderness is localized higher in the abdomen than usual.

c. Laboratory tests   The leukocyte count averages between 10,000 and 16,000/mm^3 with a 'shift to the left' (more than 75% neutrophils) in 75% of cases. 96% have leukocytosis or an abnormal differential white cell count. Urinalysis may show small numbers of erythrocytes or leukocytes.

d. X-ray findings   There are no specific abnormalities on plain abdominal films. Barium enema may be diagnostic but is reserved for doubtful cases.

2. Differential diagnosis

a. Gastroenteritis and mesenteric lymphadenitis usually occur in children or young adults. Nausea and vomiting precede abdominal pain; high fever, malaise, and other symptoms of viral illness are prominent. Pain and tenderness are poorly localized and vary during a period of observation.

b. Gynecologic diseases

(1) Acute salpingitis begins in the lower abdomen without the characteristic shift. High fever, diffuse bilateral lower abdominal tenderness, cervical tenderness, and vaginal discharge containing gram-negative intracellular diplococci are clues to the diagnosis.

(2) Mittelschmerz is pain caused by rupture of an ovarian follicle at the time of ovulation; sudden pain in the middle of the menstrual cycle, minimal gastrointestinal symptoms, and spontaneous improvement are the rule.

(3) Ruptured ectopic pregnancy causes sudden pain, shock (if blood loss is massive), and diffuse pelvic tenderness. The enlarged tube may be palpable; culdocentesis returns bloody fluid.

(4) Twisted ovarian cyst causes sudden pain and simultaneous vomiting; an anesthetic may be required to detect the mass.

c. Urinary tract diseases

(1) Ureteral colic radiates into the groin; there is no muscular rigidity and little direct tenderness. The urine contains erythrocytes. Intravenous urography makes the diagnosis.

(2) Acute pyelonephritis is associated with high fever, chills, and tenderness in the costovertebral angle. Pyuria, white cell casts, and gross bacteria are seen in the urine.

d. Meckel's diverticulitis is rare; associated symptoms of bowel obstruction, vaguely localized pain, and tenderness near the umbilicus are hints to this diagnosis.

e. Other surgical disease include perforated peptic ulcer, cholecystitis, sigmoid diverticulitis, etc.

f. Systemic diseases include basilar pneumonia, diabetic ketoacidosis, acute porphyria, and tabetic crisis. In most cases, abdominal pain and tenderness are diffuse.

3. Complications

a. Perforation occurs in 20% of patients (80-90% in infants and 30% or more in the elderly). Increased pain, high fever, diffuse tenderness, and high leukocyte counts suggest that perforation has occurred.

b. Peritonitis, diffuse or generalized, is one consequence of perforation. Diagnosis and treatment are discussed below.

c. Appendiceal abscess is another result of perforation. A tender mass is palpable in the right lower quadrant or in the pelvis. The mass is a phlegmon initially but later it contains pus.

d. Pylephlebitis (septic thrombophlebitis of the portal vein) causes high fever, shaking chills, and jaundice.

4. Treatment
a. Preoperative preparation

(1) If the diagnosis is uncertain, the patient should be observed and examination of the abdomen and pelvis repeated at intervals. Little is gained by prolonging observation beyond a few hours. Nothing is given by mouth and analgesics are withheld until a decision is reached.

(2) A nasogastric tube is inserted if the abdomen is distended or the patient is toxic.

(3) IV fluid and electrolyte repletion is not required in young adults with simple appendicitis. Infants, the elderly, and the severely ill must have deficits replaced before operation.

(4) Antibiotics are administered IV if perforation or pylephlebitis are suspected.

(5) High fever, particularly in children, must be lowered before anesthesia is induced.

b. Operation

(1) Appendectomy is the only acceptable treatment for simple appendicitis or perforated appendicitis with peritonitis if adequate facilities and personnel are available. If not, large doses of IV antibiotics should be given instead.

(2) The appendix is removed. If the appendix has perforated, the abdomen is lavaged with saline or antibiotics. Drains are not useful unless there is a well-defined abscess.

(3) Appendiceal abscess is treated expectantly with IV antibiotics; the mass may subside, or the abscess may need drainage in a few days. Appendectomy is performed when the abscess is drained or electively after an interval of 6 weeks to 3 months.

c. Postoperative care

(1) *Simple appendicitis* Ambulation is begun on the first day. Nasogastric suction is unnecessary. Antibiotics are not required. IV fluids are discontinued when oral fluids are begun on the second or third day; diet is advanced rapidly. Strong cathartics and enemas are contraindicated. Patients leave the hospital in 3–5 days and are back to full activity in 3 weeks.

(2) *Perforated appendicitis* Treatment varies with the severity of the illness. Nasogastric suction, antibiotics for 5–7 days, and prolonged IV fluids are usually necessary. Critically ill patients require intensive care.

d. Complications
Wound infection occurs in 10% or more of patients with perforated appendicitis if the skin incision is closed primarily. Abdominal abscesses, particularly in the pelvis or subphrenic space, result from perforation with peritonitis. Small bowel obstruction from adhesions may occur. Hepatic abscesses are consequences of pylephlebitis.

5. Prognosis
The mortality rate is 0–0.3% in simple appendicitis and 2% or more in perforated cases. In infants and the elderly, perforation causes death in 10–15% of patients. Perforation (and death) result from delay by the patient or the surgeon. There is an inverse correlation between the rate of perforation and the rate of negative abdominal exploration. If appendicitis cannot be excluded, it is advisable to operate and accept a negative exploration rate of 20% (10% in men and 30% in women).

B. NEOPLASMS

1. **Adenocarcinoma** of the appendix is rare and seldom is diagnosed preoperatively. Right colectomy is required.

2. **Carcinoid** tumor is fairly common. If it does not involve the cecum or regional lymph nodes and is less than 2 cm in diameter, appendectomy is sufficient. Right colectomy is advisable for larger or metastatic tumors.

3. **Mucocele** of the appendix is a simple cyst in some cases, resulting from previous appendicitis. Other mucoceles are malignant, and if they perforate, pseudomyxoma peritonei may develop.

XIV. LIVER AND BILIARY TRACT

A. HEPATIC TRAUMA

1. Diagnosis Blunt or penetrating trauma to the liver causes intraabdominal bleeding. The symptoms and signs depend upon the amount of blood loss; severe injuries produce hypovolemic shock. Occasionally the liver is ruptured centrally with little or no bleeding into the abdomen; hepatic scan or arteriography is useful in these cases. Fractured ribs on the right should raise the suspicion of hepatic injury.

2. Treatment All patients with suspected hepatic trauma should have laparotomy.

a. Small lacerations or penetrating wounds may have stopped bleeding by the time operation is performed. These wounds require no treatment other than external drainage; Penrose drains or sump drains should be placed through a separate stab wound. The hepatic wounds should **not** be sutured.

b. Actively bleeding wounds are explored and the bleeding points ligated or coagulated. Large sutures to approximate the edges of the liver are ill-advised because of the risk of creating a closed space in which a bile collection, abscess, or hematoma can develop. Devitalized tissue should be debrided and external drainage provided.

c. The Pringle maneuver (occlusion of the hepatic artery and portal vein in the duodenohepatic ligament) is useful for temporary control in patients with massive hemorrhage. The Pringle maneuver plus cannulation of the inferior vena cava through the right atrial appendage are used to isolate the liver from its vascular supply temporarily to facilitate suture of lacerations of the hepatic veins.

d. Large stellate lacerations should be debrided and drained after bleeding is controlled.

e. Subcapsular hematomas should be opened and explored because they often mask extensive disruption of hepatic parenchyma.

3. Prognosis The overall mortality rate for hepatic injuries is 10% or more; most of the deaths follow blunt trauma. Postoperative complications include the following:

a. Recurrent bleeding requires reoperation.

b. Infection within the hepatic parenchyma and/or in the subphrenic or subhepatic spaces is common. External drainage is necessary.

c. Hematobilia is bleeding into the bile duct, the cause is inadequately treated hepatic parenchymal disruption. Patients have gastrointestinal hemorrhage, often with biliary colic, jaundice, and fever. Surgical treatment consists of ligating the artery that feeds the bleeding site, or, in some cases, lobectomy.

B. HEPATIC NEOPLASMS

1. Primary malignant tumors Primary malignant hepatic tumors are common in Africa and the Orient and uncommon in the USA and western Europe. Young children and older adults are affected. Cirrhosis predisposes to hepatic malignancy.

a. Types

(1) Hepatocellular carcinoma (hepatoma) comprises 80% of primary hepatic cancers. Metastases to extrahepatic lymph nodes, lung, and other sites occur early in the course. In children, this type of tumor is also known as hepatoblastoma.

(2) Cholangiocellular carcinoma (cholangiocarcinoma) spreads throughout the liver and metastasizes early.

(3) Mixed cell type (hepatocholangioma).

b. Diagnosis

(1) *Symptoms* Abdominal pain, anorexia, weight loss, fullness or distention, and jaundice (in some cases) is the most common group of symptoms. Massive intraabdominal hemorrhage from rupture of the tumor may be the

initial manifestation. Fever and severe pain due to necrosis of tumor may occur. Obstruction of the hepatic veins produces the Budd–Chiari syndrome.

(2) *Signs* Hepatomegaly; bruit or friction rub over the liver; ascites in 30%.

(3) *Laboratory tests* Elevated serum alkaline phosphatase and/or serum bilirubin in 60%. Alpha-fetoprotein is elevated in the serum of 50–80% of patients with hepatomas.

(4) *X-rays* Arteriography is essential to evaluate patients for surgical treatment. Most hepatomas are supplied by the hepatic artery and are demonstrated by this study. Ultrasound and CT examinations have an uncertain role in the diagnostic evaluation.

(5) *Special tests* Liver scan is abnormal in most cases. Percutaneous needle biopsy is diagnostic if it is positive, but benign tissue may simply reflect failure to sample the malignant focus. Peritoneoscopy with biopsy may prove the presence of tumor in both lobes and thus avoid a futile operation.

c. Differential diagnosis Primary hepatic malignancy must be differentiated from benign tumors, metastatic cancer, and hepatic abscesses and cysts.

d. Complications Intraabdominal hemorrhage, Budd–Chiari syndrome, acute portal hypertension, and necrosis of the tumor.

e. Treatment Chemotherapy delivered systemically or into the hepatic artery is the treatment in most cases because surgical resection is seldom possible. Favorable patients, with tumor localized to one lobe, can undergo lobectomy.

f. Prognosis Patients live an average of about 6 months after diagnosis. Long-term survivors after lobectomy are uncommon.

2. Metastatic malignant tumors Cancers of the GI tract, lung, breast, ovary, uterus and kidney commonly spread to the liver by hematogenous or lymphatic routes. More than 90% of patients with hepatic metastases have metastases elsewhere.

a. Diagnosis

(1) *Symptoms and signs* Most patients have symptoms and signs of the primary tumor. Weakness, anorexia, and weight loss. Right upper quadrant abdominal discomfort. Ascites and/or jaundice in advanced cases. A large, irregular liver is palpable in about 60% of patients. A friction rub may be audible over the liver.

(2) *Laboratory tests* Anemia is common. Elevated serum alkaline phosphatase and bilirubin.

(3) *Other tests* Liver scan reveals defects. Needle biopsy is diagnostic. Peritoneoscopy with biopsy is gaining popularity for patients with nondiagnostic percutaneous biopsies. Angiography is seldom necessary unless operation is planned.

b. Treatment Partial hepatectomy is performed in highly selected patients with apparently solitary metastases. This operation is most often done for metastatic cancer of the colon or rectum.

Chemotherapy is delivered systemically or directly into the hepatic artery. The latter approach is experimental.

c. Prognosis Life expectancy depends upon the type of metastatic tumor. Cancer of the large bowel permits longer survival than other primary malignancies. Most patients are dead by 2 years after hepatic metastases are diagnosed, and many die within a few months.

3. Benign tumors

a. Adenomas Hepatic adenomas occur mainly in young women, and oral contraceptives are believed to be important etiologic factors. About one-third of patients have multiple adenomas.

Hepatic adenomas are asymptomatic until they reach 10 cm in diameter or larger. Spontaneous rupture of these large tumors produces acute abdominal pain that mimics other acute upper abdominal diseases, or they can bleed massively into the peritoneal cavity. Asymptomatic lesions may be discovered during abdominal operations for other reasons.

Hepatic scan and angiography are useful diagnostic tests unless the patient is bleeding massively.

These tumors probably have no malignant potential, but the complications associated with continued enlargement make it advisable to resect even the asymptomatic ones if it can be accomplished with low morbidity and mortality. Acutely symptomatic adenomas require urgent or emergency resection.

The prognosis is excellent if the patient survives hepatic resection.

b. Hemangiomas Small hemangiomas are found beneath the liver capsule in many patients undergoing abdominal operation. These incidental lesions can be ignored; large lesions may rupture or cause symptoms and signs of an arteriovenous fistula and should be resected.

c. Cysts Congenital solitary hepatic cysts are usually asymptomatic, but in some instances they cause pain or are palpable. Symptomatic cysts should be drained into the peritoneal cavity or into the intestine (Roux-en-Y).

Congenital polycystic liver is associated with polycystic kidneys in one-half of patients. No treatment is required in most cases, although symptoms caused by progressive enlargement may be relieved by operation.

C. HEPATIC ABSCESS

1. Pyogenic (bacterial) abscess usually follows an acute abdominal infection (e.g., appendicitis, diverticulitis) in which the liver becomes infected via the portal vein. Abscesses may also develop by direct extension, by bacteremia from distant sites, or as a consequence of cholangitis. Rarely, a pyogenic abscess has no apparent underlying cause and is termed 'cryptogenic'.

a. Diagnosis
(1) *Symptoms and signs* Evidence of the underlying disease. Fever, toxicity, chills, jaundice, and right upper abdominal pain referred to the right shoulder. Instead of this acute onset, some patients develop malaise, anorexia, and persistent fever over a period of weeks. Large, tender liver.
(2) *Laboratory tests* Leukocytosis, anemia, elevated alkaline phosphatase, elevated bilirubin (in some cases). Blood cultures may identify the responsible organism(s).
(3) *X-rays* Chest films show elevation of the right diaphragm and pleural effusion in 30% of patients. Abdominal films may show a gas-fluid level in the liver. Ultrasound is very useful. CT scan may reveal the abscess cavity but is unnecessary if the ultrasound study is diagnostic. Angiography is seldom required.
(4) *Special tests* Hepatic scan may reveal small abscesses and is one of the first tests to obtain.

b. Differential diagnosis Hepatic tumor is distinguishable from abscess because it is solid. Patients with vague complaints have various other diagnoses considered before the hepatic abscess is recognized.

Amebic abscess is very difficult to exclude, although a positive blood culture is strong presumptive evidence of pyogenic abscess (see below).

c. Complications Persistent hepatic abscess may rupture, cause septic shock, bleed into the bile ducts, or progressively impair hepatic function.

d. Medical treatment If amebic abscess is a strong possibility, antiamebic therapy should be given. IV antibiotics in large doses are required for pyogenic abscess.

e. Surgical treatment Multiple tiny abscesses are not amenable to surgical drainage. Solitary or multiple large abscesses must be drained through an abdominal approach. The abscess cavity is aspirated, and a sump drain is placed into it and led to the exterior through a separate stab wound, preferably posteriorly.

f. Prognosis Solitary abscess has an excellent prognosis if diagnosed and treated promptly. Multiple abscesses are a grave complication and often prove fatal.

2. Amebic abscess appears in the absence of amebic dysentery in 50% of cases. The abscess is solitary and in the right lobe usually.

Fever, pain, and tenderness in the right upper quadrant are typical manifestations. Alkaline phosphatase is elevated; bilirubin is normal. Studies show a fluid-filled mass in the liver.

Treatment is medical. Metronidazole (Flagyl) 750 mg orally, 3 times a day for 10 days is preferred. Alternatively, dehydroemetine (1-1.5 mg/kg IM daily for 10 days) and chloroquine (500 mg orally daily for 10 weeks) plus diiodohydroxyquin (650 mg orally, 3 times a day for 20 days) is effective treatment. Percutaneous aspiration of amebic abscess prevents rupture and speeds healing. Surgical drainage is rarely necessary or advisable.

3. Echinococcus cyst (hydatid disease) Echinococcosis of the liver produces a cyst which is manifested by pain, hepatomegaly, and (if the cyst has ruptured into the bile ducts) fever, jaundice, and biliary colic. Most cysts are solitary and in the right lobe. They are demonstrated by hepatic scan.

Surgical excision is the treatment of choice. Care must be taken to avoid spilling the contents into the peritoneal cavity.

D. PORTAL HYPERTENSION is present when the portal venous pressure equals or exceeds 20 cm water (15 mm Hg). Collateral channels dilate between portal and systemic venous circulations; the most important of these routes is at the gastroesophageal junction, leading to formation of **esophageal varices** which may rupture and bleed into the GI tract. Ascites, hepatic encephalopathy, and hypersplenism are other consequences of portal hypertension.

Surgical treatment of portal hypertension is directed at decompressing the portal vein by anastomosis to a systemic vein **(portosystemic shunt).** If this effort is successful, the risk of subsequent variceal bleeding is small. However, portosystemic shunts may impair hepatic function and may precipitate encephalopathy, so selection of patients is essential.

1. Causes Increased portal blood flow (Banti's syndrome, certain types of splenomegaly) is rarely the cause of portal hypertension. Increased resistance to portal flow is much more often responsible; the site of high resistance may be at prehepatic, hepatic, or posthepatic levels.

a. Prehepatic (obstruction of the portal vein) Congenital atresia, thrombosis, or extrinsic compression.

b. Hepatic Cirrhosis (alcoholic, postnecrotic, biliary, hemochromatosis, etc.), congenital fibrosis, schistosomiasis, acute alcoholic hepatitis, or idiopathic.

c. Posthepatic Budd–Chiari syndrome or constrictive pericarditis.

2. Cirrhosis and variceal hemorrhage Cirrhosis is responsible for 85% of cases of portal hypertension in the USA, and alcoholism is the most common cause of cirrhosis. About 30% of patients with cirrhosis die of variceal hemorrhage or hepatic failure within a year after the diagnosis is established. The first episode of variceal bleeding is fatal to 50-80% of cirrhotic patients, and two-thirds of those who survive the first episode will bleed again with about the same risk of death from the recurrent episode as from the initial one.

Since about 40% of cirrhotic patients experience variceal hemorrhage eventually, a portosystemic shunt could be done to prevent this complication. However, **prophylactic portosystemic shunt** (a shunt performed in a patient who has never bled from varices) does not improve long-term survival. In studies of this operation, shunted patients died of hepatic failure, nonshunted cirrhotics died of bleeding or hepatic failure, and the overall survival rates were about the same. Prophylactic shunt is not recommended for this reason.

Therapeutic portosystemic shunt is performed in a patient who is bleeding from varices (emergency shunt) or has bled from varices (elective shunt). These indications for portal decompression are discussed below.

3. Acute variceal hemorrhage Assessment and initial treatment of massive upper GI hemorrhage is discussed in Section IV of this chapter.

a. Diagnosis History may disclose chronic alcoholism, acute alcoholic binge, known cirrhosis, previous episodes of bleeding, or ingestion of drugs (e.g., aspirin) that bear on the acute bleeding problem.

Physical examination may reveal stigmata of cirrhosis (spider angiomata, palmar erythema, testicular atrophy, gynecomastia, hepatomegaly) or portal hypertension (ascites, splenomegaly, venous collaterals radiating from the umbilicus). Jaundice is an important finding.

Liver function tests are usually deranged in acutely bleeding alcoholics regardless of the source of bleeding.

One cannot assume that patients with varices are bleeding from that source, so **endoscopy** is essential to identify the bleeding site. Upper GI series should be done if the bleeding site is not found endoscopically.

b. Treatment Specific measures for the treatment of variceal hemorrhage include vasopressin infusion, balloon tamponade, and emergency portosystemic shunt. In general, these three methods are used in sequence so that shunting is done only in patients who are uncontrolled by the first two measures. Some surgeons, however, operate almost immediately on all reasonable candidates without a trial of vasopressin or balloon tamponade. The correct choice between these policies has not been determined.

(1) *Vasopressin infusion* Vasopressin constricts mesenteric arterioles and lowers portal venous pressure by about 25%. The drug is given into a peripheral vein at the rate of 0.4-0.6 units/minute for 1 hour, and the treatment can be repeated every 3 hours if needed.

(2) *Balloon tamponade* A Sengstaken-Blakemore tube is a triple lumen tube with a gastric balloon, an esophageal balloon and a lumen for suction of gastric contents. Before placement, a nasogastric tube is tied to the Sengstaken-Blakemore tube with its tip just proximal to the esophageal balloon to permit suction of esophageal secretions. The Minnesota tube is a newer version; it contains 4 lumens with a tube for esophageal aspiration incorporated into it.

(a) *Placement* (1) Check the tube under water for leakage from the balloons. (2) Pass the tube through the **mouth** into the stomach; be certain the tube has entered the stomach by injecting air through the gastric balloon and listening for borborygmi in the epigastrium. (3) Inflate the gastric balloon with 250 ml of air (Sengstaken-Blakemore) or 450 ml of air (Minnesota). (4) Apply traction to the tube until resistance is felt, and fasten a mouth guard to maintain tension as shown in Fig. 10-2. Check position with an x-ray. (5) The esophageal balloon is inflated only if bleeding continues. Use a manometer to maintain 25-45 mm Hg pressure in the esophageal balloon; use the least amount of pressure necessary to control the hemorrhage.

(b) *Maintenance and complications* (1) The patient must be monitored closely in an intensive care unit. (2) Proximal displacement of the tube may cause sudden obstruction of the airway. The entire tube should be transected where it emerges from the mouth to rapidly deflate the balloons should this serious problem develop. (3) Aspiration of esophageal secretions causes pneumonia. The problem is avoided by adding the nasogastric tube as described or by using the Minnesota tube. (4) Rupture of the esophagus is a complication of excessive inflation of the esophageal balloon.

(c) *Results* Bleeding from varices is controlled, at least temporarily, in 85% of patients. Deflate the balloons 24 hours after bleeding stops and

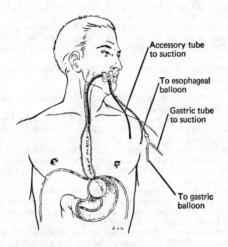

Fig. 10-2. Sengstaken–Blakemore tube with both gastric and esophageal balloons inflated. (Reproduced with permission from Dunphy JE, Way LW (Eds.) *Current Surgical Diagnosis & Treatment*, 3rd Ed. Lange 1977)

remove the tube after another 24 hours if bleeding does not recur. If it recurs, reinflate the balloons or consider an emergency shunt.

(3) *Emergency portosystemic shunt*   Ligation of varices is seldom useful because bleeding recurs in most cases. Emergency control of variceal bleeding, therefore, requires decompression of the hypertensive portal venous system.

In the presence of acute massive bleeding, the surgeon usually chooses one of the types of shunt that can be performed quickly (see below). Results vary widely, depending upon the patient population. Poor liver function, encephalopathy, ascites, malnutrition, and acute alcoholic liver disease indicate a poor prognosis. Overall operative survival rates are about 50%; good-risk patients do much better than the average.

4. Elective portosystemic shunt   Patients who survive an episode of documented variceal hemorrhage should be considered for an elective portosystemic shunt. Prime candidates are patients under the age of 60 with good liver function, although patients who lack these attributes are also shunted in some centers. Portosystemic shunt is followed by only marginally improved long-term survival, but recurrent bleeding, with its attendant demands on blood banks and other resources, is effectively prevented.

a. Preoperative evaluation and preparation   Alcoholic patients should abstain from alcohol and should consume a nutritious diet in preparation for elective operation. The goal is to allow the liver to recover from acute damage inflicted by alcohol, malnutrition, hypotension, and massive transfusion. Operative mortality correlates with preoperative liver function (Table 10-3).

Selective splenic and superior mesenteric arteriography is performed, and films are exposed until the portal venous anatomy is demonstrated. This information is essential in planning the operation. If the proposed shunt involves anastomosis to the left renal vein, a catheter is inserted percutaneously into the femoral vein and advanced into the vena cava; contrast is injected into the left renal vein to document its presence, size, and position.

Liver biopsy should be done to diagnose acute alcoholic hepatitis, schistosomiasis, hepatoma, and other lesions that influence the decision to perform a shunt or the type of shunt.

Preoperative measurement of portal pressure is recommended by some surgeons. Wedged hepatic vein pressure is the safest to obtain; alternatives are direct percutaneous splenic puncture and umbilical vein cannulation.

b. Choice of shunt   There are three types of portosystemic shunt in physiologic terms.

(1) *End-to-side portacaval shunt*   The portal vein is divided, the hepatic stump is oversewn, and the splanchnic end is anastomosed to the side of the vena cava. This has long been the standard operation against which all others are measured.

(2) *Side-to-side shunts*   There are many variations on this theme: side-to-side portacaval, mesocaval, central splenorenal, and renosplenic. All share the problem of permitting blood to flow away from the liver through the portal vein (hepatofugal flow) and via the anastomosis into the systemic circulation; this may impair liver function to a greater extent than the end-to-side shunt, but the subject is still debated.

One type of mesocaval shunt is constructed by anastomosing a dacron graft between the side of the vena cava and the side of the superior mesenteric vein. This 'H-mesocaval shunt' is preferred by some surgeons in emergency cases because it is quickly and easily performed.

Side-to-side shunts are preferred when ascites is present, because they reduce sinusoidal pressure.

Mesocaval shunts are necessary when the portal and splenic veins are too small to work with (e.g., in children).

Table 10-3. Relation of hepatic function and nutrition to operative mortality after portacaval shunt*

Group	A	B	C
Operative Mortality	**2%**	**10%**	**50%**
Serum bilirubin (mg/100 ml)	< 2.0	2.0–3.0	> 3.0
Serum albumin (g/100 ml)	> 3.5	3.0–3.5	< 3.0
Ascites	None	Easily controlled	Poorly controlled
Encephalopathy	None	Minimal	Advanced
Nutrition	Excellent	Good	Poor

*Reproduced with permission from Dunphy JE, Way LW (Eds.) *Current Surgical Diagnosis & Treatment*, 3rd Ed. Lange, 1977

(3) *Distal splenorenal (Warren) shunt*   The splenic vein is divided and the end nearest the portal vein is oversewn. The splenic end is anastomosed to the side of the left renal vein. This shunt has the advantage of maintaining perfusion of the liver because pressure in the superior mesenteric vein is not affected. It is more difficult to perform than most other kinds of shunts, but the avoidance of further liver damage and encephalopathy make it attractive.

c. Prognosis   The operative mortality rate in elective portosystemic shunts is 5–10%. Bleeding recurs in only about 5% of patients, usually because the shunt has thrombosed. Hepatic failure and encephalopathy are the most important complications.

5. Ascites is usually controllable by restriction of sodium and water intake and by the use of diuretics; spironolactone is the diuretic of choice. If a portosytemic shunt is to be undertaken because of variceal bleeding, one of the side-to-side types is selected. Ascites alone is rarely an indication for a portosystemic shunt.

The **peritoneal-jugular (LeVeen) shunt** is a relatively recent innovation for the treatment of ascites. One end of a plastic tube is inserted into the peritoneal cavity, and the other end is placed into the jugular vein. The entire tubing is placed subcutaneously, and the flow of ascites from peritoneal cavity to jugular vein is regulated by a valve. Peritoneal infection and recent variceal hemorrhage are contraindications. Early results are good; long-term evaluation is awaited.

6. Encephalopathy   Hepatic encephalopathy is a major complication of portosystemic shunts; encephalopathy also occurs in nonshunted patients, particularly during acute bleeding episodes. Factors which contribute to the appearance of encephalopathy include age, poor liver function, azotemia, the type of portosystemic shunt, the amount of protein in the diet (or in blood within the gut lumen), the intestinal flora, and many others.

Symptoms vary from mild lethargy or personality changes to psychosis or coma.

Encephalopathy precipitated by acute variceal hemorrhage is treated by laxatives (to remove blood from the gut) and antibiotics (e.g., neomycin) administered orally or through a gastric tube.

After portosystemic shunt, protein intake is limited to 40 gm/day initially to minimize the incidence of encephalopathy. Protein restriction is eased gradually if symptoms do not develop. Chronic encephalopathy is treated by laxatives and antibiotics in addition to protein restriction. Lactalose is a disaccharide which lowers pH in the colon and prevents absorption of ammonia. Give 20–30 gm orally 3–4 times daily. Rarely, surgical procedures to exclude the colon are performed in refractory cases of encephalopathy.

E. EVALUATION OF OBSTRUCTIVE JAUNDICE Jaundice may be due to prehepatic, hepatic, or posthepatic causes. Prehepatic jaundice is usually the result of hemolysis. Hepatic jaundice may arise from hepatocellular disease (e.g., viral hepatitis, alcoholic cirrhosis) or intrahepatic cholestasis (e.g., primary biliary cirrhosis, toxic effects of drugs). Posthepatic jaundice is caused by obstruction of the bile ducts; extrahepatic jaundice and obstructive jaundice are synonyms. In general, obstructive jaundice requires surgical treatment, and the prehepatic and hepatic varieties are managed medically. The goal of the evaluation, therefore, is to identify patients with biliary obstruction.

Specific disease entities are described individually later in this section. Some general guidelines are discussed here.

1. History

a. Age and sex Older people are more likely to have obstructive jaundice. Primary biliary cirrhosis is almost exclusively limited to women.

b. Drugs Alcohol, phenothiazines, and sex hormones are among the drugs which may cause jaundice. Viral hepatitis is common among people who inject illicit drugs.

c. Pain beginning in the epigastrium or right upper quadrant and radiating to the right scapula is typical of acute biliary obstruction (biliary colic). Chronic, dull, aching upper abdominal pain suggests malignancy. Diffuse pain in the right upper quadrant may result from distention of the hepatic capsule by hepatitis, acute alcoholic injury, or passive congestion from cardiac disease.

d. Fever High fever, especially when accompanied by shaking chills (rigors), is characteristic of cholangitis from biliary obstruction.

e. Light stools and dark urine are more common in patients with extrahepatic obstruction.

f. Pruritus Severe itching of the extremities may precede jaundice or coincide with it. Pruritus is due to deposition of bile salts in the skin and is a symptom of cholestasis from any cause.

2. Physical examination Hepatomegaly is not a distinguishing feature. Stigmata of cirrhosis (spider angiomata, etc.) may be found. Splenomegaly suggests the presence of portal hypertension. A nontender palpable gallbladder indicates that the cause of jaundice is malignant obstruction of the common duct (Courvoisier's law). It is erroneous to conclude, however, that obstruction has a benign cause if the gallbladder is not palpable.

3. Liver function tests Standard liver function tests usually permit separation of patients into two groups: those with prehepatic or hepatocellular jaundice, and those with cholestatic jaundice. Since cholestasis may be hepatic (medical) or posthepatic (surgical), these tests merely identify patients who need further evaluation for biliary obstruction.

Cholestatic jaundice is typically associated with an elevated direct (conjugated) fraction of bilirubin, normal or mildly elevated SGPT and SGOT, elevated alkaline phosphatase, elevated leucine aminopeptidase, normal albumin, and prolonged prothrombin time. Many variations occur, and there is substantial overlap of cholestatic and hepatocellular jaundice.

Hepatitis-associated antigen and antimitochondrial antibodies (elevated in primary biliary cirrhosis) may be helpful.

4. Plain abdominal x-rays About 10–15% of gallstones are radiopaque and thus are visible on plain abdominal films. An enlarged gallbladder may be seen as a soft tissue mass.

5. Ultrasound is a safe, simple, inexpensive, and fairly reliable method of demonstrating the bile ducts in obstructive jaundice. Dilated ducts and gallstones may be evident. If ducts are dilated, biliary obstruction is present. If ducts are not dilated, obstruction is not ruled out.

6. Liver biopsy   Percutaneous needle biopsy of the liver is generally reserved for patients with nondilated ducts in whom a medical cause of jaundice is likely. It should not be performed in the presence of coagulation defects, thrombocytopenia, or ascites. The histologic findings may confirm a diagnosis of viral hepatitis or tumor.

7. Percutaneous transhepatic cholangiography   This is an especially good way to demonstrate the upper level of obstruction if the ducts are dilated, although even ducts of normal caliber can be entered with the new 'skinny' needle. Coagulation defects, ascites, and cholangitis are contraindications.

8. Endoscopic retrograde cholangiopancreatography (ERCP)   Cannulation of the common bile duct and/or the pancreatic duct through the ampulla of Vater can be accomplished endoscopically. The lower end of obstructing lesions is demonstrated. In some cases, additional valuable information is obtained (e.g., ampullary tumor, stone eroding through the ampulla, carcinoma invading the duodenum, etc.) This technic is more difficult and more expensive than transhepatic cholangiography. Cholangitis and pancreatitis are complications. It is very useful in patients with nondilated ducts or contraindication to transhepatic cholangiography. The potential for treating the cause of obstruction at the same time (e.g., sphincterotomy for retained common duct stones) makes ERCP even more attractive.

9. Other studies

a. Intravenous cholangiography (IVC) does not opacify the bile ducts if the serum bilirubin is greater than 4 mg/100 ml because the contrast medium is not excreted into the bile in sufficient concentration. IVC may be successful if the bilirubin is less than 4, especially if it is dropping rapidly, but IVC has largely been replaced by more direct methods. Oral cholecystography (OCG) has no value in the jaundiced patient.

b. Upper GI series   The standard barium study of the stomach and duodenum may yield indirect evidence of biliary obstruction (e.g., widening of the duodenal loop suggestive of pancreatic neoplasm).

c. Transjugular cholangiography   A catheter is passed into the jugular vein and into the liver via the hepatic veins. A bile duct may be punctured and contrast instilled. The risk of bacteremia is great if the bile is infected. The method is seldom used.

d. CT scan   Computerized tomography may demonstrate dilated bile ducts, hepatic masses, and retroperitoneal (e.g., pancreatic) masses. It is more expensive than ultrasound and may not offer much more information; its role is under investigation.

e. Hepatic scan   Radionuclide scan of the liver may show hepatic masses. It is useful as a guide to the site of percutaneous biopsy in patients with suspected tumor.

f. Peritoneoscopy   The role of this modality is being explored. It probably has value in cases of suspected neoplastic involvement of the liver.

g. Angiography is important in hematobilia and in some cases of neoplasm.

10. Selection of studies   A large number of diagnostic methods are available for the evaluation of obstructive jaundice, and redundant studies should be avoided. The most important question to be answered is: **are the bile ducts obstructed?** In some cases, e.g., the patient with suppurative cholangitis, an ultrasound study which gives a positive answer to this question is sufficient, and one should proceed directly to surgical exploration.

The **level of obstruction** and the **cause of obstruction** are secondary issues which usually can be resolved by an experienced surgeon at the operating table.

Nevertheless, delineation of the ductal anatomy by transhepatic cholangiography or ERCP can help the surgeon plan the operation, and for that reason one or the other of these cholangiographic procedures is usually performed preoperatively. The other studies listed above are useful occasionally.

F. CHOLELITHIASIS is the presence of gallstones in the gallbladder. Gallstones are composed predominantly of cholesterol in 75% of patients in the USA. The incidence of stones increases with age and is associated with race (highest in American indians, lowest in blacks), sex (more common in women until menopause, thereafter about equal in men and women), multiparity, obesity, oral contraceptives, and certain intestinal diseases (e.g., inflammatory bowel disease).

The remaining 25% of gallstones are composed of calcium bilirubinate and bile acids (pigment stones). Hemolytic diseases, biliary stasis, and cirrhosis are the usual predisposing conditions.

a. Diagnosis About 50% of pigment stones are radiopaque and can be seen on plain films; most cholesterol stones are radiolucent, and they are diagnosed by **oral cholecystography**. The contrast medium (Tryopanoate or iopanoic acid) is ingested, absorbed, extracted by hepatocytes, secreted in bile, and concentrated in the gallbladder where it is evident on x-rays taken about 15 hours after ingestion. Gallstones appear as radiolucent defects in the opaque gallbladder. Failure to opacify the gallbladder indicates that one of these steps from ingestion to concentration in the gallbladder did not occur. If a second dose is given and the study repeated the next day, persistent nonopacification is a reliable indication of gallbladder disease, provided that failures of ingestion, absorption and extraction can be excluded.

b. Complications Gallstones cause problems eventually in 30-50% of patients. Chronic cholecystitis, acute cholecystitis, obstruction of the common bile duct, cholangitis, gallstone ileus, carcinoma of the gallbladder, and pancreatitis are among the complications of cholelithiasis.

c. Medical treatment Dissolution of cholesterol gallstones by the oral administration of chenodeoxycholic acid is undergoing clinical trial. Thus far, chenodeoxycholic acid appears to eradicate stones in about one-third of patients, but the side-effects and the long-term consequences (e.g., formation of new stones when the treatment is stopped) need careful study before the method can be applied widely.

d. Surgical treatment Prophylactic cholecystectomy for asymptomatic cholelithiasis is recommended in diabetics, in any patient whose gallbladder does not opacify, in patients with large gallstones or multiple tiny gallstones, and in patients with a calcified gallbladder. The wisdom of prophylactic cholecystectomy in the absence of these factors is debated. In general, elderly and poor-risk patients should not have prophylactic cholecystectomy, but it should be considered in young patients.

G. CHRONIC CHOLECYSTITIS is the most common manifestation of gallstones. The term is imprecise and is often applied to symptomatic gallbladders containing stones, whether or not there is inflammation or scarring.

1. Diagnosis

a. Symptoms Pain (biliary colic) is the characteristic symptom and is due to transient obstruction of the cystic duct by stones. Although it is termed biliary 'colic', the pain is steady. Often it begins abruptly after a meal, is centered in the epigastrium or right upper quadrant, and radiates to the right scapula. Other pain patterns occur. The pain intensifies and then subsides over a few minutes to a few hours. Attacks may be frequent or separated by long asymptomatic intervals.

Nausea and vomiting in some patients.

'Fatty food intolerance' bears no specific relationship to gallstones. Flatulence, eructation, dyspepsia, etc. occur just as often in patients with other upper gastrointestinal diseases or even with no demonstrable organic disease.

b. Signs There are usually no abdominal findings. Tenderness in the right upper quadrant is present occasionally.

c. X-rays Oral cholecystogram shows gallstones, or it fails to opacify the gallbladder. If two oral cholecystograms do not opacify the gallbladder, the diagnosis of gallbladder disease is likely. Ultrasound may be obtained to demonstrate the stones if doubt remains.

2. Differential diagnosis Chronic cholecystitis should be differentiated from other upper gastrointestinal diseases. An upper GI series is recommended. Radicular pain, angina pectoris, pancreatitis, irritable colon, and carcinoma of the cecum can mimic biliary colic.

3. Complications Acute cholecystitis, choledocholithiasis, and carcinoma of the gallbladder.

4. Treatment Cholecystectomy with operative cholangiography is the treatment of choice. The common bile duct should be explored if there is a history of cholangitis, a palpable stone in the duct, a stone shown by cholangiography preoperatively or intraoperatively, or jaundice with a bilirubin greater than 7 mg/100 ml.

5. Prognosis The operative mortality rate for elective cholecystectomy is much less than 1%. Failure to relieve symptoms usually means that the symptoms were due to some condition other than gallstones. Postoperative jaundice may be due to retained common duct stone or operative injury to the bile ducts.

H. ACUTE CHOLECYSTITIS Cholelithiasis is responsible for 98% of cases of acute cholecystitis. A stone impacts in the cystic duct, inflammation develops, and bacterial infection supervenes in some instances. Acalculous cholecystitis (2% of cases) is due to obstruction of the cystic duct by another mechanism (e.g., tumor), occlusion of the cystic artery, or it occurs in association with prolonged fasting (e.g., in patients receiving total parenteral nutrition).

1. Diagnosis

a. Symptoms Past history of biliary colic in 75% of cases. Pain is typical of biliary colic initially, but it persists. Nausea and vomiting in about 50% of patients. Fever up to 38.5°C; rigors indicate a complication or some other diagnosis.

b. Signs Tenderness and spasm in the right upper quadrant. Murphy's sign: arrest of a deep inspiratory effort as the examiner palpates the right upper quadrant. An enlarged, tender gallbladder is palpable (and sometimes visible) in about 35%. Mild jaundice is noted in 10%.

c. Laboratory tests Leukocytosis in the range of 12-15,000/μl. Mild elevation of bilirubin (rarely over 4 mg/100 ml with acute cholecystitis alone). Serum amylase may be elevated.

d. X-rays Plain abdominal films may show radiopaque gallstones or a mass. Oral cholecystogram does not opacify the gallbladder. IVC classically opacifies the common duct but not the gallbladder; this is diagnostic of cystic duct obstruction. Ultrasound demonstrates gallstones; the gallbladder may be dilated or not, depending upon the amount of fibrosis in its wall.

2. Differential diagnosis Other acute gastrointestinal diseases: perforated peptic ulcer, acute appendicitis, acute pancreatitis.

Acute distention of the liver by viral hepatitis, passive congestion, or alcoholic hepatitis.

Gonococcal perihepatitis (Curtis and Fitz-Hugh syndrome) is associated with high fever and pelvic findings of salpingitis. Gonococci are seen in the cervical smear.

Acute pneumonitis or myocardial infarction.

3. Complications

a. Empyema The gallbladder is filled with pus. The patient is toxic, with a high fever and sometimes rigors. The leukocyte count is high.

b. Perforation The gallbladder becomes focally or diffusely gangrenous and perforates in about 10% of cases. The interval from onset to perforation is seldom less than 72 hours.

(1) *Localized perforation* Perforation is contained by surrounding omentum, duodenum, and colon, and a *pericholecystic abscess* is formed. High fever, toxicity, and leukocytosis are usually present, but the development of this complication is sometimes insidious.

(2) *Free perforation* Perforation into the general peritoneal cavity. It occurs in about 1% of patients. Spreading or generalized peritonitis and deterioration of the patient's overall condition suggest the diagnosis.

(3) *Cholecystoenteric fistula* The gallbladder perforates and fistulizes into adjacent duodenum, colon, or stomach. The obstructed gallbladder is thus decompressed, and the cholecystitis may subside. Few symptoms are attributable to chronic cholecystoenteric fistulas; the main clinical problem occurs when a gallstone passes through the fistula and obstructs the intestine (gallstone ileus).

Gallstone ileus The symptoms are those of mechanical obstruction of the small intestine (rarely the colon). More than half of patients have no history suggesting recent acute cholecystitis. The diagnosis is made by plain abdominal x-rays; a radiopaque stone may be seen in the mid or lower abdomen, and gas is seen in the biliary tree in about 50% of cases. Treatment is simply to open the intestine and extract the stone; cholecystectomy is not performed at the same operation but may be required subsequently. The mortality rate is high because the patients are elderly and in poor condition.

4. Treatment

a. IV fluids, nasogastric tube, and analgesics are given routinely. Antibiotics are indicated if complications develop, otherwise they are unnecessary since the inflammation is not bacterial.

b. If the diagnosis is securely established, operation should be performed at an early convenient time. It need not be done at awkard hours unless complications occur, but it should be performed during the same hospitalization. Although acute cholecystitis usually resolves without operation, permitting cholecystectomy to be done electively later, this policy prolongs the total illness without much benefit. There is room for flexibility, however, and the patient's vocational, social and other commitments must be considered.

c. If the diagnosis is unclear or the patient is in poor general condition, expectant management can be used until a diagnosis is reached or the associated problems are corrected.

d. A true emergency exists, and operation must be done immediately, in patients with empyema or perforation. *Emphysematous cholecystitis* (anaerobic infection producing gas bubbles in the wall and lumen of the gallbladder) is a virulent form of cholecystitis, and it also should be treated by urgent operation.

e. Choice of operation

(1) *Cholecystectomy* is definitive treatment and should be performed in patients who are in good condition. Operative cholangiography is recommended. These operations may be difficult and should be undertaken only by experienced surgeons.

(2) *Cholecystostomy* is selected in elderly or poor risk patients. It may be done under local anesthesia. The gallbladder is approached through a small subcostal incision, opened, the stones extracted if possible, and a large tube sutured into the gallbladder. Cholecystectomy is necessary later if tube cholecystography demonstrates obstruction of the cystic duct or stones in the gallbladder or common duct. In other patients, the tube can be removed and cholecystectomy performed if symptoms recur.

5. Prognosis is excellent in young patients who have uncomplicated acute cholecystitis. Advanced age, associated diseases (especially diabetes), perforation, and other complications of gallstone disease (e.g., choledocholithiasis and pancreatitis) are responsible for the overall mortality rate of 5%.

I. CHOLEDOCHOLITHIASIS AND CHOLANGITIS   In about 15% of patients with cholelithiasis, gallstones pass from the gallbladder, through the cystic duct, and into the common bile duct. Stones also may form in the common bile duct itself; with rare exceptions, this is a consequence of stasis in the common duct.

Stones may pass through the ampulla of Vater into the duodenum, or they may lodge in the ampulla causing obstruction. About 50% of patients with choledocholithiasis have no symptoms related to the common duct. In the other 50%, choledocholithiasis causes biliary colic, cholangitis, obstructive jaundice, pancreatitis, or a combination of these problems.

1. Syndromes

a. Biliary colic   Episodes of biliary colic due to intermittent obstruction of the common duct by gallstones are similar to the attacks seen in patients with chronic cholecystitis. If the stone passes through the ampulla, or if it slips upward into the duct, thus relieving obstruction, pain subsides. If obstruction persists, the pain of biliary distention persists.

b. Cholangitis is infection of the biliary tree. There are three requirements: bacteria, obstruction, and increased pressure. Cholangitis is most commonly caused by choledocholithiasis, although other types of ductal obstruction may also be responsible. Septicemia is the result of cholangiovenous reflux of bacteria from the obstructed bile duct into the hepatic venous circulation.

Fever and chills, jaundice, and biliary colic are the classical symptoms of cholangitis (Charcot's triad), although the symptom complex is incomplete in many patients. If cholangitis is very severe (**acute suppurative cholangitis**), hypotension and mental confusion may occur. Leukocytosis is present.

c. Obstructive jaundice   Jaundice is the prominent abnormality in some patients with choledocholithiasis. A history of biliary colic or cholangitis is strong evidence for this diagnosis, but the absence of such history does not exclude the possibility of obstruction by gallstones. Fluctuating jaundice, due to intermittent obstruction, is common with choledocholithiasis. The gallbladder usually is not dilated because its wall is thickened by chronic inflammation, in contrast to neoplastic obstruction of the common duct (Courvoisier's law).

d. Pancreatitis is discussed under Pancreas in this chapter.

2. Treatment   Patients with choledocholithiasis should have evaluation of liver function; depressed prothrombin time is treated with parenteral vitamin K preoperatively.

a. Asymptomatic choledocholithiasis is detected by palpation of a stone or cholangiographic demonstration of a stone in the common duct during cholecystectomy. Treatment is cholecystectomy and choledocholithotomy.

Routine use of a **choledochoscope** is recommended, and a T-tube cholangiogram is mandatory before the operation is terminated. Postoperatively, the T-tube is connected to gravity drainage and another T-tube cholangiogram is performed 7-10 days later. If the duct is normal, the tube is removed.

b. Retained stones demonstrated on the postoperative study may be extracted by passing a ureteral stone basket through the T-tube tract under fluoroscopic control about 6 weeks after operation. Endoscopic sphincterotomy (division of the sphincter of Oddi) is a new technic that is especially useful if the basket method fails or if the ampulla is stenotic. Dissolution of retained stones by perfusion of the duct (through the T-tube) with sodium cholate or other solutions is still another possibility. Few patients require reoperation for retained common duct stones.

c. Biliary colic due to common duct obstruction by gallstones is treated by cholecystectomy and choledocholithotomy.

d. Acute cholangitis usually responds to IV antibiotics, which should be directed against gram-negative aerobic and anaerobic bacteria. Blood cultures reflect the bacteria present in the obstructed bile duct, but pending the results of cultures, ampicillin, cephalosporin, and gentamicin are useful agents. Operation is then performed electively.

e. Acute suppurative cholangitis is an indication for emergency operation to decompress the obstructed duct. This diagnosis may be obvious from the patient's toxic condition at the outset, or it may be suspected from failure to respond to antibiotic therapy.

f. Obstructive jaundice due to gallstones is evaluated as described earlier, and treated by cholecystectomy and choledocholithotomy.

g. Pancreatitis associated with gallstones is cured by operation (see Pancreatitis in this chapter).

3. Prognosis   Choledocholithiasis is a life-threatening complication of gallstones. Mortality rates depend upon the syndrome, age, general condition, etc. The overall operative mortality rate for choledocholithotomy is about 4%.

J. CARCINOMA OF THE GALLBLADDER   Adenocarcinoma of the gallbladder is associated with gallstones in most cases. It occurs in elderly patients and causes persistent biliary colic, acute cholecystitis, or obstruction of the common duct. The gallbladder may be palpable.

Cure is seldom possible because the cancer has metastasized or extended by the time of operation. Palliation is offered by cholecystectomy or by relief of common duct obstruction. Occasionally, a small cancer is found incidentally in a gallbladder removed for symptomatic chronic cholecystitis, and long-term survival is possible in such cases.

K. MALIGNANT TUMORS OF THE BILE DUCT are rare. They cause obstructive jaundice, usually without cholangitis. The gallbladder is palpable if obstruction is distal to the cystic duct. The diagnosis is suggested by preoperative transhepatic cholangiography or ERCP and confirmed at operation.

Tumors at the confluence of the hepatic ducts are often overlooked at operation; with findings of a collapsed gallbladder and common duct, the surgeon may conclude that the diagnosis of extrahepatic obstruction was erroneous. Exploration of the duct, including choledochoscopy and operative cholangiography, should lead to discovery of the lesion. Tumors more distally are less often a diagnostic problem. Sclerosing tumors may contain few malignant cells, and biopsies occasionally are falsely negative.

Excision of the tumor (Whipple procedure for distal lesions) is the optimal treatment, but it seldom is curative because of early metastasis or extension. Palliation is provided by placement of a T-tube or U-tube through the obstructing point, or by diverting the bile (e.g., cholecystojejunostomy, choledochoduodenostomy, choledochojejunostomy Roux-en-Y). Radiation therapy may be beneficial.

Average survival after diagnosis is 1 year, but occasional patients survive for much longer periods.

L. STRICTURE OF THE BILE DUCT is iatrogenic in 95% of cases. Strictures caused by gallstones or nonsurgical trauma comprise the remainder. The bile ducts are especially liable to injury when cholecystectomy is performed by an incompletely trained surgeon who does not appreciate the variability of ductal and vascular anatomy.

Injuries take the form of division, ligation, or excision of part or all of a segment of the duct. Postoperative fever, jaundice, and prolonged drainage of bile are indications of injury to the duct. If definitive repair is not performed at the moment of injury, stricture formation is nearly inevitable.

Cholangitis weeks to months after cholecystectomy is the typical manifestation. Sometimes the transhepatic or endoscopic cholangiogram suggests that the injured area has a rather large lumen which should not be responsible for obstruction. Cholangitis, however, **always** implies obstruction, and at operation such patients invariably have a tight narrowing of the duct despite the cholangiographic appearance.

Untreated stricture leads to secondary biliary cirrhosis and portal hypertension. Repeated cholangitis may result in hepatic abscesses and death from sepsis.

Treatment is by surgical repair. These procedures are technically difficult and should be attempted only by experienced surgeons. A variety of technics is available, and the surgeon must select the one most suitable for the conditions encountered. One common method is anastomosis of the end of the divided duct above the stricture to the side of a Roux-en-Y jejunal loop.

Operation is successful in 75% of patients. The morbidity and mortality rates are high in patients with long-standing strictures.

M. OTHER DISEASES OF THE BILE DUCTS

1. Sclerosing cholangitis Inflammation and fibrosis of the bile ducts occurs as a primary phenomenon in rare instances; there is a strong association with ulcerative colitis. Most patients have diffuse involvement of the major ducts within and outside the liver, although occasionally the process is localized, at least initially. The wall is thickened and the lumen is narrowed greatly.

Cholestatic jaundice is the clinical presentation. Transhepatic cholangiography may be unsuccessful because the ducts have a small caliber. ERCP shows multiple constrictions and areas of mild dilatation.

Operation is performed in most cases. Primary sclerosing cholangitis should be distinguished from malignant biliary tumor by biopsy. The lumen should be dilated by passing graded probes. A T-tube is inserted and often left in place for months. Corticosteroids may be helpful.

Relief of jaundice and pruritus is the objective of these palliative procedures. The disease is chronic, and biliary cirrhosis usually develops over the long term.

2. Congenital anomalies

a. Choledochal cyst is a congenital developmental abnormality which may not cause symptoms of jaundice and cholangitis until adulthood. Excision or decompression of the cyst is the treatment of choice.

b. Caroli's disease is congenital dilatation of the intrahepatic ducts. Jaundice or portal hypertension may be the first manifestation. Surgical treatment is difficult; antibiotics are used to control cholangitis.

3. Oriental cholangiohepatitis Parasitic infestation of the biliary tree may become secondarily infected by bacteria. Multiple sequential strictures of the intrahepatic ducts, hepatic abscesses, and obstruction by sludge and stones are the consequences. Patients have pain, fever, jaundice, and right upper quadrant tenderness. Treatment is by cholecystectomy, extraction of stones, and diversion of bile by choledochoduodenostomy. Results are poor because the intrahepatic ducts are strictured and filled with stones that cannot be removed. Death is from persistent sepsis.

XV. PANCREAS

A. TRAUMA Damage to the pancreas from blunt or penetrating trauma varies in severity from mild contusion to extensive disruption of the parenchyma and necrosis of the duodenum. Clinical findings may be mild and delayed; abdominal or back pain, abdominal tenderness, and elevated serum amylase are clues to the presence of pancreatic injury.

Surgical management of one common type of blunt injury, fracture of the body of the gland where it crosses the spine, consists of distal pancreatectomy and splenectomy. Minor contusions are treated by external drainage. Extensive disruption of the pancreatic head, with preservation of blood supply to the duodenum, is sometimes treated by subtotal pancreatectomy; antrectomy, gastrojejunostomy, tube duodenostomy, and external drainage is an alternative combination of maneuvers. If the duodenum is ischemic, a Whipple procedure may be necessary.

External pancreatic fistula, infection, and traumatic pancreatitis are sources of morbidity and mortality in these difficult cases.

B. ACUTE PANCREATITIS is inflammation caused by escape of active pancreatic enzymes into the interstitial tissues of the gland. Acute **edematous pancreatitis** is characterized by marked edema of the gland and surrounding structures. **Hemorrhagic pancreatitis** is a more severe manifestation of the same process in which there is necrosis of pancreatic tissue and bleeding into the pancreas and the retroperitoneal space.

1. Causes

a. Alcohol is responsible for about 40% of cases in the USA, and in certain hospitals, the majority of cases are due to alcohol. An interval of 6 years or more from the beginning of excessive drinking to the first attack of pancreatitis is typical. Microscopic changes of chronic pancreatitis already have developed by the time of the initial attack of acute pancreatitis.

b. Gallstones are the cause of acute pancreatitis in about 40% of cases. The attack is precipitated by passage of a stone through the ampulla.

c. Hyperlipidemia, either primary or secondary to alcoholism, is a cause of pancreatitis. Lactescent serum is diagnostic.

d. Hyperparathyroidism and other causes of hypercalcemia may lead to pancreatitis.

e. Postoperative pancreatitis may result from direct trauma to the gland, but some cases develop after remote (e.g., pelvic) surgery.

f. External trauma causes acute pancreatitis, especially if there is disruption of the pancreatic duct.

g. Familial pancreatitis is a rare cause of pancreatitis beginning in childhood.

h. Miscellaneous Corticosteroids, protein deficiency, and others. 10–15% of cases are idiopathic.

2. Diagnosis

a. Symptoms Postprandial, severe, unrelenting epigastric pain radiating through to the back. Nausea, vomiting, and persistent retching. Hematemesis of a mild degree is present occasionally.

b. Signs Shock in severe cases. Mild fever. Epigastric tenderness; sometimes generalized abdominal tenderness. Epigastric mass (edematous pancreas in the early stages). Ecchymosis in the flank (Grey-Turner's sign) or umbilicus (Cullen's sign) in hemorrhagic pancreatitis. Pleural effusion.

c. Laboratory tests

(1) Leukocytosis.

(2) Hematocrit may be high as a result of dehydration or low because of bleeding.

(3) Bilirubin and alkaline phosphatase may be mildly elevated.

(4) Serum calcium is low in severe cases.

(5) Serum may be lactescent to gross inspection.

(6) *Serum amylase* is greater than 200 IU/100 ml in most cases. The rise is detected 6 hours after onset, and levels return to normal in about 48 hours. Lactescent serum interferes with amylase determination, and values may

be normal in these patients. Amylase may be elevated in many other acute abdominal conditions.

(7) *Serum lipase* is elevated, but the test is seldom obtained because it is difficult to perform.

(8) *Urine amylase* is a more accurate test than the serum amylase. Timed collection of urine permits determination of urinary excretion of amylase; greater than 5000 IU/24 hours is abnormal. The ratio of amylase clearance to creatinine clearance is calculated by this equation:

$$\frac{\text{Urine amylase concentration}}{\text{Serum amylase concentration}} \times \frac{\text{Serum creatinine concentration}}{\text{Urine creatinine concentration}} \times 100\%$$

Spot samples of serum and urine are sufficient because the values are expressed as concentrations and the volumes cancel one another.

Pancreatitis is the likely cause of hyperamylasemia if this ratio is 5–10% or greater. Other causes of hyperamylasemia are associated with values of 5% or less.

d. X-rays Plain abdominal films may show a dilated loop of small or large bowel (sentinel loop); distention of the right colon with no gas beyond that point (colon cutoff sign); radiopaque gallstones; pancreatic calcification in some patients with disease of long standing. Chest film may show a pleural effusion, especially on the left. Upper GI series often demonstrates pancreatic enlargement.

e. Special tests Paracentesis, ultrasound, and other studies seldom contribute to the diagnosis of the acute attack.

3. Differential diagnosis Acute pancreatitis must be distinguished from perforated ulcer, mesenteric vascular occlusion, strangulated small bowel obstruction, and acute cholecystitis. Some of these conditions are fatal if operation is not performed, and if there is any doubt about the diagnosis of pancreatitis, laparotomy must be done.

Macroamylasemia is excluded by the amylase : creatinine clearance ratio.

4. Complications Pseudocyst and abscess are discussed below. Gastrointestinal bleeding may result from gastritis, peptic ulcer, or Mallory-Weiss tear. Respiratory complications are frequent in severe attacks.

5. Medical treatment

a. Establish and maintain an airway. Endotracheal intubation and ventilatory support may be required.

b. Replace fluid and electrolyte losses, with alertness to the appearance of hypocalcemia. This indicates a poor prognosis and must be treated aggressively.

c. Insert a nasogastric tube to relieve the pancreas of further stimulation by gastric acid entering the duodenum.

d. Analgesics Pentazocine is preferred because morphine and meperidine cause contraction of the sphincter of Oddi.

e. Anticholinergics have no proved value.

f. Antibiotics should not be given prophylactically.

g. Peritoneal lavage removes active enzymes and necrotic debris and may avoid some of the systemic toxicity from absorption of these substances. If lavage is planned, it should be instituted promptly. Instill 1 liter of lactated Ringer's rapidly through a peritoneal dialysis catheter, and allow the fluid to return by gravity. Repeat every hour. Response should be noted within 8 hours if this treatment is to be effective.

h. Other measures IV glucagon and IV trasylol (an inhibitor of proteolytic enzymes) have been advocated. Glucagon probably has no benefit; the value of trasylol is not established.

6. Surgical treatment

a. Most operations in this condition are performed to exclude some other acute abdominal disease. If acute edematous pancreatitis is found, external drainage of the pancreatic surface may be beneficial; if the bile duct appears obstructed, a T-tube should be inserted.

b. Operation for treatment of gallstone pancreatitis by cholecystectomy and common duct exploration is deferred until the acute attack resolves, if possible; on the other hand, long delays should be avoided because pancreatitis may recur in the interval.

c. Patients with hemorrhagic pancreatitis which is not responding to medical treatment should undergo abdominal exploration to debride necrotic pancreas and provide external drainage.

Patients should be investigated for the cause of pancreatitis after the initial attack resolves.

7. Prognosis The mortality rate of acute pancreatitis is about 10% overall and 50% in cases of hemorrhagic pancreatitis. Some patients develop chronic pancreatitis, and others have repeated attacks of acute pancreatitis without chronic changes (acute relapsing pancreatitis). Surgical treatment is curative of biliary pancreatitis.

C. PANCREATIC PSEUDOCYST About 2% of patients with acute pancreatitis develop a collection of enzyme-rich fluid in or near the pancreas. The pseudocyst is bounded by a capsule of inflamed peritoneum and adjacent structures (e.g., stomach, mesocolon, colon, liver, and diaphragm). Pseudocysts may also form, without antecedent acute pancreatitis, as a result of ductal obstruction (e.g., in alcoholics) or trauma. Pseudocysts are usually single; multiple cysts occur in 15% of cases.

1. Diagnosis

a. Symptoms and signs Persistent or recurrent pain and fever after an attack of acute pancreatitis; appearance of epigastric pain with no history of pancreatitis in some cases. A tender epigastric mass represents swollen pancreas in the early stages of pancreatitis, but a persistent mass is likely to be a pseudocyst. Weight loss and vomiting, especially if the mass compresses the gut. Jaundice in some cases.

b. Laboratory tests The serum amylase is elevated in 50% of patients. Leukocytosis and increased serum bilirubin are other findings.

c. X-rays Upper GI series shows a pancreatic mass that may displace the stomach forward or widen the duodenal loop. The findings are the same whether the mass is edematous pancreas, pseudocyst, or abscess.

d. Special tests Ultrasound distinguishes between solid and cystic masses; CT scan has the same capability. ERCP may demonstrate communication between the duct and a cyst, but the risks of precipitating acute pancreatitis and introducing infection into the cyst limit the usefulness of this test.

2. Differential diagnosis Edematous pancreas (pancreatic phlegmon) is not a fluid-filled mass. Abscess must be distinguished from pseudocyst (see below). Cystic neoplasm should be suspected in patients with no antecedent history of pancreatitis; arteriography may be diagnostic, but often the presence of neoplasm is not established until the cyst wall is biopsied at operation.

3. Complications

a. Rupture of a pseudocyst into the peritoneal cavity causes generalized chemical peritonitis. It complicates 5% of cases and is fatal in many. Operation consists of draining the pseudocyst.

b. Infection of a pseudocyst results in fever and toxicity. Surgical drainage is required.

c. Hemorrhage from erosion of the cyst into adjacent major vessels is a very serious complication. Emergency operation is required, but control of the bleeding site in the midst of severe inflammation is difficult.

4. Treatment Uncomplicated pseudocysts developing after acute pancreatitis should be observed for about 4 weeks to allow resolution (uncommon) or thickening of the wall of the cyst. Operation is then performed.

Small cysts can be excised, but larger ones must be drained externally or internally. External drainage is less satisfactory because 30% of such patients have prolonged drainage from a pancreatic fistula. Internal drainage may take the form of anastomosis to the stomach (cystogastrostomy) or anastomosis to a Roux-en-Y loop of jejunum.

5. Prognosis Internally drained pseudocysts resolve and the cavity becomes obliterated over several weeks. Pseudocysts recur in 10% of surgically treated cases. Deaths are consequences of the complications described above.

D. PANCREATIC ABSCESS is a collection of necrotic pancreas and pus as a result of severe pancreatitis.

1. Diagnosis Toxicity is the hallmark of pancreatic abscess. High fever, persistent severe pain and tenderness, and leukocytosis develop about 10 days to 2 weeks after the acute attack. A mass may be palpable. Multiple small bubbles in the region of the pancreas on plain x-ray is very suggestive of abscess. Upper GI series, ultrasound, or CT scan show a mass.

Treatment is by surgical drainage and debridement of necrotic pancreas. Multiple external drains are placed; internal drainage of the abscess should not be attempted. Repeated operations often are necessary.

Untreated pancreatic abscess is uniformly fatal. Delayed treatment and the difficulty of controlling the infection contribute to the mortality rate of 30%.

E. PANCREATIC ASCITES Chronic leakage of pancreatic fluid from a pseudocyst or the pancreatic duct is responsible for this condition. The enzymes are inactive, and peritonitis does not occur. Most adults with pancreatic ascites are alcoholics.

The ascites may be mistaken for cirrhotic ascites, but paracentesis reveals fluid with high amylase levels and protein >3 gm/100 ml. ERCP should be done to demonstrate the site of ductal disruption. Treatment is surgical after correction of malnutrition. Internal drainage is preferred.

F. CHRONIC PANCREATITIS Alcohol is the most common cause of chronic pancreatitis; biliary tract disease rarely progresses to this stage despite recurrent acute attacks.

1. Diagnosis

a. Symptoms and signs Persistent pain in the epigastrium and back; the intensity of pain varies during the day and from one day to another. Addiction to narcotics is common. Diabetes mellitus. Steatorrhea and malnutrition.

b. Laboratory tests Serum amylase is not elevated if the pancreas is extensively destroyed. Bilirubin may be elevated from obstruction of the common duct by fibrosis in the head of the pancreas. Diabetes mellitus is demonstrable chemically in many cases. Steatorrhea can be proved by measuring fecal fat content over a 3-day period with the patient consuming 100 gm fat/day. Secretin stimulation of the pancreas may disclose abnormal secretion, but the test usually is unable to differentiate among various diseases.

c. X-rays Plain abdominal films show pancreatic calcification in 50% of patients with chronic alcoholic pancreatitis. Oral cholecystography or other cholangiographic studies should be done.

d. Special tests ERCP reveals strictures, dilatation, calculi, etc. in the pancreatic duct. Ultrasound may demonstrate pseudocyst.

2. Differential diagnosis Other diseases of the upper GI tract should be excluded. The possibility of factitious pain for the purpose of obtaining narcotics is a frequent concern. Objective evidence of pancreatic abnormality should be sought.

3. Complications Diabetes, malnutrition, and narcotic addiction are common. Adenocarcinoma of the pancreas develops in up to 10% of patients with chronic alcoholic pancreatitis.

4. Medical treatment Abstention from alcohol is essential. Diabetes requires insulin replacement. Steatorrhea responds to oral pancreatic enzymes (e.g.,

Viokase or Cotazym) given 1 hour before and with each meal for a total daily dose of 4–12 gm.

5. Surgical treatment   Persistent pain despite abstention from alcohol is an indication for operation. Surgical treatment takes many forms, but the procedures fall into two categories:

a. Drainage   Obstruction of the duct is relieved by providing some type of internal drainage.

Obstruction at the ampulla with uniform distal dilatation is treated by sphincteroplasty.

Focal obstruction in the body of the gland responds to distal pancreatectomy and anastomosis of the pancreatic stump to a Roux-en-Y loop of jejunum (DuVal procedure).

Multiple constrictions and dilatations of the duct are often managed by the Puestow procedure. The duct is incised longitudinally through the anterior surface of the gland from the head to the tail, and a Roux-en-Y loop of jejunum is anastomosed to the full length of the opened duct.

b. Resection   Removal of the pancreas is necessary if the duct is not dilated. Pancreatectomy is limited to the distal gland in selected cases, but more often 90–95% of the pancreas must be removed (subtotal or near-total pancreatectomy). Rarely, a Whipple procedure is performed.

6. Prognosis   About 75% of patients are relieved of pain by properly performed surgery. Continued consumption of alcohol makes recurrent problems likely. Narcotic addiction is difficult to correct. Diabetes and steatorrhea must be treated if they were present preoperatively or if they develop after operation (especially after pancreatectomy).

G. ADENOCARCINOMA OF THE PANCREAS   Cancer of the pancreas is increasing in frequency. It usually develops between age 40 and 60. The disease is rarely curable because it has extended or metastasized by the time it is detected. Two-thirds of cancers arise in the head of the gland.

1. Diagnosis

a. Symptoms and signs   Pain in the epigastrium and back is deep-seated, dull, and often is exacerbated by recumbency. Anorexia and weight loss are characteristic.

Obstructive jaundice is caused by cancer arising in the head of the gland. The evaluation of jaundiced patients is discussed in the Hepatic and Biliary Section. The gallbladder often is palpable in accordance with Courvoisier's law. Cholangitis is uncommon. Migratory thrombophlebitis occasionally. Epigastric mass and hepatomegaly (from ductal obstruction or metastases).

Signs of distal spread (e.g., enlarged Virchow's node, umbilical metastases, rectal shelf).

b. Laboratory tests   Liver function tests reflect metastases or ductal obstruction. Occult blood is found in the stool in most cases of pancreatic cancer. Cytologic examination of duodenal aspirates may reveal malignant cells.

c. X-rays   Upper GI series demonstrates a pancreatic mass. Angiography may show the tumor itself or distortion of pancreatic vessels by neoplastic invasion.

d. Special tests   ERCP sometimes shows the tumor and is very useful in cases of obstruction of the common duct. Ultrasound and CT scan are other means of identifying a mass in the pancreas.

2. Differential diagnosis   Malignant obstructive jaundice may also be due to cancer arising in the common duct, ampulla of Vater, or duodenum. Benign biliary masses and fibrosis from chronic pancreatitis can obstruct the duct. Pancreatic masses may be benign lesions (pseudocysts, pancreatitis) or other types of pancreatic neoplasm (cystadenoma, cystadenocarcinoma).

3. Treatment   The diagnosis of cancer is confirmed by biopsy at operation. A zone of pancreatitis surrounds most cancers, and the biopsy may be falsely negative. Some surgeons proceed with resection even if the biopsy is negative.

About 15% of cancers of the head of the pancreas can be resected; the remainder have extended locally or metastasized so that resection offers no possibility of cure. Resection of cancers arising in the body or tail is rarely possible.

Resection of cancer in the head requires removal of the pancreas (the portion to the right of the superior mesenteric vessels), the duodenum, the distal stomach (with vagotomy to avoid peptic ulcer), the distal common bile duct, and the gallbladder (Whipple procedure). Total pancreaticoduodenectomy is performed by some surgeons in the hope that local recurrence will be less common.

Unresectable tumors of the head are palliated by biliary diversion (e.g., cholecystojejunostomy) and, if the duodenum is obstructed, gastrojejunostomy.

4. Prognosis Survivals for 5 years after radical resection are rare. Most patients die within a year after the diagnosis is made. Management of diabetes and exocrine insufficiency are required after pancreatectomy.

H. ENDOCRINE TUMORS OF THE PANCREAS
Gastrinoma produces Zollinger-Ellison syndrome (see Stomach and Duodenum in this chapter). Two other types of islet cell tumor are discussed here.

1. Insulinoma Neoplasms (or hyperplasia) of the beta cells produce hyperinsulinism. 80% of insulinomas are solitary benign lesions, 10% are malignant, and the remaining 10% are multiple benign adenomas or diffuse hyperplasia.

Whipple's triad consists of hypoglycemic symptoms with fasting, blood glucose below 50 mg/100 ml during symptoms, and relief of symptoms by IV glucose. Other causes of hypoglycemia produce Whipple's triad, but high serum insulin levels in the presence of hypoglycemia are diagnostic. Arteriography may localize the tumor.

Medical measures include diazoxide and streptozotocin. Surgical treatment is recommended. Solitary tumors are excised. If no tumor is found, the distal pancreas should be removed and sectioned. If no tumor is present, up to 80% of the gland can be excised.

Results depend upon removal of the abnormal source of insulin. Multiple tumors or diffuse hyperplasia may improve after 80% pancreatectomy. Total pancreatectomy is required occasionally.

2. Pancreatic cholera is also known as the WDHA syndrome (watery diarrhea, hypokalemia, and achlorhydria). It is caused by excessive production of a hormone or hormones by the pancreas; VIP (vasoactive intestinal polypeptide) is the substance most often implicated. Other causes of diarrhea must be excluded. Principles of surgical treatment are the same as for insulinoma.

XVI. SPLEEN

A. TRAUMA The spleen is frequently injured by blunt trauma, penetrating wounds, and, occasionally, by surgical manipulation. The spleen may rupture spontaneously in certain diseases (e.g., leukemia, malaria, and mononucleosis).

Rupture of the splenic capsule produces intraabdominal bleeding. In some cases, a blow may contuse the spleen, a subcapsular hematoma forms, and **delayed rupture** occurs days to weeks later.

Left upper abdominal pain and tenderness should raise the suspicion of splenic rupture. Fractures of the lower ribs on the left are an important sign of trauma to the splenic region. Some patients are in shock, and others have no hemodynamic instability. Pain in the left shoulder (Kehr's sign) is accentuated by the Trendelenburg position or by palpation of the left upper quadrant.

Peritoneal lavage is useful to detect blood in the peritoneal cavity (see Section I of this chapter). Splenic scan and arteriography may be helpful in obscure cases.

Table 10-4. Indications for splenectomy*

Splenectomy always indicated
    Splenic injury (common)
    Primary splenic tumor (rare)
    Splenic abscess (rare)
    Hereditary spherocytosis (congenital hemolytic anemia)

Splenectomy usually indicated
    Primary hypersplenism
    Chronic idiopathic thrombocytopenic purpura

Splenectomy sometimes indicated
    Autoimmune hemolytic disease
    Ovalocytosis with hemolysis
    Nonspherocytic congenital hemolytic anemias (e.g., pyruvate
       kinase deficiency)
    Hemoglobin H disease
    Hodgkin's disease (for staging)

Splenectomy rarely indicated
    Chronic lymphatic leukemia
    Lymphosarcoma
    Hodgkin's disease (except for staging)
    Macroglobulinemia
    Myelofibrosis
    Thalassemia major
    Splenic artery aneurysm
    Sickle cell anemia

Splenectomy not indicated
    Asymptomatic hypersplenism
    Splenomegaly with infection
    Splenomegaly associated with elevated IgM
    Hereditary hemolytic anemia of moderate degree
    Acute leukemia
    Agranulocytosis

*Reproduced with permission from Dunphy JE, Way LW (Eds.) *Current Surgical Diagnosis & Treatment*, 3rd Ed. Lange 1977

    Splenectomy is the only acceptable treatment for splenic rupture. Efforts to preserve the spleen by suturing or coagulating large capsular tears are ill-advised. Very tiny tears of the capsule, as sometimes occur from surgical trauma, may respond to application of microcrystalline collagen.
    The mortality rate of splenic rupture in the absence of other injuries is about 10%

B. HYPERSPLENISM is abnormal splenic sequestration and destruction of red cells, leukocytes, and platelets.
    1. Causes
    a. Splenic enlargement A large spleen is capable of greater destruction of blood cells than a normal size spleen.
    (1) *Primary hypersplenism* is enlargement of the spleen for no apparent reason. It is rare.
    (2) *Secondary hypersplenism* is enlargement of the spleen as a feature of some disease. Portal hypertension is the most common, and neoplastic involvement of the spleen (e.g., by lymphoma) is also frequent. Less common in

the USA are tuberculosis, malaria, mononucleosis, and sarcoidosis. Rheumatoid arthritis may be associated with hypersplenism (Felty's syndrome).

b. Defects of red cells   Defective red blood cells are trapped and destroyed in the spleen, leading to splenic enlargement and still more destruction of red cells and other blood cells. Spherocytosis, thalassemia, and G6PD deficiency are among these conditions.

c. Immunologic disorders in which splenic destruction of blood cells leads to hypersplenism include autoimmune hemolytic anemia and thrombocytopenic purpura.

2. Diagnosis and treatment   Anemia, leukopenia, and thrombocytopenia are characteristic. Treatment depends upon the underlying disease. Splenectomy is required in some hypersplenic states and recommended occasionally in others (see Table 10-4). A few of these conditions are discussed in the following section.

C. SPLENECTOMY FOR HEMATOLOGIC DISORDERS

1. Hereditary spherocytosis is the most common type of congenital hemolytic anemia. It is transmitted as an autosomal dominant trait.

a. Diagnosis   Anemia, jaundice, fatigue, and splenomegaly are usually apparent in childhood or early adulthood. Asymptomatic cases are detected when a patient's relatives are surveyed.

Mild to moderate anemia (Hgb 9–12 gm/100 ml) and reticulocytosis are present. Spherocytes are seen on smear of the peripheral blood. Bilirubin (indirect fraction) may be elevated. Special tests reveal abnormal red cell fragility. The Coombs test is negative.

b. Differential diagnosis   Spherocytes are found in the blood in other conditions, including autoimmune hemolytic anemias.

c. Complications   Gallstones form in 85% of adults with spherocytosis.

d. Treatment   Splenectomy is required. Operation should be deferred in children until age 5 years or older. Cholecystectomy is indicated for cholelithiasis.

e. Prognosis   Splenectomy is curative if the diagnosis is correct. Persistent hemolysis is due to an overlooked accessory spleen.

2. Acquired hemolytic anemia   Hemolytic anemia may be acquired by exposure to drugs, chemicals, and other agents. Nonsurgical treatment (removal of the causative agent, corticosteroids) is usually sufficient. **Autoimmune hemolytic anemia** is due to formation of antibodies against one's own red cells. This condition, if caused by warm antibodies, may require splenectomy.

Abrupt onset of anemia, fever, and jaundice in women over age 50 is the usual presentation. The spleen is enlarged in 50% and gallstones are present in 25%. Hemolytic anemia is normochromic and normocytic. Reticulocytosis and a positive direct Coombs test are present.

Corticosteroid therapy leads to permanent remission in 25% of cases; splenectomy is performed in the remainder. Splenectomy is successful in 50% of patients overall, and in 80% of patients with preoperative proof (using ^{51}Cr tagged red cells) that the spleen is the site of sequestration.

3. Idiopathic (immunologic) thrombocytopenic purpura (ITP) may be primary or secondary (to drugs, infection, lymphoproliferative disorders, etc.) Splenic destruction of platelets causes ecchymoses, petechiae, and bleeding from gingiva, gut, vagina, or urinary tract. Chronic ITP occurs mainly in women; an acute variety appears in children.

Thrombocytopenia (less than 100,000/μl) is demonstrable on peripheral smear. Abundant megakaryocytes are found in the marrow. A large number of other disorders must be excluded by special studies. Some cases resolve spontaneously, and others improve with corticosteroid treatment.

Splenectomy is done if steroids cannot be given, if they are ineffective, or if relapse occurs. Long-term remission is produced by splenectomy in 70% of patients, and another 15% have some favorable response.

4. Myeloid metaplasia Agnogenic myeloid metaplasia is a myeloproliferative disorder related to polycythemia vera and myelogenous leukemia. Anemia, bleeding, and infection are common. The spleen is greatly enlarged and may cause local symptoms. Symptomatic cases are improved by splenectomy.

5. Hodgkin's disease Splenectomy is performed as part of a laparotomy to stage Hodgkin's disease in certain patients.

D. SPLENIC ABSCESS An abscess may develop in the spleen from hematogenous seeding, by direct extension from an adjacent infection, or by secondary infection of a traumatic hematoma. Abscesses elsewhere are common in these patients. Splenic abscess should be suspected in a patient with unexplained sepsis, abdominal pain, and splenomegaly. Splenic scan or arteriogram reveals a filling defect. Splenectomy is the treatment.

E. COMPLICATIONS OF SPLENECTOMY
   1. Thrombocytosis Platelet counts routinely rise after splenectomy, and sometimes they exceed 1 million/μl. The peak response is about 7–10 days after operation. There is little apparent risk of thromboembolic complications, and anticoagulation is not warranted, but antiplatelet aggregating agents (e.g., aspirin) are advisable if thrombocytosis reaches very high levels.
   2. Immune deficiency Splenectomy places the patient at an increased risk of infection by encapsulated bacteria. The risk is greatest in children, but fulminant pneumococcemia has been reported after splenectomy in adults. It is recommended that patients be immunized against pneumococcus after splenectomy; a polyvalent vaccine (Pneumovax) is now available for this purpose.

XVII. EXTERNAL ABDOMINAL HERNIAS

Internal abdominal hernias include diaphragmatic hernia (see Chapter 18), acquired hernias caused by adhesions, and congenital hernias into the foramen of Winslow, paraduodenal spaces, etc. Intestinal obstruction is the usual manifestation, and treatment is by surgical repair.

   An **external abdominal hernia** is an abnormal protrusion of intraabdominal tissues through a congenital or acquired defect in the abdominal wall. Various types are discussed individually in this section.

A. DEFINITIONS
   1. Reducible The contents of the hernia sac return to the abdomen spontaneously or with manual pressure.
   2. Incarcerated (irreducible) The contents of the sac cannot be returned to the abdomen with manual pressure.
   3. Strangulated The blood supply to the contents of the sac is compromised.
   4. Richter's hernia Part of the circumference of a loop of bowel becomes incarcerated in the hernia sac.

B. INGUINAL HERNIAS An **indirect inguinal hernia** is a protrusion of peritoneum, with or without abdominal viscera, through the internal inguinal ring. The defect is congenital and is due to persistence of the processus vaginalis peritonei. The hernia may be apparent in infancy, or it may not become evident until later; most are diagnosed before age 50. Cryptorchidism and hydrocele are commonly associated with indirect hernias in male infants. Indirect inguinal hernia is more common in males than in females, but it is nevertheless the most common type of hernia of the groin in females.

   Direct inguinal hernia is a protrusion through **Hesselbach's triangle,** which is bounded by the inguinal ligament inferiorly, the inferior epigastric vessels laterally and superiorly, and the border of the rectus muscle medially. Direct hernia is an acquired diffuse weakness of the transversalis fascia in the floor of the inguinal canal; it is often bilateral, and it is related to older age, obesity, persistent cough, and other conditions that chronically raise intraabdominal pressure. Direct hernia is rare in women, young men, and children of either sex.

In some patients, both an indirect and direct inguinal hernia are present on the same side (pantaloon or saddlebag hernia).

1. Diagnosis

a. Symptoms Asymptomatic hernias are discovered on routine examination. A bulge or lump in the groin, accentuated by coughing, defecation, lifting, or other physical activity; the mass extends into the scrotum in some cases. Discomfort in the groin, especially as the hernia enlarges.

b. Signs

(1) A mass in the groin, reducible or incarcerated, sometimes extending into the scrotum. In infants and women, the presence of a mass is the only finding. Small asymptomatic hernias may not be visible.

(2) In older boys and in men, the following maneuver should be performed. The scrotum is invaginated with the index finger, and the finger is placed against or through the external inguinal ring. Instruct the patient to bear down (strain) as though to defecate; this provides a sustained increase in intraabdominal pressure. The hernia sac is a balloon-like structure which impresses upon the pulp of the finger directly or from the lateral aspect. **An enlarged external ring is not a hernia,** although it is likely that a hernia is the cause of the enlargement, and a hernia must be carefully sought if the ring is large enough to admit the index finger. Inguinal hernia is most easily demonstrable with the patient standing, but examine the patient both standing and supine.

(3) *Indirect vs direct* An indirect hernia is an elliptical mass descending obliquely in the inguinal canal. It may enter the scrotum. The mass strikes the lateral aspect of the examining finger. Pressure over the internal ring with one hand prevents the hernia from entering the inguinal canal.

A direct hernia is a spherical mass which rarely descends into the scrotum. The mass impresses on the examining finger from directly in front. Manual pressure over the internal ring does not reduce the hernia.

c. Contributory factors The history and physical examination should include a search for causes of increased intraabdominal pressure that may have contributed to development of the hernia. Bladder outlet obstruction, chronic cough, and ascites are among these underlying problems. Contrary to previous belief, there is no correlation between carcinoma of the colon and development of an inguinal hernia. Routine barium enema, therefore, is not recommended, but digital rectal examination, including palpation of the prostate and tests for occult blood in the stool, should be done as part of a thorough physical examination.

2. Differential diagnosis Femoral hernia (see below). 'Lipoma of the cord': properitoneal fat entering the spermatic cord resembles a hernia and may not be recognized until operation. Hydrocele and varicocele (see Chapter 12). Lymphadenopathy.

3. Complications

a. Incarceration does not imply intestinal obstruction or strangulation. It is not by itself a complication.

b. Obstruction of bowel in the sac has the clinical features of any other form of small or large intestinal obstruction. Strangulation is a risk with obstructed bowel, but it is not necessarily present.

c. Strangulation causes symptoms and signs of intestinal obstruction if the strangulated viscus is bowel. Omentum may also strangulate. There may be erythema, edema, and tenderness over the hernia, but often the abdominal findings mask the inguinal manifestations, especially in obese patients.

4. Treatment All indirect inguinal hernias, regardless of age, and large or symptomatic direct hernias should be repaired. Coexistent respiratory and obstructive urologic disease should be improved or corrected first. Acutely incarcerated hernias should be reduced or operated on immediately. Obstruction or strangulation requires emergency operation.

Common methods of surgical repair are as follows:

a. High ligation of the sac is the procedure of choice for indirect inguinal hernias in infants and children.

b. Bassini repair The indirect sac is opened, explored, and ligated; the inguinal floor is strengthened by suture of transversalis fascia to the inguinal ligament behind the cord. Direct sacs are usually imbricated and not opened. This method is popular for indirect hernias in adults.

c. Halstead repair is similar to Bassini, but the external oblique aponeurosis is also sutured to the inguinal ligament behind the cord, thus placing the cord in the subcutaneous tissue. Some surgeons prefer this method for direct hernias.

d. McVay or Lotheissen repair Transversalis fascia is sutured to Cooper's ligament behind the cord after ligation of any indirect sac. This operation is often used for direct and femoral hernias.

e. Shouldice repair The transversalis fascia is divided longitudinally and the two flaps are imbricated to the inguinal ligament. Suture of the internal oblique muscle and the conjoined tendon to the external oblique aponeurosis reinforces the repair. This technic is applicable to indirect or direct hernias.

5. Prognosis Healing is promoted by avoidance of heavy lifting or straining. Manual laborers should not return to work for 4–6 weeks; people in sedentary occupations may return to work in a few days.

Indirect inguinal hernias recur in 2–3% of patients. Direct hernias recur in up to 10% of cases. Repair of a recurrent hernia is followed by another recurrence in 10–20% of patients.

B. SLIDING INGUINAL HERNIA is one in which a viscus forms part of the wall of the hernia sac. The viscus may be cecum, sigmoid colon, bladder, or ovary. Sliding hernias may be indistinguishable from other types preoperatively, but large size and chronic incarceration should raise the suspicion of sliding hernia.

Because the viscus invariably comprises the posterior wall, all indirect inguinal hernia sacs should be opened anteriorly to avoid accidental entry into bowel or bladder. Standard texts should be consulted for special technics of repair of sliding hernias.

C. FEMORAL HERNIA In this type of hernia, the sac enters the femoral canal on the medial side of the femoral vein deep to the inguinal ligament. The sac then may curve anteriorly and superiorly around the inguinal ligament to present in the inguinal area. Femoral hernia is more common in women than in men or children.

The mass is visible or palpable in the upper medial thigh, or it may appear to reside above the inguinal ligament where it is difficult to distinguish from inguinal hernia. Femoral hernia must also be distinguished from lymphadenopathy and saphenous varix.

Because the neck is narrow, femoral hernia is prone to incarceration and strangulation. The hernia is often overlooked in obese patients with intestinal obstruction on this basis.

Treatment is by surgical repair through a standard inguinal incision. If it is difficult to reduce the hernia through the small neck, special maneuvers are required. Strangulated bowel is an indication to open the abdomen through a separate incision. Recurrences develop in about 10% of patients.

D. UMBILICAL HERNIA in children is discussed in Chapter 18. After spontaneous closure of the umbilical ring in infancy, some adults gradually develop widening of the ring and formation of an umbilical hernia. Increased intraabdominal pressure is responsible (e.g., obesity, pregnancy, ascites, tumors).

The hernia is diagnosed by inspection and palpation. Omentum is the usual content of the sac, although bowel is present in large ones. Strangulation is common because of the unyielding fascia and small size of the defect.

Surgical repair should be done to prevent strangulation. Small hernias can be sutured transversely under local anesthesia. The skin should be tacked to the fascia to preserve the umbilicus. Large umbilical hernias require general anesthesia and more elaborate repair.

E. EPIGASTRIC HERNIA is protrusion through the linea alba in the upper abdomen. A mass (usually properitoneal fat, sometimes omentum and bowel) is palpable in the midline or just to the left. Many are asymptomatic, but epigastric hernia can be the source of unexplained pain and gastrointestinal symptoms. Repair under local anesthesia is simple and effective for small hernias; larger ones are best repaired under general anesthesia.

F. INCISIONAL (VENTRAL) HERNIA Dehiscence of fascia in an abdominal incision results in a hernia. Infection, technical errors, and associated diseases (obesity, malnutrition) account for most incisional hernias. Dehiscence may be a dramatic event in the early postoperative period (see Wound Complications in Chapter 2), or it may develop slowly over a period of weeks.

Incisional hernia is an uncomfortable and unsightly protrusion which is prone to incarceration and strangulation, especially if the defect is small. Repair is recommended for most of them. Care must be taken to excise attenuated fascia and to approximate healthy structures with nonabsorbable sutures; tension on the suture line should be avoided.

Large ventral hernias pose technical problems. The contents of the hernia cannot be returned to the peritoneal cavity in extreme cases; preoperative injections of air (pneumoperitoneum) may expand the peritoneal cavity and aid in surgical reduction. The same factors which contributed to the dehiscence initially may still be present (e.g., obesity, chronic respiratory disease), and, in some of these cases, it is wise to avoid repair unless or until the associated problems can be corrected. Marlex mesh may be needed to bridge the fascial defect if wide mobilization and relaxing incisions do not bring the margins together without tension. The recurrence rate is high after repair of large defects.

G. OTHER HERNIAS

1. Spigelian hernia This is a hernia through the linea semilunaris (where the layers of investing fascia of the oblique muscles fuse to form the rectus sheath). The most common site is in the lower abdomen at the junction of the linea semilunaris and the semicircular line of Douglas; at this point, all of the fascia of the oblique muscles passes anterior to the rectus muscle, and the posterior rectus sheath is deficient.

Spigelian hernia causes discomfort and is prone to strangulation. The sac often protrudes laterally between deep layers and is difficult to palpate. For this reason, the diagnosis is frequently missed.

Spigelian hernia should be repaired.

2. Lumbar hernia is a hernia through one of the lumbar triangles in the posterior abdominal wall.

3. Littre's hernia This oddity is an external abdominal hernia (at any site) containing only a Meckel's diverticulum.

11

GYNECOLOGY

Edward C. Hill, MD

I. EXAMINATION OF THE GYNECOLOGIC PATIENT

A. HISTORY   A complete history should be taken on all gynecologic patients with particular emphasis on the menstrual history, sexual activity, past pregnancies, previous gynecologic disorders, vaginal bleeding or discharge, and pelvic pain.

B. PHYSICAL EXAMINATION   The physical examination should also be complete. In addition to a speculum and bimanual examination, the pelvic examination includes a careful combined rectovaginal palpation to detect small lesions occupying the cul-de-sac and the rectovaginal septum.

C. GYNECOLOGIC LABORATORY TESTS
   1. Wet smear   A suspension of vaginal discharge in a drop of isotonic saline solution placed on a slide and cover-slipped will confirm the diagnosis of Trichomonas vaginalis vaginitis or Corynebacterium (Hemophilus) infections. A suspension in 10% KOH solution should be done for suspected Monilial vulvovaginitis.
   2. Exfoliative cytology   Sampling of the squamocolumnar junction of the cervix for cytologic examination is a vital part of the routine pelvic examination to screen for early neoplastic lesions (dysplasia and carcinoma-in-situ). The exocervix is scraped with an appropriately designed spatula, and an endocervical sample is obtained with a pipette aspirator or cotton-tipped applicator. The material is spread uniformly on a slide and fixed immediately.
   3. Tissue biopsy   Samples of tissue may be obtained from the vulva with a dermatologist's skin punch under local anesthesia. A punch biopsy forceps may be used to obtain tissue from the vagina or exocervix; local anesthesia usually is not necessary in these locations. The endocervix and endometrial cavity can be sampled with small curettes specifically designed for this purpose.
   4. Tests of endocrine function   Hormonal studies include vaginal cell maturation index on cytological specimens obtained from the lateral vaginal wall at the level of the cervix, fern test of cervical mucus, biologic tests for pregnancy, and a variety of special hormone assays.

D. SPECIAL TESTS
   1. Schiller test   When neoplastic disease is suspected, the cervical and vaginal mucosa is painted with a strong iodine solution such as Lugol's. Nonstaining areas represent nonglycogenated cells which should be biopsied.
   2. Colposcopy   The colposcope is a low-power microscope with a long focal distance used to identify areas of intraepithelial neoplasia. This examination requires special training.
   3. Culdocentesis   Needle aspiration of the peritoneal cul-de-sac through the posterior vaginal fornix is a simple but informative procedure in a variety of clinical circumstances, such as suspected intraperitoneal bleeding or pelvic infection.
   4. Laparoscopy   Examination of the internal genitalia and surrounding organs with a fiberoptic instrument after the introduction of CO_2 or NO_2 gas

is a useful diagnostic procedure.

   5. Hysteroscopy Inspection of the endometrial cavity with a specially-designed fiberoptic instrument has limited value at present.

   6. Pelvic sonography The use of high-frequency sound waves to outline pelvic structures has proved extremely useful as a gynecologic diagnostic aid.

   7. Tubal insufflation (Ruben's test) Carbon-dioxide gas is insufflated through a cannula placed in the cervical canal; tubal patency is resumed if auscultation of abdomen reveals gas passing into the peritoneal cavity.

E. X-RAY STUDIES

   1. Hysterosalpingography A contrast medium is introduced through the cervical canal to outline radiographically the endometrial cavity and fallopian tubes. It is the test most frequently used to determine patency of the fallopian tubes in patients who are infertile.

   2. Pelvic pneumography A gas such as CO_2 or NO_2 is introduced into the peritoneal cavity to outline the pelvic viscera. X-rays are obtained with the patient in Trendelenburg position so that the gas is displaced into the pelvis.

   3. Computerized tomography (CT scan) This highly specialized radiographic technique affords accurate cross-sectional examination of the abdomen and pelvis.

II. LEUKORRHEA

Leukorrhea is excessive nonbloody vaginal discharge. It may be mucoid or purulent, thick or thin, malodorous or inoffensive, nonirritating or accompanied by itching or burning. The causes are numerous:

   1. Excess mucus due to hyperestrinism Mid-cycle production; pregnancy; exogenous hormone; foreign bodies in the vagina.

   2. Infection Trichomonas vaginitis; moniliasis; Corynebacterium (Hemophilus) vaginitis; Herpes hominis type 2 infection (see Section IV.D); gonorrhea; mixed infections (atrophic vaginitis).

   3. Cervical Inflammation (see Section V) Cervicitis due to old obstetric lacerations; ectopy (columnar epithelium on exocervix).

A. FOREIGN BODIES Forgotten tampons are a frequent cause of foul, purulent discharge in adults. Crayons, safety pins, paper clips, and beans may be deposited in the vagina by children. Speculum examination reveals the source. An anesthetic may be required in children. Removal of the foreign body is definitive treatment.

B. TRICHOMONAS VAGINALIS VAGINITIS Trichomonas vaginalis causes a thick, yellow-to-green, frothy discharge with vulvar itching or burning. The vaginal mucosa may show typical punctate, erythematous 'strawberry' marks. Diagnosis is confirmed by a microscopic wet smear examination.

   Metronidazole (Flagyl) is the treatment of choice. Because the organism is transmitted by sexual congress, both partners should be treated simultaneously with 250 mg orally, 3 times daily for 7 days. A second course can be given if the infection recurs. Metronidazole is contraindicated during pregnancy and lactation. Vaginal suppositories of furazolidone-nifuroxime (Tricofuron) may be inserted twice daily for 8 weeks in patients who cannot use metronidazole.

C. MONILIASIS Vaginal yeast infections usually are caused by Candida albicans. Diabetics and women who eat many sweets are particularly susceptible. Other predisposing factors include pregnancy, oral contraceptives, and administration of antibiotics for some unrelated condition. Vulvar itching and a non-odorous discharge like cottage cheese are common symptoms. The vulvar mucosa is fiery red, and a thick white exudate is present in the vagina.

The exudate or scrapings from the vulva are suspended in 10% KOH to reveal the spores and/or mycelia of the organism. Nickerson's medium is best for culturing Candida; typical brown colonies develop.

Any of the following therapeutic agents usually is effective: (1) nystatin (Mycostatin) vaginal tablets (100,000 units) twice daily for 2 weeks; (2) candicidin (Candeptin, Vanobid), 1 applicatorful of ointment or 1 vaginal tablet twice daily for 2 weeks; (3) miconazole nitrate (Monistat) 2% vaginal cream, 1 applicatorful each night at bedtime for 2 weeks; (4) chlordantoin and benzalkonium chloride (Sporostacin) vaginal cream, 1 applicatorful twice daily for 2 weeks; (5) clotrimazole (Gyne-lotrimin), 1 vaginal tablet each night at bedtime for 1 week.

D. CORYNEBACTERIUM (HEMOPHILUS VAGINALE) VAGINITIS This is a specific coccal infection producing an offensive, thin, grey discharge, often without local irritation. The diagnosis is made by finding the so-called 'clue cell' (a squamous epithelial cell speckled by numerous dark cocci) or clumps of the organisms in a saline wet smear.

Triple sulfa (Sultrin)—sulfathiazole, sulfacetamide, sulfabenzamide—cream or tablets should be used in treatment. The cream is introduced by vaginal applicator twice daily for 4 - 6 days, then once daily for 10 days. 1 vaginal tablet may be inserted twice daily for 10 days as an alternative.

E. GONORRHEA Neisseria gonorrhoeae infection of the cervix produces a creamy yellow discharge. A history of exposure to gonorrhea frequently is absent. A gram stain of the exudate may show the typical coffee bean shaped, gram-negative, intracellular diplococci. Culture is essential for a definitive diagnosis because of similar nonpathogenic diplococci found in the lower reproductive tract. Thayer-Martin and blood agar are the best culture media.

Cervical gonorrhea may lead to ascending infection, producing acute and chronic salpingitis and pelvic peritonitis (see Section VII). A serologic test for syphilis should be obtained whenever a diagnosis of gonorrhea is made.

Treatment of gonorrheal cervicitis is best carried out by giving probenecid (1 gm orally) 30 minutes before the IM injection of aqueous procaine penicillin G (4.8 million units in 2 or more divided doses at different sites). If the patient is allergic to penicillin, oral tetracycline HCl (1.5 gm initially followed by 500 mg 4 times daily for 4 days) should be administered. Follow-up cultures should be obtained 7 - 14 days after the completion of treatment.

F. ATROPHIC VAGINITIS This condition is encountered in postmenopausal women, whether the menopause is natural or secondary to surgical or radiation castration. The discharge often is thick and yellow and accompanied by vulvar burning and dyspareunia. Examination reveals a diffusely erythematous, smooth, atrophic mucosa. Pap smear for estrogen effect (best taken from the lateral vaginal wall at the level of the cervix) shows a predominance of immature squamous epithelial cells and few superficial cells.

Treatment with either of the following topical estrogen preparations is effective: (1) diethylstilbestrol vaginal suppositories, 0.1 mg each night at bedtime for 2 weeks, then twice weekly; (2) dienestrol vaginal cream, ½ applicatorful each night at bedtime for 2 weeks, then twice weekly.

III. ABNORMALITIES OF MENSTRUATION

A. DYSFUNCTIONAL UTERINE BLEEDING This disorder is irregular, frequent or prolonged bleeding due to chronic failure to ovulate (progesterone deficiency), resulting eventually in endometrial hyperplasia. It occurs most often in adolescents and premenopausal women. It is also encountered in association with polycystic ovaries (Stein-Leventhal syndrome) and with the uncommon

granulosa-theca cell tumors of the ovary.

1. Diagnosis Organic causes of bleeding must be excluded. A sample of the endometrium obtained either by dilatation and curettage or endometrial biopsy reveals proliferative endometrium in the second half of the menstrual cycle or cystic and/or adenomatous hyperplasia of the endometrium.

2. Complications Anemia secondary to acute or chronic blood loss. Hypovolemic shock in patients with acute severe bleeding episodes. Hyperplasia (in a small number of patients) is a premalignant condition leading to the development of endometrial carcinoma.

3. Treatment

a. Mild to moderate bleeding is treated according to one of the following programs: (1) Hydroxyprogesterone caproate (Delalutin): 125-250 mg, IM at monthly intervals. (2) Medroxyprogesterone acetate (Provera): 10 mg by mouth daily for 5 days at monthly intervals. (3) Combination estrogen-progestin (norethindrone with mestranol or ethinyl estradiol): 1 tablet daily for 21 days beginning with the fifth day of bleeding.

b. Severe bleeding Transfuse if hypovolemic shock is present. Conjugated estrogens (20 mg IV) to control acute bleeding, then oral estrogen-progestin combination by mouth daily for 3 weeks. Dilatation and curettage.

B. DYSMENORRHEA (PRIMARY) is incapacitating painful menstruation in the absence of organic disease. The condition always is preceded by ovulation and may be related to increased amplitude of uterine contractions associated with progesterone effect on the myometrium. There may be some degree of myometrial ischemia.

1. Diagnosis *Symptoms:* Intermittent cramping lower abdominal pain radiating to the back and thighs beginning with or just prior to the onset of menstruation. *Signs:* Absence of organic disease, e.g., pelvic endometriosis or chronic salpingo-oophoritis.

2. Treatment Simple analgesics (aspirin or acetaminophen, with or without codeine) every 3 to 4 hours. Antispasmodic: adiphenine HCl (Trasentine), 75-150 mg 3 times daily. Suppression of ovulation: estrogen-progestin contraceptive routine.

C. PREMENSTRUAL TENSION SYNDROME In many women, combinations of the following symptoms appear regularly several days prior to the onset of menses: headache, nervousness, irritability, insomnia, lethargy, depression, weight gain, bloating, and breast tenderness. The cause is unknown, but sodium and water retention appear to contribute.

Treatment is symptomatic and takes the form of office psychotherapy with reassurance, tranquilizers such as meprobamate (400 mg 3 times daily) or diazepam (2-5 mg 3 times daily), and diuretics (e.g. hydrochlorthiazide, 50 mg daily).

D. AMENORRHEA The failure to menstruate may be either primary or secondary. **Primary amenorrhea** is the failure of menstruation in a postpubertal female. Causes include congenital abnormalities (imperforate hymen and congenital absence of the vagina and/or uterus) and inherited endocrine disorders such as gonadal dysgenesis (Turner's syndrome) and testicular feminization syndrome. **Secondary amenorrhea** is the cessation of menses once menstrual function has become established. Pregnancy is by far the most common cause. Other causes are polycystic ovary (Stein-Leventhal) syndrome, premature menopause, cervical stricture, and intrauterine synechiae secondary to trauma (Asherman's syndrome).

Amenorrhea is merely a symptom and not a disease. The diagnosis often can be made on the basis of a careful history and physical examination. In some instances, a host of laboratory tests and special procedures will be required to arrive at the correct diagnosis.

IV. DISORDERS OF EXTERNAL FEMALE GENITALIA

A. IMPERFORATE HYMEN is a developmental failure of the vagina to canalize at the hymeneal ring.

    1. Diagnosis *Symptoms:* usually not recognized until the menarche; amenorrhea with cyclic lower abdominal cramping pain. *Signs:* hymeneal bulge may be evident on physical examination; a tender lower abdominal and pelvic cystic mass (hematometra and hematocolpos).

    2. Treatment Surgical incision of the imperforate hymen under local anesthesia is definitive.

B. BARTHOLIN GLAND ABSCESS AND CYST Acute bartholinitis results from pyogenic infection by Neisseria, Staphylococci, Streptococci, or coliform

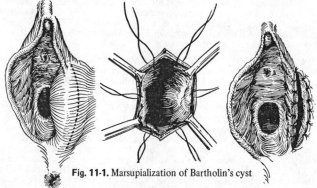

Fig. 11-1. Marsupialization of Bartholin's cyst

organisms. Inflammatory occlusion of the duct leads to an abscess. Closure of the duct in the absence of infection produces mucus retention and cyst formation.

    1. Diagnosis

    a. Abscess pain and swelling in the area of the posterior portion of the labium minus; dyspareunia; examination reveals a tender, fluctuant mass with surrounding cellulitis.

    b. Cyst a mass noted by the patient; a soft, nontender, fluctuant mass on examination.

    2. Treatment

    a. Abscess: incision and drainage, culture and sensitivity should be obtained and appropriate antibiotic therapy begun.

    b. Cyst: no treatment if small and asymptomatic; large symptomatic cysts require marsupialization (see Fig. 11-1), it is rarely necessary to excise the gland and duct.

C. SEBACEOUS CYSTS are common on the vulva. Small cysts require no treatment; large ones may be excised under local anesthetic.

D. HERPES GENITALIS Venereal infection by Herpesvirus hominis, type 2, is an increasingly common vulvar disease. During pregnancy it may be responsible for stillbirth and neonatal death. It has been associated with cervical intraepithelial neoplasia and may be a carcinogen.

    1. Diagnosis

    a. Painful, erythematous papules, vesicles and/or superficial ulcers of the vagina, vulva, and cervix; malaise, fever, anorexia, dysuria, urinary retention, and inguinofemoral adenopathy in severe cases, particularly first infections.

b. Laboratory tests Cytologic smears of the lesions often are diagnostic; the organism can be cultured, but this is rarely necessary; serum antibodies are indicative of previous infection.

2. Treatment is nonspecific and symptomatic. Spraying the lesions with ethyl chloride gives immediate, but transient relief. 2.5% lidocaine (Xylocaine) ointment relieves the discomfort for longer periods.

E. CONDYLOMATA ACUMINATA (VENEREAL WARTS) are warty excrescenses of viral origin involving the vulvar and perianal skin and mucous membranes of the vulva, vagina, and cervix. The growths may coalesce to produce large conglomerations, particularly during pregnancy. Condylomata are often associated with leukorrhea-producing conditions. The diagnosis is made by inspection, but in doubtful cases biopsy may be done.

Treatment Podophyllum resin (10-25% solution in tincture of benzoin) is applied topically to the warts, protecting the surrounding skin and mucous membrane with petrolatum; patient should be instructed to wash the area with soap and water 6 hours after application. Electrodessication in extensive lesions. Treat the cause of the leukorrhea.

F. SOLID BENIGN TUMORS OF THE VULVA Papillomas, fibromas, lipomas, hidradenomas, angiomas, and leiomyomas may be found on the vulva. Small, asymptomatic tumors may require no treatment. Any tumor should be biopsied and/or excised if there is suspicion of malignancy.

G. MALIGNANT CONDITIONS OF THE VULVA

1. Squamous cell carcinoma is the most common malignancy of the vulva. In its early stages, it appears as dysplasia or carcinoma-in-situ, often in the presence of long-standing vulvar irritation with pruritus (chronic vulvar dystrophy).

a. Diagnosis (1) Any chronic, irritating lesion of the vulva may represent a malignancy, **biopsy is essential** if malignancy is to be recognized early. (2) Dysplasia and carcinoma-in-situ often appear as red or white patches (**leukoplakia**); a benign lesion, lichen sclerosis et atrophicus, is a more common cause of white patches; biopsy is necessary to differentiate these lesions. (3) Squamous cell carcinoma occurs most often after the menopause; the lesions are papillary, cauliflower-like, nodular, or ulcerative; metastases are found in the inguinofemoral lymph nodes in 45% of patients; biopsy is diagnostic.

b. Treatment (1) simple vulvectomy prevents progression of dysplasia or carcinoma-in-situ to invasive carcinoma; (2) carcinoma requires radical vulvectomy with bilateral inguinofemoral and iliac-obturator lymph node dissection.

c. Prognosis The 5-year survival rate for squamous cell carcinoma of the vulva varies from 95% in lesions less than 2 cm in diameter without lymph node metastases to about 60% in more extensive lesions localized to the vulva and the superficial inguinal lymph nodes. When the process has extended to the deep pelvic (iliac and obturator) lymph nodes, the chances of cure are poor.

2. Paget's disease of the vulva is an in-situ malignancy. Chronic, red, weeping, scaling, eczematoid lesions should be biopsied to make the diagnosis. Simple vulvectomy is adequate treatment.

3. Other malignancies, including melanoma, basal cell carcinoma, Bartholin's gland cancer, and sarcoma, are rare in the vulva. The vulva may be the site of secondary cancer from the endometrium, cervix, vagina, or distant sites (e.g., lymphoma and leukemia).

V. DISORDERS OF THE CERVIX

A. CERVICITIS

1. Acute gonorrheal cervicitis is infection of the columnar epithelium of the endocervix by Neisseria gonorrhoeae. The primary symptom is a purulent, thick, creamy yellow discharge, although many infections are asymptomatic. Cervicitis is often associated with infection of the periurethral (Skene's) glands. (See Section II for treatment).

2. Chronic nonspecific cervicitis In the majority of adolescents the columnar epithelium of the endocervix is found on the portio vaginalis of the cervix surrounding the external os. This epithelium is gradually undergoing transformation to a metaplastic type of squamous epithelium, but it is only a single cell layer in thickness, so infection of the underlying cervical stroma by organisms which normally inhabit the vagina is common. The transformation process leads to a plugging of the numerous crypts and tunnels of endocervical mucosa by squamous epithelium, giving rise to **nabothian cysts.**

a. Diagnosis Symptoms: many patients are asymptomatic; a mucoid type of diarrhea is frequently the only symptom.

Signs: a red, granular, friable area surrounding the external cervical os; excessive mucus production.

Laboratory tests: cytologic examination reveals columnar and metaplastic squamous epithelial cells scattered among the normal squamous epithelial cells; biopsy demonstrates endocervical type of mucosa.

b. Treatment No treatment is required in asymptomatic patients. The endocervical mucosa will eventually be replaced physiologically by a stratified squamous epithelium. If leukorrhea is a complaint, cryosurgery or electrocoagulation of the columnar epithelium is beneficial. Malignant disease should be excluded by biopsy beforehand.

3. Chronic cervicitis secondary to old obstetric lacerations

a. Diagnosis Leukorrhea is the chief symptom. The discharge varies from thick, white mucus to frank pus; lower abdominal and low back discomfort, dyspareunia, infertility, and urinary symptoms (frequency, urgency, dysuria) occur sometimes; the cervix is distorted by old lacerations and is erythematous and edematous; cervical hypertrophy occurs in long-standing cases. Must be distinguished from early neoplastic disease by cytological examination and punch biopsy.

b. Treatment Medical: antibiotic therapy guided by culture and sensitivity may be helpful in chronic cervicitis associated with infertility. Surgical: electrocoagulation, cryosurgery, repair of deep cervical lacerations, or partial cervicectomy may be required.

B. CERVICAL POLYPS These benign neoplasms usually arise from the endocervix and present as fleshy, polypoid structures at or near the external cervical os.

1. Diagnosis

a. Symptoms May be asymptomatic and discovered during a routine pelvic examination; intermenstrual or postcoital bleeding.

b. Signs A red, polypoid structure in the cervical canal at or near the external cervical os.

c. Differential diagnosis Distinguish from polypoid cancers and sarcomas arising from the cervix or endometrial cavity.

2. Treatment Most polyps are pedunculated and have a small base; they can be removed by grasping the pedicle with a clamp and rotating the polyp until it separates. All polyps should be submitted for pathologic examination because of the small risk of malignancy (less than 1%). All cervical polyps are infected. Acute salpingitis rarely follows polypectomy. Antibiotic therapy should be given if it occurs.

C. DYSPLASIA AND CARCINOMA-IN-SITU OF THE CERVIX Dysplasia is a disorder in the maturation of the squamous epithelium of the cervix which in some patients becomes progressively more severe and results in malignancy. It is graded cytologically and histologically as mild, moderate, or severe. The end-stage of the dysplastic process is carcinoma-in-situ which will eventually lead to invasive squamous cell cancer of the cervix if it is not treated (see Fig. 11-2).

1. Diagnosis   Usually there are no symptoms or signs of dysplasia or carcinoma-in-situ. The cervix appears normal to gross inspection. The mucosa involved in the intraepithelial neoplastic process will be nonstaining to strong iodine (Lugol's) solution (Schiller test).

Colposcopic findings are often abnormal: white epithelium, coarse punctation, mosaicism, and atypical blood vessels.

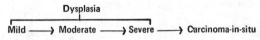

Fig. 11-2. The spectrum of intraepithelial
neoplasia of the cervix

Cervical punch biopsy of nonstaining areas on the Schiller test is moderately accurate. Colposcopically-directed biopsies are more accurate. Cold-knife cone biopsy (Fig. 11-3) with dilatation and curettage may be necessary if the process extends into the endocervical canal.

2. Treatment   **Mild dysplasia** is managed by careful observation with repeated clinical and cytologic examinations every 6 months in the expectation of spontaneous regression.

Moderate and **severe dysplasia** and **carcinoma-in-situ** should be treated by eradication of the abnormal epithelium. This requires accurate identification of the involved area. Colposcopy is helpful in this regard. Small areas may be completely removed with the punch biopsy forceps. More extensive lesions require electrocoagulation, cryosurgery, or cold-knife cone biopsy. The latter is considered preferable in severe dysplasia and carcinoma-in-situ because it affords accurate histological assessment of the extent and degree of neoplasia.

Warning   Dysplasia and carcinoma-in-situ may be found on the periphery of an invasive carcinoma. The accepted treatment of intraepithelial neoplasia is totally inadequate for invasive cancer of the cervix.

D. CANCER OF THE CERVIX   This is the second most common malignancy of the female reproductive tract (after endometrial carcinoma). It is rare before 20 years of age and reaches a peak between the ages of 45 and 55. Squamous cell cancer comprises 90% of cervical cancers. The remainder are adenocarcinomas, mixed types (adenosquamous), sarcomas, and metastatic neoplasms. Squamous cell cancer is related to sexual activity; early sexual exposure and promiscuity are prominent factors in the epidemiology. An association has been established between cancer of the cervix and infection with Herpesvirus hominis, type 2. The neoplasm extends directly to adjacent structures and metastasizes via lymphatics to the pelvic lymph nodes and thence to the para-aortic lymph nodes.

1. Diagnosis

a. Symptoms   Abnormal vaginal bleeding or discharge, particularly intermenstrual or postcoital bleeding, is often the only symptom. Pain, anorexia, and weight loss are manifestations of far-advanced disease.

b. Signs   A papillary or ulcerative lesion on the cervix; induration of the adjacent vagina and parametria if the cancer spreads beyond the cervix.

c. Laboratory tests   Cytologic examination (6% of Pap smears are falsely negative in patients with invasive cancer), histopathologic examination of a punch biopsy is usually diagnostic.

d. X-rays   Intravenous urography may show ureteral obstruction with hydronephrosis or a nonfunctioning kidney in advanced disease. Chest x-ray may show metastases. Pelvic lymphangiography is helpful if it is unequivocally positive, but a negative lymphangiogram does not eliminate the possibility of microscopic involvement of the pelvic lymph nodes.

   e. Special tests Cystoscopy to evaluate the degree of bladder involvement. Proctosigmoidoscopy to determine if there is invasion of the bowel wall.

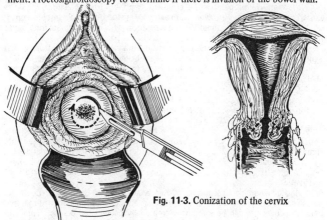

Fig. 11-3. Conization of the cervix

   2. Stage-grouping of cervical cancer is judged clinically and is defined according to the following International Classification:

Stage 0	Carcinoma-in-situ.
Stage I	Carcinoma strictly confined to the cervix.
I_a	Microinvasive carcinoma.
I_b	Frank stromal invasion (occult cancer should be labelled 'occ.').
Stage II	Carcinoma extends beyond the cervix but not onto the pelvic wall. The carcinoma involves the vagina, but not the lower third.
II_a	No obvious parametrial involvement. The vagina is invaded, but not the lower third.
II_b	Obvious parametrial involvement.
Stage III	Carcinoma extends onto the pelvic wall; on rectal examination, there is no cancer-free space between the tumor and the pelvic wall. Or, the tumor involves the lower third of the vagina. Or, hydronephrosis or nonfunctioning kidney.
III_a	No extension onto the pelvic wall. Vaginal involvement of the lower one-third.
III_b	Extension onto the pelvic wall and/or hydronephrosis or nonfunctioning kidney.
Stage IV	Carcinoma extends beyond the true pelvis or clinically involves the mucosa of the bladder or rectum.
IV_a	Spread of growth to adjacent organs (bladder or rectum with positive biopsy).
IV_b	Spread of growth to distant organs.

   3. Treatment

   a. Stage I Radiation therapy or radical hysterectomy with bilateral pelvic lymph node dissection can be used in Stage I disease. The surgical approach is preferable in the young patient because of the possibility of ovarian preservation and freedom from the interference with sexual function which frequently follows radiation therapy. Hysterectomy is also the treatment of choice in patients who are poor candidates for radiotherapy (e.g., those with ulcerative colitis, chronic pelvic infections, pelvic endometriosis with bowel adhesions, diverticulitis, or pregnancy).

Preoperative preparation: a complete work-up for metastatic disease is carried out (chest x-ray, intravenous urography, cystoscopy, and sigmoidoscopy); the patient must be in optimal general condition with normal circulating blood volume and laboratory values.

Postoperative care: particular attention must be paid to monitoring vital signs, urinary output, and retroperitoneal suction-drainage output. The bladder should be decompressed by indwelling catheter (urethral or suprapubic) until bladder function returns.

Complications of radical hysterectomy include: fistulas (ureterovaginal, vesicovaginal, rectovaginal), urinary tract infection, lymphocysts in the retroperitoneal space, and postoperative hemorrhage. The operative mortality is < 1%.

b. Stages II, III, IV   Radiation therapy is the treatment of choice for cervical cancer beyond Stage I as well as many cases of Stage I disease. Both external therapy and intracavitary radiation are required. About 8000 rads are administered over a period of 6–8 weeks in order to deliver a cancericidal dose.

Complications of radiation therapy are castration, radiation bowel injury (see Chapter 10), radiation cystitis, vaginal stenosis, and radiation necrosis of soft tissues.

4. Recurrent cervical cancer   Most recurrences are peripheral (in the regional pelvic lymph nodes or at distant sites) and are not amenable to therapy. Central recurrences can be effectively treated by **pelvic exenteration.** Total pelvic exenteration involves the surgical removal of the bladder and urethra, rectum and anus, vagina and part of the vulva, along with a radical hysterectomy and pelvic lymph node dissection. The patient is left with 2 abdominal stomas, one for the elimination of urine and the other for the fecal stream (colostomy). This operation has an operative mortality of 2–5%, and the morbidity is high with complications of intestinal obstruction, hemorrhage, sepsis, fistulas, pyelonephritis, thromboembolism, and electrolyte disturbances.

5. Prognosis   With optimal therapy, 5-year survival rates are as follows: Stage I, 85–90%; Stage II, 50%; Stage III, 30%; Stage IV, 10%.

E. CLEAR-CELL CARCINOMA OF THE CERVIX OR VAGINA   The en-utero exposure to DES (diethylstilbestrol) or related nonsteroidal estrogens has been cited recently as producing, in the majority of such young women, benign vaginal and cervical anomalies such as cervical hoods or collars, ridges and furrows, cockscomb appearance of the anterior cervical lip, vaginal septa, and vaginal adenosis (columnar epithelium containing mucin or metaplastic squamous epithelium). These abnormalities usually require no treatment.

A small number of these patients (estimated at less than 1/1000 exposed individuals) have developed clear-cell adenocarcinomas of the vagina or cervix. All exposed female offspring should be carefully examined for evidence of malignancy at intervals of not less than 6 months. The examination should include cytologic sampling of the vagina and cervix, careful palpation for evidence of submucosal nodules or induration, iodine staining, and colposcopy if available. Suspicious areas should be biopsied. Clear cell cancers should be treated by radical surgery or irradiation.

F. SARCOMA OF THE CERVIX   These malignancies are rare connective tissue tumors arising from mullerian duct elements which differentiate into mesodermal structures. Sarcoma botryoides, mixed mesodermal tumors, leiomyosarcoma, lymphosarcoma, and angiosarcoma are varieties. They may be encountered at any age but most often occur in postmenopausal women.

1. Diagnosis   *Symptoms:* abnormal vaginal bleeding or discharge. *Signs:*

a polypoid, fleshy tumor protruding from the cervix. *Laboratory tests:* biopsy of the lesion confirms the diagnosis.

2. Treatment These tumors respond poorly to radiation therapy. Surgical excision is preferred and may vary from simple hysterectomy to total pelvic exenteration, depending upon the extent of disease.

3. Prognosis Leiomyosarcoma arising in a cervical myoma carries the best prognosis, with 5-year survival rates in excess of 50%. Survival figures in the other sarcomas are considerably lower.

VI. DISORDERS OF THE CORPUS UTERI

A. LEIOMYOMA (FIBROID, FIBROMYOMA) These benign smooth muscle tumors arise from the myometrial cells. They are found in about one fifth of women over 35 years of age. Leiomyomas are more frequent in blacks than whites by a ratio of 3:1. They are usually multiple and are classified by their location in the uterine wall: submucous, intramural, or subserous. The submucous and subserous varieties may become pedunculated. Degenerative changes (hyalin, cystic, carneous, myxomatous, calcific, septic, and atrophic) may occur within the tumor. Because estrogens stimulate growth, and progestins predispose to carneous degeneration, oral contraceptive agents should be used with caution in patients with leiomyomas. Malignant degeneration (leiomyosarcoma) is rare, occurring in 0.1 to 0.5% of cases. The tumors undergo atrophy with the menopause.

1. Diagnosis

a. Symptoms Often asymptomatic. Abnormal bleeding (hypermenorrhea or intermenstrual bleeding). Symptoms due to pressure on neighboring structures, e.g., urinary frequency and urgency, constipation and pain on defecation. Severe pain is unusual and often is associated with carneous degeneration (during pregnancy), infection, or torsion of a pedunculated tumor. Large tumors may produce a sense of pressure or pelvic heaviness. Infertility (submucous myomas interfere with implantation).

b. Signs Enlarged, irregular contour of the uterus on bimanual examination. Pedunculated subserous myomas are palpable as adnexal masses. Pedunculated submucous myomas may be extruded through the cervix and come to lie in the upper part of the vagina.

c. Laboratory tests Chronic excessive blood loss may lead to anemia. Carneous degeneration and infection cause leukocytosis and elevation of the sedimentation rate.

d. X-ray findings Plain abdominal films may show a soft tissue tumor displacing bladder and/or rectum. Characteristic calcifications appear in the pelvis in some cases. Intravenous urography may demonstrate hydronephrosis and hydroureter due to compression by a large myomatous uterus.

e. Special tests Sonography defines a solid tumor enlarging the corpus. Sounding of the uterus confirms enlargement with elongation of the endometrial cavity. Exploration with a curette in the endometrial cavity outlines submucous tumors. Hysterography demonstrates enlargement and/or distortion of the endometrial cavity.

2. Differential diagnosis A myoma which is single and soft (due to cystic degeneration) may produce a symmetrical uterine enlargement simulating intrauterine pregnancy. Laparoscopic examination may be necessary to distinguish a pedunculated subserous myoma from a solid ovarian tumor.

3. Treatment Small asymptomatic leiomyomas require no treatment other than periodic examinations to estimate the growth rate. Myomectomy should be considered in the young, infertile woman who wishes to preserve reproductive function. Total hysterectomy is curative. The indications for hysterectomy are: evidence of rapid growth; hypermenorrhea producing anemia; pressure symptoms.

B. SARCOMA OF THE UTERUS (LEIOMYOSARCOMA, MIXED MESODER-MAL TUMOR, STROMAL-CELL SARCOMA

These rare connective tissue tumors arise from mesodermal differentiation of mullerian duct origin. Sarcoma botryoides occurs in infancy; the other sarcomas occur at any age, but are more frequent in postmenopausal women. A number of varieties of sarcoma are encountered in the uterus: leiomyosarcoma, mixed mesodermal tumors, stromal-cell sarcoma (including endolymphatic stromal myosis), carcinosarcoma, reticulum cell sarcoma, and angiosarcoma.

1. Diagnosis

a. Symptoms Abnormal bleeding or vaginal discharge; abdominal distention; urinary frequency and urgency; pelvic pressure.

b. Signs A fleshy, polypoid tumor protruding from the cervical canal; a rapidly enlarging myomatous uterus.

c. Laboratory tests Anemia and elevated sedimentation rate. Cytological examination may show sarcoma cells. Histopathologic examination of a biopsy or curettings is usually diagnostic.

d. X-ray findings Chest x-ray may demonstrate pulmonary metastases.

2. Differential diagnosis Rapidly growing leiomyomas and endometrial carcinoma simulate uterine sarcoma.

3. Treatment

a. Surgical Leiomyosarcoma: total hysterectomy and bilateral salpingo-oophorectomy. Mixed mesodermal tumors: preoperative irradiation followed by total abdominal hysterectomy and bilateral salpingo-oophorectomy. Stromal cell sarcomas: preoperative irradiation followed by total abdominal hysterectomy and bilateral salpingo-oophorectomy.

b. Radiation therapy may be of some palliative value in advanced disease.

c. Chemotherapy has palliative benefit only.

4. Prognosis Leiomyosarcomas arising in preexisting leiomyomas have a relatively good prognosis, particularly if they are 'low grade.' Mixed mesodermal tumors and stromal cell sarcomas carry a poor prognosis with less than 20% 5-year survival.

C. ENDOMETRIAL CARCINOMA

This lesion is an epithelial malignancy arising from the columnar cells of the endometrium; it represents the most common cancer of the female reproductive tract. It occurs primarily in postmenopausal women; in premenopausal women, it usually is associated with chronic anovulation (Stein–Leventhal syndrome). Adenomatous hyperplasia of the endometrium appears to be a precursor in some women. Chronic endogenous or exogenous estrogen stimulation of the endometrium in the absence of progesterone has been postulated as a possible cause. Obesity, hypertension and diabetes are frequent related conditions.

Histologically the tumor varies from slight atypia (carcinoma-in-situ) to large masses of poorly differentiated malignant endometrium deeply invading the myometrial wall, cervix, and adnexa. Metastases occur via the lymphatics to the regional pelvic and para-aortic lymph nodes, by peritoneal implantation, and by hematogenous spread to the lungs, liver, bone, and brain.

1. Diagnosis

a. Symptoms Postmenopausal bleeding; serous or sanguineous vaginal discharge; hypermenorrhea (prolonged bleeding) in the premenopausal patient.

b. Signs Uterus may be normal size or enlarged. Symmetrical enlargement suggests myometrial involvement. Bloody discharge from cervical canal.

c. Laboratory tests Cytologic examination is positive in only 40-80%.

d. X-ray findings Hysterosalpingography can be suspicious for endometrial carcinoma, but this test is unnecessary in most cases.

e. Special tests Cytologic sampling of the endometrial cavity. Endometrial biopsy. Fractional D and C is the most definitive diagnostic procedure.

2. Differential diagnosis Bleeding due to hormonal therapy. Cervical polyps. Cervical cancer. Atrophic vaginitis with bleeding. Uterine sarcoma.

3. Clinical staging (classification adopted by ACOG, 1976):

Stage 0	Carcinoma-in-situ. Histologic findings are suggestive of malignancy.
Stage I	Carcinoma is confined to the corpus.
I_a	Length of the uterine cavity is 8 cm or less.
I_b	Length of the uterine cavity is more than 8 cm.
G_1	Highly differentiated adenomatous carcinomas.
G_2	Differentiated adenomatous carcinomas with partly solid areas.
G_3	Predominantly solid or entirely undifferentiated carcinomas.
Stage II	Carcinoma involves the corpus and the cervix.
Stage III	Carcinoma extends outside the uterus but not outside the true pelvis.
Stage IV	Carcinoma extends outside the true pelvis or obviously involves the mucosa of the bladder or rectum. Bullous edema as such does not permit allotment of a case to Stage IV.

4. Treatment

a. Stage I_aG_1 Total abdominal hysterectomy with bilateral salpingo-oophorectomy.

b. Stage I_aG_2, Stage $I_bG_{1,2}$ Preoperative intracavitary radiation followed by total abdominal hysterectomy and bilateral salpingo-oophorectomy. Postoperative external radiation to the full pelvis should be added if there is myometrial penetration more than one third the thickness of the myometrium.

c. Stage $I_{a,b}G_3$ Preoperative intracavitary and external radiation therapy to the full pelvis and the para-aortic lymph nodes followed by total abdominal hysterectomy and bilateral salpingo-oophorectomy.

d. Stage II Preoperative intracavitary and external radiation therapy to the full pelvis followed by total abdominal hysterectomy and bilateral salpingo-oophorectomy. Radical hysterectomy with bilateral pelvic lymph node dissection may be done in patients in good general condition as an alternative if radiation therapy is contraindicated.

e. Stage III May require pelvic exenteration.

f. Stage IV Progestin therapy in high doses provides effective palliation in the majority of patients with widespread metastases. One treatment schedule is: medroxyprogesterone acetate (Depo-Provera) 400 mg IM, 3 times weekly for 6–8 weeks followed by 400 mg monthly.

5. Prognosis Small, well-differentiated lesions confined to the endometrium have 5-year survival rates in the 95% range. Anaplastic lesions with extrauterine spread have less than 10% 5-year survival.

VII. DISORDERS OF THE FALLOPIAN TUBES

A. ACUTE SALPINGITIS Acute infection of the oviducts (and adjacent ovaries and pelvic peritoneum) most often is due to Neisseria gonorrhoeae ascending via the endometrial cavity. Initially the endosalpinx is involved with a purulent exudate which escapes from the fimbriated extremity and bathes the ovaries and pelvic peritoneum in pus. Infection by secondary organisms may complicate the clinical picture.

1. Diagnosis

a. Symptoms Insidious onset of bilateral lower abdominal and pelvic pain, often following a menstrual period; fever with or without chills; nausea with or without vomiting; fatigue and general malaise.

b. Signs Temperature elevation up to 40° C; bilateral lower abdominal tenderness, rigidity and rebound tenderness; abdominal distention with hypoactive peristalsis; purulent cervical discharge; pain on motion of the cervix; bilateral adnexal tenderness on bimanual examination.

    c. Laboratory tests Leukocytosis with a shift to the left; elevated sedimentation rate; gram stain of a cervical smear may show gram-negative intracellular diplococci, but culture identification of N. gonorrhoeae is necessary (see Section II).

    d. X-ray findings Plain films of the abdomen are nonspecific; ileus usually is present.

    e. Special tests Culdocentesis produces cloudy fluid with numerous polymorphonuclear leukocytes on microscopic examination. This material should be cultured.

    2. Differential diagnosis includes: acute appendicitis; ectopic pregnancy; septic abortion; endometriosis; acute gastroenteritis; regional ileitis; and diverticulitis.

    3. Treatment Uncomplicated mild infections may be treated on an outpatient basis with bed rest at home and a single injection of aqueous penicillin G (4.8 million units) 1 hour after the oral administration of 1 gm of probenecid. Alternatively, oral tetracycline HCl (500 mg 4 times daily for 10 days) may be used.

    Patients with severe infections should be hospitalized at bed rest in semi-Fowler's position. IV fluids are necessary to correct dehydration. Aqueous penicillin G is given IV (10 million units every 8 hours), and kanamycin sulfate is injected IM (15 mg/kg of body weight daily in 3 divided doses). With improvement in the clinical condition, parenteral antibiotics may be discontinued and oral antibiotics (e.g., ampicillin, 500 mg 4 times daily) substituted for a total course of 10 days.

    Superimposed anaerobic infection or pelvic abscess formation should be suspected in patients who fail to respond. Anaerobic culture and sensitivity studies may reveal Bacteroides fragilis in which case clindamycin, chloramphenicol, or carbenicillin should be added to the treatment regimen. Pelvic (tubo-ovarian) abscess can be palpated as a mass in the adnexa or cul-de-sac. Failure of the mass to regress under intensive antibiotic therapy requires laparotomy. A total hysterectomy and bilateral salpingo-oophorectomy usually are necessary.

B. CHRONIC SALPINGITIS Low-grade infection of the fallopian tubes results from recurrent acute infections producing altered pathophysiologic states such as pyosalpinges, hydrosalpinges, extensive pelvic adhesions, and fibrosis.

    1. Diagnosis

    a. Symptoms A history of previous pelvic infections; chronic pelvic pain; dysmenorrhea of an acquired type; dyspareunia; infertility.

    b. Signs Fever is absent or minimal; tenderness on motion of the cervix; adnexal masses or thickening.

    c. Laboratory tests Leukocyte count and sedimentation rate are normal unless there is an acute reinfection.

    d. Special tests Laparoscopic examination may be necessary to make the diagnosis.

    2. Differential diagnosis Chronic pelvic pain of obscure etiology. Ectopic pregnancy, ovarian neoplasm. Pelvic endometriosis, and inflammatory bowel disease should be considered.

    3. Treatment Mild to moderate cases may be treated symptomatically with bed rest, heat to the abdomen, and mild analgesics. The relief of infertility due to bilateral tubal occlusion requires tuboplastic surgery.

    Severe cases resulting in incapacitating pain require laparotomy. Total hysterectomy with bilateral salpingo-oophorectomy usually is necessary. Estrogen replacement therapy (conjugated estrogens 0.625 mg daily for 25 days each month) should be given postoperatively to prevent menopausal atrophy of the vulva and vagina and loss of mineral from the bones.

VIII. OVARIAN TUMORS

The ovary gives rise to a greater variety of tumors than any other organ in the body. These tumors may develop at any time in life, although they are more frequent in peri- and postmenopausal women. They may be cystic or solid, benign or malignant (or of borderline malignancy), and hormonally active or inactive. One of the best classifications of these tumors is based on their cell or tissue origin in the ovary:

Coelomic (surface) epithelium Serous cystadenoma–cystadenocarcinoma; endometrioid cystadenoma (endometrial cyst)–endometrioid carcinoma; mucinous cystadenoma–cystadenocarcinoma.

Specialized stroma Granulosa-theca cell tumor; Sertoli-Leydig cell tumor; thecoma (luteoma).

Nonspecialized stroma Fibroma; fibromyoma; Brenner tumor; fibroadenoma; cystadenofibroma; sarcoma.

Germ cell Dysgerminoma. Teratoma: benign cystic (dermoid); malignant (embryonal carcinoma, endodermal sinus tumor, choriocarcinoma, various mature and immature teratomas). Gonadoblastoma.

Parovarian tumors Parovarian cyst; mesonephroma; hilar cell tumor; adrenal rest tumor.

Functional cysts of the ovary (follicular and corpus luteum cysts) are the most frequent cause of ovarian enlargement in women during the reproductive years. They rarely are larger than 5 cm in diameter and usually regress within 1 menstrual cycle. They are not true neoplasms.

Ovarian cysts larger than 5 cm in diameter or smaller cysts which enlarge or fail to regress after 2 months' observation should be considered neoplastic in women during the reproductive years. Any degree of ovarian enlargement in the prepubertal or postmenopausal patient should be considered neoplastic. Cancer of the ovary, although it is third in the order of frequency of female genital malignancies, is the leading cause of death.

1. Diagnosis

a. Symptoms The ovary is a 'silent organ'; small tumors are usually asymptomatic and are discovered during the routine physical examination. Larger tumors may produce abdominal distention or a sense of weight or pressure in the pelvis. Symptoms of ovarian cancer often do not appear until there are widespread peritoneal metastases which cause malignant ascites with abdominal distention and interference with bowel function. Menstrual disturbances secondary to ovarian tumors are infrequent (17%). Torsion of an ovarian tumor may cause sudden, severe abdominal and pelvic pain.

b. Signs Cystic or solid adnexal mass on pelvic examination. Bilaterality, nodularity, and fixation are signs suspicious for malignancy. Ascites accompanying a pelvic mass suggests malignancy with peritoneal spread. (exception: Meigs' syndrome is ascites and right hydrothorax secondary to benign ovarian tumors such as fibroma or thecoma). Huge ovarian tumors, particularly those of the mucinous variety, may distend the entire abdomen and simulate ascites.

c. Laboratory tests There are no specific abnormalities.

d. X-ray findings Chest x-ray may show metastases or hydrothorax. A plain film of the abdomen may demonstrate a benign cystic teratoma (dermoid) with tooth structure or relative radiolucency of the contents (sebum) (it also helps to demonstrate ascites). Intravenous urography defines the course of the ureters and detects bladder compression. Barium enema shows the relationship of the large intestine to the lesion and excludes primary disease of the colon (e.g., diverticulitis and primary bowel cancer). Upper GI and small bowel series help in certain cases by demonstrating small bowel involvement by the tumor; it also excludes gastric carcinoma with metastases to the pelvis (Krukenberg tumor). Computerized tomography is useful in selected cases.

e. Special tests Sonography may define the nature of an adnexal mass, whether solid or cystic, and its relationship to the uterine corpus. Laparoscopy. Paracentesis or thoracentesis with examination of cell button for malignant cells may be diagnostic.

2. Differential diagnosis includes; leiomyomata uteri; chronic salpingo-oophoritis; diverticulitis; colon cancer; pelvic kidney; and metastatic cancer to the ovaries from the breast, endometrium, GI tract, pancreas thyroid, kidney, or adrenal.

3. Treatment Surgical removal is the primary treatment of all ovarian neoplasms. Preservation of ovarian tissue is desirable in young women with benign or 'borderline' tumors. Malignant tumors require total hysterectomy, bilateral salpingo-oophorectomy and removal of as much extra-ovarian neoplastic tissue as possible. Adjunctive therapy includes chemotherapy and radiation to the pelvis or entire abdomen.

4. Stage-grouping of patients with ovarian cancer is based upon the findings at the time of operation:

Stage I	Growth limited to ovaries.
I_a	Growth limited to one ovary, no ascites.
I_b	Growth limited to both ovaries, no ascites.
I_c	Growth limited to one or both ovaries; ascites present with malignant cells.
Stage II	Growth involving one or both ovaries with pelvic extension.
II_a	Extension or metastases to uterus or tubes only.
II_b	Extension to other pelvic tissues.
Stage III	Growth involving one or both ovaries with widespread intraperitoneal metastases to the abdomen (omentum, small intestine, or its mesentery).
Stage IV	Growth involving one or both ovaries with metastases outside the peritoneal cavity.
Special Category	Cases which are thought to be ovarian carcinoma (surgery or therapy not yet performed).

5. Prognosis Benign tumors are cured by surgical removal. The overall survival for ovarian cancer, however, is only 20-30% because most are diagnosed in the late stages. Survival rates in the range of 80% can be expected if ovarian cancer is detected when it is confined to one ovary (Stage I).

IX. ENDOMETRIOSIS

Endometriosis is the occurrence of functional endometrial tissue outside the uterus, usually involving the pelvic peritoneum (cul-de-sac, ovaries, serosa of the uterus, bladder, or colon), although it may be found at distant sites (umbilicus, cesarean section scars, perineum, inguinal canal).

There are 3 theories of pathogenesis, all of which may be operative: retrograde flow of endometrial fragments through the fallopian tubes at the time of menstruation (Sampson's theory); differentiation of the peritoneum into endometrium (coelomic metaplasia); and vascular dissemination (endometrial tissue has been found in lymph nodes as well as in the lung suggesting spread via lymphatic and venous channels).

The disease is diagnosed most often in women during the fourth decade, although it is seen as early as the second decade. It occurs more often in the higher socioeconomic levels (college graduates), and the ratio of whites to blacks is 2 : 1.

The ectopic endometrium is responsive to cyclic hormonal stimulation by the ovaries with periodic micromenstruation causing inflammation and dense adhesions. Grossly, the lesions are small, dark blue or purplish areas on the peritoneal surfaces resembling 'powder burns' or 'blueberry spots.' Large endometriotic cysts of the ovary, filled with chocolate-brown old blood, are often called 'chocolate cysts.' Microscopically, endometrial tissue (glands and stroma) can often be identified. Malignant change in peritoneal endometriosis is not common

1. Diagnosis

a. Symptoms May be asymptomatic and found incidentally at laparotomy for some other condition. Acquired dysmenorrhea is the most frequent symptom—typically, severe, disabling pain of a grinding character starts several days prior to the onset of menses and reaches a peak during menstruation; as the process progresses, the pain may be present throughout the menstrual cycle. Rectal or bladder tenesmus (rarely, there is rectal bleeding). Deep dyspareunia. Infertility is a frequently associated problem.

b. Signs Shotty, tender nodules in the cul-de-sac are best appreciated by combined rectovaginal examination just prior to menstruation. Large adherent, cystic adnexal masses (unilateral or bilateral) may be palpable bimanually.

c. Laboratory tests are not distinctive.

d. X-ray findings Barium enema may reveal a constricting or submucosal lesion of the colon.

e. Special tests Sigmoidoscopy or colonoscopy may show extrinsic compression; cystoscopy; laparoscopy is helpful sometimes.

2. Differential diagnosis includes: salpingitis; ovarian cancer; colon cancer; diverticulitis; and inflammatory bowel disease.

3. Complications Infertility. Rupture of endometrioma produces a chemical peritonitis (15% of female patients who enter the hospital with acute abdominal pain have endometriosis). Obstruction of the small or large intestine. Ureteral obstruction.

4. Treatment

a. Medical Mild endometriosis may require only analgesics during periods of dysmenorrhea.

Pregnancy is beneficial because it interrupts the cyclic hormonal stimulus and episodic micromenstruation.

Hormonal treatment (pseudopregnancy) produces several months of amenorrhea: (a) Norethynodrel with mestranol (Enovid): 2.5 mg daily for 1 week, 5 mg daily for 1 week, 10 mg daily for 2 weeks, then 20 mg daily for 6–9 months. (b) Danazol: 400 mg twice daily for 3 to 9 months (this agent inhibits pituitary gonadotrophins and has possible side effects of masculinization and fluid retention).

X-ray castration is no longer considered appropriate therapy.

b. Surgical Conservative—excision or cauterization of implants, suspension of retroverted uterus in the young patient who desires preservation of childbearing potential.

Modified radical—hysterectomy with ovarian preservation.

Radical—hysterectomy with bilateral salpingo-oophorectomy. This operation is required in very extensive endometriosis or in symptomatic patients over 35 years of age.

5. Prognosis Hormonal therapy will not cure endometriosis but the majority of patients are 'improved' and some may be able to conceive. However, a significantly higher proportion of infertile patients will conceive after conservative surgery, so this approach is preferable. 50% of patients undergoing conservative surgery require subsequent therapy for symptoms due to progression of the disease. Surgical castration is curative but is a drastic step in the younger woman with endometriosis. Only 6% of patients have further difficulties after hysterectomy alone, so preservation of the ovaries is desirable in patients under 40 years of age unless the ovaries are involved in large endometriotic cysts.

X. PELVIC FLOOR RELAXATION

Weakening of the connective and muscular tissues supporting the pelvic viscera results in various combinations and degrees of prolapse of the uterus, vagina, bladder, urethra, rectum and peritoneum of the cul-de-sac (uterine descensus, cystocele, urethrocele, rectocele, and enterocele).

The etiologic factors are: childbirth injuries (submucosal stretching and tearing) to the supporting structures during childbirth in multiparas; the forces of gravity imposed by the upright position; increased intraabdominal pressure with various physical activities such as climbing, lifting, coughing, straining, sneezing; obesity; loss of hormonal influence on the tissues postmenopausally; congenital weaknesses (the condition is occasionally encountered in nulligravidas and spina bifida occulta is often an associated anomaly in these patients).

1. Diagnosis

a. Symptoms Sense of pelvic pressure or 'falling-out.' Mass protruding from the vaginal introitus. Various urinary complaints in patients with cystourethrocele (incomplete emptying; loss of urine with coughing, straining, sneezing [stress incontinence]; inability to void without digital pressure against the vagina). Problems associated with defecation in those with rectocele (constipation, incomplete evacuation without digital compression against the vagina). Low backache.

b. Signs A soft, compressible mass which bulges through the vaginal introitus with straining may represent the anterior vaginal wall (cystourethrocele) or posterior vaginal wall (rectocele and/or enterocele).

A firm mass presenting at or protruding through the vaginal introitus usually represents the cervix (and corpus) uteri. A first-degree prolapse is one in which the cervix descends to the lower third of the vagina. In second- and third-degree prolapse, the cervix protrudes through the vaginal introitus, and a fourth-degree prolapse involves a protrusion of the entire uterus.

There may be ulceration of the vaginal and/or cervical mucosa due to pressure and vascular stasis.

Stress incontinence of urine can be demonstrated by having the patient cough during the examination.

A rectocele is diagnosed by finding a large anterior sacculation of the rectum on combined rectovaginal examination. The external anal sphincter muscle may be disrupted.

Enterocele is a downward herniation of the cul-de-sac peritoneum into the rectovaginal septum and is best demonstrated as a bulge in the septum which will not admit the rectal finger. The detection of a small, high enterocele may require examining the patient rectovaginally in the standing position. A large enterocele may present as a soft, compressible mass bulging through the vaginal introitus. Small bowel may occupy the mass.

c. Laboratory tests Urinalysis may reveal evidence of cystitis due to infection of residual urine in large cystoceles.

d. X-ray findings A bead-chain cystogram may be helpful in demonstrating cystocele, urethrocele and loss of the vesicourethral angle. Small bowel series may demonstrate intestine in an enterocele when the diagnosis is in doubt.

e. Special tests Cystoscopy. Cystometrogram helps distinguish atonic and hypertonic (neurogenic) bladder problems. Cine studies with intravesical and intraurethral pressure studies at rest, while straining, and during micturition may be required in some individuals with complex voiding problems (combined urge and stress incontinence). Biopsy of ulcerating lesions in prolapsed tissues should be done to rule out neoplastic disease.

2. Complications

Chronic urinary tract infection in large cystoceles with large volumes of residual urine. Acute urinary retention. Fecal impaction. Rupture of enterocele with evisceration. Trophic ulceration of cervical and/or vaginal mucosa.

3. Treatment

a. Medical Kegel exercises to strengthen the levator ani and perineal muscles. Correct obesity and chronic cough. Treat urinary tract infections. Topical estrogens (conjugated estrogen or dienestrol cream applied to the vagina each night at bedtime) if the patient is postmenopausal and the mucosa is estrogen deficient. Pessaries, in patients who are poor surgical risks.

b. Surgical Operative intervention is best deferred in the young individual until there is no longer a desire for childbearing.

Vaginal hysterectomy with anterior colporrhaphy and posterior colpoperineoplasty is the operation most commonly performed because the condition is usually a combination of uterine prolapse, cystourethrocele and rectocele. Any portion of this operation can be omitted if the condition does not warrant it.

Vaginal obliterative procedures, such as the LeFort colpocleisis, should be avoided.

Retropubic urethral suspension (Marshall-Marchetti-Krantz operation) is indicated in patients with severe stress incontinence; it may be combined with vaginal repair when necessary.

4. Prognosis
A properly selected and executed surgical procedure will provide good support with relief of symptoms and maintenance of sexual function. A frequent cause of recurrence is the failure to recognize and repair an enterocele at the time of the operative procedure.

XI. DISORDERS OF PREGNANCY

A. ECTOPIC PREGNANCY is the implantation of a fertilized ovum outside the endometrial cavity. The majority (90%) occur in the fallopian tube; the remainder are in the uterine cornu, cervix, ovary, or peritoneal cavity (abdominal pregnancy).

The incidence is about 1 in 150 pregnancies. Factors which favor extrauterine implantation are previous salpingitis or tuboplastic surgery, congenital abnormalities, and endometriosis.

When an ovum implants in the fallopian tube, the invading trophoblast weakens the thin wall of the tube and rupture occurs, or the pregnancy separates intraluminally leading to tubal abortion into the peritoneal cavity. This usually takes place before the twelfth week of gestation. Cornual pregnancies may develop for 4 or 5 months, and rupture of such a pregnancy is often catastrophic because of massive hemorrhage. The rare abdominal pregnancy results from primary implantation of the egg or from peritoneal reimplantation of a conceptus following tubal abortion. Abdominal pregnancies may progress to term although the vast majority of such fetuses succumb and undergo calcification with the formation of a lithopedion, or they become necrotic and infected.

Decidual and myometrial changes occur in the uterus even though the pregnancy is extrauterine.

1. Diagnosis

a. Symptoms Amenorrhea—one or two missed periods or a scanty last menstrual period. Irregular vaginal bleeding. Abdominal pain—usually unilateral (pain may be absent or mild and cramping in unruptured tubal pregnancy, sudden and severe pain occurs with rupture); extravasation of blood within the peritoneal cavity causes upper abdominal or shoulder pain (referred from diaphragmatic irritation).

b. Signs Presumptive signs of pregnancy—
      Chadwick's sign—bluish discoloration of the vaginal mucosa
      Hegar's sign—softening of the uterine isthmus
      slight enlargement and softness of the uterine corpus
Pain on palpation of the adnexal area or on motion of the cervix; cul-de-sac

or adnexal mass (usually soft and ill-defined); afebrile or low-grade fever (usually less than 38° C); signs of hypovolemia in the presence of intraperitoneal hemorrhage; Cullen's sign—bluish discoloration around the umbilicus—is sometimes present in ruptured ectopic pregnancies.

c. Laboratory tests No specific abnormal tests in unruptured cases. Pregnancy test may be positive or negative; it is not very helpful. In ruptured cases mild leukocytosis and acute anemia from blood loss.

d. Special tests Sonography may identify an ectopic pregnancy. Laparoscopy may be required for the diagnosis of unruptured ectopic pregnancy. Nonclotting blood is obtained by culdocentesis in the presence of rupture. Laparotomy is indicated as a diagnostic step when ectopic pregnancy is suspected but cannot be proved.

2. Differential diagnosis Ruptured corpus luteum cyst with intraperitoneal bleeding. Abortion of uterine pregnancy. Salpingitis. Appendicitis. Twisted ovarian cyst.

3. Complications Exsanguination and death may occur if ruptured ectopic pregnancy is not recognized and treated.

4. Treatment Unruptured: operation is required; salpingectomy usually is necessary, but the tube can be salvaged in some cases.

Ruptured ectopic pregnancy: transfuse as necessary; immediate laparotomy to control the bleeding; rupture of an interstitial (uterine portion of fallopian tube) pregnancy may call for massive blood replacement and hysterectomy if the defect in the ruptured uterus cannot be rapidly and safely repaired.

B. ABORTION is the termination of pregnancy before viability of the fetus (about 24 weeks gestation). Between 10 and 15% of all intrauterine pregnancies abort spontaneously, usually before the 16th week of pregnancy. The majority of these are related to anomalous development of the fertilized egg. Often only the trophoblastic elements develop and the embryo is absent (blighted ovum). Late (second trimester) abortion, on the other hand, is frequently related to uterine factors, e.g., incompetent internal cervical os, congenital anomalies, or uterine tumors (myomas).

1. Diagnosis **Threatened abortion**—slight bleeding or cramping. **Inevitable abortion**—bleeding, cramping, and cervical effacement and dilatation. **Incomplete abortion**—expulsion of a portion of the products of conception, usually accompanied by heavy bleeding. **Complete abortion**—expulsion of the entire conceptus with cessation of cramping and marked diminution in bleeding.

2. Differential diagnosis includes: ectopic pregnancy; hydatidiform mole; leiomyomata uteri; and membranous dysmenorrhea.

3. Complications Anemia, hypovolemic shock (if bleeding is severe), and sepsis (if secondary infection occurs).

4. Treatment Threatened abortion should be treated conservatively with bed rest and analgesics. 50% will progress to inevitable, incomplete, or complete abortion.

Inevitable and incomplete abortions are potentially serious. Blood should be typed and cross-matched if the bleeding is severe. The uterus should be evacuated by suction or by dilatation and curettage. Oxytocin should be administered (10 to 20 units in an IV infusion of 5% dextrose in 0.9% saline).

C. HYDATIDIFORM MOLE This is a degenerative process in the developing trophoblast characterized by trophoblastic proliferation and hydropic enlargement of the chorionic villi producing many grape-like vesicles. The embryo is usually absent. Bilateral theca-lutein cysts of the ovaries are a frequent accompaniment due to the stimulus of excessive chorionic gonadotrophin.

1. Diagnosis

a. Symptoms Presumptive symptoms of pregnancy (missed menses, nausea, urinary frequency, breast tenderness). Vaginal bleeding (usually begins by

6-8 weeks). Grape-like tissue may be expelled.

b. Signs Uterus is larger than expected in 50% of patients. Bilateral cystic enlargement of ovaries in 50% of patients. Clusters of grape-like tissue may be found in vagina. Toxemia of pregnancy (hypertension, edema, and proteinuria) may occur in the second trimester.

c. Laboratory tests Pregnancy test is positive. Human chorionic gonado trophin (HCG) titer in the urine is markedly elevated, it may be as high as 1-2 million IU/24 hours. Anemia if bleeding is prolonged.

d. X-ray findings Percutaneous hysterography using urographin will show a typical honeycomb appearance and absence of the amniotic sac.

e. Special tests Uterine sound introduced gently through the cervical canal will meet no resistance because of the absence of membranes. Ultrasonography is the most easily performed and reliable diagnostic test.

2. Differential diagnosis Intrauterine pregnancy with twins, polyhydramnios, or leiomyomata uteri. Ovarian tumors complicating intrauterine pregnancy.

3. Complications Hemorrhage; infection; or malignant change, 20% progress to chorioadenoma destruens (invasive mole) or choriocarcinoma.

4. Treatment Suction evacuation of the uterus with simultaneous IV infusion of oxytocin (40 to 50 units/liter of 5% dextrose). Dilatation and curettage one week post-evacuation. Follow-up: contraception for at least 1 year; HCG titers weekly until negative for 3 weeks, then monthly for 6 months, and bimonthly for another 6 months; periodic chest x-ray.

D. CHORIOADENOMA DESTRUENS (INVASIVE MOLE) AND CHORIOCARCINOMA

Chorioadenoma destruens exists when chorionic tissue capable of forming villi remains in the uterine wall or elsewhere following evacuation of a hydatidiform mole. If only proliferating trophoblastic cells without villi are found after a mole or a 'normal' pregnancy, the process is classified as a choriocarcinoma.

1. Diagnosis

a. Symptoms Recent term pregnancy, abortion or mole; persistent bleeding; failure to resume normal menstrual pattern.

b. Signs Persistent bilateral ovarian cystic enlargement.

c. Laboratory tests Persistence of HCG titers or reappearance of abnormal titers after a period of normalcy.

d. X-ray findings Pulmonary metastases.

e. Special tests to search for metastases: liver-spleen scan; CT scan; brain scan, EEG, cerebral arteriogram.

2. Complications Massive bleeding from invasion of the uterine wall or from metastatic deposits. Widespread metastases.

3. Treatment

a. Chemotherapy is the treatment of choice.

Single-agent therapy is used except in the 'high-risk group' (see below) and is continued until the HCG titer has been normal for 12 consecutive weeks. Either of these regimens is recommended:

(1) Methotrexate: 0.4 mg/kg/day IM for 5 days; repeated at intervals of 2-4 weeks, depending upon the recovery from toxic side effects (bone marrow depression).

(2) Actinomycin D: 12 μg/kg/day by IV infusion daily for 5 days; repeated at intervals of 2-4 weeks as above.

In the high-risk group (those in whom therapy has been delayed for more than 4 months, or HCG titers are greater than 100,000 IU/24 hours, or metastases have occurred to brain, liver, or bowel, or the tumor is resistant to single-agent therapy), combination therapy with methotrexate, actinomycin-D, and chlorambucil should be used.

4. Prognosis Before chemotherapy, choriocarcinoma was a uniformly fatal disease. Now survival rates of greater than 50% can be expected.

12

UROLOGY

Emil A. Tanagho, MD

I. GENERAL PRINCIPLES OF DIAGNOSIS

Essential steps for the evaluation of a urologic patient include:
- Complete history with emphasis on urologic symptoms.
- Complete physical examination with emphasis on the abdomen, external genitalia, and rectum.
- Examination of the urine and prostatic or urethral secretions.
- Kidney function tests, especially the PSP (phenolsulfonphthalein) test.
- Radiographic studies, including excretory urography.
- Special tests: cystography, urethrography, retrograde pyelography, or endoscopic examinations.

A. COMMON SYMPTOMS OF GENITOURINARY DISORDERS

1. Pain   One must differentiate between kidney pain (dull, aching pain in the costovertebral angle) and ureteral pain (acute, colicky, radicular pain referred from the costovertebral angle to the pubic region or the scrotum). Suprapubic pain in spasms is typical of excessive bladder distention; this pain can be extremely severe. Prostatic pain is sensed as heaviness in the perineum or discomfort deep in the rectum. Testicular pain is felt in the scrotum (unilaterally or bilaterally).

2. Hematuria   This symptom can be initial (blood at the start of voiding), terminal (blood at the end of voiding), or total (blood throughout the voiding).

3. Voiding symptoms are: frequency, difficulty in initiation of urination, hesitancy, terminal dribbling, burning, urgency, urge incontinence, and interrupted, weak stream.

4. Other symptoms   Urinary incontinence, retention of urine, pyuria, hematuria, chyluria, oliguria, or anuria. Genital symptoms in the male include partial or unsustained erection, penile curvature, premature ejaculation, or hemospermia. In the female, genital symptoms are primarily vaginal pain, urethral pain, and dyspareunia.

B. UROLOGIC LABORATORY EXAMINATION

1. Examination of the urine is essential. In the male, one should examine a clean midstream specimen; in the female, it is best to obtain a specimen by catheterization.

Test the urine for pH, albumin, sugar, and ketones.

Microscopic examination   Place a drop of the centrifuged urine sediment under a cover slip on a glass slide and examine microscopically. Normal urine contains no red blood cells, no pus cells, no bacteria, and no crystals.

A drop of the sediment is spread on a slide, dried lightly under medium heat, flooded with triple strength methylene blue for about 20 seconds, washed, then dried again, and examined under the microscope. Look particularly for **bacteria** or **pus cells** (white blood cells). The presence of either requires further evaluation. Bacteria on the stained smear indicates that there are at least 10,000 organisms per ml of urine; this is pathognomonic of clinical infection. (If infection is suspected, obtain a urine culture.) The stained specimen should also be scrutinized for epithelial cells and possibly **malignant cells.**

Urine can be tested for its **calcium content** by the Sulkowitch test. 2 ml of Sulkowitch reagent are added to 5 ml of urine, and the amount of calcium is estimated by the speed of precipitation and the intensity of the cloud. It is graded from 0 to 4.

2. Renal function and transport of urine along the urinary tract are evaluated by the PSP test.

Immediately after the patient has voided, exactly 1 ml of the PSP dye is injected intravenously; urine specimens are collected 30 and 60 minutes after injection.

Each urine specimen is alkalinized using 10% sodium hydroxide to bring out the red color, diluted to 1000 ml, and the percentage of dye is measured against a standard colorimeter. If the concentration of dye is low, the specimen is diluted only to 500 or 250 ml (this is taken into consideration in calculating the percentage).

Interpretation:

a. Normally, the PSP concentration is about 50-60% in the first half-hour and 10-15% in the second half-hour. The normal total is about 60-75% in 1 hour.

b. If kidney function is reduced, both values will be lower than normal.

c. If there is residual urine or stasis, the curve is flat, and the total in 1 hour is slightly below normal if kidney function is not impaired. Stasis might be due to vesical or bilateral ureteral obstruction. The amount of residual urine can be calculated.

d. Any abnormality in the PSP test requires further evaluation.

C. X-RAY EXAMINATION

1. A plain film of the abdomen, also called KUB (kidney, ureter, and bladder), is an essential preliminary step to rule out calcifications within the system and to delineate the kidneys (their position, shape, size, outline, and axis).

2. Excretory urography (IVP) is fundamental; it is a test of kidney function as well as a means of delineating the anatomy of the urinary system. It is indicated whenever uropathology is suspected, especially obstruction, tumors, infection, congenital anomalies, neuropathy, or trauma. **Tomograms** may be required to see details. The only contraindication to excretory urography is allergy to the contrast medium. If the study must be done in allergic patients, hydration, antihistaminics, and steroids might be helpful.

3. Renal angiography is used for the diagnosis of kidney masses and to outline the renal vasculature in hypertensive patients.

4. Instrumental x-ray studies

a. Urethrograms are done by injecting contrast medium through the external meatus to opacify the entire urethra.

b. Cystograms are obtained by filling the bladder with contrast medium under gravity flow until full capacity is reached. Bladder contour, vesicoureteral reflux, diverticula, and trabeculation can be assessed. A voiding film outlines the bladder outlet and the urethral canal, and a postvoiding film demonstrates residual urine.

c. Retrograde pyelograms are done by passing a ureteral catheter through a cystoscope and injecting contrast; the outline of the pelvicalyceal system and the ureteral lumen are clearly seen. This test is necessary in patients with impaired renal function, poor concentration of contrast, and incomplete filling of the collecting structures.

D. ENDOSCOPY   Endoscopic evaluation includes cystoscopy, urethroscopy, and any associated procedures such as biopsy or retrograde injection of contrast medium.

Urinary instrumentation is sometimes a therapeutic maneuver, e.g., to ma nipulate and extract ureteral stones, to crush and evacuate vesical calculi, to fulgurate sites of bleeding, to resect tumors, to dilate urethral strictures, or to treat urethral stricture by urethrotomy or endoscopic incision.

II. TRAUMA

A. KIDNEY   The kidney is protected by the rib cage and the strong posterior abdominal muscles. Injuries to the kidney range in severity; contusion, parenchymal tear (partial or complete), or even rupture of the renal pedicle may occur.

1. Diagnosis

a. Symptoms and signs: hematuria; pain in the flank; shock, especially with multiple injuries; nausea and vomiting; abdominal distention (ileus); ecchymosis and a mass in the flank by percussion.

b. Laboratory tests: blood in the urine; falling hematocrit on serial tests if bleeding is active.

c. X-ray findings   Plain film reveals a large area of grayness in the region of the injured organ with absence of the psoas line because of hematoma, extravasation of urine, or both.

Excretory urogram might show impaired function or evidence of extravasation. It is important to note that the contralateral kidney is normal. Retrograde urograms are rarely indicated.

Renal angiograms sometimes help make the diagnosis and plan the surgical reconstruction.

d. Special tests   Radioisotope scan of the kidneys may be valuable in doubtful cases of renal injury.

2. Differential diagnosis   Vertebral or rib fractures and retroperitoneal hematoma cause similar symptoms. Hematuria may be due to injury of some other part of the genitourinary tract.

3. Complications   *Early:* Infection, secondary hemorrhage, and progressive renal damage. *Late:* Fibrotic stenosis of the renal artery, hypertension, and hydronephrosis due to ureteral stricture.

4. Treatment   Treat **expectantly** with blood transfusion and complete bed rest (until hematuria subsides) unless there is an indication for operation (persistent bleeding or infection). **Surgical** procedures include suture of a laceration, amputation of the upper or lower pole, heminephrectomy, and total nephrectomy.

B. URETER   The ureter is rarely injured by external trauma; most ureteral injuries occur during pelvic or abdominal surgery. A ureter (sometimes both ureters) is inadvertently cut, leading to extravasation of urine, or ligated, causing obstruction.

1. Diagnosis

a. Symptoms and signs: Anuria or severe oliguria following pelvic surgery mean **bilateral ureteral obstruction until proved otherwise;** flank pain; persistent ileus; drainage of urine from the abdominal wound or the vagina.

b. Laboratory and x-ray findings   Abnormal renal function tests if the injury is bilateral. Excretory urography shows partial or complete obstruction or extravasation. Retrograde urography defines the site and nature of the injury.

2. Differential diagnosis   Prerenal causes of oliguria and anuria. Vesicovaginal and urethrovaginal fistulas are distinguished from ureterovaginal leakage by instillation of methylene blue into the bladder. Retrograde urography proves the injury is ureteral.

3. Complications   Ureteral fistula, retroperitoneal infection, pyelonephritis, and ureteral obstruction from stenosis. Peritonitis develops if urine leaks into the peritoneal cavity.

4. Treatment The best 'treatment' is **prevention**. Catheterization of the ureters before extensive pelvic surgery may help identification during operation.

If ureteral injury is recognized immediately, the edges should be trimmed and anastomosed over a stent with proximal drainage ('T' tube). Reimplantation into the bladder is preferable if the injury occurs close to that structure.

Methods of late repair depend on the level of the injury and the status of the ureter distal to the damaged area.

5. Prognosis The results of immediate repair are good. Late repairs are also successful if properly done.

C. BLADDER Blunt trauma to the full bladder is the most common cause of injury; it is frequently associated with pelvic fractures. The bladder also may be injured during pelvic surgery or during endoscopic instrumentation. Bladder rupture can be intraperitoneal or extraperitoneal.

1. Diagnosis

a. Symptoms and signs: suprapubic pain; hematuria; inability to void; suprapubic tenderness and muscle rigidity; intraperitoneal rupture (rebound tenderness and ileus); extraperitoneal rupture (mass or dullness in the suprapubic region).

b. Laboratory tests Blood in the urine; falling hematocrit if bleeding is active.

c. X-ray findings *Cystography* demonstrates extravasation of urine. The bladder may be displaced or compressed.

2. Differential diagnosis Excretory urography and cystography differentiate extraperitoneal bladder rupture from urethral or renal injuries.

3. Treatment The peritoneal cavity is explored in all cases, the injury is repaired, and a suprapubic cystostomy tube is inserted. The site of extraperitoneal rupture is drained externally. The prognosis is good.

D. URETHRA

1. Membranous urethra The membranous urethra is fixed to the genitourinary diaphragm and is most commonly injured in association with pelvic fractures.

Urinary retention, bleeding from the urethra, and pain and fullness in the lower abdomen are the usual symptoms. Rectal examination reveals a boggy mass anteriorly; sometimes the back of the pubic bone and displacement of the prostate upward are palpable. The diagnosis is established by urethrography.

If the tear is partial, a catheter might pass into the bladder; it should be left in place for 10-14 days. If the tear is complete, no instrumentation should be done, and suprapubic cystostomy is required. Some surgeons attempt immediate repair and others defer repair until later. There is a high incidence of stricture after these injuries.

2. Bulbous urethra A straddle injury compresses the bulbous urethra between a firm object and the pubic arch causing a partial or complete tear. Instrumentation is also a cause of trauma to this structure.

Urethral bleeding and hematuria are common. Extravasation of urine with voiding might fill the perineum, ascend to the scrotum, spread to the penis, and extend to the lower abdominal wall and upper thigh (areas limited by the attachment of Colles' fascia). Urethrography is diagnostic.

If the tear is partial, a catheter might be passed to the bladder; it remains in place as a stent. Catheterization usually is impossible in patients with complete rupture; suprapubic cystostomy, drainage of extravasated urine, and antibiotic coverage are required.

These injuries invariably result in strictures which must be repaired later.

3. Pendulous urethra The pendulous urethra is most often injured by instrumentation and occasionally by trauma to the erect penis. Bleeding per urethra without urination is the usual symptom. Mild injuries heal promptly without treatment; more severe injuries heal if the urethra is stented with a catheter. Associated tears of the cavernosus tissue must be repaired to avoid formation of extensive hematoma around the penis, scrotum, and perineum. Strictures are a consequence of severe injuries.

E. PENIS   Trauma to the erect penis ruptures the cavernosus tissue. A rubber band or other constricting device can cause necrosis; these objects must be removed. Avulsion of the penile skin occurs rarely in industrial accidents; skin grafting may be required.

F. SCROTUM   Injury to the freely mobile testes is uncommon. Severe pain, vomiting, and even shock occur when the testes are contused, lacerated, or completely ruptured. Scrotal exploration may be necessary; lacerations should be sutured. Healing following severe injury is usually accompanied by testicular atrophy.

III. OBSTRUCTIVE UROPATHY

1. Classification   Urinary obstruction is classified according to:
a. Level   Upper tract (supravesical). Lower tract (vesical and infravesical).
b. Completeness   Partial; complete.
c. Acuteness   Acute; gradual, progressive.
d. Congenital or *acquired.*
2. Etiology
a. Congenital   Meatal stenosis, posterior urethral valves, congenital lower ureteral obstruction, ureteropelvic junction obstruction.
b. Acquired   Urethral or ureteral stricture, bladder outlet (usually prostatic disease), stones, neurogenic dysfunction, and extrinsic obstruction by tumors, inflammation, or fibrosis. Obstruction may also be iatrogenic.
3. Diagnosis
a. Symptoms and signs   Upper tract obstruction: abdominal pain (renal or ureteral type); gastrointestinal symptoms; tenderness and fullness in the costovertebral angle; flank mass if hydronephrosis is marked; fever and chills if infection is present. *Lower tract obstruction:* difficulty initiating voiding (hesitancy); weak, interrupted stream; urinary frequency; distended bladder; rectal examination may show prostatic enlargement.
b. Laboratory tests   Pyuria, hematuria, crystalluria. Impaired renal function (elevated serum creatinine and BUN) in chronic severe obstruction. PSP is normal in unilateral obstruction, possibly abnormal if obstruction is bilateral or if the volume of residual urine is large.
c. X-ray findings   Plain abdominal films may show enlargement of the kidney shadows or opaque calculi.
Excretory urography: (1) Establishes the diagnosis of obstruction unless renal function is markedly impaired. (2) May show the cause of obstruction (e.g., stone, tumor). (3) May show the level of obstruction. (4) Demonstrates the extent of hydroureteronephrosis above the obstruction. (5) May show trabeculation of the bladder and residual urine (in the postvoiding film) in cases of bladder outlet obstruction. (6) High-dose infusion pyelography, delayed films, and tomograms may be needed to opacify the collecting structures if renal function is impaired.
Retrograde ureterography defines the exact site of ureteral obstruction. *Retrograde cystography* may show the cause of bladder outlet obstruction; trabeculation and diverticula of the bladder are also seen.
d. Special tests   (1) Urethral calibration, retrograde urethrography. (2) Endoscopy: may identify urethral causes of obstruction; reveals changes in the bladder resulting from outlet obstruction; evaluates competency of the ureteral orifices; permits ureteral catheterization.

4. Differential diagnosis   Must rule out other causes of kidney enlargement (cysts, tumors) or other abdominal masses.

5. Complications   Complete loss of renal function if persistent bilateral obstruction is not relieved. Infection. Stones.

6. Treatment

a. Relief of obstruction occurs spontaneously in some cases (e.g., passage of a ureteral stone), but instrumental or surgical procedures are required in most patients.

b. The presence of acute infection or marked impairment of renal function demands immediate, aggressive measures to decompress the urinary tract above the obstructing point. Nephrostomy, ureterostomy, suprapubic cystostomy, or placement of urethral or ureteral catheters are methods of decompression.

7. Prognosis   The prognosis depends on the duration and severity of obstruction. Results are excellent if acute obstruction is relieved promptly and infection is eradicated completely.

IV. VESICOURETERAL REFLUX

The lower end of the ureter is protected by a valve mechanism which permits free flow of urine from the upper tract into the bladder but prevents regurgitation in the other direction. The well-developed longitudinal muscle of the submucosal ureter continues uninterrupted to the base of the bladder at the trigone. When the trigone is stretched, it tightens the closure of the lower end of the ureter, and when the trigone contracts, the contraction extends into the submucosal ureter and seals it. Thus, ureteral tonus closes the ureteral orifice when the bladder is empty. As the bladder distends, the trigone is stretched, and the ureteral closure is tightened still further. With voiding (the time of maximal intravesical pressure), the trigone and submucosal ureter actively contract, and the ureter remains occluded by this mechanism.

Primary reflux, by far the most common type, is a developmental weakness of the ureterotrigonal musculature. It probably occurs with equal frequency in children of both sexes, but because girls have a shorter urethra, the clinical manifestations of reflux (infection of the upper tract) appear earlier in them. **Secondary reflux** is acquired from infravesical obstruction, neurogenic dysfunction, inflammatory diseases, or iatrogenic causes. A third-category of reflux is due to congenital ureteral anomalies (e.g., ectopic orifices).

1. Complications   (1) Damage to the renal parenchyma from the high pressures of bladder contraction during voiding. (2) Infection in residual urine. (3) Infection is carried from the lower urinary tract to the upper tract. Reflux is found in about 50% of children with acute pyelonephritis and in 70% of patients with radiographic evidence of chronic pyelonephritis. (4) Dilatation and tortuosity of the ureters resulting from the greatly increased work load; the ureters must transport the refluxing urine as well as the newly excreted urine. (5) Stone formation.

2. Diagnosis

a. Symptoms and signs and laboratory tests are characteristic of acute pyelonephritis (see Section V.B) in children and in some adults. Other adults have the history and findings of chronic pyelonephritis (see Section V.C). The PSP test is abnormal depending on the volume of residual urine and the extent of renal damage.

b. X-ray findings   Excretory urography may show dilated ureters or the scarring of pyelonephritis. Voiding cystography demonstrates reflux conclusively.

c. Special tests   Endoscopy evaluates the trigone and the position, fixation, configuration, and orientation of the ureteral orifices. The length of the submucosal ureter can be estimated.

3. Differential diagnosis Pyelonephritis from other causes. Ureteral dilatation due to other organic or functional causes.

4. Treatment Conservative management (treat infection, dilate distal strictures) permits about one-third of patients to undergo spontaneous reversal of the reflux.

Another one-third are treated conservatively for prolonged periods; many of these patients eventually require operation.

Immediate surgical repair is indicated in the one-third with advanced disease. The weak distal ureter is excised, and the ureter is reimplanted into the bladder through a long submucosal tunnel by one of several techniques.

5. Prognosis The prognosis is good if reflux is detected early and poor if extensive renal damage has occurred. Surgical repairs succeed in preventing reflux, infection, and progression of renal injury in 90–96% of patients.

V. INFECTIONS

Urinary tract infections are categorized as specific or nonspecific. **Specific** infections are caused by specific bacteria, each of which is associated with a unique clinical disease. Examples are tuberculosis, gonorrhea, and syphilis. **Nonspecific** infections have similar manifestations regardless of the causative bacteria. They are much more frequent than the specific types. Gram-negative rods (Escherichia coli, Proteus mirabilis, Proteus prodigalis, and Pseudomonas aeruginosa) are frequently responsible; gram-positive cocci (Streptococcus faecalis and Staphylococcus aureus) occasionally cause urinary infections.

Because the urinary tract has defenses against infection (the complete washout mechanism and the bacteriostatic properties of the urothelium), infection usually has an underlying cause such as stasis, residual urine, foreign bodies, trauma, or a continuous source of infection.

The ascending route of infection is the most common. It occurs more often in females because of the short urethra and the potential source of infection in the vagina. Ascending urinary tract infection is frequent in girls under age 10 and in young women as they begin sexual activity. Hematogenous or descending infection is less common; it is associated with underlying urologic diseases such as stones, tumors, or vesicoureteral reflux. Lymphatic spread of infection to the urinary tract from the gastrointestinal tract or genital system takes place occasionally. Extension of infection from a nearby organ (e.g., in salpingitis, appendiceal abscess, vesicoenteric fistula) may occur also.

A. TUBERCULOSIS This is a specific infection that reaches the genitourinary tract by hematogenous spread. The kidney is affected most often; tubercles in the parenchyma caseate and eventually communicate with the pelvicalyceal system. The lower tract (ureter, bladder, prostate, epididymis) is affected secondarily by descending infection; the fibrosis typical of healing tuberculosis may obstruct the ureter or urethra or cause contracture of the bladder. Vesicoureteral reflux results if bladder involvement is severe. Bilateral epididymitis may cause infertility, and the testis may be destroyed by direct extension.

1. Diagnosis

a. Symptoms and signs The renal lesion is usually silent. Symptoms of cystitis are the common complaint (frequency, urgency, and sometimes hematuria). Thickened, nontender epididymis or an indurated, nodular prostate reflect tuberculosis of those structures, draining scrotal sinuses are seen sometimes.

b. Laboratory tests 'Sterile' pyuria (no organisms on stained smear or routine culture) means tuberculosis until proved otherwise. Acid-fast stains of the urine and cultures for tubercle bacilli are positive.

c. X-ray findings Chest film may show tuberculosis. Plain abdominal film may show punctate calcifications in the renal parenchyma. Excretory urography reveals ulcerated calyces, obliterated calyces, or fibrotic contracture of the ureters or bladder; vesicoureteral reflux may be present.

 d. Special tests Cystoscopy reveals tubercles if the bladder is involved; biopsy should be obtained.

 2. Treatment

 a. Medical Genitourinary tuberculosis must be treated as a systemic disease (see Chapter 4); treatment is usually successful.

 b. Surgical Must be preceded by at least 3 months of medical treatment. Nephrectomy, repair of stricture, reimplantation of refluxing ureters, epididymectomy, or augmentation cystoplasty may be necessary.

 c. Urine must be examined and cultured at intervals for years; relapse may occur.

 3. Prognosis is excellent with modern antituberculous therapy.

B. ACUTE PYELONEPHRITIS This disease is a combined infection of the renal pelvis and the renal parenchyma; the former seldom occurs alone. Bacteria reach the kidney by the ascending route most commonly; vesicoureteral reflux plays a major role. Hematogenous infection occurs in the presence of stones or other obstructions. Pyelonephritis, especially on the right side, may also be associated with atony and stasis in pregnancy.

 1. Diagnosis

 a. Symptoms and signs High fever ($39°$–$40°C$) and chills. Flank pain and lower abdominal pain (localized flank pain is uncommon in children with acute pyelonephritis). Nausea and vomiting. Tenderness in the costovertebral angle (may have abdominal distention and tenderness).

 b. Laboratory tests Leukocytosis with shift to the left. The urine is cloudy (white cells, white cell casts, and bacteria are seen). Urine culture identifies the organism and its sensitivity to antibiotics.

 c. X-ray findings Excretory urography is normal or there is delay in secretion and haziness of the outline of the calyceal system. Obstruction or vesicoureteral reflux may be demonstrated. Voiding cystography shows reflux in many cases; it should be obtained after the infection subsides.

 2. Differential diagnosis Appendicitis, cholecystitis, pancreatitis, diverticulitis, and lobar pneumonia.

 3. Complications The infection may become chronic.

 4. Treatment Antibacterial therapy is begun with sulfonamides or broad-spectrum antibiotics. The sensitivity of the organism should be determined and the treatment altered if necessary.

 If the infection does not respond within 48 hours, obstruction must be ruled out by excretory urography.

 Underlying disease (especially vesicoureteral reflux) must be sought in boys after a single episode of pyelonephritis and in girls after a second episode of infection.

 Follow-up: after clinical response, the urine should be examined at intervals for 2 months to be certain the infection has been eradicated.

 5. Prognosis is good if infection is controlled promptly and predisposing factors are identified and treated.

C. CHRONIC PYELONEPHRITIS Vesicoureteral reflux is the most common cause of this disease.

 1. Diagnosis

 a. Symptoms and signs May be asymptomatic except during acute exacerbations. Hypertension. Renal failure may be the presenting problem.

 b. Laboratory tests Absent, mild, or moderate pyuria. Bacteriuria is always present. Impaired renal function in advanced bilateral disease.

 c. X-ray findings (1) Excretory urograms are normal in the early stages. Progressive parenchymal scarring leads to shrinkage of the kidney, delayed excretion, and poor concentration of the contrast medium. Narrowing of the infundibula and clubbing of the calyces also are typical. (2) Voiding cystography may reveal reflux and hydroureteronephrosis.

    d. Special tests   Endoscopy and retrograde studies may demonstrate the underlying cause of chronic pyelonephritis.

    2. Differential diagnosis   Chronic cystitis, tuberculous pyelonephritis, glomerulonephritis, and renal atrophy from vascular insufficiency.

    3. Complications   Hypertension, stone formation, renal failure.

    4. Treatment

    a. Medical   Intensive antimicrobial therapy guided by culture and sensitivity tests. After infection is controlled, suppressive therapy is given for months using small daily divided doses of nitrofurantoin, sulfonamides, or acidified methenamine. Infection sometimes continues to recur (in these patients, suppressive therapy is continued for years).

    b. Surgical correction of predisposing factors is very important.

    5. Prognosis for chronic recurrent infections is guarded unless a correctable underlying disease is found and treated.

D. CYSTITIS   Acute cystitis is a common ascending infection in females—it may appear 36–48 hours after sexual intercourse. In men, cystitis is never primary; it occurs only as a complication of bladder outlet obstruction, prostatitis, or pyelonephritis. Because there is intermittent complete emptying of the bladder contents, acute cystitis is self-limited in the absence of stasis, a constant source of infection, or both.

    1. Diagnosis

    a. Symptoms and signs   Frequency, urgency, urge incontinence, urethral burning on urination, pyuria, and terminal hematuria. Cystitis is not associated with fever. The underlying disease (e.g., prostatic enlargement) may be found.

    b. Laboratory tests   Pyuria, bacteriuria, and hematuria.

    2. Complications   Ascending infection to the kidney may develop if the ureterovesical junction is marginally balanced; reflux occurs in the presence of infection and ceases when the infection clears in these patients.

    3. Treatment with antimicrobial agents should eradicate the infection promptly and the urine should be sterile in 14 days. If infection persists, complete urologic evaluation is essential.

E. URETHRITIS   Acute nonspecific urethritis is an ascending infection in women; in men, it usually is associated with prostatitis. Trichomonads, gonococci, viruses, and chemical irritants also cause acute urethritis.

    1. Diagnosis

    a. Symptoms and signs   Urethral discharge. Burning on urination. Evidence of prostatitis.

    b. Laboratory tests   Urethral discharge is examined in saline (wet smear) to look for trichomonads. Methylene blue and gram stains of the discharge reveal clumps of white cells, nonspecific bacteria, or gonococci. Some patients have no bacteria (viral, chemical, or *Mycoplasma pneumoniae* infection).

    2. Treatment   Nonspecific urethritis is treated with antibiotics, e.g., tetracycline or erythromycin for 1 week. If the discharge contains pus but no bacteria, assume that *Mycoplasma pneumoniae* is responsible and treat as nonspecific urethritis.

    Gonococcal urethritis responds to penicillin (1.2 million units IM in each buttock 1 hour after probenecid 1 gm orally) or tetracycline. Many patients have associated nonspecific urethritis that must be treated also.

    Treat trichomonal urethritis with metronidazole (250 mg orally for 10 days).

    Gonococcal and trichomonal urethritis require treatment of the sexual partner and discontinuance of intercourse (or the use of a condom) until the infection clears.

Associated prostatitis should be treated.

F. PROSTATITIS is most common in young adults. It usually is a hematogenous infection, but it may follow inadequately treated urethritis.

    1. Diagnosis

        a. Symptoms and signs (1) *Acute prostatitis:* severe vesical irritability, urethral discharge, perineal heaviness and pain, fever, and sometimes urinary retention. Enlarged, edematous, tender prostate. Prostatic massage is contraindicated. (2) *Chronic prostatitis:* usually asymptomatic. Prostate normal or indurated and irregular.

        b. Laboratory tests Leukocytosis in acute phase. White cells and bacteria in first-glass specimen of urine. Prostatic massage (in chronic phase only) yields secretions containing clumps of pus cells but usually no bacteria.

    2. Complications

        a. Acute prostatitis Prostatic abscess, which may rupture into the urethra or perineum. Chronic prostatitis.

        b. Chronic prostatitis Acute epididymitis. Secondary cystitis.

    3. Treatment Antimicrobial therapy for acute prostatitis. Response is usually prompt. Abscess may require surgical drainage. Residual chronic prostatitis must be treated.

    Antibiotics are less effective in chronic prostatitis, but they should be used. Prostatic massage (2-3 times at intervals of 10-14 days), and hot sitz baths are helpful. Sexual activity is encouraged to promote drainage. Chronic prostatitis in itself causes little harm, but its complications may be serious.

G. EPIDIDYMITIS Acute nonspecific epididymitis is usually secondary to prostatitis or urethritis. Occasionally it is caused by reflux of sterile urine into the ejaculatory ducts; recurrent epididymitis may be due to this mechanism.

    1. Diagnosis

        a. Symptoms and signs History of instrumentation, catheterization, urethritis, or prostatitis. Acute severe pain and swelling in the scrotum extending into the inguinal canal in some cases. Fever. The epididymis is enlarged and tender; except in the early stages, it cannot be felt separate from the testis; the scrotal skin is reddened and adherent to the inflammatory mass.

    2. Differential diagnosis Tuberculous epididymitis is usually not painful or tender. Torsion of the spermatic cord: pain is not relieved by lifting and supporting the testis; the pain of acute epididymitis is improved by this maneuver. Testicular tumor. Mumps orchitis.

    3. Treatment Infiltration of the spermatic cord with 15-20 cc of 1% procaine hydrochloride relieves the pain and speeds resolution. Antibiotics (e.g., tetracycline). Scrotal support, bed rest, cold compresses, and analgesics.

    4. Prognosis Acute epididymitis resolves slowly over 2-3 weeks, often with some residual induration and swelling. Sterility may result from bilateral severe cases that block the epididymal ductal system.

H. ORCHITIS is usually a complication of mumps parotitis. Very rarely, orchitis is a consequence of severe epididymitis.

    Painful swelling of the testicle (usually unilateral), fever, and associated parotitis are the usual findings. Laboratory tests are normal except for leukocytosis. Acute epididymitis and torsion of the spermatic cord must be differentiated.

    Infiltration of the spermatic cord with 1% procaine, bed rest, analgesics, and scrotal support are helpful. Testicular atrophy and, if bilateral, infertility are the main complications. Androgenic function is maintained.

VI. URINARY STONES

Urinary calculi often are idiopathic. Other stones are secondary to stasis and infection, and some calculi occur in association with metabolic diseases (e.g., cystinuria, gout, and hyperparathyroidism). Stones are more frequent in men; they are rare in children and in blacks.

A. RENAL AND URETERAL CALCULI

1. Diagnosis

a. Symptoms and signs Nonobstructive stones are asymptomatic in most cases. Flank discomfort and hematuria occur occasionally. Obstructive stones cause severe flank pain and agonizing colic that radiates along the course of the ureter to the scrotum or medial thigh. Gross hematuria is not uncommon. Tenderness in the flank and signs of ileus are noted.

b. Laboratory tests

(1) Urinalysis: proteinuria if hematuria is present; pH higher than 7.6 indicates the presence of urea-splitting organisms (low pH [6 to 6.5] is associated with uric acid calculi or renal tubular acidosis); erythrocytes, white cells, and bacteria are seen in the sediment; crystals (oxalate, phosphate, uric acid, cystine) should be sought in the sediment; Sulkowitch test may reveal hypercalciuria; qualitative test for cystine should be done in cases of recurrence or family history.

(2) Quantitative analysis of calcium, oxalates, uric acid, and cystine should be done in a 24-hour specimen of urine. Urinary calcium (on a low calcium diet—no dairy products) should not exceed 175 mg/24 hours. Higher values suggest hyperparathyroidism or idiopathic hypercalciuria.

(3) Renal function tests are normal unless there is bilateral obstruction, infection, or chronic underlying urologic disease.

(4) Essential blood chemistries include calcium, phosphate, uric acid, and proteins. Parathormone assays are indicated if hyperparathyroidism is suspected (see Chapter 5).

(5) Every recovered stone should be analyzed for chemical composition.

c. X-ray findings Plain abdominal films may show the stone (90% are radiopaque). Excretory urography localizes stones in the urinary tract, shows the level and degree of obstruction, and demonstrates renal damage.

d. Special tests Cystoscopy and retrograde urography are seldom necessary for diagnostic purposes.

2. Complications Infection, obstruction, and progressive renal damage.

3. Treatment

a. Conservative Renal stones that are asymptomatic, unassociated with reinfection, and nonobstructive require no treatment. Ureteral stones are small and smooth (most pass spontaneously).

b. Instrumental or surgical Renal stones that obstruct or cause recurrent infection are removed surgically (pyelotomy, nephrotomy, or even nephrectomy may be necessary); Ureteral stones that remain impacted in the lower ureter should be removed by cystoscopic manipulation or operation (ureterolithotomy) if hydronephrosis progresses or infection persists.

4. Prophylaxis against recurrence is very important.

a. General measures Large fluid intake to prevent precipitation of solutes (especially avoid nocturnal dehydration); treatment of infection; correction of obstruction and stasis.

b. Specific measures

(1) Calcium stones: parathyroidectomy for hyperparathyroidism; eliminate milk and cheese from the diet; potassium acid phosphate (3–6 gm daily) reduces urinary excretion of calcium; a diuretic (e.g., hydrochlorothiazide 50 mg twice daily) reduces calcium content in the urine; ascorbic acid (1 gm 4 times a day) or cranberry juice (200 ml, 4 times a day) acidifies the urine and makes calcium more soluble.

(2)   Oxalate stones: low oxalate and low calcium diet; phosphates (potassium acid phosphate 3-6 gm daily); pyridoxine (100 mg, 3 times a day).

(3)   Metabolic stones: cystine and uric acid precipitate in acid urine, (the urine pH should be raised to greater than 7.5 by giving 50% citrate solution, 4-8 ml, 4 times a day) and prescribing an alkaline-ash diet; limit purines in the diet of uric acid stone formers (also give allopurinol [Zyloprin] 300 mg once or twice daily); in cystinurics, low methionine diet and penicillamine (4 gm daily).

5. Prognosis   The high recurrence rate is minimized by correcting obstruction, treating infection, and using the prophylactic measures described above. Progressive renal damage is the worst danger. Prolonged follow-up is necessary.

B. VESICAL CALCULI   Primary vesical stones are very rare in the USA but are not uncommon in developing countries. Vitamin B6 deficiency may have an etiologic role. **Secondary vesical stones** are usually a consequence of infection by urea-splitting organisms in patients with neurogenic bladder or outlet obstruction. Stones entering the bladder from the ureter pass through the urethra unless the bladder outlet is obstructed. **Foreign bodies in the bladder,** whether self-introduced or a result of instrumentation, may serve as a nidus for stone formation. 95% of vesicle calculi occur in men.

1. Diagnosis

a. Symptoms and signs   Urinary frequency and occasional interruption of the urinary stream with pain radiating to the tip of the penis.

b. Laboratory tests reveal pyuria, bacteriuria, and hematuria; PSP test is consistent with residual urine.

c. X-ray findings   Opaque stones are visible on a plain film; radiolucent stones are filling defects in the bladder on excretory urography or cystography.

d. Special tests   Cystoscopy reveals the number, size, and shape of stones; it is essential before a decision is made about the method of treatment.

2. Treatment   Small stones are removed cystoscopically after they are crushed with a lithotrite or disintegrated by means of an electrohydraulic lithotrite. Large, hard stones are removed by suprapubic cystotomy. Some stones (especially those that form in the presence of infection) can be dissolved by chemicals such as Renicidin or Solution G.

3. Prognosis   Recurrence is uncommon if the predisposing factors are corrected.

VII. TUMORS

Neoplasms of the prostate, bladder and kidneys are among the most common tumors in humans. Testicular tumors are uncommon but highly malignant. Other genitourinary organs rarely give rise to neoplasia.

A. KIDNEY*   Benign renal tumors are rare. **Adenocarcinoma** (Hypernephroma, Grawitz's tumor), arising from tubular cells, is the most common of the kidney. It is more frequent in males. Adenocarcinoma invades blood vessels early and spreads to liver, lungs, and long bones. It also invades and distorts the renal pelvis and calyces, and it can metastasize to regional lymph nodes.

1. Diagnosis

a. Symptoms and signs   Painless gross total hematuria. Firm, irregular, nodular mass in the flank. Recent appearance of a varicocele in the left side of the scrotum if the left renal vein is involved. Symptoms and signs of metastases (weight loss, anemia, bone pain, fever of unknown origin).

b. Laboratory tests   Gross or microscopic hematuria. Renal function not impaired. Hypercalcemia in some cases.

---

*See Chapter 18 for Wilms' tumor

c. X-ray findings Plain film may show an enlarged, irregular kidney. Excretory urograms show calyceal distortion and a space-occupying mass. Renal angiography distinguishes tumor from cyst.

d. Special tests Immediate cystoscopy if the patient has gross hematuria when first seen (blood from one ureter localizes the problem to one side). Retrograde study may rule out epithelial tumors.

2. Differential diagnosis Renal cysts, metastases to the kidneys, hydronephrosis.

3. Treatment Radical nephrectomy with regional lymphadenectomy. The primary tumor is radioresistant, but radiotherapy may palliate local recurrence or bony metastases.

4. Prognosis The 5-year survival rate is 35%. Positive lymph nodes or involvement of the renal vein or vena cava worsens the prognosis. Tumor may recur as long as 10–15 years after removal of the primary.

B. RENAL PELVIS AND URETER These epithelial tumors comprise about 10% of kidney tumors. The most common variety is the transitional cell carcinoma, histologically similar to bladder tumors. Squamous cell carcinoma occurs in 15% of cases, commonly in association with chronic obstruction and irritation. Tumor metastasizes via lymphatics to regional lymph nodes. Secondary tumors may develop in the urinary tract distal to the primary.

1. Diagnosis

a. Symptoms and signs Painless gross total hematuria. Colicky pain if the tumor obstructs or if clot passes down the ureter.

b. Laboratory tests Hematuria. Malignant cells on stained smear of the sediment.

c. X-ray findings Irregular filling defect in the renal pelvis or calyx on excretory urography. Retrograde urograms confirm the diagnosis.

d. Special tests Cystoscopy shows unilateral hematuria (secondary tumors may be seen in the bladder). Cytologic study of unilateral urine or after ureteral brushing specimens yield a high rate of positives.

2. Treatment Nephroureterectomy with excision of a cuff of bladder wall.

3. Prognosis Good if the tumor does not extend through the pelvic or ureteral muscle, poor in anaplastic tumors.

C. BLADDER The bladder is the second most frequent site of genitourinary tumors (after the prostate). Bladder tumors are more common in males and usually occur after age 50. Known carcinogenic associations include industrial aromatic amines (many years of exposure) and smoking.

Most bladder tumors are transitional cell carcinomas. Epidermoid cancer (5%) and adenocarcinoma comprise the remainder. Transitional cell carcinomas are categorized histologically by their degree of differentiation ('grade' I to IV, IV being anaplastic) and the depth of penetration ('stage' 0 to D). The staging system is as follows:

Stage O: Papillary tumor not invading the lamina propria.

Stage A: Invasion of the lamina propria but not the muscle.

Stage B: Superficial (B_1) or deep (B_2) invasion of the bladder muscle.

Stage C: Tumor extending outside the bladder wall to perivesical fat or overlying peritoneum.

Stage D: Distant metastases.

1. Diagnosis

a. Symptoms and signs Hematuria is the most common symptom. Symptoms of secondary infection. Suprapubic pain if tumor extends beyond the bladder wall. Abdominal examination is negative unless the bladder outlet is obstructed (palpable bladder), the ureteral orifice is occluded (palpable kidney), or large bladder mass.

b. Laboratory tests Hematuria and sometimes infected urine. Malignant cells on methylene blue or Papanicolaou stain of the sediment.

c. X-ray findings Excretory urograms may show ureteral obstruction. In the cystogram phase, large tumors create a filling defect in the bladder.

d. Special tests Cystoscopy with biopsy makes the diagnosis.

2. Treatment

a. Surgical Transurethral resection for low grade superficial tumors. Partial bladder resection for localized lesions situated away from ureteral orifices and the base. Radical cystectomy, urethrectomy, and bilateral pelvic lymphadenectomy for high grade invasive tumors, urinary diversion (e.g., ileal conduit, ureterosigmoidostomy) is required.

b. Radiation therapy is effective for high grade tumors with the objective of cure or as an adjunct to radical cystectomy.

c. Topical chemotherapy (e.g., 60 mg of thiotepa in 60 ml of water instilled into the bladder once a week for 6 weeks) may control differentiated superficial tumors.

3. Prognosis Well-differentiated tumors frequently recur; cystoscopy at intervals is essential. Repeated transurethral resection often is successful. Anaplastic, deeply invasive cancers have a poor prognosis.

D. ADENOMATOUS HYPERPLASIA is a benign lesion that arises in the periurethral glands, not the prostate gland proper. It grows within the prostate, however, compressing and displacing it laterally to form the 'surgical capsule.' It affects men over the age of 50.

1. Diagnosis

a. Symptoms and signs 'Prostatism': hesitancy, frequency, nocturia, weak stream, terminal dribbling. Acute urinary retention. Hematuria from rupture of dilated veins at the bladder neck; palpable bladder sometimes; prostate normal sometimes (usually enlarged, soft to firm).

b. Laboratory tests Urine infection, hematuria, abnormal PSP test due to residual urine.

c. X-ray findings Excretory urography may show elevation of the bladder base, trabeculation, evidence of residual urine, and mild bilateral hydroureteronephrosis.

d. Special tests Catheterization measures the volume of residual urine. Endoscopy shows enlargement of the prostate (lateral lobes, middle lobe, or trilobar) and the effects of obstruction on the bladder.

2. Differential diagnosis Prostatic cancer, neurogenic bladder, acute prostatitis, and urethral stricture.

3. Complications Acute retention, chronic retention, infection, calculi, diverticula, back pressure on the kidney, and progressive renal failure.

4. Treatment Conservative treatment for the phase of irritative voiding symptoms: prostatic massage, sexual activity, and treatment of infection. The patient should void as soon as the urge is noted, and he should not drink large volumes of fluid in a short time.

Acute retention is treated by catheterization. If the catheter is left indwelling for several days, acute congestion may reverse and normal voiding becomes possible.

The phase of obstructive voiding symptoms, with progressively increasing residual urine and back pressure on the kidney, requires prostatectomy. Prostatectomy (actually, excision of the adenomatous periurethral growth) may be done by the transurethral, suprapubic, retropubic, or perineal approach. Transurethral resection is preferred for glands under 50-60 gm in size.

5. Prognosis is good if the adenoma is removed. Operative mortality is low.

E. CARCINOMA OF THE PROSTATE is rare before age 60, but by the eighth decade it affects 25% of men. It is frequently associated with benign hyperplasia;

in such cases, it arises in the 'surgical capsule' (the true prostatic tissue surrounding the hyperplastic periurethral glands). The posterior lobe is the most common site of origin. It metastasizes via lymphatics and through the blood stream to vertebrae and pelvic bones. The following staging system is used:

Stage A: Incidental focal malignant tumor noted in tissue removed by transurethral resection for benign hyperplasia. Rectal examination is normal.

Stage B: Localized induration of prostate confined within capsule. Normal serum acid phosphatase.

Stage C: Extracapsular extension of tumor. Elevation of serum acid phosphatase.

Stage D: Distant metastasis.

1. Diagnosis

a. Symptoms May be asymptomatic, found on routine rectal examination. 'Prostatism' (as in benign hyperplasia) in 95%. Bone pain, pathologic fracture, radicular pain from vertebral involvement.

b. Signs by rectal examination Early—firm nodule on lateral edge of prostate. Late—prostate is stony hard, fixed, with extension of tumor to the seminal vesicles.

c. Laboratory tests No abnormalities in early stages. Anemia from metastases to bone marrow or uremia. Infected urine. PSP shows residual urine. Deteriorating renal function with chronic obstruction. Serum acid phosphatase often is elevated with local extension or metastases; alkaline phosphatase is elevated with osseous metastases.

d. X-ray findings Sclerotic (osteoblastic) bony metastases; excretory urography may show vesical neck or ureteral obstruction.

e. Special tests Catheterization measures residual urine. Cystoscopy shows an irregular prostate and evidence of bladder outlet obstruction. Needle biopsy (transperineal or transrectal) proves the presence of malignancy; transurethral resection of obstructing tissue also may reveal carcinoma.

2. Differential diagnosis Biopsy differentiates carcinoma from benign hyperplasia, chronic prostatitis, tuberculous prostatitis, and prostatic calculi.

3. Treatment

a. Surgical Radical prostatectomy for early lesions. Transurethral resection palliates obstruction.

b. Endocrine These tumors are hormone-dependent, and the following measures are palliative: Orchiectomy; estrogen (e.g., diethylstilbestrol 1-2 mg/day); corticosteroids or hypophysectomy when the tumor becomes androgen-independent.

c. Radiation therapy (external, or interstitial with iodine-125) may be curative or palliative. Osseous metastases also respond to radiation therapy.

4. Prognosis The 5-year survival rate is 65% for early lesions treated by radical prostatectomy. Palliative measures relieve symptoms and prolong life for 10 years or more in a few patients, but most die within 5 years.

F. TESTIS Testicular tumors comprise 4% of tumors of the genitourinary tract. They occur most frequently between ages 20 and 35. The incidence is higher in undescended testes. These malignancies metastasize via lymphatics to periaortic nodes and through the blood stream to the liver and lungs.

Seminoma is the most common malignant testicular tumor, followed by embryonal carcinoma, teratoma, and choriocarcinoma. Many tumors have mixed patterns. Secretion of chorionic gonadotropins is associated with hyperplasia of the Leydig cells.

Benign (Sertoli cell and interstitial cell) testicular tumors are rare. They elaborate androgens and estrogens causing precocious sexual maturation in boys and gynecomastia in men.

The following staging system is used:

Stage 1:   Tumor confined to testis. No clinical or radiological evidence of spread.

    1A: Iliac and periaortic nodes uninvolved (determined by retroperitoneal lymphadenectomy).

    1B: Iliac or periaortic nodes involved.

Stage 2:   Clinical or radiographic evidence of metastases to nodes below the diaphragm. No metastases above the diaphragm.

Stage 3:   Metastases above the diaphragm or to the viscera.

1. Diagnosis

a. Symptoms and signs   Painless enlargement of the testicle. Gynecomastia if the tumor secretes gonadotropins or estrogens. Symptoms and signs of metastases. Testis enlarged, heavy, firm, irregular, with loss of sensation. May be associated hydrocele (10%) or hematocele.

b. Laboratory tests   Elevated urinary gonadotropins means that a chorioepithelioma is present (the degree of elevation and the response to orchiectomy are important prognostic signs). Elevated urinary 17-ketosteroids with interstitial cell tumors.

c. X-ray findings   Chest x-ray may show metastases. Excretory urograms may show ureteral displacement or obstruction from periaortic lymph node involvement.

2. Differential diagnosis   Hydrocele (transilluminates), hematocele, spermatocele, epididymitis, gumma.

3. Treatment

a. Surgical   Immediate operation through the inguinal canal to clamp and divide the spermatic cord and perform a radical orchiectomy. Bilateral radical retroperitoneal lymphadenectomy for all tumors except seminoma; this is done even if nodes are known to be involved preoperatively.

b. Radiation therapy   The treatment of choice for seminoma. An adjunct to lymphadenectomy in other tumors (may be used alone in Stage 1 tumors).

c. Chemotherapy is an effective palliative measure.

4. Prognosis   Seminoma has the best prognosis. Other Stage 1 lesions, except choriocarcinoma, have an 85–90% 5-year survival rate. Choriocarcinoma is usually fatal.

G. PENIS   Tumors of the penis are epidermoid lesions similar to epidermoid tumors elsewhere. Most arise on the glans under redundant preputial skin. Chronic inflammation and irritation in uncircumcised men is causally related. Metastases go to inguinal lymph nodes initially, then into the iliac nodes.

A firm, ulcerated, painless lesion of the glans is the usual clinical presentation. Secondary infection produces pain and a foul discharge. Biopsy of the penile lesion differentiates carcinoma from chancre, chancroid, and condyloma acuminatum. Inguinal lymph nodes may be enlarged from infection or metastases.

Partial amputation of the penis or radiation therapy gives good results in small lesions. Groin dissection (inguinal lymphadenectomy) is performed only if the nodes are enlarged.

VIII. NEUROGENIC BLADDER

Intact innervation is necessary for the bladder to function normally. The detrusor muscle is innervated by parasympathetic pelvic nerves S_2–S_4. The sensory supply for pain, touch, and temperature in the bladder is carried by sympathetic fibers arising in the lower thoracic and upper lumbar segments. The motor and sensory supply of the trigone comes from the same sympathetic nerves. The striated external sphincter and urogenital diaphragm receive somatic motor and sensory fibers via the pudendal nerves from S_2–S_4.

Normally, when the bladder fills to its maximum capacity (about 400-500 ml), a sensation of fullness and a desire to urinate are experienced. The pelvic floor and voluntary external sphincter relax, the detrusor contracts, and the bladder empties completely. The bladder generates a voiding pressure of about 20 cm of water, and the urine flow rate is 20-25 ml/second. After voiding, the bladder relaxes and the sphincter contracts to ensure continence.

Cystometry yields information about bladder capacity, completeness of emptying, and the bladder's ability to accommodate increasing volumes without increasing its pressure, thus indicating whether sensation is intact and whether the bladder can initiate and sustain a contraction. A catheter is passed into the bladder, and the volume of residual urine is measured. The catheter is attached to a water manometer and the intraluminal pressure is measured after instillation of increments of fluid. A **cystometrogram** is a graph with pressure (in cm) plotted on the ordinate and volume (in ml) on the abscissa.

Neurogenic bladder is divided into two groups, depending on the level of the lesion in relation to the micturition center (S_2-S_4).

A. UPPER MOTOR NEURON LESION (SPASTIC NEUROGENIC BLADDER)

Lesions above S_2-S_4 are usually due to trauma. The micturition center loses its communication with the midbrain and cerebral cortex, but the reflex arc between the bladder and the spinal cord remains intact. The bladder wall becomes spastic, the ability to accommodate is lost, and frequent uninhibited detrusor contraction occurs in response to bladder distention or extraneous stimuli. Detrusor contractions are ineffective, despite the high pressures generated, because simultaneous contraction of the pelvic floor and voluntary sphincter prevents adequate emptying. Contraction of the detrusor is elicited by trigger mechanisms, e.g., stimulation of the abdominal skin, genitalia, or thighs.

The bladder is hypertrophied and trabeculated. Eventually, vesicoureteral reflux occurs with progressive deterioration of the upper tract. Cystometry reveals a hyperactive detrusor, high intravesical pressure, diminished vesical capacity, and some residual urine.

If bladder capacity is adequate, the patient can be trained to empty the bladder by the trigger mechanism and thus minimize uncontrolled contractions and incontinence. The resistance of the bladder outlet can be reduced (by transurethral resection of the prostate or by pudendal neurectomy) to help the bladder empty completely. If bladder capacity is small, an indwelling catheter may be needed. Urinary diversion is indicated in cases of progressive renal damage.

B. LOWER MOTOR NEURON LESION (FLACCID NEUROGENIC BLADDER)

Lesions involving the spinal cord micturition center, the cauda equina, the sacral roots, or the peripheral nerves lead to an atonic or flaccid bladder. Trauma is the most common cause. Meningomyelocele and disc disease also can be responsible.

The bladder is areflexive since its connections to the micturition center are lost; any detrusor activity is on a myogenic basis with weak and unsustained contractions. Cystometry reveals a low pressure curve, increased capacity, no sensation of fullness, absent detrusor contraction, and a large volume of residual urine.

Urinary tract infections, stone formation, reflux, and impaired renal function are the main complications. Incontinence of the overflow type is a problem.

The patient is instructed to empty the bladder regularly by manual suprapubic compression (Crede maneuver) to avoid overflow incontinence. Surgical reduction of outlet resistance sometimes helps completeness of emptying. Intermittent self-catheterization may be of great value in controlling infection and protecting the upper tract, especially if instituted early.

IX. OTHER DISORDERS OF THE KIDNEY*

A. POLYCYSTIC KIDNEY   This familial disorder is usually bilateral and may also involve the liver and pancreas. Multiple cysts scattered throughout the kidneys compress the parenchyma and cause atrophy and renal failure. Death occurs during infancy in severe cases, but most patients become symptomatic in the 30-40 age group.

   1. Diagnosis
   a. Symptoms and signs   Hypertension, renal insufficiency, renal pain; one or both kidneys may be palpable.
   b. Laboratory tests   Hematuria, proteinuria, pyuria, bacteriuria. Anemia due to uremia. Impaired renal function.
   c. X-ray findings   Enlarged kidneys with calyceal distortion. Sonography reveals the cystic lesions.
   2. Differential diagnosis   Bilateral hydronephrosis, renal tumors, simple cysts, and tuberous sclerosis.
   3. Complications   Pyelonephritis, hypertension, renal failure.
   4. Treatment is medical (treat infection and renal failure—see Chapter 2). Surgical intervention is done in rare instances when a cyst compresses the ureter. Renal transplantation should be considered in end-stage patients.
   5. Prognosis   Death in 5-10 years after the diagnosis is made unless transplantation is successful.

B. SIMPLE SOLITARY CYST   Simple renal cysts are much more common than polycystic kidneys. The cyst is unilateral, simple, and usually is discovered incidentally on urologic evaluation. Flank pain occurs occasionally. Spontaneous rupture, infection, or hemorrhage into the cyst are possible complications.

   The most important differential diagnosis is between cyst and tumor. Sonography and angiography usually distinguish the two. Fluid can be aspirated through a percutaneous needle; it should be studied cytologically because 5% of cysts have associated malignancy in the wall. Surgical exploration is indicated in doubtful cases; simple unroofing is curative for benign cysts.

C. RENAL FUSION   Horseshoe kidney is the most common type of renal fusion. It usually is asymptomatic, but it can result in hydronephrosis (from ureteral compression), stone formation, or infection. No treatment is indicated unless complications occur.

X. OTHER GENITOURINARY DISORDERS

A. URETER
   1. Duplication   Incomplete duplication (Y-type) seldom requires treatment. Complete duplication needs surgical correction if it is associated with vesicoureteral reflux or obstruction; hydronephrosis and infection occur in both instances.
   2. Ureterocele   This is a cystic expansion of the submucosal segment of the intravesical ureter. Large ureteroceles obstruct the ipsilateral ureter, and sometimes the contralateral ureter or the bladder outlet are obstructed. These complications are indications for operation.

B. BLADDER
   1. Bladder extrophy   The syndrome includes absence of the anterior bladder wall and lack of union of the pubic bones. The posterior bladder wall is continuous with the abdominal skin. The penis in males is rudimentary. Permanent urinary diversion is usually required.

---

*See Chapter 13 for renal hypertension.

2. Vesical fistulas Fistulas between the bladder and the skin, bowel, or vagina are most often acquired from malignancy, radiation, or operative injury. Symptoms of vesicointestinal fistulas include fecaluria and pneumaturia (air bubbles in the urine). Urine drains constantly through the vagina in vesicovaginal fistulas. Treatment is surgical.

C. PENIS AND MALE URETHRA

1. Posterior urethral valves Abnormal congenital mucosal folds in the prostatic urethra balloon with voiding and occlude the urethral lumen. Obstruction and infection are the consequences; newborns with severe valves may have renal insufficiency. Voiding cystourethrograms are diagnostic. Treatment is transurethral resection of the valves.

2. Hypospadias and epispadias

a. Hypospadias is lack of development of the distal urethra, usually associated with ventral curvature of the penis distal to the hypospadic meatus. The meatus may open as far back as the perineum; partial or complete bifid scrotum is present in the scrotal or perineal types, and undescended testes are not uncommon. Hypospadias may preclude sexual intercourse or may prevent deposition of semen deep in the vagina. Treatment entails correction of the penile curvature and urethral reconstruction in one or two stages.

b. Epispadias is less common than hypospadias. More disabling and more difficult to correct, it can extend all the way to the bladder neck and be associated with urinary incontinence. The penis is small and has a dorsal curvature. Treatment consists of correction of the penile curvature, penile lengthening, urethral reconstruction, and correction of urinary incontinence if present. Urinary diversion might be needed.

3. Phimosis and paraphimosis

a. Phimosis is a narrow preputial opening. One cannot retract the foreskin over the glans. Treatment is by circumcision. If inflammation is present, preliminary incision of the dorsal foreskin under local anesthesia might be necessary.

b. Paraphimosis occurs when the foreskin is retracted behind the glans and cannot be pulled back again because of a tight preputial ring. A dorsal slit gives temporary relief; circumcision must be done later.

4. Priapism Priapism is an uncommon disease in which prolonged painful erection is not associated with sexual desire. About 25% of cases are associated with leukemia, metastatic carcinoma, or sickle cell disease; the majority are idiopathic.

Priapism may subside spontaneously, and it may recur. If persistent, ice water enemas and manual compression may relieve the erection. If erection still persists, sludged blood is aspirated from the corpora cavernosa through a large-bore needle, and the corpora are irrigated with heparinized solution. Occasionally, a venous shunt must be surgically constructed between the cavernosa and the corpus spongiosum. If decompression is not achieved promptly, the consequence is impotence from fibrous obliteration of the corpora cavernosa.

5. Urethral strictures in the male Congenital urethral strictures are rare; acquired strictures are secondary to trauma or gonococcal urethritis.

a. Diagnosis *Symptoms and signs:* weak, narrow, sprayed stream; acute urinary retention; recurring cystitis and pyelonephritis; periurethral inflammation, abscess, or fistula. *Laboratory tests:* Infected urine. *X-ray findings* urethrography shows the stricture and any associated fistula. *Special tests:* calibration with sounds of average size localize the obstruction (filiforms and dilators may be needed to enlarge the stricture for further study); endoscopy verifies the extent of stricture and evaluates the bladder for obstructive changes.

b. Differential diagnosis Prostatic enlargement, urethral carcinoma, and dysfunction of the voluntary sphincter.

c. Treatment Mild stricture—dilatation; severe stricture—intestinal urethrotomy or urethroplasty.

D. TESTIS, SCROTUM, AND SPERMATIC CORD

1. Cryptorchidism The **cryptorchid** testis has been arrested along its normal path of descent (in the abdomen, inguinal canal, or prepubic region). The **ectopic** testis has wandered off the normal pathway (e.g., in the perineum, femoral area, or prepenile region). 10% of newborns have cryptorchidism, but only 3% still have undescended testes at puberty.

Cryptorchidism may be unilateral or bilateral. The scrotum on the affected side is underdeveloped. The testis may be palpable above the scrotum but it cannot be pushed down to the scrotum. In **retractile testes,** the scrotum is normally developed, and the testes may be manipulated into the scrotum; this is best demonstrated when the child is asleep or in a hot bathtub. An inguinal hernia is associated with cryptorchidism in 75% of patients.

Progressive damage to spermatogenic cells (but not the Leydig cells) results from exposure to body temperature; it is demonstrable from age 6 years and after. Bilateral cryptorchidism (if untreated) leads to complete infertility; unilateral cryptorchidism is associated with low sperm counts. Undescended testes are more susceptible to development of tumors.

Treatment with chorionic gonadotropin (5000 IU, IM daily for 5 days) should be instituted by age 5. If this fails to induce descent, or if an inguinal hernia is present, operation is indicated. Orchiopexy may preserve spermatogenesis if done early enough.

2. Spermatocele A spermatocele is a small painless cystic mass situated just above the testis. It arises from the tubules that connect the testis to the epididymis. No treatment is needed unless the patient complains about its large size.

3. Hydrocele A hydrocele is a collection of fluid within the tunica vaginalis. It is a painless cystic mass that transilluminates. It is commonly idiopathic, but it also can be associated with injury, epididymitis, or a testicular tumor. In newborns and infants, spontaneous resolution is the rule. In young males, the hydrocele should be aspirated to permit proper palpation of the testes to rule out a testicular tumor. Surgical excision is indicated only if the patient complains of dragging heaviness from the large mass.

4. Varicocele Varicocele is dilatation and tortuosity of the pampiniform plexus, usually on the left side. A heavy sensation in the scrotum may be noted; low sperm counts are associated in some men. Asymptomatic varicocele requires no treatment. Symptomatic varicoceles are treated by ligation of the external spermatic vein at the internal inguinal ring or by ligating individual veins in the scrotum.

5. Torsion of the spermatic cord A rare condition, also named 'torsion of the testis,' it must be diagnosed and treated in 3–4 hours in order to save the testis from necrosis. It occurs just after puberty. The cryptorchid testis is more prone to undergo torsion. The testis can rotate within the tunica vaginalis or the entire cord may rotate on itself. The left testis usually rotates counterclockwise and the right turns clockwise, an important fact to remember when one must undo the torsion. Symptoms include local pain and swelling, and sometimes nausea and vomiting. Scrotal edema is common. A torsed spermatic cord must be differentiated from acute epididymitis; the latter condition is relieved by support of the testis, the former is not.

Treatment is surgical detorsion and orchiopexy. The contralateral testis should also be explored and the parietal tunica vaginalis excised to prevent torsion later.

13

VASCULAR SURGERY

Edwin J. Wylie, MD & Cornelius Olcott IV, MD

I. EVALUATION OF THE VASCULAR SURGICAL PATIENT

The history and physical examination are extremely important in the management of vascular surgical patients because the correct diagnosis can usually be made on the basis of information obtained from these two modalities.

A. HISTORY A careful history should be taken. Inquiry should be made into all aspects of vascular disease—occlusive arterial disease, venous disease, thoracic outlet syndrome, portal hypertension and so on.

Most patients have problems related to arterial occlusive disease. The examiner should look for symptoms involving any segment of the vascular system: cardiac (myocardial infarction, angina); cerebrovascular (stroke, transient ischemic attacks); visceral (abdominal pain, weight loss); renal (hypertension); and extremity (claudication, rest pain). Questions should also be asked about the presence or absence of atherosclerotic risk factors: smoking, hyperlipidemia, hypertension, and diabetes.

B. PHYSICAL EXAMINATION Both the arterial and venous systems should be examined carefully. Specific points relating to the arterial system include the following:

1. All pulses should be palpated and graded from 0 (absent) to 4+ (normal). The following pulses should be examined: carotid, superficial temporal, subclavian, brachial, radial, ulnar, abdominal aorta, femoral, popliteal, dorsalis pedis, and posterior tibial.

2. Arteries should be examined for: quality of pulse; size and quality of artery (e.g., is the vessel soft, or hard and calcified; is it aneurysmal?)

3. Bruits reflect turbulent flow from stenosis of the vessel. Auscultation should be carried out over the carotid, subclavian, abdominal aorta, iliac, and femoral vessels.

4. A thrill is a palpable bruit and is a manifestation of severe stenosis.

5. Elevation pallor (paleness of the feet when elevated) indicates significant ischemia.

6. Dependent rubor (a violaceous color to the feet when dependent) denotes severe ischemia.

7. Other signs of severe ischemia are skin ulceration and gangrene.

C. NONINVASIVE TESTS New methods are being developed to aid in the diagnosis and quantification of the severity of vascular disease.

1. Cerebrovascular disease Phonoangiogram determines the location and intensity of cervical bruits. Ocular plethysmography (OPG) is useful for determining 'forward' or 'stump' pressure (Gee-OPG), or degree of stenosis (Kartchner-OPG).

2. Lower extremity Doppler ultrasound allows one to hear blood flow, either arterial or venous, and permits quantification of blood supply by measuring arterial pressures.

D. ARTERIOGRAPHY is the mainstay of vascular diagnostic tests. It is used to delineate accurately the arterial anatomy, the presence of occlusive lesions, and the degree of stenosis.

II. PREOPERATIVE PREPARATION AND POSTOPERATIVE CARE

Attention to detail in preparing patients and caring for them postoperatively can prevent many surgical and angiographic complications. The following routine orders are suggested as guidelines for some of the common procedures.

A. ROUTINE ADMITTING ORDERS
    1. CBC, urinalysis, VDRL, EKG, and chest x-ray.
    2. If surgery is contemplated, serum electrolytes, SMA-12, prothrombin time, PTT, and platelet count should also be determined.
    3. Discontinue any antiplatelet medication (e.g., aspirin).
    4. Type and cross-match for blood as necessary.

B. ARTERIOGRAPHY
    1. Preparation (1) Informed consent is obtained. (2) NPO after midnight. (3) Start IV with D_5 ½ NS and run 50–75 cc/hour after NPO to maintain hydration. (4) Shave the groin or axilla if study will be transfemoral or transaxillary. (5) Abdominal angiography: clear liquid diet on the night before arteriograms; 1 bottle of magnesium citrate to be given by 4 pm on the day prior to study; give tapwater enema (TWE) on the night before study. (6) Translumbar aortography (TLA), give Fleet's enema on the night before study. (7) Prearteriogram medications (if study is to be done without general or regional anesthesia): carotid—atropine 0.8 mg IM, no sedatives; abdominal—atropine 0.8 mg IM, valium 5–10 mg IM. (8) Contrast solutions are powerful osmotic diuretics: Patients should void before leaving the ward for any arteriographic study.
    2. Care after the study
      a. Transaxillary or transfemoral arteriogram (1) Bed-rest for 4–6 hours. (2) Ice-bag to groin or axilla. (3) Check for distal pulses and hematoma. (4) Discontinue IV after oral liquids are tolerated.
      b. Translumbar aortogram (1) Hct that night. (2) Ambulate that night. (3) Continue IV if operation is contemplated within 24 hours.
      c. Urinary retention due to diuretic effect in an elderly or sedated patient should be guarded against.

C. CAROTID TEA's AND ARCH RECONSTRUCTIONS
    1. Preoperative Male patients should shave neck on the morning of surgery. Shave chest if sternotomy or thoracotomy is anticipated. Start IV with large-bore needle and infuse D_5 ½ NS at 50–75 cc/hour overnight. Discontinue antihypertensive medications the morning of operation. Give no sedatives.
    2. Postoperative Monitor blood pressure closely; if postoperative pressure is 20 mm Hg above or below preoperative levels, treatment may be necessary; high pressure is lowered with nitroprusside, and hypotension is treated with plasmanate. Neurological checks at frequent intervals for 48 hours. Check the neck closely for signs of expanding hematoma, tracheal deviation, or respiratory embarrassment. Vital signs should be recorded hourly for 24 hours after operation.

D. MAJOR ABDOMINAL CASES
    1. Preoperative Clear liquids for 24 hours prior to operation; NPO after midnight. Shave from the nipple to the knees. 1 bottle of magnesium citrate should be given by 4 pm on the day prior to operation. TWE on the night before operation. Start IV with D_5 ¼ NS and infuse at 50–75 cc/hour to maintain hydration overnight. Note: A patient undergoing a renovascular reconstruction or a procedure which may require aortic occlusion above the renal arteries (e.g.,

thoracoabdominal aneurysm) should have a Foley catheter inserted in the morning, and a urine output of 60-100 ml/hour should be established before the patient is taken from the ward; be certain the urine output is adequate before induction of anesthesia. Prophylactic antibiotics should be started before the operation is begun. Weigh preoperatively.

2. Postoperative In addition to the usual care after major abdominal operations, the appropriate pulses are checked every hour for 24 hours. Ambulation begins when the patient is stable, but sitting is prohibited if grafts extend below the inguinal ligament.

E. FEMORAL-POPLITEAL BYPASS, PROFUNDAPLASTY

1. Preoperative Regular diet; NPO after midnight. Shave from nipples to toes. TWE the night before surgery. Start IV with large angiocath: D_5 ¼ NS at 50-75 cc/hour overnight. Give prophylactic antibiotics.

2. Postoperative Monitor distal pulses carefully and restrict flexion of knees or hips.

F. LUMBAR SYMPATHECTOMY

All patients having a sympathectomy, alone or as part of an arterial reconstruction, should be given Dilantin (100 mg tid for 10 days) as soon as oral diet is begun.

III. TRAUMA

Penetrating wounds perforate arteries or veins directly or from blast effect. Blunt trauma disrupts vessels completely, or only the intima of arteries may be torn, causing subsequent thrombosis.

1. Diagnosis

a. Symptoms and signs Arterial bleeding at any time after the injury. Hypotension and shock. Large or expanding hematoma. Diminished or absent distal pulses (the presence of normal pulses does not rule out an arterial injury). Bruit at the site of the injury. Injury to anatomically related nerves.

2. X-rays Plain films help delineate the tract of a bullet or other penetrating missile and will reveal associated injuries to bones. Arteriograms help determine the presence or extent of injury; they are useful when the diagnosis is in doubt, and in situations where exploration may be difficult or hazardous, e.g., the base of the skull or the arch of the aorta. However, arteriography necessitates delay and should not be done if the patient is bleeding actively. Arteriography may be performed on the operating table if needed.

3. Complications Hemorrhage and shock. False aneurysm. Arteriovenous fistula. Distal ischemia due to interruption of blood flow from immediate disruption or later thrombosis of the artery. Venous thrombosis and late insufficiency. Bullet embolization.

4. Treatment

a. Emergency measures Control of hemorrhage is best achieved by direct pressure, manually or with dressings. Tourniquets should **not** be used. Resuscitate from shock (see Chapter 1) and transfuse blood as necessary. The extremity should be splinted if fractures accompany the vascular injuries.

b. Surgical treatment of arterial injuries has two objectives: to control the bleeding and to repair the blood vessel so that distal blood flow is reestablished. In venous injuries, control of bleeding is the principal goal.

Methods of repair: (1) Direct suture of the injured blood vessel should be done only when it can be accomplished without stenosis of the lumen. (2) Excision of the injured area with primary end-to-end vascular anastomosis. (3) Excision of the injured area and replacement with an autogenous graft (e.g., saphenous vein or an artery excised from another site); prosthetic grafts should not be used because of the risk of infection. (4) Ligation seldom is acceptable management of major arterial injuries, with one important exception: injuries of the carotid artery which produce fixed neurological deficits are best treated by ligation to avoid converting ischemic infarcts to hemorrhagic ones.

If an arteriovenous fistula exists, both the artery and vein should be repaired if possible.

Accompanying venous injury should be repaired if possible, otherwise ligation is acceptable.

At the conclusion of the procedure, an operative arteriogram should be taken to ensure that the reconstruction is satisfactory.

Vascular suture lines should be covered by fascia or subcutaneous tissue in addition to skin.

Penetrating wounds should be debrided to prevent infection.

Fasciotomy should be avoided if possible. In most cases, prompt vascular reconstruction will prevent severe edema in the muscle compartments.

5. Prognosis Simple ligation of a major artery has a very high rate of subsequent amputation (as high as 85% following popliteal artery ligation). Arterial reconstruction performed soon after injury, before tissue ischemia becomes irreversible, has an excellent prognosis for limb salvage.

IV. ARTERIOVENOUS FISTULAS

Arteriovenous fistulas are abnormal communications between arteries and veins. They may be congenital or acquired.

A. CONGENITAL ARTERIOVENOUS FISTULAS typically are multiple, small lesions that are present from birth, but do not become clinically manifest until age 10 to 20 years. They most frequently occur in the lower or upper extremity, female pelvis, or head and neck. The central nervous system may also be involved. They range in size from small (1-2 cm) to very large lesions that fill the entire pelvis or involve most of an extremity.

1. Diagnosis

a. Symptoms Pain and swelling in the area of the arteriovenous fistula. Bleeding. Cardiac failure.

b. Signs Enlarged, tortuous arteries and veins. Mass. Increased skin temperature over fistula. Continuous machinery murmur over the fistula. Thrill over the fistula. Venous hypertension distally, possibly associated with chronic venous insufficiency. Increased limb length if extremity is involved. Nicoladoni-Branham sign: prompt decrease in heart rate upon digital closure of the fistula; less likely to be elicited in congenital than in acquired fistula.

c. X-rays Chest x-ray may show a cardiac enlargement due to cardiac failure. Extremity x-rays may show elongation of bones. Arteriograms document the anatomical connections and extent of the arteriovenous malformation.

2. Differential diagnosis Congenital fistulas must be differentiated from traumatic fistulas. This can usually be done on the basis of history, and the fact that a traumatic AV fistula typically has only a single communication. Hemangiomas are benign tumors derived from newly formed blood vessels; they are composed of dilated thin-walled vessels, but they do not have true arteriovenous communications and the symptoms and signs of high rates of blood flow through the lesion are absent.

3. Complications These lesions may be entirely asymptomatic. They may, however, become so large that they interfere with function of an extremity or are cosmetically displeasing. Other complications include bleeding (e.g., pelvic lesions may present with uncontrolled menorrhagia), congestive heart failure, pain, and distal digital gangrene when an extremity is involved.

4. Treatment

a. If the lesions are small and easily accessible, they should be excised completely.

b. Simple ligation of afferent, or feeding, vessels is inadequate treatment and early recurrence is the rule.

c. Large, unresectable but localized lesions may be controlled by embolization. Angiography is preferred to locate the feeding vessels, and small emboli of gelfoam pellets, cotton or autogenous muscle are injected into these vessels. This method is not applicable to diffuse limb bud congenital AV fistulas.

d. Large lesions that are amenable to excision are more easily removed if they are embolized first and then excised within 24 hours. Embolization decreases the vascularity of the lesion.

5. Prognosis Completely excised lesions will not recur. Lesions treated by embolization may require embolization again in 1 or 2 years.

B. TRAUMATIC ARTERIOVENOUS FISTULAS result from penetrating injuries which produce a connection between an artery and an adjacent vein. Traumatic fistulas can be iatrogenic, e.g., following excision of an intervertebral disc. If not corrected, traumatic arteriovenous fistulas continue to enlarge.

1. Diagnosis History of trauma. Pain. Congestive heart failure. Venous insufficiency distally. Bruit and/or thrill. Nicoladoni-Branham sign.

2. Complications Untreated fistulas may become so large that they cause cardiac failure and ischemia of the extremity distally.

3. Treatment These lesions should be corrected as soon as possible. Surgical management requires closure of the fistula and reconstruction of the involved artery and vein.

V. ANEURYSMS

Most arterial aneurysms are atherosclerotic in western countries. They are true aneurysms (contain all layers of the vessel wall) and appear as fusiform dilatations. Mural thrombus is deposited on the inner surface of aneurysms because of eddy currents and stagnant flow. For this reason, the functional lumen of the aneurysmal vessel may not be widened.

A. THORACOABDOMINAL aneurysms involve the descending thoracic aorta (distal to the left subclavian artery) and the upper abdominal aorta. They typically involve the visceral and renal arteries and may extend to the infrarenal aorta as well.

1. Diagnosis

a. Symptoms Frequently asymptomatic; may cause back pain, chest pain or abdominal pain if they rupture or expand rapidly.

b. Signs Associated aneurysmal disease of other vessels. Pulsatile abdominal mass may be palpable if the infrarenal aorta is involved.

c. X-rays Chest x-rays demonstrate widening of the thoracic aorta. Plain films of the abdomen may show calcification of the wall of the aneurysm in a suprarenal location. Arteriograms demonstrate the extent of involvement including the status of visceral and renal arteries.

2. Complications Rupture is a risk if the diameter exceeds 7-9 cm. Embolization to distal arteries. Occlusion of visceral or renal arteries.

3. Treatment **Asymptomatic** thoracoabdominal aneurysms, particularly those in poor risk patients, should be treated expectantly. These aneurysms rarely produce complications. **Symptomatic** aneurysms should be resected and replaced with prosthetic grafts. It may be necessary to reimplant the celiac axis, superior mesenteric artery, and renal arteries in the course of the operation.

4. Prognosis Resection of thoracoabdominal aneurysm is a high risk procedure. The prognosis is good after reconstruction if the entire aneurysm can be resected.

B. ABDOMINAL ANEURYSMS involve the subdiaphragmatic aorta. Typically, the aneurysm is limited to the infrarenal aorta, although rarely the suprarenal aorta also is involved. The common iliac vessels often are included in the aneurysmal dilatation.

1. Diagnosis

a. Symptoms Intact aneurysms are usually asymptomatic, except for the rare 'inflammatory' aneurysms (atherosclerotic aneurysms surrounded by inflammatory reaction) which may cause abdominal pain. Rapidly expanding or rupturing aneurysms produce abdominal and/or back pain. Occasionally, an aneurysm presses on adjacent nerves and the patient senses pain along the distribution of the femoral nerve.

b. Signs Pulsatile abdominal mass just superior to the umbilicus. There may be associated aneurysmal dilatation of other vessels. The width of the mass (diameter of the aneurysm) should be measured.

c. X-rays Plain films of the abdomen may show calcification in the outer wall of the aneurysm; a cross-table lateral view is especially useful to assess size. Arteriograms are not helpful in the diagnosis of aneurysm because mural thrombosis maintains the lumen at normal caliber. Arteriograms are indicated if one suspects suprarenal or renal artery involvement or associated occlusive vascular disease.

d. Special tests Ultrasound and CT scans have been used to document the size and extent of aneurysms.

2. Differential diagnosis Other abdominal masses usually enveloping or behind the aorta, may have a transmitted pulse. Examples include lymphomas, pancreatic lesions and mesenteric masses.

3. Complications Rupture causes death from hemorrhage. Bleeding may be contained in the retroperitoneal tissues at first, but eventually it breaks into the peritoneal cavity and the patient exsanguinates. Pain in the back or flank indicates rupture. Examination may reveal a hypotensive patient, a mass in the abdomen or flank, and subcutaneous ecchymosis. Other complications are embolization and thrombosis.

4. Treatment

a. Asymptomatic aneurysms under 5 cm in diameter may be treated expectantly, particularly if the patient is a poor operative candidate. Aneurysms 6 cm in size or greater should be considered for resection because of the risk of rupture.

b. Immediate abdominal exploration is indicated whenever rupture of an aortic aneurysm is suspected. The patient may be in shock upon entry to the hospital. The patient should be taken to the operating room immediately and resuscitated from shock there, while preparations are made for emergency operation to control the hemorrhage.

c. Standard aneurysmectomy involves replacement of the aneurysmal aorta with a prosthetic (Dacron) graft. Normally the graft extends to the common iliac arteries; however, if the common iliac arteries are involved as well, the graft may need to be extended to the external iliac arteries. Following replacement grafting, the aneurysm wall is wrapped around the graft to protect it from the abdominal viscera.

C. FEMORAL ANEURYSMS involve the common femoral artery and occasionally the proximal portion of the profunda or superficial femoral artery as well.

1. Diagnosis Femoral aneurysm is usually asymptomatic and is discovered on physical examination. **Note:** an associated abdominal aneurysm should be sought in any patient with femoral aneurysm. Laboratory tests and x-rays are not necessary, although arteriography may be helpful in defining associated occlusive disease.

2. Differential diagnosis Other types of groin masses usually are differentiated easily from the pulsatile mass of femoral aneurysm. False aneurysms are the result of disruption of the arterial wall allowing blood to extravasate into surrounding tissues; false aneurysms, therefore, are not lined by arterial wall. Common causes of false femoral aneurysm include percutaneous catheterization or separation of a Dacron graft from the anterior surface of the common femoral artery.

3. Complications Thrombosis; embolization; rupture (rare in the true aneurysm).

4. Treatment Most femoral artery aneurysms do not require treatment, but symptomatic or complicated aneurysms should be repaired by resection and replacement with a Dacron or autogenous graft. False aneurysms have a high risk of rupture and should be repaired.

5. Prognosis is good.

D. POPLITEAL ANEURYSM

1. Diagnosis A pulsatile mass is palpable in the popliteal fossa; it may be associated with aneurysms elsewhere. Arteriography helps delineate the extent of the aneurysm and the presence or absence of associated occlusive disease. A negative arteriogram does not exclude the diagnosis of popliteal aneurysm. Ultrasound technics have also been used to define these lesions.

2. Differential diagnosis Adventitial cystic disease of the popliteal artery and Baker's cyst should be considered.

3. Complications Thrombosis is the main complication; it results in severe ischemia of the lower extremity. Embolization from a mural thrombus may occur. Rupture is rare.

4. Treatment Most popliteal artery aneurysms can be treated expectantly. Symptomatic aneurysms should be resected and replaced by grafts. Because of the location of the aneurysm opposite a joint space, the graft material should be autogenous (saphenous vein or autogenous artery).

5. Prognosis is good.

E. VISCERAL ARTERY ANEURYSM

Aneurysms may arise in the celiac axis or its branches, the superior mesenteric artery, or the renal arteries. Aneurysms of the superior mesenteric artery are usually mycotic. Renal artery aneurysms are atherosclerotic or associated with fibromuscular dysplasia.

1. Diagnosis Visceral aneurysms may produce abdominal or flank pain. Aneurysms of the renal arteries may cause hematuria or hypertension. Mycotic aneurysms may be associated with symptoms of systemic infection—fever, chills. The aneurysms usually cannot be detected by physical examination. The diagnosis is made by arteriography.

2. Complications Mycotic aneurysms will almost always rupture if untreated, and they are a source of chronic septicemia. Other visceral aneurysms may also rupture, especially splenic artery aneurysms in pregnant women. Visceral aneurysms may give rise to distal emboli, or they may compress adjacent structures, e.g., common bile duct or ureter.

3. Treatment

a. All mycotic aneurysms require operation for resection or endoaneurysmorrhaphy with excision of as much of the infected aneurysm wall as possible.

b. Renal artery aneurysms only occasionally require surgical treatment—if they are symptomatic, greater than 2.5 cm in diameter, or lack a calcified wall. The operation is resection of the aneurysm with autogenous reconstruction. Ex-vivo perfusion of the kidney is necessary if the aneurysm involves small branches of the renal artery.

c. Other visceral aneurysms are operated on only if they cause symptoms.

4. Prognosis The prognosis for mycotic aneurysms is poor because these patients frequently succumb to complications of septicemia. Also, it is not infrequent for other mycotic aneurysms to develop. Surgical correction of atherosclerotic aneurysms is usually curative.

VI. ARTERIAL OCCLUSIVE DISEASE

A. AORTO-ILIO-FEMORAL DISEASE Arteriosclerosis may involve singly, or in combination, any of the arteries supplying the lower extremities. Typical patterns include aorto-common iliac disease, aorto-iliac and common femoral disease, and superficial femoral disease alone. Arteriosclerosis of the popliteal and trifurcation vessels or the profunda femorus artery indicates very advanced disease. Occlusion may occur gradually (secondary to progressive atherosclerosis) or suddenly (from embolus or acute thrombosis of an atherosclerotic lesion). Chronic progressive lesions permit enlargement of collateral blood supply which, for a time, minimizes the severity of symptoms. Acute occlusion causes severe ischemia because collaterals have not been developed.

1. Diagnosis

a. Symptoms

Claudication—Ischemic muscle pain occurring with exercise. Pain begins after a variable amount of exercise; the more extensive the occlusive disease, the more prompt the onset of pain. It is characteristically relieved by rest. Lesions of the femoral system produce calf claudication; lesions of the aorto-iliac system may also produce buttock and thigh claudication.

Rest pain—Severe aching pain in the toes and forefoot which appears when the patient lies in the horizontal position; it is relieved by hanging the foot over the side of the bed or by standing. Rest pain is a symptom of advanced ischemia.

Ischemic ulcers and gangrene—Tissue loss secondary to advanced occlusive disease.

b. Signs Diminished or absent pulses distal to a lesion. Pulses are graded from 0 to 4+. The more severe the lesion, the weaker the pulse.

Bruit—An audible systolic sound over and distal to an arterial stenosis. The more severe the stenosis, the louder and higher pitched the bruit.

Thrill—A palpable bruit; it denotes severe stenosis.

Elevation pallor—Paleness of the feet with elevation of the lower extremities; it reflects significant ischemia.

Dependent rubor represents advanced ischemia.

Ischemic ulcers or gangrene is frank tissue loss and therefore indicates the most severe ischemia.

c. Arteriography is the most reliable diagnostic test for occlusive lesions. Two methods of arteriography are employed. (1) Translumbar aortography: a needle is placed percutaneously into the aorta at the level of the renal arteries; contrast medium is injected and serial films are obtained to delineate the pathologic anatomy of the aorto-ilio-femoral system. The advantage is that it can be performed relatively quickly and safely. (2) Transfemoral-Seldinger technic: an angiographic catheter is inserted into one of the common femoral arteries and advanced to the appropriate level, contrast is injected, and serial x-rays are taken. The placement of a transfemoral catheter in a patient with occlusive vascular disease carries a small but definite risk of causing acute occlusion at the puncture site; the catheter also may dislodge atherosclerotic debris which embolizes distally.

d. Special tests A number of noninvasive tests have been developed over the past several years to diagnose occlusive lesions. The most popular of these methods is Doppler ultrasound; this test employs a Doppler flowmeter and blood pressure cuff. The Doppler allows one to actually hear blood flow in vessels where pulses are not palpable. Using a standard blood pressure cuff, the

Doppler permits measurement of blood pressure in the thigh, calf, and ankle; at rest and after exercise. Pressure in these areas is expressed as a fraction of the brachial artery pressure, i.e. ankle/brachial ratio. Normal levels are 0.9–1; pressure ratios under 0.9 are thought to be compatible with claudication, and levels under 0.5 are thought to be compatible with rest pain and severe ischemia.

2. Differential diagnosis   The signs and symptoms of ischemia are fairly typical and diagnostic. One entity which can cause confusion is neurogenic claudication due to abnormalities in the spinal canal which compress the cauda equina. Typically, these symptoms are more prominent when the patient is upright with the lumbar area straightened, and can be relieved by bending over. Neurogenic claudication is not exacerbated when the patient walks uphill, but ischemic claudication is much worse during this sort of vigorous exercise.

3. Complications   Marked disability due to diminished exercise tolerance. Potential limb loss.

4. Treatment

a. Medical   Various medical regimens have been aimed at arresting the progression of atherosclerosis, by controlling cholesterol and triglyceride abnormalities and regulating hypertension. Drugs have also been used to produce vasodilatation but have not been effective treatment for atherosclerotic occlusive disease of the lower extremities. Cigarette smoking should be discouraged.

b. Surgical   Operations for occlusive disease of the aorto-ilio-femoral system have the goal of restoring blood flow through or around the diseased area. Two methods are in use: (1) Endarterectomy—removal of the diseased stenotic intima to produce a normal vessel lumen. (2) Bypass grafting from the normal proximal vessel around the diseased area to a normal vessel distally. Examples are aortofemoral bypass graft, or femoral-popliteal bypass graft.

Lumbar sympathectomy is usually added to arterial reconstruction; it may provide some improvement if done alone in patients whose vessels are not suitable for reconstruction.

5. Prognosis   Reconstructive vascular surgery for occlusive disease yields satisfactory results in 95% of patients. The long-term prognosis for any patient with atherosclerosis is guarded, however, because atherosclerosis is a progressive, generalized disease that may develop elsewhere or extend distally beyond the point of reconstruction. The number of vessels involved and the rate of progression varies; the younger the patient at the age of onset and the more vessels affected by atherosclerosis the worse the prognosis.

B. VISCERAL arteries may become occluded, usually by atherosclerosis. The celiac artery may be compressed by the median arcuate ligament, and emboli may cause acute occlusion of the superior mesenteric artery or celiac axis.

1. Diagnosis

a. Symptoms   The symptoms of chronic visceral arterial insufficiency are referrable to the GI tract. Typically, the patient complains of cramping, postprandial epigastric abdominal pain that begins within a half hour after eating and lasts from 1–3 hours. Weight loss is a prominent symptom because eating produces pain. Acute embolic occlusion produces sudden, severe abdominal pain (see Chapter 10).

b. Signs   An upper abdominal bruit is audible in about 80% of patients. The bruit is made louder by having the patient exhale. There may be findings of occlusive vascular disease, elsewhere, e.g., diminished pulses in the vessels of the lower extremities.

c. Laboratory tests   Malabsorption of fat may be demonstrated.

d. X-rays   Arteriography is the definitive diagnostic test for occlusive lesions of the visceral arteries. It is best performed by the transfemoral or transaxillary Seldinger technic so that biplane views may be obtained of the visceral vessels.

2. Differential diagnosis The patient with abdominal pain and weight loss may have other abdominal diseases, e.g., carcinoma of the pancreas. However, the pattern of postprandial abdominal pain and weight loss is fairly characteristic, and visceral ischemic syndromes should be placed high on the list of possible explanations.

3. Complications Intractable abdominal pain resulting in malnutrition from unwillingness to eat. Acute intestinal infarction and death.

4. Treatment

a. Medical There is no medical therapy for the relief of occlusive vascular disease in the intestinal tract. In fact, many of the drugs used by patients in the atherosclerotic age group (diuretics, propanolol, digitalis) have an adverse effect upon visceral perfusion.

b. Surgical treatment involves the restoration of blood flow to at least 2 of the 3 visceral arteries (celiac, superior mesenteric, inferior mesenteric). Endarterectomy is the preferred method, but interposition or bypass grafts are also used. Compression of the celiac artery by the median arcuate ligament is relieved by division of the ligament and mechanical dilatation of the celiac artery.

Acute embolic occlusion should be treated by embolectomy and resection of nonviable bowel. A 'second look' operation at 24 hours is recommended, to evaluate the viability of remaining bowel.

5. Prognosis is good following restoration of blood flow in patients with chronic intestinal ischemia. The prognosis of acute ischemia is poor (see Chapter 10).

C. CEREBROVASCULAR Lesions of the extracranial cerebral vessels are responsible for approximately 80% of vascular neurological problems. Symptoms may arise from decreased cerebral perfusion due to single or multiple occlusive lesions, thrombosis of an extracranial cerebral vessel, or embolization from a proximal lesion.

Diseases affecting the extracranial system include atherosclerosis, fibromuscular dysplasia, spontaneous or traumatic dissection, and Takayasu's arteritis.

1. Diagnosis

a. Symptoms (1) Transient ischemic attacks: transient focal neurological deficits, e.g., paresis or numbness of the contralateral arm or leg, or loss of vision (amaurosis fugax). By definition, all symptoms must resolve within 24 hours; however, these attacks characteristically last only 15-30 minutes. (2) Stroke: permanent neurological deficit. (3) Symptoms due to decreased cerebral perfusion: deficits in mentation or memory; light-headedness; fainting. (4) Vertebral-basilar insufficiency: ataxia, vertigo, drop attacks, diplopia, bilateral visual blurring.

b. Signs (1) Reduced pulses: common carotid, superficial temporal, subclavian; the internal carotid pulse cannot be palpated. (2) Bruits: Carotid bifurcation occlusive lesions characteristically produce a bruit just inferior to the angle of the mandible. Common carotid lesions produce a bruit audible along the entire length of the artery. Innominate lesions produce a bruit at the base of the right neck and along the right carotid and subclavian arteries. Lesions involving the subclavian or vertebral arteries may produce a bruit audible in the ipsilateral supraclavicular fossa.

c. X-rays Angiography remains the best test for determining the location and severity of extracranial vascular disease.

d. Special tests Noninvasive tests are also used (1) Ocular plethysmography (OPG): Gee-OPG determines 'forward' and 'stump' pressures as reflected in the ocular globe from the ophthalmic arterial supply. Kartchner-OPG detects a delay in the internal carotid waveforms and therefore assists in diagnosing carotid stenosis. (2) Doppler ultrasound detects the direction of blood flow in collateral facial arteries.

2. Differential diagnosis Other causes of decreased perfusion, e.g., heart failure, orthostatic hypotension secondary to antihypertensive medications, cardiac arrhythmias. Emboli from the heart. Intracranial vascular or neoplastic disease.

3. Complications Stroke, death.

4. Treatment

a. The object of treatment is to prevent stroke or relieve disability (e.g., prevent symptoms of low perfusion). A fixed neurologic deficit cannot usually be reversed. Medical therapy (anticoagulation) does not correct the responsible lesion(s) and therefore is not effective.

b. Endarterectomy is the preferred treatment for atherosclerotic lesions of the common carotid, carotid bifurcation, innominate, subclavian, or vertebral arteries.

c. Fibromuscular dysplasia may be treated by resection and autograft replacement. Usually, however, these lesions extend too far distally to be resectable, and in these cases mechanical arterial dilatation is used.

5. Prognosis The incidence of neurological deficit caused by the operation is less than 2%. Only 2% of patients develop recurrent disease in an operated vessel.

D. RENOVASCULAR LESIONS
Hypertension may be caused by decreased renal blood flow which stimulates the juxtaglomerular cells of the kidney to secrete renin. Renin is converted to angiotensin, and hypertension results. The most common diseases producing renovascular hypertension are atherosclerosis and fibromuscular dysplasia. Atherosclerosis characteristically involves the proximal third of the renal artery and occurs in males over 45; it is bilateral in 35% of cases. Fibromuscular dysplasia usually affects the middle and distal third of the renal arteries and often extends into the branch vessels. This disease typically occurs in middle-age females, and is bilateral in 50% of patients.

1. Diagnosis

a. Signs and symptoms Hypertension and symptoms related to it (e.g., headache). An upper abdominal bruit may be heard to one or both sides of the midline. Patients with atherosclerosis may have evidence of occlusive disease elsewhere (e.g., aortoiliac or carotid system).

b. X-rays Intravenous pyelography may demonstrate a small kidney or a delay in excretion on the affected side. Arteriography shows the location and extent of occlusive lesions.

c. Special tests (1) *Renal vein renin studies.* Renin concentration is determined in blood samples obtained from each renal vein. If the ratio of renin from the involved kidney to the uninvolved one is 1.5 or greater, the diagnosis of unilateral ischemia is suggested. (2) *Renal artery blood flow.* Nuclear scanning of the kidneys after intravenous injection of [131]hippurate allows measurement of the relative blood flow to each kidney. (3) *Split-function studies.* The affected kidney may demonstrate reduction in sodium concentration and increased concentration of para-amino hippurate and insulin in urine obtained by bilateral retrograde ureteral catheterization. These tests are seldom performed now because of unreliability and morbidity.

2. Treatment

a. The usual indications for operation are: diastolic blood pressure greater than 110 mm Hg; failure to control blood pressure with usual medical management; a significant lesion demonstrated angiographically.

b. Since the disease may develop or progress on the presently uninvolved side, surgical repair should be performed whenever possible. If arterial repair is impossible or particularly hazardous and the disease is unilateral, nephrectomy may be considered.

c. Atherosclerotic lesions are best managed by transaortic endarterectomy.

d. Replacement grafting using autogenous tissue (preferably the hypogastric artery) is the preferred treatment for fibromuscular dysplasia. If the disease extends into branch vessels, reconstruction should be performed ex vivo with constant perfusion of the kidney.

3. Prognosis Surgical arterial reconstruction is successful and blood pressure is lowered in 90% of patients with fibromuscular dysplasia, and in 60% with atherosclerosis.

E. ACUTE ARTERIAL OCCLUSION Sudden occlusion of a previously patent artery is usually a dramatic event producing severe ischemia of the distal tissues. Recovery depends upon the development of collateral vessels; collateral supply is good with occlusion of the brachial or superficial femoral artery, but it is poor with occlusion of the terminal aorta or common femoral artery.

1. Diagnosis

a. Symptoms and signs The characteristic symptoms and signs are the '5 P's': pallor; pain; paresthesia; paralysis; pulselessness. Pallor and pain (and coolness of the limb) appear early; loss of motor and sensory nerve function occurs later and represents irreversible ischemia.

b. X-rays Arteriography shows the site of occlusion and the potential for reconstruction.

2. Differential diagnosis The primary problem is to determine the cause of the sudden occlusion. Possibilities include:

a. Embolus may come from the heart (e.g., atrial thrombus in fibrillating patient, mural thrombus, atrial myxoma, valvular disease) or from atherosclerotic lesions, either occlusive or aneurysmal, in proximal arteries.

b. Thrombosis at the site of an atherosclerotic lesion, usually caused by hemorrhage beneath an atherosclerotic plaque.

c. Trauma in the form of contusion or laceration, or as a complication of arterial catheterization.

3. Complications Irreversible ischemia and gangrene resulting in amputation. Revascularization of severely ischemic limbs may flood the circulation with toxic substances resulting in myoglobinuria and pulmonary insufficiency.

4. Treatment

a. Immediate anticoagulation with intravenous heparin to prevent propagation of the thrombus.

b. Upper extremities Sudden occlusion of the axillary or brachial artery is usually well tolerated. If signs or symptoms of severe ischemia do not improve, surgical intervention is indicated.

c. Lower extremities Emergent restoration of blood flow by operation may be essential to prevent limb loss. Traumatic occlusion must be repaired within a few hours to avoid gangrene (see section on Trauma). Embolus is treated by embolectomy with a balloon (Fogarty) catheter. The source of the embolus should be found and corrected to prevent future emboli. Thrombosis of an atherosclerotic lesion requires reconstruction of the involved arterial segment by endarterectomy or bypass grafting.

5. Prognosis is good if blood flow is reconstituted before ischemia becomes irreversible. Delayed operations have a high morbidity and mortality rate.

F. THROMBOANGITIS OBLITERANS (BUERGER'S DISEASE) This obliterative disorder affects the small vessels of the extremities distal to the brachial or popliteal arteries. It may be associated with migratory phlebitis. It occurs almost exclusively in young males who are heavy cigarette smokers.

1. Diagnosis

a. Symptoms and signs (1) Foot claudication. (2) Severe digital ischemia—pain, cyanosis, gangrene. (3) Loss of ankle or wrist pulses, normal proximal pulses. (4) Allen's test, this test has several variations. One method is to compress the radial and ulnar arteries at the wrist, elevate the arm, and have the patient open and close the hand until it blanches. Release of one vessel allows blood to fill all or part of the hand. The test is repeated but with release of the other vessel. The relative importance of the radial and ulnar arterial supply and the adequacy of anastomosis between them is assessed in this way. In Buerger's disease, delayed filling of affected digital arteries is seen.

b. X-rays Discrete foci of occlusion alternating with apparently uninvolved arterial segments.

2. Differential diagnosis Atherosclerosis usually involves larger arteries. Vasospastic disorder (e.g., Raynaud's) is more prevalent in females, is associated with connective tissue disorder, and does not show focal defects on arteriography.

3. Complications Progressive digital ischemia with eventual loss of hands and feet.

4. Treatment

a. Stop cigarette smoking This is essential to avoid progression of the disease.

b. Sympathectomy is very helpful in improving collateral blood flow in this condition.

c. Amputation may be necessary for persisting pain or gangrene.

d. Reconstructive surgery is rarely possible because the disease is confined to small, distal vessels.

5. Prognosis If the patient stops smoking, the disease will usually stabilize; if the patient continues to smoke, progression of the disease is inevitable.

VII. VASOSPASTIC (VASOCONSTRICTIVE) DISORDERS

Vasospastic disorders are due to abnormal lability of the sympathetic nervous system. Constriction of tiny arteries and veins produces sluggish flow of deoxygenated blood through the capillary bed, and results in cutaneous cyanosis, coldness, and (in the severe state) pain.

1. Diagnosis

a. Raynaud's phenomenon Sequential pallor, cyanosis, and rubor (i.e., vasoconstriction followed by reflex vasodilatation) after exposure to cold. It frequently occurs in association with a connective tissue disorder such as scleroderma. Raynaud's disease is a term applied to the same findings in the absence of an identifiable underlying cause.

b. Acrocyanosis A vasoconstrictive disorder characteristically occurring in young women and manifested by persistent cyanosis of the hands and feet. The findings may be exacerbated by exposure to cold. There may be hyperhidrosis, and patchy cyanosis of the forearm, calves, and thighs (livedo reticularis) is seen.

c. Posttraumatic vasomotor dystrophy This pain syndrome follows injury to the distal upper or lower extremities. Pain is associated with chronic cyanosis and coldness due to vasoconstriction. Spotty, bony atrophy (Sudeck's atrophy) may develop.

Another related posttraumatic disorder involving the upper extremity is termed **causalgia**. It is a very severe burning pain which may be precipitated by even minor stimuli. The extremity has the signs of vasoconstriction (cold, cyanotic, moist).

2. Complications Patients with Raynaud's phenomenon or disease may develop progressive small vessel occlusion in addition to vasoconstriction; digital gangrene may result. Acrocyanosis is a chronic, although benign, disorder; tissue loss is extremely rare. Posttraumatic vasomotor dystrophy and causalgia may cause severe disabling pain, although tissue loss is rare.

3. Treatment Acrocyanosis or Raynaud's phenomenon without incapacitating symptoms can be treated conservatively (e.g., avoid cold, wear gloves and warm stockings). If symptoms are severe or the onset of gangrene is imminent, sympathectomy is indicated. Sympathectomy is the treatment of choice for posttraumatic vasomotor dystrophy and causalgia. Results are excellent.

VIII. THORACIC OUTLET SYNDROME

Thoracic outlet syndrome refers to a constellation of symptoms and signs resulting from compression of the neurovascular bundle as it exits from the chest. Compression occurs in a small area bounded by the first rib, the clavicle, and the anterior scalene muscle.

1. Diagnosis

a. Symptoms and signs   Pain, paresthesias, or numbness in the arm and hand, especially over the distribution of the ulnar nerve. Adson's maneuver (abduction of the arm with the head turned to the opposite side) and abduction with external rotation produce a diminution of the radial pulse. A bruit may be audible over the subclavian artery with these maneuvers. Venous hypertension in the arm secondary to compression of the subclavian vein.

b. X-rays   Cervical spine films may show a cervical rib or an abnormal transverse process on the fifth or sixth cervical vertebrae. Arteriography may demonstrate subclavian artery stenosis. Arteriography is particularly indicated if the thoracic outlet syndrome is believed to be responsible for arterial disease more distally, e.g., embolization from an area of dilatation just beyond a subclavian artery compression.

2. Differential diagnosis   Cervical spine disease. Carpal tunnel syndrome.

3. Complications   Incapacitating pain. Subclavian vein thrombosis. Severe stenosis or occlusion of the subclavian artery; it may produce poststenotic dilatation with embolization from this area. Muscle atrophy, particularly the thenar muscles.

4. Treatment   Conservative—shoulder girdle exercises. Surgical decompression of the thoracic outlet; this requires removal of the first rib and cervical rib if present; the transaxillary approach is preferred.

IX. VENOUS DISEASE

A. VARICOSE VEINS are dilated, tortuous superficial veins in the lower extremity. They may be either **primary** (associated with a normal deep venous system) or **secondary** (associated with a diseased deep venous system).

1. Diagnosis

a. Symptoms and signs   (1) Elongated, tortuous veins of the greater or lesser saphenous system of the thigh and/or leg. (2) Dull, heavy, aching discomfort which progresses during the day and is relieved by elevation. (3) May have findings associated with deep venous disease (see postphlebitic syndrome, below).

b. Special test   Brodie–Trendelenberg test determines competence of perforating veins and the saphenofemoral junction. With the patient supine, the leg is elevated and the saphenous vein is compressed in the thigh with a tourniquet. The patient then stands erect for 30 seconds and the tourniquet is removed. If the saphenous veins fill rapidly from below with the tourniquet in place, the perforators (communications with the deep system) are incompetent. If the greater saphenous fills rapidly from above after the tourniquet is removed, the valves at the saphenofemoral junction are incompetent.

2. Differential diagnosis   The examiner should determine if varicosities are primary or secondary. Edema, pigmentation, and ulceration are signs of deep venous disease and the varicose superficial veins are merely another manifestation of this more important underlying problem (see postphlebitic syndrome, below).

3. Complications Superficial thrombophlebitis. Dermatitis. Bleeding from variceal rupture.

4. Treatment

a. Elastic stockings, periodic elevation, and exercise are sufficient treatment for most patients.

b. Sclerosing injections are not recommended, except to obliterate small residual varicosities after surgical ligation and stripping; otherwise, the sclerosing fluid may precipitate deep thrombophlebitis.

c. Severe aching discomfort at the end of the day, or episodes of superficial thrombophlebitis (see below) are indications for surgical treatment. Most patients who request the operation for cosmetic reasons are disappointed with the results. Either external or internal ligation and stripping of the greater and lesser saphenous veins can be performed.

d. **Warning:** Varicose veins secondary to deep venous disease should **not** be treated by ligation and stripping.

B. DEEP THROMBOPHLEBITIS Acute inflammation and thrombosis of the deep veins of the lower extremity resulting in pain, swelling, and warmth of the involved area. (See Chapter 2.)

C. SUPERFICIAL THROMBOPHLEBITIS Acute inflammation and thrombosis of the saphenous system. Pain, tenderness, and induration are present along the course of the involved veins. Edema is notably absent. (See Chapter 2.)

D. POSTPHLEBITIC SYNDROME This syndrome is the consequence of deep thrombophlebitis. Persistent obstruction of the deep venous system, incomplete recanalization of thrombosed veins, valvular destruction, and reflux of blood through incompetent perforators results in high pressure in the superficial venous system. Periodic bleeding and chronic edema in the soft tissues of the lower leg and ankle cause inflammation and fibrosis; the overlying skin is easily traumatized, leading to ulceration that becomes infected and heals slowly.

1. Diagnosis

a. Symptoms and signs (1) Edema of the distal leg and ankle; it is progressive during the day and resolves with elevation. (2) Stasis dermatitis is a pruritic eczematous reaction. (3) Hyperpigmentation: brownish discoloration secondary to hemosiderin deposition from extravasated red blood cells. (4) Ulceration, most commonly over the medial malleolus, and associated with edema, induration, and cellulitis. (5) Pain associated with swelling and ulceration, relieved by elevation.

b. Special tests Phlebograms document deep venous abnormalities, but they may induce phlebitis and are rarely indicated. Doppler ultrasound may be used to detect occlusion of major deep veins.

2. Treatment

a. The goal is to control venous hypertension and avoid edema and ulceration. This can be accomplished by: custom fitted, heavy duty, knee length elastic stockings; intermittent leg elevation; avoiding sitting or prolonged standing.

b. Stasis ulcers Control edema with elevation; apply a compressive dressing (Unna boot) and change weekly until the ulcer is healed; large ulcers require hospitalization for control of edema and infection; skin grafting may be necessary.

c. In rare instances all conservative measures fail, and a subfascial ligation of the incompetent perforating veins must be carried out (Linton procedure).

3. Prognosis Postphlebitic syndrome is a chronic disease requiring close attention to avoid edema and ulceration. Elastic support is required indefinitely.

X. LYMPHEDEMA

Edema from lymphatic obstruction may be classified as **primary** or **secondary**.

PRIMARY   Congenital lymphedema is present at birth. Lymphedema praecox becomes evident in teens or twenties. Lymphedema tarda develops after age 25.
SECONDARY   Lymphatic obstruction secondary to another disease process, e.g., neoplasm, infection, surgical removal of lymphatics (groin or axillary dissection).
    1. Diagnosis
    a. Symptoms and signs   Progressive swelling of one or both extremities; it begins in the lower leg, but gradually involves the entire extremity. Edema is nonpitting and does not resolve with overnight elevation. The involved leg has a dull burning sensation or tightness but no pain. Recurrent cellulitis is common. ,
    b. Special test   Lymphangiogram may demonstrate the site of obstruction.
    2. Differential diagnosis includes other causes of lower extremity swelling: venous disease, congestive heart failure, hypoproteinemia, myxedema, cirrhosis Lymphedema is characteristically firm, rubbery and nonpitting.
    3. Complications   Recurrent cellulitis and lymphangitis, usually caused by streptococci. Lymphangiosarcoma.
    4. Treatment
    a. Medical   The goal is to control edema and prevent infection (good foot-hygiene). Elevation of the lower extremity at night and at intervals during the day. Custom fitted elastic stocking. Compression device to milk edema from the leg (pneumatic pump). Antibiotics when infection develops.
    b. Surgical   Various procedures have been proposed to improve lymphatic drainage; most are only rarely successful. Kondoleon procedure—excision of skin and subcutaneous tissues. Thompson procedure—a flap of dermis is buried beneath the skin to improve lymphatic drainage.
    5. Prognosis   Most patients have steady progression of swelling and recurrent infections.

XI. ACCESS FOR HEMODIALYSIS

Access to the vascular system is imperative for the increasing number of patients that are maintained on hemodialysis. These procedures also are useful for patients undergoing prolonged intravenous feeding or for patients receiving chemotherapy for malignancies. Many different technics have been developed.

A. SCRIBNER SHUNTS   External prosthetic shunts inserted into an artery and adjacent vein. They are indicated for patients in need of emergency dialysis or in patients who are unable to tolerate a more prolonged operation requiring anesthesia.
    1. Advantages   Can be used immediately after insertion. Can be inserted under local anesthesia. Useful in small children because the shunt can be inserted into small vessels, and venipuncture is not necessary to use the shunt.
    2. Disadvantages   Remains patent a relatively short time. High incidence of infection. Shunt is external.

B. ARTERIOVENOUS FISTULA   A variety of technics provide a subcutaneous arteriovenous fistula that can be cannulated percutaneously when dialysis is required. AV fistulas most commonly are constructed in the upper extremity, although the lower extremity can also be used.

C. CHOICE OF ACCESS PROCEDURE

1. A plan should be devised for each patient which will provide the best possible access, but will also keep open as many options as possible for future procedures.

2. The location of fistulas should begin distally and work proximally.

3. Autogenous technics are preferred; autogenous materials have a lower incidence of infection and a higher patency rate.

4. The upper extremity is preferable to the lower extremity.

5. Based on these considerations, our choice of access procedure for chronic dialysis in adults is:

a. Radial-cephalic arteriovenous fistula This is autogenous and has a long patency rate. It can be performed under local anesthesia. It requires 2–3 weeks to 'mature'.

b. Saphenous arteriovenous fistula This is autogenous, with a good patency rate, and a low incidence of infection. It requires a general anesthetic. A saphenous vein of good quality is required.

c. Bovine or Gore Tex fistula Nonautogenous grafts with a slightly lower patency rate and a higher incidence of infection. Can be performed under regional anesthesia. Can be used immediately if necessary.

14

PLASTIC SURGERY

William J. Morris, MD

I. PRINCIPLES

The objective of plastic and reconstructive surgery is the repair of congenital or acquired defects to improve function and appearance. The plastic surgeon is called upon to treat a wide variety of deformities, not only those of the surface tissues but, also, the deeper structures of all parts of the body.

A. PLANNING A RECONSTRUCTIVE OPERATION

1. Make an accurate diagnosis of the deformity. From the standpoint of plastic surgery, this includes a determination of the amount of tissue loss and the degree of distortion, separation, and atrophy or hypertrophy.

2. Consider all possible methods of repair and select one which will achieve the best possible result in the simplest and most direct manner, using neighboring tissues whenever possible.

3. In multiple stage procedures, plan in detail the entire sequence in advance. Pedicle grafts which are to be transferred should be designed to avoid scarring or deformity at the donor site.

B. TECHNIC

1. Gentleness in handling tissues is essential in reconstructive surgery. Only fine instruments and materials that inflict minimal trauma are used.

2. Incisions are made at right angles to the surface, not on the bevel. They should not cross normal flexion or expression creases but should conform to skin lines of minimal tension whenever possible. (Fig. 14-1).

3. Elliptical excisions are planned whenever possible so that the closure will be smooth and without 'dog ears' (Fig. 14-1).

4. Hemostasis must be meticulous. Fine 'mosquito' forceps are used to clamp vessels so that no more tissue than necessary is grasped. Fine ligatures (0000 or 00000 catgut or polyglycolic acid) or the electrocautery are used.

5. The skin is manipulated only with fine-tooth forceps or skin hooks to prevent crushing.

6. Subcutaneous tissues are closed with fine catgut or polyglycolic acid sutures to eliminate 'dead space' which leads to subsequent scarring and scar depression. Knots are tied on the deep surface avoiding tension (Fig. 14-2). Undermining in the subcutaneous plane is done only when necessary to permit relaxed closure (Fig. 14-3).

7. Skin sutures are placed for accurate surface approximation after the wound edges have been brought together with fine catgut or polyglycolic acid. The simplest suture is preferred: interrupted, running, or subcuticular, according to the situation and the surgeon's preference (Fig. 14-4). 00000 or 000000 silk or nylon with an atraumatic needle is used. The needle should enter and emerge at right angles to the skin, close to the wound margins. To avoid cross-hatching, sutures should not be tied tightly and should be removed within 4 or 5 days whenever possible.

Fig. 14-1. Sites of elliptical incisions corresponding to wrinkle lines in the face. (Reproduced with permission from Dunphy JE, Way LW (Eds.): *Current Surgical Diagnosis & Treatment*, 3rd Ed. Lange 1977

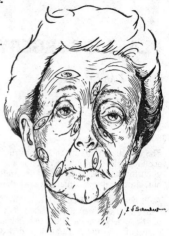

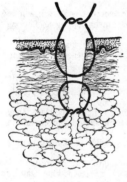 

Fig. 14-2. Wound closure in layers

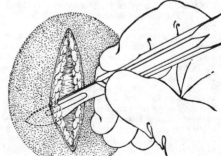

Fig. 14-3. Undermining and wound closure. (Stippling shows area to be undermined)

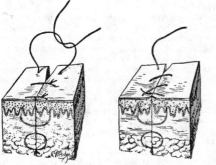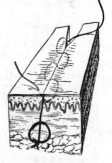

a. Interrupted   **b.** Over and over running   **c.** Subcuticular continuous

Fig. 14-4. Skin sutures (Reproduced with permission, from Grabb and Smith (Eds) *Plastic Surgery*, 2nd ed. Little, Brown, 1973.)

II. CLEFT LIP AND PALATE

Cleft lip and cleft palate occurring either separately or together are the most common congenital anomalies of the head and neck and are among the most common of all congenital anomalies, occurring as often as once in every 650–750 births.

A. CLASSIFICATION   The cleft may vary greatly in severity, involving any part or all of the floor of the nostril, the lip, the alveolus and the hard and soft palates. A useful classification divides the structures involved into the primary and secondary palates.

   1. The primary palate includes the lip, the floor of the nose, the alveolus and the hard palate back to the incisive foramen.

   2. The secondary palate includes the hard and soft palate posterior to this foramen.

   3. A cleft may involve either or both the primary or secondary palates in any degree from incomplete to complete and may be either unilateral or bilateral.

   4. Occasionally a **submucous cleft** is seen, in which case the mucosa is intact with the cleft involving the bone and muscular tissues of the palate.

B. TREATMENT
   1. Feeding   Prior to closure of the cleft lip the infant may have problems with sucking, making breast feedings or ordinary bottle feedings impossible. Generally, this problem can be overcome by enlarging the holes in an artificial nipple, by using a Breck feeder, or by using a short soft rubber tubing attached to a syringe. Gavaging is dangerous and is almost never necessary. Feed in an upright position to help prevent regurgitation.
   2. Timing of the operation
   a. Cleft lip   Clefts of the lip are ideally repaired when the infant reaches 9–10 pounds in weight (usually about 5–6 weeks of age). Surgical closure in smaller infants is more difficult and may be less accurate.
   b. Cleft palate   It is preferred to repair the cleft of the palate when the child is as large as possible, but before he learns to speak. This is usually at 18 months of age.

3. General principles of repair

a. Cleft lip   There is no actual tissue loss in cleft lip; the problem is to re-form the available lip tissue, which is present but separated. Numerous procedures have given excellent results in experienced hands, notably the procedures of Tennison and Millard. Incisions are planned to give a full, normal-appearing lip, correcting much of the nostril deformity at the same time.

b. Cleft palate   In the repair of a cleft palate it is not necessary to obtain bony union but merely to shift the two halves of the palatal mucoperiosteum to the midline and suture them together. The objective is not only to obtain closure of the cleft but also to ensure adequate length of the soft palate for proper velopharyngeal closure. If the palate is long enough, approximation of the two halves of the palate in the midline will suffice. However, in most cases a palate-lengthening operation such as the 'V–Y' flap technic is necessary.

4. Secondary and supplementary procedures

a. Nose and lips   Revision of the nostril deformity may be required. The usual defect is a flattening of the nostril on the cleft side. Minor revision of the vermilion border or cupid's bow may be desirable. In the case of bilateral clefts of the lip, a revision of the nose is probably necessary since the nasal columella is shortened and the nasal tip is pulled downward. Occasionally, in addition to the nasal deformity, the upper lip is tight and the maxilla underdeveloped. In such cases, rotation of the central portion of the full lower lip into the central portion of the upper lip produces marked improvement (Abbe flap procedure).

b. Palate and pharynx   Secondary procedures on the palate are indicated when rhinolalia (nasal speech) is not correctible by speech therapy. Shortening of the palate with inadequate velopharyngeal closure is the primary cause of typical cleft palate speech. In cases of a very minor degree of velopharyngeal incompetence, a 'V–Y' pushback procedure on the palate may correct the speech problem. In most cases, however, it is necessary to perform a pharyngeal flap operation. This consists of raising a flap of mucosa and muscle on the posterior pharyngeal wall and attaching it to the upper surface of the soft palate which has been prepared surgically to receive it.

III. SKIN GRAFTS

A. CLASSIFICATION

1. Free skin grafts
When a graft is completely removed from one part of the body and applied to another, it is termed a 'free' graft. Since its blood supply has been completely separated, its **survival depends upon its being placed on a healthy vascular bed to provide for the ingrowth of blood vessels into the graft.**

Free skin grafts are generally used to replace skin losses only, but, on occasion, they may be used to replace mucous membranes (e.g., in the oral cavity or the vagina.)

There are two types of free skin grafts.

a. Split thickness grafts   These are classified as thin, intermediate, or thick depending upon how much of the dermis is included in the graft. Thin split grafts include only the uppermost layer of dermis, intermediate thickness grafts include approximately 1/3 to 1/2 of the dermis, and thick split grafts contain approximately 2/3 of the dermis. (Fig. 14-5). Skin varies greatly in thickness according to its site on the body (from 0.009 inch on the eyelids to as much as 0.150 inch on the back). If the most common donor sites (such as the anterior or lateral thigh or the lateral buttocks) are used as reference points, the average thin split graft will measure 0.010–0.012 inch in thickness, the intermediate graft 0.016–0.018, and the thick graft 0.022–0.024 inch.

b. Full thickness grafts   These grafts include the full thickness of the epidermis and dermis (Fig. 14-5). If removed from areas of thin skin, such as the

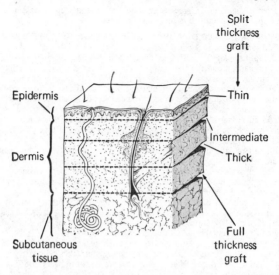

Fig. 14-5. Depths of split thickness and full thickness grafts. (Reproduced with permission from Dunphy JE, Way LW (Eds.): *Current Surgical Diagnosis & Treatment*, 3rd Ed. Lange 1977

eyelid, they will be as thin as 0.009 inch, whereas they may be as thick as 0.025-0.030 inch if removed from an area such as the supraclavicular region.

2. Pedicle grafts A pedicle graft (or flap) is made up of skin and subcutaneous tissue that is raised on one portion of the body and transferred to another. Their thickness makes it impossible for them to survive free transfer since vascular elements cannot grow throughout the graft in time to prevent their death. **Their survival depends upon a circulatory attachment to the body at all times.** This pedicle attachment must be maintained until a new circulation has developed from the recipient site, a process which usually requires 2-3 weeks.

Pedicle grafts may be classified into several general categories:

a. Local or distant—obtained from tissues adjacent to the wound or from distant areas.

b. Single or double—having either 1 or 2 points of attachment (bases).

c. Open or closed—having an exposed raw surface on the underneath side or having the underneath side completely closed.

d. They may also be classified as advancement flaps, transposed flaps, rotation flaps, tubed pedicle flaps, or island flaps (Fig. 14-6).

3. Composite grafts are free grafts that contain more than one tissue element, usually skin with its underlying adipose tissue, or skin with its underlying adipose tissue and cartilage. Composite grafts are used in special situations, such as the repair of a full thickness loss of a portion of the nostril border by a full thickness section of skin, fat, and cartilage from the rim of the ear.

Since their survival depends upon the establishment of an early circulation through the ingrowth of vascular tissue, they usually are limited in size to less than 1 cm in diameter. If larger composite grafts are attempted, vascularization does not occur soon enough to maintain viability.

B. ADVANTAGES AND DISADVANTAGES OF VARIOUS TYPES OF GRAFTS (See Tables 14-1 and 14-2)

1. Split thickness Each type of split graft has definite characteristics that depend primarily upon the thickness of the dermis in the graft. Each thickness has certain advantages and disadvantages. The major advantage in the use of thinner grafts is that they become vascularized more rapidly and thus survive transplantation more readily. This is of importance in grafting less than ideal recipient sites such as infected wounds, burn surfaces, and poorly vascularized surfaces. A second advantage is that donor sites for these thinner grafts heal more rapidly, so that they can be reused within a relatively short period of time (7-10 days) in critical cases such as major burns.

In general, the disadvantages of the thin grafts outweigh the advantages. Thin grafts exhibit the highest degree of postgraft contracture, offer the least amount of resistance to surface trauma, and possess the fewest cosmetically desirable properties that are present in normal skin (natural texture, suppleness, pore pattern, and hair growth).

The advantages of the thicker grafts are that they contract less, are more resistant to surface trauma, and possess to a greater degree the desirable elements of normal skin. They are cosmetically more acceptable than thin grafts, though they are not as acceptable as full thickness grafts.

The disadvantages of thick grafts are relatively few. They are less easily vascularized than thin grafts so there are fewer successful 'takes' when they are used on less than ideal surfaces. Their donor sites are slower to heal (requiring 10-18 days) and heal with more scarring than the donor sites for thin split thickness grafts.

2. Full thickness skin grafts are the most cosmetically desirable of all free grafts since they include the greatest number of normal skin elements. They also undergo the least amount of contracture and have a greater ability to withstand trauma.

There are several factors that limit the use of full thickness grafts: the limited availability of donor sites; the necessity for surgically closing the donor site since no epidermal elements remain to produce epithelization; and the difficulty in obtaining successful transplantation.

Only areas of **thin skin** can be used as donor sites because adequate vascularization of thick grafts will not occur before the graft dies. These areas of thin skin include the eyelids and the skin of the postauricular, supraclavicular, submammary, antecubital, inguinal, and genital areas. In grafts thicker than approximately 0.030 inch, the probability of a good take may be poor.

3. Pedicle grafts Because pedicle grafts possess their own blood supply and because they consist of thick layers of skin and subcutaneous tissue, their use is usually necessary when the areas to be grafted are avascular (exposed bone without periosteum, exposed joint surfaces, areas of radiation necrosis), or where thick coverage is necessary to protect the underlying structures from trauma (weight-bearing surfaces, decubitus ulcers with exposed bone, densely scarred areas).

Pedicle grafts maintain all the characteristics of normal skin including normal thickness, color, texture, hair growth, and sensation. Proper choice of the donor site for a pedicle graft will take advantage of these characteristics, and improper choice will make them a detriment. Some examples are:

a. Adjacent pedicle grafts of facial skin provide the best cosmetic appearance in reconstructing facial defects. Abdominal pedicles are not desirable on the face since they will continue to look like abdominal skin being different in color, bulkiness, and texture.

Table 14-1. Advantages and disadvantages of various types of skin grafts.

Type of Graft	Advantages	Disadvantages
Thin split thickness	Survive transplantation most easily. Donor sites heal most rapidly.	Fewest qualities of normal skin. Maximum contracture. Least resistance to trauma. Sensation poor. Cosmetically poor.
Thick split thickness	More qualities of normal skin. Less contracture. More resistant to trauma. Sensation fair. Cosmetically more acceptable.	Survive transplantation less well. Donor site heals slowly.
Full thickness	Nearly all qualities of normal skin. Minimal contracture. Very resistant to trauma. Sensation good to excellent. Cosmetically excellent.	Survive transplantation least well. Donor site must be closed surgically. Donor sites are limited.
Pedicle	Possess all qualities of normal skin. Minimal to no contracture. Greatest resistance to trauma. Sensation excellent to normal. Cosmetically may be excellent. Maximal padding over long bony surfaces. Will survive transplantation over avascular surfaces.	Transplantation requires highest degree of technical skill. Cosmetically may be poor. May be too bulky. Usually require multiple operative procedures.

Reproduced with permission from Dunphy JE, Way LW (Eds.): *Current Surgical Diagnosis & Treatment*, 3rd Ed. Lange 1977

Table 14-2. Indications for various types of skin grafts.

Type of Wound	Type of Graft	Reason for Choice
Infected wounds (including burns)	Thin split thickness	Difficulty in obtaining successful take of thicker grafts.
Wounds with poorly vascularized surfaces	Thin split thickness or pedicle	Difficulty in obtaining successful take of thicker grafts.
Small superficial facial wounds	Full thickness or local pedicle	Produces best cosmetic result.
Large superficial facial wounds	Thick split thickness or pedicle	Cannot use full thickness graft because of limited size of donor sites.
Noninfected wounds on a flexor surface	Thick split thickness, full-thickness, or pedicle	Produces minimal contracture.
Full thickness eyelid loss	Local pedicle or composite	Repair requires more than one tissue element.
Deep loss of nasal tip	Local pedicle or composite	Repair requires thicker tissue than present in split or full thickness grafts.
Avulsive wounds with exposed tendons and nerves	Pedicle	Requires thick protective coverage without graft adherence to tendons and nerves.
Exposed avascular cortical bone or cartilage	Pedicle	Free grafts will not survive on avascular recipient site.
Wounds resulting from excision of deep x-ray "burn"	Pedicle	Free grafts will not survive on avascular recipient site.

Reproduced with permission from Dunphy JE, Way LW (Eds.): *Current Surgical Diagnosis & Treatment*, 3rd Ed. Lange 1977

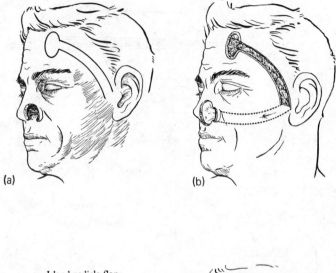

(a)

(b)

Island pedicle flap

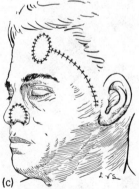

(c)

Fig. 14-6. Reproduced with permission from Dunphy JE, Way LW (Eds.): *Current Surgical Diagnosis & Treatment,* 3rd Ed. Lange 1977

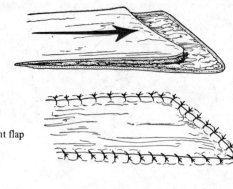

Advancement flap

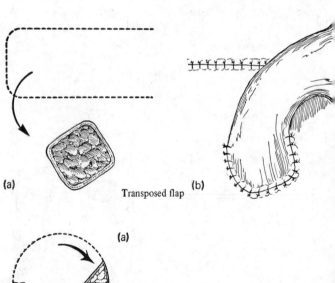

(a)   Transposed flap   (b)

(a)

Relaxing
incision

(b)

Rotation flap

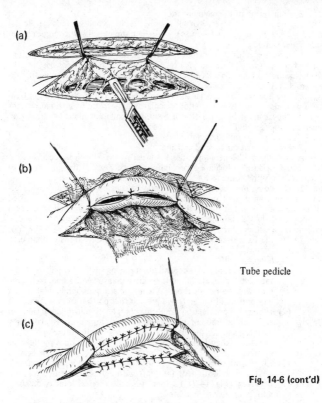

(a)

(b)

Tube pedicle

(c)

Fig. 14-6 (cont'd)

b. Grafts of abdominal or chest skin will not provide adequate sensation to the fingertip, but island pedicles (with the neurovascular bundle included) from adjacent fingers will provide nearly normal sensation.

c. The thickness of pedicle grafts obtained from the abdomen is desirable in covering bony prominences or decubitus ulcers, but the excess bulk is undesirable on the face or neck where it obliterates normal contours and features.

C. SKIN GRAFTING TECHNICS

1. Choice of donor sites

a. Follow the principles outlined in Section B for the proper selection of the type of graft needed.

b. Whenever possible choose sites for split grafts where the scar will be inconspicuous or can be easily covered by clothing (lateral buttock and hip, upper thighs).

2. Preparation of the recipient site

   a. The site must be free of all necrotic tissue. Small wounds can be debrided by enzymatic agents (Travase), but it is more expedient to surgically debride larger wounds.

   b. Infection must be controlled by meticulous wound care. (1) Irrigations and wet dressings of saline aid greatly. Change every 6 hours for best results. 0.5-1% acetic acid may be added to help control the growth of Pseudomonas organisms. (2) Antibiotics locally or systemically may be indicated.

   c. For free grafts, a vascular surface must be present. Fresh surgical or traumatic wounds usually have a healthy vascular bed, necrotic or infected wounds do not. They cannot be grafted until healthy granulation tissue has been produced by proper wound care.

   d. Hemorrhage must be controlled.

3. Procedure at the time of grafting

   a. Anesthesia   General anesthesia is usually used. However, local anesthesia with 0.5% lidocaine is quite acceptable for small cases. If the graft is not to be sutured, only the donor site needs to be anesthetized.

   b. Obtaining the graft   When the graft is to be cut with the Brown electric dermatome or the Hall air dermatome, a routine surgical preparation is carried out at the donor site and then a thin layer of mineral oil is applied to the skin surface to aid the dermatome in sliding more easily. If the Padgett or Reese dermatome is used, the natural oils are cleansed from the skin surface with Freon or ether to provide for better adherence of the special adhesive tapes that are used with these machines.

   c. Applying the graft
   (1) Since free skin grafts depend upon the ingrowth of capillaries to establish their circulation, it is essential that the **entire graft be in contact with the recipient bed.** A hematoma or purulent exudate under any portion of the graft will prevent that portion from surviving.
   (2) If bleeding or infection cannot be completely controlled, it is better to leave the graft completely exposed without a dressing so that any secretions under the graft can be expressed with cotton applicators as soon as they form. Meshing the graft aids in removing these secretions.
   (3) In areas where movement cannot be controlled (e.g., neck, extremities) immobilization of the graft with a tie-over stent dressing is necessary (Fig. 14-7). Further immobilization with bulky dressings and splints may be required.
   (4) Very thick split grafts and full thickness grafts will usually not survive without pressure being applied to their surfaces for several days.

   d. Care of the donor site
   (1) Split thickness donor sites are covered with a single layer of sterile nonadherent gauze (Xeroform) over which several layers of sterile absorbent gauze are placed.
   (2) Donor sites heal by the growth and spread of epithelium from the epithelial structures that remain at the site (hair follicles, sweat, and sebaceous glands and their ducts). Infection and excessive moisture are the main conditions that delay healing. Meticulous dressing technic using only sterile materials helps prevent infection. Donor sites become moist because of the exudation of blood or serum from the wound. This is controlled by changing the absorbent gauze daily until the wound is dry; the single layer of nonadherent gauze is left in place. Exposing the donor site to the air or to a heat lamp for several hours each day facilitates drying.

Fig. 14-7. Tie-over stent dressing.

e. Dressing the graft
  (1) When purulent drainage or bleeding is present, a dressing is usually not used unless one is necessary to hold the graft in place. When dressings are used in these circumstances, they are removed no later than 24-48 hours after operation so that any exudate beneath the graft can be removed.
  (2) In cases where the wound is clean and dry, the dressing is left in place for 5-7 days.
  (3) New grafts are easily traumatized, so a protective covering is used for 3-4 weeks.

IV. SOFT TISSUE TRAUMA

Proper primary care of soft tissue wounds minimizes the need for later revision of scars. Whenever the general condition of the patient permits, a meticulous repair should be carried out under either local or general anesthesia. Primary repair may be performed as late as 18-24 hours after injury except in the case of heavily contaminated wounds which are closed after several days of wound care.

A. CLEANSING AND DEBRIDEMENT Wounds are cleansed by thorough irrigation with saline. Skin flaps are lifted up to expose pockets, and foreign bodies are searched for and removed. Dirt or grease is removed from the tissues, at times with the aid of dermabrasion.

Ragged edges and obviously devitalized tissue should be excised. However, one should be **conservative in debriding tissues of the face** because the excellent blood supply to this area reduces the threat of infection. Bone should be conserved even if it is detached. Portions of facial skin which have lost their blood supply may sometimes be converted to full-thickness grafts and used in the repair. Portions of the ears, nose, or eyelids, if not too badly traumatized, should be trimmed, gently washed in saline, and used in the repair; many times these will survive as composite grafts. Suturing conforms to the principles described in Section I.B.7. Drainage is usually not required. If there are abraded surfaces, a layer of nonadherent gauze should be applied to the wound. An evenly applied pressure dressing using stockinette, Kerlix, or Cling gauze is usually advantageous.

B. REPAIR Uneven or beveled edges are excised to make right angles with the surface of the skin.

Suturing conforms to the principles described in Section I.B.7.

If the suture line crosses a flexion crease which will produce webbing after healing, a small Z-plasty may be done to avoid the necessity of later revision.

When tissue is lost on the face, distortion of features by the wound closure should be avoided. Several procedures are available for repair of tissue-loss injuries.

1. Undermining adjacent skin edges to provide sufficient relaxation for the closure of wounds of moderate size.

2. Trimming avulsed skin and using it as a free full-thickness graft.

3. Using local rotated or transposed flaps.

4. Transplanting full-thickness skin grafts taken from suitable donor areas.

5. Using split-thickness grafts in large defects. These may be revised or replaced later if necessary.

6. Portions of ear or nasal cartilages are saved by temporarily burying them in a subcutaneous pocket on the thorax or abdomen.

7. Avulsed parts of the facial features are sutured back in place if the avulsed part is available and not too badly traumatized.

When facial lacerations sever the lacrimal or parotid duct, both ends are identified and repaired immediately. Later they may be unidentifiable in the scar that forms.

Severed nerves are repaired immediately, but if a section of nerve is missing a nerve graft is done later. In this case the nerve ends are tagged with a suture or small metal clip to make them easier to identify.

C. POSTOPERATIVE CARE OF THE WOUND

1. Examine the wound after 24-48 hours. Look for hematomas or evidence of infection. If a hematoma is present, sufficient sutures are removed so that the trapped blood can be expressed. If infection is present, sutures are removed to permit drainage; culture and sensitivity studies are obtained. The appropriate antibiotic should be given in large doses and discontinued as soon as the infection is under control.

2. Sutures are removed early to prevent suture marks from forming. If no tension is present, facial sutures are removed by the fourth or fifth day. The incision line is then supported by adhesive paper tapes for another 3-4 days.

V. HYPERTROPHIC SCARS AND KELOIDS

When the skin is injured it heals by scar formation. Under ideal circumstances a fine, flat, hairline scar will result. When circumstances are not ideal, scar hypertrophy may occur or a keloid may develop during the second and third phases of scar formation.

A. DEFINITIONS It is incorrect to regard all thickened scars as keloids and to label as 'keloid formers' all patients with unattractive scars. The two conditions are different entities, and the clinical course and prognosis are quite different.

1. Hypertrophic scar is a thickened and raised scar. The overreactive process that results in thickening of the hypertrophic scar ceases within a few weeks, before it extends beyond the limits of the original scar, and in most cases some degree of maturation occurs and gradual improvement takes place.

2. Keloid is a tumor-like condition that grows beyond the limits of the original scar. The overreactive proliferation of fibroblasts continues for weeks or months. By the time it ceases, an actual tumor is present that typically extends well beyond the limits of the original scar, involves the surrounding skin, and may become quite large. Maturation with spontaneous improvement does not usually occur.

B. TREATMENT

1. Hypertrophic scars Since nearly all hypertrophic scars undergo some degree of spontaneous improvement, they do not require treatment in the early phases. If the scar is still hypertrophic after 6 months, surgical excision and primary closure of the wound may be indicated. Improvement may be expected when the hypertrophic scar was originally produced by excessive endothelial and fibroblastic cell proliferation, as is present in the healing of open wounds, burns, and infected wounds. However, little or no improvement can be anticipated if the hypertrophic scar followed uncomplicated healing of a simple surgical incision. Hypertrophic scars that cross flexion surfaces such as the anterior elbow or the fingers cannot be improved unless a procedure such as a Z-plasty (Fig. 14-8) is performed to change the direction of the scar.

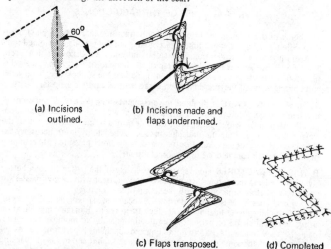

(a) Incisions outlined.

(b) Incisions made and flaps undermined.

(c) Flaps transposed.

(d) Completed closure.

Fig. 14-8. Z-plasty (Reproduced with permission from Dunphy JE, Way LW (Eds.): *Current Surgical Diagnosis & Treatment*, 3rd Ed. Lange 1977)

2. Keloids   The treatment of choice for keloids is the injection of triamcinolone acetonide, 10 mg/ml (Kenalog-10 Injection), directly into the lesion. In the case of larger lesions, injection is made into more than one site. There is evidence that keloids may respond better to early than to late treatment.

Lesions are injected every 3-4 weeks, and treatment should not be carried out longer than 6 months. The following dosage schedule should not be exceeded:

Size of lesion	Dose per injection
1-2 cm²	20-40 mg
2-6 cm²	40-80 mg
6-10 cm²	80-110 mg

For larger lesions, the maximum dose should be 120 mg. The maximum dose for each treatment for children are as follows:

Age	Maximum dose
1-2 years	20 mg
3-5 years	40 mg
6-10 years	80 mg

There is a tendency to inject the drug into the scar too often or in too high a dosage. Either may produce too vigorous a response, resulting in excessive atrophy of the skin and subcutaneous tissues surrounding the lesion and in depigmentation of darker skins. Both of these adverse effects improve spontaneously in 6-12 months.

The response varies greatly; some lesions become flat after 2-3 injections, and some fail to respond at all.

Surgical excision of keloids should be avoided since it almost invariably leads to the recurrence of a larger lesion.

VI. FRACTURES OF THE FACIAL BONES

The bones of the nose are the most commonly fractured facial bones. Next in order of frequency are the mandible, the zygoma, and the maxilla. Combined fractures of these bones are common as a result of automobile collisions at high speed.

Soft tissue edema may develop rapidly, making it difficult to palpate a displaced facial fracture. X-ray examination, including the Waters view, basal view, and oblique views of the mandible, is imperative for accurate diagnosis.

A. EMERGENCY CARE is directed toward maintaining the airway and controlling hemorrhage. Remove blood clots from the airway manually and by suctioning. Position unconscious patients on the side or in a prone position, so that the tongue does not occlude the oral pharynx. A tracheostomy is not necessary except in some very severe cases. Control bleeding by direct pressure until clamping of severed vessels can be done under direct vision.

B. NASAL FRACTURES are treated immediately if the patient is seen before significant edema has formed. If edema is marked, treat with ice compresses for several days before proceeding with reduction of the fractures.

Local anesthesia is preferred using 4% cocaine intranasally and ½-1% xylocaine with epinephrine in the skin. Reduce fractures by bimanual manipulation using a surgical clamp or periosteal elevator intranasally to mobilize and disimpact the bony fragments. External molding and alignment is performed by external pressure at the same time. Use an external nasal splint and intranasal packing of nonadherent gauze to maintain alignment. The splint is left in place for 1 week. Additional fixation with stainless steel wires or surgical pins may be indicated in cases of severe comminution.

C. MANDIBULAR FRACTURES most commonly occur in the midbody at the mental foramen, at the angle of the ramus, or through the neck of the condyle. Bilateral fractures are common and are accompanied by displacement of the bony fragments and disturbance of dental occlusion. **Restoration of normal occlusion is the most important consideration in treating these fractures.**

When teeth are present, dental arch bars are attached to both the mandibular and maxillary arches by wiring them to the teeth. Intermaxillary fixation between the upper and lower jaws is accomplished by connecting the arch bars together. Elastic traction bands between the arch bars are used to align fragments that are displaced. When normal occlusion is established, the elastic bands are removed and stainless-steel wires are used for fixation. Fixation is necessary for 6 weeks to allow for solid union of the bony fragments.

In cases of inadequate dentition, severe comminution, or severe displacement of the fracture fragments, open surgical reduction and direct fixation may be necessary.

D. ZYGOMATIC FRACTURES Fractures of the zygomatic bones may involve just the arch or the entire body (the malar eminence) along with the lateral wall and floor of the orbit. Displacement of the zygoma results in flattening of the cheek and depression of the orbital rim and floor.

Important diagnostic signs are subconjunctival hemorrhage, disturbances of extraocular muscle function (usually accompanied by diplopia), and loss of sensation on the involved side as a result of injury to the infraorbital nerve.

Reduction of a displaced zygomatic fracture is seldom an emergency procedure and may be delayed until the patient's general condition is satisfactory for anesthesia.

E. MAXILLARY FRACTURES range from partial fractures through the alveolar process to extensive displacement of the midfacial structures in conjunction with fractures of the frontonasal bones and the orbits.

Hemorrhage and airway obstruction require emergency care, and in severe cases tracheostomy may be indicated.

Mobility of the fragments is usually present. 'Dish-face' deformity of the retruded displaced maxilla may be disguised by edema, so that careful x-ray studies are necessary to determine the extent and complexity of the midfacial fracture.

Treatment may have to be delayed because of other severe injuries. A delay of as long as 10-14 days may be safe before reduction and fixation, but the earliest possible restoration of maxillary position and dental occlusion is desirable to prevent late complications.

In fractures with little or no displacement, splinting by arch bars and intermaxillary fixation for 4 weeks is all that is necessary. When fractures are displaced severely or are impacted, surgical disimpaction and reduction are usually necessary.

Treatment is directed toward restoring normal occlusion and maintaining reduction for 4-6 weeks by intermaxillary fixation to the mandible and by direct fixation to intact facial or cranial bones. Complicated fractures may require external fixation using a head-cap and intraoral splints in conjunction with multiple surgical incisions for direct wire fixation. Coexisting mandibular fractures usually necessitate open reduction and fixation at the same time.

VII. SYNTHETIC IMPLANTS

Several synthetic materials have been developed in recent years as substitutes for autogenous tissue grafts in reconstructive surgery. These include dimethyl siloxanes (Silicone—solid block, sponge, and gel), halogenated carbons (Teflon—solid block or felt), and polyvinyl alcohol sponge. They have the advantages of being nonreactive and nonabsorptive, and they are available in any desired size and shape. Also, their use eliminates the need to make a second incision to obtain an autogenous graft.

Silicone in its solid form has been used successfully for a long period to reconstruct contour defects such as saddle-nose deformity or micrognathia. Soft silicone gel contained within a thin silicone bag has also been used successfully for many years to augment hypoplastic breasts and, more recently, in the reconstruction of patients who have undergone a radical mastectomy. Flexible silicone prostheses have been developed to replace joints, tendons, and tendon sheaths.

Synthetic implants may become exposed or extruded in certain cases if: they are not absolutely inert; infection should occur; sharp edges are present that work through the skin; they are exposed to trauma; or they are not well covered with normal surface tissues. Sponge implants have a tendency to harden and shrink in time. Some of these disadvantages will no doubt be eliminated as research continues.

Research is now being conducted into the use of injected Dow Corning 360 Fluid Silicone for soft tissue augmentation. The use of this fluid is at present restricted to certain centers for the purpose of controlled experimentation; recommendations for its use will eventually be made by these research groups. **The use of injected silicone liquid for breast augmentation is a hazardous procedure which has been condemned.**

VIII. SKIN TUMORS

Tumors of the skin are by far the most common of all tumors. Since they arise from any of the histologic structures that make up the skin, they are quite numerous in type. They are conveniently classified as benign, premalignant, and malignant. Only those tumors that are commonly seen by the plastic surgeon will be discussed here.

A. BENIGN SKIN TUMORS The many benign tumors that arise from the skin rarely interfere with function. Since most are removed for cosmetic reasons, they are quite commonly treated by the plastic surgeon. The majority are small and can be excised quite simply under local anesthesia following the principles of elliptical excision and wound closure discussed earlier. General anesthesia may be necessary for larger lesions that require excision and repair with skin grafts or for those occurring in young children.

Most superficial lesions (seborrheic keratoses, actinic keratoses, squamous cell papillomas) can be easily treated by simpler technics such as electrodesiccation, curettage and electrodesiccation, cryotherapy, and topical cytotoxic agents.

1. Seborrheic keratoses are superficial noninvasive tumors that originate in the epidermis. These lesions appear in older people as multiple, slightly elevated, yellowish, brown, or brownish-black, irregularly rounded plaques with waxy or oily surfaces. They are most commonly present on the trunk and shoulders but are frequently seen on the scalp and face.

Curettage and electrodesiccation is usually the treatment of choice.

2. Cysts Although sebaceous cyst is the commonly used term, these lesions more properly should be called epidermal or keratinous cysts since they are composed of thin layers of epidermal cells and are filled with epithelial debris. (True cysts arising from sebaceous epithelial cells are uncommon.)

Epidermal cysts are soft to firm, usually spherical, and are filled with an odorous cheesy material. Their most common sites of occurrence are the scalp, face, ears, neck, and back. They are usually covered by normal skin, which may show dimpling at the site of skin attachment.

Treatment consists of surgical excision.

3. Lipomas do not arise from the skin but are included here because they are so common and are frequently mistaken for cysts. Like cysts, they may be soft or firm, and they are spherical or discoid in shape. Unlike cysts, they arise in the subcutaneous tissues and have no skin attachment.

Treatment is surgical excision.

4. Pigmented nevi

a. Junction nevi are well-defined pigmented lesions appearing in infancy. They are usually flat or slightly elevated, light to dark brown in color, and have no hair. They may appear on any part of the body, but most nevi seen on the palms, soles, and genitalia are junction nevi.

Histologically, a proliferation of melanocytes is present in the epidermis at the epidermal-dermal junction. A varying amount of cellular activity in the form of cellular division with mitotic figures may be seen. Partly because of this, it has been widely accepted that junction nevi give rise to malignant melanoma and that all junction nevi should be excised for prophylactic reasons. However, most investigators now feel that they are not precancerous. If there is no change in their appearance, treatment is unnecessary. Any change such as inflammation, darkening in color, halo formation, increase in size, bleeding, or ulceration calls for immediate treatment.

Surgical excision is the treatment of choice.

b. Intradermal nevi are the typical dome-shaped, sometimes pedunculated, fleshy to brownish pigmented 'moles' that are characteristically seen in adults. They frequently contain hairs and may occur anywhere on the body.

Microscopically, melanocytes are present entirely within the dermis and, in contrast to junction nevi, show little activity. They are rarely if ever malignant and require no treatment except for cosmetic reasons.

Surgical excision is nearly always the treatment of choice.

c. Compound nevi exhibit the histologic features of both junction and intradermal nevi in that melanocytes lie both at the epidermal-dermal junction and within the dermis. They are usually elevated, dome-shaped, and light to dark brown in color.

Because of the presence of nevus cells at the epidermal-dermal junction, the indications for treatment are the same as for junction nevi. If treatment is indicated, surgical excision is the method of choice.

d. Benign juvenile melanomas are rapidly growing pigmented lesions that appear in children and exhibit some of the microscopic and clinical features of malignant melanoma. They usually appear on the face as distinctive small, pinkish or reddish, soft, nodular lesions. They increase in size rapidly, but the average lesion reaches only 6-8 mm in diameter, remaining entirely benign without invasion or metastases. Microscopically, the lesion can be confused with malignant melanoma by the inexperienced pathologist.

The usual treatment is excisional biopsy.

e. Giant hairy nevi Unlike most nevi arising from melanocytes, giant hairy nevi are congenital. They occur anywhere on the body and frequently cover large areas such as the entire trunk. They are of special significance for several reasons: their large size is especially deforming from a cosmetic standpoint; they show a definite predisposition for developing malignant melanoma; and they may be associated with neurofibromas or melanocytic involvement of the leptomeninges and with other neurologic abnormalities.

Microscopically, a varied picture is present. All of the characteristics of intradermal and compound nevi may be seen, along with those associated with juvenile melanoma. Neurofibromas may also be present within the lesion. Malignant melanoma may arise anywhere within the lesion; the rate of occurrence of malignant melanoma is as high as 15-20%. Malignant melanoma with metastases can arise in childhood and even in infancy.

The only treatment is complete excision and skin grafting. Large lesions may require excision and grafting in stages. Some lesions are so large that excision is not possible.

5. Hemangiomas are quite common, especially in children, occurring once in every 10 births. Some are true neoplasms arising from endothelial cells or other vascular elements (involuting hemangiomas of childhood, endotheliomas, pericytomas) while others are not true neoplasms but, rather, malformations of normal vascular structures (port-wine stains, cavernous hemangiomas, arteriovenous fistulas).

A simple classification based upon whether or not the hemangioma undergoes spontaneous involution can be used.

a. Involuting hemangiomas are the most common tumors that occur in childhood and comprise at least 95% of all the hemangiomas that are seen in infancy and childhood. They are true neoplasms of endothelial cells, but they are unique among neoplasms in that they undergo complete spontaneous involution.

Typically, they are present at birth or appear during the first 2-3 weeks of life. When they first appear, they are bright red in color, raised above the surface of the skin, and have a roughened uneven surface which has been compared to a ripe strawberry. Occasionally they are entirely subcutaneous, being covered by normal skin and presenting as firm bluish masses. They grow at a rather rapid rate for 4-6 months, when growth ceases and spontaneous involution begins. Involution progresses slowly but is complete by 5-7 years of age.

Treatment is not usually indicated since the cosmetic appearance following spontaneous regression is nearly always superior to the scars that follow surgical excision. Complete surgical excision of lesions that involve important structures such as the eyelids, nose, or lips results in the unnecessary destruction of these structures.

Partial resection of a portion of a hemangioma of the brow or eyelid is indicated when the lesion is large enough to prevent light from entering the eye—**a condition that will lead to blindness.** The same type of treatment may be necessary for lesions of the mucosal surfaces of the lips when they project into the mouth and are traumatized by the teeth. In these cases, surgery should be very conservative, resecting only enough of the lesion to alleviate the problem and leaving the remaining portions to involute spontaneously.

After involution of large lesions, superficial scarring may be present or the involved skin may be thin, wrinkled, or redundant. These conditions may require conservative plastic surgical procedures.

b. Noninvoluting hemangiomas Most noninvoluting hemangiomas are present at birth. In contrast to involuting hemangiomas, they do not undergo rapid growth during the first 4-6 months of life but grow in proportion to the growth of the child. They persist into adulthood, when they may cause severe cosmetic and functional problems. Some, such as arteriovenous fistulas, may cause death due to cardiac failure.

Unfortunately, treatment of noninvoluting hemangiomas is difficult and usually far from satisfactory.

Port wine stains are by far the most common of the noninvoluting hemangiomas. They may involve any portion of the body, but most commonly they appear on the face as very superficial flat patchy lesions that are reddish to purple in color.

Microscopically, port wine stains are made up of thin-walled capillaries that are arranged throughout the dermis.

If the lesion is small, surgical excision with primary closure may be indicated. Unfortunately, most lesions are large, and surgical excision requires split-thickness skin grafting. Because of the scar present around the edge of the graft and the loss of normal skin texture, along with the inability to obtain a good color match between the graft and the facial skin, the results of excision with skin grafting are far less than ideal.

c. Cavernous hemangiomas are bluish or purplish lesions that are usually deep to the surface but cause the overlying skin to bulge. At times the skin itself is involved. They may occur anywhere on the body but, like other hemangiomas, are more common on the head and neck. They are composed of mature, fully formed venous structures that are present in tortuous masses which have been described as feeling like 'a bag of worms.'

Microscopically, cavernous hemangiomas are made up of large, dilated, closely packed vascular sinuses that are engorged with blood.

Treatment is difficult. In only a few cases is the lesion small enough or superficial enough to permit complete surgical excision. Most lesions involve deeper structures, including muscle and bone, so that complete excision is impossible without radical surgery. Since most lesions are just cosmetic problems, radical surgery is rarely indicated.

Other forms of treatment such as x-ray and radium therapy are of no value in treating noninvoluting lesions since they are made up of mature vessels not sensitive to radiation. Suture ligation of surrounding vessels, multiple intralesional ligations, and injections of sclerosing solutions usually have no effect upon the lesions and have been discarded.

B. PREMALIGNANT SKIN LESIONS

1. Actinic keratoses are the most common of the precancerous skin lesions. They appear as small, single or multiple, slightly elevated, scaly or warty lesions ranging in color from red to yellow, brown, or black. Since they are related to sun exposure, they occur most frequently on the face and the back of the hands in fair-skinned Caucasians whose skin shows evidence of actinic elastosis.

Microscopically, actinic keratoses consist of well-defined areas of abnormal epithelial cells limited to the epidermis. Approximately 15% of these lesions become squamous cell carcinomas which invade the dermis.

Since the lesions are limited to the epidermis, superficial treatment in the form of curettage and electrodesiccation or the application of chemical agents such as liquid nitrogen, phenol, bi- or trichloroacetic acid, or fluorouracil is curative. The application of fluorouracil (5-FU) cream is of particular benefit in preventive treatment in that it will destroy lesions of microscopic size even before they can be detected clinically and without causing damage to uninvolved skin.

2. Chronic radiation dermatitis Radiation dermatitis may result from high doses of ionizing radiation administered over short periods of time or from chronic exposure to low doses over a prolonged period.

The clinical picture is one of scarring, characterized by atrophy of the epidermis and dermis along with loss of skin appendages (sweat glands, sebaceous glands, and hair follicles). Marked fibrosis of the dermis occurs, with gradual endarteritis and occlusion of the dermal and subdermal vessels. Telangiectasia of the surface vessels is seen, and areas of both hypo and hyperpigmentation occur. Drying of the skin may become pronounced and deepening of the skin furrows is typically present.

In radiation dermatitis, **late changes** may occur: hyperkeratotic growths may appear on the skin surface; chronic ulceration may form; and **either basal cell or squamous cell carcinoma** may develop. When malignant growths appear, basal cell carcinomas are seen more frequently on the face and neck and squamous cell carcinomas more frequently on the hands and body.

Treatment of chronic radiation dermatitis or the malignant lesions that develop is complicated by the marked scarring that is present and by the avascularity of the involved tissues secondary to endarteritis.

Surgical excision is the treatment of choice. Primary wound closure is feasible for only the smallest lesions. Free skin grafting can be performed only for the most superficial lesions, where damage to the vascular supply of the subcutaneous structures is not advanced. Lesions that involve the deeper subcutaneous tissues require surgical excision followed by pedicle skin grafting.

3. Bowen's disease is characterized by single or multiple, brownish or reddish plaques that may appear anywhere on the skin surface but often arise in areas that are covered by clothing. The typical plaque is sharply defined, slightly raised, scaly, and slightly thickened. The surface is often keratotic, and crusting and fissuring may be present. Ulceration is not common, but when present it suggests malignant degeneration with dermal invasion. Some authorities believe that all cases of Bowen's disease are secondary to the ingestion of arsenic. (A significant number of cases are related to arsenic-induced malignancies of internal organs).

Treatment of small or superficial lesions consists of total destruction by curettage and electrodesiccation or by any of the other superficially destructive methods (cryotherapy, cytotoxic agents). Excision and skin grafting is preferred for larger lesions and for those that have undergone early malignant degeneration with invasion of the dermis.

C. MALIGNANT SKIN TUMORS

1. Basal cell carcinoma is the most common skin cancer. Since exposure to ultraviolet rays of the sun is a major causative factor, the lesions usually appear on the face. Basal cell carcinoma is more common in people whose skin is susceptible to damage from sun exposure, i.e., fair skinned individuals with blue eyes and blond hair. It may occur at any age but is uncommon before age 40.

The growth of basal cell carcinoma is usually slow but nearly always steady and insidious. Several months or years may pass before the patient becomes concerned. Without treatment, widespread invasion and destruction of adjacent tissues may occur, producing massive ulceration. Penetration into the deeper tissues, even the bones of the facial skeleton and the skull, can occur. Basal cell carcinomas rarely metastasize, but death can result from direct intracranial extension or erosion of major blood vessels.

a. Orthodox Typical individual lesions appear as small, translucent or shiny elevated nodules with central umbilication and rolled, 'pearly' edges. Telangiectatic vessels are commonly present over the surface, and pigmentation is sometimes present. Superficial ulceration occurs early. When invasion of the dermis and subcutaneous tissues occurs along with deeper ulceration, the lesion is termed a 'rodent ulcer'. Pigmented basal cell carcinomas may be mistaken for melanomas because of the large number of melanocytes present within the tumor. They may also be confused with seborrheic keratoses.

b. Sclerosing A less common type of basal cell carcinoma is the sclerosing or morphea type consisting of elongated strands of basal cell cancer which infiltrate the dermis, with the intervening corium being unusually compact. These lesions are usually flat and whitish or waxy in appearance and firm to palpation.

c. Body The superficial erythematous basal cell cancers (body basal) occur most frequently on the trunk. They appear as reddish plaques with atrophic centers and smooth, slightly raised borders. These lesions are capable of peripheral growth and wide extension but do not become invasive until late.

Treatment There are several methods of treating basal cell carcinoma, but no one method is applicable to all patients. The special features of each individual lesion must be considered before proper treatment can be selected.

Since most lesions occur on the face, cosmetic and functional results of treatment are important. However, the most important consideration is whether or not therapy is curative. **If the basal cell carcinoma is not eradicated by initial treatment, continued growth and invasion of adjacent tissues will occur.** This results not only in additional tissue destruction but also in penetration of the tumor into deeper structures, sometimes making cure impossible.

The principal methods of treatment are curettage and electrodesiccation, surgical excision, and radiation therapy. Chemosurgery, topical chemotherapy, and cryosurgery are not often used but may have value in selected cases.

2. Squamous cell carcinoma is the second most common cancer of the skin. As with basal cell carcinoma, exposure to sun is the most common causative factor, and most lesions occur in fair-skinned individuals whose skin is sensitive to the sun. Other causative factors are chemical and thermal burns, scars, chronic ulcers, chronic granulomas, draining sinuses, contact with tars and hydrocarbons, and exposure to ionizing radiation.

Most of the lesions are preceded by actinic keratosis on areas of the skin showing chronic solar damage, especially the ears, cheeks, the lower lip and the backs of the hands.

The course of squamous cell carcinomas may vary considerably. They may present as slowly growing, locally invasive lesions without metastases or as rapidly growing, widely invasive tumors with early metastatic spread. In general, squamous cell carcinomas that develop from actinic keratoses are of the slowly growing type, whereas those that develop from Bowen's disease, erythroplasia of Queyrat, chronic radiation dermatitis, scars, and chronic ulcers tend to be more aggressive in nature.

Early squamous cell carcinoma usually appears as a small, firm, erythematous plaque or nodule with indistinct margins. The surface may be flat and smooth, or it may be verrucous. As the tumor grows it becomes raised; because of progressive invasion, it becomes fixed to surrounding tissues. Ulceration may occur early or late but tends to appear earlier in the more rapidly growing lesions.

Treatment As with basal cell carcinomas, there is no single method of treatment that is applicable to all squamous cell carcinomas.

Since basal cell carcinomas are relatively nonaggressive lesions that very rarely metastasize, failure to eradicate the lesion will result only in local recurrence. **Aggressive squamous cell carcinomas,** on the other hand, may metastasize to any part of the body, so that **failure of treatment may have fatal consequences.** For this reason, total eradication of each lesion is imperative.

Factors that determine the optimal method of treatment include the size, shape, and location of the tumor as well as the histologic pattern that determines its aggressiveness. Although small very superficial lesions may be treated by electrodesiccation, surgical excision or radiation therapy are the treatments of choice for nearly all squamous cell carcinomas.

Because the overall incidence of lymph node metastasis is relatively low, most authorities agree that node dissection is not indicated in the absence of palpable regional lymph nodes except in the case of very aggressive carcinomas of the genitalia and anal regions.

3. Malignant melanomas are not nearly as common as basal cell or squamous cell carcinomas, but they have a far greater potential for widespread invasion, metastasis, and subsequent mortality.

a. Clinical and histologic classification Although all melanomas arise from the common melanocyte, 3 distinct clinical lesions are seen. Each presents with different shapes, sizes, and shades of color and with different potentials for aggressive behavior.

(1) *Lentigo maligna melanomas* usually occur on exposed surfaces of the body in older individuals (65-70 years). They are large (3-5 cm), flat, freckle-like lesions with multicolored surfaces composed of light brown, dark brown, or black areas. Depigmented areas are

sometimes present, and the dark brown or black areas are sometimes raised. Usually they are preceded by lentigo maligna.

(2) *Superficial spreading melanomas* are smaller than lentigo maligna melanomas (2-3 cm), and they occur in a slightly younger age group (50-60 years). The surface tends to be flat or slightly elevated with irregular and indented edges. As with lentigo maligna melanomas, bizarre combinations of light brown, dark brown, black, red, or pink lesions may be seen. Numerous small nodules may also be present.

(3) *Nodular melanomas* tend to occur in a younger age group (30-60 years). They are smaller than the other 2 types and are elevated above the surface of the surrounding skin. They are almost always uniformly dark brown or black, not showing the variations in color that are present in the other lesions. At times they exhibit a very rapid rate of growth and may become quite large.

b. Treatment of malignant melanoma is surgical excision. Nearly all lesions except small lentigo maligna melanomas must be excised widely enough so that skin grafting is necessary.

There is considerable controversy regarding the value of prophylactic node dissection for melanoma. At present, most authorities feel it is not indicated for lentigo maligna melanoma or superficial spreading melanoma unless palpable nodes are present, since excellent results follow wide excision alone. In nodular melanoma with invasion to level III or IV, (see Prognosis) the regional nodes are nearly always involved so that therapeutic dissection is indicated. Unfortunately, the prognosis with this lesion is so poor that genuine benefit from removal of clinically uninvolved nodes (prophylactic node dissection) is difficult to establish.

Regional perfusion with antitumor drugs has been performed both by arterial and endolymphatic routes. Remarkable regressions have followed such therapy, but adequate clinical trials to establish its exact place are needed.

Malignant melanoma sometimes regresses spontaneously. Moreover, dramatic regressions have followed a variety of immunologic treatments such as vaccination with smallpox vaccine, transfusion of blood from patients whose tumors have previously undergone spontaneous regression, and nonspecific stimulation of the immune system with BCG. A circulating tumor-specific antibody has been identified in cases of malignant melanoma, and there is evidence to suggest that a common antigen is shared by most, if not all, malignant melanomas. The prospect of controlling the disease by immunotherapy appears promising.

c. Prognosis An accurate estimation of the prognosis of a patient with malignant melanoma can be made by correlating the clinical appearance of the lesion with its histologic picture. In general, lentigo maligna melanomas are less aggressive and less apt to metastasize than superficial spreading melanomas, and both of these lesions tend to be less aggressive than nodular melanomas.

A helpful classification of malignant melanomas is based on their clinical and pathologic features correlated with the level of histologic invasion of the lesion: Level I, in situ melanoma, with no extension through the basement membrane. Level II, invasion through the basement membrane into the papillary level of the dermis. Level III, filling the papillary layer of the dermis and extending to the junction of the papillary and reticular layers but not into the reticular layer. Level IV, invasion into the reticular layer of the dermis. Level V, invasion into the subcutaneous adipose tissue.

Lentigo maligna and superficial spreading melanomas that do not invade the dermis below level II do not cause death in more than 10% of cases. When nodular melanoma is first treated, it usually extends at least to level III and causes death in approximately 45% of cases. Regardless of the type of tumor, the mortality rate increases with the depth of invasion at the time of treatment.

IX. MICROVASCULAR SURGERY

In microvascular surgery, the operating microscope and ultra-fine instruments and sutures are used to anastomose blood vessels and nerves that are as small as 1 mm or less in diameter.

The salvage of amputated digits and hands has been made possible by the availability of surgical teams trained in the technics of microvascular surgery. Replantation is discussed in Chapter 15.

Microsurgical technics may also be used in the reconstruction of congenital and acquired deformities in which other modes of treatment such as primary closure, skin grafts, and local or distant pedicles are not available or have been attempted without success. Many of these cases can be reconstructed by the immediate transfer of a free composite graft from a distant source using microsurgical anastomoses.

The graft most commonly used at present is the groin flap, based on the superficial circumflex iliac artery. Other flaps which may be considered are the deltopectoral flap and the dorsalis pedis flap. A composite flap, such as a rib with the intercostal vessels and the overlying skin, or a groin flap with the underlying iliac crest are considered where a bony defect is present in the area to be reconstructed. The only major contraindication to the use of these flaps is the absence of a suitable recipient vascular pedicle.

15

HAND

Eugene S. Kilgore jr., MD &
William L. Newmeyer III, MD

Any severe hand disorder should be referred to a general, plastic, or orthopedic surgeon who specializes in the hand, if one is available. Only a specialist can adequately manage all of the tissues and structures (skin, muscles and tendons, nerves, vessels, bones, and joints) and give the expert care necessary to preserve or restore the function of all systems of this complex mechanism. Most hand problems are caused by trauma, but tumors, neurologic disorders, congenital anomalies, and rheumatic joint and tendon afflictions also need treatment. The functional outcome depends on the quality of immediate and subsequent surgical treatment.

I. TRAUMA

Management of the injured hand requires constant attention to the components of hand function (sensibility, mobility, placement, and power) and knowledge of how such function may be compromised or threatened by trauma or its treatment. A thorough understanding of the functional anatomy of the upper extremity is crucial to a successful outcome.

A. EVALUATION OF THE INJURED HAND Careful records of history and examination—including, in many instances, a diagram detailing the problem—are invaluable aids in the initial and subsequent treatment as well as in preparing reports on temporary and permanent disability. It is essential to record in precise language everything that one knows about, plans, and actually does for the injured hand. Accurate reports can be prepared only if these details are recorded immediately at the time of evaluation and treatment.

1. History Repeat the history-taking procedure once or twice to make certain that the data from the patient, family, employer, etc. are accurate and complete. The following information is required.

a. Age, occupation, hand dominance, and pre-existing hand problems, if any.

b. Chief complaint, its duration, its previous occurrence, and whether or not it is getting worse, getting better, or remaining static.

c. The how, where, when, and why of the injury. A detailed history must be taken of the mechanism of injury, the interval between injury and treatment, factors of contamination, and treatment rendered to date.

d. The status of tetanus prophylaxis and allergies.

e. A review of the patient's past and current state of health and treatment given.

2. Physical examination The examination of the total patient may be cursory or complete depending on whether the history raises relevant questions or whether the patient is to be admitted to the hospital for care.

The examination of the extremity should determine the following:

a. Pain or anesthesia Note the presence, type, and severity of pain. Throbbing pain implies venous congestion and must be relieved by mechanical means rather than by drugs. The patient must be made as comfortable as possible during the examination, often by recumbency. Anesthetic areas should be mapped and confirmed by retesting later.

b. Viability of tissues Compare capillary filling, color, and temperature with normal skin and the opposite hand; note the quality of the pulse.

c. Deformity Note any distortion of form by soft tissue swelling (edema, hemorrhage, infection), tumor, or bone displacement.

d. Mobility Note the status of active and passive mobility. Division of motor nerves or tendons creates characteristic deficits in active motion. Selective testing of muscle units should be done.

e. Wounding Is the wound tidy or untidy, new or old, bleeding, blood-logged or dry, clean or infected, punctured or incised, deep or superficial, with or without foreign body? Probing should not be done by inexperienced surgeons or in circumstances where help is inadequate, lighting is poor, tourniquet ischemia is not instituted, or proper instruments and facilities are not available. Bleeding can usually be controlled by direct pressure on the bleeding point and the release of tight garments and jewelry. If not, the bleeding point may be isolated under tourniquet (blood pressure cuff) control and carefully ligated without injury to an adjacent nerve. Loupe magnification is often indispensable for this purpose.

f. X-rays X-rays (postero-anterior, lateral, and special views) should be taken to determine any abnormality of bone or the presence of a radiopaque foreign body.

3. Referral and deferral of treatment The freshly injured hand should be made as comfortable as possible, usually by splinting and elevation. Constrictive dressings must be avoided. A well-padded, light cast around the forearm and hand (like a boxing glove) with the wrist slightly extended and a large soft roll of gauze in the palm between the thumb and fingers often gives the greatest comfort. Pain should also be controlled by analgesics if necessary. Surgical toilet (irrigation and skin preparation) may be rendered and wounds closed loosely and covered with sterile dressings. If there will be more than 2 or 3 hours of delay before definitive care of an open injury, tetanus prophylaxis together with prophylactic IM or IV broad-spectrum antibiotics should be administered. Injections and IVs should not be given in the injured extremity in case congestion results. Nothing should be given by mouth. An amputated part should be placed in a sterile waterproof bag or other container, cooled on ice, and transferred with the patient. A detailed record of the initial diagnosis and treatment should accompany the patient.

B. MANAGEMENT OF THE INJURED HAND

1. Surgical facilities An operating table, arm board, good light, a magnifying loupe, specialized fine instruments, a pneumatic gauged cuff, and surgical assistance are essential for hand surgery. Inexperience, haste, and fatigue are serious handicaps.

2. Preparation for surgery

The patient should be supine and comfortable, with a well-padded pneumatic tourniquet on the arm. Many surgeons sit, but it is better to elevate the table and stand so that the surgeon can readily shift his position as circumstances require. However, microsurgery of nerves and vessels is done sitting.

If pain is not severe, anesthetic paralysis of the whole upper extremity should be withheld until the skin preparation and draping are completed since the patient's cooperation greatly facilitates these procedures. Skin preparation consists of one paint brush coating of 1–2% iodine, which is then neutralized with alcohol. These solutions should be kept out of the wound and off of the tourniquet and its padding. Sterile waterproof draping is applied, and general or regional anesthesia can be administered.

The freshly injured or infected extremity may then be passively elevated and the tourniquet inflated (to 300 mm Hg for adults or to 150-250 mm Hg for infants and persons with very thin arms). Uncontrolled bleeding may necessitate tourniquet control before the anesthesia and skin preparation. In elective surgical cases which are not infected, the extremity is usually exsanguinated with an elastic roll (e.g., Esmarch bandage) before inflation of the tourniquet. The patient will generally tolerate tourniquet ischemia on the unanesthetized upper arm for 20-30 minutes. When the arm is anesthetized, the tissue tolerance for ischemia is 2-2½ hours. The tourniquet manometer should be tested for accuracy before use since paralyses have occurred as a result of excessive tourniquet pressure. The tourniquet may be released and reinflated after the reactive hyperemia subsides in procedures demanding prolonged tourniquet time.

3. Anesthesia General anesthesia (or axillary block or IV 0.5% lidocaine block) is preferred for procedures which last for over 20-30 minutes. Premedication with morphine sulfate and scopolamine (when not contraindicated by allergy or glaucoma) is ideal for its tranquilizing and analgesic effect.

Lidocaine (1-2%) **without** epinephrine injected slowly through a fine needle (e.g., No. 26-30 gauge for the digit) is used for local blocks (into the wound) or nerve blocks (axillary, radial, ulnar, median, or digital nerve (see Fig. 3-4). Avoid excessive amounts which will congest the nerve, the hand, or the digit. The skin and fat should still be soft and pliable after the injection. The most one should inject at the base of an adult digit is 2.5 ml. Large caliber needles may cut nerve tissue and should not be used.

4. Surgical technics for fresh injuries* Anything that touches the wound must be aseptic and both chemically and mechanically atraumatic. Starch powder should be wiped off of sterile gloves. Sponging should be by dabbing, not wiping. Instruments must be in the best condition and should consist of a selection of fine plastic hooks, retractors, forceps, clamps, scissors, needle holders, atraumatic sutures, and Kirschner wires and drill. Nonreactive material should be stipulated for sutures and ligatures. Catgut should be avoided. Monofilament nylon is preferred. The tissues must be kept moist, preferably with lactated Ringer's solution. Hemostasis must be complete.

a. The 6 fundamental precepts of dissection in the hand are as follows: (1) Dissect with at least 2 x magnification, tourniquet ischemia, and a needle-point electrocautery available. (2) Dissect from normal tissue into abnormal. (3) Keep the tissues dissected under tension. (4) Keep the margins of the wound suspended by hooks or stay sutures. (5) Once through the dermis with a scalpel, use short-bladed, sharp, fine scissors for dissection and identify and coagulate or ligate all vessels that need to be divided. (6) Spread the tissue gently before cutting, and then cut with precision only the tensed white fascial or fibrous tissue. This will prevent the inadvertent severing of nerves or vessels, which are identifiable by their soft and lax consistency.

b. Irrigation Gross dirt on the skin should be washed off with soap and water. Skin stains do not necessarily have to be washed off. If the skin is coated with oil, grime, or tar, ether or benzine may be necessary to remove it, but such solutions must be kept out of the wound. Dried blood is most easily removed with hydrogen peroxide. An open wound may be irrigated with lactated Ringer's solution or antibiotic solution.

c. Debridement is the removal of blood clots, nonviable tissue, and foreign bodies which will constitute dead space. Thus, living tissue can be coapted and grafted tissue can be nourished by capillary invasion. It is occasionally necessary to debride without tourniquet ischemia so that the level of viability can be determined by the scalpel. The hand specialist will know when and how to save debrided tissue for primary or secondary use in reconstructive surgery. The objective of debridement in the primary care of injuries is to preserve function by

---

*Management of injured nerves, tendons, etc. are discussed individually later in this chapter.

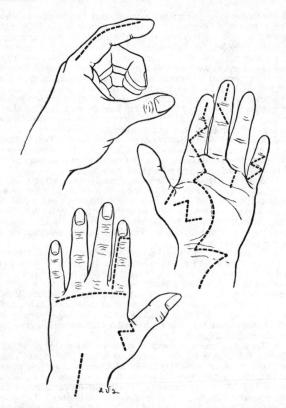

Fig. 15-1. Proper placement of skin incision. (Reproduced, with permission, from Dunphy and Way (Eds.), *Current Surgical Diagnosis & Treatment.* Lange, 1977.)

preserving circulation and curtailing edema and infection. Closing a wound with irregular but viable margins or with primary or delayed split thickness grafting is far preferable to trimming the edges and forcing the closure with tight sutures. Stained but viable tissue and minute fragments of foreign material should not be removed unless the foreign material is known to be caustic.

d. Exposure (see Fig. 15-1) Evaluation and repair demand identification of the anatomic relationships. Incisions often must be extended beyond scar or blood-discolored tissue. This should be done without injury to the blood supply, nerves, and tendons and should not predispose to secondary disabling contractures (e.g., scars crossing at right angles to flexion skin creases).

e. What to repair After debridement and exposure, the surgeon's experience and facilities will determine how much to repair deep to the skin. Skilled primary reparative or reconstructive hand surgery will go far to spare function, time, and expense. Unskilled efforts may do just the opposite. Generally speaking, skeletal distortion should be gently corrected, and if the tissues are not congested and the circulation is good, structures that are easily identifiable and clearly matched should be approximated. Unstable bone alignment often requires Kirschner wires or screws for adequate fixation. Sutures of nylon vary in caliber from 8·0 to 11·0 for digital nerves and from 4·0 to 6·0 for tendons and skin. All ligatures are preferably of 4·0 to 6·0 nylon. (Catgut is reactive and therefore should not be used except to close the skin of infants.)

Given satisfactory skeletal stability, the circulation has first priority, skin and fat second, tendons (e.g., long flexor tendons) third, and nerves the last priority in primary repair. One must avoid overloading the already injured tissues with the trauma of surgery itself.

Primary repair is that which is done within the first 24–72 hours. If circumstances of wounding suggest heavy contamination (e.g., a tooth, a farmyard, or a sewer inflicted wound), it is probably best to drain the wound and repair nothing primarily. When contamination is minimal but the circulation is impaired (e.g., much swelling)—or if over 8 hours have passed without any surgical toilet or splinting—then it is best to prepare, dress, splint, and elevate the part and administer prophylactic broad-spectrum antibiotics. If within the first 2 weeks there is no evidence of inflammation and the tissues are soft and pliable, delayed primary repair may be considered.

Secondary repair is that which follows the first 2 weeks after injury and is usually undertaken after resolution of the swelling and induration that followed the injury.

5. Wound closure and drainage A rubber drain prevents the accumulation of serum and blood and forestalls the development of 'dead space' and infection or cicatrix. Therefore, drainage should be selectively used in contaminated wounds and severe compound crushing wounds. Drains should be inserted in such a way as to favor gravity drainage from the elevated extremity.

Wounds should never be closed with tension. If tension is unavoidable, it is best to leave the wound open or to graft it. When tension has already built up and uncontrollable throbbing pain has developed, it should be treated by adequate slitting of the skin and slitting the fascia of all tight compartments.

Most wounds of the hand can be closed with one layer of interrupted or running everting skin sutures. Interrupted sutures are preferred if motion is to start early.

6. Prophylaxis against infection This involves prophylaxis against tetanus (see Chapter 4) and against streptococcal and staphylococcal infections. If the wound is contaminated (not necessarily clinically infected), it should be irrigated with penicillin or bacitracin solution at surgery and systemic antibiotics should be given for 48–72 hours afterward. The systemic drugs of choice for gram-positive organisms are penicillin, methicillin, erythromycin, cephalosporin, or oxacillin; for gram-negative organisms, kanamycin or gentamicin. Antibiotics must not be regarded as a substitute for the more important fundamental principles of surgical technic and protection of circulation (especially venous return).

7. Dressings and splints The dressing should serve to keep the soft tissues at rest and prevent the development of 'dead space' by gentle compression that does not obstruct venous return. Sopping wet dressings facilitate drainage of blood and serum. A single layer of fine mesh gauze smoothed out flush with the wound prevents granulation tissue from invading the dressing and facilitates the search for sutures when the dressing is removed. On top of this should be placed wet, loose-meshed gauze which should be tailored to lie flat without folds and ridges. Up to this point nothing is wrapped circumferentially around the digit, hand, or forearm. Over this should then be placed a carefully tailored sheet of sponge rubber or plastic (e.g., Reston) to prevent congestion by the dressing. This in turn is held in place with circumferentially wrapped, loose-meshed gauze (e.g., Kling, Kerlix). Care should be taken not to wrap the part too snugly.

Immobilization is mandatory initially in most cases of hand trauma, bearing in mind that prolonged immobilization involves a risk of stiffness. The position in immobilization must never be at the extreme of joint extension or flexion but must generally serve its need, e.g., to relieve tension on a tendon or nerve suture line. Whenever possible, immobilization should be in the **position of function** (see Fig. 15-2). This favors circulation and promotes comfort as well as

Fig. 15-2. Position of function of the hand: wrist extended 30° and fingers semi-flexed with thumb pronated. (Reproduced, with permission, from Dunphy and Way (Eds.), *Current Surgical Diagnosis & Treatment,* 3rd Ed. Lange, 1977).

early reestablishment of unimpaired function. It is the posture assumed when the hand holds a small drinking glass and is most readily achieved by putting a soaking-wet roll of gauze (e.g., Kerlix) in the palm between the thumb and fingers and molding it to them. Loosely wrapped dry cast padding covered with a volar plaster splint (12-16 thicknesses, 1-2 inches wide and 6-8 inches long) from the midpalm across the wrist to the midforearm and held in place with one 3-4 inch wide roll of circumferentially wrapped plaster makes a light and effective splint (see Fig. 15-3).

After extensive hand trauma, infection, or surgery, a softly padded boxing-glove forearm cast is preferred. One may put only part of the hand in such a cast—e.g., the thumb alone, or a combination of any 2 or 3 adjacent fingers. Generally speaking, such splinting is preferred for even severe fingertip injuries (e.g., amputation or crush). The wrist must be immobilized to adequately splint any part of the hand. Flat splints (e.g., tongue blade) and single digit splinting for an extensive injury impose a risk of distortion and stiffness and often fail to relieve pain. Infants and irresponsible adults usually need a long arm cast rather than a forearm cast. The elbow is immobilized at 90°.

The duration of splinting will vary with the problem and the age of the patient. Repair of nerves and tendons and fractures of phalanges and metacarpals usually require immobilization for 3-4 weeks, whereas ganglionectomy and fingertip grafting require only 6-8 days of casting.

8. Postinjury and postoperative care

a. Control of circulation In serious cases where microcirculation is threatened by tissue trauma and congestion, sludging and microthrombosis may be curtailed by administering 1 unit of low molecular weight dextran (dextran 40) daily. It is essential that the hand be constantly elevated in comfort above the heart. There must be no compression or constriction by clothing, jewelry, dressings, casts, or even skin or fascia. Throbbing and brawny induration must be mechanically (not medicinally) relieved—if necessary, by slitting skin and fascia.

b. Movement The patient must understand that motion inside a splint is undesirable even though possible and that vigorous movement of **any** part of the upper extremity may disrupt the tissues being splinted. On the other hand, gentle movement of all unsplinted joints helps the circulation of the whole upper extremity. When immobilization is discontinued, active exercise should be started on an organized routine (e.g., 4 times daily for 15 minutes). The frequency and duration of rehabilitative exercises of the injured part should steadily increase. The more the patient can do on his own and the less he needs the crutch of physical therapy, the better.

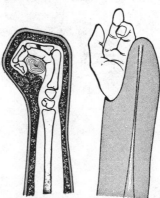

Fig. 15-3. Keeled cast. (Reproduced, with permission, from Dunphy and Way (Eds.), *Current Surgical Diagnosis & Treatment*, 3rd Ed. Lange, 1977.)

c. Chronic stiffness Pain is often the chief deterrent to overcoming stiffness caused by tight scar tissue and contracted ligaments. This can sometimes be relieved around joints by the intra-articular and peri-articular injection of a small amount of lidocaine mixed with triamcinolone. Passive stretching is also possible by the use of dynamic splints carefully adjusted and tailored to the needs of the specific problems, but these must be worn intermittently rather than continuously and should not be permitted to cause pressure sores, nerve injury, or edema. In selected intractable cases, arthrolysis, tenolysis, or modification of skin scars may be required.

d. Care of the paralyzed hand During the recovery stage following nerve injury, the patient must take care not to injure anesthetic skin by burns or cuts, or pain-free joints by sprains and subluxations. Splints should be used to keep paralyzed muscles from being overstretched and uninvolved muscles from overcontracting without antagonism. An example is the cock-up splint for the wrist and metacarpophalangeal joints in radial nerve palsy.

C. CONTUSION AND COMPRESSION INJURIES A crushing or compressive force to the forearm, hand, or digit can result in severe stiffness and even impairment of nerve function. Impaired circulation in such cases results from bleeding and serous effusion, then swelling, and finally venous obstruction and microvascular thrombosis caused by tissue tension. This can lead to irreversible ischemic fibrosis, as in Volkmann's ischemic paralysis and contracture. This process can occur in any fascial compartment of the upper extremity—even that of any of the intrinsic muscles. It can usually be prevented by attending promptly to throbbing pain and relieving it mechanically. Brawny (rocky hard) congestion must be prevented even if it means slitting the skin and fascia extensively. It is both useless and harmful to try to squeeze infiltrated blood out of tissues, though clearly defined clots can occasionally be extracted.

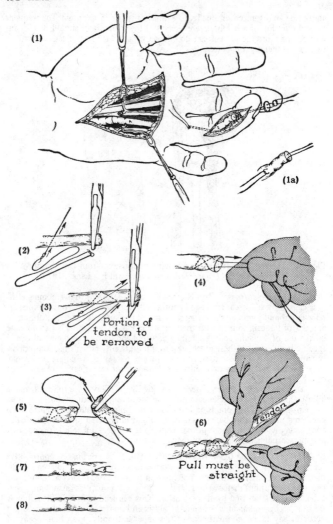

(1)

(1a)

(2)

(3)

Portion of
tendon to
be removed

(4)

(5)

(6)

Tendon

Pull must be
straight

(7)

(8)

Fig. 15-4. Methods of flexor tendon repair. (1) Exposure and suture of flexor tendons. Within the finger, the pull-out method is used. In the palm, the buried suture technic is used. (1a) Enlarged view of suture placement in finger. (2, 3, 4) Details of suture placement in the proximal tendons. (5, 6, 7, 8) Details of suture placement in the distal end of tendon for buried suture.

D. LACERATIONS AND SKIN AVULSIONS All wounds should be inspected and closed under tourniquet control. A magnifying loupe should be available. Blood clots should be gently removed, and easily accessible foreign bodies should be searched for by inspection or probing. It is often impractical and unnecessary to remove all foreign bodies; secondary removal is often preferable after the surrounding blood has been absorbed. Vessels that need ligation must be identified and isolated, and ligatures must be placed accurately to avoid damage to an adjacent nerve. If continued oozing is expected after the wound is closed, a drain should be inserted. If a full thickness of skin has been lost, the wound may be primarily closed with a skin graft. If oozing is too great, grafting should be delayed for 1 or 2 days. Split-thickness grafts are the most certain to take, but a full-thickness graft may be prepared by defatting an avulsed piece of skin or by taking some from the hairless portion of the groin. Very long reverse flaps and flaps that have been significantly traumatized are preferably defatted and applied as free full-thickness grafts or replaced by a split-thickness graft. Immobilization is crucial to the healing of lacerations and grafts.

II. TENDON INJURIES

Any laceration must be assumed to have divided a tendon until proved otherwise by inspection of the wound under tourniquet ischemia with prior or simultaneous systematic testing of all tendons as they are actively tensed. An abnormal digital stance created by a tendon injury can often be demonstrated by extreme passive flexion or extension of the wrist. Penetrating glass and metal wounds can damage tendons far in excess of what is apparent and at sites far removed from the skin wound.

Tendon constriction is a common cause of pain at the site of the offending tendon sheath (pulley). The pain may coincide with a jog in the excursion of the tendon (usually a flexor tendon, e.g., trigger finger); or it may be merely associated with stretch and tension of the synovial sheath when the tendon is tensed (e.g., DeQuervain's stenosing tenosynovitis of the abductor pollicis longus). Tendon rupture is uncommon, but tendon adherence due to adhesions (tenodesis) is common.

A. TREATMENT Because of the complexity of restoring tendon and joint function after injury or other impairment, most problems of the flexor or extensor musculotendinous systems should be referred to the hand specialist for definitive treatment.

Stenosing tenosynovitis or trigger finger is usually treated first by injecting a small amount of lidocaine mixed with triamcinolone into the tendon sheath at the trigger point. If that fails, the tendon must be liberated surgically. Ruptures that materially affect digital function often present complex reconstruction problems. Tenolysis can be effective in restoring tendon glide if early active postoperative movement is instituted.

The restoration of function after division of tendons requires surgical judgment and skill and the subsequent perseverance of the patient in the rehabilitation effort. Tendon repair must not be at the expense of mobility of uninjured tendons and joints. The surgeon may appropriately elect no treatment, tenorrhaphy, tendon transfer, tenodesis, or arthrodesis. Tenorrhaphy may be done primarily or secondarily by direct suture, by tendon graft, or by tendon transfer, followed by immobilization for 3-4 weeks. Cases referred to the specialist should receive primary wound toilet, closure, splinting, and prophylactic antibiotics. Joints must be freely mobile and skin- and fat-cover healthy and pliable before tenorrhaphy or tendon transfer is undertaken.

The handling of tendons and their fibro-osseous sheaths should be atraumatic. Sponges, forceps, clamps, and needles all invite adhesions where they contact these structures. The long flexor tendons require pulleys for mechanical efficiency and to prevent bowstringing; however, in order to make certain that this pulley system does not choke and prevent excursion of a tenorrhaphy callus, enough fibro-osseous sheath must be removed to correspond with the expected amplitude of glide of the callus; or the tendon(s) should be transposed superficial to the retinaculum.

The technic of suturing a tendon must be meticulous. The amount of suturing required depends on the amount of separation of the proximal stump from its distal attachment and the force necessary to hold the suture line. Retraction of the proximal stump may be prevented while placing the tendon suture by skewering the stump with a straight needle. Atraumatic nonreactive 4-0 to 5-0 sutures (e.g., monofilament nylon) should be used and can be threaded (see Fig. 15-4) in a mattress, figure-of-eight, or once or twice crisscrossing fashion through the tendon stumps. The rim of a tendon juncture may be reinforced and evened up by a 6-0 or 7-0 running once-and-over suture. Nylon sutures are usually buried except when anchoring a tendon into bone, in which case the suture ends may pass through the bone and overlying epithelial layer (e.g., fingernail) to be tied over a cotton dental roll and then withdrawn in 3-4 weeks (Fig. 15-5). When the size of 2 tendons to be joined is disproportionate, the smaller one may be woven once or twice through the larger one.

Immobilization should be in a position that takes tension off the tendon wound without putting any joints in extreme flexion or extension. The wrist is most often the principal joint to be positioned.

1. Extensor tendon injury If injury to an extensor tendon is recognized immediately and proper treatment is given, the prognosis for recovered function is usually more favorable than is the case with flexor tendons. This is because there is less sheath to contend with and, over the digit, less glide. The danger with the extensor system lies in the fact that it is very complex and at first may fully compensate for a major interruption only to decompensate insidiously later, due to inadequate treatment.

Exposure (often by proximal and distal extension of the wound) is important for the proper assay and repair of the injury. Because retraction of the proximal stump may be physically negligible but functionally significant, reapproximation of ends and immobilization are usually essential.

Positioning alone may satisfactorily restore the continuity. If not, buried 4-0 to 6-0 monofilament nylon sutures are placed as figure-of-eight, horizontal mattress, or (on the dorsum of the hand and forearm) crisscross weaving sutures. Immobilization should be maintained for 3-6 weeks.

a. Mallet (baseball) finger (Fig. 15-6) is a flexion stance of the distal joint resulting from separation of the attachment of the extensor to the distal phalanx. Bone or tendon may be separated, and active extension may be partially or completely lost. A dorsal or volar padded splint across the distal joint for 6 weeks may be all that is needed in fresh cases. Hyperextension and excessive skin pressure must be avoided. Intractable cases may cause a secondary change in the middle finger joint, which goes into hyperextension (recurvatum), resulting in 'swan neck' deformity.

b. Buttonhole (boutonniere) deformity (Fig. 15-7) is the converse of the swan neck habitus. It results from blunt or sharp injury to the dorsum of the middle finger joint (or metacarpophalangeal joint of the thumb). By attenuation of the extensor hood, the injured joint fails to extend while the distal joint overextends. Anticipation of the deformity and immobilization of the injured joint in full extension by a padded dorsal or volar splint or by Kirschner wires for 4-6 weeks is the recommended treatment.

2. Flexor tendon injury Anatomic zones of injury that have important implications for prognosis and management are shown in Fig. 15-8. The principal difference between the zones is not only the existence or nonexistence of a fibrous flexor sheath and its nature but also the number of tendons within it.

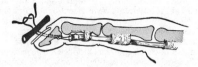

Fig. 15-5. Flexor tenorrhaphy by reattachment, advancement or graft.

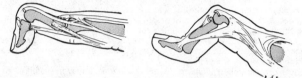

Fig. 15-6. Mallet finger with swan-neck deformity.

Fig. 15-7. Buttonhole deformity.

Fig. 15-8. Flexor tendon zones.

Illustrations at the top of the page are reproduced, with permission, from Dunphy and Way (Eds.), *Current Surgical Diagnosis and Treatment,* 3rd Ed. Lange, 1977.

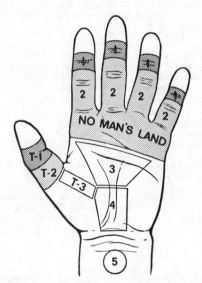

Thus, in zone 2 of the finger ('no man's land') there is a tight sheath around 2 tendons, one of which (the superficialis) forms a tunnel around the other (the profundus). Because of the unselective involvement of all structures in reparative scar, tendon injuries in this zone often defy subsequent excursion by virtue of intractable tenodesis. Consequently, considerable experience and judgment are required for successful management of such tendon injuries.

Instead of stump-to-stump approximation tendon advancement (Fig. 15-5) with sacrifice of the distal stump is occasionally favored for division of the flexor within 1 cm of the distal phalanx (i.e., zone 1). It may be combined with tendon lengthening in the case of the flexor pollicis longus. The other alternatives are tenodesis of the distal stump, arthrodesis of the distal joint, or no treatment.

Primary tendon repair (within 72 hours) or delayed primary repair (within 2 weeks) is favored for midpalm (zone 3), wrist (zone 4), and forearm (zone 5) injuries. It is also favored selectively in tidy injuries in the proximal portion of the finger (zone 2). When the wound in this area is untidy or when several weeks or months have elapsed since the injury, a tendon graft is generally preferred in zone 2. Secondary tendon repair (more than 2 weeks after surgery) is frequently possible in zones 3, 4, and 5.

When multiple tendons are divided in one zone, it may be preferable to re-pair only the more important ones. This is especially true in injuries in zone 2, where the profundus is usually the only one that should be repaired.

Lateral digital incisions may be made to connect the ends of the flexion creases, or volar incisions may cross the fat pads obliquely in a zigzag fashion. Zigzagging is also preferred for opening the palm or wrist. Damage to neurovas-cular bundles must be avoided. (See Fig. 15-1.)

Priority should be given to repairing flexor tendons before repairing nerves. When dealing with a very bloody palm or digit with both nerve and flexor ten-don injury, neurorrhaphy often demands such excessive surgical dissection to even identify a nerve that it is contraindicated as a primary procedure.

Movement of digits within 3 weeks after flexor tenorrhaphy, if permitted at all, must be done very guardedly. After 3 weeks, active motion may progress in a graded fashion.

B. PROGNOSIS Excursion after tenorrhaphy or tenolysis depends on the mobility of joints, the remodeling of scar tissue so that it yields to the glide of tendons, adequate strength of muscles, and perseverance by the patient. It often takes many months—even up to a year—to regain maximal tendon excursion and joint motion and for the collagen of scar tissue to attenuate and adapt. The pa-tient must be encouraged to persevere and must be made aware of the difficulty and sometimes impossibility of recovering completely normal excursion. Prog-ress may be gauged by serial records of the distance by which digital tips fail to reach points in space (e.g., a straight line in extension or the midpalm in flexion). If there is no sign of improvement during a period of 4 weeks of close super-vision beginning 2–3 months after surgery, further spontaneous improvement is most unlikely.

III. NERVE INJURIES

The interruption of nerve conduction following injury may be merely physio-logic (i.e., neurapraxia) or it may be anatomic. The distinction can be made by repeated examination in the first few hours after an open injury and before any anesthetic is administered if the neurapraxia is transient.

The median, ulnar, and radial nerves are vital to the function of the hand. They are all mixed (sensory and motor) at the elbow, and the median and ulnar nerves are mixed up to the heel of the hand. A knowledge of innervation is essen-tial to determine the level of an injury. (See Figs. 15-9 and 15-10.) Pain and failure to cooperate may lead to a false diagnosis of motor paralysis, whereas absence of sweating over the distribution of an injured nerve objectively identifies sensory paralysis. Two-point discrimination 3-4 mm apart also signifies good sensory function.

Bleeding should be initially controlled by compressing and not by clamping. 'Blind' clamping of bleeding points leads to iatrogenic nerve injury and must

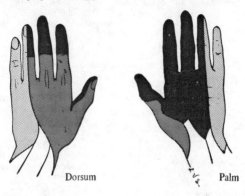

Dorsum   Palm

Fig. 15-9. Sensory distribution in the hand. Dotted area, ulnar nerve; diagonal area, radial nerve; darker area, median nerve. (Reproduced, with permission, from Dunphy and Way (Eds.), *Current Diagnosis & Treatment.* Lange, 1977.)

be avoided. Before clamping or ligating, the vessel must be clearly distinguished from a nearby nerve by accurate dissection under tourniquet control (arm blood pressure cuff at 100 mm Hg above systolic pressure) with loupe magnification and ideal facilities. The patient should be supine.

When blood prevents meticulous exploration, the dissection should extend to normal tissue and then reverse into the zone of injury.

Motor and sensory nerve conduction studies occasionally help to clarify difficult diagnostic problems in chronic cases.

A. TREATMENT

1. Neurapraxia is treated expectantly. How long to defer the exploration of a nerve depends on the mechanism of injury and the surgeon's estimate of its physical impact on the nerve. If there is no sign of regeneration (i.e., return of muscle function and advancement of Tinel's sign) in 4-6 months, surgical measures (if applicable) should no longer be deferred. Surgical measures (singly or in combination) may consist of neurolysis, resection of scarred nerve and neurorrhaphy, nerve graft, tendon transfer, tenodesis, arthrodesis, and neurovascular island pedicle flaps.

2. The sooner a divided nerve is repaired, the better. Regeneration takes months, and after 2 months the motor end plates of the small intrinsic muscles become increasingly resistant to recovery. Neurorrhaphy more than a year after injury gives generally poor return of sensory function.

Peripheral neurorrhaphy is highly specialized surgery which can only be done properly by the experienced hand surgeon. Fresh cases being referred should have a surgical skin preparation and the extremity should be immobilized and elevated with or without temporary wound closure and prophylactic antibiotics.

Wrist drop in radial
nerve injury

Forceful extension of
thumb tip is lost in
radial nerve injury

Radial nerve

Ape hand deformity in
median nerve injury

Unopposed thumb

Thenar atrophy (espe-
cially the abductor
pollicis brevis which is
the thenar muscle
closest to the meta-
carpal)

Forceful flexion of tip
of thumb and index is
lost in high median
nerve injury

Median nerve

Thumb web atrophy
and clawing of ring and
little fingers

Loss of abduction and
adduction in ulnar
nerve injury

Ulnar nerve

Fig. 15-10. Findings in nerve injuries.

3. Technic of nerve suture. (See Fig. 15-11.) All peripheral nerve surgery
requires loupe or microscopic magnification as well as microsurgical instruments and suture material (i.e., 8-0 to 12-0 atraumatic nylon).

Freshly incised nerves should be approximated without further surgical
section of the stumps. Macerated and scarred nerves require razor blade section
across normal nerve tissue before approximation. The minimal amount of nerve
should be resected.

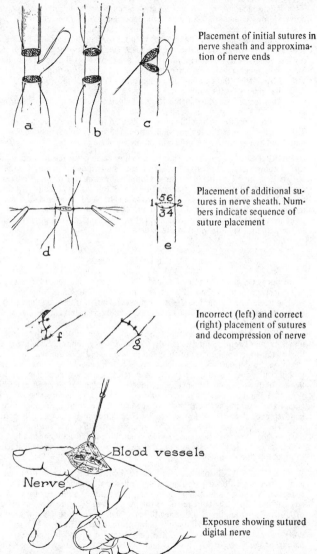

Placement of initial sutures in nerve sheath and approximation of nerve ends

Placement of additional sutures in nerve sheath. Numbers indicate sequence of suture placement

Incorrect (left) and correct (right) placement of sutures and decompression of nerve

Exposure showing sutured digital nerve

Fig. 15-11. Methods of neurorraphy.

Anatomic matching of fascicles and epineural vessels in proximal and distal nerve stumps is essential. Sutures should be atraumatic, fine caliber, as few as possible, and placed into the epineurium or perineurium in such a way as to accurately approximate fascicular stumps without overlap, telescoping, furling, and protrusion from the connective tissue sleeve. Tension must be avoided; if it can not be overcome by the positioning of joints, a nerve graft should be considered. Tension of edema within a nerve after epineural approximation should be prevented by slitting the epineurium of the proximal and distal stumps a distance from the epineural suture line.

The use of local corticosteroids has helped to reduce neuromal scar formation.

Tension on the suture line must be avoided for 3-4 weeks postoperatively. This usually requires plaster immobilization. Thereafter, joints may be gradually mobilized at a rate inverse to the tension on the nerve juncture.

B. PROGNOSIS A nerve that has been reunited can never regain normal innervation completely. Compensatory factors may substitute adequately for the deficit so that function may be nearly normal. The principal factors that restrict quantitative and qualitative reinnervation are as follows: (1) Inability to reunite and match all divided axons. (2) Distortion due to bleeding, edema, and scar formation. (3) Impairment of circulation and the lack of soft tissue about the injured nerve. (4) Delay in neurorrhaphy. (5) Inexperience in hand surgery. (6) Age of the patient. (7) Motivation of the patient.

IV. BURNS OF THE HANDS

Hand burns occur in the following order of decreasing incidence: thermal, friction, electric, chemical, and radiation. The impact on function may be catastrophic. The overall economic loss due to deep second and third degree thermal burns of the hand is a staggering burden. Preventive safety measures and proper primary therapy can reduce this toll.

While instituting lifesaving measures in the severely burned patient, the upper extremity must simultaneously receive urgent attention. Swelling and the loss of the functional arches of the hand must be avoided as much as possible by elevation, by dermatomy and fasciotomy if brawny edema develops, and by immobilization and positioning (wrist in extension, metacarpophalangeal joints flexed, and, in certain instances, proximal interphalangeal joints in extension). A swollen hand is a claw hand in disguise. Therefore, swelling must be controlled and 'fixed' clawing avoided. High voltage electrical current in contact with the hand spreads deep tissue destruction by coagulation as it passes to its point of exit. The 'entry' wound may be far removed from the 'exit' burn. The elbow must not be allowed to become fixed in extension and the shoulder in adduction. Whenever possible (and as soon as possible), all joints must be moved actively— often before the burn wound is reepithelialized.

A. TREATMENT Burns that do not need debridement and grafting (e.g., first and second degree burns) may be treated initially with an ice-water bath and analgesics followed by a soothing cream (e.g., zinc oxide or a proprietary burn remedy such as Kip First Aid Cream). If the burn is deep second degree, is infected, or is already granulating but not healthy and 'clean' enough to graft, it should be coated twice a day with zinc oxide, silver-sulfadiazine (Silvadene) cream, povidone-iodine (Betadine), or an ointment consisting of 1 part silver nitrate, 5 parts balsam of Peru, 30 parts hydrous lanolin, and 30 parts amber petrolatum. Chemical burns are treated initially by copious and sometimes prolonged (e.g., 12-24 hours) irrigation with tapwater or weak acid (alkali burns) or alkaline (acid burns) solutions. Hydrofluoric acid burns may be neutralized by the local injection of small amount of 10% calcium gluconate.

The chief objective of therapy of deep or extensive burns is to restore effective skin cover and the integrity of deep tissue as rapidly as possible without infection, so that muscle and joint use may be started early and maximal function spared. There is no one rule or one method of accomplishing this, but delay and neglect in the implementation of these principles may lead to permanent disability.

As long as swelling does not prevent active motion and there is no sign of infection, debridement and grafting are not urgent. However, the converse is equally true, and in urgent cases it makes little difference if, during debridement, a small amount of equivocally viable skin is removed in continuity with unequivocally lifeless eschar.

Debridement should be followed by a biologic dressing (autograft, homograft, or heterograft) as soon as hemostasis is adequate to prevent dead space under the graft—this may be immediate or may require waiting for 12-24 hours. Immobilization and protection of the hand for 24-48 hours is essential so that there will be no shift of the graft on its bed. Sutures may not be needed to hold the graft in place. Continuous wet dressings inside a waterproof seal (e.g., plastic bag) often avoid the need for 'rolling out' grafts in the first 24-48 hours.

The thinner (i.e., 0.002 mm) and smaller (i.e., 4-10 mm square) the grafts are, the surer they are to take. 'Mesh' grafts are suitable substitutes for postage stamp grafts, but they must be sutured in place. Sheets of skin are favored for 'clean' wounds with good hemostasis. If the margins lie along lines of stretch, they should be zigzagged with skin darts.

B. FUNCTIONAL DISABILITIES DUE TO HAND BURNS   Scar leads to a host of characteristic digital deformities (e.g., clawing, buttonhole, swan neck, mallet), adduction contracture of the thumb, and a multitude of other extension and flexion joint contractures. Proper splinting may prevent and reconstructive procedures may correct many deformities.

V. FRACTURES, DISLOCATIONS, AND LIGAMENT INJURIES

A. GENERAL PRINCIPLES

1. The history of the degree of force and the mechanism of injury to the hand is essential to the evaluation of these injuries. X-rays in the anteroposterior and lateral and even oblique planes as well as comparative views of the opposite hand are often indispensable. Pain, distortion, or abnormality of motion (hypermobility or reduced mobility) are usually but not always present. Swelling may mask distortion, and distortion may be mistaken for swelling. To diagnose unexplained continuing skeletal pain one must obtain follow-up x-rays at intervals of 7-10 days initially, then monthly.

2. Treatment should be directed at restoration of proper alignment, painless movement, and stability with forceful use of the involved parts. Ultimate function of the hand, not radiologic perfection, is what is most important, and functional considerations must dictate the timing and choice of treatment. For example, irreversible and disabling stiffness may be the price of a 'perfect' reduction and union of a fracture that has been manipulated too much and immobilized too long. For this reason, in selected cases, it is best to start guarded movement early, particularly in 'heavy handed' and older individuals. Instead of using any force to effect a needed reduction it is often best to do an open reduction or settle for imperfect alignment.

3. Initial immobilization should assume the position of maximal function in order to minimize the impact of stiffness. The test of adequate immobilization is freedom from pain. With few exceptions, if one finger needs immobilization, one or more adjacent fingers should also be splinted as well as the wrist. Cast padding, soft gauze, or a spongy cushion such as Reston, and plaster are generally far better for making a custom-fitting splint than boards, sticks, or metal or plastic material. The surgeon must avoid splinting all joints of a digit in extension for fear of stiffness and rotational deformities, and must guard against the hazards of traction technics, i.e., stiffness and pressure necrosis.

Internal fixation with fixation screws or Kirschner wires and occasionally with compression technics should be considered when there is marked instability and when one wishes to allow motion of neighboring tendons and joints. Joints are usually secured with one oblique wire, whereas bones often need one longitudinal wire with another one placed obliquely to prevent rotation.

4. Open bone and joint injuries should be treated with prophylactic local or systemic antibiotics (or both). When skin and fat cover is lost, it should be replaced by free grafts or pedicle transfer of local or distant skin.

5. Fracture treatment generally takes precedence over tendon repair, but this does not mean that easily accessible tendon ends should not be reapproximated as a primary procedure.

B. FRACTURES

1. Wrist fractures Every apparent sprain of the wrist should be considered a fracture until shown to be otherwise by total subsidence of pain or negative follow-up x-rays in 8-10 days. The 3 most common fractures of the wrist are the result of sudden forceful hyperextension or radial deviation.

a. Colles' fracture The deformity consists of dorsal displacement of the joint surface of the radius, recession of the radial styloid, and fracture of the ulnar styloid. One must watch for compression of the median nerve with numbness over its distribution in the hand. Reduction requires anesthesia and should be gentle. It need not be radiologically perfect. The wrist should generally be in the neutral position, not flexed. Immobilization in a long arm cast for 4 weeks and a forearm cast for 2 weeks is usually adequate. Digital motion with full amplitude of metacarpophalangeal joint and thumb web should be started immediately. Temporary disability commonly persists for 4-6 months or more. Residual traumatic arthritis may be unavoidable and require surgery (e.g., ulnar styloidectomy or wrist fusion).

b. Navicular (scaphoid) fracture Special x-ray views are essential to rule out these fractures. Pain is maximal in the anatomic snuff box and on radial deviation of the wrist. Reduction is seldom necessary. Immobilization is usually maintained by means of a long arm cast that includes the metacarpophalangeal joint of the thumb for 4 weeks and a short arm cast for an additional 2 weeks. Many patients are then ready to return to work. When there is no x-ray evidence of union, months of immobilization may be necessary. If union does not occur or if aseptic necrosis develops, surgery must be considered and may consist of bone grafting, radial styloidectomy, silicone implant substitution, wrist fusion, or other procedures. Such cases may have traumatic arthritis and 6-12 months of disability.

c. Triquetral fracture Fracture of the triquetrum is usually a small chip dorsal fracture seen only on the lateral x-ray view. Pain and tenderness are localized to the dorsal-ulnar aspect of the carpus and are often of short duration, requiring only a forearm cast for 1-3 weeks.

2. Metacarpal fractures are often undisplaced. When displacement does occur, the distal segment is usually pulled volarward so that the fracture is bowed to the dorsum (see Fig. 15-12). Manipulation and reduction are often difficult and are not necessary for minor distortions (e.g., 20-40° of bowing). Rotation at the fracture site must be prevented by keeping adjacent fingers furled side by side in functional flexion for 3-4 weeks. Open reduction and internal fixation are advocated for unstable fractures. A forearm cast may be necessary to the metacarpophalangeal joint level or may involve the entire length of the digits. Metacarpophalangeal joints must be splinted in flexion to avoid disabling stiffness.

Bennett's fracture is one at the base of the thumb metacarpal.

3. Proximal and middle phalangeal fractures The most common distortion of these fractures is opposite to that of metacarpal fractures. Here the distal segments are pulled dorsally, causing a volar bowing of the fracture site (see Fig. 15-13). Extension of the wrist and flexion of the metacarpophalangeal joint give the relaxation needed for reduction. This, together with side-to-side splinting to the adjacent finger and forearm boxing glove casting for 3 weeks, usually gives sufficient immobilization. Internal fixation with Kirschner wires—and even open reduction—may be necessary for accuracy of reduction and for very unstable fractures and intra-articular fractures. If joint integrity cannot be reestablished in articular fractures, positioning for a 'spontaneous' functional fusion is required

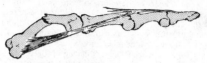

Fig. 15-12. Dorsal bowing of metacarpal fracture.

or, occasionally, silicone implant joint-spacer arthroplasty is undertaken. Very small chip fractures are only treated for the pain they cause. Intra-articular fracture fragments involving less than a third of the articular surface are often resected.

4. Distal phalangeal fractures These present the least hazard to function once pain has subsided (usually in 3-4 weeks). They are often comminuted and open. Intramedullary fixation with a No. 18 or 19 hypodermic needle on a 10 ml syringe barrel is sometimes necessary for displaced shaft and intra-articular fractures, but most cases require only external splinting. This may be achieved by forearm-to-fingertip casting for several days, followed by a digital guard.

Fig. 15-13. Volar bowing of phalangeal fracture.

Open 'bursting' type injuries are often too tense to tolerate sutures and should be simply 'molded' with fine mesh, dressed with wet gauze, and casted.

C. DISLOCATIONS Most dislocations occur as a result of hyperextension injuries and can be reduced by a combination of traction and hyperextension and by manipulating the displaced parts back into position. If reduction is impossible without force, open reduction is required.

1. Dislocations of the wrist Severe injuries of the wrist may cause dislocations about the navicular and lunate bones. The inexperienced eye may easily fail to notice the abnormality in the x-ray unless it is compared with exactly the same view of the opposite wrist. The navicular is often fractured as well as dislocated, whereas the lunate is simply dislocated volarward, where it tends to compress the median nerve and cause dysesthesia. Primary closed reduction under anesthesia is usually successful, but open reduction must be resorted to if this fails. Immobilization is generally for 4-6 weeks.

2. Finger dislocations may occur at any joint and usually involve the dorsal displacement of the distal bone on the proximal one. The proximal interphalangeal joint is most commonly dislocated. The patient often reduces it immediately himself. An unsatisfactory reduction is usually associated with some restrained active or passive motion and imperfect digital stance. When closed reduction is not possible in a fresh case, it means that the head of the more proximal bone has become trapped in a noose formed by displaced tendons, ligaments, and even bands of fascia. The volar plate occasionally fails to clear the joint during reduction and blocks flexion. In other instances, the volar plate has been avulsed so that the phalanx of its origin tends to redislocate. All such difficulties can only be managed surgically. Simple dislocations which are easily reduced and do not tend to redislocate (as verified by x-ray) need very little or no splinting beyond the patient's own tendency to favor the part.

D. LIGAMENTOUS INJURIES (Sprains and ruptures) Any ligament may be sprained or torn. However, before making a diagnosis of a sprain of the wrist, one must rule out fracture by repeated x-rays. Desmitis (inflammation of a ligament) is a common cause of wrist pain and responds well to rest and trigger-point lidocaine and triamcinolone injections.

Abduction force to the metacarpophalangeal joints and abduction or adduction force to the proximal interphalangeal joints are the most common sources of such injuries. Local pain and evidence of relaxation by clinical and x-ray examination under stress are diagnostic. A small piece of bone is sometimes avulsed. If large, it may require reduction or removal.

Most of these injuries are treated by splinting. An injured finger may be strapped to the adjacent normal one. Prolonged immobilization invites stiffness, which itself is a cause of pain.

Total avulsions of the collateral ligaments of the metacarpophalangeal joint of the thumb should be repaired if fresh and reconstructed if old.

VI. AMPUTATIONS

Loss of all or part of a digit is always a shocking experience for the patient, who often brings in the amputated part in the hope that it can be reimplanted. This is seldom feasible or indicated. Reimplantation may be considered by the experienced hand surgeon when the injury is tidy, the patient young, multiple digits and/or the thumb are involved, and the injury is proximal to the distal interphalangeal joint. Any amputation composed of more than just skin requires anastomosis of an artery and vein if it is to survive. The amputated part should be kept sterile and dry over ice if a patient is referred to a hand surgeon for possible reimplantation.

The functional impact of an amputation depends on the digits involved and the plane and extent of the loss. Thus, volar-radial fingertip loss and volar-ulnar thumb tip loss (the surfaces that oppose for pinch) are often disabling amputations. The concepts of (1) hand breadth for stability of grasp, and (2) digital length (especially of the thumb and the finger closest to it) for effectiveness of pinch must always be considered in planning salvage and reconstruction. Above all, the amputation stump must be rendered pain-free and with durable skin cover. Fingers that are intractably stiff, anesthetic, painful, or too short are often amputated by the surgeon if that will enhance overall function of the hand. Custom molded prosthetic devices that provide a hook or enhance pinch may be used in selected cases. Other prostheses worn for their cosmetic value have no functional usefulness and are generally discarded by the patient after a time.

A. STUMP CLOSURE Clots and nonviable or usable tissue should be debrided, but any part or tissue of reconstructive value should be saved. Closure should never be under tension. Bleeding vessels should be meticulously distinguished and separated from nerves by the use of loupe magnification and tourniquet control. Ligatures should be of nonreactive material such as fine nylon. Protruding bone should either be covered with a pedicle flap or rongeured back. Cartilage does not have to be removed. Nerve stumps must be recessed or transferred (preferably into a bed of fat or muscle) well away from bone stumps or pressure points. Tendons should not be sutured over amputation stumps. Local and systemic antibiotics should be used freely.

The loss of a fingertip is the most common amputation. The surest closure of such wounds is by means of a *thin* (0.002 mm) split thickness onlay graft.* Grafting should be done primarily unless active bleeding prevents it, in which case grafting must be deferred for 24–48 hours. The donor site is most often the volar-ulnar aspect of the proximal forearm, which is regionally anesthetized and

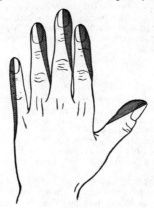

Fig. 15-14. Areas requiring padded skin with sensibility.

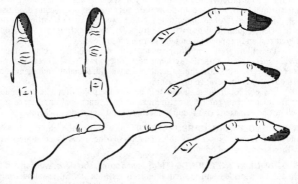

Fig. 15-15. Planes of distal digit amputation.

---

*The graft should be so thin that writing on the blade can be easily read through it.

then stretched tightly as the graft is taken with a razor blade. Anesthesia is required for the digit only if it must be debrided of clots and other debris. The procedure is done using loupe magnification and tourniquet control (blood pressure cuff at 300 mm Hg). The graft may be held in place with narrow strips of fine mesh gauze which is covered with wet gauze carefully tailored to the size of the grafted wound. Deadspace is closed by applying two narrow strips of plastic foam (e.g., Reston) at right angles to one another across the digit tip and down the sides and held in place with tubular gauze (i.e. Tubegauz). The digit is then immobilized—alone if it is the thumb, or with an adjacent finger if it is a finger—by a well-padded forearm circumferential cast which is worn for a week. Constrictive dressings and garments are avoided, and the extremity is kept elevated. Such grafts survive more often than full thickness skin grafts and invariably take on a satisfactory recipient bed. In time they shrink 50% or more so as to draw normal skin over the defect for satisfactory function.

The experienced hand surgeon may selectively employ other grafting technics consisting of local or distant pedicle flaps. When amputation stumps remain sensitive, the pain may subside with fingertip percussion. If not, surgical revision may be necessary.

VII. INFECTIONS

The most common hand infections are caused by gram-positive cocci and develop out of ignorance or neglect of the pathogenic factors. Tissues and structures whose blood supply is limited or easily impaired (e.g., nail folds, digital fat pads, bones, joints, and tendon sheaths) have the least resistance to infection. Constricting fascia, garments, and jewelry, wounds closed under tension, and dependent position of the hand all favor congestion and the formation of dead space (i.e., seroma and hematoma) which greatly enhance the likelihood of infection of any wound.

Most hand infections can be avoided if proper early treatment is given. The most important preventive measures in the case of hand injuries are (1) preservation of circulation by elevation and immobilization and the avoidance of tension by sutures, dressings, garments, or swelling; (2) facilitation of drainage of potential dead space or contaminated wounds by drains, wet dressings, or zinc oxide; (3) the liberal prophylactic use of local and systemic antibiotics, along with tetanus prophylaxis; and (4) debridement of clots, foreign bodies, and dead tissue.

Rapid onset of an infection, marked swelling, or unrelenting, throbbing pain often requires bed rest with the trunk flat so the extremity can be continually at rest and propped up on pillows above heart level.

Penicillin, erythromycin, cephalosporin, methicillin, oxacillin, and lincomycin are currently effective systemic antibiotics for staphylococcal and streptococcal infections. Bacitracin is useful in the wound. Kanamycin or gentamicin is effective for gram-negative organisms.

Incision for drainage should be done over the point of maximum tenderness or fluctuancy and parallel to structures of vital functional importance so they will not be damaged. This requires anesthesia and tourniquet ischemia.

A. FURUNCLE AND CARBUNCLE   These are common about hair follicles and often require only a very thick coating of zinc oxide as a compress with or without incision and drainage.

B. GRANULATING WOUNDS (Third degree burns, abrasions, avulsions)   These should be debrided and grafted as quickly as possible. Silver-sulfadiazine and Povidone-iodine compresses are useful antibacterial topical agents.

C. CELLULITIS is characterized by throbbing pain, local heat, redness, swelling, and tenderness. Elevation, immobilization, empirical antibiotic treatment, and frequent observation are the crucial elements of care. Surgical release of tension on skin and fascia must be done before brawny induration occurs.

Lymphangitis and lymphadenitis are treated in the same way as cellulitis.

D. PYOGENIC GRANULOMA Granulation tissue that forms on wounds should be scraped off flush with the skin and compressed to control bleeding for 12–24 hours. It is then left exposed to the air to dry up if it is less than 6 mm in diameter or grafted with a thin shaving of skin if it is larger. No sutures are needed.

E. PYODERMA is a pus-filled blister which often has a central sinus to a collar-button abscess. Treatment consists of unroofing the abscess and applying a bulky zinc oxide compress.

F. EPONYCHIA, PARONYCHIA, AND SUBEPONYCHIAL ABSCESS Incipient cases may respond to rest, elevation, and antibiotics. When drainage is spontaneous, resolution may be expedited by zinc oxide compresses. Surgical drainage of the nailfold can usually be done with a No. 11 pointed scalpel placed flat against the surface of the nail and advanced slowly in a scratching fashion into the point of maximum fluctuancy and tenderness. If this is done properly, it is not painful and no blood is drawn—only pus (see Fig. 15-16). When the base of the nail floats in pus, it is best to resect it.

G. SPACE INFECTIONS These include infections of the pulp (e.g., felon) and web and of the thenar, hypothenar, midpalmar, dorsal subcutaneous, dorsal subaponeurotic, and quadrilateral (Perona) spaces. It also includes infections of the sheaths of the flexor tendons (digital, radial, and ulnar bursae) and the extensor tendons (6 compartments at the wrist). If pain, tissue tension, and tenderness are minimal or slight, incision and drainage may not be necessary and there may be a rapid response to rest, elevation, and antibiotics. The chief function of incision is the release of tension. If pus is drained and if there is involvement over a signi-

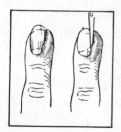

Fig. 15-16. Incision and drainage of paronychia

Fig. 15-17. Incision of felon

ficantly broad or long space (e.g., tendon sheath), catheter-drip administration of local antibiotics (e.g., bacitracin, 50,000 units in 500 ml Ringer's lactate) should be considered.

    1. Felon (see Fig. 15-17) The best drainage of a felon is through a midline longitudinal incision, often only 1–2 cm long. The vertical strands of fascia (septae) should not be divided. This technic spares the important blood and nerve supply to the digital tip, which may be iatrogenically damaged by the traditional fishmouth and lateral incisions.

    2. Flexor tenosynovitis The diagnosis is established if pain can be elicited by making the tendon move actively or passively within its sheath. The examiner may passively do this by handling (picking up) **only** the patient's finger nail as he extends the distal digital joint. If this can be done painlessly, then the site of infection rests in the skin or subcutaneous fat and spares the sheath.

Most cases of tenosynovitis that require incision and drainage need only a short volar longitudinal incision in the midline of the middle phalanx of the finger (proximal phalanx of the thumb) that does not cross the skin flexion

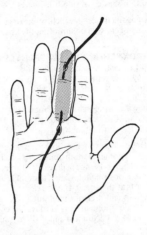

Fig. 15-18. Drainage and irrigation for septic tenosynovitis

creases, with a similarly directed counterincision in the palm. A fine catheter for antibiotic drip (5-10 ml/hour) is placed into the distal wound and another catheter (for drainage) into the proximal wound (see Fig. 15-18). These are usually removed in 24-72 hours.

Phlegmonous tenosynovitis often destroys digital function unless the flexor sheath is widely opened. This is done through a lateral midaxial incision.

H. BONE AND JOINT INFECTIONS   These structures have particularly low resistance to infection because circulation is limited. All open wounds of bone and joint must be treated as if infection were present, i.e., with local and systemic antibiotics, immobilization, and elevation. Established osteomyelitis may require hyperbaric oxygen treatments for 1-2 hours daily at 2 atmospheres.

I. HUMAN BITE INJURIES   Most of these are into the knuckles as a result of fist-fights and should be considered emergencies for prophylactic treatment. When infections become established, they are apt to be very disabling. Wounds of the soft parts should be drained and never fully closed.

J. MISCELLANEOUS INFECTIONS
    1. Streptococcal gangrene requires prompt fasciotomy, debridement, and antibiotic treatment.
    2. Tuberculosis   This is an indolent process which most often involves the synovial tissues of joints and tendons. Cultures may take months to be diagnostic. Good response follows synovectomy and antituberculosis drug therapy.

3. Fungal infections involve primarily the nail area. The response to antifungal agents may be good, e.g., griseofulvin systemically and diamthazole (Asterol), 0.5% ointment locally. In chronic cases the nail plate should be removed.

4. Herpes simplex usually presents as multiple tiny, quite painful vesicles about the distal phalanx which may become purulent and even coalesce into a pyoderma. It may need no treatment since it is self-limiting in about 3 weeks. Topical diethyl ether or 4% thymol in chloroform 3 or 4 times a day are the best forms of treatment. Idoxuridine, a specific antiviral agent, may be useful.

5. Other infections Gas gangrene, syphilis, deep fungal infections (coccidioidomycosis, blastomycosis, actinomycosis, sporotrichosis), tularemia, yaws, and glanders are rare infections diagnosed by history, chronicity, and identification of stigmas and pathogens.

Leprosy is not so much an infection of the hand as it is a motor and sensory paralyzer requiring extensive prophylactic education against trophic ulceration and sometimes reconstructive surgery.

VIII. MISCELLANEOUS DISORDERS

A. DESMITIS, TENDONITIS, AND MYOSITIS Inflammation of ligaments, tendons, or muscles may cause pain and tenderness in many areas of the elbow, forearm, wrist, and hand. Examples of this are **lateral** (tennis elbow) and **medial epicondylitis** and **myositis crepitans.** Repetitive or excessively vigorous effort often initiates the process, but in some cases no cause can be identified. Treatment includes local slow injection of a mixture of lidocaine and triamcinolone, systemic anti-inflammatory agents, rest, and, in acute severe cases, temporary immobilization. If long-acting steroid is injected, the patient should be warned that it may cause depigmentation and local tissue atrophy which may or may not be reversible.

Constrictive conditions commonly impair nerve and tendon function. **Carpal tunnel syndrome** is characterized by pain and numbness radiating along the median nerve and even up to the shoulder or chest due to its compression in the carpal tunnel. The cause is most commonly nonspecific and consists of an anatomic predilection combined with factors of aging or a shift in the water content of tendons and ligaments. However, it may also result from swelling and space consumption by repetitive effort, trauma, rheumatoid disease, tumor, etc. A similar state may affect the ulnar nerve in its tunnel at the elbow or the carpal level.

Constriction of tendons occurs for similar reasons where they are most snugly tethered by the sheath-pulley systems. The most common stenosing tenosynovitis occurs at the level of the proximal pulleys of the digital flexors in the distal palm as a **trigger finger or thumb,** and about the radial styloid as **DeQuervain's tenosynovitis.**

Initial treatment for most of these conditions is local injection of a mixture of lidocaine and triamcinolone (3:1) into the affected space but not into a nerve. Failure to respond after 2 or 3 injections combined with appropriate rest of the part (e.g., splinting) justifies surgical release of the constriction.

B. GOUT AND OSTEOARTHRITIS Pain, limitation of motion, and deformity are the complaints that lead to treatment of these conditions. Gout is most often controlled by colchicine or allopurinol (Zyloprim). Tophi are sometimes resectable. The pain of osteoarthritis can be helped by local triamcinolone and systemic anti-inflammatory agents. Intractable pain or stiffness can often be corrected by surgery (e.g., joint fusion or implant arthroplasty).

C. RHEUMATOID HAND DISORDERS This disease of unknown cause affects the hand in many ways. The hand surgeon is able to improve its appearance and function, and, in many instances, can forestall disabilities by excisional, incisional, and reconstructive technics. These include the resection of nodules, synovectomy, tenovaginotomy, and a host of tenoplasty and arthroplasty procedures to correct such deformities as ulnar drift, swan neck, buttonhole, intrinsic plus, etc.

D. DUPUYTREN'S CONTRACTURE   This is a thickening of the palmar fascia of unknown cause. It is commonly mistaken for a callus or tendon problem. It may involve any portion of the fascia and may develop insidiously over years or rapidly in weeks. It may be tender, but the most common complaint is of a lump in the palm or inability to extend the involved digits (usually the ring and little fingers). Treatment is surgical and for the most part consists of excision of the involved fascia. Skill is important to avoid neurovascular injury and postoperative stiffness (e.g., a frozen hand). Occasionally, one may prefer a subcutaneous fasciotomy of a discreet longitudinal band if the skin around it is soft and pliable. Recurrences are not uncommon.

E. TUMORS   Malignancies in the hand are rare. The most common one is squamous carcinoma of the dorsal skin in Caucasians with chronic exposure to sunlight. It can generally be cured with local excision.

Warts (verrucca vulgaris), ganglions, inclusion cysts, soft tissue giant cell tumors (xanthomas), and enchondromas of bone are the most common tumors. All may recur if inadequately treated. Warts may be electrodesiccated or treated with a 40% salicylic acid pad. The others should be meticulously operated on under tourniquet and magnification conditions in the operating room.

F. FOREIGN BODIES   The necessity to remove a foreign body will depend on its size, depth, location and the symptoms and signs it may cause. Unless superficial and easily seen or felt, it is often best to splint the hand and give antibiotics and tetanus prophylaxis and wait several days or weeks. This makes the need for removal a certainty, and the cystic pocket that forms around it helps greatly in finding it by dissection with tourniquet control and magnification technic. Multiple x-rays or xenograms in different planes should be taken to help localize the foreign body, and the image intensifier will sometimes facilitate its removal.

16

NEUROSURGERY

Julian T. Hoff, MD &
Lawrence H. Pitts, MD

I. GENERAL PRINCIPLES

A. EVALUATION OF THE NEUROSURGICAL PATIENT   Neurosurgical diagnosis is based upon a detailed history and a careful physical examination. Headache, visual disturbance, altered consciousness, memory impairment, weakness, paresthesia, incoordination, and speech difficulty are symptoms suggesting disease of the central nervous system. The physical examination should include specific assessment of mentation, sensory and motor testing, and a thorough cranial nerve examination, including optic fundoscopy. These steps detect clinical signs that permit accurate anatomic localization of the lesion. For patients with nervous system disorders, an accurate history need be taken once, but the physical examination must be repeated and recorded often to gauge the course of the illness and to judge the urgency of other diagnostic steps to be taken before treatment can be given.

1. Plain and tomographic x-rays

a. Plain skull films should be obtained if an intracranial problem is suspected. Standard views include an AP, both laterals, a basal view and a Townes' projection. Intracranial calcifications suggesting tumors or aneurysms can be seen. Tomograms are more precise, but they are useful only when plain films suggest that a specific area requires more detailed scrutiny.

b. X-rays of the cervical, thoracic, and/or lumbosacral spine are ordered if clinical assessment indicates disease or injury in these areas. AP, lateral, and right and left oblique views should be obtained. Spine injury is often overlooked, particularly when it is associated with head injury, and tumors of the spine (especially metastatic) are frequently missed also. Where one spine lesion exists, suspect another! Tomograms are accurate in diagnosing infection, tumor, and fracture-dislocation, but tomograms must be directed to some specific focus suggested by plain films or clinical evaluation.

c. Films of the chest, pelvis, and long bones may clarify the neurosurgical problem. For example, long bone fractures may suggest that a child's subdural hematoma is the result of abuse; or, a mass in the lung may explain hemiparesis and aphasia on a metastatic basis; or, the cause of a peripheral nerve lesion may become obvious with findings on x-rays of that extremity. In short, CNS lesions may be primary or secondary, and both possibilities should be considered.

2. Lumbar puncture (LP) is **indicated** whenever analysis of CSF constituents is likely to help in the diagnosis and treatment. LP is **contraindicated** when an intracranial mass may be or is present because of the risk of tentorial or foraminal herniation in patients with elevated intracranial pressure. LP is rarely indicated in the diagnosis of head injury unless meningitis is strongly suspected. If a spinal cord tumor is believed present, LP should be done at the time of myelography; LP done earlier may reduce the accuracy of the myelogram and can worsen the neurological deficits by altering intraspinal CSF pressure around the tumor.

During the spinal tap, the initial pressure should be measured accurately and the appearance of the fluid recorded. Normal CSF is clear and colorless; yellow staining (xanthochromia) suggests a recent subarachnoid hemorrhage (jaundice also causes xanthochromia). Since several hours must elapse before erythrocytes lyse and xanthochromia appears, the absence of xanthochromia in the presence of red-tinged fluid usually reflects bleeding from the puncture site ('traumatic tap'). Additional evidence that the tap was traumatic is obtained if the erythrocyte count decreases as more fluid is collected; i.e., compare the first tube of CSF with the third or fourth.

CSF should be analyzed for cell count and type, protein, glucose, and bacterial content.

3. CT scan This noninvasive, safe, and accurate test makes the diagnosis of intracranial lesions substantially easier than it was before. Hematomas, neoplasms, strokes, abscesses, and even aneurysms can be diagnosed rapidly. Motion artifact, occasionally a problem in agitated patients or in children, can be reduced by pretest sedation (10–20 mg diazepam [Valium]) in adults; 1 mg/kg Demerol plus 1 mg/kg Phenergan in children.

4. Angiography Cerebral angiography can be done with minimal risk (1%) of a neurological complication. Radiopaque contrast is injected into the carotid or vertebral arteries, usually by a transfemoral route, and x-rays of the head are taken in rapid sequence as the contrast passes through the brain. Arterial, capillary, and venous phases (usually within 8 seconds of injection) can be seen. Vascular lesions (aneurysms, arteriovenous malformations, vascular tumors) and strokes are readily identified.

5. Air studies involve the replacement of CSF with air, injected either by lumbar puncture or direct ventricular cannulation. X-rays of the head or spine are made with the patient in various positions to locate air selectively in the ventricular system and/or the subarachnoid spaces. This test is usually painful, and it is now reserved to outline in sharp detail lesions near the ventricular system, particularly the third and fourth ventricles. Normally, air is absorbed within hours after the study.

6. Radionuclide scan The brain may be scanned after intravenous injection of radionuclide. Technetium pertechnetate is commonly used; it gives qualitative information about cerebral perfusion, and it identifies defects in the blood-brain barrier. Radionuclide scans are especially useful for detecting neoplasms, infarcts, and abscesses.

7. Other tests

a. Echoencephalography uses the sonar principle, projecting a radiofrequency beam across the skull and detecting its echo. The test is most effective for localization of normal midline structures (e.g., the third ventricle).

b. Cisternography consists of injection of a radionuclide directly into the CSF and tracking its flow from the lumbar sac to the arachnoid granulations over the brain cortex, where the isotope is absorbed into venous blood. Impaired flow of CSF through the basal cisterns and/or reflux of isotope into the ventricles are common pathological patterns that appear on the radionuclide image.

B. SPECIAL CONSIDERATIONS IN NEUROSURGERY

1. Seizures are useful clinical signs, because the aura, onset, type of seizure, and the postictal state may provide clues to the location of a lesion. Seizures are particularly common in patients with neoplasms, abscesses, and cortical injuries.

Repetitive seizures should be treated vigorously. Phenytoin (Dilantin) is the drug of choice. 750–1000 mg may be given IV over 1 hour as a loading dose. Supplemental doses are usually 100 mg, 3 or 4 times a day. Phenobarbital is also useful (32–65 mg, 3 or 4 times a day), but larger doses may depress consciousness. Diazepam (Valium) given IV (10–50 mg) is highly effective in the control of status epilepticus, but diazepam is not a good long-term anticonvulsant.

2. Raised intracranial pressure (ICP) Almost any space-occupying intracranial lesion can raise the ICP. Clinical indications of elevated ICP are headache, stupor, diplopia, nausea, vomiting, and neck stiffness. Altered blood pressure and heart rate are late signs; typically, the BP is increased and the heart rate is slowed. Apnea may occur if ICP is very high. Raised ICP may be prevented and treated by the following:

a. Hyperventilation The $PaCO_2$ should be monitored and maintained at 25-35 mm Hg. A good airway is obviously essential.

b. Hypothermia Since fever causes the brain to swell, the temperature should be controlled by alcohol sponging, antipyretics (aspirin or Tylenol), and hypothermia blankets. Thorazine (5 mg IV every 3-4 hours) minimizes shivering during these maneuvers.

c. Osmotic diuretics Mannitol (1.5 gm/kg/24 hours) causes shrinkage of the brain and reduction of the ICP. It should be used only when the clinical situation is desperate; its beneficial effect is transient, and the drug can severely alter serum electrolytes and osmolarity.

d. Steroids Dexamethasone (Decadron, 4-6 mg every 4 hours, IV or orally) or methylprednisolone (Solumedrol 125-250 mg IM or IV twice daily) lowers ICP by reducing brain edema. The drug probably acts to stabilize 'leaky' sites in the blood-brain barrier.

3. Infections CNS infections include meningitis, subdural empyema, brain abscess, and epidural abscess. Antibiotics (with the exception of chloramphenicol) penetrate the normal blood-brain barrier poorly. In the presence of meningitis, however, antibiotics are better able to penetrate the blood-brain barrier. Specific antibiotics should be given for specific documented infections. During the 1-2 days required to identify the pathogenic organism, broad-spectrum antibiotics should be given if the infection is life-threatening. Methicillin (2 gm IV every 4 hours) and either chloramphenicol (1 gm every 4 hours, IV) or gentamicin (75 mg every 8 hours, IV) are the drugs of choice while awaiting culture results.

Antibiotics for prevention of CNS infection are rarely indicated. In patients with persistent CSF leak, a broad-spectrum antibiotic may be helpful (cephalosporin or ampicillin).

4. Fluid balance Neurosurgical patients should have low-normal to normal intake and output of fluids (2000-2500 cc/24 hours for an adult). Free water (D-5-W) should be avoided because it causes brain swelling. The preferred IV solution is 5% dextrose in 0.5 normal saline with potassium supplements (40 mEq/day). Fluid balance should be monitored by daily weights and periodic measurements of serum electrolytes. Feedings by gastric lavage may be started early (2-3 days after injury or operation), provided that gastrointestinal function is normal.

Some neurosurgical patients have profound disturbances of fluid balance. Inappropriate antidiuretic hormone (ADH) secretion, which most commonly occurs after head trauma, causes retention of free water resulting in low serum Na, high urinary Na, low serum osmolarity, and high urinary specific gravity. Seizures and coma may be the first clinical signs of inappropriate ADH secretion. The best treatment is fluid restriction.

Diabetes insipidus is also common in patients with neurosurgical illnesses. Urine volume is high and specific gravity is low; serum Na and osmolarity are high. Seizures and stupor may appear. The condition is treated by administration of IV or oral fluids.

Patients who receive steroids, osmotic diuretics, anticonvulsants, and tube feedings (the typical neurosurgical patients!) are prone to develop a hyperosmolar state, sometimes leading to nonketotic coma. Consequently, careful monitoring of the fluid and electrolyte status of the neurosurgical patient is essential.

C. COMA is loss of consciousness from which the patient cannot be aroused by any stimulus. **Stupor** implies that the patient can be partially aroused by loud commands or painful stimuli but promptly lapses into unconsciousness again when the stimulus is withdrawn.

1. Diagnosis The 'diagnosis' of coma consists of determining the specific cause. This requires a careful history (generally from friends or relatives) and a complete physical examination with specific attention to the neurologic examination. Laboratory and radiologic tests of value include serum electrolytes, blood glucose, blood urea nitrogen, skull x-rays, and CSF examination (LP). Medical consultation should be sought promptly.

Coma may be caused by poisoning (e.g., alcohol, barbiturates, narcotics); cerebral lesions (e.g., trauma, vascular accidents, tumors, infections, epilepsy); metabolic disorders (e.g., diabetic coma, hypoglycemia, Addison's disease, uremia, hepatic coma, eclampsia); and other disorders such as severe infection, shock, asphyxia, heat stroke, and hypoxia.

Diagnostic features of common types of coma are listed below.

a. Acute alcoholic intoxication A history of drinking, alcoholic breath, flushed face, slow and stertorous respirations, diminished reflexes, and a blood alcohol level above 0.5% point to this diagnosis. **Caution:** always search for other causes of coma, particularly head injury, in the alcoholic patient.

b. Narcotic poisoning Even small doses of narcotics may cause respiratory depression and coma in patients with liver insufficiency, myxedema, emphysema, or head injuries, and in debilitated or elderly patients.

Findings include cold, clammy, cyanotic skin; pinpoint pupils; respiratory depression (breathing slow and irregular, sometimes Cheyne-Stokes); and a feeble and often irregular pulse.

Acute toxicity due to an overdose of a self-administered narcotic occurs commonly in some localities. The type and purity of the drug are difficult to determine, although a companion or acquaintance may know the patient's drug habits. The examiner should look for needle marks in the arms and wrists. Laboratory tests are of value in determining barbiturate, alcohol, or narcotic levels.

c. Diabetic coma Coma may be precipitated in a diabetic patient by infection or by failure to regulate insulin dosage. Diagnostic features include the following: history of diabetes, gradual onset with blurred vision and thirst, air hunger or Kussmaul breathing, dehydration (soft eyeballs), acetone breath ('fruity' odor on breath), glycosuria, acetonuria, hyperglycemia, ketonemia, and low plasma bicarbonate.

d. Hypoglycemia Hypoglycemic reactions in diabetics may be precipitated by failure to eat or by vigorous exercise. Mental confusion and bizarre behavior precede coma and convulsions. Tachycardia, perspiration, tremor, and vomiting are other manifestations. The diagnosis is confirmed by finding a low blood glucose level.

2. Treatment

a. Emergency measures (1) Identify and treat any life-threatening condition immediately. (2) Establish and maintain an **airway** to provide oxygenation. An endotracheal tube should be inserted (see Chapter 3) if the respiratory rate is less than 10/minute, or if the PaO_2 is below 70 mm Hg, or if the $PaCO_2$ is greater than 50 mm Hg with the patient breathing oxygen through a mask. Arterial blood gases should be monitored frequently. (3) Treat shock. (4) When no cause for coma is apparent, obtain blood for glucose determination and toxicologic analysis and immediately administer each of the following: 50 cc of 50% dextrose in water for possible hypoglycemia. 1 cc (0.4 mg) naloxone for possible narcotic overdose. 100 mg thiamine IV for possible Wernicke's (alcoholic) encephalitis.

b. General measures (1) Observe the patient frequently, record neurologic and vital signs at regular intervals, and change the patient's position every

30–60 minutes to avoid hypostatic pneumonitis and decubiti. A lateral and slightly head-down position is best for patients who are likely to vomit. Have a suction machine and an alert attendant near the bedside. (2) Maintain ventilation. (3) Monitor urinary output through an indwelling catheter. (4) Maintain fluid, electrolyte, and caloric intake. Tube feeding should be started if coma lasts more than 2–3 days. (5) Avoid narcotics, sedatives, and other medications until the diagnosis is established; restlessness can then be treated best by administration of parenteral diazepam (2–5 mg IV every 2 hours as needed).

II. TRAUMA

A. HEAD INJURIES: GENERAL PRINCIPLES   The extent of brain damage is the primary determinant of treatment for patients with head injuries. The prognosis is related to the type and degree of brain damage and to the number and kinds of injuries to other parts of the body.

Injury to the brain results from rapid deceleration, acceleration, and/or the shearing-rotational effects of a blow to the head. These mechanisms may produce: **concussion**, a temporary loss of consciousness with no permanent organic brain damage; **contusion**, bruising of the brain; or **laceration**, frank disruption of brain substance. The 3 types of brain injury can occur singly, but more commonly they are seen in varying combinations.

Contusion may be local, causing focal signs and symptoms (e.g., hemiparesis or aphasia), or it may be generalized, with widespread damage to the brain. Increased vascular permeability in contused brain produces cerebral edema. Decreased respiratory exchange in severely injured patients leads to anoxia and hypercapnia; the resulting cerebral vasodilation contributes still further to cerebral swelling.

1. Emergency management   (a) Establish and maintain adequate ventilation. (b) Control hemorrhage. (c) Treat shock. (d) Examine the patient quickly but thoroughly to ascertain the type and degree of all injuries. (e) Splint longbone fractures. (f) Evaluate the nervous system injury (see below). (g) Do **not** move the patient for any reason (e.g., to obtain x-rays or to transport to another hospital or to another room) until the extent of all injuries is known and the immediate threats to life (respiratory embarrassment, hemorrhage, etc.) have been controlled. (h) If the patient is comatose, assume that the cervical spine is unstable; immobilize the patient in the supine position with sandbags supporting both sides of the head until x-rays exclude a cervical fracture.

2. Evaluation of nervous system injury   Every head injury is potentially serious. A thorough neurologic examination should be performed as soon as possible, and a record should be made of the following features: (a) Direct inspection of the head for abrasions, swelling, laceration, blood behind the tympanic membranes, or CSF in the nose or ears. (b) Level of consciousness (Table 16-1). (c) Size of pupils and response to light. (d) Motor response in all 4 extremities (normal, weakness, abnormal flexion, abnormal extension, movement). (e) Eye movements (spontaneous, gaze preference or palsy, response to icewater instillation into the external ear canal if the tympanic membrane is intact and free of obstruction). (f) Corneal response. (g) Cough and gag responses. (h) Breathing pattern. (i) Tendon and plantar reflexes. (j) Ophthalmoscopic examination. **Never artificially dilate the pupils in head injury.** (k) Skull x-rays. (l) Cervical spine x-rays if there is evidence of injury to that area or if the patient is unconscious on admission. (m) Lumbar puncture should **not** be done unless meningitis is strongly suspected. (n) CT scan or cerebral angiography should be done immediately if intracranial hemorrhage is suspected.

Accurate records of the initial physical examination are essential, because decisions to operate depend to a great extent upon later variations from the baseline. Repeated examination at frequent intervals is imperative. The most sensitive signs of improvement or deterioration are changes in the level of responsiveness (Table 16-1) or the pupils.

3. Postoperative management   Hypoxia and hypercapnia must be prevented, since they cause intracranial vascular dilatation and add to cerebral swelling. Respiratory care, therefore, is very important (see Chapter 2). Measures to lower body temperature should be used (see Section I.B.2.b). Intravenous hyperosmotic solutions (e.g., mannitol 150–300 ml of 20% solution) also help reduce cerebral edema, but they should never be used until it is certain that there is no expanding intracranial hematoma; these agents may enlarge the hematoma and hasten deterioration.

Table 16-1. Evaluation of level of consciousness by responses to graded stimuli

Eye opening	Spontaneous
	To voice command
	With painful stimulus
	None
Motor response	Follows commands
	Localizes painful stimulus
	Withdraws from painful stimulus
	Abnormal flexion in response to pain
	Abnormal extension
	None
Verbal response	Oriented
	Confused
	Speaks only words
	Makes only sounds
	None

The **best** response is recorded in each of the 3 categories

B. SCALP INJURIES   The scalp is an extremely vascular structure, and injury may cause serious hemorrhage. Bleeding usually is controlled with a simple pressure dressing of several 4x4 gauze sponges placed over the wound and held firmly in place by a circumferential dressing. Arterial bleeding can be controlled by firm finger pressure along the edges of the wound, or by a hemostat that is attached to the galea and allowed to hang down over the skin edge to pull the galea firmly against the skin and compress the bleeding vessels.

All scalp wounds should be closed as soon as possible, unless they overlie a depressed fracture or a penetrating wound of the skull which requires debridement in the operating room.

1. Scalp lacerations   Shave and wash a **generous** area. If the laceration is large, a 4x4 gauze sponge in the wound will prevent debris from entering. Cleanse the wound thoroughly with repeated irrigations of saline or Ringer's solution. Infiltrate the circumference of the wound with local anesthetic about 1 inch away from the edges. Remove foreign bodies, which may lead to infection or leave unsightly tattoos. All devitalized tissue should be debrided, taking care not to cut away normal tissue.

2. Emergency management A thorough neurologic examination must be performed as soon as possible to establish the level and degree of functional loss. Examine for associated injuries. Spinal cord injury should be assumed present until there is definite proof that none has occurred. Do not move the patient until the full extent of the injury is known, since the spinal cord may be further damaged by improper management.

Obtain a detailed description of the accident, since management may depend upon whether the injury was caused by hyperflexion, hyperextension, or a direct blow.

If cervical fracture is suspected, place sandbags at both sides of the head to prevent motion and apply halter traction with 6-10 lbs of weight as emergency splinting measures. At least 4 persons are required to lift the patient onto a Stryker frame. One person directs the move; the spine should be kept aligned while applying traction on the chin and occiput.

If the patient cannot void, connect an indwelling urinary catheter to gravity drainage.

As soon as the patient's general condition warrants, obtain x-rays of the spine. The physician should accompany the patient to the x-ray department and remain there until satisfactory anteroposterior, and lateral-oblique views have been obtained without rotating the patient's head.

3. Treatment If cervical fracture or fracture-dislocation is found on the x-ray, skeletal traction should be instituted using halo or tong devices. The traction device can be applied in the x-ray department, but the procedure preferably is carried out in an operating room equipped with an x-ray unit.

Laminectomy to decompress and debride the injury should be done in the following circumstances: (a) progressive neurologic loss; (b) total block of the vertebral canal as shown by myelography; (c) x-rays show bone fragments or a foreign body in the spinal canal. If decompression is decided upon, it should be carried out as soon as the patient's condition is stable and immediately after life-threatening associated injuries have been dealt with. If the injury is cervical, skeletal tong traction should be instituted immediately and maintained during the operation.

III. CONGENITAL LESIONS

Evaluation of congenital lesions of the CNS requires an understanding of embryology. The formation of the neural groove begins at the midposition of the neural plate, and closure progresses rostrally and caudally. The neural tube gradually separates from the ectoderm and comes to lie within the mesoderm early in embryologic development. Therefore, malformations of the nervous system are frequently associated with malformations of mesodermal and ectodermal elements.

A. CRANIOSTENOSIS (Craniosynostosis) is premature bony fusion of the cranial sutures. Normally, the bones of the skull are separated at birth and become joined in a fibrous union at the suture lines after 6 months of age. In craniostenosis, closure of the sutures begins in utero and progresses after birth.

Early recognition of this condition is important because brain weight doubles in the first year of life. In the normal child, growth of the skull is stimulated by growth of the brain, but if 2 or more of the sutures fuse prematurely, brain growth will be stunted.

1. Diagnosis The principal clinical feature of craniostenosis is deformity of the cranial contour; the type of deformity is dependent upon the suture or sutures involved. Typical patterns of involvement include: sagittal suture alone; coronal suture alone; all sutures.

2. Treatment and prognosis The only treatment is surgical. Operation consists of removing a linear strip of bone, following the line of and including

The wound is closed with multiple interrupted vertical mattress sutures of stainless steel wire, or the galea and skin may be closed in separate layers. Meticulous technic should be used.

2. Avulsions of the scalp usually include all layers of the scalp down to the periosteum. These injuries should be treated only by experienced surgeons with complete operating room facilities. The surrounding area should be shaved and thoroughly irrigated. If the avulsion is small, the ragged edges can be sparingly trimmed; closure can often be accomplished by tripod extension or modified Z-plasty. If the denuded area is large, the wound is covered with a single layer of fine mesh gauze. A large dressing is placed on top of the gauze, and a firm circumferential dressing is applied to exert even pressure over the area. Delayed closure (using plastic surgical technics) can be performed 8-10 days later.

C. SKULL FRACTURES Skull fracture is no more serious than fracture of any other bone if the brain is not injured; the extent of brain damage determines the prognosis. Skull fractures can be classified according to: (1) whether the skin overlying the fracture is intact (closed) or broken (open or compound); (2) whether there is a single fracture line (linear), several fractures radiating from a central point (stellate), or fragmentation of bone (comminuted); (3) whether the edges of the fracture line have been driven below the level of the surrounding bone (depressed) or not (nondepressed).

1. Simple skull fractures (linear, stellate, or comminuted nondepressed) These fractures are serious if they cross major vascular channels in the skull, such as the groove of the middle meningeal artery or the major dural venous sinuses. If these vessels are torn, epidural or subdural hematomas may form. Patients with these types of fractures should be kept under close observation until it is certain that no such bleeding is occurring. A fracture that extends into the accessory nasal sinuses or the mastoid air cells is considered to be open, since it is in communication with an external surface of the body.

2. Depressed skull fractures Depressed stellate or comminuted fractures require a surgical procedure to elevate the depressed bone. If there are no untoward neurologic signs and the fracture is closed, operation may be delayed until a convenient time.

3. Open skull fractures As soon as the patient's general condition permits, a depressed open skull fracture should be elevated, debrided, and closed. Until that can be done, the wound is covered with a sterile compression dressing. The scalp wound should not be closed, and no attempt should be made to remove any foreign body protruding from the wound until the patient is in the operating room and all preparations have been made for craniotomy.

Linear or stellate, nondepressed, open fractures can be treated by simple closure of the skin wound after thorough cleansing. Open fractures with severe comminution of underlying bone should be treated in the operating room, where proper debridement can be carried out. If possible, the dura should be inspected to make certain that no laceration has been overlooked.

4. Basal skull fractures may cause rhinorrhea or otorrhea if the dura and arachnoid are torn; they may also cause bleeding from the nose or ears if mucous membranes or skin are lacerated. It is often difficult to tell if blood is mixed with CSF. A drop of the bloody discharge can be placed on a cleansing tissue; if CSF is present, there will be a spreading yellowish-orange ring around the central red stain of blood. If there is a leak of CSF, methicillin (2 gm IV every 4 hours) or dicloxacillin (2 gm orally, every 4 hours) should be given. The patient's head should remain elevated to 30° and fluid intake is restricted to 1200 cc/day. The patient is cautioned against blowing the nose, a maneuver which could contaminate the intracranial space. If a leak persists for longer than a week, spinal drainage and acetozolamide (250 mg orally three times a day) can be used to reduce CSF production and lower intracranial pressure. Craniotomy may be required for leaks that continue for more than 2 weeks. Less than 5% of patients with CSF leaks require surgical repair.

D. TRAUMA TO THE MENINGES Head injury, with or without skull fracture, may cause tears in the vascular channels coursing through the meninges and can lead to serious intracranial hemorrhage. Tears in the dura should be repaired to lessen the chances of infection.

E. EPIDURAL HEMATOMA Hemorrhage between the inner table of the skull and the dura mater most commonly arises from a tear of the middle meningeal artery caused by a skull fracture across the arterial groove in the temporal region. Arterial bleeding strips the dura from the undersurface of the bone and produces still more bleeding because the small bridging veins from the dura to bone are torn. The hematoma rapidly increases in size and compresses the cerebral cortex. If sufficient hemispheric compression occurs, the medial portion of the temporal lobe (uncus and hippocampal gyrus) is forced through the incisura tentorii; this causes pressure on the third cranial nerve and dilatation of the pupil on the same side. Hemispheric compression shifts the brain stem toward the opposite side of the tentorial notch; if it shifts too far, venous hemorrhages into the brain stem lead to irreparable neurologic deficits or death.

An epidural hematoma may arise from torn venous channels in the bone at a point of fracture or from lacerated major dural venous sinuses. Since venous pressure is low, epidural venous hematomas usually form only when a depressed skull fracture has stripped the dura from the bone and left a space in which the hematoma can develop.

Epidural hematoma classically follows a blow to the head that causes unconsciousness for a brief period. After the patient regains consciousness, there may be a 'lucid interval' during which there are no abnormal neurologic symptoms or signs. As the hematoma enlarges sufficiently to compress the cerebral hemisphere, there is gradual deterioration of consciousness which progresses to coma and death if the hematoma is not evacuated. As the level of consciousness deteriorates, the pupil on the side of the lesion dilates and contralateral hemiplegia occurs.

Even though epidural hematoma is a curable lesion, the mortality rate is high because patients are not seen by a physician, or the gravity of the injury is not recognized by a physician. A patient may be seen during the lucid interval and discharged. At home, the patient is assumed to be asleep when, actually, the hematoma has increased in size and caused coma instead of sleep. Considering this danger, any patient with a history of a blow to the head leading to even a brief period of unconsciousness should have a thorough neurologic examination and skull x-rays. If x-rays show a fracture, the patient should be hospitalized and the conscious level checked at least every hour. If no fracture is demonstrated, the patient may be discharged, but a reliable relative should be instructed to **awaken the patient at least hourly** to make certain that he or she is arousable and not comatose.

Impairment of sensorium is the first indication that operation may be urgently necessary. This is a **true emergency;** if operation is delayed until brain stem hemorrhages occur, the patient is likely to remain comatose even though the epidural clot is evacuated.

F. SUBDURAL HEMATOMA occurs most commonly when the veins bridging from the cortex to the superior sagittal sinus near the midline are torn, or when an intracerebral hematoma communicates with the subdural space. Bleeding occurs between the arachnoid and the dura; since the arachnoid is attached loosely to the dura, these hematomas can attain tremendous size, even though the bleeding is of venous (low pressure) origin.

1. Acute subdural hematomas are associated with severe head injuries. They arise from a combination of torn bridging veins and frank lacerations of

the pia and arachnoid of the cortex. The hematoma is usually discovered during CT scanning, angiography, or burr hole exploratory operation. Evacuation of the clot may result in significant improvement, but often a major neurologic deficit remains, due to the widespread cerebral contusion and/or laceration.

2. Subacute subdural hematomas These lesions become apparent 3-10 days after injury and are associated with progressive lethargy, confusion, hemiparesis, or other hemispheric deficits. Removal of the hematoma usually produces striking improvement.

3. Chronic subdural hematomas are most common in infants and in adults older than 60 years. They arise from tears in bridging veins after a minor head injury. The hematoma is small initially; it becomes encased in a fibrous membrane, liquefies, and gradually enlarges.

The history is usually one of progressive mental or personality changes, with or without focal symptoms (progressive hemiplegia, aphasia, etc). Papilledema may be present. These findings often suggest a diagnosis of brain tumor, and the hematoma may be discovered unexpectedly during angiography or CT scanning.

Treatment consists of drainage through multiple burr holes. If the fluid reaccumulates, craniotomy for removal of the encasing membranes may be necessary.

4. Subdural hygromas are collections of clear or yellow-stained fluid in the subdural space. They probably form through a tear in the arachnoid that allows CSF to escape into the subdural space, producing the same symptoms as a chronic subdural hematoma. The condition is treated by draining the fluid through multiple burr holes.

G. BRAIN INJURY Contusions and lacerations of the brain cannot be treated surgically as a rule, but some neurosurgeons feel that resection of the most severely contused portions of cerebrum may be indicated in selected cases. Intracerebral hematomas are usually associated with lacerations; if the hematoma is large, surgical evacuation is indicated.

H. INJURIES TO THE SPINAL CORD AND NERVE ROOTS* Laceration, disruption, or dissolution of part or all of the spinal cord or nerve roots is usually caused by penetrating wounds or severe fracture-dislocations of the bony spine. Concussion of the spinal cord produces temporary interruption of function without anatomically demonstrable changes. Contusion of the cord usually occurs at the site of a fracture-dislocation or a penetrating wound.

1. Diagnosis Neurologic deficits resulting from trauma to the spinal nervous system may be partial or complete, and transient or permanent. The diagnosis usually is not difficult, but **spinal cord injury may be overlooked** in comatose patients. It is imperative that cervical spine x-rays be obtained in all patients with severe head injuries; about 3% of such patients have injuries to the spine as well.

a. Symptoms and signs (1) Weakness or paralysis of the extremities and diminished reflexes below the level of the injury as a consequence of 'spinal shock', which may persist for hours or days. (2) Partial or complete loss of any modalities of sensation below the level of the lesion. (3) Urinary retention. (4) Paralytic ileus with abdominal distention. (5) Respiratory difficulty which frequently accompanies cervical lesions because the intercostal muscles are paralyzed and breathing is purely diaphragmatic. (6) Loss of sweating below the level of the lesion. (7) Point tenderness over the fracture site, with or without gibbus or crepitus.

b. X-rays may be negative, or they may demonstrate simple fracture or complete fracture-dislocation with marked comminution.

---

*See Chapter 15 for peripheral nerve injuries.

the involved suture. Silastic film is sutured over the edge of the bone to delay regrowth.

Operations for premature closure of a single suture (sagittal is the one most commonly affected) are mainly cosmetic. If 2 or more sutures are closed, brain growth is restricted, and operation is indicated to prevent impaired brain development.

The outlook for normal mental development is good if the diagnosis is made during the first few months of life and if the operation is done before brain growth is retarded.

B. ENCEPHALOCELE Encephaloceles are protrusions of meninges and neural tissue from their normal intracranial location. About 75% of all encephaloceles are in the occipital area. Most protrude extracranially in the midline, but they may project into the nasopharynx, nasal cavity, or orbit.

The sac may be large with a narrow stalk, but more commonly it is sessile in shape. It is often difficult to determine by examination if the mass contains neural structures, CSF, or both. Transillumination with a bright light in a darkened room may show neural tissue as a shadow against the homogeneous red glow of the fluid.

At operation, the neck of the mass and the cranial defect are exposed, the sac is opened, neural contents are replaced within the cranial cavity, and the dura is closed. The bony defect may be repaired later if it persists.

C. DERMAL SINUS tracts are due to incomplete embryonal separation of the neural tube from overlying ectoderm, creating a persistent connection between the skin and the CNS or its investing membranes or bone. Since closure and separation of the neural tube proceeds caudally and rostrally from about the midpoint of embryo, dermal sinuses occur most often at either end of the neural tube. Midline cutaneous defects are common in the sacral area; most of these are of no significance because they penetrate no deeper than the sacral fascia. If they extend into the subarachnoid space through a bony defect (spina bifida), the tract may serve as a pathway of infection.

The diagnosis is usually suggested by the cutaneous defect (dimple, port wine stain, hair tuft, etc.), and there may be a history of recurrent meningitis.

Surgical excision should be done to prevent meningitis.

D. HYDROCEPHALUS is enlargement of the ventricles of the brain due to a decrease in CSF absorption; an increase in CSF production; or obstruction of CSF flow by a lesion in the normal pathway of CSF circulation. Common sites of obstruction are the foramina of Monro, the aqueduct of Sylvius, the foramina of Luschka and Magendie, and the basilar cisterns.

E. HYDROCEPHALUS IN INFANTS

1. Diagnosis Abnormal, progressive enlargement of the head. Measurements of head circumference should be compared with standard charts. The fontanel is usually wide, tense, and nonpulsating. The fontanel bosses are prominent, and sclerae may be visible above the iris because the eyeballs are displaced downward by pressure on the thin orbital roofs ('sunset sign'). Symptoms of increased intracranial pressure: irritability, vomiting, and somnolence.

2. Differential diagnosis In **obstructive** hydrocephalus, no communication exists between the ventricular system and the subarachnoid absorptive bed. In **communicating** hydrocephalus, the ventricles communicate freely with the subarachnoid space. The following diagnostic steps should be taken to determine the type and cause of hydrocephalus: (1) If the child is moribund, subdural taps should be done bilaterally to exclude a subdural hematoma. A 20-gauge short-beveled spinal needle is inserted into the subdural space through the lateral angle of the anterior fontanel or the coronal suture well away from the midline. Fluid emerging spontaneously after the stylet is withdrawn is diagnostic of a subdural hematoma, hygroma, or empyema. Specimens should be obtained for cells, protein, and culture. Fluid should not be aspirated, but it should be allowed to flow until the fontanel becomes soft. (2) A CT brain scan, with and without contrast, should follow the subdural taps. Subdural taps may be omitted prior to CT scanning if the child is stable. Ventricular size and the presence of hematomas, neoplasms, abscesses, etc., can be recognized easily and safely. General anesthesia or sedation (Demerol 1 mg/kg plus Phenergan 1 mg/kg IM) may help to obtain a good study without motion artifact. (3) Air study may be necessary to detail the lesion causing hydrocephalus; a CT scan alone may not provide enough information. (4) Arteriography is necessary in certain cases. (5) Lumbar puncture should be done only after an intracranial mass has been excluded.

3. Treatment   Occasionally the hydrocephalus will arrest spontaneously. Ventricular hemorrhage and secondary hydrocephalus (from clogged subarachnoid CSF pathways) in premature infants may arrest after early treatment with spinal taps (to drain the bloody CSF) and Diamox (to reduce CSF formation). Repeated lumbar punctures (in communicating hydrocephalus) or ventricular taps (in obstructive hydrocephalus) may be used until definitive treatment can be given.

Several shunting procedures are available to direct the CSF to an absorptive bed. The choice of procedure depends to some extent on the type of hydrocephalus. In obstructive hydrocephalus, the fluid must be shunted directly from the ventricular system; whereas in communicating hydrocephalus, the fluid can be shunted from the lumbar subarachnoid space. In both instances, the fluid is shunted into either the peritoneal cavity or the right atrium.

F. HYDROCEPHALUS IN ADULTS

1. Diagnosis   In patients over 3 years of age the skull expands poorly to accommodate rising CSF pressure and expanding ventricles. Progressive dementia, headache, somnolence, nausea, vomiting, and occasionally visual impairment are symptoms of hydrocephalus in this group of patients. Urinary incontinence and truncal ataxia may appear as the ventricles expand, forming, in association with dementia, the 'triad' of occult hydrocephalus. CSF pressure may be nearly normal or episodically elevated and unpredictable. On the other hand, CSF pressure may be severely elevated, particularly if the ventricles are obstructed, accounting for the appearance of papilledema and visual impairment.

2. Treatment   CSF shunting is the most effective current treatment. Ventriculo-peritoneal or ventriculo-atrial shunts usually function well for all types of hydrocephalus. Lumbar-peritoneal shunts are only indicated if CSF can pass from its ventricular source freely into the lumbar subarachnoid space. Ventriculo-cisternal shunting (Torkildsen procedure) is reserved for patients with obstruction of the aqueduct or the foramina of the fourth ventricle. Drugs to reduce CSF production are usually ineffective, although Diamox (250 mg 4 times a day) may help.

G. PORENCEPHALY is a circumscribed cavity in cerebral tissue that communicates with the ventricle; it is usually caused by a stroke in utero. The most common clinical findings are seizures and, rarely, enlargement of the head. Surgical treatment is indicated only when seizures cannot be controlled by anticonvulsant drug therapy.

H. ARNOLD-CHIARI MALFORMATION consists of: elongation and caudal projection of the cerebellar tonsils through the foramen magnum; elongation and kinking of the medulla into the cervical canal so that the fourth ventricle opens into the cervical spinal subarachnoid space; and downward displacement of the cervical spinal cord so that the cervical nerve roots course upward to their respective foramina. Hydrocephalus is often present, as well as congenital anomalies of the cervical vertebrae (e.g., fusion of 1 or more cervical vertebrae), lower cranial nerve palsies, cerebellar disturbances, and long tract signs.

Hydrocephalus and other symptoms may be relieved by decompression of the posterior fossa and upper cervical laminectomy. If these measures are ineffective, a shunting procedure may be required.

I. PLATYBASIA is a developmental defect characterized by upward displacement of the cervical vertebral column into the base of the skull so that the odontoid process projects into the cranial cavity. Other bony anomalies are frequently associated, such as occipitalization of the atlas, malformation of the foramen magnum, and fusion of the cervical vertebrae.

Symptoms rarely develop before adulthood. Neurologic signs are those of cervical spinal cord compression with weakness, ataxia, sensory loss, and sphincter disturbances. The diagnosis is established by x-rays of the skull and cervical spine. Platybasia is present when the odontoid process projects more than 5 mm above a line drawn from the posterior rim of the foramen magnum to the posterior edge of the hard palate (Chamberlain's line).

Decompression of the foramen magnum by suboccipital craniectomy and cervical laminectomy may help. In most cases, arrest of progressive deficits is all that can be accomplished; occasionally, recovery of function is excellent.

J. SYRINGOMYELIA (AND SYRINGOBULBIA) A syrinx is a central cavitation of the spinal cord (syringomyelia) and/or the brain stem (syringobulbia). Syringomyelia usually occurs in the cervical and upper thoracic cord.

Examination shows dissociated loss of pain and temperature sensation involving the upper extremities, shoulder girdles, and upper thorax, with relative preservation of touch perception. This is produced when the cavitation disrupts the decussating pain fibers in the commissures around the central canal. Associated findings are weakness of the muscles of the upper extremities, particularly the intrinsic muscles of the hands, with atrophy and fasciculations. Long tract signs are often present in the lower extremities. X-rays of the cervical or thoracic spine may reveal an increase in the interpedicular distances. Myelography can demonstrate widening of the spinal cord in the upright position, and narrowing of it in the Trendelenberg position.

Laminectomy (with or without drainage of the cystic area), myelotomy, or permanent drainage of the cavity have mixed success, and the prognosis is guarded.

K. SPINA BIFIDA OCCULTA is a defect in the laminar arch, most often in the lumbosacral area. Associated anomalies are common in the skin overlying the bifid spine, and the lower extremities may be malformed. The condition usually is asymptomatic, but urinary incontinence, weakness, atrophy, and sensory loss in the lower lumbar area and along the distribution of the sacral nerve roots may be noted. Contrast myelography may demonstrate an intraspinal mass, which is usually a lipoma.

Treatment is indicated only when there are progressive neurological deficits. The operation consists of laminectomy with removal of any intraspinal mass (lipoma, dermoid, etc.).

L. MENINGOCELE AND MYELOMENINGOCELE A meningocele is a protrusion of meninges containing CSF through a defective neural arch. If neural elements are present, it is a myelomeningocele. The lesion usually is in the lumbosacral area, but it may occur at any level. Occasionally it protrudes anteriorly into the pelvic, abdominal, or thoracic cavities. Neurologic deficits (sensory, motor, and sphincter disturbances) suggest that the lesion contains neural tissue.

The objective of surgery is cosmetic removal of the mass and prevention of further neurologic deficits. The lesion should be removed if technically feasible and if the neurologic deficit does not preclude relatively normal development. A meningocele or myelomeningocele that has ruptured and is leaking CSF should be repaired emergently if the neurologic deficits are not severe. If there is no CSF leak, operation can be delayed until there is sufficient skin covering to ensure a satisfactory closure. Progressive hydrocephalus is usually treated before removal of the meningocele, since increased CSF pressure may threaten the repair.

Prognosis depends upon the extent of associated neurologic deficits and the severity of associated anomalies.

IV. NEOPLASMS OF THE CENTRAL NERVOUS SYSTEM

A. INTRACRANIAL NEOPLASMS   Brain tumors occur in all age groups with approximately equal distribution up to the age of 70 years. Two-thirds of brain tumors in children arise in the subtentorial space (posterior fossa). About 45% of brain tumors are gliomas, 15% meningiomas, 10% pituitary tumors, 5% tumors of nerve sheaths, 5% blood vessel tumors, 5% congenital, and 10% metastatic. Miscellaneous tumors account for the remainder.

Symptoms and signs are produced by the mass effect of the tumor and by secondary effects, such as brain swelling, brain shift, and CSF obstruction. Brain tumors almost never metastasize outside the CNS.

1. Local effects

a. Frontal lobe   Personality changes (inappropriate behavior, loss of social inhibitions) and mental changes may occur. If pressure is elevated, there may be headache, nausea, vomiting and papilledema also.

If the posterior portions of the frontal lobe are involved, the patient may show forced grasping; if the motor areas of the cortex or subcortical areas are involved, varying degrees of hemiparesis on the contralateral side, increased deep tendon reflexes, and a positive Babinski reflex occur.

Tumor in the dominant frontal lobe may cause expressive aphasia. If convulsions occur, they are frequently of the adversive type (head and eyes turned toward the side opposite the lesion). Tumors arising beneath the frontal lobes may cause anosmia.

b. Parietal lobe   Contralateral paralysis accompanied by defects in the appreciation of the weight, texture, size, and shape of objects. Ability to perceive and localize pinprick on the side of the body opposite the lesion may be impaired (astereognosis). Parasagittal tumors (involving the paracentral area) may cause spastic paralysis of the contralateral leg or paraplegia and urinary incontinence. Tumors low in the parietal area may produce visual field defects. If the dominant hemisphere is involved, global aphasia may be present.

c. Occipital lobe   A visual field defect is the major neurologic sign and tends to be more congruous than a visual field defect produced by a lesion in the temporal lobe. Complete homonymous hemianopsia ·has no localizing value, since it can be produced by a lesion anywhere from the chiasm to the occipital lobe. Isolated visual hallucinations may occur, or they may appear as part of a generalized seizure.

d. Middle fossa   'Temporal lobe seizures' are a common manifestation. Uncinate fits are accompanied by unpleasant olfactory sensations, often with lip-smacking and loss of contact with surroundings. A generalized seizure may follow. The seizure may take the form of momentary episodes of staring, a feeling of unreality, and extreme familiarity (déjà vu) or unfamiliarity with surroundings at the time of the attack. Distorted perceptions of sounds, objects, sizes, or shapes may be noted. Visual field defects are common and tend to be incongruous. If the dominant temporal lobe is involved, receptive aphasia or auditory agnosia may occur.

e. Posterior fossa   Early symptoms are produced by involvement of the cerebellum, brain stem, and cranial nerves, and often by obstruction of the flow of CSF. A tumor arising in a hemisphere of the cerebellum causes ataxia of gait and incoordination of the ipsilateral arm and leg. Nystagmus is common. The principal manifestation of a tumor in the midline of the cerebellum is ataxia of the trunk and legs with unsteadiness and falling even while sitting; incoordination of the arms is less frequent. Cranial nerve palsies, particularly of those nerves supplying the extraocular muscles, also occur.

f. Brain stem Multiple cranial nerve palsies, nystagmus, and incoordination and paresis of extremities. Intracranial pressure increases are late events.

g. Cerebellopontine angle tumors are situated in the angle formed by the petrous ridge, tentorium, cerebellum, and brain stem. The vast majority are neurilemmomas arising from the vestibular portion of the eighth cranial nerve. Symptoms begin with tinnitus on the involved side, followed by nerve deafness. Involvement of the seventh cranial nerve produces facial palsy; involvement of the fifth cranial nerve may cause numbness or paresthesia in the face and loss of the corneal reflex. Involvement of the cerebellum causes ataxia, dysmetria, and nystagmus.

h. Midbrain Usually involved secondarily by tumors arising from nearby structures. Tumors in the pineal region frequently press on the roof structures of the midbrain causing difficulty in upward gaze (Parinaud's syndrome) and impairment of the pupillary light reflex. Involvement of the red nucleus area produces ataxia, incoordination, and intention tremor.

i. Pituitary gland Hyperfunction of portions of the gland (acromegaly, Cushing's disease, Nelson's syndrome) or, more commonly, hypofunction leading to amenorrhea, loss of libido, pubic and axillary hair, etc. As sellar tumors enlarge, they encroach on the optic chiasm and produce a characteristic bitemporal hemianopsia.

2. General or secondary effects Increased intracranial pressure produced by any space-occupying intracranial mass leads to the classic triad of headache (commonly located in the vertex, worse in the morning after prolonged recumbency, and frequently relieved by standing up); nausea and vomiting; and papilledema. Increased intracranial pressure may also cause personality changes, convulsions, cranial nerve palsies, and even homonymous hemianopsia as the posterior cerebral artery passing over the edge of the tentorium is compressed by the tense brain.

3. Diagnosis Focal symptoms and signs of a brain tumor depend on its location, whether it is situated on the surface or in the deeper tissues, cell type, rapidity of growth, etc. It is imperative to determine if there is progression. Progression of symptoms justifies the suspicion of brain tumor and the studies outlined below should be obtained.

a. CT brain scan is an excellent initial study which usually localizes the tumor accurately, and can often differentiate tumor types.

b. Arteriography is used to localize the tumor, either by indicating a tumor 'blush,' or indirectly by distortion of arteries or veins from their normal position.

c. Pneumoencephalography may be helpful in some cases.

d. Ventriculography is used when there is increased intracranial pressure.

e. Radionuclide brain scan accurately identifies the tumor in about 85% of cases.

f. Electroencephalography is helpful in recognition of certain brain tumors involving the cerebrum, since it may indicate a focal pathologic process. Localization is never accurate enough to plan surgical treatment from EEG evidence alone.

4. Treatment of brain tumors In general, the treatment of brain tumors is surgical exploration and excision through a craniotomy. The tumor should be completely removed without producing a serious neurologic deficit if possible. If the tumor cannot be excised completely, radical subtotal removal should be done to decompress the surrounding brain. If the tumor blocks the flow of CSF, shunting is indicated. Postoperative radiation therapy has considerable value in some tumors but not in others. Chemotherapy of primary and metastatic brain tumors may also help.

B. INTRACRANIAL GLIOMAS   All tumors that arise from the interstitial cells of the CNS are included in this category.

1. Glioblastoma multiforme comprises about 25% of gliomas and is the most malignant primary tumor of the brain. It arises in the white matter, grows rapidly, and has a strong tendency to cross to the opposite hemisphere. This tumor is highly cellular and pleomorphic, with many mitoses. The most common sites of occurrence are the frontal, parietal, and temporal lobes, and the highest incidence is in the age group from 40-60. Glioblastoma multiforme can rarely, if ever, be completely removed and is resistant to radiation therapy. Most patients die within a year after diagnosis.

2. Astrocytomas account for about 35% of gliomas. They grow relatively slowly and frequently blend diffusely into the surrounding brain. In adults, they arise most often in the frontal, parietal, and temporal lobes and are often impossible to remove completely because they extend into deep structures. Most astrocytomas are not radiosensitive, and survival is usually 3-6 years. Survival may be extended by reoperation. In children, they occur predominantly in the cerebellar hemisphere and often are cystic; cystic or solid cerebellar astrocytomas can be completely excised in many cases and recurrence is uncommon.

3. Medulloblastomas (about 10% of gliomas) occur almost exclusively in children 4-8 years of age, usually boys (3:1). They arise from the lateral wall or roof of the fourth ventricle, and frequently seed to other parts of the nervous system. Complete surgical removal is not possible. These tumors are initially radiosensitive, but they become radioresistant later and survival beyond 5 years is uncommon.

4. Ependymomas arising from the choroid plexus of the lateral ventricles or fourth ventricle may be totally removable. Often, however, they arise from the ventricular walls, rendering them difficult to remove totally. Ependymomas usually respond to radiation therapy.

5. Oligodendrogliomas (about 5% of gliomas) usually occur in the cerebral hemisphere in adults. Total removal is often impossible, and the cells are relatively radioresistant. Average survival is 3-7 years.

6. Pinealomas (2-3% of gliomas) occur in young adults and block the flow of CSF early. Some of them can be removed surgically. An alternate treatment is CSF shunting followed by radiation therapy. The prognosis for survival is 3-10 years.

C. MENINGIOMAS are benign tumors that arise from cells of the pia arachnoid and dura. They occur predominantly in the 40-60 age group. Since meningiomas involve the cerebral cortex early in their growth, convulsive seizures often herald their presence. Characteristic locations, in descending order of frequency, are as follows:

1. Parasagittal   Anterior parasagittal meningiomas produce headache and personality changes. Midparasagittal meningiomas cause paresis of the contralateral foot, with or without cortical sensory change, incontinence of urine, and seizures beginning in the contralateral foot. Posterior parasagittal meningiomas produce headache and visual field defects.

2. Convexity of the cerebral hemisphere   In general, these tumors are situated anteriorly and produce mental changes and motor weakness. Tumors in the midparietal area cause motor and sensory loss, and tumors situated posteriorly lead to sensory and visual field losses.

3. Sphenoid ridge   Meningiomas along the inner third of the sphenoid ridge cause extraocular muscle palsies and visual loss with optic atrophy. Meningiomas along the middle third of the ridge usually attain a large size before significant symptoms are produced. Ultimately, encroachment on the temporal lobe causes psychomotor fits, and involvement of the frontal lobe produces mental changes. Meningioma along the outer third of the ridge often grows as a flat plate of tumor (en plaque); progressive exophthalmos and a palpable mass in the temporal region are the consequences.

4. Olfactory groove These usually become quite large before clinical manifestations appear (anosmia and personality changes).

5. Less common locations are suprasellar, in the posterior fossa, and in the region of the gasserian ganglion.

6. Treatment Surgical removal is indicated in all cases, and complete removal is often possible. Even with subtotal removal, the prognosis is good.

D. TUMORS OF THE CRANIAL NERVES The great majority of cranial nerve tumors arise from the sheath of the eighth nerve at the internal auditory meatus (so-called acoustic tumor or cerebellopontine angle tumor). Most of them can be removed completely. Where total removal is not possible because the capsule is intimately adherent to the brain stem, the prognosis with subtotal removal may still be good. Some of these tumors grow very slowly, and reoperation can be done when symptoms recur.

E. TUMORS OF THE INTRACRANIAL BLOOD VESSELS

1. Hemangiomas are actually malformations with no neoplastic elements. They usually occur in the pons and are often clinically silent, although occasionally they may produce symptoms if the malformation ruptures or obstructs the flow of CSF.

2. Hemangioblastomas These are true neoplasms formed by proliferation of angioblasts. They are usually found in the cerebellum of adults where they produce symptoms. If there is associated hemangioblastoma of the retina, the disorder is called von Hippel–Lindau disease. Hemangioblastomas in the cerebellum frequently form a large cyst filled with thick yellow fluid. The tumor lies within the wall of the cyst (mural nodule), and surgical removal of the mural nodule is curative. Solid tumors are difficult to excise completely, and the prognosis is less favorable.

F. CONGENITAL INTRACRANIAL TUMORS

1. Craniopharyngiomas are the most common congenital brain tumors (3–4% of all brain tumors). They arise from epithelial cell rests in the region of the infundibular stalk and consist of squamous epithelium or epithelium of the type seen in developing tooth buds (also called adamantinomas). The cysts may become quite large. Deposits of calcium above the sella turcica can often be seen by x-ray. Symptoms are produced by compression of neighboring structures, and consist of endocrine disorders, visual field defects, optic atrophy, and obstruction of CSF flow.

Treatment is surgical removal, although often total removal is impossible because the capsule is adherent to the hypothalamus or the carotid artery. Aspiration of the cyst and subtotal removal of the capsule carries a low operative mortality, but symptoms soon recur. The long-term prognosis is poor.

2. Epidermoid cysts (pearly tumors, cholesteatomas) arise from embryonic epidermal cells, usually near the midline. Symptoms are usually delayed until adulthood. Treatment is surgical removal. If the wall is adherent to vital structures, complete surgical removal is not possible, but long-term survivals have been reported even with incomplete removals.

3. Dermoids These resemble epidermoids but contain dermal structures, such as sebaceous glands and hair follicles. Treatment is surgical.

4. Teratomas are derived from the 3 germinal layers and may attain huge size. Symptoms usually occur in childhood. The prognosis is good if the tumor is removed completely.

5. Chordomas These slow-growing neoplasms arise from remnants of primitive notochord along the clivus beneath the pons, and they extend into the middle fossa and cerebellopontine angle. They produce multiple cranial nerve palsies combined with long tract signs from pressure on the pons. Marked erosion of the base of the skull is usually visible on basilar x-rays. Total removal is rarely possible, and the prognosis is poor.

6. Colloid cyst of the third ventricle These cystic lesions in the anterior portion of the third ventricle cause symptoms by intermittent blockage of the CSF flow through the foramen of Monro. Since the cyst hangs from the roof of the ventricle by a stalk, changes in body position may produce, or relieve, sudden violent headache. The lesion should be removed; the prognosis is good.

G. PITUITARY TUMORS most often arise from the anterior lobe and are classified by cell type:

1. Chromophobe adenomas comprise the great majority of pituitary tumors. Most of them are composed of cells that have no known secretory function, and they produce symptoms by compressing the secretory cells of the anterior pituitary to cause hypopituitarism. Often the first symptom is bitemporal hemianopsia from compression of the optic chiasm.

Occasionally, chromophobe adenomas secrete prolactin and cause amenorrhea and galactorrhea. Functioning tumors may be so small that they are termed 'microadenomas,' becoming apparent clinically before visual fields are affected.

The diagnosis can usually be made by the physical appearance of the patient, visual field defects, and enlargement of the sella turcica on the skull x-rays. Laboratory tests confirm the presence and degree of hypopituitarism.

The primary objective of treatment is to preserve vision in patients who have large tumors. These tumors respond well to radiation therapy. A transfrontal or transsphenoidal biopsy is recommended before radiation is begun. The visual fields should be checked frequently during the course of radiation treatment; if the tumor swells and produces visual field defects, surgical removal of the tumor is indicated. The prognosis is good.

2. Eosinophilic adenomas that develop before closure of the epiphyses cause gigantism; those that begin in adult life cause acromegaly. Surgical removal by the transsphenoidal or transfrontal route is effective and is usually followed by radiotherapy.

3. Basophilic adenomas produce Cushing's disease and rarely reach sufficient size to cause local pressure symptoms. They are treated by surgery and radiotherapy.

H. INTRASPINAL NEOPLASMS occur at any level of the cord from the foramen magnum to the sacral canal; the greatest number are in the thoracic area. They may arise from the spinal cord, spinal nerves, bone, cartilage, fat blood vessels, fibrous tissue, or they may be metastatic. They are rare before age 10.

These tumors may be grouped as follows: (1) Those arising within the spinal canal, extending extraspinally through a vertebral foramen (dumbbell tumors); (2) those arising within the spinal canal but not invading the dura or cord (intraspinal extradural tumors); (3) those arising within the dura but not invading the spinal cord (intradural extramedullary tumors); and (4) those arising entirely within the substance of the cord (intramedullary tumors).

Most intraspinal tumors are benign, but early diagnosis and treatment is essential to avoid irreparable spinal cord damage.

1. Diagnosis

a. Symptoms and signs A history of pain in the back with radiation into dermatomal patterns, accompanied by sensory and/or motor root signs, and the appearance of long tract deficits suggest a spinal cord tumor.

History of progression: It is imperative to establish (1) whether symptoms began abruptly and have not changed significantly since onset, in which case an intraspinal tumor is unlikely; (2) whether symptoms began abruptly but remitted and recurred, as is typical of multiple sclerosis; or (3) whether the onset was vague, but progression since the onset has been steady, as one would expect with spinal cord tumor.

One of the earliest symptoms of spinal cord tumor is **radicular pain**—pain produced by pressure or traction on the nerve roots. The pain is often experienced in a peripheral area of the dermatome supplied by the root or roots involved; e.g., tumors of the cervical region may cause pain in the shoulder, arm, or hand.

Radicular pain has the following distinct characteristics: often restricted to the involved dermatomes; severe, sharp, stabbing, and superimposed on a background of continuous dull, aching pain; made worse by straining; worse at night after prolonged recumbency and temporarily relieved by physical activity. **Paresthesia** and/or **dysesthesia**, which are variously described as numbness, coldness, and tingling, are also in a radicular pattern.

Sensory loss, if it appears, is of a spinal cord type; i.e., a distinct level of sensory loss with greater involvement of one modality than of another. **Motor involvement** may be of the upper motor neuron type (i.e., spasticity, hyperreflexia, and extensor plantar response) or of the lower motor neuron type if the tumor involves the cauda equina.

Hesitancy in urination is an early sign of pressure on the spinal cord. Incontinence and/or retention of urine are late signs.

b. X-rays of the spine may show erosion, calcium deposition in the tumor, increase in the interpedicular distances, enlargement of the intervertebral foramina or collapse of vertebrae. The diagnosis of tumor is confirmed by myelography.

2. Treatment and prognosis When symptoms and signs progress rapidly, surgical treatment is urgent. Most benign tumors can be removed completely. The prognosis for return of function depends upon the location of the tumor, whether it can be removed completely or not, and the severity and duration of neurologic deficit before excision. The prognosis for intramedullary tumors is more guarded, since the hazard of increasing the neurologic deficit usually precludes complete removal. Postoperative radiation therapy may be beneficial in diminishing the mass effect and preventing further neurologic losses.

I. METASTATIC INTRASPINAL TUMORS The spinal cord is often compressed by metastases to the bones of the spinal column or to the epidural space. When compression of the spinal cord occurs, laminectomy and decompression should be considered, weighing also the patient's general condition and life expectancy in making the decision. Radiotherapy is usually given as a palliative measure, but a histologic diagnosis should be obtained first.

J. PERIPHERAL NERVE TUMORS
1. Neurilemmoma These are the most common tumors of the peripheral nerves; they arise in the supporting tissues. They are usually solitary, well encapsulated, of variable size, and benign. The diagnosis is suggested by a mass in the course of a peripheral nerve. Symptoms include paresthesia or hypesthesia; with tumors of mixed or pure sensory nerves, percussion over the tumor elicits tingling distally (Tinel's sign). Malignant change (sarcoma) occurs rarely. Treatment is by surgical removal, but in some cases excision is difficult and results in permanent neurologic deficit.

2. Neurofibromas are composed of all the elements of peripheral nerves (axis cylinders, myelin sheaths, and connective tissue). They may appear as solitary lesions, but most commonly they are multiple, occurring as part of Von Recklinghausen's neurofibromatosis (cafe-au-lait spots, multiple neurofibromas, and multiple brain tumors of all types). Individual tumors causing disabling symptoms can be excised.

Sarcomatous changes are more frequent in neurofibromas than in neurilemmomas. Neurofibrosarcoma may not be clinically distinguished from its benign counterpart, except for the rapidity of its growth. Surrounding structures are infiltrated, and distant metastases may occur.

V. CEREBROVASCULAR DISEASE

A. CEREBRAL ISCHEMIA Any area of the brain can become ischemic from arterial occlusion (partial or complete) or embolization. Symptoms may be slow and progressive, or sudden and catastrophic. Extracranial cerebrovascular disease is discussed in Chapter 13; intracranial atheromatous plaques most commonly form at the bifurcation of the internal carotid artery into the middle and anterior cerebral arteries.

   1. Symptoms and signs of cerebral ischemia depend upon the vessel that is affected:

   a. Internal carotid artery Occlusion usually produces contralateral weakness of the arm and leg, subjective numbness, blindness, and aphasia (if the predominant hemisphere is involved).

   b. Middle cerebral artery Usually the same as internal carotid occlusion, except that blindness does not occur, and the arm is usually weaker than the leg.

   c. Anterior cerebral artery Weakness and/or subjective numbness of the contralateral leg and occasionally the arm.

   d. Posterior cerebral artery Hemianopsia, scintillating scotomas, and (if lesions are bilateral) temporary or permanent cortical blindness.

   e. Basilar artery Usually bilateral symptoms such as quadriparesis, bilateral paresthesia, ataxia, dysarthria, diplopia, dysphagia, blindness, and frequently unconsciousness.

   2. Treatment of extracranial disease is discussed in Chapter 13. Revascularization of the brain after intracranial artery occlusion is now possible in selected cases by extracranial-intracranial arterial microanastomosis.

B. INTRACRANIAL ANEURYSM Most intracranial aneurysms are congenital lesions located on the anterior portion of the circle of Willis at points of bifurcation of major arteries. Approximately 10-15% arise in branches of the basilar artery, including the posterior cerebral arteries. About 20% of patients have multiple aneurysms.

   1. Diagnosis

   a. Intracranial aneurysms produce symptoms by one or more mechanisms: Subarachnoid hemorrhage or, less often, intracerebral or subdural hemorrhage. Pressure on adjacent structures leading to cranial nerve palsies (third, fifth, second, fourth, and sixth). Ischemia from occlusion of neighboring or parent arteries. Distention or pressure on pain-sensitive structures causing headache, usually orbital or supraorbital.

   b. Subarachnoid hemorrhage typically is a sudden, catastrophic event in a previously healthy person 20-40 years of age. Severe meningeal irritation (stiff neck, photophobia, headache), nausea and vomiting may stabilize or progress to coma and death within minutes to days.

   c. Intracerebral hemorrhage is associated with profound neurologic loss (hemiplegia, aphasia), coma, and death.

   d. The diagnosis of subarachnoid hemorrhage is established by lumbar puncture. The pressure is usually increased, the fluid is homogeneously bloody, and the supernatant is xanthochromic.

   e. Arteriograms should be obtained as soon as the patient's condition permits.

2. Treatment

a. General Absolute bed rest, maintenance of fluid and electrolyte balance, and mild analgesics to control headache and restlessness.

b. Surgical If operation is indicated, it should be done as soon as the patient's condition permits. **Direct intracranial approach:** The objective is to isolate the aneurysm from the circulation without producing a neurologic deficit. Methods include clipping the neck of the aneurysm, clipping the parent vessel proximally and distally, or reinforcing the aneurysm wall with various materials. **Indirect surgical approach:** Ligation of the carotid artery in the neck lowers the pressure in the aneurysm and may reduce the danger of subsequent hemorrhage. In general, this method of treatment is only applicable to aneurysms arising from the internal carotid artery proximal to the circle of Willis.

3. Prognosis

The mortality rate is 30% with the first episode of subarachnoid hemorrhage from ruptured intracranial aneurysm. The danger of a second hemorrhage is greatest within the first 3 weeks after the initial episode.

C. CEREBRAL ARTERIOVENOUS MALFORMATIONS (AVM)

These are congenital lesions that may cause subarachnoid or intracerebral hemorrhage, although hemorrhage is far less common with AVM than with aneurysm. Other manifestations include recurrent convulsive seizures, loss of function of adjacent brain (hemiparesis, aphasia), or progressive mental deterioration. Neurologic deficits may be caused by hemorrhage with subsequent gliosis and cyst formation, or they may result from shunting of blood directly into the venous system leading to local tissue hypoxia and eventual gliosis.

The diagnosis is suggested by the history, the presence of a bruit over the lesion, and sometimes intracranial calcification on x-ray. Cerebral angiography is diagnostic.

The only effective method of treatment is surgical removal. The prognosis depends upon the size and location of the lesion.

D. INTRACEREBRAL HEMORRHAGE

is the cause of stroke in many hypertensive patients. Hematomas develop most often in the basal ganglia, subcortical white matter, cerebellum, and brain stem. Catastrophic in onset, the lesion depresses consciousness severely and progressively. Because an intracranial mass and brain deformity result from intracerebral hemorrhage, initial diagnostic steps include CT scanning and angiography. Lumbar puncture is usually contraindicated.

Treatment consists of control of hypertension, life support, and removal of the mass by operation if the lesion is positioned in such a place that its removal will restore the patient to useful life. Deep hemorrhages are usually managed without operation. The prognosis depends upon the site and severity of the hemorrhage.

VI. INTERVERTEBRAL DISK DISEASE

A. PROTRUSION OF LUMBAR INTERVERTEBRAL DISKS

90% of protrusions occur at the L4-5 and L5-S1 interspaces.

1. Diagnosis

a. Symptoms Episodic back pain, with or without leg pain. The pain characteristically spreads to the gluteal region and then down the posterior or posterolateral aspect of the thigh and calf; it is aggravated by coughing, sneezing, or straining and may be relieved by rest. The patient will favor the painful leg, and will tend to carry himself with a 'list' either away from or toward the side of the disk protrusion.

b. Signs Spasm of the paravertebral muscles; flattening of the lumbar spine with loss of the normal lordosis; limitation of back motion, particularly forward flexion; and tenderness to deep pressure over the interspace involved.

c. Neurologic findings Straight leg-raising produces leg pain and frequently back pain which is accentuated by dorsiflexion of the foot (further stretching of the sciatic nerve and roots). The ankle reflex is diminished or absent (more common with protrusion at the L5-S1 interspace impinging on the first sacral nerve root). The knee reflex may be diminished with herniations at the L3-L4 interspace. Motor evaluation shows weakness of dorsiflexion and/or plantar flexion; weak inversion or eversion of the foot may be found also with herniations at the lower 2 lumbar interspaces. Weakness of the quadriceps may be present with L3-L4 lesions. Sensory status varies from no loss to complete analgesia in the distribution of the root involved.

d. X-rays Plain films may be normal or may show narrowing of the involved interspace, arthritic 'lipping' of the adjacent vertebral bodies, and/or arthritic changes around the zygoapophysial joints.

e. Special examinations Myelography is the most valuable test. Radiopaque dye is injected into the lumbar thecal sac and observed fluoroscopically as it flows over the suspected interspaces. Permanent films record the extent and level of the lesion. Electromyography can be used to identify the involved nerve root by demonstrating fibrillation potentials in the muscles supplied by the root.

2. Differential diagnosis Lumbar disk disease must be differentiated from tumors, congenital bony abnormalities (spondylolisthesis, spina bifida), and inflammatory disease (abscess, osteomyelitis, rheumatoid disease).

3. Treatment

a. Supportive Analgesics, strict bed rest with boards between springs and mattress to prevent sagging, local heat, and muscle 'relaxants' (Valium, 10 mg 3 times a day). The patient is often more comfortable in the modified Fowler's or contour position. 1 or 2 weeks of strict bed rest may be necessary before improvement is noted.

After the acute pain subsides, a progressive physical therapy program should be instituted to strengthen the back, abdominal, and leg muscles and to instruct the patient in the proper way to use the back muscles to prevent straining. Support of the back with a corset or brace may be useful when pain is severe and chronic.

b. Surgical Operation is indicated when pain is intractable or when neurologic signs appear. Excision of a diseased disk usually helps. Education of the patient and a well-directed exercise program are essentials of management, whether medical or surgical.

B. PROTRUSION OF CERVICAL INTERVERTEBRAL DISKS

1. Diagnosis

a. Symptoms Patients with lateral cervical protrusions have frequent bouts of pain involving the neck, shoulder, and scapular region, accompanied by lancinating root pain into the arm or hand, and accentuated by straining. Paresthesias into the fingers are common: into the first and second digits if C6 is involved, the third digit if C7, and the fourth and fifth digits if C8 is involved.

b. Signs Restricted neck motion, absence of cervical lordosis, spasm of the neck muscles, hypesthesia in a dermatomal pattern in the arm and hand, and weakness in the muscles supplied by the involved root. Arm reflexes are often decreased; diminished biceps reflex if C6 is involved and diminished triceps reflex if C7 is involved.

c. X-rays may be normal if the protrusion is recent, or x-rays may show a narrowed interspace and/or hypertrophic lipping with narrowing of the root foramina. Myelography reveals a defect of the root sleeve.

d. With *midline protrusions,* there may be no history of root pain; a common presenting complaint is spastic paraparesis with or without urinary hesitancy or incontinence. Signs of pyramidal tract involvement are apparent in the lower extremities. X-rays reveal interspace narrowing, with or without osteophytic spurring at the posterior edges of the vertebrae. Myelography shows an anterior deformity.

2. Treatment   Bed rest with intermittent halter traction (5-10 lbs) initially; as symptoms subside, a neck brace may be helpful.

If symptoms fail to improve and/or neurologic deficits are present, operation to remove the offending disk may be necessary. Myelography should precede operation in order to localize the lesion precisely. In midline or lateral protrusions, the operation of choice is anterior diskectomy with or without intervertebral fusion. A foraminotomy by a posterior approach is an effective alternative for laterally placed disk fragments. Surgery usually prevents progression of neurologic loss and may partially restore lost function.

VII. INFECTIONS OF SCALP, BONE, AND BRAIN

A. PYOGENIC SCALP INFECTIONS should be treated vigorously, as there are abundant communications from the venous channels of the scalp to the diploic spaces of the calvaria and from these spaces to the underlying dura. Treatment of scalp infections includes appropriate antibiotics, drainage of abscesses, and debridement of necrotic tissue.

B. OSTEOMYELITIS OF THE SKULL occurs most commonly after implantation of bacteria into bone by trauma or by extension of infection in contiguous structures such as scalp or sinuses. The appearance of signs and symptoms of osteomyelitis may be delayed for weeks to months after the initial trauma or neighboring infection. Typical manifestations are headache, local evidence of inflammation (with or without a draining sinus), and tenderness. Systemic effects such as fever, leukocytosis, and cervical or suboccipital lymphadenopathy may not be present. X-rays may be negative early in the course, but later they reveal a characteristic mottled appearance to the bone.

Vigorous antibiotic therapy should be based on results of cultures and sensitivity tests. If inflammation or drainage persist despite antibiotics and initial debridement, infected bone should be excised. Cranioplasty to repair the defect should be deferred until at least 6-12 months after all evidence of infection has disappeared.

C. EPIDURAL ABSCESS usually develops by direct extension from an adjacent infection, although hematogenous spread of bacteria can give rise to this lesion also. The classical findings in cranial epidural abscess are those of a rapidly enlarging space-occupying lesion in association with the symptoms and signs of systemic infection. Acute or chronic spinal epidural abscesses cause cord compression. Pain is prominent, and bony tenderness is always present.

Epidural abscesses require immediate surgical drainage and antibiotics. Closed irrigation of the infected space with antibiotics is often employed.

D. SUBDURAL ABSCESS is usually the result of direct extension from an overlying area, but they may occur from rupture of an intracranial abscess into the subdural space. Since there are no limiting structures in the subdural space, these abscesses extend over the entire hemisphere, under the brain, and into the interhemispheral fissure.

The abscess is a rapidly enlarging space-occupying lesion and causes lethargy, obtundation, paresis, coma, and papilledema. The diagnosis is based upon a history of primary infection and the findings of subdural pus on exploration. Treatment is essentially the same as for epidural abscesses.

E. INTRACEREBRAL ABSCESS   A variety of bacteria and parasites cause intracerebral abscesses. Until recently most abscesses were associated with sinusitis or mastoiditis, but now only about one-third arise from these sources. Pulmonary infection accounts for 30%, and the remainder result from head injury or bacteremia due to congenital heart disease, drug addiction or other systemic infection. Abscesses are multi-focal in 10-15% of cases resulting from hematogenous seeding.

1. Diagnosis   A history of infection (ear, sinuses, or elsewhere) is important. Convulsions, headache, and paresis with progressive lethargy are the symptoms and signs. In the acute phase, the patient may have fever, leukocytosis, and an elevated CSF cell count. In the chronic phase, as the infection is walled off by formation of a capsule, toxic symptoms are replaced by signs of a mass. Lumbar puncture may be dangerous and should be preceded by other studies if an abscess is suspected.

CT scan often shows a characteristic lucent area surrounded by a dense capsule which enhances with iodinated contrast medium, the so-called 'donut sign'. Radionuclide brain scan is positive in over 90% of cases of brain abscess, and the scan demonstrates a defect in the blood/brain barrier.

2. Treatment   In the acute phase, broad spectrum antibiotics must be given until the causative organism has been identified, then specific antibiotics are given. If the patient is lethargic or has focal neurologic findings, dexamethasone (6 mg IV every 6 hours) usually controls the cerebral edema surrounding the abscess.

Surgical treatment consists of aspiration or total excision of the abscess. The mortality rate varies from 15-50%; the worst results occur in patients who are comatose before operation.

VIII. PAIN

The neurosurgeon is frequently called upon to carry out procedures for relief of chronic pain of known or unknown origin. Every effort must be made to determine the cause of the pain, and every patient who complains of chronic pain that has no apparent cause or is atypical must be thoroughly evaluated psychiatrically before operation is considered.

The most common pain syndromes requiring surgical intervention are trigeminal neuralgia, glossopharyngeal neuralgia, postherpetic neuralgia, and pain produced by advanced malignancies.

A. TRIGEMINAL NEURALGIA

1. Diagnosis   Trigeminal neuralgia is a disorder characterized by severe lancinating pain occurring without warning in the distribution of any of the major branches of the trigeminal nerve. Each pain is a brief stabbing sensation with frequent paroxysms. Attacks are most frequent in the spring and fall, and there may be periods of remission lasting for many months. Many patients describe a 'trigger area' somewhere about the face, mouth, or tongue, where stimulation produces the stabbing pain, and the patient may refuse to eat, shave, or talk, to avoid stimulating the trigger area. There is no pain between attacks, and there is no loss of sensation in the distribution of the trigeminal nerve. If there is loss of sensation, a tumor in or near the gasserian ganglion should be suspected.

2. Treatment   Carbamazepine (Tegretol) relieves the pain in approximately 80% of patients with trigeminal neuralgia. In a few cases, phenytoin (Dilantin), 300 mg daily, may be effective.

If the pain persists despite adequate medical therapy or if medications are not tolerated, a variety of surgical procedures are available. (1) The peripheral branch of the trigeminal nerve innervating the trigger area can be surgically excised. (2) Passage of a radiofrequency current through a needle stereotactically placed in the trigeminal ganglion. The ganglion is coagulated by transfer of heat. The radiofrequency lesion can be graded to preserve some sensation in the trigeminal nerve distribution. Of particular importance is preservation of sensation from the first branch of the trigeminal nerve, which is necessary for corneal protection. (3) Craniotomy, either via the temporal fossa (to section or decompress the ganglion) or through the posterior fossa (to section portions of the nerve between the brain stem and the gasserian ganglion). (4) Arteries that cause trigeminal neuralgia by compressing the nerve can be freed and the disorder cured.

B. GLOSSOPHARYNGEAL NEURALGIA The pain of glossopharyngeal neuralgia is similar to that of trigeminal neuralgia, but it is located in the distribution of the ninth cranial nerve: in the tonsillar fossa and deep in the neck at the angle of the jaw on the affected side. The diagnosis is confirmed by application of topical anesthetic to the tonsillar fossa on the affected side; in true glossopharyngeal neuralgia, pain is relieved immediately but returns after the local anesthetic has worn off. Intracranial section of the ninth cranial nerve and the upper 2 filaments of the tenth through a posterior fossa approach gives permanent relief.

C. POSTHERPETIC NEURALGIA In a few cases of herpes zoster, severe burning pain persists in the involved area after the infection has run its course. Chronic inflammatory changes are present in the posterior root ganglion and in the ascending pathways of the spinal cord and brain stem carrying pain impulses.

A variety of medications has been used. One combination which is often successful is amitriptyline (Elavil) (initial dose 75 mg daily in divided doses, increased to a maximum of 150 mg daily) and fluphenazine (Prolixin) (2 mg daily in divided dosage initially, increased to a maximum of 10–15 mg/day). Transcutaneous stimulators have limited success. Undermining of the skin in a wide margin around the involved area occasionally brings relief. Peripheral neurectomies are sometimes useful, but because of the widespread inflammatory changes in the pain-conducting pathways, these procedures may not eliminate the pain; in addition, painful neuromas may develop postoperatively. Therefore, the simplest procedure should be used before resorting to more complicated and dangerous procedures. In severe cases unresponsive to other therapy, cordotomy, thalamatomy or frontal leukotomy may be required.

D. PAIN PRODUCED BY ADVANCED MALIGNANCIES Severe pain becomes a problem as inoperable malignancies invade sensitive structures. The pain is deep, boring, and steady, with sharp, stabbing pains at times superimposed.

Operations for relief of pain in cancer patients should not be considered a last resort. Large doses of narcotics often produce mental dullness and disinterest in life. As a general rule, if the patient's life expectancy is longer than 3–6 months, a pain-relieving surgical procedure should be carried out as soon as the pain becomes significant.

Relief can be given without loss of vital neurologic function by cutting the fibers responsible for pain transmission at an appropriate level in the peripheral or central nervous system. The operation most frequently used is a **cordotomy** (spinothalamic tractotomy). The spinothalamic tract in the anterior quadrant of the spinal cord on the side opposite the pain is sectioned at the high thoracic or high cervical level causing loss of pain and thermal sensation on the contralateral side below the level of the section. For pelvic pain involving the midline or for bilateral pain, bilateral cordotomy is indicated. Thoracic cordotomy can be performed by laminectomy and open section, or cordotomy can be done in the awake patient by passage of radiofrequency current through a small needle placed percutaneously into the spinothalamic tract at the C1-C2 level.

Pain involving the face, jaw, neck, or brachial plexus can be relieved by sectioning the pain fibers in the medulla at the level of the obex. An alternative procedure is section of the trigeminal, glossopharyngeal, and upper filaments of the vagus nerves intracranially and the upper 3 or 4 posterior cervical roots on the side of the pain.

17

ORTHOPEDICS

Floyd H. Jergesen, MD

I. INJURIES TO THE SPINE

A. GENERAL PRINCIPLES Depending upon the severity and the mechanism of the trauma and the anatomic location of the lesion, these injuries may vary from minor affections of soft tissue (e.g., contusion, muscle strain, or joint sprain) to extensive fracture-dislocation with severe neurologic impairment.

The specific site of fracture is indicated by the structure involved (i.e., body, pedicle, lamina, or muscle process). Dislocations are described by direction and by magnitude (complete or incomplete) of displacement and by the degree of complexity (i.e., unilateral or bilateral). Pathologic fracture may occur without evident episodic trauma.

1. Types of injury

a. Direct

(1) Closed: Caused by trauma applied through overlying soft tissues without open wounds communicating with the axial skeleton; usually fracture of spinous or transverse processes and rarely the lamina.

(2) Open: Generally due to penetrating injuries such as those inflicted by firearms, military missiles, or knives.

b. Indirect When these injuries are extensive, they are likely the result of complex combinations of varied basic stresses (e.g., compression, traction, bending, shearing, and torsion) rather than a single stress.

2. Neurologic injury Most skeletal injuries of the spine do not involve the cord or nerves. Damage to the spinal cord may complicate any displacement that reduces even transitorily the diameter of the canal. Extensive neurologic harm may occur without evident osteoarticular disruption and, conversely, marked skeletal derangement may not be associated with neurologic loss. Indirect, closed injury to the spinal cord or nerves can result from displaced bone fragments, portions of vertebral disks, or dislocated vertebral segments.

Neurologic injury may be intensified by manipulation during emergency care. When the patient is unable to communicate or is likely to have sustained injury to either the cervical or thoracolumbar regions, the head and trunk should be manipulated with utmost caution until the precise involvement can be critically assessed. Multiple levels of the spine may be injured concomitantly.

3. Associated injuries Associated injury to the appendicular skeleton or to the other organ systems of the conscious patient may mask symptoms that might focus attention on spinal injuries.

4. Diagnosis A period of unconsciousness or transitory amnesia may obscure the mechanism and extent of initial injury. Determination of the earliest time of onset of any motor or sensory compromise gives insight of prognostic value.

a. Symptoms and signs The location and extent of superficial soft tissue lesions should be noted because they may indicate the direction and magnitude of force that was applied indirectly to the spine. Palpation of the entire spinal region without manipulation of the patient may reveal sites of deep tenderness.

tered alignment or abnormal prominence of the spinous processes may suggest the presence of occult lesions.

Careful neurologic assessment is an integral part of the general physical examination. When the anatomic site of skeletal disruption, as demonstrated by x-ray, is compared to the most proximal level of total neurologic deficit as indicated by clinical examination, that portion due solely to cord damage may be separated from that caused by root injury.

Root lesions are characterized by segmental sensory and motor deficits in peripheral nerve distributions.

During the first 24 hours after injury, a partial spinal cord lesion is manifest minimally by sacral sparing—residual perianal sensation and some voluntary motor activity of the toe flexors. Residual reflex activity during this initial period merely indicates that cord function distal to the interruption is not suppressed by spinal shock which persists, as a rule, no longer than 24 hours. Failure to recover any sensory or active motor function distal to the level of the cord lesion during this period suggests complete and permanent spinal cord damage. Return of the bulbocavernosus reflex indicates recovery from spinal shock and precedes the return of deep tendon reflexes.

b. X-rays When the patient is unconscious, a preliminary x-ray or fluoroscopic survey of the spine and appendicular skeleton may aid in establishing a more precise initial diagnosis. After a tentative diagnosis has been made and protective measures have been taken against unintentional injury, more extensive investigation by routine x-rays can be undertaken. Preexisting skeletal displacement may not be apparent because of spontaneous reduction.

Laminagraphy may demonstrate occult bone lesions, especially in the region of the spinal canal.

When available, computerized tomography (CT) may localize structures that intrude on the spinal canal.

c. Special tests (1) Determination of spinal fluid dynamics can help to differentiate partial from complete blockage of the canal. (2) Myelography localizes precisely the level of spinal canal compromise and, when partial, its configuration.

5. Treatment Prime objectives of early treatment are to protect the spinal cord and nerves from further damage and to minimize discomfort during transportation of the patient to a hospital. This can be accomplished most simply by removal of the injured on a flat surface in the supine decubitus position with bolsters beside the head and neck. As soon as medically oriented help is available, stabilization of proximal spine injuries, especially when there is apparent neurologic loss, can be enhanced by head halter traction directed axially to the spine while maintaining the head in anatomic posture.

During initial x-ray examination, the surgeon should determine whether any manipulation or change of bodily position is advisable.

General guidelines for definitive treatment are offered under specific lesions.

6. Prognosis The presence and extent of neurologic damage, the level and severity of skeletal disruption, the age of the patient, and the presence of associated injuries are factors that bear on the prognosis.

B. SPRAIN OF THE CERVICAL SPINE The injuries considered here involve supporting muscles and ligaments. Motor vehicle accidents are the common cause, while a smaller number is due to sports mishaps. 'Whiplash' is a nonspecific term employed (especially by the laity) to refer to the protean and frequently bizarre posttraumatic syndromes that follow automobile accidents.

When a stationary motor vehicle is struck from the rear by another, the unsupported head and neck of the occupant can be initially extended and then reversed immediately into forced flexion. Conversely, sudden deceleration of a vehicle by a front-end collision can cause initial forced flexion of the cervical spine followed by extension. More complex variants of these mechanisms may operate depending upon the attitude of the head at the instant of impact and the direction, magnitude and rate of application of stresses.

1. Diagnosis The diagnosis is established by critical differentiation from structural osteoarticular derangements and from traumatic lesions of the brain, spinal cord, and nerves. Obtain a detailed history of the accident.

a. Symptoms and signs The onset of symptoms may be immediate or delayed. In the absence of other more serious injury, delay of onset is often an indication of less severe neck injury. The principal symptom is pain that is poorly localized and is likely to be distributed to the posterior cervical, occipital, and trapezius regions. It is commonly accentuated by neck movements and relieved somewhat by rest. A sensation of stiffness may be associated. Physical findings that require active patient participation require critical evaluation by the examiner. Symmetric restriction of active neck movements is to be expected and may be caused by unconscious muscle guarding or conscious inhibition. Tenderness is

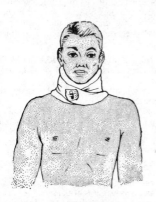 

Fig. 17-1. Cervical collar   **Fig. 17-2.** Minerva jacket

commonly diffuse and not precisely and consistently localized on repeated examination. The significance of muscle spasm is difficult to assess especially when associated with deep, diffuse tenderness.

b. X-rays X-ray examination of the cervical spine must be thorough because differentiation of sprain from other conditions may depend upon its reliability. In addition to the standard projections which include the lateral projections in flexion and extension, laminagraphy and cineradiography may help to differentiate sprain from fracture or dislocation.

c. Special tests Myelography may be necessary to determine intervertebral disk derangements. Electromyography may aid in the identification of nerve root lesions.

2. Differential diagnosis Radiation of pain or altered sensation in a dermatomal pattern associated with motor dysfunction in the corresponding myotome should immediately suggest the possibility of a focal lesion of a spinal nerve root. Persistent and severe headache requires search for intracranial sources. Difficulty swallowing associated with pharyngeal edema points to a more serious condition than sprain. If blurring of vision or diplopia do not subside promptly they require ophthalmologic investigation. Complaints of dizziness or tinnitus that are not transient suggest eighth cranial nerve dysfunction. Both hemorrhage in the labyrinth and transient ischemia due to vertebral artery compression have been suggested as causes of posttraumatic vertigo. Persistent asymmetric restriction of active movement suggests the presence of an anatomic osteoarticular lesion. Bizarrely performed active neck movements through a near-average range suggests malingering especially when accompanied by theatric grimaces. Emotionally labile and apprehensive patients may manifest anxiety, depression, loss of memory, or inability to concentrate mentally.

3. Treatment   The treatment of cervical sprain is essentially symptomatic. Pain is likely to be intensified by neck movement. Restriction of movement by any method such as external cervical support by a felt collar (Fig. 17-1) or brace, or by recumbency in bed may provide comfort. Light cervical traction (2-3 kg) by head halter may give additional relief. Analgesics and sedatives (for apprehensive patients) relieve mild pain. Local application of heat or cold, depending upon the patient's preference, may offer additional comfort.

4. Prognosis   If litigation or emotional lability are not factors, symptoms generally respond promptly to conservative measures. Younger patients become asymptomatic more rapidly than older ones with joint disease that existed prior to injury. Neck pain and headache may be aggravated by prolonged treatment with heat, diathermy, ultrasonics, or traction.

C. FRACTURES, DISLOCATIONS, AND FRACTURE-DISLOCATIONS OF THE CERVICAL SPINE   These lesions account for about 15% of all derangements of the spine caused by severe trauma.

The type and extent of injury is suggested by the history and is established by physical examination, x-rays, and other tests.

In addition to the diagnostic evaluation described above, neurologic findings peculiar to injuries of the cervical portion of the spinal cord bear emphasis. The body of the third cervical vertebra marks the approximate level of the fourth cervical cord segment. A **complete** lesion at this site or more proximally causes death by respiratory paralysis. The most common **partial** lesion involves the central region of the cord which causes flaccid paralysis of the upper extremities and spasticity distally. A lesion of the anterior cord results in partial paralysis and anesthesia. Loss of deep pain and proprioception indicates a lesion posteriorly. Involvement of a lateral half of the cord results in paralysis of the same side of the body with hypalgesia and absence of temperature perception of the opposite side (Brown-Sequard syndrome).

1. Proximal cervical spine

a. Fracture of the atlas (Jefferson's fracture)   An axial blow to the top of the head may drive the condyles of the occiput into the lateral masses of the first cervical vertebra causing fracture of the arches and displacement of the masses. Routine x-rays may demonstrate displacement of the lateral masses while occult fracture may be revealed only by tomography or computerized tomography. When the spinal cord has not been injured and the fragments are not markedly displaced, immobilization in a Minerva jacket (Fig. 17-2) for 12-16 weeks may be all that is required. Otherwise, skull traction for 4-8 weeks is advisable before plaster immobilization. Persistently unstable fractures require posterior occipito-axial fusion.

b. Fracture of the axis (epistropheus)   The most common fracture of the proximal cervical spine involves the odontoid (which should be differentiated from os odontoideum). Subluxation or dislocation of the atlantoaxial joint may complicate. Displacement of the odontoid fragment with the atlas partially protects the cord from injury. When necessary, reduction can be accomplished by skull traction which should be maintained until stabilization by preliminary healing permits transfer to plaster. Fracture at the base of the odontoid heals more rapidly than at the middle.

Fracture of the body of the axis may be manifest as a vertical or oblique cleft that extends in the lateral mass or the lamina. When neurologic injury does not complicate, treatment by Minerva jacket is adequate because of inherent stability.

An avulsion fracture of the anteroinferior margin of the body suggests injury due to hyperextension and infers an associated lesion of the disk. It may accompany fracture-dislocation of the second and third cervical segments.

c. Occipitoatlantal dislocation This extremely rare lesion is generally fatal because of spinal cord injury. Because extensive ligamentous disruption causes gross instability, treatment by traction should be avoided. Stabilization may be provided by a Minerva cast or preferably by a cranial halo attached to a plaster body jacket. Persistent instability requires posterior occipitoaxial fusion.

d. Atlantoaxial dislocation Traumatic anterior dislocation of the atlas without fracture of the odontoid is very rare and because of spinal cord injury, is likely to be fatal. The transverse ligament must rupture to permit dislocation. Persistent instability is likely because of failure of ligamentous healing. Posterior atlantoaxial fusion may be required to provide reliable stability.

Pathologic anterior subluxation or dislocation may complicate rheumatoid arthritis or may occur without any identifiable cause.

Posterior dislocation of the atlas without fracture of the odontoid is rare. It is caused by displacement of the arch upward over the tip of the odontoid. Reduction is accomplished by cranial traction followed by immobilization in a Minerva jacket with the head in anatomic position.

e. Atlantoaxial dislocation in children Spontaneous forward dislocation of the atlas on the axis may occur in children as a complication of upper respiratory tract infection. Irritability associated with restriction of active neck motions should focus attention to the cervical spine and suggest examination by x-ray. Initial treatment is by head halter traction until painful restriction of active motion is relieved. Cervical support by brace or collar should continue until recovered stability can be demonstrated by x-ray.

f. Fracture-dislocation of the axis Bilateral fracture through the pedicles with forward displacement of the body of the axis on that of C3 (hangman's fracture, traumatic spondylolisthesis) may occur as the result of motor vehicle accidents or legal hanging. Displacement of the segments may be corrected by carefully controlled cranial traction until stabilization occurs. External immobilization by a Minerva jacket should be afforded until bony healing occurs—generally a period of 12–16 weeks.

2. Lower cervical spine

a. Compression fracture of the vertebral body Uncomplicated compression fracture is rare with comparison to its counterpart in the thoracic spine and is more likely to occur in the inferior half of the cervical spine. Injury to the spinal cord or nerve roots is unlikely. Because the posterior ligaments are not disrupted and the fragments are impacted, the lesion is mechanically stable and prompt healing is to be expected. Critical study by x-ray is necessary to differentiate this lesion from fracture-dislocation. Deformity is not marked and attempted reduction is not indicated. Treatment is conservative by external support until symptoms subside.

b. Comminuted fracture of the vertebral body Comminution results from driving the respective disks of the segments above and below into the affected centrum (burst fracture, tear-drop fracture). The posterior ligaments are not disrupted. Bone fragments are not impacted and are likely to be displaced. The high incidence of neurologic damage results from compression of the cord by fragments posteroinferiorly and injury to the roots by fragments displaced laterally.

When damage to the spinal cord is not a factor, sustained cranial traction in the anatomic position is necessary until reliable stabilization is provided by initial healing—usually 2–3 months. When cord damage is evident, early laminectomy is liable to increase instability by disrupting undamaged posterior ligaments.

Concomitant posterior fusion is unlikely to provide adequate stability for early mobilization of the patient. Compression of the cord unrelieved by traction may be treated more effectively by combined anterior debridement of offending fragments followed by fusion. Any persisting instability may be treated subsequently by posterior fusion without laminectomy.

   c. Fracture of spinous processes Episodic fractures of spinous processes occur more frequently in the lower than the upper cervical spine and may be isolated or may accompany more serious lesions. Fracture is usually caused by indirect violence, such as avulsion by forced flexion or impingement on adjacent spines during forced extension. Clinical findings may be accentuated pain during cervical movement and localized tenderness. The lesion generally can be identified in the lateral x-ray film, but in the cervicothoracic region oblique views can be helpful. Treatment is symptomatic and failure of healing is unlikely.

   Fatigue fracture of a spinous process occurs in the distal cervical or proximal thoracic region ('clay shoveler's disease'). It has been postulated that arduous and repetitive physical activity such as shoveling causes avulsion by action of the trapezius and rhomboid muscles. The counterpart of this lesion occurs in adolescents prior to fusion of the spinous apophysis.

   d. Forward bilateral dislocation Complete bilateral forward dislocation (luxation) without fracture is more apt to occur in the lower than in the upper cervical spine. Both inferior articular processes of the segment above are displaced anterior to the superior ones of the segment below. This infers disruption of the intervertebral disk and tearing of the apophyseal joint capsules and the longitudinal and posterior ligaments. Damage to the spinal cord and nerves is likely to complicate. Locked facets may be demonstrated by standard or stereo x-ray examination.

   When neurologic damage is evident (especially an incomplete spinal cord lesion), prompt reduction is necessary to prevent further injury from pressure. Although locked facets make reduction difficult by skull traction alone, it should be tried with the neck slightly flexed and the patient awake. Freeing of locked facets may be apparent visually by elongation of the neck and by x-ray examination. Traction force is then gradually increased until both facets are minimally distracted. Reduction is completed by extending the head to neutral position and decreasing the distracting force. The course of further treatment is moot because of indolent and unreliable ligamentous healing which may permit redislocation or subluxation even though immobilization is not discontinued prematurely. Anterior or posterior arthrodesis has been advocated early in the course, especially when quadriparesis or quadriplegia complicate, to facilitate nursing care and to expedite rehabilitation. When extensive neurologic damage is not a factor, a more conservative program is reasonable.

   e. Forward unilateral dislocation Complete unilateral dislocation anteriorly below the level of the axis is characterized by torsional displacement whereby one facet joint remains essentially undisturbed while the other is completely displaced and usually locked. Less extensive disk and ligamentous damage is probable than that of the bilateral lesion. When present, neurologic findings may be asymmetric and involve predominantly the side of displacement. Routine x-rays demonstrate the spinous process of the dislocated segment above to be displaced toward the side of the more involved facet and the body displaced anteriorly less than half of its diameter. Stereo or tomographic x-ray studies may provide confirmatory evidence.

   Reduction may be accomplished by cranial traction with the patient awake, the head being flexed slightly and tilted to the side opposite the dislocated facet joint. When reduction has been effected, the head is placed in anatomic position which is mechanically stable. Early open reduction is indicated when closed methods fail and especially when neurologic injury complicates.

   f. Forward bilateral subluxation (incomplete dislocation) may occur alone or it may complicate compression fracture. Neurologic damage is not likely but when it is evident other accompanying lesions should be sought. Uncomplicated bilateral subluxation can be treated by gentle manual traction with the patient awake, letting the head extend over a mattress so that its weight can provide the traction force or by head halter with 2-3 kg of weight. The neck should be protected by a felt collar for 2-3 weeks. Resubluxation may occur.

g. Forward unilateral subluxation below the level of the C2 may be caused by minimal injury; it may occur spontaneously, especially during sleep. Younger persons are affected more commonly than older ones. Pain may not be a prominent feature. Tilting of the head away from the side of the lesion with rotation of the chin slightly toward the unaffected side are the chief physical signs. The lesion is best demonstrated by stereo lateral x-rays or laminagraphy.

Reduction can frequently be accomplished by gentle manual traction or by head halter using 2-3 kg of force for 12-24 hours. After reduction, the neck should be protected by a felt collar until discomfort and any restriction of active movement disappear. Recurrence is possible. Any persistence of symptoms requires search for other causes.

h. Extension dislocation The diagnosis is often difficult and at times must rest on speculation because of the inherent stability of the cervical spine, the likelihood of spontaneous reduction, and the paucity of evidence from standard x-ray examination. Dislocation without significant fracture implies rupture of the anterior longitudinal ligament and disruption of the disk. Injury to the cord may be caused by infolding of the posterior longitudinal ligament and by hypertrophic spurs of the posterior body that encroach upon the canal anteriorly. The neurologic pattern of incomplete deficit may conform to that of an acute central cord lesion.

Standard x-ray studies may show only widening of the disk space or avulsion of a bit of bone from the body of an adjacent vertebra by the anterior longitudinal ligament.

This lesion is stable when the cervical spine is in slight flexion. Treatment by prolonged neck support is adequate. The major therapeutic challenge is care of any neurologic complication.

i. Fracture-dislocation Compression fracture of the vertebral body may occur as an isolated lesion (see above) or it may be associated with varying degrees of forward (anterior) dislocation. Compression of the superior plate of the body, with disruption of the intervertebral disk, displacement of the facet joints, and tearing of the posterior supporting ligaments, account for the major components of this lesion complex. Even though the facet joints do not displace, fracture of the lateral mass can permit subluxation. Injury to the spinal cord and nerve roots may complicate. Because of impaction of the bone fragments, fracture healing is not a problem. Treatment is directed to the accompanying dislocation (see above).

Stresses that cause chiefly lateral flexion may produce compression fracture of the lateral mass or adjacent segment of the vertebral body. Contralateral facet subluxation by distraction, with or without avulsion of an adjacent transverse process may be associated. Injury to roots of the brachial plexus on the distracted side may complicate. Associated damage to the cord of varying severity may obscure the root lesion initially. Because of inherent stability of the lesion, treatment by external support alone is apt to be adequate; traction may be harmful.

D. FRACTURES OF THE THORACIC SPINE The thoracic spine is comparatively stable. Fracture results either from direct violence, which may involve only a spinous process; or indirect violence, which may result in compression of the body of the vertebra.

Compression fractures of the thoracic vertebrae are rare in young children and are caused only by severe trauma in older children. In this age group, therefore, unless there is a positive history of severe trauma, a wedge-shaped deformity in the thoracic spine should suggest pathologic fracture. This must not be confused with Calve's or Scheuermann's disease.

Minimal (frequently unrecognized) trauma may cause compression fracture of the body of the thoracic vertebrae in adults with osteoporosis. Disability is not great, and reduction is not indicated. If rest in bed for 3-4 days does not relieve the pain, a surgical corset with shoulder restraints or brace (Taylor or Arnold type) may provide comfort and permit early ambulation.

Compression fractures of the thoracic spine caused by severe trauma are characterized by wedge-shaped deformity of the vertebral body. No adequate closed method has been devised for the reduction of these injuries. However, because of the inherent stability of the thoracic spine, prolonged immobilization is not necessary. In fracture of the upper thoracic region, if immobilization is required for relief of pain, a long plaster Minerva jacket that includes the iliac crests may be the only adequate method of external support that will provide relief from pain.

Rotational fracture-dislocations near the thoracolumbar junction and shear fractures of the thoracic spine are commonly associated with paraplegia. Rotational fracture-dislocation is inherently unstable because of extensive rupture of supporting ligaments, fracture of the vertebral body in the transverse plane, and disruption of the articular facet joints by fracture or dislocation. These fractures may or may not be stable, and fusion may be necessary to minimize injury to the cord.

Shear fracture is a term used to describe a fracture-dislocation of the thoracic spine whereby dislocation takes place at or near the intervertebral disk with fracture of the articular processes or the pedicles. Forward displacement takes place in the transverse plane.

E. FRACTURES AND FRACTURE-DISLOCATIONS OF THE LUMBAR SPINE

1. Uncomplicated compression fractures Compression fractures of the vertebral bodies caused by hyperflexion injury are the most common fractures of the lumbar spine and occur most often near the thoracolumbar junction. The widespread use of seat belts in automobiles has been accompanied by an increasing incidence of fractures that occur near the lumbosacral level as the result of accidents. Often more than one vertebral body is involved, but deformity may be greatest in one segment. Acute angulation of the spine caused by compression fracture of the body of a vertebra may be associated with varying degrees of disruption of the facet joints, from sprain to complete dislocation.

Standard x-rays demonstrate the characteristic lesions such as wedge-shaped deformity of the body and the presence of dislocation of the facets, comminuted fracture of the body, and fracture of the pedicle. Laminagraphy is a useful adjunctive technic.

In older patients with preexisting degenerative arthritis where there is mild deformity involving no more than one-fourth of the anterior height of the body of the vertebra, the surgeon may elect merely to place the patient at bed rest for a few days. As soon as acute pain is relieved, the back should be braced and increasing physical activity encouraged within the tolerance of pain. In the more active age group, and when the compression deformity involves more than one-half of the anterior height of the body of the vertebra, reduction by hyperextension and immobilization in a plaster jacket is the preferred treatment (Fig. 17-3).

2. Comminuted fractures of the vertebral body are characterized by disruption of the adjacent intervertebral disks and varying degrees of displacement of bone fragments. The end-plates of the body are forced into the centrum together with the disk. A large fragment of the body may be displaced anteriorly. Posteriorly displaced fragments are apt to cause compression of the cord or cauda equina; and the facet joints may be fractured or dislocated. Therefore, careful physical and x-ray examinations are mandatory before treatment is instituted.

The method of **treatment** may be dictated by the extent of bone injury and the presence of neurologic complications. When neurologic involvement is absent and comminution is not manifest by extensive fragmentation, reduction may not be necessary. Under these circumstances, immobilization in a plaster jacket may be sufficient. It must be determined whether dislocation has occurred or is likely because of posterior element injury (see below). Mobilization of the patient from recumbency should be controlled by periodic physical and x-ray examinations to determine incipient displacement of fragments which may herald

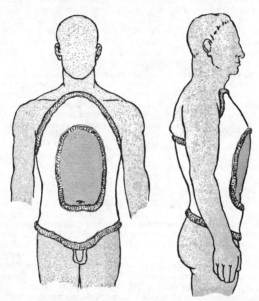

Fig. 17-3. Hyperextension plaster for compression fracture of the lumbar spine

or accompany the onset of neurologic deficit. When the posterior elements are intact and compression of the body has been greater than one-fourth to one-third its former height, reduction by extension of the spine and immobilization in a plaster jacket should be considered in young adults. When cauda equina injury has occurred, laminectomy may also be necessary. Bone healing is likely to be slow, and immobilization should be prolonged until stabilization has occurred. Cautiously executed biplane bending x-ray studies give helpful guidance in determining the soundness of healing and the extent to which mechanical stability is restored.

3. Fracture of the transverse processes may result from direct violence, such as a crushing injury, or may be incidental to a more serious fracture of the lumbar spine. It may result also from violent muscle contraction alone. One or more segments may be involved. If displacement is minimal, soft tissue injury is likely to be minor. Extensive displacement of the fragments indicates severe soft tissue tearing and hematoma formation.

Treatment depends upon the presence or absence of associated injuries. If fracture of the transverse process is the sole injury, and if pain is not severe upon guarded motions of the back, strapping and prompt ambulation may be sufficient. If displacement and soft tissue injury are extensive, bed rest for a few days followed by prolonged support in a corset or brace may be necessary and slow symptomatic recovery may be anticipated.

4. Fracture-dislocation of the lumbar spine Severe compression trauma may cause fracture-dislocation with rupture of one disk or, if comminution occurs, rupture of two disks. Varying degrees of injury to the posterior elements occur, including unilateral or bilateral dislocation of the facets or fracture of the pedicles or facets. Accompanying fractures of spinous and transverse processes, and tearing of the posterior ligaments and adjacent muscles can add to the complexity of this severe lesion. The dislocation of the upper segment may be solely in the anteroposterior plane, or it may be complex, with additional displacement in the coronal plane with torsion around the longitudinal axis of the spine.

Treatment depends upon the type of injury. If there is no neurologic involvement and dislocation was associated with fracture of the pedicles or facets, reduction may be attempted by cautious extension with traction on the lower extremities under x-ray control without anesthesia. When dislocation has been corrected, immobilization in a plaster body cast with a spica extension to incorporate at least one thigh may be necessary for adequate support. Mobilization of the patient from the recumbent position should be accomplished slowly because displacement of fragments can occur and neurologic complications may result. When reasonable doubt exists, it is preferable to continue recumbency for 8-12 weeks until initial healing has provided mechanical stability. If closed reduction is not successful, or if extension causes neurologic symptoms, the attempt should be abandoned at once in favor of open reduction.

In complete dislocation of one or both facets, open reduction may be necessary.

F. FRACTURE OF THE SACRUM may accompany fracture of the pelvis. It may also appear as an isolated lesion as a result of direct violence. Linear fracture of the sacrum without displacement should be treated symptomatically. Strapping of the buttocks of males and the wearing of a snug girdle by females can provide some comfort during the acutely painful stage. If the fracture extends through a sacral foramen and is associated with displacement, there may be injury to one of the sacral nerves and consequent neurologic deficit. If the sacral fragment is displaced anteriorly, reduction should be attempted by means of bimanual manipulation. Great care should be exercised to prevent injury to the rectal wall by pressure of the palpating finger against a sharp spicule of underlying bone.

G. FRACTURE OF THE COCCYX is usually the result of a blow on the buttock. No specific treatment is required other than protection. Strapping the buttocks together for a few days may minimize pain. Pressure on the coccygeal region can be avoided by selecting a firm chair in which to sit or placing a support beneath the thighs to relieve pressure. The patient should be warned that pain may persist for many weeks. Fracture-dislocation can be reduced by bimanual manipulation, but recurrence of the deformity is likely. Every effort toward conservative management should be made before coccygectomy is considered for treatment of the painful unhealed or malunited fracture.

II. FRACTURES OF THE PELVIS

A. AVULSION FRACTURES OF THE PELVIS include those involving the anterior superior and anterior inferior iliac spines, a portion of the iliac crest apophysis anteriorly, and the apophysis of the ischium. The ischial apophysis may be avulsed indirectly by violent contraction of the hamstring muscles in the older child or adolescent. If displacement is minimal, prompt healing without disability is to be expected. If displacement is marked (i.e., more than 1 cm), reattachment by open operation is justifiable.

B. FRACTURE OF THE WING OF THE ILIUM Isolated fracture without involvement of the hip or sacroiliac joints most often occurs as a result of direct trauma. With minor displacement of the free fragment, soft-tissue injury is usually minimal and treatment is symptomatic. Wide displacement of the free fragment may be associated with extensive soft-tissue injury and hematoma formation. Healing may be accompanied by ossification of the hematoma with exuberant new bone formation.

C. ISOLATED FRACTURE OF THE OBTURATOR RING involving either the pubis or ischium with minimal displacement, is associated with little or no injury to the sacroiliac joints. This is also true of minor subluxation of the symphysis pubis. Initial treatment consists of bed rest for a few days followed by ambulation on crutches. A sacroiliac belt or pelvic binder may give additional comfort. As soon as discomfort disappears, unsupported weight-bearing may be permitted.

D. COMPLEX FRACTURES OF THE PELVIC RING are due either to direct violence or to force transmitted indirectly through the lower extremities. They are characterized by disruption of the pelvic ring at two points: (1) anteriorly, near the symphysis pubis, manifested either by dislocation of that joint or by fracture through the body of the pubis, by unilateral or bilateral fracture through the obturator ring, or by fracture through the acetabulum; and (2) disruption of the pelvic ring through or in the vicinity of the sacroiliac joint. The disruption can extend partially through the sacroiliac joint as a dislocation and extend into the sacrum or into the adjacent ilium as a fracture. The magnitude of displacement of the fragments may indicate the severity of soft tissue injury. These complex injuries are often associated with extensive hemorrhage into the soft tissues or injury to the bladder, urethra, or intraabdominal organs. When anterior and posterior disruptions are ipsilateral, the entire involved hemipelvis and extremity may be displaced proximally. Anterior disruption may occur on one side, and posterior disruption on the opposite side with wide opening of the pelvic ring.

When severe and complex fractures of the pelvic ring are suspected, the extent of associated injuries must be determined at once by physical and x-ray examination. Shock due to blood loss may be present. Treatment of the fracture by reduction should not be instituted until the extent of associated injuries has been determined. Treatment of some of those injuries may be more urgent than that of the fracture lesion. A careful search must be made for possible injury to bowel, bladder, ureters, and major blood vessels.

If displacement and soft tissue injury are minimal, a pelvic sling to facilitate nursing care may be all that is required. When the hemipelvis has been displaced proximally, skeletal traction on the distal end of the femur on the affected side with suspension of the extremity may permit reduction.

If the sacroiliac joint has been dislocated and the ilium is rotated posterior to the sacrum, with opening of the anterior fracture, closed reduction can be attempted. Postmanipulation maintenance of reduction is accomplished by a pelvic sling or a short bilateral thigh spica.

III. INJURIES TO THE SHOULDER GIRDLE

A. FRACTURE OF THE CLAVICLE may occur as a result of direct trauma or indirect force transmitted through the shoulder. Most fractures of the clavicle are seen in the distal half, commonly at the junction of the middle and distal thirds. About two-thirds of clavicular fractures occur in children. Birth fractures of the clavicle vary from greenstick to complete displacement and must be differentiated from congenital pseudarthrosis.

Because of relative fixation of the medial fragment and the weight of the upper extremity, the distal fragment is displaced downward, forward, and toward the midline. Anteroposterior x-rays should always be taken, but oblique projections are occasionally of more value. Although injury to the brachial plexus or subclavian vessels is not common, such complications can usually be demonstrated on physical examination.

1. Treatment

a. Without displacement Immobilization of greenstick fractures is not required in children, and healing is rapid. Complete fractures should be immobilized for 10–21 days. A figure-of-eight dressing made of sheet cotton and an elastic bandage is adequate (Fig. 17-4). In adolescents and adults, treatment is by immobilization in a sling and swathe for 4–6 weeks.

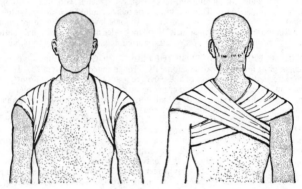

Fig. 17-4. Figure-of-eight dressing

b. With displacement In infants and small children, apply a figure-of-eight dressing of sheet cotton and elastic bandage reinforced with adhesive tape. Healing usually takes 2–4 weeks. Older children and adolescents require reduction by closed manipulation and immobilization with a figure-of-eight dressing reinforced with plaster. Reduction need not be exact, since exuberant callus formation will be partially or completely obliterated by remodeling of bone architecture incidental to the late stage of the fracture reparative process.

c. With displacement or comminution (in adults)

(1) *Closed reduction* Comminuted fractures of the clavicle with displacement can usually be managed successfully by closed reduction, although in women greater effort must be made to secure accurate realignment without deformity. Fractured surfaces of displaced fragments which cannot be reduced closed can sometimes be manipulated into apposition by seizing the main fragments percutaneously with large towel clamps. A plaster shoulder spica (Fig. 17-5) gives more secure immobilization than the figure-of-eight dressing. Immobilization must be maintained for 6–12 weeks. The patient should remain ambulatory if possible, but in some cases the position of the fragments requires bed rest initially, with skin traction applied to the abducted upper arm (Fig. 17-6) and a sandbag between the shoulders to permit the distal fragment to fall into position and to aid in maintaining re-

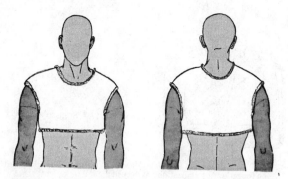

Fig. 17-5. Plaster shoulder spica for fracture of clavicle (Reproduced with permission from Dunphy JE, Way LW (Eds.) *Current Surgical Diagnosis & Treatment,* 3rd Ed. Lange 1977)

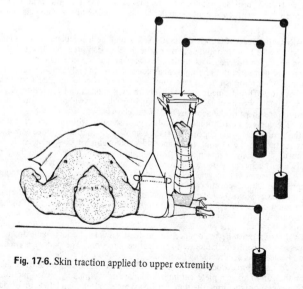

Fig. 17-6. Skin traction applied to upper extremity

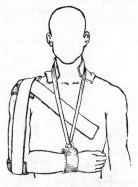

Fig. 17-7. Stimson's dressing

duction. Recumbency in this position may be necessary for 5-6 weeks or even longer until stabilization has occurred.

(2) *Open reduction* may be justifiable occasionally to prevent delay of healing where there is interposition of soft tissue.

d. Fracture of the outer third of the clavicle distal to the coracoclavicular ligaments is comparable to dislocation of the acromioclavicular joint, (see below). If the coracoclavicular ligaments are intact and the fragments are not widely displaced, immobilization in a sling and swathe is adequate. If the coracoclavicular ligaments have been lacerated and extensive displacement of the main medial fragment is present, treatment is similar to that advocated for acromioclavicular dislocation.

B. ACROMIOCLAVICULAR DISLOCATION may be incomplete or complete. A history of a blow or fall on the tip of the shoulder can often be obtained. The acromial end of the clavicle is displaced upward and backward; the shoulder falls downward and inward. Careful physical examination generally demonstrates this deformity. Anteroposterior x-rays should be taken of both shoulders with the patient erect. Displacement is more likely to be demonstrated when the patient holds a 5-8 kg weight in each hand. An axillary projection will demonstrate backward displacement of the acromial end of the clavicle.

Incomplete dislocation (subluxation) is associated with only minor tearing of the acromioclavicular ligaments, since complete dislocation requires concomitant rupture of the conoid and trapezoid components of the coracoclavicular ligament. These ligaments may be torn within their substance, or they may be avulsed with adjacent periosteum from the acromial end of the clavicle.

1. Treatment In general, reduction is indicated for both complete and incomplete acute dislocations.

a. Incomplete dislocation When displacement is minimal, initial treatment may be by sling until acute pain from movement and the weight of the upper extremity has been relieved. Stimson's dressing (Fig. 17-7) can be used for injuries of intermediate severity, where displacement is greater but not complete. This dressing must be maintained for at least 4 weeks; frequent adjustment is necessary to maintain reduction in the correct position. The patient is encouraged to sleep in a semireclining position.

b. Complete dislocation It is difficult to maintain reduction and adequate immobilization of complete acromioclavicular dislocations by closed methods. Open operation performed within the first 3 weeks after complete acromioclavicular dislocation offers the best hope of restoring anatomic alignment. If it is deferred longer, the ligaments will have partially healed with elongation, and the deformity can be expected to recur when immobilization is discontinued unless the ligaments have been reconstructed. Open reduction, should be supplemented by temporary internal stabilization of either the acromioclavicular joint or the coracoclavicular relationship even though there has not been major ligamentous damage. Torn ligaments should be repaired by suture or reconstructive technics.

  c. Old and unreduced dislocations with painful secondary osteoarthritis can be treated by resection of the segment of the clavicle between the acromio-clavicular joint and the conoid and trapezoid ligaments; when gross displacement and marked instability are present, supplementary reconstruction of the damaged coracoclavicular ligament is indicated.

C. STERNOCLAVICULAR DISLOCATION
Displacement of the sternal end of the clavicle may occur superiorly, anteriorly, or, less commonly, inferiorly. Retrosternal displacement is rare and may be complicated by injury to the great vessels. Complete dislocation can be diagnosed by physical examination. Antero-posterior and oblique x-rays confirm the diagnosis. Laminagraphy may also be helpful.

  For incomplete dislocation, a plaster shoulder spica is adequate. Open reduction with repair of the torn sternoclavicular and costoclavicular ligaments, with or without internal fixation, are normally required to maintain adequate reduction of complete dislocations. Additional protection by external immobilization should be continued at least while the internal fixation apparatus is in situ.

  Extraperiosteal resection of the medial two-thirds of the clavicle may be necessary for relief of persistently painful posttraumatic arthritis.

D. FRACTURE OF THE SCAPULA
Fracture of the neck of the scapula is most often caused by a blow on the shoulder or by a fall on the outstretched arm. The degree of fragmentation varies from a crack to extensive comminution. The main glenoid fragment may be impacted into the body fragment. The treatment of impacted or undisplaced fractures in patients 40 years or older should be directed toward the preservation of shoulder joint function, since stiffness may cause prolonged disability. In young adults especially, unstable fractures require arm traction with the arm at right angles to the trunk for about 4 weeks and protection in a sling and swathe for an additional 2–4 weeks. Open reduction is rarely required even for major displaced fragments except for those involving the articular surface when associated with dislocation of the humeral head. These fractures are likely to involve only a segment of the articular surface and may be impacted. When it is displaced, accurate reposition of the minor fragment is desirable because of the likelihood of secondary glenohumeral osteoarthritis (see below).

  Fracture of the acromion or spine of the scapula requires reduction only when the displaced fragment is apt to cause interference with abduction of the shoulder. Persistence of an acromial apophysis should not be confused with fracture.

  Fracture of the coracoid process may result from violent muscular contraction or, rarely, may be associated with anterior dislocation of the shoulder joint.

  When fracture of the body of the scapula is caused by direct violence, fractures of underlying ribs may be associated. Treatment of uncomplicated fracture should be directed toward the comfort of the patient and the preservation of shoulder joint function.

E. FRACTURE OF THE PROXIMAL HUMERUS
occurs most frequently during the sixth decade. Swelling of the shoulder region with visible or palpable deformity and restriction of motion due to pain are the most prominent clinical features. The precise diagnosis is established by x-rays prepared perpendicular to the plane of the scapula and a lateral view made at a right angle to the former, tangential to the body of the scapula. The transthoracic projection may be inadequate to

demonstrate detail because of interference by the ribs and spine. Axillary x-rays are helpful to demonstrate the direction of any displacement of the head of the humerus from the glenoid or infractions involving the articular surfaces of the shoulder joint.

The classification of proximal humeral fractures is based on the presence or absence of displacement of the articular surface of the humeral head, greater tuberosity, lesser tuberosity, and shaft.

1. Undisplaced fractures of the proximal humerus or minimally displaced fractures of the proximal humerus—with the exception of those of the anatomic neck—require little treatment beyond guarding of the shoulder by the use of a sling until discomfort is tolerable and, subsequently, judicious exercise. Restoration of firm bone continuity occurs in about 8–12 weeks.

2. Single fractures of the proximal humerus

a. Fracture of the anatomic neck   Isolated fracture of the anatomic neck of the humerus is uncommon and may be followed by avascular necrosis of the articular fragment even in the absence of displacement. Malhealing of displaced fractures may cause limitation of shoulder motion. When displacement is the determinant of open operation, primary humeral prosthetic arthroplasty is likely to provide a more satisfactory long-term result than anatomic replacement of the devascularized articular fragment.

b. Fracture of the surgical neck   The main fracture cleft is distal to the tuberosities. Minor comminution of the proximal segment can be disregarded when displacement of those fragments does not occur. Some angulation is likely to accompany any displacement in the transverse plane of the humerus. The apex of angulation is generally directed anteriorly, but its direction should be accurately determined by biplane x-rays. When angulation greater than 45° occurs in the active person, it should be corrected to avoid subsequent restriction of abduction and elevation. Lesser degrees of deformity do not require manipulation, especially when encountered in elderly persons. Impacted and minimally angulated fractures can be treated by means of a sling.

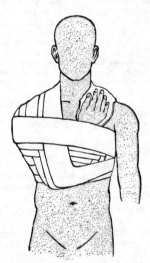

Fig. 17-8. Velpeau dressing

When displacement at the fracture site is complete, the free end of the distal fragment lies medially and anteriorly (in relation to the proximal fragment).

Neurovascular injury is not a common complication. Closed manipulation is justifiable, but, because persistent instability is a frequent complication, impaction or locking of the fragments is desirable. If reduction is stable, a Velpeau

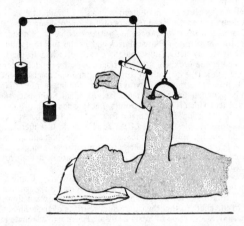

Fig. 17-9. Method of suspension of upper extremity with skeletal traction on olecranon

dressing (Fig. 17-8) provides reliable immobilization after correction of anterior angulation. Redisplacement may occur when reduction is not stable or when the arm is immobilized in abduction. Continuous traction by a Kirschner wire through the proximal ulna with the arm at right angle elevation (Fig. 17-9) is advisable when the fracture cannot be maintained in reduction by a dressing such as a Velpeau. Traction must be continued for about 4 weeks before partial healing provides stability. This closed method of traction treatment is commonly required also for comminuted fractures of the surgical neck. When comminution is not extensive, the fracture that has been adequately reduced by closed methods may be stabilized by one or two heavy Kirschner wires introduced percutaneously and obliquely in the deltoid region through the distal fragment into the head of the humerus. With the fragments fixed, the arm is then brought to the side and immobilized either by a sling and swathe or by a plaster Velpeau dressing. Open reduction and internal fixation of uncomplicated fractures of the surgical neck are not commonly required.

    c. Fracture of the greater tuberosity generally is a component of a complex injury, either comminuted fracture of the proximal humerus or anterior dislocation of the shoulder joint. Fracture of the greater tuberosity with no associated injury is apt to be undisplaced. When isolated and displaced fracture does occur, it is likely to be associated with persistent or spontaneously reduced anterior dislocation of the humeral head and longitudinal tear of the capsulotendinous cuff.

When accurate repositioning of the greater tuberosity fragment does not occur following closed reduction of the dislocated humeral head, open operation is desirable to fix anatomically the avulsed fragment and to repair any capsulo-tendinous tear.

d. Fracture of the lesser tuberosity is generally a part of comminuted fracture of the proximal humerus. Isolated fracture is rare and is due to avulsion by the subscapularis muscle. Because of the broad insertion of that muscle which extends to the adjacent humeral shaft inferiorly, displacement of the bony fragment is unlikely to be marked.

Treatment consists of immobilization in a sling for about 4 weeks.

3. Combined and displaced fracture of the proximal humerus

a. Fracture of the surgical neck and greater tuberosity   Combined and displaced fractures involving the surgical neck and greater tuberosity are unique because the persistently active subscapularis muscle attached to the intact lesser tuberosity causes the proximal articular fragment to be rotated internally in relation to the shaft. It is difficult to correct this torsional displacement by closed methods. It may be accomplished with the aid of the image intensifier by initially inserting, percutaneously and transversely, a small Steinmann pin into the proximal segment which is used to derotate that fragment and to stabilize it while completing the reduction. The two major fragments are then fixed percutaneously as described for unstable fractures of the surgical neck. If reduction of displacement at both fracture sites is not adequate, open reduction and internal fixation of the bone fragments and repair of any rotator cuff tear is indicated. This combined lesion may be complicated by anterior dislocation of the proximal head fragment from the glenoid.

b. Fracture of the surgical neck and lesser tuberosity   Combined and displaced fracture of the surgical neck and lesser tuberosity are significant because the external rotators cause the proximal fragment to be externally rotated with reference to the shaft so that the cartilaginous surface of the humeral head is directed anteriorly. Correction of torsional displacement and adequate reduction is difficult by closed methods but may be achieved by appropriate modification of the technic described for combined fracture of the surgical neck and greater tuberosity. If satisfactory reduction cannot be attained, open reduction with fixation of the bone fragments and repair of any coexisting laceration of the capsulotendinous cuff is appropriate. Posterior dislocation of the head fragment from the glenoid may complicate this combined lesion.

c. Fracture of the surgical neck and both tuberosities   This uncommon but serious lesion is generally complicated by displacement of one or all of the component fragments. Dehiscence of the tuberosities and displacement of the shaft provide a mechanism for subluxation or dislocation of the main articular fragment which may be anterior, posterior, lateral, or inferior. Shattering of the articular segment provides the opportunity for multidirectional displacement of component fragments. Extensive laceration of the rotator cuff is a part of the total lesion.

Because of comminution and displacement of component fragments of the proximal segment, satisfactory functional results are unlikely and delay of bone healing is probable after any type of closed treatment. Avascular necrosis of the articular fragment is an anticipated sequel because of its inherently jeopardized blood supply. Open operation offers the best chance for preservation of some function with tolerable discomfort. Removal of the articular segments and repair of the remaining structures cannot be expected to be as successful in the treatment of recent lesions of this type as replacement arthroplasty of the humeral head and fixation of the tuberosities to each other and to the distal shaft fragment.

A sequel of articular fractures of the proximal humerus is secondary glenohumeral osteoarthritis.

d. Separation of the epiphysis of the head of the humerus   When this injury occurs as a result of birth trauma, it is difficult to recognize because of the absence of a bony nucleus in the capital epiphysis. Even though x-ray examination is negative, the injury should be suspected when there is swelling of the shoulder region and limitation of active movements of the arm. Fracture through the epiphyseal plate may be encountered in older children. The principles of treatment are the same as for fracture of the surgical neck of the humerus. Open reduction is rarely desirable, and every effort should be made to obtain reduction by manipulation or traction.

F. DISLOCATION OF THE SHOULDER JOINT Over 95% of all cases of shoulder joint dislocation are anterior or subcoracoid. Subglenoid and posterior dislocations comprise the remainder.

1. Anterior dislocation presents the clinical appearance of flattening of the deltoid region, anterior fullness, and restriction of motion due to pain. Both anteroposterior and axillary x-rays are necessary to determine the site of the head and the presence or absence of complicating fracture which may involve either the head of the humerus or the glenoid. Anterior dislocation may be complicated by (1) injury to major nerves arising from the brachial plexus; (2) fracture of the upper extremity of the humerus, especially the head or greater tuberosity; (3) compression or avulsion of the anterior glenoid; and (4) tears of the capsulotendinous rotator cuff. The most common sequel is recurrent dislocation. Before manipulation, careful examination is necessary to determine the presence or absence of complicating nerve or vascular injury. Under general anesthesia, reduction can usually be accomplished by simple traction on the arm for a few minutes or until the head has been disengaged from the coracoid. If reduction cannot be achieved in this way, the surgeon should apply lateral traction manually to the upper arm, close to the axilla, while the assistant continues to exert axial traction on the extremity. This is a modification to Hippocrates' manipulation in which the surgeon exerts traction on the arm while the heel of his unshod foot in the axilla provides countertraction and simultaneously forces the head of the humerus laterally from beneath the acromion.

If neither of the foregoing technics proves successful, Kocher's method may be useful. This maneuver, however, must be carried out gently or spiral fracture of the humerus may result. The elbow is flexed to a right angle and the surgeon applies traction and gentle external rotation to the forearm in the axis of the humerus. The surgeon continues traction to the arm while gentle external rotation about the longitudinal axis of the humerus is applied, using the forearm flexed to a right angle at the elbow as a lever. The maneuver can be completed by shifting the elbow across the anterior chest while traction is continuously exerted and, finally, slow internal rotation of the arm until the palm of the affected side rests on the opposite shoulder.

After closed reduction of an initial dislocation the extremity is immobilized in a sling and swathe for 3 weeks before active motion is begun. If a second episode is the result of minor trauma, the lesion is considered permanent and treated accordingly.

2. Subcoracoid dislocation Uncomplicated subcoracoid dislocation can almost always be reduced by closed manipulation. With associated fracture, or when the dislocation is old, open reduction may be necessary. Even when the dislocation is old, however, closed reduction by skeletal traction should be tried before open reduction is elected.

3. Posterior dislocation is characterized by fullness beneath the spine of the scapula and by restriction of motion in external rotation. An axillary x-ray view demonstrates the position of the head of the humerus in relationship to the glenoid. This uncommon lesion may be reduced by the same combination of coaxial and transverse traction as described for anterior dislocation. Immobilization following an initial episode should be accomplished by plaster spica, with the arm in approximately 30° external rotation and the elbow flexed to a right angle.

4. Recurrent dislocation of the shoulder is almost always anterior. Various factors can influence recurrent dislocation. Avulsion of the anterior and inferior glenoid labrum or tears in the anterior capsule remove the natural buttress that gives stability to the arm with abduction and external rotation. Other lesions which impair the stability of the shoulder joint are fractures of the posterior and superior surface of the head of the humerus (or of the greater tuberosity) and longitudinal tears of the rotator cuff between the supraspinatus and subscapularis. Reduction of the acute episodic dislocation is by closed manipulation. Immobilization does not prevent subsequent dislocation, and it should be discontinued as soon as acute symptoms subside, usually within a few days.

Adequate curative treatment of recurrent dislocation of the shoulder, so that unrestricted normal use of the joint is possible, almost always requires plastic repair of the anterior capsulotendinous cuff by an operation.

Although reparative operations for recurrent dislocation of the shoulder joint may prove successful in preventing further episodes, a late sequel is secondary osteoarthritis. Complicating fractures of the articular surfaces of either the humeral head or the glenoid (or both) which cause incongruity may hasten the onset and intensify the symptoms of the complication. Other contributing factors include axillary nerve lesions with loss of deltoid muscle function and laxity of the capsulotendinous cuff with episodes of transient subluxation.

IV. FRACTURES OF THE SHAFT OF THE HUMERUS

Fracture of the shaft of the humerus is more common in adults than in children. Direct violence is accountable for the majority of such fractures, although spiral fracture of the middle third of the shaft may result from violent muscular activity such as throwing a ball. X-rays in two planes are necessary to determine the configuration of the fracture and the direction of displacement of the fragments. Documentation of torsional displacement about the longitudinal axis of the shaft of transverse and comminuted fractures requires inclusion of the shoulder and elbow in the anteroposterior view. Before initiating definitive treatment, a careful neurologic examination should be done (and recorded) to determine the status of the radial nerve. Injury to the brachial vessels is not common.

A. FRACTURE OF THE UPPER THIRD Fracture through the metaphysis proximal to the insertion of the pectoralis major is classified as fracture of the surgical neck of the humerus.

Fractures between the insertions of the pectoralis major and the deltoid commonly demonstrate adduction of the distal end of the proximal fragment, with lateral and proximal displacement of the distal fragment. Medial displacement occurs with fracture distal to the insertion of the deltoid in the middle third of the shaft.

Treatment depends upon the presence or absence of complicating neurovascular injury, the site and configuration of the fracture, and the magnitude of displacement.

In infants, skin traction for 1–2 weeks will permit sufficient callus to form so that immobilization can be maintained by a sling and swathe or a Velpeau dressing. Open reduction for the sole purpose of accurate positioning of the fragments is rarely justified in children and adolescents, since slight shortening and less than 15° of angulation will be compensated during growth. Torsional displacement, however, will not be compensated and must be corrected initially.

In the adult, an effort should be made to reduce completely displaced transverse or slightly oblique fractures by manipulation. A local anesthetic solution injected directly into the hematoma at the fracture site will provide adequate anesthesia for manipulation. To prevent recurrence of medial convex angulation and maintain proper alignment, it may be necessary to bring the distal fragment into alignment with the proximal by bringing the arm across the chest and immobilizing it with a plaster Velpeau dressing (Fig. 17-8). If the ends of the fragments cannot be approximated by manipulative methods, traction on the skin (Fig. 17-6) or skeletal traction with a wire through the olecranon (Fig. 17-9) is indicated. In young patients, the olecranon wire should be placed opposite the coronoid process to avoid injury to the epiphysis. Traction should be continued for 3–4 weeks until stabilization occurs, after which time the patient can be ambulatory with an external immobilization device.

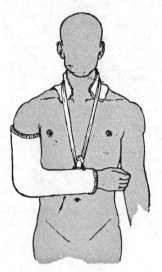

Fig. 17-10.
Caldwell's hanging cast

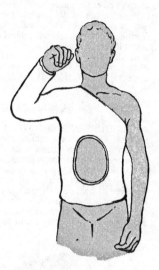

Fig. 17-11.
Plaster shoulder spica
for fracture of humerus

B. FRACTURE OF THE MIDDLE AND LOWER THIRDS Spiral, oblique, and comminuted fractures of the shaft below the insertion of the pectoralis major may be treated by Caldwell's hanging cast (Fig. 17-10) which consists of a plaster dressing from the axilla to the wrist with the elbow in 90° of flexion and the forearm in midposition. The cast is suspended from a bandage around the neck by means of a ring at the wrist. Alignment should be verified on anteroposterior and transthoracic x-rays with the patient standing. Angulation may be corrected by lengthening or shortening the suspension bandage. When lateral convex angulation cannot be corrected by adjustment of the bandage, moving the suspension ring closer to the elbow may be effective. Traction is afforded by the weight of the plaster. The patient is instructed to sleep in the semireclining position. As soon as clinical examination demonstrates stabilization (in about 6–8 weeks), the plaster may be discarded and a sling and swathe substituted.

When fracture of the shaft of the humerus is associated with other injuries which require confinement to bed, initial treatment may be by skin or skeletal traction.

Fractures of the shaft of the humerus—especially transverse fractures—may heal slowly. If stabilization has not taken place after 6-8 weeks of traction, more secure immobilization, such as with a plaster shoulder spica, (Fig. 17-11) must be considered. It may be necessary to continue immobilization for 6 months or more.

When complete loss of radial nerve function is apparent immediately after injury, open operation is indicated to determine the type of nerve lesion or to remove impinging bone fragments. Internal fixation of the fragments can be accomplished at the same time. If partial function of the radial nerve is retained, exploration can be deferred since spontaneous recovery sometimes occurs and may be complete by the time the fracture has healed. Open reduction of closed fractures is indicated also if arterial circulation has been interrupted or (in the adult) if adequate apposition of major fragments cannot be obtained by closed methods, as is likely to be the case with transverse fractures near the middle third of the shaft. When 4-5 months of treatment by closed methods have not resulted in clinical or x-ray evidence of healing, operative treatment should be considered.

V. INJURIES TO THE ELBOW REGION

A. FRACTURE OF THE DISTAL HUMERUS is most often caused by indirect violence. Therefore, the configuration of the fracture cleft and the direction of displacement of the fragments are likely to be typical. Injuries of major vessels and nerves and elbow joint dislocation are apt to be present.

Clinical findings consist of pain, swelling, and restriction of motion. Minor deformity may not be apparent because swelling usually obliterates landmarks. The type of fracture is determined by x-ray examination. Especially in children, it is advisable to obtain films of the opposite elbow for comparison.

Examination for peripheral nerve and vascular injury must be made and all findings carefully recorded before treatment is instituted.

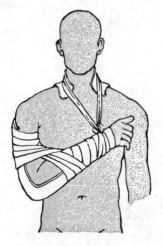

Fig. 17-12.
Posterior plaster splint
for supracondylar fracture

1. Supracondylar fracture of the humerus occurs proximal to the olecranon fossa; transcondylar (diacondylar) fracture occurs more distally and extends into the olecranon fossa. Neither fracture extends to the articular surface of the humerus. Treatment is the same for both types.

Supracondylar fractures are observed more commonly in children and adolescents, and they may extend into the epiphyseal plates of the capitellum and trochlea. Transcondylar fracture is very rare in children.

The direction of displacement of the distal fragment from the midcoronal plane of the arm serves to differentiate the 'extension' from the less common 'flexion' type. This differentiation has important implications for treatment.

a. Extension-type fracture In the extension type of supracondylar fracture, the usual direction of displacement of the main distal fragment is posterior and proximal. The distal fragment may also be displaced laterally and, less frequently, medially. The direction of these displacements is identified easily on biplane x-ray films. Internal torsional displacement, however, is more difficult to recognize; and unless torsional displacement is reduced, relative cubitus varus with loss of carrying angle will persist.

Displaced supracondylar fractures are surgical emergencies. Immediate treatment is required to avoid occlusion of the brachial artery and to prevent or to avoid further peripheral nerve injury. If hemorrhage and edema prevent complete reduction of the fracture at the first attempt, a second manipulation will be required after swelling has regressed.

(1) *Manipulative reduction* Minor angular displacements (tilting) may be reduced by gentle forced flexion of the elbow under local or general anesthesia, followed by immobilization in a posterior plaster splint in 45° of flexion (Fig. 17-12). If displacement is marked but normal radial pulsation indicates that circulation is not impaired, closed manipulation under general anesthesia should be done as soon as possible. If radial pulses are absent or weak on initial examination and do not improve with manipulation, traction is indicated (see below). Capillary flush in the nail beds cannot be relied on as the sole indication of competency of deep circulation. After reduction and casting the patient should be placed at bed rest, preferably in a hospital, with the elbow elevated on a pillow and the dressing arranged so that the radial pulse is accessible for frequent observation. Swelling can be expected to increase for 24-72 hours. During this critical period, continued observation is necessary so that any circulatory embarrassment which may lead to Volkmann's ischemic contracture can be identified at once. The circular bandage must be adjusted frequently to compensate for initial increase and subsequent decrease of swelling. If during manipulation it was necessary to extend the elbow beyond 45° to restore radial pulses, the joint should be flexed to the optimal angle as swelling subsides to prevent loss of the reduction.

In children, stabilization will take place in 4-5 weeks, after which time the plaster splint may be discarded and a sling worn for another 2 weeks before active motion is permitted. In adults, healing is less rapid and immobilization must be continued for 8-12 weeks or even longer before active exercise is permitted.

(2) *Traction and immobilization* In certain instances, supracondylar fractures of the humerus with posterior displacement of the distal fragment should be treated by traction (Fig. 17-13): (a) If comminution is marked and stability cannot be obtained by flexion of the elbow, traction is indicated until the fragments have stabilized. (b) If two or three attempts at manipulative reduction have been unsuccessful, continuous traction under x-ray control for 1-2 days is justifiable before further manipulation. (c) If the radial pulse is absent or weak when the patient is examined initially and does not improve with manipulation, traction may be necessary to pre-

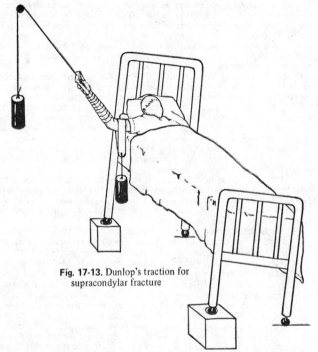

Fig. 17-13. Dunlop's traction for supracondylar fracture

vent displacement of the fracture and further embarrassment of circulation. During the early phase of treatment by continuous traction, flexion of the elbow beyond 90° should be avoided since this may jeopardize circulation.

b. Flexion-type fracture of the humerus is characterized by anterior and sometimes also torsional and lateral displacement of the main distal fragment. Treatment is by closed manipulation. A posterior plaster splint is then applied from the axillary fold to the level of the wrist, with the forearm in supination and the elbow in full extension. Elevation is advisable for at least 24 hours or until soft tissue swelling has reached the maximum, after which time the patient may be ambulatory. Immobilization is then continued for 4-6 weeks. When satisfactory reduction cannot be accomplished by closed manipulation, treatment should be by traction with the elbow in full extension until the fragments become stabilized.

2. Separation of the distal humeral epiphyses is an uncommon variation of supracondylar fracture, with or without appreciable displacement. Sprains of the elbow do not commonly occur in children; injury more often involves the distal humeral epiphyses. X-ray comparison of the injured elbow with the uninjured elbow may show no deviation, but careful physical examination may demonstrate posterior tenderness over the lower epiphyses and also swelling. This combination of swelling and tenderness should suggest epiphyseal separation, and warrants protection from further injury by means of a sling worn for about 3 weeks.

The direction of displacement is determined by careful clinical and radiographic examinations. Depending upon the direction of angulation of the osseous nuclei of the capitellum and trochlea (as demonstrated in the lateral x-ray), immobilization is as described for supracondylar fractures.

3. Intercondylar fracture of the humerus is classically described as being of the T or Y type (or both), according to the configuration of the fracture cleft observed on an anteroposterior x-ray. This fracture is usually seen in adults, commonly as the result of a blow over the posterior aspect of the flexed elbow. Open fracture and other injuries to the soft tissues are frequently present. The fracture often extends into the trochlear surface of the elbow joint, and unless the articular surfaces of the distal humerus can be accurately repositioned, restriction of joint motion, pain, instability, and deformity can be expected.

a. Closed reduction If the fragments are not widely displaced, closed reduction may be successful. Since comminution is always present, stabilization is difficult to achieve and maintain by manipulation and external immobilization.

(1) *Anterior displacement* may be treated first by a combination of continuous skin traction with the elbow in full extension and closed manipulation of the main fragments. If adequate positioning can be achieved in this manner, traction is continued until stabilization occurs. The extremity may then be immobilized in a tubular plaster cast.

(2) Significant *posterior displacement* requires overhead skeletal traction by means of a Kirschner wire inserted through the olecranon. It may be necessary to apply a swathe around the arm or body for simultaneous transverse traction (Fig. 17-14).

b. Open reduction may be indicated if adequate positioning cannot be obtained by closed methods. A requirement for acceptable results of open reduction and internal fixation is that the fragments be sufficiently large so that they can be fixed to one another. Comminution may be so extensive that satisfactory stabilization cannot be accomplished by current technics of internal fixation. Under such circumstances, it is better either to abandon open operation and to accept the imperfect results of closed treatment, or, if the proximal radius and ulna are intact, to plan subsequent replacement arthroplasty by means of a custom-made lower humeral prosthesis. Total elbow replacement technics are currently in the developmental stage.

4. Fracture of the lateral condyle of the humerus The three major varieties of this fracture are: (a) fracture of a portion of the capitellum in the coronal plane of the humerus, with or without extension into the trochlea (seen only in adults); (b) isolated fracture of the lateral condyle without extension into the trochlea; and (c) separation of the capitellar epiphysis (in children).

a. Fracture of the capitellum This is characterized by proximal displacement of the anterior detached fragment, and probably occurs as one component of a spontaneously reduced incomplete dislocation of the elbow joint. The lesion is most clearly demonstrated on lateral x-rays. Closed reduction should be attempted by forcing the elbow into acute flexion. After reduction, the extremity is immobilized in a posterior plaster splint with the elbow in full flexion to prevent displacement of the small distal fragment.

When accurate reduction cannot be accomplished by closed technics, open operation may be desirable to avoid subsequent restriction of elbow movement. If the small distal fragment retains sufficient soft tissue attachment to assure adequate blood supply, it may be temporarily fixed to the main fragment in anatomic position by a Kirschner wire. If the articular fragment lacks significant soft-tissue bonds, removal is recommended since avascular necrosis is likely to follow.

b. Isolated complete fracture of the lateral condyle without extension into the trochlea is uncommon and is not usually associated with major displacement of the detached fragment. The extremity should be supported by a sling. If tense

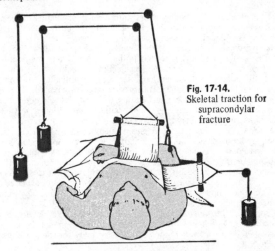

Fig. 17-14.
Skeletal traction for supracondylar fracture

hemarthrosis is present, aspiration may minimize pain. Guarded active motions of the elbow should be initiated as soon as pain subsides. Fracture which involves the entire capitellum and extends into the trochlea is discussed below.

c. Separation of the capitellar epiphysis Fracture of the lateral condyle of the humerus in children is essentially separation of the capitellar epiphysis, even though the fracture may extend into the metaphysis and the trochlear epiphysis. If the center of ossification of the capitellum is small, minor displacement may be missed on initial examination; further displacement will then result from unguarded use. The fact that a part of the extensor muscles originates on the fragment is an important factor in displacement.

(1) *Closed reduction* Minor displacement may be treated by manipulative reduction and external immobilization in a posterior plaster splint which extends from the posterior axillary fold to the level of the heads of the metacarpals. X-rays are taken at least twice a week for the first 3 weeks to determine whether displacement has occurred.

(2) *Open reduction* When anatomic reduction cannot be achieved by one or two manipulations, open reduction is indicated.

d. Avulsion of the medial epicondylar apophysis in children may occur without dislocation of the elbow. Minor displacement causing localized tenderness and swelling over the medial aspect of the elbow can be treated by immobilization in a sling and swathe for a few days. More extensive injury should be suspected if tenderness and swelling are diffuse. When separation is greater than 1–2 mm, treatment is similar to that for dislocation of the elbow associated with separation of the apophysis.

B. FRACTURE OF THE PROXIMAL ULNA Common fractures of the proximal ulna include fracture of the olecranon and fracture of the coronoid process. Fracture of the coronoid process is a complication of posterior dislocation of the elbow joint, and is discussed below.

Fracture of the olecranon which occurs as the result of indirect violence (e.g., forced flexion of the forearm against the actively contracted triceps muscle) is typically transverse or slightly oblique. Fracture due to direct violence is usually comminuted and associated with other fracture or anterior dislocation of the joint. Since the major fracture cleft extends into the elbow joint, treatment should be directed toward restoration of anatomic position to afford maximal recovery of range of motion and functional competency of the triceps.

The method of **treatment** depends upon the degree of displacement and the extent of comminution. Minimal displacement (1-2 mm) can be treated by closed manipulation with the elbow in full extension, assisted by digital pressure over the proximal fragment, and immobilization in a volar plaster splint which extends from the anterior axillary fold to the wrist. X-rays should be taken twice weekly for 2 weeks after reduction to determine whether reduction has been maintained. Immobilization must be continued for at least 6 weeks before active flexion exercises are begun.

Open reduction and internal fixation are indicated if closed methods are not successful in approximating displaced fragments and restoring congruity to articular surfaces.

C. FRACTURE OF THE PROXIMAL RADIUS

1. Fracture of the head and neck of the radius may occur in adults as an isolated injury uncomplicated by dislocation of the elbow or the superior radio-ulnar joint. This fracture is caused by indirect violence, such as a fall on the out-stretched hand, when the radial head is driven against the capitellum. Care must be taken to obtain true anteroposterior and lateral x-rays of the proximal radius as well as of the elbow joint, since minor lesions may be obscured by a change from midposition to full supination during exposure of the films.

a. Conservative measures Fissure fractures and those with minimal displacement can be treated symptomatically, with evacuation of tense hemarthrosis by aspiration to minimize pain. The extremity may be supported by a sling or immobilized in a posterior plaster splint with the elbow in 90° of flexion. Active exercises of the elbow are to be encouraged within a few days. Recovery of function is slow, and slight restriction of motion (especially extension) may persist.

b. Surgical treatment When the fracture involves the articular surface and is comminuted, or when displacement is greater than 1-2 mm, excision of the entire head of the radius is generally recommended. However, simple removal of a minor fragment of the head which comprises less than a quarter of the articular surface is compatible with recovery of satisfactory elbow function.

2. Fracture of the upper epiphysis of the radius in a child is not a true epiphyseal separation since the fracture cleft commonly extends into the neck of the bone. Because the articular surface of the proximal fragment remains intact, the prominent features of displacement are angulation and impaction. Wide displacement of the minor proximal fragment may mean that the elbow joint was dislocated but has reduced spontaneously since the injury.

a. Closed reduction Every effort should be made to reduce these fractures by closed manipulation. Several x-rays taken with the forearm in various degrees of rotation should be examined so that the position can be selected which is best suited for digital pressure on the proximal fragment. Anteroposterior and lateral x-rays with the elbow in flexion are then taken; if angulation has been reduced to less than 45°, the end result is likely to be satisfactory.

b. Open reduction If closed reduction is not successful, open reduction and repositioning under direct vision is indicated even in the child.

D. SUBLUXATION AND DISLOCATION OF THE ELBOW JOINT

1. Subluxation of the head of the radius This injury occurs most frequently in infants between the ages of 18 months and 4 years, usually when the child is suddenly lifted by the hand with the forearm in pronation. Because of comparative laxity of the interosseous membrane and other supporting ligamentous structures, the direction of displacement of the radial head is distal in the direction of the longitudinal axis of the shaft. It has been suggested that this permits the proximal part of the annular ligament to become infolded between the radial head and the capitellum. In unreduced subluxations, in addition to tenderness about the radial head and restriction of supination, swelling and tenderness may be present in the region of the ulnar head at the level of the inferior radioulnar joint. The infant holds the forearm semiflexed and pronated. If spontaneous reduction has occurred, diagnosis is dependent upon finding slightly restricted supination associated with discomfort. X-rays are generally not helpful, but in the older child the distance between the radial head and the capitellum may be increased in comparison to the uninjured side.

Reduction by forced supination of the forearm can usually be accomplished easily without anesthesia. The extremity should be protected in a sling for 1 week. Rarely, in an older child, closed manipulation may be unsuccessful and open release of the annular ligament may be necessary.

2. Dislocation of the head of the radius Isolated dislocation of the radius at the elbow is a rare lesion which implies dislocation of the proximal radioulnar and radiohumeral joints without fracture. This lesion, which occurs in children older than 5 years or occasionally in adults, should be differentiated from subluxation of the head of the radius. To cause dislocation, the injury must be sufficiently severe to disrupt the capsulotendinous support—especially the annular ligament—of the proximal radius. The direction of displacement of the radial head is usually anterior or lateral, but it may be posterior.

Reduction can usually be accomplished by forced supination of the forearm under anesthesia. The extremity should be immobilized for 3-4 weeks with the elbow in flexion and the forearm in supination.

3. Dislocation of the elbow joint without fracture is almost always posterior. It may be encountered at any age but is most common in children. Complete backward dislocation of the ulna and radius implies extensive tearing of the capsuloligamentous structures and injury to the region of insertion of the brachialis muscle. The coronoid process of the ulna is usually displaced posteriorly and proximally into the olecranon fossa, but it may be displaced laterally or medially. Biplane x-rays of the highest quality are necessary to determine that no fracture is associated.

Peripheral nerve function must be carefully assessed before definitive treatment is instituted. The ulnar nerve is most likely to be injured.

In recent dislocations, closed reduction can be achieved (under general anesthesia) by axial traction on the forearm with the elbow in the position of deformity. Hyperextension is not necessary. Lateral or medial dislocation can be corrected during traction. As soon as proximal displacement is corrected, the elbow should be brought into 90° of flexion and a posterior plaster splint applied which reaches from the posterior axillary fold to the wrist. Active motion is permitted after 3 weeks.

Closed reduction should be attempted even if unreduced dislocation has persisted for 2 months following the injury.

Myositis ossificans of the brachialis anticus muscle is a rare sequel.

E. FRACTURE-DISLOCATION OF THE ELBOW JOINT
Dislocation of the elbow is frequently associated with fracture. Some fractures are insignificant and require no specific treatment; others demand specialized care.

1. Fracture of the coronoid process of the ulna is the most frequent complication of posterior dislocation of the elbow joint. Treatment is the same as for uncomplicated posterior dislocation of the elbow joint (see above).

2. Fracture of the head of the radius with posterior dislocation of the elbow joint This injury is treated as 2 separate lesions. The severity of comminution and the magnitude of displacement of the radial head fragments are first determined by x-ray. If comminution has occurred or the fragments are widely displaced, the dislocation is reduced by closed manipulation; the head of the radius is then excised.

If fracture of the head of the radius is not comminuted and the fragments are not widely displaced, treatment is as for uncomplicated posterior dislocation of the elbow joint.

3. Fracture of the olecranon with anterior dislocation of the elbow joint This very unstable injury usually occurs from a blow on the dorsum of the flexed forearm. Fracture through the olecranon permits the distal fragment of the ulna and the proximal radius to be displaced anterior to the humerus, and may cause extensive tearing of the capsuloligamentous structures around the elbow joint. The dislocation can be reduced by bringing the elbow into full extension, but anatomic reduction of the olecranon fracture by closed manipulation is not likely to be successful and immediate open reduction is usually indicated. Recovery of function is likely to be delayed and incomplete.

4. Fracture of the medial epicondylar apophysis with dislocation of the elbow joint Dislocation of the elbow joint in children may be complicated by avulsion of the medial epicondylar apophysis. The direction of dislocation may have been lateral, posterior, or posterolateral. Physical and x-ray examination may not demonstrate the extent of displacement at the time of injury since partial reduction may have occurred spontaneously. X-rays of the uninjured elbow in similar projections are desirable to compare the exact locations of the 2 apophyses. The free fragment is normally displaced downward by the action of the flexor muscles. If partial spontaneous reduction of the elbow dislocation has occurred, the detached apophysis may be found incarcerated within the elbow joint between the articular surfaces of the trochlea and the olecranon. This may happen also during manual reduction. Ulnar nerve function must be evaluated before definitive treatment is given.

Dislocation of the elbow joint may be reduced by closed manipulation, but accurate repositioning of a widely separated apophysis cannot be achieved by closed methods. Opinion differs concerning the necessity for anatomic reduction of the apophysis if it is not incarcerated within the elbow joint. Some authorities maintain that fibrous healing of the apophysis causes no disability; others anticipate weakness of grasp or subsequent pain as the result of development of a pseudarthrosis between the apophysis and the medial condyle. Exuberant bone formation around the apophysis may cause tardy ulnar paralysis. If it is elected not to reduce displacement of an apophysis outside the elbow joint, the extremity should be immobilized at a right angle for 3 weeks in a tubular plaster cast before active motion is permitted.

If the ulnar nerve has been injured, or if the apophysis cannot be displaced from the elbow joint by closed manipulation, open reduction is advisable.

5. Fracture of the lateral condyle with lateral dislocation of the elbow joint must be differentiated from fracture of the lateral condyle with or without posterior dislocation of the joint (see below). Neither lesion is common. A complicating feature of fracture of the lateral condyle with lateral dislocation is inclusion not only of the entire capitellum but also extension of the fracture cleft into the trochlea. This creates an unstable mechanism which cannot be reliably immobilized in either flexion or extension even though closed reduction has been successful. If closed methods of treatment are not adequate, open reduction is recommended.

6. Fracture of the lateral condyle with posterior dislocation of the elbow joint Treatment should be divided into 2 phases. The dislocation should be reduced first by closed manipulation. This maneuver may also simultaneously accomplish adequate reduction of the condylar fracture. If the condylar fragment cannot be adequately repositioned by closed manipulation, open reduction and internal fixation are justifiable to assure anatomic restoration of the articular surfaces.

VI. FRACTURES OF THE SHAFTS OF THE RADIUS AND ULNA

A. GENERAL CONSIDERATIONS

1. Causative injury Spiral and oblique fractures are likely to be caused by indirect injury. Greenstick, transverse, and comminuted fractures are commonly the result of direct injury.

2. Radiography

a. In addition to anteroposterior and lateral films of the entire forearm, including the elbow and wrist joints, oblique views are often desirable.

b. The lateral projection is usually taken with the forearm in midposition (between complete pronation and supination).

c. For the anteroposterior projection, care must be taken to prevent any change in relative supination of the radius; if this happens, the distal radius will be the same in both views and fracture may not be demonstrated.

d. Especially in children, films of the uninjured forearm are desirable for comparison of epiphyses and for future reference if growth is impaired.

3. Anatomic peculiarities Both the radius and the ulna have biplane curves which permit 180° of rotation in the forearm. If the curves are not preserved by reduction, full rotatory motion of the forearm may not be recovered or derangement of the radioulnar joints may follow.

Torsional displacement by muscle activity has important implications for manipulative treatment of certain fractures of the radial shaft. The direction of torsional displacement of the distal fragment following fracture of the shaft is influenced by the location of the lesion in reference to muscle insertion. If the fracture is in the upper third (above the insertion of the pronator teres), the proximal fragment will be drawn into relative supination by the biceps and supinator and the distal fragment into pronation by the pronator teres and pronator quadratus. The relative position in torsion of the proximal fragment may be determined by comparing the position of the bicipital tubercle of an anteroposterior film with similar projections of the uninjured arm taken in varying degrees of forearm rotation. In fractures below the middle of the radius (below the insertion of the pronator teres), the proximal fragment characteristically remains in midposition and the distal fragment is pronated; this is due to the antagonistic action of the pronator teres on the biceps and supinator.

4. Closed reduction and splinting With fracture and displacement of the shaft of either the radius or the ulna, injury of the proximal or distal radioulnar joints should always be suspected. The presence of swelling and tenderness around the joint may aid in localization of an occult injury when x-rays are not helpful.

In both adults and children, closed reduction of uncomplicated fractures of the radius and ulna should be attempted. The type of manipulative maneuver depends upon the configuration and location of the fracture and the age of the patient. The position of immobilization of the elbow, forearm, and wrist depends upon the location of the fracture and its inherent stability.

B. FRACTURE OF THE SHAFT OF THE ULNA

Isolated fracture of the shaft of the proximal third of the ulna (above the insertion of the pronator teres) with displacement is often associated with dislocation of the head of the radius. Reduction of an undislocated transverse fracture may be achieved by axial traction followed by digital pressure to correct displacement in the transverse plane. With the patient supine, the hand is suspended overhead and countertraction is provided by a sling around the arm above the flexed elbow. After the fragments are distracted, transverse displacement is corrected by digital pressure. With the elbow at a right angle and the forearm in midposition, the extremity is then immobilized in a tubular plaster cast extending from the axilla to the metacarpophalangeal joints. During the first month, weekly examination by x-ray is necessary to determine whether displacement has occurred. Immobilization must be maintained until bone continuity is restored (usually in 8-12 weeks).

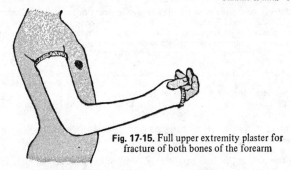

Fig. 17-15. Full upper extremity plaster for fracture of both bones of the forearm

Fracture of the shaft of the ulna distal to the insertion of the pronator teres is apt to be complicated by angulation. The proximal end of the distal fragment is displaced toward the radius by the pronator quadratus muscle. Reduction can be achieved by the maneuver described above. To prevent recurrent displacement of the distal fragment, the plaster cast must be carefully molded so as to force the mass of the forearm musculature between the radius and ulna in the antero-posterior plane. Care should be taken to avoid pressure over the subcutaneous surfaces of the radius and ulna around the wrist. Healing is slow, and frequent radiologic examination is necessary to make certain that displacement has not occurred. Stabilization by bone healing may require more than 4 months of im-mobilization.

An oblique fracture cleft creates an unstable mechanism with a tendency toward displacement, and immobilization in a tubular plaster is not reliable. Open reduction and rigid internal fixation with bone plates or an intramedullary rod are indicated.

Open reduction of uncomplicated fracture of the ulna in children is rarely justifiable because accurate reduction is not imperative; in children under 12 years of age an angular deformity as great as 15° may be corrected by growth. Torsional displacement of uncomplicated fractures of the shaft is not likely to occur. Deformity caused by transverse displacement will be corrected by growth and remodeling.

C. FRACTURE OF THE SHAFT OF THE RADIUS Isolated closed fracture of the shaft of the radius can be caused by direct or indirect violence; open fracture usually results from penetrating injury. Closed fracture with displacement is usu-ally associated with other injury (e.g., fracture of the ulna or dislocation of the distal radioulnar joint). X-rays may not reveal dislocation, but localized tender-ness and swelling suggest injury to the distal radioulnar joint.

If the fracture is proximal to the insertion of the pronator teres, closed re-duction is indicated. The extremity should then be immobilized in a tubular plaster cast which extends from the axilla to the metacarpophalangeal joints, with the elbow at a right angle and the forearm in full supination (Fig. 17-15).

If the fracture is distal to the insertion of the pronator teres, manipulation and immobilization are as described above except that the forearm should be in midrotation rather than full supination. Since injury to the distal radioulnar joint is apt to be associated with fracture of the radial shaft below the insertion of the pronator teres, weekly anteroposterior and lateral x-ray projections should be taken during the first month to determine the exact status of reduction.

If the configuration of the fracture cleft is transverse rather than oblique, displacement is less apt to take place following anatomic reduction. In the adult, if stability cannot be achieved or if reduction does not approach the anatomic, open reduction and internal fixation are recommended since deformity as a result of displacement of fragments is likely to cause limitation of forearm and hand movements. Children under 12 years of age are likely to recover function provided that torsional displacement has been corrected and angulation does not exceed 15°. Especially if it is convex anteriorly, angulation greater than 15° should be corrected in children even though open reduction is required.

In adults, a snug plaster should be maintained for 8-12 weeks or even longer, since healing may be slow. Healing is rapid in children even though reduction is not anatomic; open reduction to promote bone healing in children is not necessary.

D. FRACTURE OF THE SHAFTS OF BOTH BONES The management of fractures of the shafts of both bones of the forearm is essentially a combination of those technics which have been described for the individual bones. If both bones are fractured at the same time, dislocation of either radioulnar joint is not likely to occur. If the configuration of the fracture cleft is approximately transverse, stability can be attained by closed methods provided reduction is anatomic or nearly so. Oblique or comminuted fractures are unstable.

Treatment depends in part upon the degree of displacement, the severity of comminution, and the age of the patient.

1. Without displacement In adults, fracture of the shaft of the radius and ulna without displacement can be treated by immobilization in a tubular plaster cast extending from the axilla to the metacarpophalangeal joints with the elbow at a right angle and the forearm in supination (fractures of the upper third) or midposition (fractures of the mid and lower thirds). Immobilization for 8-12 weeks is generally sufficient for restoration of bone continuity in children; immobilization for a longer time is necessary for adults. To avoid late angulation or refracture, the elbow should be included in the plaster until the callus is well mineralized.

2. Greenstick fractures of both bones of the forearm are common in children. With fractures of the lower third in children under 12 years of age, if angulation is greater than 15° or if the apex is directed anteriorly, deformity should be corrected and the extremity immobilized in a tubular plaster cast extending from the axilla to the bases of the fingers, the elbow at a right angle, the forearm in pronation, and the wrist in the neutral position. Reduction is maintained by snug anteroposterior molding of the plaster over the distal third of the forearm rather than placing the wrist in volar flexion.

Greenstick fracture of both bones proximal to the distal third of the shaft can cause a tendency toward increased angular deformity if angulation alone is corrected without completion of the fracture. It is recommended that the fracture be completed by sharply reversing the direction of angulation until a palpable 'snap' indicates that intact fibers of bone and periosteum on the convex surface have ruptured. The extremity is then immobilized in a plaster cast similar to that used for lower third fractures, with the forearm in semisupination.

3. With displacement Although it is not always possible to correct displaced fractures of both bones of the forearm by closed methods, an attempt should be made to do so both in adults and in children if x-ray studies show a configuration whereby stabilization can be accomplished without operation. Manipulative reduction is recommended if the patient is treated soon after injury and overriding is less than 1 cm. It is essential that good apposition of the fragments of each bone be obtained. Once adequate reduction has been achieved, and while traction is maintained, a padded tubular plaster cast is applied from the bases of the fingers to the axilla.

If treatment is delayed until hemorrhage and swelling have caused induration by infiltration of the soft tissues, or if overriding is more than 1 cm, sustained traction for 2-3 hours will probably be necessary to overcome shortening.

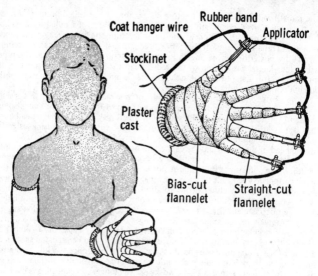

Fig. 17-16. Banjo splint and skin traction for fracture
of the forearm in children (Blount)

Traction on the skin with countertraction on soft tissues is hazardous in these circumstances because of the possibility of decubiti or vascular injury. Skeletal traction is indicated. When correction of the overriding is demonstrated by x-ray, the fragments are manipulated into position under local or general anesthesia. A plaster cast with wires incorporated is then applied and the tension bows maintained to keep the wires taut.

Persistent overriding without angulation in children is not a problem since 0.5 cm of shortening may be corrected by growth. If overriding of more than 0.5 cm is demonstrated, continuous skin traction upon the fingers with elastic bands attached to a banjo loop incorporated into the tubular plaster is indicated (Fig. 17-16).

In adults, if accurate apposition of fragments or stability cannot be achieved in fractures of both bones, open reduction and internal fixation are recommended provided that experienced personnel and adequate equipment are available. Persistent displacement of the fragments of one or both bones may be associated with delay of healing, restriction of forearm movements, derangement of the radioulnar joints, and deformity. In those fractures in which open reduction is justifiable in the adult, rigid internal fixation is indicated; technical pitfalls to be avoided are the use of a single wire loop or transfixation screw, a short bone plate attached with unicortical screws, or small intramedullary wires. Even though excellent stability is achieved at operation with internal devices, the extremity should be protected by external fixation until bone healing is well under way.

E. FRACTURE-DISLOCATIONS OF THE RADIUS AND ULNA

1. Fracture of the ulna with dislocation of the radial head (Monteggia's fracture) Fracture of the ulna, especially when it occurs near the junction of the middle and upper thirds of the shaft, may be complicated by dislocation of the radial head. This unstable fracture-dislocation, the so-called Monteggia fracture, is categorized commonly under three types. When the radial head is dislocated anteriorly, angulation at the ulnar fracture site is convex in the same direction (type I). In type II, posterior dislocation of the radial head is accompanied by posterior convex angulation at the fracture site of the ulna. The type III lesion—lateral dislocation of the radial head with fracture of the ulna in its proximal third, distal to the coronoid process—is rare. All three types occur both in children and in adults.

a. Anterior dislocation of the head of the radius   Although this lesion can be caused by direct violence upon the dorsum of the forearm, it may also be caused by forced pronation. The annular ligament may be torn, or the head may be displaced distally from beneath the annular ligament without causing a significant tear. The injured ligament may be interposed between the articular surface of the head of the radius and the capitellum of the humerus or the adjacent ulna.

Adequate reduction can usually be achieved by closed manipulation in children and sometimes in adults. A posterior plaster splint is applied from the axillary fold to the heads of the metacarpals with the elbow in 110-130° of flexion and the forearm either in midrotation or slight supination. If reduction is satisfactory, the extremity is elevated and observed frequently for signs of circulatory embarrassment for at least 72 hours. Bandages must be adjusted at appropriate intervals to accommodate for changes of soft-tissue swelling which may embarrass circulation soon after reduction and later may cause displacement of the splint and loss of reduction. X-ray examination should be repeated as soon as the dressings are applied, on the third day, and at least once weekly during the first month. Immobilization is continued until bone continuity of the ulna is restored; this usually requires 10-12 weeks or even longer, since healing is likely to be slow. Acute flexion of the elbow in plaster should not be decreased before the eighth week.

b. Posterior dislocation of the head of the radius   This lesion is caused by direct violence to the volar surface of the forearm. Treatment is by closed reduction. Anteroposterior and lateral x-rays are then taken, and a tubular plaster cast or stout posterior plaster splint is applied from the metacarpal heads to the axilla with the elbow in full extension and the forearm in midposition. Careful postreduction observation as for anterior dislocation (see above) is essential.

c. Open reduction   If accurate reduction of the fracture and the dislocation cannot be achieved by closed methods, open reduction is indicated. Plaster immobilization is indicated until bone healing is well under way.

2. Fracture of the shaft of the radius with dislocation of the ulnar head   In fracture of the shaft of the radius near the junction of the middle and lower thirds with dislocation of the head of the ulna (Dupuytren's fracture, Galeazzi's fracture), the apex of major angulation is usually directed anteriorly while the ulnar head lies volar to the distal end of the radius. (Convex dorsal angulation with the ulnar head posterior to the lower end of the radius is rare.)

a. Closed reduction   Anatomic alignment is difficult to obtain by closed manipulation and difficult to maintain in plaster, but these technics should be tried before open reduction is used. After reduction, anteroposterior and lateral x-rays should be prepared before application of the cast. If reduction is adequate, a tubular plaster cast is applied from the axilla to the knuckles with the elbow at a right angle, the forearm in pronation, and the wrist in neutral position. Weekly x-ray examination is indicated during the first month. Immobilization in a snug tubular plaster cast is continued until healing of the radius is complete.

Immobilization of the rare posterior type is with the forearm in supination.

b. Open reduction   If anatomic reduction cannot be achieved by closed methods, open reduction of recent fracture of the radius is the recommended method of treatment.

VII. INJURIES OF THE WRIST REGION

A. SPRAINS OF THE WRIST Isolated severe sprain of the ligaments of the wrist joint is not common, and the diagnosis of wrist sprain should not be made until other lesions, e.g., injury to the lower radial epiphysis (in children) and carpal fractures and dislocations (in adults), have been ruled out. If symptoms persist for more than 2 weeks, and especially if pain and swelling are present, x-ray examination should be repeated.

Treatment may be by immobilization with a volar splint extending from the palmar flexion crease to the elbow. The splint should be attached with elastic bandages so that it can be removed at least 3 times daily for gentle active exercise and warm soaks.

B. COLLES' FRACTURE Abraham Colles described the fracture that bears his name as an impacted fracture of the radius 4 cm above the wrist joint. Modern usage has extended the term Colles' fracture to include a variety of complete fractures of the distal radius characterized by convex volar angulation and by varying degrees of dorsal displacement of the distal fragment.

The fracture is commonly caused by a fall with the hand outstretched, the wrist in dorsiflexion, and the forearm in pronation, so that the force is applied to the palmar surface of the hand. Colles' fracture is most common in middle life and old age.

The fracture cleft may be transverse or oblique, and it extends across the distal radius. It may be comminuted, extending into the radiocarpal joint. Displacement is often minimal, with dorsal impaction caused by tilting of the distal fragment and volar convex angulation. As displacement becomes more marked, dorsal and radial tilt of the distal fragment causes increased angulation and torsional displacement in supination of the distal fragment. The normal volar and ulnar inclination of the carpal articular surface of the radius is reduced or reversed.

Avulsion of the styloid process is the usual injury to the distal ulna. Extension of the fracture cleft into the ulnar notch may injure the distal radioulnar articulation. The carpus is displaced with the distal fragment of the radius. Marked displacement at the fracture site causes dislocation of the distal radioulnar and ulnocarpal articulations, and tearing of the triangular fibrocartilage, both radioulnar ligaments, and the volar ulnocarpal ligament. If the ulnar styloid is not fractured, then the collateral ulnar ligament is torn. The head of the ulna lies anterior to the distal fragment of the radius.

1. Symptoms and signs Clinical findings vary according to the magnitude of injury, the degree of displacement of fragments, and the interval since injury. If the fragments are not displaced, examination soon after injury will demonstrate only slight tenderness and insignificant swelling; pain may be absent. Marked displacement produces the classic 'silver fork' or 'bayonet' deformity, in which a dorsal prominence caused by displacement of the distal fragment replaces the normal convex curve of the lower radius and the ulnar head is prominent on the antermedial aspect of the wrist. Later, swelling may extend from the fingertips to the elbow.

2. Complications Derangement of the distal radioulnar joint is the most common complicating injury. Direct injury to the median nerve by bone spicules is not common. Compression of the nerve by hemorrhage and edema or by displaced bone fragments is frequent and may cause all gradations of sensory and motor paralysis. Initial treatment of the fracture by immobilization of the wrist in acute flexion can be a significant factor in aggravation of compression. Persistent compression of the nerve creates classic symptoms of the carpal tunnel syndrome, which may require operative division of the volar carpal ligament for relief. Other complicating injuries are fractures involving the carpal navicular, the head of the radius, or the capitellum. Dislocation of the elbow and shoulder and tears of the capsulotendinous cuff of the shoulder may be associated.

3. Treatment Complete recovery of function and a pleasing cosmetic result are goals of treatment which cannot always be achieved. The patient's age, sex, and occupation, the presence of complicating injury or disease, the severity of comminution, and the configuration of the fracture cleft govern the selection of treatment.

Open reduction of recent closed Colles' fracture is rarely indicated. Many technics of closed reduction and external immobilization have been advocated; the experience and preference of the surgeon determine the choice.

a. Minor displacement Colles' fracture with minimal displacement is characterized by absence of comminution and slight dorsal impaction. Deformity is barely perceptible, or may not be visible even to the trained observer. In the elderly patient, treatment is directed toward early recovery of function. In young patients, prevention of further displacement is the first consideration.

Reduction is not necessary. The wrist is immobilized for 3-5 days in a volar plaster splint extending from the distal palmar flexion crease to the elbow. Thereafter the splint may be removed periodically (4-5 times daily) to permit active exercise of the wrist. Soaking the hand and forearm for 15-20 minutes in warm water 2-3 times a day tends to relieve pain and stiffness. The splint can usually be discarded within 2 weeks.

b. Marked displacement Early reduction and immobilization are indicated. When reduction has been delayed until preliminary healing is advanced, open reduction may be elected or correction of the deformity can be deferred until healing is sound. The malunion can then be corrected by osteotomy and bone grafting.

In an elderly person with complicating arthritis, when impaction causes stability, the mild deformity may be accepted in favor of early restoration of function.

Stable fractures Colles' fracture is characterized by comminution of the dorsal cortex. Correction of the deformity creates a wedge-shaped area of fragmented and impacted cancellous bone. The base of the wedge is directed dorsally, and there is no buttress to prevent recurrence of displacement. In part, stability is attained by bringing the volar cortices of the fragments into anatomic apposition.

Muscular relaxation of the extremity can usually be attained more readily under general anesthesia, but local anesthesia is commonly the better choice for the elderly patient.

Reduction is by manipulation. Success of manipulation is determined by clinical examination. Swelling is dissipated by massaging the volar and lateral aspects of the radius until the subcutaneous border can be palpated. Restoration of the normal convex curve of the distal radius implies that transverse displacement and angulation are absent. Proximal displacement has been reduced if the radial styloid process can be palpated 1 cm distal to the ulnar styloid.

A lightly padded tubular cast extending above the elbow or a 'sugar tong' splint (Fig. 17-17) is preferred. The plaster should extend distally only to the palmar flexion crease, with the forearm in midposition and the wrist in slight volar flexion and ulnar deviation. In obese patients, immobilization is more reliable if the elbow is included in the plaster. After the plaster has been applied, it is molded carefully around the wrist until it has set. X-rays are taken while anesthesia is continued. If x-rays show that reduction is not adequate, remanipulation is carried out immediately.

X-ray examination is repeated on the third day and thereafter at weekly intervals during the first 3 weeks. The plaster must remain snug; if loosening occurs after absorption of hematoma, a new cast should be applied.

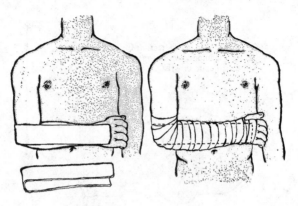

Fig. 17-17. 'Sugar tong' plaster splint

Unstable fractures If x-rays show extensive comminution with intraarticular extension and involvement of the volar cortex, the fracture is likely to be unstable and skeletal distraction is probably indicated by means of traction in Kirschner wires (Fig. 17-18). Traction is continued while the plaster is applied. To ensure maximal external support, the extremity is immobilized in a tubular plaster cast extending from the axilla to the palmar flexion crease, with the elbow at a right angle, the forearm in midposition, and the wrist in slight ulnar deviation and volar flexion. The Kirschner wires are incorporated in the plaster, and the bows are maintained to hold the wires taut (Fig. 17-19). The wires are left in place for 6 weeks. The fracture is protected for an additional 2 weeks following removal of the wires by a gauntlet or a 'sugar tong' splint.

4. Postreduction treatment Frequent observation and careful management can prevent or minimize some of the disabling sequelae of Colles' fracture. The patient's full cooperation in the exercise program is essential. If comminution is marked, if swelling is severe, or if there is evidence of median nerve deficit, the patient should remain under close observation (preferably in a hospital) for at least 72 hours. The extremity should be elevated to minimize swelling, and the adequacy of circulation determined at frequent intervals. Active exercise of the fingers and shoulder is encouraged. In order that the extremity can be used as much as possible, the plaster should be trimmed in the palm to permit full finger extension.

As soon as the plaster is removed, the patient is advised to use the extremity for customary daily care but to avoid strenuous activity that might cause refracture.

5. Complications and sequelae Joint stiffness is the most disabling sequel of Colles' fracture. Derangement of the distal radioulnar joint may be caused by the original injury and perpetuated by incomplete reduction; it is characterized by restriction of forearm movements and pain. Late rupture of the extensor pollicis longus tendon is relatively uncommon. Symptoms of median nerve injury due to compression caused by acute swelling alone usually do not persist more than 6 months. Prolonged symptoms can cause carpal tunnel syndrome. Failure to perform shoulder joint exercises several times daily can result in disabling stiffness.

Fig. 17-18. Skeletal distraction for closed manipulation of fracture of the forearm or wrist.

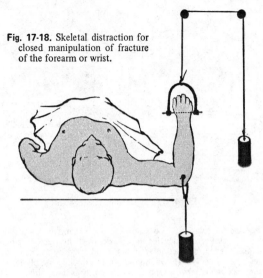

Fig. 17-19. Full upper extremity plaster with Kirschner wires incorporated.

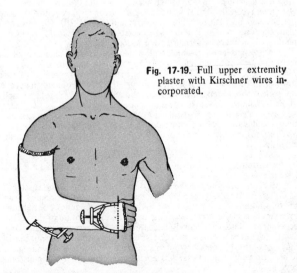

C. SMITH'S FRACTURE (REVERSED COLLES') The fracture site of the radius is 1–2.5 cm above the wrist joint in this lesion. The normal volar concavity of the lower radius is accentuated because the apex of angulation at the fracture site is posterior. The ulnar head is prominent dorsally, and there may be derangement of the inferior radioulnar joint. This lesion should be differentiated from Barton's fracture-dislocation.

The fracture can be reduced by closed manipulation and immobilized with the wrist in dorsiflexion. Unstable fractures may require initial skeletal distraction (see above for unstable Colles' fracture). Fractures which cannot be reduced adequately by closed methods may require open reduction and bone plating.

D. FRACTURE OF THE RADIAL STYLOID Forced radial deviation of the hand at the wrist joint can fracture the radial styloid. A large fragment of the styloid is usually displaced by impingement against the carpal navicular. Avulsion of the tip of the styloid by the radial collateral ligament occurs less frequently, and it may be associated with dislocation of the radiocarpal joint. If the fragment is large, it can be displaced farther by the brachioradialis muscle, which inserts into it.

Because the fracture is intraarticular, reduction of large fragments should be anatomic. If the styloid fragment is not displaced, immobilization in a plaster gauntlet for 3 weeks is sufficient. If the fragment is displaced, manipulative reduction should be tried. If the distal, smaller fragment tends to displace but can be apposed by digital pressure, percutaneous fixation can be achieved by a medium Kirschner wire inserted through the proximal anatomic snuffbox so as to transfix both fragments. The wrist is then immobilized in a snugly molded plaster gauntlet for 6 weeks. X-ray examination is repeated every week for at least 3 weeks.

If closed methods fail, open reduction is indicated since persistent displacement is likely to cause posttraumatic degenerative arthritis relatively early.

E. FRACTURE OF THE DISTAL RADIAL EPIPHYSIS Fracture through the distal radial epiphyseal plate in children is the counterpart of Colles' fracture in the adult. Wrist sprain is rare in childhood and should be differentiated as early as possible from fracture of the distal epiphysis. Such an injury is usually caused by indirect violence due to a fall on the outstretched hand. The magnitude of displacement of the epiphyseal fragment varies.

In some cases, separation and displacement of the epiphysis cannot be demonstrated by radiologic studies and may be quite difficult to identify on clinical examination. The patient may complain of pain in the region of the wrist joint, and slight swelling may be present. Pressure with a blunt object, e.g., the eraser of a lead pencil, may demonstrate maximal tenderness at the epiphyseal plate instead of at the wrist joint. Buckling of the adjacent metaphyseal cortex manifests greater displacement.

Displacement is posterior and to the radial side. Marked displacement may be accompanied by crushing of the epiphyseal plate, tear of the triangular fibrocartilage of the distal radioulnar articulation, displacement of the distal ulnar epiphysis, or avulsion of the ulnar styloid.

Both wrists should be examined by x-ray if injury to the distal radial epiphysis is suspected. Severe injury, crushing the epiphyseal cartilage and fracturing the epiphysis, is likely to impede growth and may even lead to early epiphyseal fusion; continued growth of the distal ulnar epiphysis produces derangement of the distal radioulnar joint.

Open reduction is rarely necessary. The trauma of the operation superimposed on the injury is likely to cause early arrest of epiphyseal growth. Closed reduction by manipulation is usually successful if it can be done within the week following injury. Immobilization is with a plaster gauntlet or 'sugar tong' splint.

The plaster should be worn for 4-6 weeks. Permanent stiffness due to immobilization of the wrist is not to be feared.

The child should be examined yearly to determine whether there is any growth disturbance.

F. FRACTURE-DISLOCATIONS OF THE RADIOCARPAL JOINT   Dislocation of the radiocarpal joint without fracture is rare. Dislocation without injury to one of the carpal bones is usually associated with fracture of the anterior surface of the radius or the ulna. Comminuted fracture of the distal radius may involve either the anterior or posterior cortex and extends into the wrist joint. Subluxation of the carpus may occur at the same time. The most common fracture-dislocation of the wrist joint involves the posterior or anterior margin of the articular surface of the radius.

1. Anterior fracture-dislocation of the radiocarpal joint (Barton's fracture) is characterized by fracture of the volar margin of the carpal articular surface of the radius. The fracture cleft extends proximally in the coronal plane in an oblique direction, so that the free fragment has a wedge-shaped configuration. The carpus is displaced volar and proximally with the articular fragment. This uncommon injury should be differentiated from Smith's fracture by x-ray examination.

Treatment by closed reduction may be successful, especially in cases in which the free fragment of the radius does not involve a large portion of the articular surface. Immobilization is with a tubular plaster cast extending from the palmar flexion crease to above the elbow with the wrist in volar flexion and the elbow at a right angle. Immediate x-rays are taken in two projections. If reduction is not anatomic and the fracture is unstable, skeletal distraction may be necessary. Weekly x-ray examination should be repeated during the first month. Skeletal distraction should be continued for 6 weeks or until preliminary bone healing has stabilized the fracture.

2. Posterior fracture-dislocation of the radiocarpal joint should be differentiated from Colles' fracture by x-ray. In most cases the marginal fragment is smaller than in anterior injury and often involves the medial aspect where the extensor pollicis longus crosses the distal radius. If reduction is not anatomic, fraying of the tendon at this level may lead to late rupture.

Treatment is by manipulative reduction as for Colles' fracture and immobilization in a snug plaster gauntlet with the wrist in dorsiflexion.

G. DISLOCATION OF THE DISTAL RADIOULNAR JOINT   The triangular fibrocartilage is the most important structure in preventing dislocation of the distal radioulnar joint. The accessory ligaments and the pronator quadratus muscle play a secondary role. Complete anterior or posterior dislocation implies a tear of the triangular fibrocartilage and disruption of accessory joint ligaments. Tearing of the triangular fibrocartilage in the absence of major injury to the supporting capsular ligaments causes subluxation or abnormal laxity of the joint. Since the ulnar attachment of the triangular fibrocartilage is at the base of the styloid process, x-rays may demonstrate associated fracture. Widening of the cleft in comparison with the opposite radioulnar joint, which is apparent by x-ray examination, demonstrates diastasis of the radius and ulna if frank anterior or posterior displacement is not present.

Complete anterior or posterior dislocation of the distal radioulnar joint is rare. Medial dislocation is associated with fracture of the radius. The direction of dislocation is indicated by the location of the ulnar head in relation to the distal end of the radius.

H. FRACTURES AND DISLOCATIONS OF THE CARPUS   Injury to the carpal bones occurs predominantly in men during the most active period of life. Because it is difficult to differentiate these injuries by clinical examination, it is im-

perative to obtain x-ray films of the best possible quality. The oblique film should be taken in midpronation, the anteroposterior film with the wrist in maximal ulnar deviation. Special views, such as midsupination to demonstrate the pisiform, and carpal tunnel views for the hamate, may be necessary.

1. Fracture of the carpal navicular   The most common injury to the carpus is fracture of the navicular. Fracture of the carpal navicular should be suspected in any injury to the wrist in an adult male unless a specific diagnosis of another type of injury is obvious. If tenderness on the radial aspect of the wrist is present and fracture cannot be demonstrated, initial treatment should be the same as if fracture were present (see below) and should be continued for at least 3 weeks. Further x-ray examination after 3 weeks may demonstrate an occult fracture.

Three types of fracture are distinguished:

a. Fracture of the tubercle   This fracture usually is not widely displaced, and healing is generally prompt if immobilization in a plaster gauntlet is maintained for 2-3 weeks.

b. Fracture through the waist is the most common type. The blood supply to the proximal fragment is usually not disturbed, and healing will take place if reduction is adequate and treatment is instituted early. If the nutrient artery to the proximal third is injured, avascular necrosis of that portion of the bone may occur.

X-ray examination in multiple projections is necessary to determine the direction of the fracture cleft and displacement of the proximal fragment. If the proximal fragment is displaced, it can be reduced under local anesthesia by forced dorsiflexion and radial deviation of the wrist. Immobilization in a plaster gauntlet with the wrist in slight dorsiflexion is necessary. The plaster should extend distally to the palmar flexion crease in the hand and to the base of the thumbnail. If reduction has been anatomic and the blood supply to the proximal fragment has not been jeopardized, adequate bone healing can be expected within 10 weeks. However, such healing must be demonstrated by the disappearance of the fracture cleft and restoration of the trabecular pattern between the two main fragments. X-ray examination to verify healing should be repeated 3 weeks after removal of the cast.

c. Fracture through the proximal third of the navicular is likely to be associated with injury to the arterial supply of the minor fragment. This can be manifested by avascular necrosis of that fragment. If the lesion is observed soon after injury, reduction and immobilization in a plaster gauntlet will promote healing. The plaster gauntlet should be applied snugly and must be changed if it becomes loose; it is usually necessary to renew the gauntlet every 4 weeks. X-rays should be taken once a month to determine the progress of bone healing; it may be necessary to prolong immobilization for 4-6 months. The same criteria of radiographic examination as are used for healing of fractures through the waist are used in fractures of the proximal third. It is advisable to make an additional x-ray examination 3-4 weeks after removal of the cast.

If evidence of healing is not apparent after immobilization for 6 months or more, further immobilization will probably not be effective. This is especially true if x-rays show that the fracture cleft has widened and if sclerosis is noted adjacent to the cleft. If the interval between the time of injury and the establishment of a diagnosis is 3 months or more, a trial of immobilization for 2-3 months may be elected. If obliteration of the fracture cleft and evidence of bone continuity are not visible in x-rays after this trial period, some form of operative treatment will be necessary to initiate bone healing. Bone grafting is probably more successful. Prolonged immobilization in a plaster gauntlet is necessary before bony continuity is restored.

If avascular necrosis has occurred in the proximal fragment, bone grafting is less likely to be successful. Although excision of the avascular fragment may relieve painful symptoms for a time, the patient usually notes weakness of grasp and discomfort after prolonged use. Postraumatic arthritis is apt to develop late.

Prolonged failure of bone healing predisposes to posttraumatic arthritis. Bone grafting operations or other procedures directed toward restoration of bone continuity may be successful, but arthritis causes continued disability. Arthrodesis of the wrist gives the best assurance of relief of pain and a functionally competent extremity.

2. Fracture of the lunate may be manifested by minor avulsion fractures of the posterior or anterior horn. Careful multiplane x-ray examination is necessary to establish the diagnosis. Either of these lesions may be treated by the use of a volar splint for 3 weeks.

Fracture of the body may be manifested by a crack, by comminution, or by impaction. A fissure fracture can be treated by immobilization in plaster for 3 weeks.

Complications of this fracture are persistent pain in the wrist, slight restriction of motion, and tenderness over the lunate. X-ray examination can demonstrate areas of sclerosis and rarefaction. Impaction or collapse can be accompanied by arthritic changes surrounding the lunate. This x-ray appearance is referred to as Kienbock's disease, osteochondrosis of the lunate, or avascular necrosis.

3. Fracture of the hamate may occur through the body and is shown on x-ray as a fissure or compression. Fracture of the base of the hamulus is less common and more difficult to diagnose; special projections are necessary to demonstrate the cleft. If the hamulus is displaced, closed manipulation will not be effective. Prolonged painful symptoms or evidence of irritation of the ulnar nerve may require excision of the loose fragment.

4. Fracture of the triquetrum is caused commonly by direct violence and is often associated with fracture of other carpal bones. Treatment is by immobilization in a plaster gauntlet for 4 weeks.

5. Dislocation of the lunate is the second most common injury of carpus. Dislocation is caused by forced dorsiflexion of the wrist, and the direction of dislocation is almost always anterior. The diagnosis is usually made by x-ray examination. Dislocation may be manifest by dorsal displacement of the capitate while the lunate retains contact with the radius. A further degree of injury is manifested by complete displacement of the lunate from the radius, so that it comes to lie anterior to the capitate and loses its relationship to the articular surface of the radius. If x-ray examination is adequate, the diagnosis can be established easily.

Reduction may be achieved by closed manipulation. X-rays are then taken to determine the success of treatment. If reduction is adequate, the extremity is immobilized in a plaster gauntlet with the wrist in full volar flexion for about 2 weeks. The plaster is then removed and another applied with the wrist in neutral position for an additional 2 weeks. If x-rays show that this manipulative manuever has not caused reduction, skeletal distraction by means of Kirschner wires may separate the radiocarpal joint sufficiently to permit manipulative reduction. If closed methods are not successful, open reduction should be done promptly.

6. Dislocation of the capitate is most often associated with other lesions of the carpus and is commonly called transcarpal or midcarpal dislocation. The most frequent accompanying injury is fracture of the carpal navicular, in which case the lunate and the proximal fragment of the navicular retain their relationship to the articular surface of the radius whereas the distal fragment of the navicular, the capitate, and the remainder of the carpus are displaced dorsally. Thus, the dislocation is retrolunar.

Subluxation of the navicular is less often associated with dislocation of the lunate. The direction of this dislocation is also retrolunar. Fracture of the radial or ulnar styloid process is likely to be present also.

X-rays of poor technical quality may not demonstrate the lesion satisfactorily; anteroposterior and true lateral projections are necessary.

The comparatively uncommon midcarpal dislocation can be reduced by closed manipulation if the lesion is uncomplicated and recognized within 10–14 days after injury. Immobilization in a plaster gauntlet with the wrist in slight dorsiflexion for 4 weeks is sufficient for stabilization by early ligamentous healing. If fracture complicates the dislocation, treatment is divided into 2 phases: reduction of the fracture-dislocation is accomplished by closed manipulation; the navicular fracture is then treated as outlined above.

VIII. INJURIES OF THE HIP REGION

A. BIRTH FRACTURE OF THE UPPER FEMORAL EPIPHYSES is rare, and the diagnosis by physical examination alone is difficult because the skeletal structures involved are deeply situated. Swelling of the upper thigh and pseudoparalysis of the extremity following a difficult delivery suggest injury. X-ray examination may demonstrate outward and proximal displacement of the shaft of the femur. Formation of new bone in the region of the metaphysis may be demonstrated in 7–10 days. If displacement has occurred, treatment for 2–3 weeks by Bryant's traction (Fig. 17-20) is recommended. Otherwise, protection by a perineal pillow splint for the same length of time is adequate.

B. DISPLACEMENT AND SEPARATION OF THE CAPITAL FEMORAL EPIPHYSIS Displacement of the capital femoral epiphysis due to trauma in the normal child should be differentiated from idiopathic slipped epiphysis (epiphysiolysis, adolescent coxa vara) due possibly to endocrine or metabolic dysfunction. However, between the ages of 10 and 16 years, differentiation may be impossible. Mild injury may cause sudden separation and displacement because of weakening of the plate by antecedent idiopathic disturbance of cartilage growth.

Traumatic separation of the capital femoral epiphysis is rare in normal children, but it may occur as a result of a single episode of severe trauma which otherwise might cause fracture of the femoral neck. The direction of displacement is likely to be the same as in adolescent coxa vara. Although anatomic reduction can be obtained by closed manipulation, immobilization in a plaster spica should not be trusted since redisplacement is possible; internal fixation is more reliable. Traumatic separation of the capital epiphysis associated with dislocation of the hip joint (epiphysis and proximal femur) is a rare lesion with an unfavorable prognosis. Avascular necrosis of the epiphysis is almost certain.

C. FRACTURE OF THE FEMORAL NECK occurs most commonly in patients over the age of 50. If displacement has occurred, the extremity is in external rotation and adduction. Leg shortening is usually obvious. Motion of the hip joint causes pain. If the fracture is impacted in the valgus position, the injured extremity may be slightly longer than the opposite side and active external rotation may not be possible. If the fragments are not displaced and the fracture is stable, pain at the extremes of passive hip motion may be the only significant finding. The fact that the patient can actively move the extremity often interferes with prompt diagnosis.

Before treatment is instituted, anteroposterior and lateral films of excellent quality must be obtained. Gentle traction and internal rotation of the extremity while the anteroposterior film is exposed may provide a more favorable relation of fragments to demonstrate the fracture cleft.

Fractures of the femoral neck may be classified as abduction or adduction fractures.

1. Abduction fracture of the femoral neck Abduction describes the relationship between the neck and shaft fragment and the head, which creates a coxa

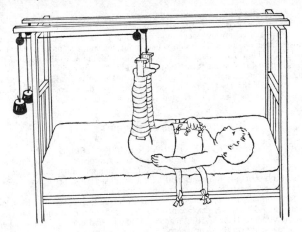

Fig. 17-20. Bryant's traction

valga deformity. Abduction fractures occur most often in the proximal femoral neck adjacent to the head. Displacement is apt to be minimal, and impaction is often present. The direction of the fracture cleft approaches the transverse plane of the body, and the angle is 30° or less. The anteroposterior x-ray may show a wedge-shaped area of increased density whose base is directed superiorly. A good lateral film will demonstrate both the anterior and posterior cortices of the femoral neck. In this plane the neck and shaft fragment may be angulated slightly, so that only the posterior cortex appears to be impacted and the anterior cortices of the fragments appear to be separated.

Impaction is precarious and undependable as a fixation mechanism; if internal fixation is not used, separation may occur before healing is sound. If firm impaction can be demonstrated in both the anterior and posterior x-rays, some surgeons recommend conservative treatment, i.e., bed rest with the extremity in balanced suspension for 4–8 weeks. The patient is then permitted to be ambulatory with crutches, but full weight-bearing is not permitted until complete healing can be demonstrated by x-rays (usually 4–12 months after injury). Other surgeons prefer internal fixation because it permits the patient to be out of bed soon after the operation even though unsupported weight-bearing is not permitted any sooner than after nonoperative treatment.

If examination in the lateral projection does not show firm impaction of both cortices at the fracture site, closed manipulation and internal fixation are indicated.

2. Adduction fracture of the femoral neck is characterized by coxa vara deformity. The fracture may be at any level of the neck, and the direction of the fracture cleft approaches that of the sagittal plane of the body. Displacement is usually present. The relatively vertical configuration of the fracture cleft favors proximal displacement of the distal fragment by the force of any axial thrust transmitted through the extremity. The fracture should be considered unstable if the angle between the fracture cleft and the transverse plane of the body is greater than 30° (Fig. 17-21).

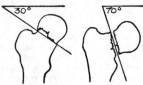

Fig. 17-21. Pauwels' angles

Adduction fracture of the femoral neck can be a life-endangering injury, especially when it occurs in elderly persons. Treatment is directed toward the preservation of life and restoration of function to the hip joint. In most cases, when the life expectancy of the patient is more than a few weeks, open operation is the treatment of choice. Immobilization of this unstable fracture by means of a plaster spica is unreliable. Definitive treatment by skeletal traction requires prolonged recumbency with constant nursing care and is associated with more numerous complications than early mobilization. Some surgeons believe that immediate operative treatment is required after fracture; others reply that 1-2 days of evaluation of the general health status of the patient is rewarded by a lower mortality rate. Operative treatment usually consists of internal fixation or primary prosthetic arthroplasty.

a. Internal fixation The goal is to preserve the capital fragment by providing a setting for bony healing of the fracture. The objective is to allow the patient as much general physical activity during healing as is compatible with the mechanics of fixation. To permit necessary preoperative evaluation of the patient when internal fixation is elected, initial treatment may be by balanced suspension, skeletal traction, and prompt closed reduction of the fracture. Persistent displacement may cause further compromise of the retinacular blood supply to the articular fragment.

Anatomic or near anatomic reduction and firm fixation are desirable to provide optimal circumstances for bone healing. Comminution at the fracture site, injury to the retinacular blood supply of the capital fragment, excessive stressing of the fracture site, and insecure fixation are some of the factors that lead to failure.

The wide variety of surgical technics that make use of the many fixation appliances available testifies to the multiplicity of problems that can be encountered and the variability of opinion concerning treatment. When the fragments are undisplaced or minimally displaced, manipulation is unnecessary. When displacement occurs, reduction may be closed as a preliminary step to fixation or can be accomplished by surgical exposure of the fracture site, especially when determination of competency of blood supply of the proximal fragment is necessary. The fixation apparatus may consist of multiple pins applied percutaneously or more elaborate implants that require open operation. In addition to reduction and internal fixation of the fracture, some surgeons believe that either displacement or valgus osteotomy in the trochanteric region enhances the chances of osseous healing of the fracture and minimizes the incidence of ischemic osteonecrosis of the articular fragment. After operation, the patient may be free in bed and may be mobilized at an early date. To salvage the operative effort if fixation is precarious, traction in balanced suspension or immobilization in a plaster spica for 1-4 months may be necessary until preliminary healing gives additional stability.

Depending upon the relative security of fixation, the extent of early weight-bearing must be regulated until bone continuity is restored to the point where displacement of fragments is unlikely. The agile and cooperative patient may be ambulatory on crutches (but within the limitations of acceptable weight-bearing) within a few days after operative treatment. Crutch walking is hazardous in elderly patients since inadvertent loading may disrupt the fracture relationship.

b. Primary arthroplasty   In selecting primary arthroplasty, the surgeon realizes that the main proximal fragment must be sacrificed because of injury to the blood supply, preexisting disease, or the intent to permit early unrestricted weight-bearing with stability of the coxofemoral relationship. When the acetabulum is undamaged or is not the site of preexisting disease, the commonly accepted technic is hemiarthroplasty using a femoral component (generally of the intramedullary type) which may or may not be stabilized by a grouting substance such as methyl methacrylate. In the rare circumstance when there is concomitant involvement of the acetabulum, total joint replacement may be justified. Primary head and neck resection may be indicated when there is preexisting infection or local tumor.

The most common sequelae of cervical fracture of the femur are redisplacement after reduction and internal fixation, failure of bone healing, and osteonecrosis (avascular, aseptic, or ischemic necrosis) of head fragment. Secondary osteoarthritis (posttraumatic arthritis) appears somewhat later and may be complicated by any of the common sequelae mentioned above. The most serious complication of any open operative treatment is infection.

3. Femoral neck fracture in childhood (rare) must be differentiated from congenital coxa vara. Traumatic fracture is usually caused by severe injury. Anatomic reduction by closed manipulation and immobilization in a plaster spica are necessary to prevent deformity. Internal fixation with wires or screws may be necessary. Removal of the fixation apparatus after healing may prevent early fusion of the epiphysis.

Osteonecrosis of the capital epiphysis is a frequent sequel.

D. TROCHANTERIC FRACTURES

1. Fracture of the lesser trochanter is quite rare but may develop as a result of the avulsion force of the iliopsoas muscle. It occurs commonly as a component of intertrochanteric fracture.

2. Fracture of the greater trochanter may be caused by direct injury, or it may occur indirectly as a result of the activity of the gluteus medius and gluteus minimus muscles. It occurs most commonly as a component of intertrochanteric fracture.

If displacement is less than 1 cm and there is no tendency to further displacement (determined by repeated x-ray examinations), treatment may be by bed rest with the affected extremity in balanced suspension until acute pain subsides. As rapidly as symptoms permit, activity can increase gradually to protected weight-bearing with crutches. Full weight-bearing is permitted as soon as healing is apparent, usually in 6-8 weeks. If displacement is greater than 1 cm and increases on adduction of the thigh, extensive tearing of surrounding soft tissues may be assumed and open reduction is indicated, followed by internal fixation with 2-3 loops of stainless steel wire.

3. Intertrochanteric (including pertrochanteric) fractures   These fractures occur most commonly among elderly persons. The cleft of an intertrochanteric fracture extends upward and outward from the medial region of the junction of the neck and lesser trochanter toward the summit of the greater trochanter. Pertrochanteric fracture includes both trochanters, and is likely to be comminuted.

It is important to determine whether comminution has occurred and the magnitude of displacement. These fractures may vary from fissure fracture without significant separation to severe comminution into four major fragments: head-neck, greater trochanter, lesser trochanter, and shaft. Displacement may be so marked that the head-neck fragment forms a right angle with the shaft fragment and the distal fragment is rotated externally through an arc of 90°.

Failure of restoration of bone continuity by healing of intertrochanteric fractures is unlikely and, when it occurs, the causes are usually apparent. Of the many factors that influence the rate of healing, those of particular significance are inadequate treatment as manifested by incomplete reduction with unsatisfactory apposition of fragments and unsustained immobilization, comminution, and osteopenia (osteoporosis and disuse atrophy). Healing in malposition (varus and external rotation) is abetted by the major stresses that cause displacement (gravity and muscle activity).

Initial treatment of the fracture in the hospital can be by balanced suspension and, when indicated, by the addition of traction. The selection of definitive treatment—closed or operative technics—depends in part upon the general condition of the patient. Because of the elderly age group in which intertrochanteric fracture is likely to occur, multiple system disease is a determinant of the mortality rate and for that reason the incidence of complications is diminished by the avoidance of prolonged recumbency in bed. Some surgeons are of the opinion that delay in open treatment is hazardous to the life of the patient, and they prefer to operate promptly. Others believe than an evaluation of the general health status of the patient should be made and that preliminary treatment of the fracture—reduction by closed technics—can proceed simultaneously.

Undisplaced fractures can be treated by balanced suspension of the lower extremity until the fragments are stabilized by preliminary bone healing. These fractures can also be treated initially by immobilization in a plaster spica. Sufficient healing generally occurs within 2-3 months to permit the patient to follow a bed and wheelchair existence until partial weight-bearing with crutches can be initiated. Unsupported weight-bearing should not be resumed until the fracture cleft has been obliterated by healing.

If comminution is present and displacement is significant, skin or (preferably) skeletal traction by a Kirschner wire through the tibial tubercle must be added to provide immobilization and to accomplish reduction. Definitive treatment of the fracture can be given in this way or it can be used as a preliminary to open operation.

Open operation may be done electively or may be mandatory for optimal treatment. Reduction of the fracture can be accomplished by closed technics, or it can be an integral part of the open operation. Some surgeons prefer not to anatomically reduce unstable fractures caused by comminution of the medial femoral cortex. It is maintained that medial displacement of the upper end of the main distal fragment enhances mechanical stability (although it may cause concomitant varus deformity), and this advantageously permits earlier weight-bearing and more prompt healing. The chief intent of open operation is to provide sufficient fixation of the fragments by a metallic surgical implant so that the patient need not be confined to bed during the healing process.

Intertrochanteric fracture during childhood can be treated by skeletal traction with a Kirschner wire inserted through the lower femur above the epiphyseal line or by closed reduction and internal fixation. Varus deformity should be avoided if possible.

E. SUBTROCHANTERIC FRACTURE due to severe trauma occurs below the level of the lesser trochanter at the junction of cancellous and cortical bone. It is most common in men during the active years of life. Soft tissue damage is extensive. The direction of the fracture cleft may be transverse or oblique. Comminution occurs and the fracture may extend proximally into the intertrochanteric region or distally into the shaft. Muscle is often interposed between the major fragments.

Closed reduction should be attempted by continuous traction to bring the distal fragment into alignment with the proximal fragment. If comminution is not extensive and the lesser trochanter is not detached, the proximal fragment is often drawn into relative flexion, external rotation, and abduction by the predominant activity of the iliopsoas, gluteus medius, and gluteus minimus muscles.

Prolonged skeletal traction by means of a Kirschner wire inserted through the supracondylar region of the femur (with the hip and knee flexed to a right

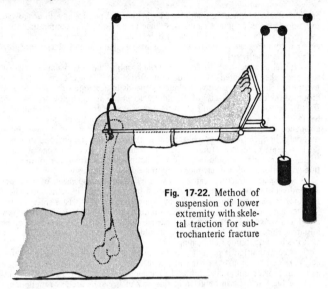

Fig. 17-22. Method of suspension of lower extremity with skeletal traction for subtrochanteric fracture

angle) is necessary (see Fig. 17-22). X-ray is repeated every 4–8 hours until reduction has been accomplished. If soft tissue interposition is not a factor, reduction can be achieved within 48 hours. Thereafter the extremity is left in this position with an appropriate amount of traction until stabilization occurs, usually in 8–12 weeks. The angle of flexion is then reduced by gradually bringing the hip and knee into extension. After 2–3 months of continuous traction, the extremity can be immobilized in a plaster spica provided stabilization of the fracture has occurred. Weight-bearing must not be resumed for 6 months or even longer, until bone healing obliterates the fracture cleft.

Interposition of soft tissue between the major fragments may prevent closed reduction. Open reduction of this fracture is difficult and should be undertaken early; if treatment is delayed until the third week following injury, extensive bleeding at the fracture site is likely to be encountered.

After open reduction has been performed, internal fixation is required to prevent redisplacement. If comminution is present, or if it is important to avoid prolonged immobilization, biplane fixation is recommended.

The activity status after operation depends upon the adequacy of internal fixation. If fixation is precarious, skeletal traction in balanced suspension should be continued until healing is well under way. Otherwise, if the patient is agile and cooperative, he may be ambulatory on crutches (but without weight-bearing) a few days after the operation.

F. TRAUMATIC DISLOCATION OF THE HIP JOINT may occur with or without fracture of the acetabulum or the proximal end of the femur. It is most common during the active years of life and is usually the result of severe trauma unless there is preexisting disease of the femoral head, acetabulum, or neuromuscular system. The head of the femur cannot be completely displaced from the normal acetabulum unless the ligamentum teres is ruptured or deficient because of some unrelated cause. Traumatic dislocations can be classified according to the direction of displacement of the femoral head from the acetabulum.

1. Posterior hip dislocation   The head of the femur is usually dislocated posterior to the acetabulum while the thigh is flexed, e.g., as may occur in a head-on automobile collision when the passenger's knee is driven violently against the dashboard.

The significant clinical findings are shortening, adduction, and internal rotation of the extremity. Anteroposterior, transpelvic, and, if fracture of the acetabulum is demonstrated, oblique projections are required. Common complications are fracture of the acetabulum, injury to the sciatic nerve, and fracture of the head or shaft of the femur. The head of the femur may be displaced through a rent in the posterior hip joint capsule, or the glenoid lip may be avulsed from the acetabulum. The short external rotator muscles of the hip joint are commonly lacerated. Fracture of the posterior margin of the acetabulum can create an unstable mechanism.

If the acetabulum is not fractured or if the fragment is small, reduction by closed manipulation either by Bigelow's or Stimson's method is indicated.

The success of reduction is determined immediately by anteroposterior and lateral x-rays. Interposition of capsule substance will be manifest by widening of the joint cleft. If reduction is adequate, the hip will be stable with the extremity in extension and slight external rotation.

Postreduction treatment may be by immobilization in a plaster spica or by balanced suspension. Since this is primarily a soft tissue injury, sound healing should take place in 4 weeks. Opinion differs on when unsupported weight-bearing should be resumed. Some surgeons believe that disability caused by ischemic osteonecrosis of the femoral head is less likely when complete weight-bearing is deferred for 6 months after injury; others are of the opinion that early loading is not harmful.

If the posterior or superior acetabulum is fractured, dislocation of the hip must be assumed to have occurred even though displacement is not present at the time of examination. Undisplaced fissure fractures may be treated initially by bed rest and avoidance of full weight-bearing for 2 months. Frequent examination is necessary to make certain that the head of the femur has not become displaced from the acetabulum.

Minor fragments of the posterior margin of the acetabulum may be disregarded unless they are in the hip joint cavity. Larger displaced fragments often cannot be reduced adequately by closed methods. If the fragment is large and the hip is unstable following closed manipulation, open operation is indicated. If the sciatic nerve has been injured it should be exposed and treated by appropriate neurosurgical technics when the posterior hip joint is exposed. The fragment is then placed in anatomic position and fixed with 1–2 bone screws.

After the operation the patient is placed in bed with the extremity in balanced suspension under 5–8 kg of skeletal traction on the tibial tubercle for about 6 weeks or until healing of the acetabular fracture is sound. Full weight-bearing is not permitted for 6 months or more.

2. Anterior hip dislocation   In anterior hip dislocation the head of the femur may lie medially on the obturator membrane, beneath the obturator externus muscle (obturator or thyroid dislocation), or, in a somewhat more superior direction, beneath the iliopsoas muscle and in contact with the superior ramus of the pubis (pubic dislocation). The thigh is classically in flexion, abduction, and external rotation, and the head of the femur is palpable anteriorly and distal to the inguinal flexion crease. Anteroposterior and lateral films are required; films prepared by transpelvic projection are likely to be helpful.

Closed manipulation with general anesthesia is usually adequate. Postreduction treatment may be by balanced suspension or by immobilization in a plaster spica with the hip in extension and the extremity in neutral rotation. Active hip motion is permitted after 3 weeks.

3. Central dislocation of the hip with fracture of the pelvis Central dislocation of the head of the femur with fracture of the acetabulum may be caused by crushing injury or by an axial force transmitted through the abducted extremity to the acetabulum. Comminution is commonly present. There are usually two fragments; superiorly, the ilium with the roof of the acetabulum; inferiorly and medially, the remainder of the acetabulum and the obturator ring. Fracture occurs near the roof of the acetabulum, and the components of the obturator ring are displaced inward with the head of the femur. Extensive soft tissue injury and massive bleeding into the soft tissues are likely to be present. Intraabdominal injury must not be overlooked. Initially, stereoanteroposterior and oblique x-rays are required.

In the absence of complicating injury or immediately after such an injury has received priority attention, closed treatment of the fracture-dislocation by skeletal traction should be tried. Open reduction is hazardous and technically difficult; it should not be attempted except by the expert. Bidirectional traction is likely to achieve the most satisfactory results in all but the exceptional case. For the average adult, approximately 10 kg of force is applied axially to the shaft of the femur, in neither abduction nor adduction, through a Kirschner wire placed preferably in the supracondylar region. A second Kirschner wire is inserted in the anteroposterior plane between the greater and lesser trochanters (in substantial cortical bone). Force is applied at a right angle to the direction of axial traction and the magnitude is the same. The extremity is placed in balanced suspension. Progress of reduction is observed by portable x-rays made three times a day until adequate positioning is manifested by relocation of the head of the femur beneath the roof of the acetabulum. Bidirectional traction is maintained for 4-6 weeks. Thereafter, the transverse traction component is gradually diminished under appropriate x-ray control until it can be discontinued. Axial traction is maintained until stabilization of the fracture fragments by early bone healing has occurred, usually about 8 weeks after injury. During the next 4-6 weeks, while balanced suspension is continued, gentle active exercises of the knee and hip are encouraged. After discontinuation of balanced suspension, more elaborate exercises designed to aid recovery of maximal hip function are performed frequently during the day. Full and unprotected weight-bearing should not be advised before 6 months.

Sequelae are common, and the patient should be warned of their probable occurrence. Anatomic reduction is an unattainable goal in most severely comminuted and widely displaced fractures of this type. Scarring within and around the hip joint, with or without ectopic bone and exuberant callus formation, is incidental to the healing process and can be a significant factor in restriction of motion in varying degrees. Osteonecrosis of the femoral head and secondary osteoarthritis are common sequelae that appear somewhat later.

IX. FRACTURE OF THE SHAFT OF THE FEMUR

A. IN ADULTS Fracture of the shaft of the femur usually occurs as a result of severe direct trauma. Indirect violence, especially torsional stress, is likely to cause spiral fractures that extend proximally or, more commonly, distally into the metaphyseal regions. These fractures are likely to be encountered in bone that has become atrophic as a result of disuse or senescence. Most are closed fractures; open fracture is often the result of compounding from within. Extensive soft tissue injury, bleeding, and shock are commonly present.

If the fracture is through the upper third of the shaft, the proximal fragment is apt to be in flexion, external rotation, and abduction, with proximal displacement or overriding of the distal fragment. In mid-shaft fracture the direction of displacement is not constant, but the distal fragment is almost always displaced proximally if the fracture is unstable; and angulation is commonly present with the apex directed anterolaterally. In complete fracture of the lower third of the shaft the distal fragment is often displaced proximally; the upper end of the distal fragment may be displaced posteriorly to the distal end of the upper fragment.

1. Diagnosis The most significant features are severe pain in the thigh and deformity of the lower extremity. Hemorrhagic shock is likely to be present. Careful x-ray examination in at least two planes is necessary to determine the exact site and configuration of the fracture cleft. Emergency splints should be removed either by the surgeon or by a qualified assistant so that manipulation will not cause further damage. The hip and knee should be examined for associated injury.

Injuries to the sciatic nerve and to the superficial femoral artery and vein are not common but must be recognized promptly. Hemorrhagic shock is the most important early complication. Later complications are essentially those of prolonged recumbency, e.g., the formation of renal calculi.

2. Treatment depends upon the age of the patient and the site and configuration of the fracture. Displaced, oblique, spiral and comminuted fractures are unstable and can rarely be treated successfully by closed manipulation and external plaster fixation. Traction followed by closed manipulation should be tried. Skeletal traction is generally the most effective form of closed treatment.

After preliminary traction, biplane x-rays are made to determine the progress of correction of overriding. If alignment and apposition of fragments are not satisfactory, closed manipulation, preferably under general anesthesia, should be carried out while traction is continued.

If soft tissue interposition prevents reduction by closed methods, open reduction may be required in the adult to avoid delay of bone healing.

a. Fracture of the upper third The treatment of subtrochanteric fracture is discussed above. If a comminuted subtrochanteric fracture extends into the upper third of the femoral shaft, it may be necessary to use skeletal traction through the supracondylar region of the femur and suspend the extremity with the hip and knee at a right angle. Otherwise, skeletal traction can be through either the lower femur or the tibial tubercle with the extremity at a less acute angle in balanced suspension. Russell's traction can be used if the patient is small and muscular development is not great (see Fig. 17-23). External rotation and abduction of the extremity are usually required to bring the lower fragment into alignment with the proximal fragment.

b. Fracture of the middle third The deformity caused by fracture at this level is not constant. Angulation is commonly present with the apex directed anterolaterally. Treatment may be by skeletal traction through the tibial tubercle or the lower end of the femur. Traction in the transverse plane by a swathe around the thigh may be necessary to prevent recurrence of angulation.

c. Fracture of the lower third In transverse and comminuted fractures, the proximal end of the distal fragment is likely to be displaced posterior to the distal end of the proximal fragment. The same displacement is likely to be encountered in supracondylar fracture. Russell's traction should not be used for comminuted or widely displaced fractures since it may injure the femoral or popliteal vessels. Simultaneous skeletal traction through the distal femur at right angles to the tibial tubercle can correct displacement of the distal fragment. The same mechanism of traction is used for supracondylar fracture.

After reduction has been accomplished by traction, biplane x-ray examination should be repeated at least weekly to determine maintenance of reduction and the progress of healing. When sufficient callus has formed to assure stabilization of the fragments, generally after 12 weeks or more, further immobilization

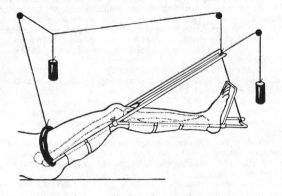

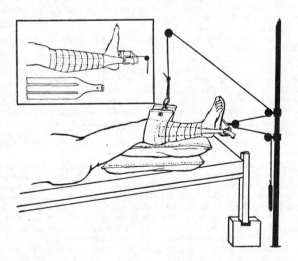

Fig. 17-23. Methods of traction for lower extremity fractures. *Top:* Method of suspension of lower extremity with skeletal traction on tibial tubercle. *Bottom:* Russel's traction. Inset shows method of application of skin traction.

can be given by a one and one half plaster spica. Prior to application of the spica, there should be a period of observation in balanced suspension without traction to determine whether displacement of the fracture fragments by overriding will occur. Angulation can generally be corrected in plaster by appropriate wedging.

Elective indications for open reduction and internal fixation may be based upon the desire to avoid prolonged recumbency in bed and hospitalization. Some mandatory indications include inability to obtain adequate reduction by closed technics and delay of bone healing. The purpose of open reduction is generally to provide anatomic reposition and clinically rigid fixation that will permit the patient to be ambulatory without such external supportive apparatus as casts, splints, or braces. Unprotected weight-bearing without crutches until restoration of bone continuity should not be a goal of open operation of most fractures.

B. IN INFANTS AND CHILDREN Femoral fracture at birth occurs most often in the middle third. Comminution is usually not present.

Skin traction and plaster immobilization are adequate, although skeletal traction may be necessary in older children. Open reduction is rarely necessary.

Fracture of the proximal or middle third of the femur in a child under 5 years of age can be treated with Bryant's traction (see Fig. 17-20). Adhesive strips are applied to both extremities from the upper thirds of the thighs to the supramalleolar regions, and held firm by circular bandages. Both hips are flexed to a right angle, and the knees are maintained in full extension. Sufficient traction force is applied to raise the buttocks free of the bed. Circulatory adequacy must be observed carefully and another method substituted if swelling, cyanosis or pallor of the foot, or obliteration of pedal pulsations cannot be managed by adjustment of dressings.

As a rule, sufficient callus is present at the fracture site after 3-4 weeks so that traction can be discontinued. If callus formation is adequate, infants who have not yet begun to walk need no further protection; walking infants may require a single plaster hip spica for an additional 4-6 weeks.

Preliminary treatment of unstable fracture of the femur in children over 5 years of age can be by Russell's traction (see Fig. 17-23). If the child is uncooperative, or if adequate correction cannot be obtained, it may also be necessary to place the sound extremity in traction. Traction should be continued until the fracture is stabilized; if traction is discontinued before the reparative callus is sufficiently mature, the deformity (especially angulation) may recur even though the extremity is protected by a plaster spica. Correction of angulation and torsional displacement around the long axis of the femur are mandatory. Slight shortening (1-2 cm) can be compensated by growth. Close apposition of fragments is not necessary, since healing will take place in spite of minimal soft tissue interposition.

It is usually necessary to continue traction for 6-8 weeks or until sufficient callus has formed to prevent recurrence of the deformity. Immobilization in a plaster spica should be maintained for another 2 months. Weight-bearing must not be resumed until x-rays show that healing is sound.

X. INJURIES OF THE KNEE REGION

A. FRACTURES OF THE DISTAL FEMUR

1. Supracondylar fracture of the femur This comparatively uncommon fracture (at the junction of cortical and cancellous bone) may be transverse, oblique, or comminuted. The distal end of the proximal fragment is apt to perforate the overlying vastus intermedius, vastus medialis, or rectus femoris muscles, and may penetrate the suprapatellar pouch of the knee joint to cause hemarthrosis. The proximal end of the distal fragment is usually displaced posteriorly and slightly laterally.

Since the distal fragment may impinge upon the popliteal vessels, circulatory adequacy distal to the fracture site should be verified as soon as possible. Absence of pedal pulsations is an indication for immediate reduction. If pulsation does not return promptly after reduction, immediate exploration and appropriate treatment of the vascular lesion is indicated.

A less frequent complication is injury to the peroneal or tibial nerve.

If the fracture is transverse or nearly so, closed manipulation under general anesthesia will occasionally be successful. Stable fractures with minimal displacement can be treated in a single plaster hip spica with the hip and knee in about 30° of flexion. Frequent x-ray examination is necessary to make certain that displacement has not occurred.

Stable or unstable uncomplicated supracondylar fracture is best treated with biplane skeletal traction if soft tissue interposition does not interfere with reduction. If adequate reduction cannot be obtained, it may be necessary to manipulate the fragments under general anesthesia, using skeletal traction to control the distal fragment.

Traction must be continued for about 6 weeks or until stabilization occurs. The wires can then be removed and the extremity immobilized in a single plaster spica for an additional 2-3 months.

An alternative method of treatment (applicable only to stable fractures) is to incorporate the wires into a plaster spica after reduction.

Supracondylar fracture is likely to be followed by restriction of knee motion due to scarring and adhesion formation in adjacent soft tissues.

2. Intercondylar fracture of the femur This uncommon comminuted fracture, which occurs only in older patients, is classically described as T or Y according to the x-ray configuration of the fragments. Closed reduction is difficult when the proximal shaft fragment is interposed between the two main distal fragments. Maximal recovery of function of the knee joint requires anatomic reduction of the articular components. If alignment is satisfactory and displacement minimal, immobilization for about 4 months in a plaster spica will be sufficient. If displacement is marked, skeletal traction through the tibial tubercle (with the knee in flexion) is required. Manual molding of the distal fragments may be necessary. Open reduction and bolt fixation of the distal fragments may be indicated to restore articular congruity. Further treatment is as described for supracondylar fracture.

3. Condylar fracture of the femur Isolated fracture of the lateral or medial condyle of the femur is a rare consequence of severe trauma. Occasionally only the posterior portion of the condyle is separated. The cruciate ligaments or the collateral ligament of the opposite side of the knee are often injured.

The objective of treatment is restoration of anatomic intraarticular relationships. If displacement is minimal, the knee can be manipulated into varus or valgus (opposite the position of deformity). If anatomic reduction cannot be obtained by closed manipulation, open reduction and fixation of the minor fragment with 2-3 bone screws is recommended. The ligaments must be explored, and repaired if found to be injured.

4. Separation of the distal femoral epiphysis Traumatic separation of the distal femoral epiphysis in children is the counterpart of supracondylar fracture in the adult. The direction of displacement of the epiphyseal fragment is most commonly anterior. Torsional displacement around the long axis of the femur may be associated.

Reduction of anterior displacement can be achieved by closed manipulation. After reduction is complete, the knee is flexed to a right angle and a tubular plaster cast is applied from the inguinal region to the toes. If the thigh is obese, the plaster should be extended proximally to include the pelvis in a single hip spica.

Peripheral circulation must be observed carefully. After 4 weeks the plaster is changed and flexion of the knee reduced to 45°. At the end of the second month the patient may be permitted to be free in bed until he regains complete knee extension.

B. FRACTURE OF THE PATELLA

1. Transverse fracture of the patella is the result of indirect violence, usually with the knee in semiflexion. Fracture may be due to sudden voluntary contraction of the quadriceps muscles or sudden forced flexion of the leg when these muscles are contracted. The level of the fracture is most often in the middle. The extent of tearing of the patellar retinacula depends upon the degree of force of the initiating injury. The activity of the quadriceps muscles causes displacement of the proximal fragment; the magnitude of displacement is dependent upon the extent of the tear of the quadriceps expansion.

Swelling of the anterior knee region is caused by hemarthrosis and hemorrhage into the soft tissues overlying the joint. If displacement is present, the defect in the patella can be palpated and active extension of the knee is lost.

Open reduction is indicated if the fragments are separated more than 2-3 mm. The fragments must be accurately repositioned to prevent early posttraumatic arthritis of the patellofemoral joint. If the minor fragment is small (no more than 1 cm in height), it may be excised and the rectus or patellar tendon (depending upon which pole of the patella is involved) sutured directly to the major fragment. If the fragments are approximately the same size, repair by wire cerclage is preferred.

Removal of 50% of the patella causes incongruity of joint surfaces, and posttraumatic arthritis may occur early.

2. Comminuted fracture of the patella is caused only by direct violence. Little or no separation of the fragments occurs because the quadriceps expansion is not extensively torn. Severe injury may cause extensive comminution of the articular cartilages of both the patella and the opposing femur. If comminution is not severe and displacement is insignificant, plaster immobilization for ° weeks in a cylinder extending from the groin to the supramalleolar region is sufficient.

Severe comminution requires excision of the patella and repair of the defect by imbrication of the quadriceps expansion.

C. TEAR OF THE QUADRICEPS TENDON occurs most often in patients over 40 years of age. Preexisting attritional disease of the tendon is apt to be present, and the causative injury may be minor. The tear commonly results from sudden deceleration, such as stumbling, or slipping on a wet surface. A small flake of bone may be avulsed from the superior pole of the patella, or the tear may occur entirely through tendinous and muscle tissue.

Pain may be noted in the anterior knee region. Swelling is due to hemarthrosis and extravasation of blood into the soft tissues. The patient is unable to extend the knee completely. X-rays may show avulsion of a bit of bone from the superior pole.

Operative repair is required for complete tear. If treatment is delayed until partial healing has occurred, the suture line can be reinforced by transplantation of the iliotibial band from the upper extremity of the tibia.

D. TEAR OF THE PATELLAR LIGAMENT The same mechanism which causes tears of the quadriceps tendon, transverse fracture of the patella, or avulsion of the tibial tuberosity may also cause tear of the patellar ligament. The characteristic clinical finding is proximal displacement of the patella. A bit of bone may be avulsed from the lower pole of the patella if the tear takes place in the proximal patellar tendon.

Operative treatment is necessary for complete tear. The ligament is resutured to the patella and any tear in the quadriceps expansion is repaired. The extremity should be immobilized for 8 weeks in a tubular plaster cast extending from the inguinal to the supramalleolar region. Guarded exercises may then be started.

E. DISLOCATION OF THE PATELLA Traumatic dislocation of the patello-femoral joint may be associated with dislocation of the knee joint. When this injury occurs alone it may be due to direct violence or muscle activity of the quadriceps, and the direction of dislocation of the patella may be lateral. Spontaneous reduction is apt to occur if the knee joint is extended; if so, the clinical findings may consist merely of hemarthrosis and localized tenderness over the medial patellar retinaculum. Gross instability of the patella, which can be demonstrated by physical examination, indicates that the injury to the soft tissues of the medial aspect of the knee has been extensive. Recurrent episodes require operative repair for effective treatment.

F. DISLOCATION OF THE KNEE JOINT is uncommon in adults and extremely rare in children. It is caused by severe trauma. Displacement may be transverse or torsional. Complete dislocation can occur only after extensive tearing of the supporting ligaments, and is apt to cause injury to the popliteal vessels or the tibial and peroneal nerves.

Signs of neurovascular injury below the site of dislocation are an absolute indication for prompt reduction under general anesthesia, since failure of circulation will undoubtedly result in gangrene of the leg and foot. Axial traction is applied to the leg and a shearing force is exerted over the fragments in the appropriate direction. If pedal pulses do not return promptly, arteriograms should be performed and the vascular injury repaired immediately.

Anatomic reduction of uncomplicated dislocation should be attempted. If impinging soft tissues cannot be removed by closed manipulation, arthrotomy is indicated. After reduction, the extremity is immobilized in a tubular plaster cast extending from the inguinal region to the toes with the knee · in slight flexion. (In the obese patient, a single hip spica should be applied.) A window should be cut in the plaster over the dorsum of the foot to allow frequent determination of dorsalis pedis pulsation. After 8 weeks' immobilization the knee can be protected by a long leg brace. Intensive quadriceps exercises are necessary to minimize functional loss.

G. INTERNAL DERANGEMENTS OF THE KNEE JOINT mechanism may be caused by trauma or attritional disease. Although ligamentous and cartilaginous injuries are discussed separately, they commonly occur as combined lesions.

Arthroscopy and newer technics of arthrography using single or double contrast media can be valuable adjuncts in establishing a precise diagnosis when the usual diagnostic methods are inconclusive.

1. Injury to the Menisci Injury to the medial meniscus is the most frequent internal derangement of the knee joint. Any portion of the meniscus may be torn. A marginal tear permits displacement of the medial fragment into the intercondylar region ('bucket-handle tear'). A fragment of cartilage displaced between the articular surfaces of the femur and tibia prevents either complete extension or complete flexion.

The significant clinical findings after acute injury are swelling (due to hemarthrosis) and varying degrees of restriction of flexion or extension. Motion may cause pain over the anteromedial or posteromedial joint line. Tenderness can often be elicited at the point of pain. Forcible external rotation of the foot with the knee flexed to a right angle may cause pain over the medial joint line. If symptoms have persisted for 2-3 weeks, weakness and atrophy of the quadriceps femoris may be present.

Injury to the lateral meniscus less often causes mechanical blockage of joint motion. Pain and tenderness may be present over the lateral joint line. Pain can be elicited by forcible rotation of the leg with the knee flexed to a right angle.

Initial treatment may be conservative. Swelling and pain caused by tense hemarthrosis can be relieved by aspiration. If pain is severe, the extremity should be immobilized in a posterior plaster splint with the knee in slight flexion. Younger patients usually prefer to be ambulatory on crutches, but immediate weight-bearing must not be permitted. As long as acute symptoms persist, isometric quadriceps exercises should be performed frequently throughout the day with the knee in maximum extension (as a 'straight leg lift'). Unrestricted activity must not be resumed until complete motion is recovered and healing is complete.

Exploratory arthrotomy is advisable for recurrent 'locking', recurrent effusion, or disabling pain. Isometric quadriceps exercises are instituted immediately after the operation and gradually increased in frequency. As soon as the patient is able to perform these exercises comfortably, graded resistance maneuvers should be started. Exercises must be continued until all motion has been recovered and the volume and competency of the quadriceps are equal to those of the uninjured side.

2. Injury to the collateral ligaments The collateral ligaments prevent excursion of the joint beyond normal limits. When the knee is in full extension, the collateral ligaments are taut; in flexion, only the anterior fibers of the tibial collateral ligament are taut.

a. Tibial collateral ligament Forced abduction of the leg at the knee, which is frequently associated with torsional strain, causes injury varying from tear of a few fibers to complete rupture of the ligament. A bit of bone may be avulsed from its femoral or tibial attachment.

A history of twisting injury at the knee with valgus strain can usually be obtained. Pain is present over the medial aspect of the knee joint. In severe injury, joint effusion may be present. Tenderness can be elicited at the site of the lesion. When only an isolated ligamentous tear is present, x-ray examination may not be helpful unless it is made while valgus stress is applied to the extended knee. Under local or general anesthesia the extremities are bound together in full extension at the knee joint, and an anteroposterior film is made with the legs in forced abduction. Widening of the medial joint cleft suggests complete rupture.

Treatment of incomplete tear consists of protection from further injury while healing progresses. Painful hemarthrosis should be relieved by aspiration. The knee may be immobilized in a posterior plaster splint or a tubular cast extending from the inguinal to the supramalleolar region.

Complete rupture should be surgically repaired immediately so that healing will take place without ligamentous elongation and subsequent instability of the knee joint. Tear of the medial collateral ligament is frequently associated with other lesions, such as tear of the medial meniscus, rupture of the anterior cruciate ligament, or fracture of the lateral condyle of the tibia.

b. Fibular collateral ligament Tear of the fibular collateral ligament is often associated with injury to surrounding structures (e.g., the popliteus muscle tendon and the iliotibial band). Avulsion of the apex of the fibular head may occur, and the peroneal nerve may be injured.

Pain and tenderness are present over the lateral aspect of the knee joint, and hemarthrosis may be present. X-rays may show a bit of bone avulsed from the fibular head. If severe injury is suspected, x-ray examination under stress, using local or general anesthesia, is required. A firm, padded, nonopaque object about 20-30 cm in diameter is placed between the knees and the legs are forcibly adducted while an anteroposterior exposure is made. Widening of the lateral joint cleft indicates severe injury.

The treatment of partial tear is similar to that described for partial tear of the medial collateral ligament. If complete tear is suspected, and especially if the peroneal nerve has been injured, exploration is indicated. The extremity is protected for 8 weeks in a plaster cylinder extending from the inguinal region to above the ankle.

    3. Injury to the cruciate ligaments The function of the anterior and posterior cruciate ligaments is to restrict anterior and posterior gliding of the tibia when the knee is flexed. If the tibia is rotated internally at the femur, the ligaments twist around themselves and become taut; if the tibia is rotated externally, they become lax.

    a. Anterior cruciate ligament Injury to the anterior cruciate ligament is usually associated with injury to the medial meniscus or the tibial collateral ligament. The cruciate ligament may be avulsed with a part of the medial tibial tubercle, or at the femoral attachment, or may rupture within the substance of its fibers.

    The characteristic clinical sign of tear of either cruciate ligament is a positive 'drawer' sign: the knee is flexed at a right angle and pulled forward; if excessive anterior excursion of the proximal tibia (in comparison with the opposite normal side) can be noted, a tear of the anterior ligament is likely.

    Complete recent rupture of the anterior cruciate ligament within its substance can occasionally be repaired with stout sutures. When manifest by avulsed tibial bone that is displaced, attachment of the fragment in anatomic position by arthrotomy is necessary. When the fragment of bone is large, displaced, and not treated until 4 weeks or more after injury, excision of the fragment and reinsertion of the ligament may be necessary to eliminate the blocking effect of the bone fragment and to permit recovery of function. Old tears may require reconstructive procedures.

    b. Posterior cruciate ligament Tear of the posterior ligament may occur within its substance or at its femoral attachment, or may be manifest by avulsion of a fragment of bone of variable size at its tibial attachment. Tear of the posterior cruciate ligament can be diagnosed by the 'drawer' sign: the knee is flexed at a right angle and the upper tibia is pushed backward; if excessive posterior excursion of the proximal tibia can be noted, tear of the posterior ligament is likely.

    Treatment is directed primarily at the associated injuries and maintenance of the competency of the quadriceps musculature. Primary repair of tears within the fibers is difficult and of dubious value. Open reduction and fixation of a fragment of tibia with the attached ligament is feasible and is likely to restore functional competency of the ligament.

H. FRACTURES OF THE PROXIMAL TIBIA

    1. Fracture of the lateral tibial condyle is commonly caused by a blow on the lateral aspect of the knee with the foot in fixed position, producing an abduction strain. Hemarthrosis is always present, as the fracture cleft involves the knee joint. Soft tissue injuries are likely to be present also. The tibial collateral and anterior cruciate ligaments may be torn. A displaced free fragment may tear the overlying lateral meniscus. If displacement is marked, fracture of the proximal fibula may be present also.

    The objective of treatment is to restore the articular surface and normal anatomic relationships, so that torn ligaments can heal without elongation. In cases of minimal displacement where ligaments have not been extensively damaged, treatment may be by immobilization for 6 weeks in a tubular plaster cast extending from the toes to the inguinal region with the knee in slight flexion. Reduction of marked displacement can be achieved by closed manipulation unless comminution is severe. After x-ray verification of reduction, the extremity can be immobilized in a tubular plaster cast extending from the inguinal region to the toes, preferably with the knee in full extension.

    Many fractures of the lateral condyle of the tibia, especially comminuted fractures, cannot be reduced adequately by closed methods. Open reduction and stabilization with a bolt or multiple bone screws may be necessary.

2. Fracture of the medial tibial condyle is caused by the adduction strain produced by a blow against the medial aspect of the knee with the foot in fixed position. The medial meniscus and the fibular collateral ligament may be torn. Severe comminution is not usually present, and there is only one major free fragment.

Treatment is by closed reduction to restore the articular surface of the tibia so that ligamentous healing can occur without elongation. After reduction the extremity is immobilized for 10–12 weeks in a tubular plaster cast extending from the inguinal region to the toes with the knee in full extension. Weight-bearing is not permitted for 4 months at least.

3. Fracture of both tibial condyles Axial force, such as may result from falling on the foot or sudden deceleration with the knee in full extension (during an automobile accident), can cause simultaneous fracture of both condyles of the tibia. Comminution is apt to be severe. Swelling of the knee due to hemarthrosis is marked. Deformity is either genu varum or genu valgum. X-ray examination should include oblique projections.

Severe comminution makes anatomic reduction difficult to achieve by any means and difficult to maintain following closed manipulation alone. Sustained skeletal traction is usually necessary. When stability has been achieved, the extremity can be immobilized for another 4–6 weeks in a tubular plaster cast extending from the toes to the inguinal region with the knee in full extension. Unassisted weight-bearing is not permitted before the end of the fourth month.

If closed methods are not effective, open reduction must be attempted.

Instability and restriction of motion of the knee are common sequelae of this type of fracture. If reduction is not adequate, posttraumatic arthritis will appear early.

4. Fracture of the tibial tuberosity Violent contraction of the quadriceps muscle may cause avulsion of the tibial tuberosity. Avulsion of the anterior portion of the upper tibial epiphysis, uncommon in childhood, must be differentiated from Osgood–Schlatter disease (osteochondrosis of the tibial tuberosity).

When avulsion of the tuberosity is complete, active extension of the knee is not possible.

If displacement is minimal, treatment is by immobilization in a tubular plaster cast extending from the inguinal to the supramalleolar region with the knee in full extension. Immobilization is maintained for 8 weeks or until stabilization occurs.

A loose fragment which has been displaced more than 0.5 cm can be treated either by closed reduction and percutaneous fixation, with plaster immobilization, or by open reduction.

5. Fracture of the tibial tubercle This injury usually occurs in association with comminuted fracture of the condyles. The medial intercondyloid tubercle may be avulsed with adjacent bone attached to the anterior cruciate ligament, and injury to that structure is of greater importance. In addition to avulsion of the anterior cruciate ligament, there may also be injury to the tibial collateral ligament and the medial knee joint capsule. Hemarthrosis is always present.

Isolated and undisplaced fracture may be treated by immobilization of the extremity for 6 weeks in a tubular plaster cast extending from the inguinal region to the toes with the knee in slight flexion. The treatment of displaced fracture is the same as that of rupture of the anterior cruciate ligament (see above).

6. Separation of the proximal tibial epiphysis Complete displacement of the proximal tibial epiphysis is rare; partial separation due to forceful hyperextension of the knee is more common. The distal metaphyseal fragment is displaced anteriorly.

If no circulatory or neurologic deficit is present, immediate treatment by closed manipulation is indicated. Reduction can be accomplished by forced flexion of the knee. Anteroposterior films are then exposed by holding the plate against the anterior surface of the leg with the beam directed through the lower thigh. A lateral film is also prepared. If x-rays show that reduction is adequate, a heavy anterior plaster splint is applied from the inguinal region to the bases of the toes, with the knee in acute flexion. The splint is maintained in position with circular bandages around the foot, ankle, and upper thigh. The bandages are wrapped in figure-of-eight fashion around the thigh and leg (as is done for supracondylar fracture of the humerus). Peripheral circulation must be observed frequently for at least 72 hours. After 3 weeks the knee may be brought to a right angle and a tubular plaster cast applied from the inguinal region to the toes for another 3–4 weeks. Even guarded weight-bearing must be avoided until the end of the second month.

Injury to the proximal tibial epiphyseal plate as a result of a blow on the lateral aspect of the knee causes compression but only minor displacement. This lesion, analogous to fracture of the lateral condyle in the adult, is apt to retard or arrest the growth of the lateral aspect of the tibia and thus cause tibia valga, or knock-knee. Surgical arrest of the growth of the medial tibial epiphysis may be necessary to prevent this deformity.

I. FRACTURE OF THE PROXIMAL FIBULA   Isolated fracture of the proximal fibula is uncommon; this fracture is usually associated with fracture of the femur or of the tibia or fracture-dislocation of the ankle joint. The apex of the fibular head may be avulsed by the activity of the biceps femoris muscle or detached with the fibular collateral ligament by an adduction strain of the knee.

The fracture usually requires no treatment, but avulsion of the apex of the head may necessitate operative repair of the ligament or tendon.

Fracture in this region may be associated with paralysis of the common peroneal nerve.

J. DISLOCATION OF THE PROXIMAL TIBIOFIBULAR JOINT   This extremely rare lesion is caused by the activity of the biceps femoris muscle. Displacement is posterior, and can be reduced by digital pressure over the head of the fibula in the opposite direction.

XI. FRACTURES OF THE SHAFTS OF THE TIBIA AND FIBULA

Fracture of the shaft of the tibia or fibula occurs at any age but is most common during youth and active adulthood. In general, open, transverse, comminuted, and segmental fractures are caused by direct violence. Fracture of the middle third of the shaft (especially if comminuted) is apt to be complicated by delay of bone healing.

If fracture is complete and displacement is present, clinical diagnosis is not difficult. However, critical local examination is of utmost importance in planning treatment. The nature of the skin wounds which may communicate with the fracture site often suggests the mechanism of compounding, whether it has occurred from within or from without. A small laceration without contused edges suggests that the point of a bone fragment has caused compounding from within. A large wound with contused edges, especially over the subcutaneous surface of the tibia, suggests compounding from without. The presence of abrasions more than 6 hours old, blebs, pyoderma, and preexisting ulcers precludes immediate open treatment of closed fracture. Extensive swelling due to hemorrhagic exudate in closed fascial compartments may prevent complete reduction immediately. Extensive hemorrhagic and edematous infiltration can complicate satisfactory closure of the subcutaneous tissue and skin incidental to elective open reduction. Neurovascular integrity below the level of the fracture must be verified before definitive treatment is instituted.

X-rays in the anteroposterior and lateral projection of the entire leg, including both the knee and ankle joints, are always necessary, and oblique projections are often desirable. The surgeon must know the exact site and configuration of the fracture, the severity of comminution, and the direction of displacement of fragments. Inadequate x-ray examination can lead to an incomplete diagnosis.

A. FRACTURE OF THE SHAFT OF THE FIBULA   Isolated fracture is uncommon and is usually caused by direct trauma. Fibular shaft fracture is usually associated with other injury of the leg, such as fracture of the tibia or fracture-dislocation of the ankle joint. If no other lesion is present, immobilization for 4 weeks in a plaster boot (equipped with a walking surface) extending from the knee to the toes is sufficient for displaced, painful fractures. Undisplaced fractures require no immobilization, but discomfort can be minimized during the early days after injury by the use of crutches or a cane. Complete healing of uncomplicated fracture can be expected.

B. FRACTURE OF THE SHAFT OF THE TIBIA   Isolated fracture is likely to be caused by indirect injury, such as torsional stress. Because of mechanical stability provided by the intact fibula, marked displacement is not apt to occur. Marked overriding suggests a lesion of either tibiofibular joint.

If the fragments are not displaced, reliable treatment may be given by immobilization in a tubular plaster cast extending from the inguinal region to the toes with the knee in flexion and the foot in neutral position. The plaster should be changed at appropriate intervals to correct the loosening which will occur as a result of absorption of hemorrhagic exudate and atrophy of the thigh and calf muscles. Immobilization should be continued for at least 10 weeks, or until early bone healing is demonstrated by x-ray.

If the fragments are displaced, manipulation under anesthesia may be necessary. Fractures with a comparative transverse cleft tend to be stable after reduction. Oblique and spiral fractures tend to become displaced unless the fragments are locked.

A tubular plaster cast is applied as for undisplaced fracture. If x-rays do not show satisfactory apposition of fragments, alternative methods of treatment should be used (see below).

C. FRACTURE OF THE SHAFTS OF TIBIA AND FIBULA IN ADULTS
Simultaneous fracture of the shafts of both bones are unstable lesions which tend to become displaced following reduction. Treatment is directed toward reduction and stabilization of the tibial fracture until healing takes place. For adequate reduction, the fragments must be apposed almost completely, and angulation and torsional displacement of the tibial fracture must be corrected.

If reduction by closed manipulation is anatomic, transverse fractures tend to be stable. Repeated x-rays are necessary to determine whether displacement has recurred. The plaster must remain snug at all times. Recurrent angular displacement can be corrected by dividing the plaster circumferentially and inserting wedges in the appropriate direction. If apposition is disturbed, another type of treatment must be substituted.

If oblique and spiral fractures are unstable following manipulation and immobilization, internal fixation, percutaneous fixation, or skeletal traction is usually required. Percutaneous fixation (osteotaxis) can be accomplished either by incorporation of pins or wires into the cast which transfix the major bone fragments or by the use of an extraskeletal apparatus such as that of Anderson, Stader, or Haynes.

An alternative method is continuous skeletal traction, which must be continued for about 6 weeks or until preliminary healing causes stabilization. The extremity is then immobilized in plaster for at least 12 weeks until bone continuity has been restored.

If adequate apposition and correction of the deformity cannot be achieved by closed methods, open reduction and internal fixation are required.

The blood supply to intermediate fragments is likely to be disturbed in comminuted and segmental fractures. These unstable fractures can usually be treated successfully only by closed reduction and external immobilization. If the patient wishes to remain ambulatory, percutaneous fixation of the major fragments with Steinmann pins or Kirschner wires will maintain reduction and alignment. However, continuous skeletal traction in plaster with a Kirschner wire inserted through the calcaneus is usually preferred until stabilization occurs (Fig. 17-24).

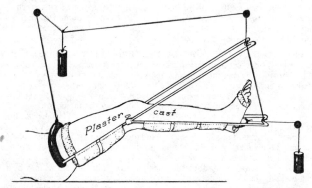

Fig. 17-24. Calcaneal skeletal traction and full lower extremity plaster for unstable fracture of tibia and fibula.

D. FRACTURE OF THE SHAFTS OF TIBIA AND FIBULA IN CHILDREN

Open reduction and internal fixation of closed fractures of the tibia or fibula in children are rarely necessary. If a tibial fracture is stable because of the configuration of the ends of the fragments, or if the fibular shaft is intact, closed reduction of axial displacement (overriding) is desirable; angular and torsional displacement must be corrected also. If proper alignment is secured, 1 cm of overriding is acceptable.

Comminuted or oblique tibial fractures with displacement or fractures of both bones require continuous skeletal traction by means of a Kirschner wire inserted through the calcaneus until early bone healing stabilizes the fragments. Further immobilization in a tubular plaster cast is necessary until bone healing is sufficiently well along to permit weight-bearing.

XII. INJURIES OF THE ANKLE REGION

A. ANKLE SPRAIN during childhood is rare. In the adult, ankle sprain is most often caused by forced inversion of the foot, as may occur in stumbling on uneven ground. Pain is usually maximal over the anterolateral aspect of the joint; greatest tenderness is apt to be found in the region of the anterior talofibular and talocalcaneal ligaments. Eversion sprain is less common; maximal tenderness and swelling are usually found over the deltoid ligament.

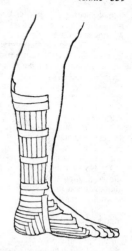

Fig. 17-25. Gibney ankle strapping

Sprain is differentiated from major partial or complete ligamentous tears by anteroposterior, lateral, and 30° internal oblique x-ray projections; if the joint cleft between either malleolus and the talus is greater than 4 mm, major ligamentous tear is probable. Occult lesions can be demonstrated by x-ray examination under inversion or eversion stress after infiltration of the area of maximal swelling and tenderness with 5 ml of 2% procaine.

If swelling is marked, elevation of the extremity and avoidance of weight-bearing for a few days is advisable. The ankle can be supported with a Gibney strapping (Fig. 17-25). Adhesive support for another 2 weeks will relieve pain and swelling. Further treatment may be by warm foot baths and elastic bandages. Continue treatment until muscle strength and full joint motion are recovered. Tears of major ligaments of the ankle joint are discussed below.

B. FRACTURES AND DISLOCATIONS OF THE ANKLE JOINT may be caused by direct injury, in which case they are apt to be comminuted and open; or by indirect violence, which often causes typical lesions (see below).

Pain and swelling are the prominent clinical findings. Deformity may or may not be present. X-rays of excellent technical quality must be prepared in a sufficient variety of projections to demonstrate the extent and configuration of all major fragments. Special oblique projections may be required.

1. Fracture of the medial malleolus may occur as an isolated lesion of any part of the malleolus (including the tip), or may be associated with (1) fracture of the lateral malleolus with medial or lateral dislocation of the talus, and (2) dislocation of the inferior tibiofibular joint with or without fracture of the fibula. Isolated fracture does not usually cause instability of the ankle joint.

Undisplaced isolated fracture of the medial malleolus should be treated by immobilization in a plaster boot extending from the knee to the toes with the ankle flexed to a right angle and the foot slightly inverted to relax the tension on the deltoid ligament. Immobilization must be continued for 6–8 weeks or until bone healing is sound.

Displaced isolated fracture of the medial malleolus may be treated by closed manipulation under general or local anesthesia. The essential maneuver consists of anatomic realignment by digital pressure over the distal fragment, followed by immobilization in a plaster boot (as for undisplaced fracture) until bone healing is sound. If anatomic reduction cannot be obtained by closed methods, open reduction and internal fixation with 1-2 bone screws are required.

2. Fracture of the lateral malleolus may occur as an isolated lesion, or may be associated with fracture of the medial malleolus, tear of the deltoid or posterior lateral malleolar ligament, or avulsion of the posterior tibial tubercle. If the medial aspect of the ankle is injured, lateral dislocation of the talus is apt to be present. The tip of the lateral malleolus may be avulsed by the calcaneofibular and anterior talofibular ligaments. Transverse or oblique fracture may occur. Oblique fractures commonly extend downward and anteriorly from the posterior and superior aspects.

If swelling and pain are not marked, isolated undisplaced fracture of the lateral malleolus may be treated by Gibney ankle strapping. Otherwise, a plaster boot should be applied for 6 weeks and an elastic bandage worn thereafter until full joint motion is recovered and the calf muscles are functioning normally.

Isolated displaced fracture of the lateral malleolus should be treated by closed manipulation. The foot should be immobilized in slight inversion, which tautens the ligaments over the lateral aspect of the ankle joint and tends to prevent displacement.

If anatomic reduction cannot be achieved by closed methods, open reduction is required.

3. Combined fracture of the medial and lateral malleoli Bimalleolar fractures are commonly accompanied by displacement of the talus, usually in a medial or lateral direction. In conjunction with dislocation in the coronal plane, concurrent displacement may take place in the sagittal plane, either anteriorly or posteriorly, or in torsion about the longitudinal axis of the tibia.

Bimalleolar fracture may be treated by closed manipulation. A tubular plaster cast is then applied from the inguinal region to the toes with the knee in about 45° of flexion and the foot in neutral position. Immediate open reduction must be resorted to if x-rays show that perfect anatomic reduction has not been achieved by closed manipulation.

4. Fractures of the distal tibia are usually associated with other lesions.

a. Fracture of the posterior margin Fracture of the posterior articular margin may involve part or all of the entire posterior half and is apt to be accompanied by fracture of either malleolus and posterior dislocation of the talus. It must be differentiated from fracture of the posterior tibial tubercle, which is usually caused by avulsion with the attached posterior lateral malleolar ligament.

Anatomic reduction by closed manipulation is required if the fracture involves more than 25% of the articular surface. The extremity is immobilized in a plaster cast extending from the inguinal region to the toes with the knee in about 45° of flexion, the ankle at a right angle, and the foot in neutral position.

Frequent x-ray examination is necessary to make certain that redisplacement does not occur. The plaster should be changed as soon as loosening becomes apparent. Immobilization must be maintained for at least 8 weeks. Weight-bearing must not be resumed until bone healing is sound, usually in about 12 weeks.

b. Fracture of the anterior margin of the tibia (rare) is likely to be caused by forced dorsiflexion of the foot. If displacement is marked and the talus is dislocated, tear of the collateral ligaments or fractures of the malleoli are likely to be present.

Reduction is by closed manipulation. If comminution is present, the extremity should be immobilized for about 12 weeks. Healing is apt to be slow.

c. Comminuted fractures Extensive comminution of the distal tibia ('compression type' fracture) presents a difficult problem of management. The congruity of articular surfaces cannot be restored by closed manipulation, and satisfactory anatomic restoration is usually not possible even by open reduction. The best form of treatment for extensively comminuted and widely displaced fractures is closed manipulation and skeletal traction. After traction has been applied and impaction of fragments has been disrupted, displacement in the transverse plane is corrected by manual molding with compression. A tubular plaster cast is applied from the inguinal region to the toes with the knee in 10-15° of flexion and the foot in neutral position. With the extremity immobilized in plaster, continuous skeletal traction can be maintained for 8-12 weeks or until stabilization by early bone healing occurs. An alternative is distraction with a wire or pin in the calcaneus and one or two wires or pins in the shaft of the tibia.

Healing is likely to be slow. If the articular surfaces of the ankle joint have not been properly realigned, disabling posttraumatic arthritis is likely to occur early. Early arthrodesis is indicated to shorten the period of disability.

5. Complete dislocation of the ankle joint The talus cannot be completely dislocated from the ankle joint unless all ligaments are torn. This lesion is rare.

6. Incomplete dislocation of the ankle joint Major ligamentous injuries in the region of the ankle joint are usually associated with fracture.

a. Tear of the deltoid ligament Complete tear of the talotibial portion of the deltoid ligament can permit interposition of the posterior tibial tendon between the medial malleolus and the talus. Associated injury is usually present, especially fracture of the lateral malleolus with lateral dislocation of the talus.

Pain, tenderness, swelling, and ecchymosis in the region of the medial malleolus without fracture suggest partial or complete tear of the deltoid ligament. If fracture of the lateral malleolus or dislocation of the distal tibiofibular joint is present, the cleft between the malleolus and talus is likely to be widened. If significant widening is not apparent, x-ray examination under stress is necessary.

Interposition of the deltoid ligament between the talus and the medial malleolus often cannot be corrected by closed manipulation. If widening persists after closed manipulation, surgical exploration is indicated so that the ligament can be removed and repaired by suture.

Associated fracture of the fibula can be treated by fixation with a coaxial intramedullary standard bone screw or a bone nail to assure maintenance of anatomic reduction.

b. Tear of the talofibular ligament Isolated tear of the anterior talofibular ligament is caused by forced inversion of the foot. X-ray examination under stress may be necessary, using local or general anesthesia. Both feet are forcibly inverted and internally rotated about 20° while an anteroposterior film is exposed. If the tear is complete, the talus will be seen to be axially displaced from the tibial articular surface.

Rupture of the anterior talofibular ligament may be associated with tear of the calcaneofibular ligament. Tear of both ligaments may be associated with fracture of the medial malleolus and medial dislocation of the talus.

Instability of the ankle joint, characterized by a history of recurrent sprains, may result from unrecognized tears of the anterior talofibular ligament.

Recent isolated tear of the anterior talofibular ligament or combined tear of the calcaneofibular ligament should be treated by immobilization for 4 weeks in a plaster boot. Associated fracture of the medial malleolus creates an unstable mechanism. Unless anatomic reduction can be achieved and maintained by closed methods, open reduction of the malleolar fragment is indicated, followed by internal fixation of the fracture and repair of the ligamentous injury.

7. Dislocation of the distal tibiofibular joint Both the anterior and posterior lateral malleolar ligaments must be torn before the distal tibiofibular joint can be dislocated. Lateral dislocation of the talus is also an essential feature, and this cannot occur unless the medial malleolus is fractured or the deltoid ligament is torn. The distal fibula is commonly fractured, but it may remain intact, and dislocation may be caused by a tear of the interosseous ligament.

Anatomic reduction by closed manipulation is difficult to achieve, but should be tried. Under general anesthesia, the foot is forced medially by a shearing maneuver and a snug plaster is applied from the inguinal region to the toes. If immediate and repeated x-ray examinations do not demonstrate that anatomic reduction has been achieved and maintained, open reduction and internal fixation should be performed as soon as possible.

8. Separation of the distal tibial and fibular epiphyses   The most common injury of the ankle region of children is traumatic separation of the distal tibial and fibular epiphyses. Sprain is rare in children. Separation of the distal fibular epiphysis may occur as an isolated injury, or it may be associated with separation of the tibial epiphysis.

If displacement has occurred, treatment is by closed manipulation and plaster immobilization. Open reduction is seldom justifiable. If injury has been severe, disturbance of growth is likely to follow.

XIII. INJURIES OF THE FOOT

A. FRACTURE AND DISLOCATION OF THE TALUS

1. Dislocation of the subtalar and talonavicular joints without fracture occasionally occurs. The talocrural joint is not injured. Displacement of the foot can be either in varus or valgus. Reduction by closed manipulation is usually not difficult. Incarceration of the posterior tibial tendon in the talonavicular joint may prevent reduction by closed manipulation. After reduction, the extremity should be immobilized in a plaster boot for 4 weeks.

2. Fracture of the talus   Major fracture commonly occurs through the body or through the neck; the uncommon fracture of the head involves essentially a portion of the neck with extension into the head. Indirect injury is usually the cause of closed fracture as well as most open fractures; severe comminution is infrequent. Compression fracture or infraction of the tibial articular surface may be caused by the initial injury or may occur later in association with complicating avascular necrosis. The proximal or distal fragments may be dislocated.

a. Fracture of the neck   Forced dorsiflexion of the foot may cause this injury. Undisplaced fracture of the neck can be treated adequately by a non-weight-bearing plaster boot for 8-12 weeks. Dislocation of the body or the distal neck fragment with the foot may complicate this injury. Fracture of the neck with anterior and frequently medial dislocation of the distal fragment and foot can usually be reduced by closed manipulation. Subsequent treatment is the same as that of undisplaced fracture.

Dislocation of the proximal body fragment may occur separately or may be associated with dislocation of the distal fragment. If dislocation of the body fragment is complete, reduction by closed manipulation may not be possible. If reduction by closed manipulation is not successful, open reduction should be done promptly to prevent or to minimize the extent of the avascular necrosis. Bone healing is likely to be retarded since some degree of ischemic necrosis is probable.

Complete dislocation of the neck fragment from the talonavicular and subtalar joints is rare; but if it does happen, avascular necrosis of the fragment is to be expected even though anatomic reduction is promptly accomplished. If satisfactory reduction by closed manipulation is not possible, immediate open operation with reduction of the fragment or its removal is advisable, since delay may cause necrosis of overlying soft tissues.

b. Fracture of the body   Closed uncomminuted fracture of the body of the talus with minimal displacement of fragments is not likely to cause disability if immobilization is continued until bone continuity is restored. If significant displacement occurs, the proximal fragment is apt to be dislocated from the subtalar and ankle joints. Reduction by closed manipulation can be achieved best by traction and forced plantar flexion of the foot. Immobilization in a plaster boot with the foot in equinus for about 8 weeks should be followed by further casting with the foot at a right angle until the fracture cleft has been obliterated by new bone formation as evidenced by x-ray examination. Even though prompt adequate reduction is obtained by either closed manipulation or by open operation, extensive displacement of the proximal body fragment is likely to be followed by avascular necrosis. If reduction is not anatomic, delayed healing of the fracture may follow and posttraumatic arthritis is a likely sequel. If this occurs, arthrodesis of the ankle and subtalar joints may be necessary to relieve painful symptoms.

  c. Compression fracture or infraction of the dome of the talus from the initial injury (which is likely to have been violent) cannot be reduced. When this lesion occurs as a separate entity or in combination with other fractures of the body, prolonged protection from weight-bearing is the major means of preventing the further collapse that is so likely to occur in the area of healing.

B. FRACTURE OF THE CALCANEUS is commonly caused by direct trauma. Since this fracture is likely to occur as a result of a fall from a height, fracture of the spine may also be present. Comminution and impaction are general characteristics. Minor infractions or impactions and fissure fractures are easy to miss on clinical examination, and x-rays must be prepared in multiple projections to demonstrate fracture clefts. In some instances, minor impactions of articular surfaces will be evident only by tomography.

  Various classifications have been advocated. Fractures that are generally comminuted and disrupt the subtalar and calcaneocuboid articulations should be distinguished from those that do not; this differentiation has important implications for treatment and prognosis.

  1. Fracture of the tuberosity Isolated fracture is not common. It may occur in a vertical or a horizontal direction.

  a. Horizontal fracture may be limited to the superior portion of the region of the former apophysis and represents an avulsion by the Achilles tendon. Where the superior minor fragment is widely displaced proximally with the tendon, open reduction and fixation with a stout wire suture may be necessary to obtain the most satisfactory functional result.

  Further extension of the fracture cleft toward the subtalar joint in the substance of the tuberosity creates the 'beak' fracture. The minor fragment may be displaced proximally by the action of the triceps surae. If displacement is significant, reduction can be achieved by skeletal traction applied to the proximal fragment with the foot in equinus. Immobilization is obtained by incorporation of the traction pin or wire in a full extremity plaster with the knee flexed 30° and the foot in plantar flexion. If adequate reduction cannot be accomplished in this way, open reduction is advised.

  b. Vertical fracture occurs near the sagittal plane somewhat medially through the tuberosity. Because the minor medial fragment normally is not widely displaced, plaster immobilization is not required. Comfort can be enhanced by limitation of weight-bearing with the aid of crutches.

  2. Fracture of the sustentaculum Isolated fracture is a rare lesion which may be caused by forced eversion of the foot. Where displacement of the larger body fragment occurs, it is lateral. Incarceration of the tendon of the flexor hallucis longus in the fracture cleft has been reported. Generally this fracture occurs in association with comminution of the body.

  3. Fracture of the anterior process is caused by forced inversion of the foot. It must be differentiated from midtarsal and ankle joint sprains. The firmly attached bifurcate ligament (calcaneonavicular and calcaneocuboid components) avulses a bit of bone. Maximum tenderness and slight swelling occur midway between the tip of the lateral malleolus and the base of the fifth metatarsal. The lateral x-ray view projected obliquely is the most satisfactory to demonstrate the fracture cleft. Treatment is by a non-weight-bearing plaster boot with the foot in neutral position for 4 weeks.

4. Fracture of the body may occur posterior to the articular sufaces, in a general vertical but somewhat oblique plane, without disruption of the subtalar joint. Most severe fractures of the calcaneal body are comminuted and extend into the subtalar and frequently the calcaneocuboid joints. Fissure fractures without significant displacement cause minor disability and can be treated simply by protection from weight-bearing, either by crutches alone or in combination with a plaster boot until bone healing is sufficiently sound to justify graded increments of loading.

a. Nonarticular fracture Where fracture of the body with comminution occurs posterior to the articular surface, the direction of significant displacement of the fragment attached to the tuberosity is proximal, causing diminution of the tuber joint angle. Since the subtalar joint is not disrupted, symptomatic posttraumatic degenerative arthritis is not an important sequel even though some joint stiffness persists permanently. Marked displacement should be corrected by skeletal traction applied to the main posterior fragment to obtain an optimal cosmetic result, especially in women. Success of reduction can be judged by the adequacy of restoration of the tuber joint angle.

b. Articular fractures are of three general types:

(1) *Noncomminuted* Fracture of the body without comminution may involve the posterior articular facet. Where displacement of the posterior fragment of the tuberosity occurs, the direction is lateral. Fractures of this category with more than minimal displacement should be treated by the method advocated for nonarticular fracture of the body.

(2) *With minor comminution* In fractures with minor comminution, the main cleft occurs vertically, in a somewhat oblique lateral deviation from the sagittal plane. From emergence on the medial surface posterior to the sustentaculum it is directed forward and rather obliquely laterally through the posterior articular facet. The sustentaculum and the medial portion of the posterior articular facet remain undisplaced with relation to the talus. The body below the remaining lateral portion of the posterior articular facet with the tuberosity are impacted into the lateral portion of the posterior articular facet. Open reduction and bone grafting is recommended. Lack of precise reduction, determined in part by restoration of the normal tuber joint angle, causes derangement of the subtalar joint, and symptomatic posttraumatic arthritis is a frequent sequel.

(3) *With extensive comminution* Fracture with extensive comminution extending into the subtalar joint may involve the calcaneocuboid joint as well as the tuberosity. Multiple fracture clefts involve the entire posterior articular surface and the facet is impacted into the substance of the underlying body. There are many variants; the clefts may extend across the calcaneal groove into the medial and anterior articular surface, and detachment of the peroneal tubercle may be a feature. This serious injury may cause major disability in spite of the best treatment since the bursting nature of the injury defies anatomic restoration.

Some surgeons advise nonintervention. Displacement of fragments is disregarded. Initially, a compression dressing is applied and the extremity is elevated for a week or so. Warm soaks and active exercises are then started, but weight-bearing is avoided until early bone healing has taken place. In spite of residual deformity of the heel, varying degrees of weakness of the calf, and discomfort in the region of the subtalar joint (which may be intensified by weight-bearing), acceptable functional results can be obtained, especially among vigorous men who are willing to put up with the discomforts involved.

Other surgeons advocate early closed manipulation which can partially restore the external anatomic configuration of the heel region, a cosmetic goal particularly desirable for women.

Persistent and disabling painful symptoms originating in the deranged subtalar joint may require arthrodesis for adequate relief. Concomitant involvement of the calcaneocuboid joint is an indication for the more extensive triple arthrodesis.

C. FRACTURE OF THE TARSAL NAVICULAR

Minor avulsion fractures may occur as a feature of severe midtarsal sprain and require neither reduction nor elaborate treatment. Avulsion fracture of the tuberosity near the insertion of the posterior tibial muscle is uncommon and must be differentiated from a persistent, ununited apophysis (accessory scaphoid) and from the supernumerary sesamoid bone, the os tibiale externum.

Major fracture occurs either through the middle in a horizontal plane, or, more rarely, in the vertical plane, or is characterized by impaction of its substance. Only noncomminuted fractures with displacement of the dorsal fragment can be reduced. Closed manipulation by strong traction on the forefoot and simultaneous digital pressure over the displaced fragment can restore it to its normal position. If a tendency to redisplacement is apparent, this can be counteracted by temporary fixation with a percutaneously inserted Kirschner wire. Comminuted and impacted fractures cannot be anatomically reduced. Some authorities offer a pessimistic prognosis for comminuted or impacted fractures. It is their contention that even though partial reduction has been achieved, posttraumatic arthritis supervenes, and that arthrodesis of the talonavicular and cuneonavicular joints will be ultimately necessary to relieve painful symptoms.

D. FRACTURE OF THE CUNEIFORM AND CUBOID BONES

Because of their relatively protected position in the midtarsus, isolated fracture of the cuboid and cuneiform bones are rarely encountered. Minor avulsion fractures occur as a component of severe midtarsal sprains. Extensive fracture usually occurs in association with other injuries of the foot and often is caused by severe crushing. Simple classification is impractical because of the complex character and the multiple combinations of the whole injury.

E. MIDTARSAL DISLOCATIONS

through the cuneonavicular and the calcaneocuboid joints or, more proximally, through the talocalcaneonavicular and the calcaneocuboid joints may occur as a result of twisting injury to the forefoot. Fractures of varying extent of adjacent bones are frequent complications. When treatment is given soon after the accident, closed reduction by traction on the forefoot and manipulation is generally effective. If reduction is unstable and displacement tends to recur upon release of traction, stabilization for 4 weeks by percutaneously inserted Kirschner wires is recommended.

F. FRACTURES AND DISLOCATIONS OF THE METATARSALS

Fractures of metatarsals and tarsometatarsal dislocations are likely to be caused by direct crushing or indirect twisting injury to the forefoot. Besides osseous and articular injury, complicating soft tissue lesions are often present. Tense subfascial hematoma of the dorsum of the forefoot, if not relieved, may cause necrosis of overlying skin or may even lead to gangrene of the toes by interruption of the arterial supply.

1. Tarsometatarsal dislocations Possibly because of strong ligamentous support and relative size, dislocation of the first metatarsal at its base occurs less frequently than similar involvement of the lesser bones. If dislocation occurs, fracture of the first cuneiform is likely to be present also. More often, however, tarsometatarsal dislocation involves the lesser metatarsals, and associated fractures are to be expected. Dislocation is more commonly caused by direct injury but may be the result of stress applied indirectly through the forefoot. The direction of displacement is ordinarily dorsal, lateral, or a combination of both.

Attempted closed reduction should not be deferred. Skeletal traction applied to the involved bone by a Kirschner wire or a stout towel clamp can be a valuable aid to manipulation. Even though persistent dislocation may not cause significant disability, the resulting deformity can make shoe fitting difficult for men and the cosmetic effect undesirable to women. Open reduction with evacuation of dorsal subfascial hematoma and Kirschner wire stabilization is a preferred alternative to unsuccessful closed treatment. When effective treatment has been deferred 4 weeks or even longer, early healing will prevent satisfactory reduction of persisting displacement by closed technics. Under such circumstances, it is better to defer open operation and to direct treatment toward recovery of function. Extensive operative procedures and continued immobilization can increase joint stiffness. Reconstructive operation can be planned more suitably after residual disability becomes established.

2. Fractures of the shafts Undisplaced fractures of the metatarsal shafts cause no permanent disability unless failure of bone healing is encountered. Displacement is rarely significant where fracture of the middle metatarsals is oblique and the first and fifth are uninjured, since they act as splints. Even fissure fractures should be treated by a stiff-soled shoe (with partial weight-bearing) or, if pain is marked, by a plaster walking boot.

Great care should be taken in displaced fractures to correct angulation in the longitudinal axis of the shaft. Persistent convex dorsal angulation causes prominence of the head of the involved metatarsal on the plantar aspect with the implication of concentrated local pressure and production of painful skin callosities. Deformity of the shaft of the first metatarsal due to convex plantar angulation can transfer weight-bearing stress to the region of the head of the third metatarsal. After correction of angular displacement, the plaster casing should be molded well to the plantar aspect of the foot to minimize recurrence of deformity and to support the longitudinal and transverse arches.

If reduction is not reasonably accurate, fractures through the shafts near the heads (the 'neck') may cause great discomfort from concentrated pressure beneath the head on the plantar surface and reactive keratosis formation. Every effort should be made to correct convex dorsal angulation by disrupting impaction and appropriate manipulation. Unstable fracture can be treated by sustained skeletal traction using a Kirschner wire inserted through the distal phalanx and traction supplied by an elastic band attached to a 'banjo' bow. The efficacy of closed treatment should be determined without delay, and, where it is lacking, open operation should be substituted.

3. Fatigue fracture of the shafts of the metatarsals has been described by various terms, e.g., march, stress, and insufficiency fracture, and by a variety of other terms in the French and German literature. Its protean clinical manifestations cause difficulty in precise recognition, even to the point of confusion with osteogenic sarcoma. Commonly, it occurs in active young adults, such as military recruits, who are unaccustomed to vigorous and excessive walking. A history of a single significant injury is lacking. Incipient pain of varying intensity in the forefoot which is accentuated by walking, swelling, and localized tenderness of the involved metatarsal are cardinal manifestations. Depending upon the stage of progress, x-rays may not demonstrate the fracture cleft and extracortical callus formation may ultimately be the only clue. More striking findings may vary from an incomplete fissure to an evident transverse cleft. Persistent unprotected weight-bearing may cause arrest of bone healing and even displacement of the distal fragment. The second and third metatarsals are most frequently involved near the junction of the middle and distal thirds. The lesion can occur more proximally and in other lesser metatarsals. Since weight-bearing is likely to prolong and aggravate symptoms, treatment is by protection in either a plaster walking boot or a heavy shoe with the sole reinforced by a steel strut. Weight-bearing should be restricted until painful symptoms subside and restoration of bone continuity has been demonstrated by x-ray examination.

4. Fracture of the tuberosity of the fifth metatarsal Forced adduction of the forefoot may cause avulsion fracture of the tuberosity of the fifth metatarsal and, where supporting soft tissues have been torn, activity of the peroneus brevis muscle may increase displacement of the avulsed proximal fragment. If displacement of the minor fragment is minimal, adhesive strapping or a stiff-soled shoe is adequate treatment. If displacement is significant, treatment should be by a walking boot until bone healing occurs. Rarely does healing fail to occur. Fracture should be differentiated from a separate ossific center of the tuberosity in adolescence and the supernumerary os vesalianum pedis in adulthood.

G. FRACTURES AND DISLOCATIONS OF THE PHALANGES OF THE TOES

Fractures of the phalanges of the toes are caused most commonly by direct violence such as crushing or stubbing. Spiral or oblique fracture of the shafts of the proximal phalanges of the lesser toes may occur as a result of indirect twisting injury.

Comminuted fracture of the proximal phalanx of the great toe, alone or in combination with fracture of the distal phalanx, is the most disabling injury. Since wide displacement of fragments is not likely, correction of angulation and support by an adhesive dressing and splint usually suffices. A weight-bearing plaster boot may be useful for relief of symptoms arising from associated soft tissue injury. Spiral or oblique fracture of the proximal phalanges of the lesser toes can be treated adequately by binding the involved toe to the adjacent uninjured member. Comminuted fracture of the distal phalanx is treated as a soft tissue injury.

Traumatic dislocation of the metatarsophalangeal joints and the uncommon dislocation of the proximal interphalangeal joint usually can be reduced by closed manipulation. These dislocations are rarely isolated and usually occur in combination with other injuries to the forefoot.

H. FRACTURE OF THE SESAMOIDS OF THE GREAT TOE is rare, but it may

occur as a result of crushing injury. It must be differentiated from partite developmental lesions. Undisplaced fracture requires no treatment other than a foot support or a metatarsal bar. Displaced fracture may require immobilization in a walking plaster boot with the toe strapped in flexion. Persistent delay of bone healing may cause disabling pain arising from arthritis of the articulation between the sesamoid and the head of the first metatarsal. If a foot support and metatarsal bar do not provide adequate relief, excision of the sesamoid may be necessary.

XIV. INFECTIONS OF BONES AND JOINTS

A. OSTEOMYELITIS is an infection of bone and is classified according to origin as primary or secondary, according to microbial flora, and according to course as acute, subacute, or chronic.

Primary osteomyelitis is caused by direct implantation of microorganisms into bone and is usually localized to that site. Open (compound) fractures, penetrating wounds (especially those due to firearms), and surgical operations on bone are the most common causes. Operative treatment is usually necessary; treatment with antimicrobial drugs is adjunctive.

Secondary (acute hematogenous) osteomyelitis is usually due to spread through the blood stream. Occasionally, secondary osteomyelitis may result from direct extension of infection in contiguous soft tissues or from septic arthritis in an adjacent joint.

1. Acute pyogenic osteomyelitis (secondary or hematogenous osteomyelitis) About 95% of cases of acute secondary osteomyelitis are caused by pyogenic organisms, usually a single strain. Secondary contamination during treatment may produce a mixed infection.

Acute hematogenous osteomyelitis occurs predominantly during the period of skeletal growth, with the peak incidence during childhood. About 75% of cases in children are due to staphylococci; group A streptococci are the next most common pathogen; and the remainder of cases are caused by a wide variety of organisms. Preexisting infection of another organ system is present in about half of cases. The tibia and femur are the most commonly involved of the long bones.

The initial lesion may become progressive or chronic, or the infection may resolve with or without treatment.

If the initial lesion is not controlled, spread of infection causes bony destruction that differs in infancy, childhood, and adulthood due to the vascular supply of bone. During infancy, terminal ramifications of the nutrient artery perforate the growth plate and end in the cartilaginous precursor of the epiphysis. This may explain both the frequency of complicating septic arthritis during infancy and subsequent disturbances of growth. There may also be rapid spread of infection throughout the entire length of the bone, but involucrum formation is not characteristic.

At about 18 months of age, the epiphyseal plate becomes a vascular barrier. The blood flow on the metaphyseal side of the growth plate reverses its direction, forming loops that empty into the large sinusoidal veins where the rate of blood flow is slower. This may explain the frequency of metaphyseal infections in the long bones during childhood. Initial localization of infection in cancellous bone is rapidly followed by edema which causes increased intraosseous pressure. Suppuration follows edema, and the escape of exudate beneath the periosteum causes elevation with disruption of vascular channels. The inflamed periosteum starts to produce a shell-like layer of new bone which can be identified by x-ray. Disturbance of blood supply to the inner surface of the cortex from thrombosed branches of nutrient vessels leads to necrosis of compact bone and sequestration. Because the epiphysis is separated from the metaphysis by the growth plate, it is protected from direct involvement.

In adulthood, metaphyseal and epiphyseal vessels communicate across the scar of the previous growth plate, and microorganisms can enter the epiphysis through the nutrient artery. This permits organisms to reach the subchondral bone of joints and precipitate a complicating septic arthritis. Since the periosteum of adults is rather fibrous and adherent, extensive subperiosteal abscess formation is not a prominent feature. However, periosteal inflammation can be identified by demineralization and absorption of the cortex. Involucrum formation and extensive cortical sequestration occur in adulthood. Involvement of the diaphysis, chronic infection of the marrow, and abscesses of the soft tissues surrounding bone are more common sequelae in adults.

a. Diagnosis

(1) *Symptoms and signs* In infants and children, the onset is often sudden, with marked toxicity; an insidious onset may produce more subtle symptoms. Voluntary movement of the extremity is inhibited. Tenderness followed by swelling and redness are the local manifestations.

The onset in adults is less striking. Generalized symptoms of bacteremia may be absent; vague, shifting, or evanescent local pain may be the earliest manifestation. Limitation of joint motion may be marked, especially in patients with spine involvement or when lesions are near joints.

(2) *Laboratory tests* The ESR and white count are often elevated. Identification of the causative organism is often possible by blood culture. Exudates may be recovered for culture by aspiration of extraosseous tissues in

areas of tenderness or directly from the involved bone. In severe infections of more than 2 days' duration, material for culture and smear is usually obtained during open surgical treatment.

(3) *X-rays* Significant changes in bone cannot be identified by x-ray before 7–10 days after onset in infants and 2–4 weeks after onset in adults, but extraosseous soft tissue swelling adjacent to the infection may appear within 3–5 days after the onset of symptoms. Xeroradiography may demonstrate subtle changes in extracortical soft tissues that are not apparent on routine x-ray films. If antimicrobial therapy was started early, x-ray changes in bone may not appear for 3–5 weeks. Subperiosteal new bone formation is a late manifestation of healing.

b. Differential diagnosis Acute local infections of bone must be differentiated from the prodromal states of acute exanthemata and from traumatic injuries.

Acute hematogenous osteomyelitis must be differentiated from suppurative arthritis, rheumatic fever, cellulitis, tuberculosis, mycotic infections, and Ewing's sarcoma. The pseudoparalysis associated with acute osteomyelitis in infancy may simulate poliomyelitis. When symptoms are mild, osteomyelitis may initially mimic Legg-Perthes disease.

c. Complications Delayed diagnosis or inadequate early treatment can lead to chronic osteomyelitis. Other complications include soft tissue abscess formation, septic arthritis, and metastatic infections to other organs. Pathologic fracture may occur at sites of extensive bone destruction.

d. Treatment Toxic patients require intravenous administration of fluid and electrolytes. Accompanying anemia should often be corrected by blood transfusion. Immobilization of the affected extremity by splinting, plaster encasement, or suspension in an orthopedic apparatus is advisable for relief of pain and protection against pathologic fracture.

Although antibiotics are of great benefit, they are not usually curative. The mainstay of therapy is surgery. Treatment must be individualized, and only broad guidelines will be given here.

(1) *Surgical* During the first 2–3 days after the onset of acute infection, open surgical treatment can be avoided in many cases, especially in infants and children. If vigorous general care and appropriate antibiotic therapy are instituted promptly, the progress of the local lesion may be controlled and spread of the infection halted before suppuration and significant tissue destruction have occurred.

If an abscess has formed beneath the periosteum or has extended into the soft tissues of infants and children, it should be drained at least once daily by aspiration. Pain and fever that persist longer than 2–3 days after initiating aspiration and antimicrobial therapy suggest spread. Surgical decompression of the medullary cavity by drilling or limited fenestration should be done promptly with the hope of minimizing progression of bone necrosis. Subsequent treatment of the local lesion may be by open or closed technics. Open treatment of the wound by packing requires multiple dressing changes, which are painful and frequently cannot be accomplished except under general anesthesia. Closed wound treatment with intermittent suction drainage provides egress of exudates and minimizes the likelihood of secondary contamination. Antibiotics can be given topically through the drainage tube in concentrations that systemically would be toxic.

Radical surgical technics such as extensive guttering and diaphysectomy should be reserved for the treatment of chronic osteomyelitis.

(2) *Antibiotics* Antibiotic therapy is aided by identification of the organism and its antibiotic sensitivities. Since acute infections in children are usually due to staphylococci or β-hemolytic streptococci, appropriate systemic

antibiotics for these organisms should be administered without waiting for culture reports. Chemotherapy should be continued for about 2–3 weeks after the patient becomes afebrile or repeated wound cultures fail to show growth.

e. Prognosis   The mortality rate in treated acute osteomyelitis is about 1%, but morbidity continues to be high. If effective treatment is instituted within 48 hours after onset, prompt recovery can be expected in about two-thirds of cases. Chronicity and recurrence of infection are likely when treatment is delayed.

2. Chronic pyogenic osteomyelitis may occur as a consequence of acute infection or may appear as an indolent, slowly progressive process with no striking symptom. Recurrent infection is manifested by exacerbation of symptoms with or without drainage after a quiescent period of days, weeks, or years.

   a. Diagnosis

(1) *Symptoms and signs*   Symptoms may be so mild and the onset so insidious that there is little or no disability, but recurrent fever, pain, and swelling are common. There may be a history of injury. The infection may communicate through a sinus to the skin surface with periodic or constant discharge of pus.

(2) *Laboratory tests*   Leukocytosis, anemia, and acceleration of the ESR are inconstant. The causative organisms should be cultured and drug sensitivity studies performed. Culture of exudates from sinus orifices may be misleading because skin contaminants are likely to be present. More reliable specimens can be obtained by taking samples of suspected tissue at operation or by deep aspiration at a distance from sinus tracts.

(3) *X-rays*   Architectural alterations of bone depend upon the stage, extent, and rate of progress of the disease. Destruction of bone may create diffuse areas of radiolucency. Bone necrosis, apparent as areas of increased density, is due in part to increased absorption of calcium from surrounding vascularized bone. Involucrum and new bone formation are healing responses which may be identified beneath the periosteum or within the bone. Subperiosteal new bone may be seen as a lamellar pattern. Progressive resorption of sclerotic bone and reformation of the normal trabecular pattern also suggest healing.

   Tomography may be helpful in identifying deep areas of bone destruction. Sinograms made with aqueous radiographic media may aid in localization of sequestra or points of persistent infection and will demonstrate the course of sinus tracts. Occasionally, bone scanning with radioisotopes will localize otherwise occult infection.

   b. Differential diagnosis   Chronic pyogenic osteomyelitis should be differentiated from benign and malignant tumors; from certain forms of osseous dysplasia; from fatigue fracture; and from specific infections discussed later in this section.

   c. Complications   The most common complication is persistence of infection with acute exacerbations. Persistent infection may cause anemia, weight loss, weakness, and amyloidosis. Chronic osteomyelitis may disseminate to other organs. Acute exacerbations can be complicated by serious effusions in adjacent joints or by frank purulent arthritis. Constant erosion and progressive destruction of bone cause structural weakening which occasionally leads to pathologic fracture.

   Before epiphyseal closure, osteomyelitis can produce overgrowth of a long bone from chronic hyperemia of the growth plate. Focal destruction of an epiphyseal plate can create asymmetric growth.

   Rarely, after many years of drainage, squamous cell carcinoma or a fibrosarcoma arises in persistently infected tissues.

d. Treatment

(1) *General* During the quiescent phase, no treatment is necessary and the patient lives an essentially normal life. Minor exacerbations accompanied by drainage may be managed adequately with dressing changes. More acute episodes may require immobilization, bed rest, local heat, and mild analgesics.

(2) *Medical* Occasionally, when the drug sensitivities of the causative organism are known, systemic antibiotic therapy without surgical intervention is advantageous. This is especially true during the early phase of a recurrence without external drainage or abscess formation.

Copious drainage and clinical and x-ray evidence of progressive bone destruction and sequestration require more aggressive treatment.

(3) *Surgical* Soft tissue abscesses without sequestration can be treated by operation and open or closed drainage. Similar treatment may also suffice for Brodie's abscess, a rare, walled-off infection of bone. Removal of a sequestrum with drainage of the abscess cavity often permits rapid healing. With the exception of the fibula, metatarsals, and possibly the metacarpals, diaphysectomy should be avoided in adults, if possible, because the resected shaft will not regenerate. More extensive and long-standing infections may require more radical surgery such as diaphysectomy or amputation.

e. *Prognosis* Even after vigorous treatment, recurrence of infection is likely. This is usually due to incomplete removal of all areas of infected soft tissue scar or necrotic and unseparated bone.

B. MYCOTIC INFECTIONS OF BONES AND JOINTS

Fungal infections of the skeletal system are usually secondary to a primary infection in another organ system, frequently the lower respiratory tract. Although skeletal lesions have a predilection for the cancellous extremities of long bones and the bodies of vertebrae, the predominant lesion—a granuloma with varying degrees of necrosis and abscess formation—does not produce a characteristic clinical picture.

The principal mycotic infections of the skeletal system are **coccidioidomycosis**, which is usually secondary to a primary pulmonary infection; **histoplasmosis** (rare), which usually represents dissemination from a primary focus in the lungs; **cryptococcosis** (torulosis or European blastomycosis), an uncommon chronic granulomatous pulmonary disease that may be disseminated to the nervous system and rarely to the skeletal system; and North American **blastomycosis** (Gilchrist's disease), which may be disseminated to skeletal structures from the lungs or, less commonly, from a cutaneous lesion.

Treatment is usually with amphotericin B (Fungizone). Surgical debridement and in some cases saucerization are often required.

C. SYPHILIS OF BONES AND JOINTS

Syphilitic arthritis or osteitis may occur during any stage of congenital or acquired infection. Neurotrophic arthropathy (Charcot's joints) can be caused indirectly by syphilitic disease of the spinal cord.

In infancy, congenital syphilis typically causes epiphysitis and metaphysitis. Radiologically, a zone of sclerosis appears adjacent to the growth plate but is separated from another similar zone by one of rarefaction. Partial replacement of the rarefied bone by inflammatory tissue precedes suppuration, which may in turn allow epiphyseal displacement because of structural weakening.

Congenital syphilis causes periostitis and osteoperiostitis in childhood and adolescence. Bone involvement is frequently symmetric, and periosteal proliferation along the tibial crest causes the classic 'saber shin.' A painless bilateral effusion of the knees (Clutton's joints) is a rare manifestation.

In adults, gumma formation is a tertiary manifestation. This granulomatous process is characterized by localized destruction of bone accompanied by surrounding areas of sclerosis. Extensive destruction with accompanying rarefaction may cause pathologic fracture. Periostitis in the adult is likely to occur in the bones of the thorax and in the shafts of long bones. The x-ray picture of syphilitic osteitis in the adult is not diagnostic, but bone production is generally more pronounced than bone destruction.

Osteoarticular lesions due to other causes must be differentiated from syphilis. Serologic studies will usually provide confirmatory evidence. Biopsy is not necessary to establish a direct diagnosis, but it may differentiate a gumma from other lesions. A favorable response to penicillin treatment supports the diagnosis.

The only local treatment necessary is immobilization to provide comfort or protection from fracture if the bone is seriously weakened. Lesions of bones and joints respond promptly to adequate chemotherapy.

D. TUBERCULOSIS OF BONES AND JOINTS
Infection of the musculoskeletal system with Mycobacterium tuberculosis is usually caused by hematogenous spread from the respiratory or gastrointestinal tract. Tuberculosis of the thoracic or lumbar spine may be associated with an active lesion of the genitourinary tract.

1. Diagnosis
a. Symptoms and signs The onset of symptoms is generally insidious. Pain in an involved joint may be mild and accompanied by a sensation of stiffness. It is commonly accentuated at night. Limping and restriction of joint motion are seen. As the disease progresses, the joint becomes fixed by muscle contractures, organic destruction of the joint, and healing in soft tissues and bone.

Local findings during the early stages may be limited to tenderness, soft tissue swelling, joint effusion, and increase in skin temperature about the involved area. As the disease progresses without treatment, muscle atrophy and deformity become apparent. Spontaneous external drainage of abscess leads to sinus formation. Progressive destruction of bone in the spine, especially in the thoracolumbar region, may cause a gibbus.

d. Laboratory tests The diagnosis rests upon recovery of acid-fast bacilli from joint fluid, tissue exudates, or tissue specimens. Biopsy of the lesion or of a regional lymph node may demonstrate the characteristic histologic picture but does not differentiate tuberculosis from other mycobacterial lesions.

c. X-ray The earliest changes of tuberculous arthritis are soft tissue swelling and distention of the capsule by effusion. Subsequently, bone atrophy causes thinning of the trabecular pattern, narrowing of the cortex, and enlargement of the medullary canal. As joint disease progresses, destruction of cartilage causes narrowing of the joint cleft and focal erosion of the articular surface, especially at the margins. Extensive destruction of joint surfaces causes deformity. As healing takes place, osteosclerosis becomes apparent around areas of necrosis and sequestration. Where the lesion is limited to bone, especially in the cancellous portion of the metaphysis, the x-ray picture may be that of single or multilocular cysts surrounded by sclerotic bone. As intraosseous foci expand toward the limiting cortex and erode it, subperiosteal new bone formation takes place.

2. Differential diagnosis
Tuberculosis of the musculoskeletal system must be differentiated from other subacute and chronic infections, rheumatoid arthritis, gout, and occasionally from osseous dysplasia. Infections caused by nontuberculous mycobacteria can be differentiated only by cultures.

3. Complications
Destruction of bones or joints may occur in a few weeks or months if adequate treatment is not provided. Deformity due to joint destruction, abscess formation with spread into adjacent soft tissues, and sinus formation are common. Paraplegia is the most serious complication of spinal tuberculosis. As healing of severe joint lesions takes place, spontaneous fibrous or bony ankylosis follows.

4. Treatment

a. General In acute infections where synovitis is the predominant feature, treatment can be conservative, at least initially; immobilization by splint or plaster, aspiration, and chemotherapy may suffice. A similar approach is used for infections of large joints of the lower extremities in children during an early stage. It may also be used in adults either as definitive treatment of mild infections or before operation.

b. Surgical Various types of operative treatment are necessary for chronic or advanced tuberculosis of bones and joints. The advent of effective drug treatment has broadened the indications for synovectomy and debridement at the expense of more radical surgical procedures such as arthrodesis and amputation. Even though the infection is active and all involved tissue cannot be removed, supplementary chemotherapy may permit healing to occur. In general, arthrodesis of weight-bearing joints is preferred when function cannot be salvaged. Reconstructive arthroplasty with prostheses to restore function has not proved reliable in eradicating disease and is not recommended at present.

c. Chemotherapy of osteoarticular tuberculosis is based on the systemic administration of drugs to which the strain of pathogen is likely to be susceptible as indicated by in vitro testing. Resistant strains may emerge during administration of single drugs; therefore, combinations of antituberculous agents are recommended (see Chapter 4).

E. PYOGENIC ARTHRITIS (suppurative, infectious, or septic arthritis) is an acute or chronic inflammation of joints which may be caused by a variety of microorganisms.

1. Classification can be based on the mechanism of introduction of the pathogen or the microbial etiology.

a. Primary pyogenic arthritis can be the result of direct implantation of microorganisms into joints through penetrating wounds or can complicate percutaneous procedures (e.g., arthrocentesis or intraarticular drug therapy). Joint infections that follow open surgical operations are discussed under acute pyogenic arthritis.

b. Secondary pyogenic arthritis is generally blood-borne; it can also result from direct extension from an adjacent focus of osteomyelitis or from an extra-articular soft tissue infection.

c. Chronic pyogenic arthritis is usually a sequel to untreated or unsuccessfully treated acute primary or secondary pyogenic arthritis.

2. Acute pyogenic arthritis Pyogenic cocci (staphylococci, streptococci, pneumococci, and meningococci) are the most frequent pathogens. Enteric gramnegative bacilli, especially Escherichia coli, may produce infection in adults. Haemophilus influenzae is a frequent pathogen in children 6 months to 2 years of age.

In acute hematogenous arthritis, the larger joints (knee, hip, elbow, shoulder, and ankle) are commonly involved. An acute or chronic infection of nearby bone or soft tissue may secondarily involve a joint. Infections of other organ systems (e.g., skin, respiratory tract, and genitourinary tract) are possible sources of blood-borne infections. Although a single joint is generally involved in adults, multiple joints may be involved by hematogenous arthritis in children. Antecedent trauma to the area may be misleading.

The initial reaction is an acute synovitis. The intraarticular fluid during this phase may show a few polymorphonuclear leukocytes. Later, the synovial fluid changes to pus; edema and cellular infiltration occurs in the subsynovial soft tissues. Destruction of cartilage follows, especially at the point of contact of opposing joint surfaces. Continued infection may produce destruction of synovia and capsular components as well as cartilage and bone. Following successfully treated early infections, there may be no permanent sequelae, but extensive tissue destruction after severe and indolent infections can only be partially repaired and fibrous or complete bony ankylosis may result.

a. Diagnosis

(1) *Symptoms and signs* Systemic disease or another serious infection may distract attention from the infected joint. Migratory polyarthralgia or multiple joint symptoms may be misleading. Systemic symptoms include fever, chills, and malaise. Pain is generally progressive and is usually accentuated by active or passive joint motions. The patient tends to limit motion of the involved joint. Local tenderness and warmth are present over the joint and are often accompanied by soft tissue swelling and joint effusion.

(2) *Laboratory tests* Examination of joint fluid is crucial. During the incipient stage of infection, the fluid may be grossly clear or only slightly turbid, but it tends to become purulent as the infection progresses. The white cell count is likely to be greater than 50,000/ml, with more than 90% polymorphonuclear neutrophils. The fasting blood glucose level is usually more than 50 mg/100 ml above that of the synovial fluid. The mucin clot produced by addition of acetic acid to the synovial fluid tends to fragment or form a flocculent precipitate (in comparison to its normal ropy consistency) which suggests an inflammatory cause of the effusion. The sedimentation rate is almost invariably accelerated.

Gram stain alone may suggest the appropriate antibiotic. Culture of the blood and synovial fluid establishes a definitive diagnosis and provides specific information on antibiotic sensitivities.

(3) *X-rays* Findings depend in part on the virulence of the infection. X-ray changes lag behind the clinical and pathologic process. During the first 2 weeks, the joint capsule can be seen on x-ray to be distended by effusion. As the inflammatory reaction spreads, demarcation between capsule and fat becomes obliterated. Increase in intraarticular pressure from effusion may cause widening of the joint cleft in hip infections, especially in infants, where subluxation can occur. Comparative x-rays of the opposite normal joint can aid in the identification of subtle changes. With persistent hyperemia and disuse, demineralization of subchondral bone occurs adjacent to the joint cleft and extends centrifugally. Trabecular detail is progressively lost and the compact subchondral bone appears accentuated. Destruction of cartilage is reflected by narrowing of the width of the joint cleft until subchondral bone is in apposition.

b. Complications

Joint infections can disseminate to other sites either via the blood stream or directly.

c. Differential diagnosis

Acute pyogenic arthritis must be differentiated from other acute arthropathies (e.g., rheumatic fever, rheumatoid arthritis, gout and pseudogout, and gonococcal arthritis). Hematogenous osteomyelitis, rheumatic fever, and epiphyseal trauma may mimic acute septic arthritis in childhood.

Acute pyogenic arthritis may complicate other types of preexisting joint disease, notably rheumatoid arthritis or neurotrophic arthropathy. Concomitant or recent systemic treatment with corticosteroids may cloud the diagnosis, especially during the prodromal stage, by modification of physical signs. Polyarthralgia may occur in systemic viral infections or allergic reactions, but other features of pyogenic arthritis are lacking. Acute infections or inflammations of periarticular structures (e.g., septic bursitis and tenosynovitis, osteomyelitis, cellulitis, and acute calcific tendinitis) may be difficult to differentiate. Transient synovitis of the hip in infancy and childhood may be especially difficult to distinguish from bacterial infection, and culture of aspirated joint fluid may be the only method of differentiation.

d. Treatment

(1) *General* Analgesics and splinting of the involved joint in the position of maximum comfort alleviate pain. Pain caused by increased intraarticular

pressure can be relieved by intermittent aspiration or surgical drainage. Bilateral suspension of the lower extremity in abduction with traction may prevent subluxation or dislocation of a septic hip joint, especially in infants and children.

(2) *Specific* Definitive treatment is based on surgery and antibiotic therapy. The specific operation depends in part upon the infecting agent, the stage of the infection, and the response of the patient.

During the first 48-72 hours after onset, intermittent aspiration relieves intraarticular tension and evacuates exudates. When the infection is due to Staphylococcus areus, open or tube drainage is preferable because of the chondrolytic nature of the altered synovial secretions. If infection is not recognized or not treated effectively within the first 72 hours, immediate drainage by open or closed tube methods is advocated for most cases. Open drainage implies arthrotomy without closure of the surgical wound, whereas closed drainage indicates closure of the surgical wound with an indwelling tube or percutaneous insertion of a tube via a small trocar into the joint cavity.

(3) *Antibiotics* should be given based on smear and culture reports.

e. Prognosis If effective treatment is instituted within the first 48-72 hours of onset, prompt response can be expected in an otherwise healthy patient. Defervescence, disappearance of pain, return of uninhibited joint motion, resorption of joint effusion, and a decreasing sedimentation rate are some of the factors that indicate a favorable response to treatment.

Prompt diagnosis and aggressive treatment can prevent the most serious sequel of acute joint infection: loss of function due to bone and soft tissue destruction during the subacute or chronic stage.

3. Gonorrheal arthritis Acute gonorrheal arthritis caused by Neisseria gonorrhoeae, is almost always secondary to infection of the genitourinary tract. Joints become infected by the hematogenous route, and symptoms appear 2-3 weeks after the onset of gonorrhea. Clinical evidence of involvement of multiple joints is often present at the onset, but symptoms are usually transient in all joints but one. Large weight-bearing joints are most often affected. Systemic symptoms may accompany acute arthritis. Initial synovitis with effusion progresses to a purulent exudate with destruction of cartilage which may lead to fibrous or bony ankylosis.

The precise diagnosis is established by recovery of the causative microorganism from the involved joint by culture, which may be successful in only a minority of acute cases. Gonorrheal arthritis must be differentiated from rheumatoid arthritis, pyogenic arthritis caused by other organisms, acute synovitis, Reiter's disease, and gout.

Nonspecific treatment includes immobilization of the joint, bed rest, and analgesics as necessary for pain. If the joint fluid is purulent and recurs rapidly, systemic antibiotic treatment can be supplemented by instillation into large joints of 25,000-50,000 units of penicillin G in 5 ml saline, repeated once or twice at daily intervals.

The prognosis for preservation of joint function is good if the diagnosis is established promptly and treatment is vigorous.

4. Chronic pyogenic arthritis may follow acute primary or secondary pyogenic arthritis. Pyogenic cocci and enteric gram-negative rods are the most common organisms. The original bacterial strain is sometimes supplanted by another during treatment, or a mixed infection may occur.

The infection can be continuously or intermittently active. Uninterrupted progress from the acute stage is characterized by local pain and swelling, restriction of joint motion, sinus formation, and increasing deformity. X-rays show progressive destruction of cartilage manifested by narrowing of the joint cleft, erosion of bone, and even infraction or cavitation. Even though the course is indolent, it is that of continued deterioration. Episodic abatement may follow treatment with antibiotics in the recurrent type. Occult infections may be unrecognized for long periods since they do not produce striking clinical findings. They may occur concomitantly with other joint diseases or may complicate surgical operations on joints, especially after surgical implants or antibiotic prophylaxis of postoperative infection.

Chronic pyogenic arthritis must be differentiated from chronic nonpyogenic microbial infections of joints, gout, rheumatoid arthritis, and symptomatic degenerative arthritis.

The goal of treatment is eradication of infection and restoration of maximum joint function. Bacterial sensitivity tests provide a basis for selection of antimicrobial drugs. Operative destruction of the joint by arthrodesis or resection is often necessary to eliminate chronic infection.

5. Salmonella osteomyelitis and arthritis Infection of bones and joints occurs as a complication in less than 1% of cases of typhoid fever. The precise diagnosis depends upon recovery of Salmonella typhi from the osteoarticular focus, and treatment is essentially the same as for other salmonella infections and osteomyelitis in general.

In otherwise healthy patients, the bone lesion of salmonellosis is more likely to be solitary and may exhibit any of the protean gross pathologic manifestations of acute or chronic pyogenic osteomyelitis. In infants and children, it commonly affects the metaphysis of a major long bone, especially the lower femur, proximal humerus, or distal tibia. In the adult, in addition to the shafts of long bones, the lesion may be found in the metaphyses or epiphyses; other probable locations include the ribs and spine.

Infants and children with sickle cell disease complicated by antecedent episodes of marrow thrombosis and bone infarction can present a somewhat different picture since there is a tendency toward diaphyseal involvement, multiple foci, and a propensity toward symmetric localization.

6. Brucella osteomyelitis and arthritis Osteoarticular infection due to brucellae is not common in the USA. The manifestations include chronic osteomyelitis, pyogenic arthritis, synovitis, and bursitis. In the USA, Brucella abortus and B suis are the usual organisms, but B melitensis is more common worldwide. Adult men employed in the meat processing or dairy industries and persons who ingest unpasteurized milk products are most likely to be infected.

The osteoarticular lesions appear histologically as caseating or noncaseating granulomas. The lesion caused by B suis is more likely to be suppurative and caseous than those caused by other species; the similarity to sarcoidosis and tuberculosis has also been emphasized.

General treatment measures are those applicable to any chronic pyogenic infection, modified when acute symptoms of septicemia are present. Tetracycline, streptomycin, or chloramphenicol is used systemically, although if the drug is administered soley by this route it may not completely penetrate all foci of bone infection.

18

PEDIATRIC SURGERY

Alfred A. deLorimier, MD &
Michael R. Harrison, MD

I. SPECIAL CONSIDERATIONS IN PEDIATRIC MANAGEMENT

Infants and young children have a relatively low tolerance to infection, trauma, blood loss, and nutritional and fluid disturbances. The management of these disorders in infants and children differs somewhat from their treatment in adults and the margin of safety is narrower. Certain unique aspects of surgical care in infants and young children deserve emphasis.

A. FLUID AND ELECTROLYTE MANAGEMENT   Parenteral fluids must be adjusted to the size of the patient.

   1. Daily maintenance fluid and electrolyte requirements may be calculated according to body weight (Table 18-1). The physiologic limits of water replacement are 30 ml/kg above or below these mean daily requirements. Maintenance electrolyte requirements may be given IV by using such solutions as 5% dextrose and 0.2% saline (D_5 ¼ N.S.) with potassium chloride added to a concentration of 20 mEq/liter.

   Maintenance requirements are higher when there is visible perspiration or abnormally high environmental temperature, fever, or hyperventilation.

   2. Previously existing deficits from external fluid losses such as vomiting, diarrhea, and third space losses into the bowel lumen, peritoneal cavity, or large wounds require rapid blood volume expansion. When a severely contracted blood volume exists, Ringer's lactate or 5% albumin solution (or both) should be given rapidly in a volume of 10-20 ml/kg. Rehydration may then be continued with 5% dextrose and 0.45% saline until the clinical status of the baby is improved.

   3. Acute blood loss is replaced by transfusion in 10-20 ml/kg increments to maintain vital signs, urine output, and normal hematocrit. Normal blood volume is 85 ml/kg in infants and 75 ml/kg in children. Chronic blood loss is replaced only when hemoglobin drops below 8-9 gm/100ml.

   4. Continuing losses such as gastrointestinal secretions, chest tube or bile drainage, and 'third space' losses require replacement along with maintenance requirements (Table 18-2).

   5. The fluid requirements should be reassessed continuously and the orders should be rewritten at intervals of not more than 8 hours. Placement of a catheter in the right atrium by a cutdown in the external jugular vein or brachial vein will allow monitoring of central venous pressure. Methods for evaluating the response to therapy include assessment of weight, skin turgor, mucous membrane moisture, pulse and central venous pressure response, skin perfusion, urine output and specific gravity, serum and urine osmolarity, hemoglobin, hematocrit, and serum electrolyte changes.

B. NUTRITION   An infant requires 100 cal/kg/24 hours and 3 gm protein/kg/24 hours to achieve a normal weight gain of 10-15 gm/kg/24 hours. These high caloric and protein requirements decline with age but increase with sepsis, stress, and trauma. The catabolic state associated with prolonged starvation and the increased energy expenditures accompanying surgical conditions should be treated by providing adequate calories and protein.

1. Gastrointestinal feeding The best means of alimentation is through the GI tract. If the GI tract is functional, standard infant formulas, blenderized meals, or prepared elemental diets can be given by mouth, through nasogastric or naso-jejunal feeding tubes, or through gastrostomy and jejunostomy tubes placed surgically.

2. Intravenous feeding When it is necessary to infuse concentrated solutions which thrombose peripheral vessels (greater than 15% glucose), a catheter is placed into the superior vena cava or right atrium where the large blood flow will dilute the solution immediately.

Table 18-1. Maintenance requirements

Age Size	Premature <2 kg	Infants 2-10 kg	Children 11-20 kg	Children >20 kg
Water (ml/kg/24h)	125-175	125	100	40-60
Sodium (mEq/kg/24h)	1-2	2-3	1-3	1-2
Potassium (mEq/kg/24h)	1-3	2-3	1-3	1-2
Calories (Cal/kg/24h)	125-150	100-125	60-100	30-60
Protein (gm/kg/24h)	3-4	3.0-3.5	2.5-3.0	1.0-2.5
Urine output (ml/kg/24h)	1-3	1-3	1-3	1-3

Newborns of any size require only half normal maintenance for the first 1-2 days.

The catheter may be placed percutaneously through the subclavian or internal jugular veins, or by cutdown over the external jugular, anterior facial, internal jugular or brachial veins. This should be performed with strict aseptic technic. The catheter should be of inert material such as silastic or polyvinyl tubing. The tubing should be sutured to the skin to prevent accidental dislodgement. Dressings should be changed daily and cleansed with iodine solution. A bacterial filter in line with the intravenous tubing will minimize the risk of infection.

Standard intravenous alimentation solutions containing an amino acid source (2-5%), glucose (10-25%), electrolytes, vitamins, and some trace elements are widely available. The electrolyte composition of each solution should be recognized and adjusted if necessary. The solution must be infused at a constant rate to prevent wide fluctuations of blood glucose and amino acid concentrations. This requires the use of an infusion pump. Complications of intravenous feeding include clotting or accidental dislodgement of the catheter requiring replacement in a new site, sepsis (particularly candidiasis), thromboembolism, acidosis, hyperammonemia, secondary liver damage, and sudden hypoglycemia following abrupt cessation of the infusion.

The risks of a central venous catheter can be avoided by using less concentrated solutions of amino acids (2-3%) and glucose (less than 12%), in combination with an emulsified fat solution (Intralipid) given through peripheral veins. Intralipid may not be mixed with other solutions and will not pass through a millipore filter. It may be given alone or concurrently with an amino acid-glucose solution by employing a 'Y' tube with the 2 columns of fluid meeting near the level of the peripheral vein needle. Intralipid 10% (1 gm = 10 ml = approximately 10 calories) is given as a continuous infusion at a rate of 10-40 ml/kg/24 hours. Large infusion volumes (100-200 ml/kg/24 hours) may be necessary to provide adequate calories through peripheral vessels. Fluid and electrolytes must be closely monitored.

When properly given, any of these technics can maintain normal growth in infants.

Table 18-2. Replacement of abnormal losses of fluids and electrolytes

TYPE OF FLUID	Na⁺ (mEq/liter)	K⁺ (mEq/liter)	Cl⁻ (mEq/liter)	HCO₃⁻ (mEq/liter)	Replacement
			ELECTROLYTE CONTENT		
Gastric (vomiting)	50 (20–90)	10 (4–15)	90 (50–150)	—	D₅ ½ N.S. + K⁺ 20–40mEq/liter
Small bowel (ileostomy)	110 (70–140)	5 (3–10)	100 (70–130)	20 (10–40)	Lactated Ringer's
Diarrhea	80 (10–140)	25 (10–60)	90 (20–120)	40 (30–50)	Lactated Ringer's ± HCO₃
Bile	145 (130–160)	5 (4–7)	100 (80–120)	40 (30–50)	Lactated Ringer's ± HCO₃
Pancreatic	140 (130–150)	5 (4–7)	80 (60–100)	80 (60–110)	Lactated Ringer's ± HCO₃
Sweat Normal	20 (10–30)	5 (3–10)	20 (10–40)		
Cystic fibrosis	90 (50–130)	15 (5–25)	90 (60–120)		

Table 18-3. Drugs useful in pediatric surgery

Drug	Dose	Notes
Emergency drugs: single IV dose		
Atropine	0.1 mg/kg	Push intracardiac or IV
Epinephrine (Adrenalin)	0.1-1 ml 1:1000	1 mg/100 ml D_5W, titrate IV drip
Isoproterenol (Isuprel)	0.1-1 mg/kg/min	40 mg/100 ml D_5W, titrate IV drip
Dopamine (Intropin)	5-40 mg/kg/min	
Lidocaine (Xylocaine)	1 mg/kg	
$NaHCO_3$	1 mEq/kg	Slow pushes prn, pH<7.2 or 2 mEq/kg/5 min arrest
Calcium gluconate 10%	10 mg(0.1 ml)/kg	Slow push
Glucose 50%	1 ml/kg	
Furosemide (Lasix)	1 mg/kg	
Mannitol	1 gm/kg	
Hydrocortisone (Solu-Cortef)	10-50 mg/kg	High dose, short course R_x
Dexamethasone (Decadron)	2 mg/kg	Slow IV to decrease BP
Hydralazine (Apresoline)	1 mg/kg	2 mg/kg IM
Succinylcholine	1 mg/kg	
Tubocurarine	0.1-0.5 mg/kg	
Ketamine	2 mg/kg	6-10 mg/kg IM
Analgesics and sedatives		
ASA (Aspirin)	5-20 mg/kg	orally, rectally; every 3-6 hours, prn
Acetaminophen (Tylenol)	5-20 mg/kg	orally, rectally; every 3-6 hours, prn
Codeine	0.5-1.5 mg/kg	IM, orally; every 4-6 hours, prn
Morphine sulfate	0.1-0.2 mg/kg	IV, IM; every 4-6 hours, prn
Meperidine (Demerol)	1-2 mg/kg	IV, IM, orally; every 4-6 hours, prn
Naloxone (Narcan)	0.005 mg/kg	IV, IM; every 5 min prn x 3
Nalorphine (Nalline)	0.1 mg/kg	IV, IM; every 15 min prn x 2

Chloral hydrate	5–20 mg/kg	orally, rectally; every 8 hours prn
Diazepam (Valium)	0.1–0.2 mg/kg	IV, IM, orally; every 6 hours prn
Secobarbital (Seconal)	1–2 mg/kg	IV, IM, orally; every 6 hours prn
Pentobarbital (Nembutal)	1–2 mg/kg	IV, IM, orally; every 6 hours prn

GI drugs

Trimethobenzamide (Tigan)	5 mg/kg	IM, orally, rectally, every 6 hours prn
Malt soup extract (Maltsupex) }	½–1 tsp, twice a day <1 year old	
Senna concentrate (Sennekot) }	1–2 tsp, twice a day >1 year old	
Bisacodyl (Dulcolax)	0.3 mg/kg	orally, rectally; every 8 hours prn
Cascara	0.2 ml/kg	orally; every 8 hours prn
Mg hydroxide (Milk of Magnesia)	0.5–1 ml/kg	orally; every 8 hours prn
Mg citrate	4 ml/kg	orally; every 8 hours prn
Dioctyl sulfosuccinate (Colace)	2 ml/kg	orally; every 8 hours prn
Mineral oil	1–2 tsp	orally; prn
Ferrous sulfate (Fer-in-Sol)	1 mg/kg	orally; every 8 hours prn

Antibiotics

Aqueous penicillin	50,000–100,000 U/kg/24 hours	IV; every 12 hours (newborn)
	25,000–400,000 U/kg/24 hours	IV, IM, orally; every 4–6 hours (infants & children)
Ampicillin	50–200 mg/kg/24 hours	IV, IM; every 4–8 hours
Methicillin and Oxacillin	100–200 mg/kg/24 hours	IV, IM; every 4–6 hours
Gentamicin	3–5 mg/kg/24 hours	IV, IM; every 12 hours (newborn)
	5–7.5 mg/kg/24 hours	IV, IM; every 8 hours (infants & children)
Kanamycin	15 mg/kg/24 hours	IM; every 12 hours
Cephalothin	50–100 mg/kg/24 hours	IV, IM; every 4–6 hours
Clindamycin	10–40 mg/kg/24 hours	IV, IM; every 6 hours
Neomycin	50–100 mg/kg/24 hours	orally; every 6 hours (bowel prep)

C. TEMPERATURE Infants lose heat rapidly from their relatively large body surface area. The infant must be kept in an incubator warmed to 32°C and with temperature monitored continuously. For operation, a warmed room, a warming mattress, and warmed humidified anesthetic gases are required.

D. PREOPERATIVE AND POSTOPERATIVE CARE All newborns receive 1 mg vitamin K (AquaMephyton), IM. Whole blood or packed red cells are cross-matched. Oxygen and humidity are used as needed. Premedication is not usually necessary. Drugs useful in the surgical care of pediatric patients are listed in Table 18-3.

II. DISORDERS OF THE NECK

A. BRANCHIOGENIC CYSTS AND FISTULAS During the first month of fetal life, the primitive neck develops 4 external branchial clefts. Each cleft overlies outpocketings of the foregut, the pharyngeal pouches, so that the external cleft is separated from the internal pouch by only a membrane. The ridges between the clefts, or branchial arches, ultimately form portions of the face and neck. Persistent branchial clefts result in cysts or fistulas lined by squamous or columnar epithelium and surrounded by lymphoid follicles.

1. Diagnosis

a. A persistent first branchial cleft may present as a cyst or fistula in front of or below the ear or below the margin of the mandible. The tract commonly extends to the external auditory canal near the facial nerve.

b. A second branchial cleft remnant may be a cyst or fistula located along the anterior border of the sternocleidomastoid muscle. The tract extends between the internal and external carotid arteries, coursing above the hypoglossal nerve to the tonsillar fossa (see Fig. 18-1).

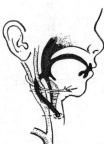

Thyroglossal duct cyst   Branchial cleft fistula

Fig. 18-1.

c. A cyst produces localized painless swelling unless secondary infection has occurred, in which case erythema and tenderness are present. If a fistula opens into the pharynx, a sour taste may be noted.

d. A fistula produces mucoid material or crusting from a pinpoint skin opening over the middle or lower third of the sternocleidomastoid muscle. Milking the tract from above downward may produce mucoid material at the orifice of the fistula. If the fistula becomes secondarily infected, symptoms of inflammation are present.

e. Branchiogenic cysts and fistulas are bilateral in approximately 10% of cases.

2. Treatment Surgical excision through a transverse incision is the treatment of choice. If the tract is long, it may be necessary to place a second or third transverse incision above the first for ease of dissection.

B. THYROGLOSSAL DUCT CYSTS, SINUSES, AND FISTULAS

Thyroglossal duct cysts and sinuses may develop from cell rests at any point along the migratory path of the thyroid gland. If the cyst suppurates and drains externally, a fistula will result. The cysts contain mucoid material and are lined by squamous or columnar epithelium. Mucous glands occur in 60% of tracts. Scattered islands of thyroid follicles may be present. Sinuses pass a variable distance upward toward the foramen cecum at the base of the tongue. Multiple tracts are common.

1. Diagnosis

a. Thyroglossal duct cysts may be asymptomatic, may be large enough to cause symptoms by pressing on adjacent structures, or, if infected, may be tender and have a discharge. They are found in the midline of the neck anywhere from the submental region to the suprasternal notch, but are most commonly located at the level of the hyoid bone. They vary in size from a barely palpable nodule to a mass 3-4 cm in diameter. Motion of the cyst during protrusion of the tongue is characteristic.

b. Thyroglossal duct fistulas usually develop after a thyroglossal duct abscess has been incised and drained. A deeply placed cord of dense tissue passing upward in the neck with attachment to the hyoid bone suggests the diagnosis.

2. Differential diagnosis Dermoid cysts may also occur in the midline. Ectopic thyroid tissue is clinically difficult to distinguish from a cyst; a radioactive scintiscan will identify thyroid tissue.

3. Treatment Cysts and sinuses should be excised because they are apt to become infected. The tracts must be completely removed, including the central portion of the hyoid bone and a block of tissue to the base of the tongue (see Fig. 18-1). Infected cysts must be drained, and definitive removal should be delayed until the inflammation has subsided. A sinus or cyst will recur if a branch of the original sinus is overlooked at the first operation.

C. CERVICAL LYMPHADENOPATHY

1. Pyogenic lymphadenitis Acute inflammation of cervical lymph nodes in the submandibular and anterior cervical triangles usually develops after a respiratory infection. These enlarged nodes ordinarily subside within several weeks. Occasionally, a streptococcal or staphylococcal abscess develops in the nodes and incision and drainage are necessary.

2. Granulomatous lymphadenitis Typical or atypical tuberculosis lymphadenitis develops slowly and may suppurate. The diagnosis is established by appropriate skin tests. These nodes should be excised rather than drained to prevent a chronically draining sinus.

3. Lymphoma Lymphomatous nodes are usually located in the posterior as well as the anterior cervical triangle. These nodes may be solitary, but they are usually multiple, rubbery-hard, matted together, and painless.

4. Metastatic tumor Metastatic cervical nodes in children are usually due to primary thyroid carcinoma or neuroblastoma.

III. RESPIRATORY DISORDERS

A. SURGICAL RESPIRATORY EMERGENCIES

1. Certain aspects of respiration peculiar to infants must be appreciated:

a. Babies are obligate nasal breathers. Mouth breathing is an acquired habit which may not be learned for days or weeks.

b. Infants breathe primarily by diaphragmatic movement. The accessory and intercostal muscles contribute little to ventilation in the newborn.

   c. An infant's response to hypoxia is an increase in respiratory rate before an increase in volume. Normal tidal volume is approximately 10 ml/kg.

   d. Infants have a flaccid chest wall and mediastinum. Paradoxical motion and increased work in breathing occur with any degree of respiratory distress.

   e. Infants have a small, flaccid airway. The tracheal cartilages are readily compressed by slight external pressure. The subglottic area is the narrowest part of the upper airway, measuring about 14 mm^2. If mucosal edema of 1 mm occurs, 1. will reduce the subglottic area to 5 mm^2.

   f. Air swallowing develops rapidly during respiratory distress and produces abdominal distention and impaired diaphragmatic excursion.

   g. During ventilatory assistance, transpulmonary pressure must be less than 30 cm of water to prevent alveolar rupture.

   2. Symptoms and signs suggestive of respiratory distress in the newborn include the following: (a) Respiratory rate greater than 40/minute. (b) Retraction of the chest wall. (c) Stridor. (d) Cyanosis. (e) Episodes of choking. (f) Episodes of apnea.

   3. Differential diagnosis of surgical respiratory emergencies The diagnosis must be established as soon as possible. Causes of airway obstruction above the thoracic inlet can be identified by physical examination, by attempting to pass a tube through the nasopharynx and esophagus, or by direct laryngoscopy. Intrathoracic lesions must be diagnosed by chest x-ray, bronchoscopy, esophagoscopy, arteriogram, and computerized axial tomography (CT).

   Surgically treatable causes are choanal atresia, Pierre Robin syndrome; congenital laryngeal obstructions due to webs, cysts, or tumors; compression of the trachea by vascular rings, neck masses and mediastinal masses; congenital lobar emphysema and lung cysts; alveolar rupture and pneumothorax; esophageal anomalies; and diaphragmatic hernia. Each of these lesions is discussed in the following sections.

B. CHOANAL ATRESIA Complete obstruction at the posterior nares due to choanal atresia may be unilateral and relatively asymptomatic. When it is bilateral, severe respiratory distress is manifest by marked chest wall retractions on inspiration and a normal cry.

   1. Diagnosis There is arching of the head and neck in an effort to breathe, and the baby is unable to eat. The diagnosis is confirmed by inability to pass a tube through the nares to the pharynx. With the baby in a supine position, radiopaque material may be instilled into the nares and lateral x-rays of the head taken to outline the obstruction.

   2. Treatment The emergency treatment of choanal atresia consists of maintaining an oral airway by placing a nipple, with the tip cut off, in the mouth. The membranous (10% of cases) or bony (90% of cases) occlusion may then be perforated by direct transpalatal excision, or it may be punctured and enlarged by using a Hegar's dilator. The newly created opening must be stented with plastic tubing for 5 weeks to prevent stricture.

C. PIERRE ROBIN SYNDROME is characterized by micrognathia, glossoptosis, and cleft palate. The small lower jaw allows the tongue to fall back and occlude the laryngeal airway.

   Treatment The infant should be kept in the prone position during care and feeding; a nasogastric or gastrostomy tube may be necessary. If conservative measures fail, tracheostomy is indicated. The tongue may be sutured forward to the lower jaw, but this frequently breaks down. In time the lower jaw develops normally. These infants eventually learn how to keep the tongue from occluding the airway.

D. CONGENITAL LARYNGEAL OBSTRUCTIONS Laryngeal obstructions may be due to intraluminal webs or cysts or to extraluminal tumors such as hemangiomas, cystic hygromas, large congenital goiters, or thyroglossal cysts.

1. Diagnosis These infants have stridor and chest wall retraction. When the vocal cords are involved the cry is hoarse or aphonic. Examination of the neck and direct laryngoscopy will usually identify the cause.

2. Treatment An airway must be established by placing an endotracheal tube through the larynx or by tracheostomy. Webs and cysts as well as extraluminal tumors must be excised.

E. TRACHEAL OBSTRUCTION BY VASCULAR RINGS AND MEDIASTINAL TUMORS Vascular rings may compress and encircle the trachea and esophagus, producing respiratory distress and dysphagia. Mediastinal tumors cause respiratory distress by displacement of the lungs or compression of the airways.

There are 5 main types of vascular rings: (1) double aortic arch; (2) right aortic arch and persistent left ligamentum arteriosum; (3) anomalous origin of the right subclavian artery; (4) anomalous origin of the innominate artery; (5) anomalous origin of the right common carotid artery.

Masses causing respiratory distress may involve the anterior, middle, or posterior mediastinum. Examples of such masses include:

Anterior mediastinum—thymoma, teratoma, lymphangioma, intrathoracic goiter.

Middle mediastinum—pathogenic lymph node enlargement (lymphoma, etc.), aneurysm.

Posterior mediastinum—neurogenic tumor (neuroblastoma), gastrointestinal duplication (neurenteric cyst), bronchogenic cyst, achalasia or hiatus hernia, mediastinal meningocele.

1. Diagnosis These infants have a characteristic inspiratory and expiratory wheeze, stridor, or crow. The head is held in an opisthotonic position to prevent compression of the trachea. If the head is forcibly flexed, the stridor is increased and apnea may be produced. There may be hesitation on swallowing with episodes of choking—so called 'dysphagia lusoria.' Chest x-rays may show compression of the trachea. A-P and lateral esophagograms may show indentation of the esophagus. When there is no esophageal indentation, a tracheogram may be necessary to demonstrate tracheal compression due to an anomalous origin of the innominate or left common carotid artery. An arteriogram is sometimes necessary. Esophagoscopy and bronchoscopy may be helpful in assessing the degree and level of compression.

2. Treatment

a. Vascular rings The aortic arch anomaly must be completely dissected and evaluated through a left thoracotomy. The smallest component of a double aortic arch must be divided. An anomalous right subclavian artery is divided at its origin. The anomalous innominate or left carotid arteries are pulled forward by placing sutures between their adventitia and the sternum. The accompanying fibrous bands and sheaths constricting the trachea and esophagus must also be divided. Occasionally, symptoms persist postoperatively because of deformed tracheal cartilage rings which require tracheostomy or nasotracheal intubation for a period of time.

b. Most *mediastinal tumors* are excised.

F. CONGENITAL LOBAR EMPHYSEMA may be due to deficient bronchial cartilage, partial obstruction by a redundant or edematous membrane, or compression of the bronchus by an anomalous pulmonary vessel. Lobar emphysema almost always involves the upper lobes or middle lobe. The emphysematous lobe becomes progressively enlarged, compresses the normal lung, and displaces the mediastinum to the opposite side.

1. Diagnosis These infants have wheezing, dyspnea, and cyanosis. The chest is hyperresonant, and the breath sounds are decreased over the involved lobe. The diagnosis is established by chest x-ray showing the overdistended lobe and compression of the normal lung. The mediastinum may be displaced and the emphysematous lobe may herniate into the opposite chest.

2. Treatment Occasionally, bronchoscopy and aspiration of mucus or removal of a foreign body are curative. In severely distressed infants, immediate thoracotomy is usually required, and the abnormal lobe must be resected. Relatively asymptomatic patients should be followed closely and may require no treatment.

G. PULMONARY CYSTS AND SEQUESTRATIONS

1. Pulmonary cysts may be congenital or acquired. They may become large enough to be confused with lobar emphysema or pneumothorax and to produce symptoms of severe pulmonary insufficiency.

2. In cystic adenomatoid malformation, usually only one lobe is involved by cysts containing proliferating respiratory epithelium but no cartilage or bronchioles.

3. Pulmonary sequestration presents as a soft, rounded mass lying between the dome of the diaphragm and the lower lobe, usually on the left side. They are usually asymptomatic. Sequestrations are supplied by an artery directly from the aorta.

4. Treatment The involved lobe should be removed to relieve the symptoms of respiratory insufficiency and to prevent pulmonary suppuration.

H. ALVEOLAR RUPTURE
Rupture of an alveolus may occur spontaneously or may be caused by excessive intratracheal pressure during resuscitation or mechanical ventilation. Initially, air dissects along the bronchovascular planes, producing pulmonary interstitial emphysema. Further dissection of the air may produce pneumomediastinum or pneumothorax. Mediastinal air does not readily dissect into the tissues of the neck and may markedly compress the trachea. An incision above the clavicles may be necessary to release mediastinal air. Pneumothorax requires tube thoracotomy.

IV. ESOPHAGEAL ANOMALIES

1. Classification There are three common types of esophageal anomaly:

a. Esophageal atresia in which there is a blind proximal pouch and the distal esophagus communicates with the trachea as a tracheoesophageal fistula (Fig. 18-2a). This anomaly accounts for 85% of cases.

b. Esophageal atresia with a blind proximal esophageal pouch, no tracheoesophageal fistula, and a rudimentary distal esophagus (Fig. 18-2b). This accounts for 10% of cases.

c. No esophageal atresia, but an H-type tracheoesophageal fistula (Fig. 18-2c). This accounts for 4–5% of esophageal anomalies.

Esophageal stenosis, esophageal web, and esophageal atresia with fistula to the proximal pouch or with multiple fistulas are all rare.

2. Diagnosis

a. Symptoms and signs The infant appears to have excessive salivation because of inability to swallow. There are repeated episodes of cyanosis, coughing, and gagging. Attempts to feed these babies results in choking and regurgitation. Pneumonia is common due to aspiration from the blind proximal pouch and/or reflux of gastric contents through the tracheoesophageal fistula. When there is a fistula to the distal esophagus, abdominal distention is common, because air is forced into the bowel during crying.

b. X-ray findings A nasogastric tube passed through the nose will not

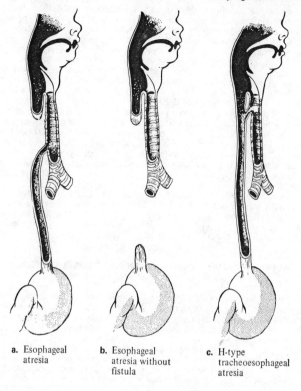

a. Esophageal atresia

b. Esophageal atresia without fistula

c. H-type tracheoesophageal atresia

Fig. 18-2. Esophageal anomalies.

traverse the expected esophageal length. If 1 ml propylidine (Dionosil) or barium is injected into the tube, followed by air, it will outline the blind pouch on a A-P and lateral chest x-ray. The contrast material should then be evacuated from the pouch to prevent aspiration. The presence or absence of air in the stomach will indicate whether a distal tracheoesophageal fistula is present. The most reliable methods of diagnosing an H-type tracheoesophageal fistula are cine-esophagography and endoscopy.

3. Treatment

a. General measures A sump catheter should be placed in the upper esophageal pouch and connected to continuous suction. The head of the bed should be elevated. The infant should be placed in a humidified incubator and should be turned from side to side every hour and stimulated to cry and cough. Antibiotic therapy is begun immediately: ampicillin, 50 mg/kg/every 6 hours IM or IV; and gentamicin, 2.5 mg/kg/every 12 hours IM.

b. Surgical treatment Infants with a tracheoesophageal fistula require emergency gastrostomy to control reflux of gastric juice. Full-term infants without severe associated anomalies may then undergo extrapleural thoracotomy for division of the tracheoesophageal fistula and primary esophageal anastomosis as soon as the lungs are clear. Definitive repair may be delayed if there is significant pneumonia or if the infant is premature or has severe associated anomalies.

In most cases of atresia without fistula and in some cases of atresia with fistula, the proximal and distal ends of the esophagus are too far apart for repair. The short proximal pouch may be elongated by daily stretching with a 22-24 French bougie over a period of 2-10 weeks. During this time, a sump suction catheter is maintained in the upper pouch and the infant is fed by gastrostomy. It may be necessary to perform a transpleural division of the tracheoesophageal fistula in order to feed the baby by gastrostomy while the pouch is being elongated. In the final stage, extrapleural thoracotomy and anastomosis of the two esophageal segments is usually possible. If the two esophageal ends cannot be brought together, a conduit between the cervical esophagus and the stomach can be constructed from either colon or the greater curvature of the stomach after 1 year of age.

In infants with H-type tracheoesophageal fistula, the fistula is located above the thoracic inlet in two-thirds of cases. These fistulas may be divided through a left transverse cervical incision. Intrathoracic fistulas may be divided by an extrapleural right thoracotomy. A gastrostomy is commonly employed for feeding until the esophageal closure is healed.

V. DIAPHRAGMATIC EVENTRATION AND POSTEROLATERAL (BOCHDALEK) DIAPHRAGMATIC HERNIA

Eventration of the diaphragm may be a congenital defect in which the diaphragm consists of a thin membrane lacking tendon and muscle, or it may be acquired by injury to the brachial plexus during birth; the latter is usually associated with Erb's palsy. The phrenic nerve may be injured during thoracotomy, producing diaphragmatic paralysis.

Posterolateral (Bochdalek) diaphragmatic hernia is a congenital defect in the posterior and lateral portion of the diaphragm caused by failure of the septum transversum to fuse with the pleuroperitoneal folds during the eighth week of fetal life. The defect occurs on the left side 3-5 times more frequently than on the right side. During fetal development, the intestinal contents are pushed into the pleural cavity by abdominal muscle tone (see Fig. 18-3). Varying degrees of pulmonary hypoplasia result, depending on the size of the defect and the amount of intestinal content compressing the lungs.

1. Diagnosis The onset and severity of symptoms are dependent upon the degree of pulmonary hypoplasia and the amount of lung compressed by the bowel. These infants have markedly labored respiration and cyanosis. The heart sounds are displaced, and there is apparent dextrocardia with left-sided hernias. The ipsilateral chest is flat to percussion and has diminished breath sounds. The abdomen is characteristically scaphoid. The diagnosis is confirmed by chest x-ray showing the bowel, spleen, and portions of the liver within the thorax. The lungs, mediastinum, and trachea are displaced to the opposite chest.

2. Treatment

a. General measures A nasogastric tube should be placed in the stomach to prevent further distention of the bowel with air. Oxygen should be given, but ventilation by mask is avoided. For severely distressed infants, an endotracheal tube should be placed and ventilation assisted with transpulmonary pressure less than 25 cm water. A catheter should be inserted into the distal aorta via the umbilical

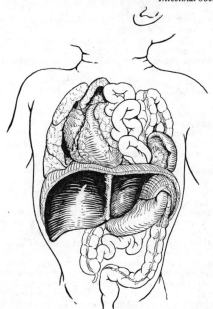

Fig. 18-3. Congenital posterolateral (Bochdalek) diaphragmatic hernia.

artery, and the blood gas and pH levels should be monitored. Metabolic acidosis due to hypoxia is corrected with sodium bicarbonate.

  b. Surgical treatment Infants with eventration may develop severe respiratory distress, and they may require a thoracotomy and plication of the diaphragm to prevent paradoxical motion of the diaphragm and mediastinum.

  For infants with a posterolateral diaphragmatic hernia, an abdominal incision is preferred. The bowel is reduced from the pleural space and a hernia sac lining the pleural space should be looked for and excised. A chest tube should be placed in the pleural space and connected to water-seal without suction. The diaphragmatic defect is closed. Forced expansion of the lung must not be attempted lest alveoli be ruptured. A gastrostomy is beneficial. A large ventral hernia may be created by closing the skin, but not the fascia, to accommodate the intestine in the small abdominal cavity.

VI. NEONATAL INTESTINAL OBSTRUCTION

A. GENERAL PRINCIPLES The cardinal symptoms and signs of neonatal intestinal obstruction are: (1) Polyhydramnios in the mother. (2) Vomiting. (3) Abdominal distention. (4) Failure to pass meconium.

  1. Polyhydramnios is related to the level of obstruction, occurring in approximately 45% of women who have infants with duodenal atresia and 15% of those who have infants with ileal atresia.

When a tube is passed into the stomach of a newborn, a residual greater than 40 ml is diagnostic of obstruction.

2. Vomiting occurs early in upper intestinal obstruction, and it is bile-stained if the obstruction is distal to the ampulla of Vater.

3. Abdominal distention is related to the level of obstruction, being most marked in distal obstructions.

4. Meconium is passed in 30-50% of newborn infants with intestinal obstruction, but the failure to pass meconium within the first 24 hours is distinctly abnormal.

Approximately one-fourth of infants with congenital intestinal obstructions weigh less than 5½ pounds.

Causes of neonatal intestinal obstruction include intestinal atresia or stenosis, annular pancreas, malrotation with peritoneal bands or volvulus, meconium ileus, Hirschsprung's disease, and imperforate anus.

B. CONGENITAL DUODENAL OBSTRUCTION   Duodenal atresia and stenosis and annular pancreas are frequently associated with other anomalies, and 30% of these patients have Down's syndrome. In 25% of the patients with duodenal atresia, the obstruction is proximal to the ampulla of Vater.

1. Diagnosis   Abdominal x-rays show gastric and duodenal distention (double-bubble sign) when obstruction of the duodenum is almost complete. Total absence of gas distal to the duodenum indicates atresia rather than stenosis. Barium enema (in saline) identifies the presence or absence of malrotation of the colon. The colon is usually very narrow (microcolon).

2. Treatment   A nasogastric tube should be placed and continuous suction applied. Dehydration should be treated preoperatively. Duodenal atresia, stenosis, and annular pancreas should be treated by a retrocolic, side-to-side duodeno-jejunostomy. The overdistended proximal duodenum frequently fails to function well for many days, and a gastrostomy is helpful for decompression and to check gastric residual during graded feedings.

C. MALROTATION OF THE MIDGUT   During the 10th week of fetal development the small bowel and colon undergo counterclockwise rotation and fixation to the posterior peritoneum. If bowel rotation fails to occur, intestinal obstruction may be produced by 2 mechanisms. First, when the cecum is arrested in the upper abdomen, filmy or dense adhesive bands from the right abdomen to the cecum may obstruct the duodenum and other portions of the small bowel. Second, the failure in fixation of the mesentery produces a narrow 'universal mesentery' based on the superior mesenteric vessels. This predisposes to volvulus of the intestine, always following clockwise torsion of the bowel and mesentery. The mesenteric blood supply then becomes compromised and may lead to infarction of the entire small and proximal large bowel if the volvulus is not reduced immediately. This is a true emergency, where time counts.

1. Diagnosis   Mesenteric bands usually produce symptoms of duodenal obstruction early in infancy. The abdomen is not distended, and abdominal x-rays show little gas in the small bowel. In contrast, when volvulus occurs, the bowel is usually distended. Bloody stools are a late sign of bowel infarction. A barium enema confirms the abnormal position of the colon and cecum. Since symptoms and abdominal findings may be minimal until bowel infarction is irreversible, emergency barium enema is mandatory if malvolation is suspected.

2. Treatment   The adhesive bands are divided through an upper abdominal transverse incision. When a volvulus is present, the torsion is reduced by counterclockwise rotation of the gut. The duodenum is mobilized and placed in the right lower quadrant, and, following appendectomy, the cecum is placed in the left lower quadrant. Frankly necrotic bowel should be resected and continuity established either by primary anastomosis or by Mikulicz enterostomy. After reduction of the volvulus, intestine with questionable viability should be left alone and the abdomen re-explored 12-24 hours later to confirm the viability of the bowel.

D. JEJUNAL, ILEAL, AND COLONIC ATRESIA OR STENOSIS
Small intestinal and colonic atresias probably follow a vascular accident in utero such as volvulus, intussusception, or gangrenous obstruction. Following aseptic necrosis and resorption of the segment of bowel, the atresia may be a membranous occlusion, may produce 2 blind ends connected by a cord, or there may be a complete separation of the bowel ends. Multiple atresias occur in 10% of cases. Infarction of long lengths of bowel in utero results in abnormally short intestine.

1. Diagnosis The vomiting, distended infant should have abdominal roentgenograms. Air is sufficient contrast to outline the presence of obstruction, and barium by mouth is not indicated. The colon cannot be distinguished from the small bowel in the newborn. Therefore, a barium enema (in saline) will demarcate the colon and determine the presence of colonic obstruction or malrotation. The colon is usually small in caliber (microcolon) because it has been unused, but it is not abnormal. The onset and severity of symptoms from intestinal stenosis is dependent upon the degree of narrowing of the lumen.

2. Treatment A transverse upper abdominal incision is used for jejunal atresia, and a transverse infra-umbilical incision is employed for ileal or colonic atresia. The bulbous dilated proximal blind end of the bowel should be resected. End-to-oblique anastomosis is preferred. A gastrostomy is valuable because prolonged postoperative functional obstruction of the dilated proximal bowel frequently occurs.

E. MECONIUM ILEUS
About 15-20% of infants born with cystic fibrosis have meconium ileus. Cystic fibrosis is an inherited disease transmitted as an autosomal recessive trait. The disease affects all the exocrine glands. The secretion from the mucous glands is abnormally viscid and produces varying degrees of obstruction of the bronchi and the pancreatic and bile ducts. Obstruction of the distal small bowel in utero occurs because of the abnormal viscosity of intestinal mucus and not because of pancreatic enzyme deficiency.

1. Diagnosis Enormous abdominal distention may produce dystocia at birth. Dilated intestinal loops are palpable, and plain abdominal x-rays show dilated loops of bowel of varying diameter. Air-fluid levels are not prominent because of delayed layering of the viscous fluid. Small 'soap' bubbles of gas can be seen in the meconium-filled bowel. Calcification in the abdomen may be seen. About 50% of cases are complicated by volvulus and atresia, with or without perforation of the bowel, and meconium peritonitis. The sodium and chloride content of sweat and fingernails is abnormally high.

2. Treatment A nasogastric tube should be placed into the stomach and connected to suction. Under fluoroscopic control, enemas containing methylglucamine diatrizoate (Gastrografin), which is hygroscopic, or acetylcysteine (Mucomyst), which is mucolytic, may effectively unplug the meconium in uncomplicated cases. Most patients require operation with Mikulicz resection of the most dilated portion of the ileum. The proximal and distal bowel loops may then be irrigated with acetylcysteine. Subsequently, the Mikulicz enterostomy is closed.

F. HIRSCHSPRUNG'S DISEASE
Congenital absence of myenteric ganglion cells, extending for a varying distance from the anus, produces functional obstruction of the colon. The normally ganglionic bowel proximal to the aganglionic segment becomes markedly dilated and hypertrophic. The transition zone between aganglionic and ganglionated bowel is at the rectosigmoid in 75% of cases. The entire colon lacks ganglion cells in 10% of cases.

1. Diagnosis Invariably, constipation begins at birth and may be obstinate enough to cause intestinal obstruction in the neonatal period. Paradoxically, symptoms of abdominal distention and diarrhea in infancy are due to Hirschsprung's disease until proved otherwise. Rectal examination may reveal a tight and narrow anus and rectum. The diagnosis is suspected by barium enema (in saline) showing a normal or small caliber distal intestine and dilatation of the bowel above the transitional zone. No effort should be made to evacuate the contents of the colon before barium enema, so that the transition zone will be retained. The infant is usually unable to evacuate the barium during the next 24 hours. Suction mucosal biopsy of the rectum is safe and simple but interpretation requires an experienced pathologist. Full thickness biopsy is definitive in confirming the absence of ganglion cells. Rectal manometry may be helpful.

Enterocolitis is a serious and often fatal complication before the first year of life.

2. Treatment Conservative measures to evacuate the colon are inadequate.

For infants less than 1 year old, colostomy should be performed at the transition zone (established by biopsy) in an area of ganglionated bowel.

When the child weighs more than 20 pounds, a choice of 3 abdominoperineal pull-through procedures is available.

a. In the *Swenson procedure* (Fig. 18-4), the overly dilated and aganglionic colon and rectum are excised to a point 1.5 cm anteriorly and 0.5 cm posteriorly from the dentate line.

b. The *Soave operation* (Fig. 18-5) consists of dissecting the mucosa out of the residual rectal stump, pulling the proximal bowel through, and suturing it to the rectal muscular sleeve.

c. In the *Duhamel procedure* (Fig. 18-6), the overly dilated and aganglionic bowel is removed down to the rectum at the level of pelvic peritoneal reflection. The proximal bowel is brought between the sacrum and rectum and sutured end-to-side to the rectum above the dentate line. The intervening spur of rectum and bowel is crushed to form a side-to-side anastomosis.

G. ANORECTAL ANOMALIES Two important types of anorectal malformations must be distinguished, depending on whether the distal rectum extends through the levator ani (puborectalis) muscle: the low (translevator) type of imperforate anus or ectopic anus; and the high (supralevator) type of imperforate anus or anorectal agenesis (see Fig. 18-7).

The low type of imperforate anus may be diagnosed by the presence of an ectopic (and usually stenotic) anal orifice or fistula tract anterior to the normal position. In the male, a fistula tract may extend along the perineal raphe; more rarely, the fistula is higher and enters the bulbous urethra. In the female, the ectopic orifice may be in the perineum, vestibule, or lower vagina.

In the high type, the distal rectum and anus fail to develop. In the female, there is usually a fistula to the upper vagina or, rarely, to the bladder. In the male, there is usually a fistula to the urethra or bladder.

1. Diagnosis The most definitive test is careful examination of the perineum for meconium. The presence of a meconium fistula from the bowel to the perineum is the most reliable indicator of a low type anomaly. It is usually safe to wait 12-24 hours to allow meconium to appear.

If a communication between the bowel and perineum cannot be seen, a lateral upside down x-ray of the infant pelvis is sometimes helpful, but may be misleading. This should be taken several hours after birth to allow time for swallowed gas to travel to the distal end of the rectum. The baby should be held upside down for several minutes, and the x-ray should be centered over the greater trochanter. X-ray studies of the spine often reveal vertebral anomalies. Intravenous urograms and voiding cystourethrograms must be done because of the frequency of associated urinary malformations, particularly with anorectal agenesis.

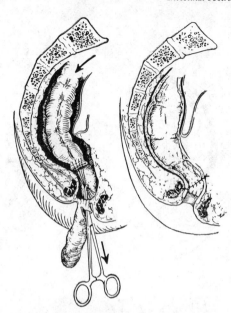

Fig. 18-4. Swenson abdominoperineal pull-through.

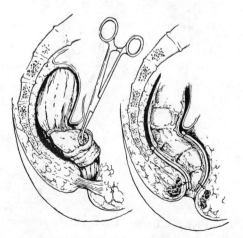

Fig. 18-5. Soave endorectal pull-through.

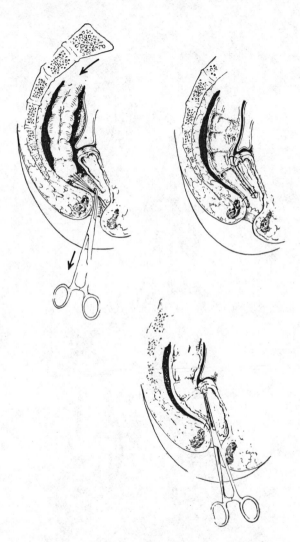

Fig. 18-6. Duhamel abdominoperineal pull-through.

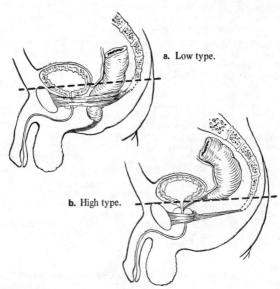

a. Low type.

b. High type.

Fig. 18-7. Imperforate anus.

2. Treatment   If a meconium-containing fistula can be demonstrated in the perineum or low vagina, the malformation is a low anomaly and can usually be surgically repaired from a perineal approach with a good prognosis for continence.

If a fistula cannot be demonstrated or is high in the vagina, the anomaly is the high type. This malformation requires a sigmoid or right transverse colostomy in the newborn period. When the infant grows to 20 pounds, the anorectal agenesis should be repaired by sacroperineal or abdominoperineal operation in which the distal colon is brought anterior to the puborectalis muscle and is sutured to the perineum. In this anomaly, the external anal sphincter is inadequate and the internal sphincter is absent. Therefore, continence is dependent upon a functional puborectalis muscle.

VII. NEONATAL JAUNDICE

The numerous medical causes of jaundice in the newborn include giant cell hepatitis, cytomegalic inclusion disease, herpes simplex, toxoplasmosis, rubella, syphilis, and galactosemia. Surgically treatable causes of jaundice are biliary atresia and choledochal cyst (see below). During the first months of life, liver function studies cannot identify these various conditions. Microcephaly, choreoretinitis, intracranial calcification, and cytomegalic inclusion bodies in the cells of urinary sediment suggest toxoplasmosis or cytomegalic inclusion disease. Excretion in the stools of more than 10% of an intravenous dose of radioactive rose bengal rules out biliary atresia but not choledochal cyst. Needle biopsy of the liver is diagnostic in 60% of cases. Surgical exploration, cholangiography, and open liver biopsy establish the diagnosis in more than 90% of cases. Since cirrhosis in surgically correctable cases of jaundice is often irreversible after 90 days of age, surgical exploration is advocated before 3 months.

A. BILIARY ATRESIA The cause of biliary atresia is unknown, but it is probably acquired after birth. Surgical correction requires a ductal structure at the hilum of the liver which drains a normal intrahepatic biliary tree. Although a hilar ductal structure may be found in 10-20% of cases, only 5% of these drain a normal intrahepatic biliary tree. The bile duct may be anastomosed to the duodenum, but recurrent cholangitis is frequent. A Roux-en-Y choledochojejunostomy or hepatic duct jejunostomy may be preferable.

Uncorrectable biliary atresia may be extrahepatic or intrahepatic. In extrahepatic atresia, both the major extrahepatic and intrahepatic ducts are obliterated, but numerous proliferating cholangioles and varying grades of cirrhosis may be seen on liver biopsy. The average life span of these infants is 19 months. Intrahepatic biliary atresia is characterized by a total absence of intrahepatic ducts with few cholangioles and little cirrhosis. These patients may live for 3-5 years.

B. CHOLEDOCHAL CYST The 3 types of choledochal cysts are cystic dilatation of the common bile duct, diverticulum of the common bile duct, and choledochocele. These cysts commonly have thick, fibrous walls which lack an epithelial lining. The onset of symptoms is usually between the age of 3 months and adulthood. Females are affected 4 times as frequently as males. The symptoms are the triad of jaundice, pain, and abdominal mass.

These cysts may be excised with Roux-en-Y choledochojejunostomy.

VIII. GASTROINTESTINAL PROBLEMS IN OLDER INFANTS AND CHILDREN

A. HYPERTROPHIC PYLORIC STENOSIS Progressive hypertrophy of the circular muscle of the pylorus produces narrowing and obstruction of the pyloric canal. The cause is unknown. There is a familial tendency, and males—particularly first-born males—predominate over females 4:1.

This disorder must be differentiated from feeding problems, gastroesophageal reflux, hiatus hernia, pylorospasm, intracranial lesions, uremia, adrenal insufficiency, duodenal stenosis, and malrotation of the bowel.

1. Diagnosis The symptoms are nonbilious projectile vomiting, failure to gain weight or weight loss, dehydration, and diminished number of stools. The onset of symptoms may occur shortly after birth but is usually delayed until 2-3 weeks after birth. Prominent gastric waves may be seen traversing from the left costal margin across the upper abdomen. A pyloric 'tumor' or 'olive' 1-2 cm in size is palpable in the upper abdomen in more than 95% of the cases. This latter finding is diagnostic, and x-ray studies to show the pyloric 'string sign' are usually not necessary.

2. Treatment A Fredet–Ramstedt pyloromyotomy through a right upper quadrant muscle-splitting incision is curative. This is an elective operation that should be performed only after dehydration and metabolic alkalosis have been treated. Postoperatively, feeding may begin within 6 hours, starting with 1 oz of 10% dextrose solution every 2 hours; increasing amounts of formula are then given every 3-4 hours. There should be no mortality in the treatment of this disease. Complications such as duodenal mucosal perforation, intra-abdominal bleeding, and aspiration of vomitus must be carefully watched for in the immediate postoperative period.

B. INTUSSUSCEPTION Telescoping of a segment of bowel (intussusceptum) into the adjacent segment (intussuscipiens) produces intestinal obstruction, and it may result in gangrene of the intussusceptum. The terminal ileum is usually telescoped into the right colon, producing ileocolic intussusception but ileo-ileal, ileo-ileocolic, jejuno-jejunal, and colo-colic intussusceptions also occur. In 95% of infants and children the cause is unknown, but this disorder may be related to adenovirus infection. The most frequent occurrence is in midsummer and mid-winter. The peak age is in infants 5-9 months old; 65% are less than 1 year old; and 80% are less than 2 years old. Causes such as Meckel's diverticulum, polyps, intramural hematoma (Henoch-Schonlein purpura), and hypertrophic Peyer's patches are reported with increasing frequency in children older than 1 year.

1. Diagnosis The typical patient is a healthy, robust child who has sudden onset of crying and doubles up his knees on the abdomen because of pain. The ratio of males to females is 3:2. The pain is intermittent, lasts for about 1 minute, and is followed by intervals of apparent well-being. Reflex vomiting is a frequent early sign, and vomiting from bowel obstruction occurs later in the course. Blood and mucus in the rectum produce a 'currant jelly' stool. In small infants, colicky pain may not be apparent; these babies become withdrawn, and the most prominent symptom is vomiting. Pallor and sweating during colic is frequent. A mass is usually palpable along the distribution of the colon. A hollow right lower quadrant (Dance's sign) may be noted. Occasionally the intussusception is palpable on rectal examination. The blood count usually shows a polymorphonuclear leukocytosis and hemoconcentration. Barium enema is diagnostic.

2. Treatment Hypovolemia and dehydration must be corrected. Barium enema reduction may be attempted if there is no evidence of advanced small bowel obstruction or perforation. The patient is sedated, and barium enema is then performed with a surgeon present. The enema bag must not be raised to more than 30 inches above the patient, and under fluoroscopic control the barium enema will distend the intussuscipiens and reduce the intussusceptum in 65-70% of cases.

If enema reduction cannot be accomplished, the patient is anesthetized and the abdomen is explored through a right lower quadrant transverse incision. The intussusception is then reduced by gentle, retrograde compression of the intussuscipiens and not by traction on the proximal bowel. Intestinal resection is indicated if the bowel cannot be reduced or if the bowel is gangrenous. Mikulicz resection may be necessary in critically ill patients. Resection of a Meckel's diverticulum, polypectomy, and incidental appendectomy may be performed.

Intussusception recurs in 1-2% of cases.

C. REFLUX ESOPHAGITIS Persistent nonbilious vomiting in infants is usually due to gastric outlet obstruction (pyloric stenosis, antral web, or duodenal obstruction proximal to the ampulla of Vater) or malfunction of the gastroesophageal junction at the diaphragmatic hiatus. CNS lesions and sepsis must be exluded. Barium studies often reveal some reflux of gastric contents up the esophagus with or without a hiatus hernia and also help rule out congenital esophageal stenosis and achalasia with megaesophagus. In the majority of infants and children with vomiting and reflux, symptoms are controlled by upright feeding and resolve spontaneously when the child begins to sit up and walk.

However, some children develop esophagitis and ulceration with bleeding, anemia, failure to thrive and subsequent stricture formation. These infants have dysphagia and frequent aspiration pneumonia. Acid reflux can be demonstrated with an esophageal pH probe. A Nissen fundoplication anti-reflux operation is indicated when sequelae of reflux are documented: esophageal ulcerations and/or stricture, refractory anemia, failure to thrive, and recurrent aspiration pneumonia.

D. OMPHALOMESENTERIC DUCT ANOMALIES When the entire duct remains intact it is called an **omphalomesenteric fistula.** When the duct is obliterated at the intestinal end but communicates with the umbilicus at the distal end, it is called an **umbilical sinus.** When the epithelial tract persists but both ends are occluded, an **umbilical cyst** or intra-abdominal **enterocystoma** may develop. The entire tract may be obliterated but form a band between the ileum and the umbilicus.

The most common remnant of an omphalomesenteric duct is a Meckel's diverticulum, which occurs in 1-3% of the population. Meckel's diverticulum may be lined in part or totally by small intestinal, colonic, or gastric mucosa, and it may contain aberrant pancreatic tissue. In contrast to duplications and pseudo-diverticula, it is located on the antimesenteric border of the ileum 10-90 cm from the ileocecal valve.

1. Diagnosis Omphalomesenteric remnants may produce symptoms of continuous mucous discharge at the umbilicus, umbilical mass, or abscess. Intestinal obstruction may develop from a persistent band occluding the bowel lumen, or by volvulus of the intestine about the band.

Meckel's diverticulum may cause painless, sudden, severe intestinal hemorrhage due to peptic ulceration of the adjacent bowel. The hemorrhage usually occurs in infants less than 2 years old. Peptic ulceration may lead to perforation and generalized peritonitis.

Meckel's diverticulum with a narrow lumen may become occluded and result in diverticulitis, with a clinical picture similar to appendicitis. A Meckel's diverticulum may also become inverted into the bowel lumen and act as a leading edge for an intussusception.

2. Treatment Umbilical fistulas, sinuses, and cysts should be excised to prevent the development of infection. Meckel's diverticulum should be considered the source of peritonitis or massive gastrointestinal bleeding when some other cause cannot be identified. Usually the omphalomesenteric remnant can be excised and the communication with the ileum oversewn. Resection of the small intestine is occasionally required.

IX. ABDOMINAL WALL DEFECTS

A. INGUINAL HERNIA AND HYDROCELE Autopsy studies have shown that the processus vaginalis remains patent in more than 80% of newborn infants. With increasing age, the prevalence of a patent processus diminishes; at 2 years, 40-50% are open, and in adult autopsy specimens, 25% are open. Actual indirect inguinal hernia develops in 1-4% of children; 45% occur in the first year of life.

1. Diagnosis The diagnosis of a *hernia* in infancy and childhood can be made only by the demonstration of an inguinal bulge originating from the internal ring. Commonly, the bulge cannot be elicited at will, and signs such as a large external ring, 'silk glove' sign, and thickening of the cord are not dependable. Under these circumstances, a reliable history alone may be sufficient. Hernias are found on the right side in 60% of cases; on the left side in 25%; and bilaterally in 15%. Bilateral hernias are more frequent in premature infants. The processus may be obliterated at any location proximal to the testes or labia. When the bowel herniates into the scrotum, it is referred to as a complete indirect inguinal hernia; when it extends to a level proximal to the testes in the male or external ring in the female, it is an incomplete inguinal hernia. Direct inguinal and femoral hernias are very rare in infancy and childhood.

Incarcerated inguinal hernia accounts for approximately 10% of childhood hernias, and the greatest incidence is in young infants. In 45% of females with incarcerated hernia, the contents of the sac consists of various combinations of ovary, tube, and uterus. These structures are usually a sliding component of the sac.

Hydroceles almost always represent peritoneal fluid trapped in a patent processus vaginalis; hence, they are commonly called communicating hydroceles. Hydrocele is characteristically an oblong, nontender, soft mass that transilluminates with light. The sudden appearance of fluid confined to the testicular area may represent a noncommunicating hydrocele secondary to torsion of the testes or testicular appendage, or epididymo-orchitis. Rectal examination and palpation of the peritoneal side of the internal ring may distinguish an incarcerated hernia from a hydrocele or other inguino-scrotal mass.

2. Treatment If expert anesthesia is available, an inguinal hernia in an infant or child should be repaired soon after diagnosis. In premature infants under constant surveillance in the hospital, hernia repair may be deferred until the baby is strong enough to be discharged home. Ordinarily, high ligation and excision of the hernia sac at the internal ring is all that is required. When there is a large internal ring, it may be necessary to narrow the internal ring with sutures placed in the transversalis fascia, but use of abdominal muscles for the repair is unnecessary.

An incarcerated hernia in an infant can usually be reduced initially before operation. This is accomplished by sedation with meperidine (Demerol), 2 mg/kg and secobarbital, 2 mg/kg, and by elevating the foot of the bed to keep abdominal pressure from being exerted on the inguinal area. When the infant is well-sedated, the hernia may be reduced by gentle pressure over the internal ring in a manner that milks the bowel into the abdominal cavity. During this time, nasogastric suction and intravenous fluids are used as required for bowel distention and fluid and electrolyte losses. If the bowel is not reduced after a few hours, operation is required. If the hernia is reduced, operative repair should be delayed for 24 hours to reduce the edema in the tissues. Bloody stools and marked edema or red discoloration of the skin around the groin suggest strangulated hernia, and reduction of the bowel should not be attempted. Emergency repair of incarcerated inguinal hernia is technically difficult because the edematous tissues are friable and tear readily. Gangrenous intestine should be resected, but black, hemorrhagic discoloration of the testis or ovary does not require excision of the gonad.

B. UMBILICAL HERNIA A fascial defect at the umbilicus is frequent in the newborn, particularly in premature infants. The incidence is higher in blacks. In most children, the umbilical ring progressively diminishes in size and eventually closes. Protrusion of bowel through this defect rarely results in incarceration. Because of these 2 factors, surgical repair is not indicated unless the intestine becomes incarcerated or unless the fascial defect is greater than 1.5 cm in diameter after the age of 3 years.

C. OMPHALOCELE occurs once in every 10,000 births. It is a defect in the periumbilical abdominal wall in which the celomic cavity is covered only by peritoneum and amnion. The omphalocele may contain small and large bowel, liver, stomach, spleen, pancreas, and bladder. This defect results from an arrest in mesoblastic infiltration of the ventral body wall. When this mesoblastic arrest takes place in the eighth to tenth week of fetal development, a small defect occurs in which the cord is at the apex of the sac; this is called a **fetal** type of omphalocele, or hernia into the cord. If arrest in mesoblastic infiltration occurs during the third week of fetal development, a large abdominal wall defect is formed and the umbilical cord is located at the edge of the omphalocele. This is called the **embryonic** type of omphalocele. Malrotation of the midgut is commonly associated with omphalocele. Associated major anomalies involving the central nervous, cardiovascular, and skeletal systems are frequent. More than half of these babies are born prematurely.

1. Treatment The conservative treatment of omphalocele consists of painting the amniotic sac with povidone-iodine every 3 hours to form a sterile eschar which becomes vascularized beneath the membrane. Over a period of time, contraction of the skin and the abdominal wall will occur and the skin will grow over the granulating portion of the omphalocele. The disadvantages of this technic are the risk of rupture of the omphalocele, the potential for infection, and the prolonged period of hospitalization required until the defect has healed. It is indicated only for patients with extremely large defects which might not be covered by a surgical approach, or for infants who are critically ill because of prematurity, pulmonary complications, or severe associated malformations.

The fetal type of omphalocele, with a small abdominal defect, can be treated by excising the omphalocele sac and by reapproximating the abdominal wall muscles and skin edges.

The large embryonic omphalocele may be treated by staged closure with a 'Silo' of prosthetic material (usually Silastic coated dacron) sutured to the abdominal wall and then removed after the viscera have been progressively reduced into the expanded abdominal cavity. If early closure by this technic is not possible due to respiratory insufficiency from impaired diaphragmatic excursion, cardiac insufficiency from compression of the inferior vena cava, or vascular insufficiency and infarction of bowel, the omphalocele can be covered with skin and the ventral hernia repaired in stages when the child is older.

The skin edges can be undermined in the plane between the subcutaneous fat and the abdominal fascia well around to the back, inguinal area, and costal margin, and then approximated in the midline to cover the abdominal wall defect. Because of the frequency of malrotation and potential duodenal obstruction, excision of the omphalocele sac is advised to allow exploration of the abdominal cavity and correction of the exisiting defects. Gastrostomy is a valuable adjunct.

D. GASTROSCHISIS This abdominal wall defect probably follows intrauterine rupture of an omphalocele. It is characterized by a full-thickness defect in the ventral abdominal wall lateral to and usually to the right of a normal insertion of the umbilical cord. There may be a bridge of skin between the defect and the cord. The small and large bowel are herniated through to the abdominal wall defect, and, having been bathed in the amniotic fluid, have a very thick, shaggy membrane covering the bowel wall. The loops of intestine are usually matted together, and the length of intestine appears to be abnormally short. Since the bowel has not been contained intra-abdominally, the abdominal cavity fails to enlarge and cannot accommodate the protuberant bowel. Over 70% of these infants are premature. Malrotation of the intestine is almost always present, and other associated anomalies are infrequent.

1. Treatment These defects can sometimes be closed primarily.

If the abdominal cavity is not large enough to accept the exteriorized bowel, a tube may be formed from Silastic-covered nylon mesh to encompass the bowel, and the tube is sutured to the abdominal wall defect. When this tube is suspended from the top of an isolette, the intestines will progressively fall into the expanded abdominal cavity. The fibro-gelatinous pseudomembrane surrounding the matted loops of bowel will resorb. Once the bowel is reduced, the Silastic 'silo' may be removed and the abdominal wall layers may be reapproximated.

A gastrostomy should be performed for gastrointestinal decompression during the period of ileus, which may be prolonged.

X. NEOPLASMS

A. NEUROBLASTOMA   Of all childhood neoplasms, neuroblastoma is second only to leukemia and brain tumors in frequency. Two-thirds of cases occur within the first 5 years of life. This tumor is of neural crest origin and may arise anywhere along the distribution of the sympathetic chain. The tumor is retroperitoneal in 65% of cases, and adrenal in 40%, posterior mediastinal in 15%, and cervical or sacral in 5% of cases. The site of origin cannot be determined in 10% of cases.

The biologic behavior of neuroblastoma is frequently different in infants under 1 year old compared with older children. The tumor is frequently localized in infants, but distant metastases have developed in more than 70% of older children at the time of diagnosis. In infants, distant metastases are commonly confined to the liver and subcutaneous tissues, whereas in older children bone and lymph node metastases are most common.

1. Diagnosis   The symptoms in infants are an isolated tumor, hepatomegaly, or subcutaneous nodules.

Older children may also have an isolated tender mass, but they frequently have pain in the bones and joints and associated malaise, fever, vomiting, and anemia, which may mimic infection or rheumatic fever.

Hypertension occurs in less than 20% of patients.

Abdominal neuroblastoma may be distinguished from other tumors by the hard, irregular surface of the tumor and the tendency to cross the midline.

X-rays and computerized axial tomography (CT scan) show a soft tissue mass displacing surrounding structures, and calcification is present in 45% of the tumors. For retroperitoneal tumors, an intravenous pyelogram shows displacement or compression of the adjacent kidney without distortion of the renal calyces.

Approximately 70% of neuroblastomas produce norepinephrine and its precursors or metabolites. The breakdown products of excess norepinephrine production, most commonly vanillylmandelic acid (VMA) and homovanillic acid (HVA), should be measured in urine specimens at intervals so that the clinical course of the patient can be followed.

2. Treatment   A localized neuroblastoma should be excised and the local area of the tumor bed should be irradiated. An unresectable primary tumor and its metastases should be treated by radiation therapy and combination chemotherapy. This may produce tumor regression which is sometimes permanent in infants but usually only temporary in older children. The two-year 'cure' rate in infants with distant metastases is 45%. Cure in older children is much less frequent.

B. WILMS' TUMOR arises within the capsule of the kidney and consists of a variety of epithelial and sarcomatous cell types such as abortive tubules and glomeruli, smooth and skeletal muscle fibers, spindle cells, cartilage, and bone. Hence the tumor is also called nephroblastoma, embryoma, carcinosarcoma, or mixed tumor of the kidney. Eighty per cent of patients are under 4 years old. Bilateral tumors occur in 5-10% of cases. Metastases most commonly occur to the liver and lungs.

1. Diagnosis   A large, firm, smooth, lateral abdominal mass is always palpable. An intravenous urogram shows distortion of the calyces and kidney silhouette. Very rarely there is nonfunction of the kidney, in which case the mass must be distinguished from hydronephrosis. Cystoscopy, retrograde urograms, and renal arteriograms are unnecessary.

2. Treatment   The preferred treatment is immediate nephrectomy and excision of all the surrounding tissues within Gerota's fascia. Radiation therapy to the tumor bed is required when regional nodes contain tumor. Very large tumors should be treated with irradiation preoperatively to reduce the size of the tumor; nephrectomy should then be performed. The nephrectomy is accomplished through an abdominal or thoracoabdominal incision. Dactinomycin and vincristine should be given postoperatively.

Patients with distant metastases are curable. Solitary liver and lung metastases should be resected. Multiple metastases should be treated with irradiation in conjunction with dactinomycin. The cure rate is more than 85% when this tumor is treated in pediatric oncology centers.

C. TERATOMAS are congenital tumors derived from pluri-potential embryonic cells. They are located in the midline or paramedian parts of the body. Teratomas consist of cells representing the 3 germ layers such as neural tissue, dermal epithelial elements and teeth, intestinal and respiratory epithelium, chorio-epithelioma, and mesenchymal tissue such as smooth and striated muscle, connective tissue, fat, cartilage, and bone. There are benign and malignant types of teratomas. Metastases may represent one cellular element but usually consist of most of the cellular types present in the primary lesion. Sites of origin in order of frequency are the ovaries, testes, anterior mediastinum, presacral and coccygeal regions, and retroperitoneum. Most ovarian teratomas are benign 'dermoid' tumors. Most testicular teratomas are malignant, and the incidence of malignancy is higher than the normal population in undescended testes and in pseudohermaphrodites. Most of the mediastinal, retroperitoneal, and coccygeal teratomas are benign. These tumors should be excised because of their malignant potential and the symptoms produced by their size.

D. RHABDOMYOSARCOMAS   The histologic varieties of rhabdomyosarcomas are the embryonal cell, the alveolar cell, and the pleomorphic types. Sarcoma botryoides is a variant of the embryonal type which is characterized by grape-like masses located in mucosal-lined cavities such as the bladder, vagina, bile ducts, middle ear, and sinuses. The embryonal type of tumor occurs primarily in infants and children and arises from the urogenital tract or the skeletal muscles of the head and neck, the extremities, and the trunk. The alveolar cell type occurs in adolescents and young adults and arises from skeletal muscles in the trunk and extremities. The pleomorphic type develops mainly in adults. Metastases spread to regional lymph nodes and to the lungs and liver. Treatment requires radical excision. Radiation therapy and dactinomycin, vincristine, and Cytoxan are supplements to surgical excision or are used for palliation of disseminated tumor.

E. CYSTIC HYGROMA AND LYMPHANGIOMA   These tumors of lymph vessels occur at the junction of large lymphatic trunks in the neck, axilla, and groin. Cystic hygromas contain large cysts with a well-defined capsule. Lymphangiomas consist of microcystic lymph masses and characteristically invade surrounding structures without respect for tissue planes. Whether these tumors are true neoplasms or whether they represent malformations of the lymphatic system is controversial. Indications for treatment are cosmetic deformity, functional impairment, and prevention of repeated lymphangitis. These lesions do not respond to drugs or injection of sclerosing agents, and they are radioresistant. Excision is the only method of treatment. Every effort should be made to spare normal structures, particularly nerves.

INDEX